THE LEGAL LEGACY OF THE SPECIAL COURT FOR SIERRA LEONE

This book examines whether the Special Court for Sierra Leone (SCSL), which was established jointly through an unprecedented bilateral treaty between the United Nations (UN) and Sierra Leone in 2002, has made jurisprudential contributions to the development of the nascent and still unsettled field of international criminal law. The work, which focuses on the main legal legacy of the SCSL, opens with an examination of the historical and political circumstances which led to the outbreak of a notoriously brutal civil war in Sierra Leone which lasted between March 1991 and January 2002 and led to the deaths of approximately 75,000 people. Following a discussion of the creation, jurisdiction, and the trials conducted by the SCSL, the author examines the SCSL's unique personal jurisdiction over persons bearing "greatest responsibility" for the serious crimes committed in Sierra Leone and the implications of its use in future ad hoc international tribunals; the prosecution of the novel crime of "forced marriage" as other inhumane acts of crimes against humanity; the prosecution of the war crime of recruitment and use of children under the age of fifteen for the purpose of using them to participate in hostilities; as well as issues of immunity for the serving head of state of Liberia, which President Charles Taylor sought to invoke to block his own trial for international crimes before the SCSL. The book then discusses the status of blanket amnesties under international law, and critically evaluates the SCSL's ruling that such a domestic measure could not block prosecution of universally condemned crimes before an independent international tribunal. Lastly, the book evaluates the tenuous interaction between truth commissions and special courts given both their simultaneous operation in Sierra Leone and distinctive mandates aimed at reconciliation and punishment. The author demonstrates that the SCSL, as the third modern international criminal tribunal supported by the UN, made some useful jurisprudential additions on many of these topics, and in some cases broke new ground, and that these represent a valuable legal and judicial contribution to the development of the nascent field of international criminal law.

Charles C. Jalloh is Professor of Law at Florida International University, USA and a member of the International Law Commission. He was formerly a legal adviser in the Special Court for Sierra Leone, and between 2018–2019, was the Fulbright Distinguished Chair in Public International Law at Lund University and Raoul Wallenberg Institute of Human Rights and Humanitarian Law, Sweden. His related books include, as (lead) editor, *Consolidated Legal Texts for the Special Court for Sierra Leone* (Brill, 2007), *The Law Reports of the Special Court for Sierra Leone* (Brill, AFRC Case, 2012; CDF Case, 2013, Taylor Case, 2015; RUF Case, 2020) and *The Sierra Leone Special Court and Its Legacy: The Impact for Africa and International Criminal Law* (Cambridge, 2014). Jalloh is Founding Editor of the *African Journal of Legal Studies* and the *African Journal of International Criminal Justice*.

The Legal Legacy of the Special Court for Sierra Leone

CHARLES C. JALLOH
Florida International University

CAMBRIDGE
UNIVERSITY PRESS

CAMBRIDGE
UNIVERSITY PRESS

University Printing House, Cambridge CB2 8BS, United Kingdom

One Liberty Plaza, 20th Floor, New York, NY 10006, USA

477 Williamstown Road, Port Melbourne, VIC 3207, Australia

314–321, 3rd Floor, Plot 3, Splendor Forum, Jasola District Centre,
New Delhi – 110025, India

79 Anson Road, #06–04/06, Singapore 079906

Cambridge University Press is part of the University of Cambridge.

It furthers the University's mission by disseminating knowledge in the pursuit of
education, learning, and research at the highest international levels of excellence.

www.cambridge.org
Information on this title: www.cambridge.org/9781107178311
DOI: 10.1017/9781316823491

First published 2020

A catalogue record for this publication is available from the British Library.

Library of Congress Cataloging-in-Publication Data
NAMES: Jalloh, Charles, author.
TITLE: The legal legacy of the Special Court for Serra Leone / Charles C. Jalloh.
DESCRIPTION: Cambridge, United Kingdom ; New York, NY, USA : Cambridge University
Press, 2020. | Based on author's thesis (doctoral – Universiteit van Amsterdam, 2016) issued
under title: Judicial contributions of the Sierra Leone tribunal to the development of
international criminal law | Includes bibliographical references and index.
IDENTIFIERS: LCCN 2020004396 | ISBN 9781107178311 (hardback) | ISBN 9781316823491 (epub)
SUBJECTS: LCSH: Special Court for Sierra Leone – Influence. | International criminal
courts – Netherlands. | International criminal law.
CLASSIFICATION: LCC KZ1208.S53 A14 2020 | DDC 341.6/9–dc23
LC record available at https://lccn.loc.gov/2020004396

ISBN 978-1-107-17831-1 Hardback
ISBN 978-1-316-63089-1 Paperback

To my parents, who gave me the education that they were promised,
but never received.

Contents

Preface and Acknowledgments

After the end of the Cold War, in the early 1990s, the United Nations established various types of ad hoc international criminal tribunals for different parts of the world to prosecute the perpetrators of crimes against humanity, genocide, war crimes, and other serious violations of international law. Although the UN Security Council–created International Criminal Tribunals for the Former Yugoslavia (ICTY) and Rwanda (ICTR) were the modern pioneers, and are therefore better known, the Special Court for Sierra Leone (SCSL) followed not long afterwards and occupied its own space in the landscape of modern international criminal tribunals.

The SCSL, which was created through a bilateral treaty that was concluded between the UN and the Government of Sierra Leone in January 2002 following the latter's request, was designed to address perceptions of shortcomings in the ICTY and ICTR models, in particular, their apparently costly nature; the relatively slow pace of their proceedings; their geographic and emotional distance from the local populations in whose names they were asked to render justice; and their seemingly unfocused prosecutions which sometimes included lower-ranking suspects that some deemed more appropriate for trial within national courts rather than before an international penal tribunal. The coercive Chapter VII legal basis of the twin UN tribunals and the consensual treaty-based character of the SCSL therefore differ markedly, reflecting the particular historical and political circumstances of their establishment.

Today, the ICTY, ICTR, and the SCSL have all completed their respective mandates. All have transformed into some type of residual mechanism, with the first two sharing a common one while the latter has its own separate body. Both residual courts are located in The Hague. Interestingly, in the lead-up to the completion of their work, the tribunals themselves as well as legal academics and others turned towards efforts aimed at evaluating the likely impact, and limitations, of these ad hoc courts using doctrinal, semi-empirical, and empirical approaches in an attempt to discern their "legacy." Though often mentioned in contemporary international criminal law discourse, but not always defined, the term "legacy" as used in this work is a narrow reference to the body of legal rules, innovative practices, and norms that the tribunal is expected to hand down to current and future generations of international, internationalized, and national courts charged with the responsibility to prosecute the same or similar international crimes. I describe this as the "legal legacy," as that term is used in the title of this book, in contrast to other possible types of sociological, political, and other legacies that the tribunals might leave behind.

This definition can be distinguished from the broader conception of legacy offered by the UN for internationalized tribunals, which encompasses their "lasting impact on bolstering the rule of law in a particular society, by conducting effective trials to contribute to ending impunity, while also strengthening domestic judicial capacity."[1] My use of the term here does not contemplate the physical infrastructure like the SCSL buildings that were left behind in Freetown or the documents and archives and records of the tribunal now officially located in The Hague, those being matters that are more appropriately considered in discussions of the residual mechanism. It also leaves out the institutional aspects of the SCSL model such as the creation of defense or outreach offices or other types of institutional innovations that were developed during the founding of the tribunal or in the course of its existence. The latter are important, but not the focus of this book.

The SCSL, though the last of the first three UN supported tribunals, became the first of the modern ad hoc international criminal tribunals since the Nuremberg Trials to complete all of its cases through to appeals and to symbolically close down its doors even as it transformed into a Residual Special Court for Sierra Leone. Perhaps unsurprisingly given that they were the first truly international criminal courts to be established, various scholarly efforts have already been undertaken to assess the legacy and impact of the ICTY, and to a lesser extent, the ICTR. Most of the attempts to evaluate the legacy of the twin UN tribunals have focused on their pioneering additions to the Nuremberg legacy and the normative advancement of the concept of individual criminal responsibility at the international level as well as on the elaboration of the substantive content of the various international crimes within their jurisdiction, in particular, genocide, crimes against humanity, and war crimes.

In contrast, between the establishment of the SCSL in January 2002 and its closure in December 2013, fewer scholarly works have studied that tribunal and its legacy to international criminal law and practice. Yet, because of the near unique fact pattern of the Sierra Leone conflict, the SCSL was often confronted with a range of novel legal issues in the course of its proceedings. This gave it the opportunity to develop some interesting jurisprudence on issues of wider significance for the field.

---

1   Office of the High Commissioner for Human Rights, *Rule-of-Law Tools for Post-conflict States. Maximizing the Legacy of Hybrid Courts* (2008), available at www.ohchr.org/Documents/Publications/HybridCourts.pdf (last accessed November 2012), at 4–5.

The Sierra Leone Court was among the first to grapple with some of the more important and recurring legal dilemmas for many modern post-conflict situations. For example, among others, the SCSL was the first international criminal court to prosecute persons bearing "greatest responsibility"; to try and convict persons for the recruitment and enlistment of children for the purposes of using them in hostilities. It was also the first international tribunal to recognize the new crime against humanity of forced marriage as an "other inhumane act," and importantly, the first to indict, fully try, and then convict an African president for planning and aiding and abetting the commission of international crimes in a neighboring state thereby getting the opportunity to pronounce on the question of his immunity.

Finally, because of some key SCSL decisions which are now frequently cited by the International Criminal Court and other national and international tribunals, future legal efforts to hold perpetrators to account may now benefit from greater clarity on, among others, the question whether blanket amnesties granted under a peace agreement barred the prosecution of universally condemned international crimes before an ad hoc international criminal court; and the question whether alternative accountability mechanisms such as special tribunals and truth commissions can coexist and complement each other where used simultaneously.

The purpose of this book is to discuss the SCSL's legacy on these legal issues on which the tribunal made some juridical contributions. It seeks to contribute to the emerging literature on the legacy of ad hoc international criminal courts by offering an assessment of the main legacy of the Sierra Leone Court from the perspective of an academic, but who because of his prior role, also had the opportunity to occupy a front row seat in the tribunal's most important trial involving Liberia's former president Charles Taylor. The focus is to analyze what I have described as the "legal legacy" of the tribunal, in particular, its key judicial decisions on the above mentioned issues and their possible contributions to the wider corpus of norms for substantive international criminal law and practice. This, of course, is not an exhaustive assessment. There are other judicial decisions on several other issues such as the role of the United Nations Security Council in creating ad hoc courts or the first prosecution of the war crime of attacks against UN peacekeepers, which due to reasons of space, are not considered in this book. Though generally positive, the evaluation was also critical; it sought to be as objective as possible and to take advantage of the distance created by many years in academia while at the same time engaging with the substance of the SCSL's work through publications and other scholarly endeavors. It is my sincere hope that, by engaging in this critical assessment focusing on the main contributions and limitations of the SCSL rather than all its possible legal legacies, this book will make a useful contribution to the legal literature on international criminal courts. It should add to the legal literature on the contributions of the somewhat understudied SCSL to the development of international law as well as to the ongoing global discussion about how best to enhance accountability for international crimes through the establishment of such special tribunals in partnership with the affected State.

As usual, with multi-year projects of this kind, this book would not have been possible without the support and encouragement of my family and various friends/ colleagues. First, to my immediate family, I am grateful to my wife Jan Osei-Tutu, and our three boys, Salieu, Chay, and Kannin, for their loving support and encouragement. Thanks also to my two kotors, Ibrahim (aka IB), Salieu (aka Sal), and my two jajas, Binta and Jarieu, for their usual moral support.

Second, because the seeds of this book were first planted as part of a doctoral dissertation completed on the Special Court for Sierra Leone at the University of Amsterdam Faculty of Law, I am indebted to Erika de Wet and Harmen van der Wilt, my two PhD supervisors, for their insightful comments on the various chapters which I wrote for the thesis. I also appreciated the incisive comments of the examining board, comprised of Y. M. Donders, P. A. Nollkaemper, G. K. Sluiter, L. J. van den Herik, and G. Werle. Grateful to them all, though of course, I take full responsibility for all arguments, errors, and omissions.

Two additional chapters were completed during my research leave as the 2018– 2019 Fulbright Distinguished Chair of Public International Law at the Faculty of Law, Lund University and the Raoul Wallenberg Institute of Human Rights and Humanitarian Law. I am grateful to the Fulbright Commission for the opportunity, and to the many academic colleagues who made my Swedish experience a very pleasant one. Although I never presented this work or asked them to comment on aspects of it, their warmth and hospitality during my stay in Lund provided a rather congenial atmosphere in which to continue my research. Most staff at both of my host institutions proved to be warm and friendly. I therefore hope they will forgive me for singling out Michael McEachrane, for our many great conversations on everything from law to politics to philosophy and Pan-Africanism; Maria Green, for helping me avoid cultural gaffes, especially for prodding me to stop and enjoy the inestimable joys of *fika*, which I have come to love; Morten Kjaerum, for always great lunches and stimulating conversations about the present and future of human rights, multilateralism, and international law; and Alejandro Fuentes, Radu Mares, Kamal Makili-Aliyev, and Rolf Ring for their generous time spent with a short-term visitor and useful tips about teaching and culture in Sweden.

In the Lund Faculty of Law, Eduardo Gill-Pedro, Xavier Groussot, Valentin Jeutner, and Ulf Linderfalk and their colleagues made me feel welcome, while Karol Nowak, who runs the LLM program in human rights, shared insights on the Swedish legal education system. It helped limit classroom culture shock, for both me and my students; and made my comparative teaching experience a rather fun experience. My excellent Swedish and other students proved to be quite open-minded, even as I introduced them to the alien Socratic Method. Fellow international law travelers Valentin Jeutner and Britta Sjöstedt helped me settle into life in

Lund, with tips on where to go and what to do, punctuated by some nice lunches and periodic evening drinks with a group of younger international faculty.

To the friendly staff at the Fulbright Commission of Sweden, in Stockholm, I especially thank Eric Jönsson and Monica Dahlen. They and their colleagues both shared richly on the Swedish culture and way of life. They also invited me to additional Fulbright events in other parts of the country, including to Uppsala and Stockholm. They generously provided guidance, as I navigated the necessary bureaucracy that came with this great intercultural exchange. I am grateful to them for helping make my fond memories of Sweden.

***

Parts of the content of this book were developed and expanded from previously published works for which I gratefully acknowledge the various publishers: The Contribution of the Special Court for Sierra Leone to the Development of International Law, *African Journal of International and Comparative Law*, Vol. 15, No. 2, pp. 165–207 (2007); Special Court for Sierra Leone: Achieving Justice?, *Michigan Journal of International Law*, Vol. 32, No. 3, pp. 395–460 (2011); Prosecuting Those Bearing "Greatest Responsibility": The Lessons of the Special Court for Sierra Leone, *Marquette Law Review*, Vol. 96, p. 863 (2013); International Decision: *Prosecutor v. Taylor*: Case No. SCSL-03–01-A: Appeals Judgment, *American Journal of International Law,* Vol. 108, p. 58 (2014); The Law and Politics of the Charles Taylor Case, *Denver Journal of International Law and Policy*, Vol. 43, No. 3 (2015); Charles Taylor, in *The Cambridge Companion to International Criminal Law*, pp. 312–332 (William A. Schabas ed., 2016).

Table of Authorities

Special Court for Sierra Leone

Prosecutor v. Brima, Case No. SCSL-03–06-PT-088, SCSL-03–06-PT-088-II, Decision and order on Prosecution motions for joinder, (Jan. 28, 2004).

Prosecutor v. Brima, Case No. SCSL-04–16-PT-006, Indictment, (Feb. 5, 2004).

Prosecutor v. Brima, Case No. SCSL-04–16-PT, Dissenting Opinion of Judge Bankole Thompson, Presiding Judge of the Trial Chamber on Prosecution's Motion for Leave to Amend Indictment Against Accused Alex Tamba Brima, Brima Bazzy Kamara and Santigie Borbor Kanu, (May 6, 2004).

Prosecutor v. Brima, Case No. SCSL-04–16-T, Prosecution Filing of Expert Report Pursuant to Rule 94(bis) and Decision on Prosecution Request for Leave to Call an Additional Expert Witness, (Aug. 8, 2005).

Prosecutor v. Brima, Case No. SCSL-2004–16-AR73, Decision on Brima-Kamara Defence Appeal Motion Against Trial Chamber II Majority Decision on Extremely Urgent Confidential Joint Motion for the Re-Appointment of Kevin Metzger and Wilbert Harris as Lead Counsel for Alex Tamba Brima and Brima Bazzy Kamara, (Dec. 8, 2005).

Prosecutor v. Brima, Case No. SCSL-04–16-T, Joint Legal Part Defense Motion for Judgment of Acquittal under Rule 98, (Dec. 13, 2005).

Prosecutor v. Brima, Case No. SCSL-04–16-T, Decision on Defense Motion for Judgment of Acquittal Pursuant to Rule 98, (Mar. 31, 2006).

Prosecutor v. Brima, Case No. SCSL-2004–16-T, Joint Defence Disclosure of Expert Report on Forced Marriages by Dr. Dorte Thorsen, (Aug. 21, 2006).

Prosecutor v. Brima, SCSL-04–16-T, Judgment, (June 20, 2007).

Prosecutor v. Brima, Case No. SCSL-2004–16-A, Separate Concurring Opinion of the Hon. Justice Sebutinde Appended to Judgement Pursuant to Rule 88(c), (June 20, 2007).

Mouvement Ivoirien des Droits Humains (MIDH) v. Cote d' Ivoire, Communication 246/02, [Afr. Comm'n H.P.R.], (July 29, 2008).

Zimbabwe Human Rights NGO Forum v. Zimbabwe, Communication 245/2002, [Afr. Comm'n H.P.R.], (May 15, 2006).

European Court of Human Rights

Abdülsamet Yaman v. Turkey, (No. 32446/96), Eur. Ct. H.R. 55 (2004).

Okkah v. Turkey, (No. 52067/99), Eur. Ct. H.R. 76 (2006).

Marguš v. Croatia, (No. 4455/10), Eur. Ct. H.R. 74 (2012).

Yesil & Sevim v. Turkey, (No. 34738/04), Eur. Ct. H.R. 38 (2007).

Extraordinary Chambers in the Courts of Cambodia

Prosecutor v. Duch, Case No. 001/18–07-2007/ECCC/TC, Judgment, (July 26, 2010).

Prosecutor v. Duch, Case No. 001/18–07-2007-ECCC/SC, Appeal Judgment, (Feb. 3, 2012).

Prosecutor v. Nuon, Case No. 002/19–09-2007-ECCC-OCIJ /No: D427, Closing Order, (Sept. 10, 2010).

Prosecutor v. Sary, Case No. 002/19–09-2007/ECCC/OCIJ (PTC75), Decision on Ieng Sary's Appeal against the Closing Order, (Apr. 11, 2011).

Prosecutor v. Sary, Case No. 002/19–09–2007/ECCC/TC, Decision on Ieng Sary's Rule 89 Preliminary Objections (Ne bis in idem and Amnesty and Pardon), (Nov. 3, 2011).

Inter-American Court of Human Rights

Almonacid Arellano v. Chile, Preliminary Objections, Merits, Reparations, and Costs, Judgment, Inter-Am. Ct. H.R. (ser. C) No. 154 (Sept. 26, 2006).

Barrios Altos v. Peru, Merits, Reparations, and Costs, Judgment, Inter-Am. Ct. H.R. (ser. C) No. 75 (Mar. 14, 2001).

Gelman v. Uruguay, Merits and Reparations, Judgment, Inter-Am. Ct. H.R. (ser. C) No. 221 (Feb. 24, 2011).

Gomes Lund ("Guerrilha Do Araguaia") v. Brazil, Preliminary Objections, Merits, Reparations, and Costs, Judgment, Inter-Am. Ct. H.R. (ser. C) No. 219 (Nov. 24, 2010).

Gomes Lund ("Guerrilha Do Araguaria") v. Brazil, Judgment, Inter-Am Ct. H.R. (ser. C) No. 219 (Nov. 29, 2010).

Massacres of El Mozote and Nearby Places v. El Salvador, Merits, Reparations, and Costs, Judgment, Inter-Am. Ct. H.R. (ser. C) No. 252 (Oct. 25, 2012).

International Criminal Court

Table of Authorities

International Criminal Tribunal for Rwanda

International Criminal Tribunal for the former Yugoslavia

Prosecutor v. Luckic, Case No. IT-98–32/1-PT, Decision on the Referral of Case Pursuant to Rule 11 bis with Confidential Annex A and Annex B, (Int'l Crim. Trib. for the Former Yugoslavia Apr. 5, 2007).

Prosecutor v. Milošević, Case No. IT-99–37, Decision on Review of the Indictment and Application for Consequential Orders, (Int'l Crim. Trib. for the Former Yugoslavia May 24, 1999).

Prosecutor v. Tadic, Case No. IT-94–1-T, Decision on Prosecutor's Motion Requesting Protective Measures for Victims and Witnesses, (Int'l Crim. Trib. for the Former Yugoslavia Aug. 10, 1995).

Prosecutor v. Tadić, Case No. IT-94–1-AR72, Judgment, (Int'l Crim. Trib. for the Former Yugoslavia July 15, 1999).

Prosecutor v. Todović, Case No. IT-97–25/1-AR11bis.1, Decision on Savo Todović's Appeal Against Decision on Referral under Rule 11 bis, (Int'l Crim. Trib. for the Former Yugoslavia Sept. 4, 2006).

International Court of Justice

Armed Activities on the Territory of the Congo (New Application: 2002) (Dem. Rep. Congo v. Rwanda), Jurisdiction and Admissibility, Judgment, 2006 I.C.J. Rep. 6 (Feb. 3).

Arrest Warrant of 11 April 2000 (Dem. Rep. Congo v. Belg.), Judgment, 2002 I.C.J. Rep. 3 (Feb. 14).

Barcelona Traction, Light and Power Company, Limited (Belg. v. Spain), Judgment, 1970 I.C.J. Rep. 3 (Feb. 5).

Certain Questions of Mutual Assistance in Criminal Matters, (Djib. v. Fr.) Judgment, 2008 I.C.J. Rep. 177 (June 4).

Interpretation of the Agreement of Mar. 25, 1951 between the WHO and Egypt, Advisory Opinion, 1980 I.C.J. Rep. 80 (May 28).

Jurisdictional Immunities of the State (Ger. v. It., Greece Intervening), Judgment, 2012 ICJ Rep. 95 (Feb. 3).

Legality of the Use by a State of Nuclear Weapons in Armed Conflict, Advisory Opinion, 1996 I.C.J. Rep. 78 (July 8).

Reparation for Injuries Suffered in the Service of the United Nations, Advisory Opinion, 1949 I.C.J. Rep. 174 (Apr. 11).

Questions relating to the Obligation to Prosecute or Extradite (Belg. v. Sen.), Judgment, 2012 I.C.J. Rep. 422 (July 20).

The International Military Tribunals

International Military Tribunal, Indictment, app. A, reprinted in 1 Trial of the Major War Criminals Before the International Military Tribunal (1945).

Nuremberg Trials Final Report (Dec. 20, 1945), http://avalon.law.yale.edu/imt/imt10.asp.

United States v. Pohl, Indictment of the International Military Tribunal, Trials of the War Criminals Before the Nuremberg Military Tribunals Under Control Council Law No. 10, vol. 5 (Jan. 13, 1947).

United States v. Araki, Indictment of the International Military Tribunal for the Far East, app. E (1946), reprinted in Documents on the Tokyo International Military Tribunal: Charter, Indictment, and Judgments (Neil Boister & Robert Cryer eds., 2008).

International Instruments

Additional Protocol I to the Geneva Conventions of Aug. 12, 1949 Relating to the Protection of Victims of International Armed Conflicts, June 8, 1977, 1125 U.N.T. S. 3.

Additional Protocol II to the Geneva Conventions of Aug. 12, 1949 Relating to the Protection of Victims of Non-International Armed Conflicts, June 8, 1977, 1125 U. N.T.S. 609.

Agreement for the Prosecution and Punishment of the Major War Criminals of the European Axis, Aug. 8, 1945, 59 Stat. 1586, 82 U.N.T.C. 279.

Agreement between the United Nations and the Government of Sierra Leone on the Establishment of a Special Court for Sierra Leone, Jan. 16, 2002, 2178 U.N.T. S. 138.

Agreement Between the United Nations and the Royal Government of Cambodia Concerning the Prosecution Under Cambodian Law of Crimes Committed During the Period of Democratic Kampuchea, June 6, 2003, 2329 U.N.T.S. 117.

Charter of the International Military Tribunal, Aug. 8, 1945, 59 Stat. 1544, 82 U.N.T. S. 279.

Charter of the International Military Tribunal for the Far East, Jan. 19, 1946, T.I.A.S. No. 1589.

Convention on Consent to Marriage, Minimum Age of Marriage and Registration of Marriages, Nov. 7, 1962, 521 U.N.T.S. 231.

Convention on the Elimination of All Forms of Discrimination against Women, Dec. 18, 1979, 1249 U.N.T.S. 13.

Convention on Non-Applicability of Statutory Limitations to War Crimes and Crimes Against Humanity, Nov. 11, 1970, 754 U.N.T.S. 73.

Convention on the Rights of the Child, Nov. 20, 1989, 1577 U.N.T.S. 3.

Geneva Convention for the Amelioration of the condition of the wounded, sick and shipwrecked members of the armed forces at sea, Dec. 8, 1949, 75 U.N.T.S. 85.

Geneva Convention for the Amelioration of the Condition of the Wounded and Sick in Armed Forces in the Field, Dec. 8, 1949, 75 U.N.T.S. 31.

Geneva Convention Relative to the Treatment of Prisoners of War, Dec. 8, 1949 75 U.N.T.S. 135.

Geneva Convention Relative to the Protection of Civilian Persons in Time of War art. 147, Dec. 8, 1949, 75 U.N.T.S. 287.

International Covenant on Civil and Political Rights, Dec. 16, 1966, 999 U.N.T.S 171.

International Covenant on Economic, Social and Cultural Rights, Dec. 16, 1996, 993 U.N.T.S. 3.

International Military Tribunal for the Far East Special Proclamation: Establishment of an International Military Tribunal for the Far East, Jan. 10, 1946, T.I.A.S. No. 1589.

International Convention against the Taking of Hostages, Dec. 17, 1979 1316 U.N.T.S 205.

Rome Statute of the International Criminal Court, July 17, 1998, 2187 U.N.T.S. 3.

Statute of the International Court of Justice, June 26, 1945, 59 Stat. 1031, 33 U.N.T.S. 993.

Vienna Convention on the Law of Treaties, May 23, 1969, 1155 U.N.T.S. 331.

Declarations, draft articles, resolutions, conclusions and recommendations

Draft Articles on the Responsibility of International Organizations with Commentaries, U.N. Doc. A/66/10 reprinted in [2011] 2 Y.B. Int'l L. Comm'n 88, U.N. Doc. A/CN.4/SER.A/2011/Add.1.

Principles of International Law Recognized in the Charter of the Nurnberg Tribunal and in the Judgment of the Tribunal, U.N. Doc. A/CN.4/22, reprinted in [1950] 2 Y.B. Int'l L. Comm'n 181, U.N. Doc. A/CN.4/SER.A/1950/Add.1.

United Nations Resolutions

G.A. Res. 217 (II) A (Dec. 10, 1948).
G.A. Res. 95(I) (Dec. 11, 1946).
G.A. Res. 177(II) (Nov. 21, 1947).
G.A. Res. 57/228 (May 13, 2003).
G.A. Res. 60/1 (Sept. 16, 2005).
G.A. Res. 52/164 (Oct. 24, 2005).
S.C. Res. 808 (Feb. 22, 1993).
S.C. Res. 827 (May 25, 1993).
S.C. Res. 955 (Nov. 8, 1994).
S.C. Res. 1260 (Aug. 20, 1999).
S.C. Res. 1315 (Aug. 14, 2000).
S.C. Res. 1343 (Mar. 7, 2001).
S.C. Res. 1503 (Aug. 28, 2003).
S.C. Res. 1534 (Mar. 26, 2004).

S.C. Res. 1593 (Mar. 31, 2005).

S.C. Res. 1664 (Mar. 29, 2006).

S.C. Res. 1757 (May 30, 2007).

S.C. Res. 1820 (June 19, 2008).

S.C. Res. 1966 (Dec. 22, 2010).

S.C. Res. 1970 (Feb. 26, 2011).

International Tribunal for the Former Yugoslavia Rules of Procedure and Evidence, U.N. Doc. IT/32/Rev. 45 (Dec. 8, 2010).

International Tribunal for Rwanda Rules of Procedure and Evidence, U.N. Doc. ITR/3/REV.1 (June 29, 1995).

Special Court for Sierra Leone Rules of Procedure and Evidence (Mar. 7, 2003), http://hrlibrary.umn.edu//instree/SCSL/Rules-of-proced-SCSL.pdf.

Domestic Legislation, Agreements, and Jurisprudence

Cambodia

Law on the Establishment of the Extraordinary Chambers in the Courts of Cambodia for the Prosecution of Crimes Committed during the Period of Democratic Kampuchea, (NS/RKM/1004/006), Oct. 27, 2004.

Kenya

Special Tribunal for Kenya Bill (2009) (Kenya).

Sierra Leone

Conakry Peace Plan, U.N. Doc. S/1997/824 (Oct. 23, 1997).

Christian Marriage Act 1907 (Sierra Leone).

Civil Marriage Act (Sierra Leone).

Lomé Peace Agreement between the Government of the Republic of Sierra Leone and the Revolutionary United Front of Sierra Leone, U.N. Doc. S/1999/777 (July 7, 1999).

Peace Agreement between the Government of the Republic of Sierra Leone and the Revolutionary United Front of Sierra Leone, U.N. Doc. S/1996/1034 (Nov. 30, 1996).

The Child Rights Act 2007 (Sierra Leone).

The Mohammedian Marriage Act 1960 (Sierra Leone).

The Customary Marriage and Divorce Act 2009 (Sierra Leone).

National Unity and Reconciliation Commission Act 1996 (Sierra Leone).

Special Court Agreement 2002 Ratification Act (Sierra Leone).

Truth and Reconciliation Commission Act, Supplement to the Sierra Leone Gazette Vol. CXXXI, No. 9, (Feb. 10, 2000) (Sierra Leone).

South Africa

The Minister of Justice and Constitutional Development v. The Southern African Litigation Center 2016, (17) SA (CC) at 3 ¶¶ 66–75 (S. Afr.).

United Kingdom

Grey v. Pearson, [1857] 6 HLC 61, 106 (Eng.).
R v. Bow Street Metropolitan Stipendary Magistrate, ex parte Pinochet Ugarte (No. 2) 1999 1 All ER 577 HL and (No. 3) 1999 2 All ER 97 (Eng.).

United States of America

Knote v. U.S., 95 U.S. 149 (1877).

Reports of International and Non-Governmental Organizations and Special Envoys

Analysis and Policy Considerations of the Government of Sierra Leone for the Special Court Planning Mission (2002).

Cassese, Antonio, Report on the Special Court for Sierra Leone (Dec. 12, 2006).

Child Soldiers Int'l, Child Soldiers Global Report 2004 – Sierra Leone (2004).

Compilation of General Comments and General Recommendations adopted by Human Rights Treaty Bodies, U.N. Doc. HRI\GEN\1\Rev. 1 (1994).

Concepcion Escobar Hernandez (Special Rapporteur on the Immunity of State officials from foreign criminal jurisdiction), Second Rep. on the Immunity of State Officials from foreign criminal jurisdiction, U.N. Doc. A/CN.4/661 (Apr. 4, 2013).

Commission on the Responsibility of the Authors of the War and on Enforcement of Penalties, Report Presented to the Preliminary Peace Conference, 14 Am. J. Int'l L. 95 (1920).

David Pratt M.P, Nepean-Carleton (Special Envoy to Sierra Leone), Sierra Leone: The Forgotten Crisis Rep. to the Minister of Foreign Affairs, the Honourable Lloyd Axworthy, P.C. (Apr. 23, 1999).

Econ. & Soc. Council, Rep. of the High Commissioner for Human Rights pursuant to Commission on Human Rights Resolution 2001/20: Situation of human rights in Sierra Leone, U.N. Doc. E/CN.4/2002/3 (Feb. 18, 2002).

Geoffrey Robertson (President of the Special Court for Sierra Leone), First Annual Report of the President of the Special Court for Sierra Leone, (Dec. 2, 2002 to Dec. 1, 2003), www.rscsl.org/Documents/AnRpt1.pdf.

Global Witness, Timber, Taylor, Soldier, Spy: How Liberia's Uncontrolled Resource Exploitation, Charles Taylor's Manipulation and the Re-recruitment of Ex-combatants are Threatening Regional Peace (2005).

Human Rights Watch, Press Release, Chad Lifts Immunity of Ex-Dictator: Green Light to Prosecute Hissène Habré in Belgium (Dec. 5, 2002), www.hrw.org/news/2002/12/05/chad-lifts-immunity-ex-dictator.

Human Rights Watch, Sierra Leone: Getting Away with Murder, Mutilation, Rape, Vol. 11, No. 3(A) (July 1999).

Human Rights Watch, Sowing Terror: Atrocities Against Civilians in Sierra Leone, Vol. 10, No. 3(A) (July 1998).

Human Rights Watch, The Interrelationship Between the Sierra Leone Special Court and Truth and Reconciliation Commission (Apr. 2002).

Human Rights Watch, "We'll Kill You If You Cry" Sexual Violence in the Sierra Leone Conflict, Vol. 15, No. 1 (A) (Jan. 2003).

International Criminal Court, Paper on Some Policy Issues Before the Office of the Prosecutor (Sept. 2003), www.icc-cpi.int/nr/rdonlyres/1fa7c4c6-de5 f-42b7-8b25-60aa962ed8b6/143594/030905_policy_paper.pdf.

International Committee of the Red Cross, Convention (IV) relative to the Protection of Civilian Persons in Time of War: Commentary of 1958 (Aug. 12, 1949).

Int'l Law Comm'n, Rep on the Work of its Fifty-First Session, U.N. Doc. A/54/10 (2011).

Permanent Rep. of Sierra Leone to the U.N., Letter dated Aug. 9, 2000 from Permanent Rep. of Sierra Leone to the United Nations addressed to the President of the Security Council, U.N. Doc. S/2000/786 (Aug. 10, 2000).

Memorandum to President Roosevelt from the Secretaries of State and War and Attorney General (Jan. 22, 1945) (on file with Yale Law School).

Michael Wood (Special Rapporteur on the Identification of Customary International Law), Second Rep. on the Identification of Customary International Law, U.N. Doc. A/CN.4/672 (May 22, 2014).

Ministry of Finance and Economic Development, Adaptation of the Goals in Sierra Leone Progress Report, (2016), https://sustainabledevelopment.un.org/content/documents/10720sierraleone.pdf.

National Electoral Commission, Statement from NEC Chairperson on the Conduct and Result of the Presidential Elections, (Dec. 4, 2012), www.nec-sierraleone.org/index_files/STATEMENT%20%20FROM%20NEC%20CHAIRPERSON%220 (press%20district).pdf.

Off. of the Att'y Gen.& Ministry of Just. Special Ct. Task Force, Briefing Paper on the Relationship Between the Special Court and the Truth and Reconciliation Commission, Legal Analysis and Policy Considerations of the Government of Sierra Leone for the Special Court Planning Mission (2002).

Off. of the Prosecutor, Report on Prosecutorial Strategy (Sept. 14, 2006).

Off. of the Prosecutor, Prosecutorial Strategy 2009–2012 (Feb. 1, 2010).

Physicians for Human Rights, War-Related Sexual Violence in Sierra Leone (2002).

President of the S.C., Letter dated 21 November 2006 from the President of the Security Council addressed to the Secretary-General, U.N. Doc. S/2006/911 (Nov. 24, 2006).

Permanent Rep. of Ghana to the U.N., Letter dated June 18, 2003 from the Permanent Rep. of Ghana to the U.N. addressed to the President of the Security Council, U.N. Doc. S/2003/657 (June 18, 2003).

Permanent Rep. of Sierra Leone to the U.N., Letter dated 9 August 2000 from the Permanent Representative of Sierra Leone to the United Nations addressed to the President of the Security Council, U.N. Doc. S/2000/786 (Aug. 10, 2000).

Post Conflict Reintegration Initiative for Development and Empowerment (PRIDE), Ex-Combatant Views of the Truth and Reconciliation Commission and the Special Court for Sierra Leone (Sept. 12, 2002).

President of the S.C., Letter dated Dec. 22, 2000 from the President of the Security Council addressed to the Secretary-General, U.N. Doc. S/2000/1234 (Dec. 22, 2000).

President of the S.C., Letter dated Jan. 31, 2001 from the President of the Security Council to the Secretary-General, U.N. Doc. S/2001/95 (Jan. 31, 2001).

Registrar of the Special Court for Sierra Leone, Practice Direction on the procedure following a request by a State, the Truth and Reconciliation Commission, or other legitimate authority to take a statement from a person in the custody of the Special Court for Sierra Leone, (Sept. 9, 2003) (amended Oct. 4, 2003).

Rep. of the Assembly of States Parties to the Rome Statute of the ICC, pt. II Elements of Crimes, ICC-ASP/1/3 (Sept. 2002).

Report of the Panel of Experts Appointed Pursuant to Security Council Resolution 1306, Paragraph 19, in Relation to Sierra Leone, U.N. Doc. S/2000/1195 (Dec. 20, 2000).

Sierra Leone Truth and Reconciliation Comm'n, Children and the Armed Conflict in Sierra Leone, in Witness to Truth: Final Report of the TRC (2004).

Sierra Leone Truth & Reconciliation Report, Witness to Truth: Report of the Sierra Leone Truth & Reconciliation Commission (2004).

U.N. Diplomatic Conference of Plenipotentiaries on the Establishment of an International Criminal Court, Rome Statute of the International Criminal Court, U.N. Doc. A/CONF.183/9 (July 17, 1998).

U.N.D.P., Evaluation of UNDP Assistance to Conflict Affected Countries-Human Security: Case Study Sierra Leone, U.N. Development Program Evaluations Office (2006).

U.N.D.P., Human Development Reports: Sierra Leone, http://hdr.undp.org/en/countries/profiles/SLE.

U.N. Secretary-General, Report of the Secretary-General Pursuant to Paragraph 2 of Security Council Resolution 808, U.N. Doc. S/25704 (May 3, 1993).

U.N. Secretary General, Report of the Secretary-General on the Establishment of a Special Court for Sierra Leone, U.N. Doc. S/2000/915 (Oct. 4, 2000).

U.N. Secretary-General, The Rule of Law and Transitional Justice in Conflict and Post Conflict Societies, U.N. Doc. S/2004/616 (Aug. 23, 2004).

U.N. Secretary General, United Nations Approach to Transitional Justice: Guidance Note of the Secretary-General (Mar. 2010), www.un.org/ruleoflaw/files/TJ_Guidance_Note_March_2010FINAL.pdf.

U.N. Sustainable Development Goals, The 2030 Agenda for Sustainable Development: Advanced Draft Report on Adaptation of the Goals in Sierra Leone (July 2016). https://sustainabledevelopment.un.org/content/documents/10720sierraleone.pdf.

World Peace Foundation, Mass Atrocity Endings, Sierra Leone (2015).

Abbreviations

ACHPR	African Charter on Human and People's Rights
AFRC	Armed Forces Revolutionary Council
APC	All People's Congress Party (Sierra Leone)
ASP	Assembly of States Parties of the International Criminal Court
AU	African Union (formerly Organization of African Unity – OAU)
CCP	Commission for the Consolidation of Peace
CDF	Civil Defense Forces
CEDAW	Convention on the Elimination of All Forms of Discrimination Against Women
CRC	Convention on the Rights of the Child
CSOs	Civil Society Organizations
DAC	Directive on the Assignment of Counsel
ECCC	Extraordinary Chambers in the Courts of Cambodia
ECHR	European Convention on Human Rights
ECOMOG	Economic Community of West African States Monitoring Group
ECOWAS	Economic Community of West African States
EIDHR	European Instrument for Democracy and Human Rights
EU	European Union
FoSL	Friends of Sierra Leone
FRY	Federal Republic of Yugoslavia
GNU	Government of National Unity
GoSL	Government of Sierra Leone
HRW	Human Rights Watch
ICC	International Criminal Court
ICC&Ts	International Criminal Courts and Tribunals
ICG	International Crisis Group
ICJ	International Court of Justice
ICCPR	International Covenant on Civil and Political Rights
ICRC	International Committee of the Red Cross

ICTR	International Criminal Tribunal for Rwanda
ICTY	International Criminal Tribunal for the former Yugoslavia
IHL	International Humanitarian Law
IMT	International Military Tribunal at Nuremberg
IMTFE	International Military Tribunal for the Far East
IOs	International Organizations
JCE	Joint Criminal Enterprise
LSC	Legal Services Contract
MICT	Mechanism for International Criminal Tribunals
NATO	North Atlantic Treaty Organization
NCDDR	National Commission for Disarmament, Demobilization and Reintegration
NCDHR	National Commission for Democracy and Human Rights
NGOs	Non-Governmental Organizations
NPFL	National Patriotic Front of Liberia
NPRC	National Provisional Ruling Council
NPWJ	No Peace Without Justice
NURC	National Unity and Reconciliation Commission
OAU	Organization of African Unity (later became the African Union)
OHCHR	Office of the High Commissioner for Human Rights (UN)
OPD	Office of the Principal Defender or Defense Office
OSIWA	Open Society Initiative for West Africa
OTP	Office of the Prosecutor
POW	Prisoner of War
RPE	Rules of Procedure and Evidence
RSCSL	Residual Special Court for Sierra Leone
RSLMF	Republic of Sierra Leone Military Forces
RUF	Revolutionary United Front
RUF/SL	Revolutionary United Front of Sierra Leone
RUFP	Revolutionary United Front Party
Rules	Rules of Procedure and Evidence
SCSL	Special Court for Sierra Leone
SCWG	Special Court Working Group
SL	Sierra Leone
SLA	Sierra Leone Army
SLPP	Sierra Leone People's Party
STL	Special Tribunal for Lebanon
TRC	Truth and Reconciliation Commission of Sierra Leone
UDHR	Universal Declaration of Human Rights
UK	United Kingdom
ULAA	Union of Liberian Associations in the Americas
UN	United Nations

UNAMIR	United Nations Assistance Mission for Rwanda
UNAMSIL	United Nations Assistance Mission in Sierra Leone
UNGA	United Nations General Assembly
UNICEF	United Nations Children's Fund
UNIOSIL	United Nations Integrated Office in Sierra Leone
UNMIL	United Nations Mission in Liberia
UNOMSIL	United Nations Observer Mission in Sierra Leone
UNSC	United Nations Security Council
UNSG	United Nations Secretary-General
US	United States of America
VCLT	Vienna Convention on the Law of Treaties
WVSS	Witness and Victims Support Section

Introduction

1.1 INTRODUCTION

On January 16, 2002, the United Nations (UN) and the Government of Sierra Leone (Sierra Leone/the GoSL) signed a historic agreement establishing the Special Court for Sierra Leone (SCSL, the Court, the Tribunal).[1] The SCSL, authorized by UN Security Council ("UNSC") Resolution 1315 (2000),[2] was mandated under Article 1 of its Statute to try those persons bearing "greatest responsibility"[3] for crimes against humanity, war crimes, and other serious violations of international humanitarian law committed in the West African nation during the latter half of a decade-long conflict involving at least four armed factions.[4] The SCSL, whose legal legacy and contributions to the development of the emerging field of international criminal law is the subject of this book, was also empowered to bring to justice those who masterminded violations of Sierra Leonean law relating to the abuse of underage girls, the wanton destruction of property and arson during what has been described as one of "the worst in the history of civil conflicts."[5] Tribunal prosecutors were directed to prioritize the investigation and prosecution of those leaders who had, in

---

[1] Agreement between the United Nations and the Government of Sierra Leone on the Establishment of a Special Court for Sierra Leone, UN-Sierra Leone, Jan. 16, 2002, 2178 U.N.T.S. 137 [hereinafter UN-Sierra Leone Agreement]. Annexed to the UN-Sierra Leone Agreement was the Statute of the Special Court for Sierra Leone, *id.* at 145 [hereinafter SCSL Statute]. Both can be found in Consolidated Legal Texts for the Special Court for Sierra Leone at 7, 19 (Charles C. Jalloh ed., 2007). For convenience, all three instruments have also been annexed to this book.

[2] S.C. Res. 1315 (Aug. 14, 2000). See Consolidated Legal Texts, *supra* note 1, at 3.

[3] SCSL Statute, *supra* note 1, at art. 1(1).

[4] Because the Sierra Leone conflict had not ended when the parties were negotiating the establishment of the SCSL, the expiry date for the temporal jurisdiction was left open-ended. Sierra Leone officially declared the war over on January 18, 2002. Thus, that date informally represents the cut-off point of the Court's jurisdiction. For a detailed discussion of the Court's various jurisdictions, *see infra,* at Chapter 4.

[5] *See* Permanent Rep. of Sierra Leone to the U.N., *Letter dated Aug. 9, 2000 from Permanent Representative of Sierra Leone to the United Nations addressed to the President of the Security Council,* annex, U.N. Doc. S/2000/786 (Aug. 9, 2000).

the course of carrying out the heinous crimes, threatened the establishment and implementation of the peace process in Sierra Leone.

Regrettably, though grave international crimes were documented by human rights groups from the start of the conflict on March 23, 1991, the temporal jurisdiction[6] of the SCSL was limited – apparently because of concerns about funding and overburdening the time-limited Court with cases – to the offenses committed in Sierra Leone after November 30, 1996.[7] The hostilities were ongoing at the time the Tribunal was created. Therefore, it made sense for the UN and the GoSL to leave open the formal end date of the temporal jurisdiction. The hope was that this would help bolster the fragile peace accord, stem the perpetration of atrocity crimes, and deter further violence. In the end, although there were a few dramatic Revolutionary United Front (RUF) rebel violations of the ceasefire which had been signed at Lomé, Togo in July 1999 with the view to ending the conflict, the government could declare the war over on January 18, 2002. The latter date thereby effectively serves as the end point for the Tribunal's temporal jurisdiction. This implied, to the concern of many Sierra Leoneans, that the SCSL would prosecute only the crimes committed in the last six years of a brutal eleven-year war.

The creation of the SCSL, which successfully prosecuted and convicted nine individuals[8] notably including former Liberian President Charles Taylor (who is currently serving a fifty-year sentence in Great Britain), was one of the most important institutional developments in international criminal law since the adoption on July 1, 1998 of the Rome Statute of the International Criminal Court (Rome Statute) and its entry into force on July 1, 2002.[9] This importance arguably derived from the SCSL's status as the first independent and consensual treaty-based international criminal tribunal with a mixed *ratione materiae* jurisdiction and composition. Indeed, while so-called "hybrid"[10] courts were set up by the UN in East Timor, Kosovo, Bosnia and Cambodia at the request of those countries, those tribunals were grafted on to the institutions and structures of those countries' legal systems. They therefore formed an integral part of their domestic legal orders. Conversely, although it exhibits some

---

[6] See U.N. Secretary-General, *Report of the Secretary-General on the Establishment of a Special Court for Sierra Leone*, ¶22–27, U.N. Docs. S/2000/915 (Oct. 4, 2000) [hereinafter Report on SCSL Establishment].

[7] See *id.* at ¶27.

[8] Besides the Taylor case, as further discussed *infra* at Chapter 3, there were three joint trials comprised of three indictees each. The nine accused are former members of the main warring parties: The Revolutionary United Front (Issa Sesay, Morris Kallon, Augustine Gbao), the Armed Forces Revolutionary Council (Alex Brima, Santigie Kanu, Ibrahim Kamara) and the Civil Defence Forces (Samuel Norman, Moinina Fofana, Allieu Kondewa). The indictment of Johnny Paul Koroma still stands though he is not, as of writing, in the custody of the SCSL. The Court closed down in December 2013. Provision was made, should he surface, for the case to be tried in the Residual Special Court for Sierra Leone. The indictments of Foday Sankoh and Sam Bockarie were withdrawn following their confirmed deaths. For further discussion of the trials and indictments, see *infra* Chapter 4.

[9] Rome Statute of the International Criminal Court, July 17, 1998, 2187 U.N.T.S. 3.

[10] See Laura Dickinson, *The Promise of Hybrid Courts*, 97 AM. J. INT'L. 297 (2003).

Sierra Leonean features in relation to its mixed material jurisdiction and staff composition, the SCSL operated independently of its mother and father (that is the GoSL and the UN). This is because it possessed the distinct legal personality of an international organization, which permitted it to operate in the sphere of international law.[11]

Significantly, only six decades after the establishment of the International Military Tribunals at Nuremberg[12] (IMT) and for the Far East (IMTFE),[13] the SCSL was widely heralded, in retrospect prematurely, as a "more cost effective"[14] and "more efficient model"[15] of the ad hoc international criminal court. Some even expected that its type and focused mandate would play a central role in future attempts to prosecute perpetrators of mass atrocities in situations where, for whatever reason, the sole use of pure domestic or pure international judicial mechanisms is deemed inadequate, ineffective or both.[16] Indeed, the establishment of what the UNSG described as a *"sui generis"*[17] court with a mixed jurisdiction *ratione materiae* and

---

[11] An international organization, of course, is an entity "established by a treaty or other instrument governed by international law and possessing its own international legal personality." The SCSL, like the Special Tribunal for Lebanon, fits into this definition since it was an entity created, on the one part, by a State (i.e. Sierra Leone), and on the other, an international organization (the UN). It is therefore a subject of international law. Of course, the classical example of an international organization with legal personality under international law is the United Nations itself. *See* Reparation for Injuries Suffered in the Service of the United Nations, Advisory Opinion, 1949 I.C.J. Rep. 174, 179 (Apr. 11). The Appeals Chamber of the SCSL has confirmed, in several decisions, that the Tribunal exists in and functions solely in the sphere of international law rather than the municipal law of Sierra Leone. *See* Prosecutor v. Kallon, Case No. SCSL-2004–14-PT, SCSL-2004–15-PT, SCSL-2004–16-PT, Decision on Constitutionality and Lack of Jurisdiction, ¶ 80 (Mar. 13, 2004); Prosecutor v. Kondewa, SCSL-2004–14-AR72(E), Decision on Preliminary Motion on Lack of Jurisdiction: Establishment of Special Court Violates Constitution of Sierra Leone, ¶ 2 (May 25, 2004) (holding that "the Special Court acts only in an international sphere."). We need not, for our limited purposes here, dwell on the debate about how an international organization acquires international legal personality. It suffices to note that the ICJ's *obiter dicta* to date have not established any stringent requirements, preferring instead an open and liberal approach to the question. *See*, in this regard, Interpretation of the Agreement of Mar. 25, 1951 between the WHO and Egypt, Advisory Opinion, 1980 I.C.J. REP. 89–90, ¶37 (May 28); Legality of the Use by a State of Nuclear Weapons in Armed Conflict, Advisory Opinion, 1996 I.C.J. REP. 78 ¶25 (July 8). *See Draft Articles on the Responsibility of International Organizations with Commentaries*, U.N. Doc. A/66/10 *reprinted in* [2011] 2 Y.B. INT'L L. COMM'N 88, U.N. Doc. A/CN.4/SER.A/2011/Add.1.

[12] After World War II, the allies set up a tribunal to try former senior Nazi officials. *See* Agreement for the Prosecution and Punishment of the Major War Criminals of the European Axis, Aug. 8, 1945, 59 Stat. 1586, 82 U.N.T.C. 279.

[13] Charter of the International Military Tribunal for the Far East, (Jan. 19, 1946, as amended, Apr. 26, 1946) T.I.A.S. 1585.

[14] *See* Antonio Cassese, *Report on the Special Court for Sierra Leone* (Dec. 12, 2006).

[15] *Id.*

[16] For example, as Cassese suggested, the mixed SCSL model could be particularly useful wherever the national judicial system is weak or has collapsed or is unable to dispense justice because of civil strife or ethnic and religious hatred. *See* Antonio Cassese, *The Role of Internationalized Courts and Tribunals in the Fight Against International Criminality, in* INTERNATIONALIZED CRIMINAL COURTS: SIERRA LEONE, EAST TIMOR, KOSOVO, AND CAMBODIA at 10 (Cesare Romano et al. eds., 2004).

[17] U.N. Secretary-General, *Report of the Secretary-General on the establishment of a Special Court for Sierra Leone*, ¶ 9, U.N. Doc. S/2000/915 (Oct. 4, 2000).

composition by the UN and Sierra Leone appeared to be a significant development in the trend towards ascribing criminal liability to perpetrators of crimes that scar the conscience of people throughout the world. Alongside the increased reliance on universal jurisdiction to investigate international crimes, which initially gained momentum in the early 1990s in countries such as Belgium, France and Spain but declined as of the 2000s, the SCSL was perceived as yet another step in the inevitable forward march against impunity for atrocity crimes. That movement had begun in the immediate aftermath of World War I when the victorious allies established a Commission on the Responsibility of the Authors of the War at the Paris Peace Conference and included in the subsequent Treaty of Versailles of June 1919 several provisions mandating the establishment of an Allied High Tribunal that would, among other things, try Kaiser Wilhelm II.[18] It became significantly reinforced by the successful completion of the unprecedented Nuremberg and Tokyo trials in the immediate aftermath of World War II.

But the SCSL may also have been part of a new cosmopolitanism premised on liberal notions of "international community."[19] That globalist attitude emphasized a common humanity and fidelity to principles of individual criminal responsibility for international crimes that was resuscitated with the UNSC's fateful decision to establish the International Criminal Tribunals for the former Yugoslavia and Rwanda (ICTY and ICTR) in 1993 to punish "ethnic cleansing" in the Balkans and the shocking genocide in Rwanda in 1994. From this perspective, the SCSL represented a new breed or a "second generation"[20] of the ad hoc international court, and importantly, preceded the formal establishment of the permanent International Criminal Court (ICC). Today, as of this writing, the world criminal court sits in The Hague and enjoys the support of 123 States Parties.[21] However, taking a historic view, the establishment of the SCSL might best exemplify the slow evolution of an international rule of law. That notion would insist on directly

---

[18]   See Commission on the Responsibility of the Authors of the War and on Enforcement of Penalties, "Report Presented to the Preliminary Peace Conference, 29 March 1919," *reprinted in* AM. J. OF INT'L LAW (1920) vol. 14, nos. 1/2, pp. 95–1. For a seminal work on the trial that never was, *see* THE TRIAL OF THE KAISER (William Schabas, 2018).

[19]   For an excellent discussion on the wide use of the phrase in international instruments and discourse and its various meanings, *see* Edward Kwakwa, *The International Community, International Law and the United States: Three in One, Two against One, or One and the Same*, *in* UNITED STATES HEGEMONY AND THE FOUNDATIONS OF INTERNATIONAL LAW 25 (Michael Byers & Georg Nolte eds., 2008).

[20]   Daphna Shraga, *The Second Generation UN-Based Tribunals: A Diversity of Mixed Jurisdictions*, *in* INTERNATIONALIZED CRIMINAL COURTS, *supra* note 16.

[21]   *See generally* U.N. Diplomatic Conference of Plenipotentiaries on the Establishment of an International Criminal Court, *Rome Statute of the International Criminal Court*, U.N. Doc. A/CONF. 183/9 (June 15–July 17, 1998). For a discussion of the initial enthusiasm of African States for the International Criminal Court, which appears to be waning and eventually led to the withdrawal of Burundi from the ICC Statute, *see* THE INTERNATIONAL CRIMINAL COURT AND AFRICA (Charles C. Jalloh & Ilias Bantekas eds., 2017). For an early warning of the potential for the ICC and Africa to clash, *see* Charles C. Jalloh, *Regionalizing International Criminal Law?*, 9 INT'L. CRIM. L. REV. 445 (2009).

imposing responsibility on individual perpetrators of atrocities. It first reached its watershed at Nuremberg in 1946, but at the same time, now seeks to account for the wider context of what Harmen van der Wilt and André Nollkaemper have described as the "system criminality"[22] which makes the commission of such crimes possible.

That said, the SCSL can also be understood as the product of a political compromise. On the one hand, it was an ambitious project of a war-weary African country that sought international assistance to break with a past full of governance, accountability and nation-building demons, all ills which seemed to have been exacerbated by a brutal fratricidal war. On the other hand, a UN reeling from David Scheffer's infamously described "tribunal fatigue"[23] and the disillusionment that quickly beset the UN when it became increasingly clear that the post–Cold War honeymoon in the Security Council could no longer be taken for granted to bankroll another full-fledged international criminal tribunal that would become a subsidiary organ and financial responsibility for the UN's wealthier Member States. Thus, with a carefully calibrated mandate to deliver a limited quantity of donations-supported justice for the widespread atrocities Sierra Leoneans experienced during the war, the Court was expected to address – and perhaps even help to remedy – some of the perceived inadequacies of the ICTY and ICTR model. It is a model that was supposed to reflect the lessons learned from the experiences of the first modern ad hoc international criminal tribunals. For these and related reasons, the SCSL contained many novel features that reflected the general malaise with Chapter VII courts with respect to the pace, cost and efficiency of their investigations and trials. It also sought to account for some of the particularly problematic features of the dirty war that nearly destroyed Sierra Leone.

The Court's founding instruments contained several innovations. Among other things, the SCSL was: (1) the first independent international penal tribunal to be endowed with a limited personal jurisdiction over a narrow class of persons "bearing greatest responsibility" for serious international/national crimes; (2) the first modern ad hoc court to sit in the *locus commissi delecti* – the place where the crimes were committed; (3) the first to be funded entirely through donations from UN Member States; (4) the first to be overseen by an independent management committee comprised of non-party states that would provide policy oversight and assist the Tribunal on non-judicial aspects of its operations; (5) the first to provide scope for the government of the affected state (that is Sierra Leone) to appoint a minority of its principal officials including judges and the deputy prosecutor; and (6) significantly for transitional justice debates on whether truth commissions and criminal courts

---

[22] *See* Andre Nollkaemper et al., *Preface, in* SYSTEM CRIMINALITY IN INTERNATIONAL LAW vii (Harmen van der Wilt & André Nollkaemper, eds., 2009) (defining "system criminality" as "situations where collective entities such as states or organised armed groups order or encourage international crimes to be committed, or permit or tolerate the committing of international crimes").

[23] David Scheffer, *Challenges Confronting International Justice Issues*, 4 NEW ENG. INT'L & COMP. L. ANN. 1 (1998).

can complement or detract from each other, the first international court to provide for prosecutions in a situation where an amnesty was already part of the negotiated end to the conflict. This meant that it would later become the first to operate alongside a national truth and reconciliation commission in a post-conflict situation anywhere in the world.

Upon its establishment, mostly due to its limited funding and its location in the "former theatre of conflict,"[24] the SCSL had to innovate in various areas of broader interest for the global anti-impunity project. Its practice in a range of areas therefore had some modeling potential. In this regard, the Tribunal became the first ad hoc court to create a Defense Office charged exclusively with ensuring that the rights and interests of suspects and accused persons are protected. This would later serve as an innovation for other similar tribunals. In this way, it provided for better equality of arms between the prosecution and defense and impacted the approach to defense rights in the courts that followed it.[25] The SCSL was also the first to create an Outreach Office unprecedented within international criminal courts for its location, depth, scope, and impact, as it sought to create a two-way communication system that enabled it to establish good rapport with the local population.

Finally, relatively early in its operations, the Court also established a Legacy Phase Working Group, which was comprised of staff from the various sections, and entrusted with devising long-term projects that were intended to assist the Tribunal to leave a lasting legacy for the host country.[26] Though there remain open questions concerning the extent of the legacy that the process actually bequeathed to Sierra Leone, the attempt to do deliberate and advance planning of a court's legacy was unique. It was also intended to go well beyond the prosecution of a few bad guys towards helping bolster the country's fledgling local justice system. Whether it could, with the limited resources it had, realistically achieve much in this area was always open to some doubt. In any case, these other legacies of the SCSL in those areas are not discussed in this work.

Once the SCSL became operational in August 2003, the Prosecutor issued thirteen indictments which generally reflected the main government, army and militia parties to the armed conflict.[27] But the indictment list did not include the peacekeepers from the West African region, under the banner of the Economic Community Of West African States Monitoring Group (ECOMOG), who were effectively excluded from the Tribunal's jurisdiction. Yet, during their time in Sierra Leone, the ECOMOG forces – mostly from Nigeria and Guinea – had actively

---

[24]   Charles C. Jalloh, *Special Court for Sierra Leone: Achieving Justice?*, 32 MICH. J. INT'L. L. 395 (2011).

[25]   The impact of the SCSL's Defense Office as a model for other courts is analyzed in Charles C. Jalloh, *The Special Tribunal for Lebanon: A Defense Perspective*, 47 VAND. J. TRANSNAT'L L. 765 (2014).

[26]   Vincent O. Nmehielle and Charles C. Jalloh, *The Legacy of the Special Court for Sierra Leone*, 30 FLETCHER F. WORLD AFF. 107 (2006). For the first comprehensive assessment of the legacy on all these components of the SCSL, *see* CHARLES C. JALLOH, *in* THE SIERRA LEONE SPECIAL COURT AND ITS LEGACY: THE IMPACT FOR AFRICA AND INTERNATIONAL CRIMINAL LAW (Charles C. Jalloh, ed., 2014).

[27]   The trials are discussed *infra* at Chapter 4.

fought against the rebels to restore the democratically elected Kabbah Government. They were later accused of engaging in wanton acts of violence against civilians that allegedly amounted to war crimes.[28] The jurisdiction also excluded mercenaries from two private companies retained by the government, first from Nepal (the Gurkhas) and then South Africa (Executive Outcomes), who had been involved at different stages of the Sierra Leonean conflict. In the end, save for the deaths of three suspects and the prosecutor's withdrawal of their indictments, the Court went on to successfully indict, arrest and try all but one of its thirteen fugitives (Major Johnny Paul Koroma). Koroma, who overthrew an elected government and served as president between May 1997 and February 1998, is presumed dead. A total of nine persons were ultimately convicted for crimes against humanity, war crimes and other serious violations of international humanitarian law that occurred in Sierra Leone. Unlike the Chapter VII courts, the SCSL did not enter any acquittals in its international crimes trials.

1.2 AIM AND SIGNIFICANCE OF THIS BOOK

Sierra Leone's request for UN assistance to create an independent special tribunal to try those most responsible for atrocity crimes during its brutal armed conflict seems remarkable considering the near paralysis of states in prosecuting individuals for international crimes between the end of World War II in 1945 and the creation of the ICTY and ICTR in the early 1990s. While partly motivated by the desire of the government of President Ahmed Tejan Kabbah to credibly punish its adversaries,[29] with the SCSL in place alongside the other international criminal courts, it appeared that international criminal justice is beginning to come of age,[30] and with it, the extension of the horizontal as well as vertical reach of international criminal and humanitarian law.

The ICTY, ICTR and SCSL characterized the international legal landscape for many years.[31] Today, all their trials and appeals have been completed. Of the three,

---

[28] Human Rights Watch, *Sierra Leone – Getting Away with Murder, Mutilation, Rape*, Vol. 11, No. 3(A) (1999); Human Rights Watch, *Sowing Terror: Atrocities Against Civilians in Sierra Leone*, Vol. 10, No. 3(A) (July 1998). The contemporaneous reports of a small percentage of peacekeeper crimes documented by human rights groups were later corroborated through the evidence heard by the Sierra Leone Truth and Reconciliation Commission as well as in the judgments of the SCSL.

[29] *See* WILLIAM SCHABAS, THE U.N. INTERNATIONAL CRIMINAL TRIBUNALS: THE FORMER YUGOSLAVIA, RWANDA AND SIERRA LEONE 507 (2006).

[30] For a thoughtful assessment of this development in international law, *see* THEODOR MERON, WAR CRIMES LAW COME OF AGE (1998).

[31] The ICTY and ICTR were supposed to complete their work by 2010 but took until 2015 to do so. *See* S. C. Res. 1534 (Mar. 26, 2004). The SCSL also had a Completion Strategy, and following its winding up in Dec. 2013, became the first of the U.N.-supported ad hoc courts to complete its work. All the courts have finished their first instance trials. The remaining cases of the Chapter VII tribunals have were transferred to the Mechanism for International Criminal Tribunals. *See* U.N. Secretary-General, Identical Letters dated May 26, 2005 from the Secretary-General addressed to the President of the

the SCSL was the last of the three ad hoc courts to be established but the first of them to finish its caseload. Irrespective of their individual number of trials, it is undisputable that all three international tribunals have left an indelible imprint on international criminal law.[32] Perhaps not surprisingly given that the ICTY and ICTR were the first truly international criminal tribunals to be ever created, there has been much scholarly commentary on their pioneering work. Much of that literature has elucidated their jurisprudential contributions to the advancement of the concept of individual criminal responsibility at the international level and on the elaboration of the substantive content of the various crimes within their jurisdiction, especially genocide, crimes against humanity and war crimes.[33]

In stark contrast, between the creation of the SCSL in January 2002 and its closure in December 2013, relatively fewer scholarly works have systematically studied that ad hoc court to discern whether it has offered any meaningful additions to the corpus of international criminal law and practice. True, there was towards the end of the SCSL's lifespan an exponential growth in the literature on the Court. Nonetheless, for a long time, the bulk of the commentary focused on the SCSL's so-called hybridity compared to the ICTY and ICTR and its potential to serve as a more cost effective nationalized-internationalized tribunal model for bringing justice to diverse post-conflict situations. Even fewer academic works have studied the case law and *judicial practice* of the Court after it began operations in 2003 to determine whether it made substantive contributions to the development of the relatively young field of international criminal law.

Yet, beyond its seeming status as a forgotten African tribunal based in what some might perceive as an uninfluential African State, an in-depth study of the SCSL and core aspects of its jurisprudence that would likely remain appears justified for at least four additional reasons. First, despite the tremendous achievements of the ICTY and ICTR and their significant contributions to international law since they were established in the early 1990s, institutional design issues are still part of the fundamental challenges facing the nascent international criminal law regime. This is evidenced by the international community's continued experimentation with different accountability models to hold responsible high-level persons who oversee the commission of serious international crimes in specific conflict situations. These range from full-fledged international criminal courts, whether ad hoc or permanent,

General Assembly and the President of the Security Council, U.N. Doc. A/59/816–S/2005/350 (May 27, 2005).

[32] *See* GERHARD WERLE & FLORIAN JESSBERGER, PRINCIPLES OF INTERNATIONAL CRIMINAL LAW 2 (3d ed. 2014) (arguing that the establishment of the ICTY and ICTR and their work is one of the three milestones of international criminal law).

[33] For examples of recent works thoughtfully addressing the issues, *see generally* SCHABAS, *supra* note 29; GUÉNAËL METTRAUX, INTERNATIONAL CRIMES AND THE AD HOC TRIBUNALS (2005); GEORGE MUGWANYA, THE CRIME OF GENOCIDE IN INTERNATIONAL LAW: APPRAISING THE CONTRIBUTION OF THE U.N. TRIBUNAL FOR RWANDA (2007); LARISSA J VAN DEN HERIK, THE CONTRIBUTION OF THE RWANDA TRIBUNAL TO THE DEVELOPMENT OF INTERNATIONAL LAW (2005); and Erik Møse, *Main Achievements of the ICTR*, 3 J. INT'L CRIM. JUST. 920 (2005).

to various types of mixed courts. Notable examples include the Serious Crimes Panels in the District Court of Dili (East Timor) through to the permanent ICC as well as other models such as the Special Tribunal for Lebanon, the special chambers within the courts of Bosnia, Cambodia, Kosovo, the International Crimes Division of the Ugandan High Court and the Extraordinary Chambers within the Courts of Senegal. The proliferation of the various types of tribunals in the past two decades, as states searched for appropriate prosecution mechanisms suitable to their individual circumstances, suggests that we are in the early days of a cottage industry of internationally supported courts. Thus, bringing to bear analysis of what worked, and what did not, in Sierra Leone's own transitional justice experiment may hold wider interest for other transitional situations especially those in Africa and perhaps even others much further afield.

Second, despite the landmark contributions of the ICTY and ICTR through their revival of what Larissa van den Herik has described as an essentially "dormant branch of public international law,"[34] the elaboration of the substantive elements of international crimes within their jurisdiction, which will likely be their primary legal legacy,[35] will necessarily continue into the future. The reason is that the limited post July 1, 2002 ICC temporal jurisdiction, and the relative immaturity and abundance of the present accountability models, will likely necessitate the continued deployment of this evolving body of law to address new situations from around the world. To fill the impunity gap would require the creation of not only new enforcement regimes, but also development of novel crimes such as the international-transnational blend recently incorporated by the African Union into a June 2014 regional treaty that would establish a criminal chamber within the African Court of Justice and Human and Peoples' Rights.[36] Over time, such institutions should help to fill the lacuna arising from the lack of a unified and comprehensive code of international/transnational crimes while speaking to the particular needs of a given region.

[34] *See* van den Herik, *supra* note 33, at 30.

[35] The "legacy" of these tribunals has been the subject of recent examination. The leading works include DIANE F. ORENTLICHER, SHRINKING THE SPACE FOR DENIAL: THE IMPACT OF THE ICTY IN SERBIA (2008); LEGACY OF THE INTERNATIONAL CRIMINAL TRIBUNAL FOR THE FORMER YUGOSLAVIA (Bert Swart et al. eds., 2011); ASSESSING THE LEGACY OF THE ICTY (Richard Steinberg ed., 2011). Of course, this legacy has been largely endorsed by others as well. *See* Rep. of The Assembly of States Parties to the Rome Statute of the ICC, pt. II B. Elements of Crimes, ICC-ASP/1/3 (Sept. 2002); Knut Dorman, *Contributions by the ad hoc tribunals for the former Yugoslavia and Rwanda to the ongoing work on elements of crime for the ICC*, 94 PROC. ANN. MEETING AM. SOC'Y INT'L L. 284 (2000).

[36] *See* Protocol on Amendments to the Protocol on the Statute of the African Court of Justice and Human and Peoples' Rights, June 27, 2014 (incorporating the following crimes in a single instrument: genocide, crimes against humanity, war crimes, aggression, piracy, mercenarism, corruption, money laundering, trafficking in persons, trafficking in drugs, trafficking in hazardous wastes, illicit exploitation of natural resources, and the crime of unconstitutional change of government). For a comprehensive overview of the promise and limits of the proposed court, *see* CHARLES C. JALLOH, *in* THE AFRICAN COURT OF JUSTICE AND HUMAN AND PEOPLES' RIGHTS IN CONTEXT: DEVELOPMENT AND CHALLENGES (Charles C. Jalloh et al. eds., 2019).

The third reason why the main aspects of the SCSL judicial legacy deserves critical scrutiny is also important. The Court benefited from, and at the same time, presumably also added to solidifying the legal foundation laid by the two Chapter VII ad hoc tribunals that preceded it. This was so not only with respect to the definition of the core international crimes within its jurisdiction, but also its rules. Thus, though in the early discussions the UN and Sierra Leone contemplated the prospect of having the SCSL share a joint appellate chamber with the ICTY and ICTR to promote a coherent development of international criminal law, this did not come to pass. The proposal for a common appeals court did not garner the support of the Chapter VII courts because of concern about possible negative effects on their Security Council-mandated Completion Strategies. For that reason, and due partly to concerns about maintaining a measure of unity of the body of international criminal law being applied by these ad hoc tribunals, the Statute of the SCSL ultimately provided that the Appeals Chamber *shall* be guided by the decisions of the Appeals Chamber of the ICTY and ICTR. The SCSL, as only the second Africa-based tribunal, was similarly instructed to apply to the conduct of its proceedings, *mutatis mutandis*, the Rules of Procedure and Evidence of the ICTR obtaining at the time.

The question therefore arises whether, when viewed in the wider context of the UN's apparent interest in the normative development of a coherent international criminal law architecture, the Court's practice reflected awareness of that edict. If so, it might have assisted towards that unifying goal either by reaffirming or strengthening the existing body of legal norms.

On the other hand, the SCSL as only the third ad hoc international penal tribunal might have had to address novel legal issues presented for the first time before such courts. If so, did the manner in which the judges resolved the relevant questions offer useful precedents which could then be developed and expanded upon by future sister courts? In that case, we could find that it might have contributed to enhancing international criminal law's certainty and predictability by exploring some of the rougher terrain of international criminal justice. Conversely, if the judges of the SCSL failed to give adequate reasoning to justify their more important rulings, we might find that it may have added to legal uncertainty and perhaps even contributed to the oft-discussed fragmentation of international (criminal) law.

Fourth, an evaluation of some of the SCSL's main contributions through this work could add value to the present literature on such courts because tribunals like the ICTY/ICTR are, as the now late Italian jurist Antonio Cassese has submitted, "no longer an option, as they are too expensive, trials are too lengthy, and they will be superfluous because of the setting up of the [ICC]."[37] While, as Cassese rightly observed, the prosecution of modern atrocities will require different types of responses for different situations and the jury is still out on the outcome of some

[37]   Cassese, in Romano et al., *supra* note 16.

of these efforts, in the long run, "resorting to mixed or internationalized criminal courts and tribunals may prove to be one of the *most effective* societal and institutional devices of the many which are at present available to international lawmakers."[38] Present state practice appears to support this contention. Nonetheless, only time will tell whether nationalized international courts similar in nature to the SCSL will likely become more prevalent given the temporal and other jurisdictional limitations of the ICC. The trend certainly seems to point in that direction.

Indeed, we are beginning to see increasing national government requests for UN assistance to establish mixed courts. This has happened, for instance, in relation to Burundi, and more recently Lebanon, the Central African Republic and the Democratic Republic of the Congo. When combined with the United States' opposition to the ICC, which gives the world's only superpower the tendency to support such ad hocs as an alternative to the permanent ICC, we might infer that we will continue to have these types of courts going forward. The present crisis of confidence in the ICC, especially among African States, and the ability of individual countries to more directly mold such tribunals to their preferences increases the likelihood that more of these special courts will be established in the future.[39]

Given the above reasons, though keeping in mind that each situation will be distinct and therefore require its own specific solutions, it appears to make general sense for the innovative judicial practices of the SCSL – which so far stands as one of the more credible examples of the special court model[40] – to be examined, and where appropriate, replicated by the international community. In fact, various aspects of the SCSL case law and institutional model have already been reproduced, albeit in a repackaged form, in other justice initiatives such as that between the UN and Lebanese authorities establishing the Special Tribunal for Lebanon. The latter is currently prosecuting, in absentia, those deemed most responsible for the February 2005 assassination of then Prime Minister Rafik Hariri and twenty-two others.[41]

---

[38] *Id.*

[39] For analysis of some of the main challenges confronting Africa and the ICC, see Charles C. Jalloh, *supra* note 21. See also GERHARD WERLE ET AL., AFRICA AND THE INTERNATIONAL CRIMINAL COURT (Gerhard Werle et al. eds., 2014) and AFRICA AND THE ICC: PERCEPTIONS OF JUSTICE (Kamari Clarke et al., eds., 2016).

[40] For example, *compare* the SCSL *with* the Serious Crimes Panels for East Timor, whose trials were marred with tremendous difficulties. *See* Sylvia de Bertodano, *East Timor: Trials and Tribulations*, in INTERNATIONALIZED CRIMINAL COURTS, *supra* note 16, at 79.

[41] The UNSC adopted Resolution 1644 (Dec. 14, 2005) under Chapter VII. Paragraph 6 of the resolution asked the U.N.S.G. to assist Lebanon in identifying the character an international special tribunal could take to try those responsible for the murder of Hariri: S.C. Res. 1664 (Mar. 29, 2006) authorized the U.N.S.G. to negotiate the establishment of the special tribunal. *See* U.N. Secretary-General, *Report pursuant to paragraph 6 of resolution 1644*, U.N. Doc. S/2006/176 (Mar. 21, 2006); U.N. Secretary-General, *Report on the establishment of a special tribunal for Lebanon*, U.N. Doc S/2006/893 (Nov. 15, 2006). *See also* President of the S.C., *Letter dated 21 November 2006 from the President of the Security Council addressed to the Secretary-General*, U.N. Doc. S/2006/911 (Nov. 24, 2006).

In terms of literature, there are many articles in scholarly journals and some in edited collections addressing aspects of the SCSL's jurisprudence on specific topics such as the crime against humanity of forced marriage, the war crime of child recruitment, the question of amnesty for international crimes, the immunity of sitting heads of state, joint criminal enterprise, command responsibility, and so on.[42] But, to date, it seems that only one (English language) monograph has attempted a big picture assessment of the SCSL's specific contributions to the substantive development of the law of armed conflict.[43] That work, by Ousman Njikam, focused on the Court's judicial contribution to the substantive law of war crimes, crimes against humanity, other serious violations of international humanitarian law as well as aspects of its legacy concerning amnesty, forced marriage, head of state immunity and the war crime of child recruitment.[44] All these issues remain important. They form part of the key legal legacy of the tribunal that requires additional scholarly engagement.

The other substantive treatment, with a similar thrust instead of the focused topical evaluations like the works of Tim Kelsall,[45] Nancy Combs[46] and Jessica Lincoln,[47] among many others, was the 2006 work of William Schabas – a prominent scholar – which engaged in a "stocktaking"[48] comparison of the ICTY, ICTR and the SCSL's jurisdiction. Schabas also sought to identify "lessons" that were of more than "academic interest" that could "help guide the [ICC] as it develops its own judicial personality."[49] But, although undoubtedly an important addition to the literature on the ad hoc tribunals, Schabas' book differed from the present study in at least three significant ways.

First, it was a much broader study of all ad hoc international tribunals instead of a selective assessment of key SCSL judicial contributions and their impact on the development of international criminal law. Second, and even more importantly, the treatise was completed around four years into what proved to be the Court's eleven-year lifespan. This was long before the completion of its most important trials. Lastly,

---

[42] A comprehensive listing of the leading works, and author references to further literature, can be found in Jalloh, *supra* note 26, and in the extensive topical bibliography selection at the back of this book.

[43] OUSMAN NJIKAM, THE CONTRIBUTION OF THE SPECIAL COURT FOR SIERRA LEONE TO THE DEVELOPMENT OF INTERNATIONAL HUMANITARIAN LAW (2013).

[44] *See infra* at Chapters 4 to 8.

[45] TIM KELSALL, CULTURE UNDER CROSS EXAMINATION: INTERNATIONAL JUSTICE AND THE SPECIAL COURT FOR SIERRA LEONE (2013) (providing an anthropological account focusing on the operation of a largely Western court in an African context).

[46] NANCY COMBS, FACT FINDING WITHOUT FACTS: THE UNCERTAIN EVIDENTIARY FOUNDATIONS OF INTERNATIONAL CRIMINAL CONVICTIONS (2013) (revealing an empirical study that international criminal trials including those at the SCSL are beset by severe fact-finding impediments thereby questioning their determinations of criminal responsibility).

[47] JESSICA LINCOLN, TRANSITIONAL JUSTICE, PEACE AND ACCOUNTABILITY: OUTREACH AND THE ROLE OF INTERNATIONAL COURTS AFTER CONFLICT (2011) (focusing on the role of outreach as carried out by the SCSL).

[48] WILLIAM SCHABAS, *supra* note 29, at ix.

[49] *Id.*

as a result of that relatively early timing, Schabas could not be expected to address some of the vital topics that scholars today tend to associate with the SCSL as part of its core contributions to the corpus of international criminal law.

The other work excavating judicial contributions, more directly on point compared to Schabas' book, is the present writer's edited volume which assembled a group of leading scholars and practitioners of international criminal law to examine the practical legacy and jurisprudential impact of the SCSL to Africa and international law.[50] Each of these works, taken alone and certainly in combination with the others, has offered useful contributions to our understanding of the Sierra Leone Tribunal and its legacy to international law more generally. Nevertheless, given the relatively small number of single-authored books on the SCSL, none of which appear to have been attempted after it completed its work in December 2013, some gaps still remain.

This book aims to be among the first to evaluate the SCSL's main judicial contributions to the evolution of modern international penal law. The study, which seeks to help fill part of the current lacuna in the literature, does so by providing a substantive analysis of some of the more well-known – but also some of the lesser known legal contributions of the SCSL – to the development of international criminal law and its practice, especially in Africa. The research benefits from the knowledge that all the Court's trials and jurisprudence are now complete. The present author also had the opportunity to be a participant in some of the trials first-hand, allowing him to draw on his practical experience to enrich the analysis.

1.3 ASSUMPTIONS

This work departs from two premises. The first is that international criminal law, by which I mean the law encompassing the principles and procedures governing the international investigation and prosecution of the "core international crimes" (that is genocide, crimes against humanity, war crimes and aggression), is still at an adolescent state of development.[51] That body of penal law, which is derived partly from domestic criminal law and partly international treaties and customary law comprised of state practice and *opinio juris*, will therefore likely continue to evolve. If this assumption is correct, it stands to reason that we can tentatively conclude that there may be something to gain from a study of how international criminal law is being applied by ad hoc international criminal courts charged with implementing that body of law, not least because the manner of application can also be a source of guidance for national courts.

---

[50] CHARLES C. JALLOH, *supra* note 26.

[51] *See* WERLE & JESSBERGER, PRINCIPLES OF INTERNATIONAL CRIMINAL LAW, *supra* note 32, at Part 1 (Foundations), for a thorough overview of the origins and development of the concept of international crimes and the notion of individual criminal responsibility in international criminal law.

Second, the work also assumes that an ad hoc international tribunal with a limited mandate and limited funding fashioned out of an unprecedented partnership between the UN and one of its Member States can impact – or at least influence – the wider development of international criminal law through sound judicial decision-making. This doctrinal attitude implicitly challenges a solely state-centered understanding of international law. In fact, under this view, it is taken as given that not only formal treaty-making processes are relevant to the development of international law. Rather, especially in a still emerging legal system such as international criminal law, law-making can take place in various and sometimes more informal ways. These, for our purposes, can occur when a judge in one court selects non-binding precedent from a prior court to apply it to resolve a legal problem. That precedent might in turn be picked up and used by others, thereby becoming part of the standard in the application of that legal doctrine.

Finally, perhaps it can be said that the above assumptions appear to rest on safe ground, since judicial decisions are formally part of the subsidiary means for determination of the law under Article 38(1)(d) of the Statute of the International Court of Justice.[52] Being subsidiary to other sources such as treaties and custom, it can be argued that such a source is not terribly important. I would disagree for various reasons. For one thing, historically, the case law has been important to the development of international law generally and international criminal law in particular. Perhaps more so than many other fields of international law, and all the more so if we consider present judicial practice and the history of the development of the field. Who can deny the importance of not only the International Military Tribunal at Nuremberg's founding instruments, but also its seminal judgment at the end of that historic trial? Indeed, if one takes as examples the more recent ICTY and the ICTR, it is clear that the judges of those courts have, collectively, helped to clarify and shape the body of modern international criminal and humanitarian law. Unsurprisingly, much like in the case law developed by the two Chapter VII courts, we are beginning to see frequent references to SCSL case law in various cases in international courts such as the ICC. Indeed, the present understanding of the importance of judicial decisions that make them worthy of study is also consistent with the types of research that scholars have carried out in relation to the contributions of other ad hoc international criminal tribunals, including the ICTY and the ICTR, to the development of the still evolving field of international criminal law.

1.4 THE SCOPE OF THE BOOK AND THE RATIONALE FOR THE CHOICE OF TOPICS

Having noted the generally immature state of modern international criminal law, and the research premise that one court may influence the law through sound rule

---

[52] Statute of the International Court of Justice art. 38(1), June 26, 1945, 59 Stat. 1031, 33 U.N.T.S. 993.

development or sound rule interpretation or sound rule application, the overarching question that I will aim to address in this work is this: What, if any, are the main judicial contributions of the SCSL to the development of international criminal law? Of particular interest will be the attempt to discern whether, given the fact that the SCSL was only the third ad hoc tribunal in modern international criminal justice and only the second in Africa after the ICTR, the Court carved out a jurisprudential space for itself on important international penal law topics, and if so, how and in what areas.

The role of judges in developing, rather than applying the law, is controversial in both domestic and international law. They are expected to neutrally apply the law made by the legislative branch of government, rather than to make that law. When they are perceived to be doing more than that, they are usually accused of acting outside the bounds of their roles and even judicial activism. Of course, at the international level, there is no centralized government. Nor is there a system of separation of powers between co-equal branches of government, with a legislature, executive and judiciary. There is, however, a rough analogy in the sense that, in the process of adjudication, international judges are expected to also neutrally apply the law found in the constitutive instruments of their tribunals and or as agreed to by states in treaties or as manifested in customary law. The latter is, of course, comprised of and is reflective of the existing state practice and *opinio juris*.

Yet, the complex process of rule application whether from a treaty or custom also entails a measure of choice in how to interpret and apply a given rule. The art of interpretation entails several steps in which a measure of discretion is available to the supposedly neutral arbiter of a given rule. In this dialectic, a narrow approach to a rule may lead to a strict construction of that rule and its potential legal effects. Conversely, a broad approach to a rule may lead to a wide construction of the content of that rule that could result in broader legal effects. The act of making the choice, either favoring a strict or broad approach, becomes a way of framing the outer bounds of the rule. It often might shape if not determine the potential scope and reach of the law. It is in those interpretive spaces that the path taken to interpret and apply a rule to a new set of facts could prove to be more influential than the simple process a pure theoretical and neutral application of the law would assume.

With the above considerations in mind, which assumes that judges may help to shape the law through the process of interpretation and application of it, the first substantive chapter of this work begins with an inquiry into the classic topic of jurisdiction under international law. In particular, focusing on jurisdiction *ratione personae*, we explore the meaning of the phrase to prosecute persons bearing "greatest responsibility" as a grant of personal jurisdiction to an ad hoc international criminal court. That phrase was first introduced by the SCSL Statute. Since then, it appears to have become the preferred way of describing the narrow jurisdictional reach of modern international criminal tribunals. This includes by prosecutors and judges at the permanent ICC, whose adoption of the terminology is based on policy rather than as a result of a formal legal requirement of the Rome Statute.

In relation to this first topic, this book will ask and seek to answer two specific sub-questions based on the judicial rulings on the matter in the SCSL. First, how should that controversial and apparently ambiguous phrase be interpreted and applied in the context of a concrete criminal case? Should it be construed as a *jurisdictional threshold* or as a requirement that prosecutors must prove beyond a reasonable doubt during the trial, or is it a *mere guideline* delimiting the exercise of prosecutorial discretion? The consequences can be quite significant. If the former, and prosecutors fail to meet the threshold, then the accused will have to be released and victims will not get an opportunity to see justice done.

Second, depending on the answers found to these two sub-issues, what types of perpetrators should fall within the ambit of a tribunal with personal jurisdiction spelled out in this rather specific way? Can it be seen as a descriptor of only those holding *leadership positions* in a given organizational hierarchy, or alternately, does "greatest responsibility" personal jurisdiction imply that prosecutors can also focus on the *worst perpetrators* in terms of the numbers of persons victimized and the cruel means employed against them? This work will explore how the SCSL judges grappled with these questions in several important decisions.

The next two chapters address the first international judicial recognition of the crime against humanity of *forced marriage*[53] and issues arising from the war crime

---

[53] See Karine Bélair, *Unearthing the Customary Law Foundations of "Forced Marriages" During Sierra Leone's Civil War: The Possible Impact of International Criminal Law on Customary Marriage and Women's Rights in Post-Conflict Sierra Leone*, 15 COLUM. J. GENDER & L. 551, 551–607 (2006); Mariane C. Ferme, *"Archetypes of Humanitarian Discourse": Child Soldiers, Forced Marriage, and the Framing of Communities in Post-Conflict Sierra Leone*, 4 HUMANITY: AN INT'L J. HUM. RTS., HUMAN'ISM, DEV. 49 (2013); Micaela Frulli, *Advancing International Criminal Law: The Special Court for Sierra Leone Recognizes Forced Marriage as a "New" Crime Against Humanity*, 6 J. INT'L CRIM. JUST. 1033, 1033–41 (2008); Elena Gekker, *Rape, Sexual Slavery, and Forced Marriage at the International Criminal Court: How Katanga Utilizes A Ten-Year-Old Rule but Overlooks New Jurisprudence*, 25 HASTINGS WOMEN'S L.J. 105, 126–32 (2014); Gong-Gershowitz, *Forced Marriage: A "New" Crime Against Humanity?* 8 NW. U. J. INT'L HUM. RTS. 53 (2009); Nicholas Azadi Goodfellow, *The Miscategorization of "Forced Marriage" as a Crime Against Humanity by the Special Court for Sierra Leone*, 11 INT'L CRIM. L. REV. 831 (2011); Neha Jain, *Forced Marriage as a Crime Against Humanity: Problems of Definition and Prosecution*, 6 J. INT'L CRIM. JUST. 1013, 1013–32 (2008); Valerie Oosterveld, *The Gender Jurisprudence of the Special Court for Sierra Leone: Progress in the Revolutionary United Front Judgments*, 44 CORNELL INT'L L.J. 49 (2011); Valerie Oosterveld, *Lessons from the Special Court for Sierra Leone on the Prosecution of Gender-Based Crimes*, 17 AM. U.J. GENDER SOC. POL'Y & L. 407, 407–30 (2009); Valerie Oosterveld, *The Special Court for Sierra Leone, Child Soldiers, and Forced Marriage: Providing Clarity or Confusion?*, 45 CAN. Y.B. INT'L L. 131, 131–72 (2007); Michael Scharf & Suzanne Mattler, *Forced Marriage: Exploring the Viability of the Special Court for Sierra Leone's New Crime against Humanity, Case Research Paper Series in Legal Studies*, (Case Law Sch. Case Research Paper Series in Legal Studies, Working Paper 05–35 2005); Rachel Slater, *Gender Violence or Violence Against Women? The Treatment of Forced Marriage in the Special Court for Sierra Leone*, 13 MELBOURNE J. INT'L L. 1 (2012); Bridgette Scharf, *What Is Forced Marriage? Towards a Definition of Forced Marriage as a Crime Against Humanity*, 19 COL. J. GENDER

prohibiting the recruitment and use of children under fifteen to participate actively in hostilities.[54]

In the first of these two chapters, concerning the crime against humanity of forced marriage, I consider whether the SCSL, like the international criminal courts that preceded it, paid attention to the gendered burden of the Sierra Leone conflict which is known to have fallen disproportionately on Sierra Leonean women and girls. This proved to be the case. The tension we have seen in other tribunals such as the ICTR is how to balance the needs of the victims, as represented by the prosecution's desire to name and shame the perpetrators, on the one hand, and on the other hand, how this could be done while ensuring the fairness of the process towards the suspects and accused persons who are entitled to certain fair trial rights under the statute of the tribunal and international law. Focusing on the practice misnamed as "forced marriage," which the prosecution belatedly decided to charge as part of the residual category of "other inhumane acts" of crimes against humanity, I address whether the SCSL solution to this peculiar feature of the Sierra Leone war contributed in some way to the treatment of gender crimes in international criminal law. In this regard, one must also analyze the fair trial implications of innovating crimes in light of the rights to which the suspects and accused persons are entitled under the statute of the SCSL and under international human rights law.

In the second of the two chapters, I examine how the adults who recruited and used children in the Sierra Leone war were prosecuted for war crimes for the first time in international criminal law for conscripting or enlisting children for the purpose of using them in hostilities. In this regard, I consider how the SCSL fleshed

---

AND L. 539, 539–91 (2010); Sara Wharton, *The Evolution of International Criminal Law: Prosecuting "New" Crimes Before the Special Court for Sierra Leone*, 11 INT'L CRIM. L. REV. 217 (2011).

[54] *See generally* Diane M. Amann, *Calling Children to Account: The Proposal for a Juvenile Chamber in the Special Court for Sierra Leone*, 29 PEPP. L. REV. 167 (2001); Stephanie Bald, *Searching for a Lost Childhood: Will the Special Court for Sierra Leone Find Justice for Its Children?*, 18 AM. U. INT'L L. REV. 537 (2002); Tracey Begley, *The Extraterritorial Obligation to Prevent the Use of Child Soldiers*, 27 AM. U. INT'L L. REV. 613 (2012); Stuart Beresford, *Child Witnesses and the International Criminal Justice System: Does the International Criminal Court Protect the Most Vulnerable?*, 3 J. INT'L CRIM. JUST. 721 (2005); Ilene Cohn, *The Protection of Children and the Quest for Truth and Justice in Sierra Leone*, 55 J. INT'L AFF. 2 (2001); Michael Corriero, *The Involvement and Protection of Children in Truth and Justice-Seeking Processes: The Special Court for Sierra Leone*, 18 N.Y.L. SCH. J. HUM. RTS. 337 (2002); Michael Custer, *Punishing Child Soldiers: The Special Court for Sierra Leone and the Lessons to be Learned from the United States' Juvenile Justice System*, 19 TEMP. INT'L & COMP. L.J. 449 (2005); Matthew Happold, *International Humanitarian Law, War Criminality and Child Recruitment: The Special Court for Sierra Leone's Decision in Prosecutor v. Samuel Hinga Norman*, 18 LEIDEN J. INT'L L. 283 (2005); Michael Hoffmann, *May We Hold Them Responsible? The Prosecution of Child Soldiers by the Special Court for Sierra Leone*, 14 INT'L CHILD. RTS. MONITOR 23 (2001); Paola Konge, *International Crimes and Soldiers*, 16 SW. J. INT'L L. 41 (2010); Noah Novogrodsky, *Litigating Child Recruitment Before the Special Court for Sierra Leone*, 7 SAN DIEGO INT'L L.J. 421, 422–26 (2006); Alison Smith, *Child Recruitment and the Special Court for Sierra Leone*, 4 J. INT'L CRIM. JUST. 1141, 1141–53 (2004). For a careful out of the box book length treatment of child soldiers, drawing partly on the SCSL and Sierra Leone experience, *see* MARK A. DRUMBL, REIMAGINING CHILD SOLDIERS IN INTERNATIONAL LAW AND POLICY (2012).

out the elements of the crime in the first tribunal to apply it in a concrete case. Since the same crime had first been included in the Rome Statute, but not yet used by the ICC, the chapter ponders on whether the SCSL application of the elements of the crimes had proved useful to the case law of the ICC. This becomes especially relevant given that the ICC's symbolically significant maiden case, involving Thomas Lubanga, relied solely on a charge of conscripting or enlisting children under the age of fifteen years into the national armed forces or using them to participate actively in hostilities.

The book then moves on to consider the SCSL jurisprudence on one of the most frequently contested issues in contemporary international criminal law: immunities. Immunities provide their beneficiaries, often the most senior of government officials, with a form of defense to criminal liability. They can therefore be used as a means to avoid individual criminal responsibility altogether. As a consequence, from the very beginnings of the field, there have been debates about how best to reconcile the immunity of officials, especially the highest ones such as sitting heads of state, which is predicated on notions of sovereignty and equality, and the logic of individual penal responsibility which underpins modern international criminal law. Immunities posed problems for the ad hoc ICTY and ICTR, and today, appears to have become a bane for the ICC. The latter's list of high profile indictees includes both incumbent and former presidents and other high officials, most of whom are not in its custody. The SCSL Appeals Chamber became one of the few to grasp the proverbial nettle of immunities when it ruled on whether Liberia's President Charles Taylor was immune from prosecution before the Court for the serious international crimes with which he had been charged. Part of the legal difficulty stemmed from the fact that Liberia, which was a *third party* to the UN-Sierra Leone treaty constituting the SCSL, had not directly participated in or explicitly consented to the establishment of the Tribunal.

Liberia, which as a State is ordinarily entitled to immunity for its officials, protested. Sierra Leone's neighbor took exception to the SCSL's purported extension of jurisdiction over its then sitting president. The thrust of Liberia's argument was that the SCSL was a national, not an international, court. Liberia consequently initiated proceedings at the International Court of Justice where it claimed that Sierra Leone, by delegating powers to the SCSL that its national courts did not have, had violated its obligation to respect the *personal* and *functional* immunities that President Taylor enjoyed under customary international law.

This book will consider whether the SCSL Appeals Chamber ruling that there was a customary international law exception permitting the trial of President Taylor was consistent with immunity law as articulated by the ICJ. The answer to that question may demonstrate whether, or not, there was a judicial contribution from the SCSL on a possible exception to the immunity of former presidents of third states whenever they are accused of involvement with the perpetration of atrocity crimes such as war crimes and crimes against humanity.

Another significant question for the present study, which was also extensively litigated before the SCSL, exposes one of the most difficult dilemmas facing countries seeking to transition from war to peace. The circumstances of the Sierra Leone conflict, which the government seemed unable to win militarily, were such that there was an initial preference to choose peace in return for truth and reconciliation instead of punishment. For the rebels, in addition to power sharing, there was a big carrot in the form of a promise of an unqualified amnesty to all the combatants for all their acts carried out in pursuit of the war. This concession was seen as necessary in order to end the fighting. The approach failed miserably as the rebels refused to keep their side of the bargain. The main issue was whether such an arrangement arising out of a peace agreement, between the government and its former enemies, would bar the prosecution of universally condemned offenses before the separate court established subsequently to prosecute the alleged perpetrators of the atrocities. I examine the SCSL's judicial rulings on that question and whether, or not, it added to the normative development of international criminal law.

In the final topic selected for this work, in the last chapter, I broaden the analysis from what we might describe as pure international criminal law topics to the wider and perhaps even more challenging context of its intersection with the field of transitional justice. Sierra Leone's initial creation of a Truth and Reconciliation Commission (TRC), which emphasized truth telling and reconciliation, was part of the bargain struck to secure peace in return for conferment of the blanket amnesty. The rebels, who split along the lines of doves who wanted peace and hawks who sought to continue the war, failed to honor the arrangement. The government, which had waffled back and forth between a hard line and an appeasement approach, unilaterally voided parts of the deal. It thereafter requested international community support to establish a credible special tribunal to prosecute the enemy rebel leadership and their collaborators.

International criminal tribunals are largely adversarial institutions. The specific role of the SCSL, of course, was to determine individual guilt of those most responsible for the war crimes, crimes against humanity and other serious violations of international humanitarian and Sierra Leonean law during the conflict. The TRC, on the other hand, was a more communal affair. Its explicit purpose was not to punish perpetrators for bad criminal conduct. Rather, it was to advance truth seeking and reconciliation instead of punishment and retribution. Through this process, of trial and error with one mechanism and then the other, Sierra Leone thus became the first country in the world to deploy a truth commission and special court alongside each other in an attempt to address the painful aftermath of mass atrocity.

Since countries in Africa and elsewhere have since contemplated following its example, it seems helpful for us to ponder whether the parallel existence of two traditionally alternative post-conflict mechanisms work well in practice in post-conflict contexts. All the more so because, largely because of the separate circumstances from which they emerged and their apparently conflicting goals, there was little clarity on how the two institutions should relate with each other under their respective founding instruments. What, if any, were the main legal concerns that affected the concurrent functioning of those two institutions? How best might those have been resolved? The original findings from this analysis of the SCSL-TRC interaction may add to present thinking on coordinating punitive criminal mechanisms with reconciliatory measures.

The critical examination of the SCSL's jurisprudence in all the above areas should help to identify some key preliminary lessons from the Sierra Leone case study. Overall, although not all its legacy will be discussed in this book due to space constraints, the contemporary relevance of the selected topics of personal jurisdiction, the crime against humanity of forced marriage, the war crime of conscripting or enlisting children under fifteen into armed forces or groups, amnesty, head of state immunity and the relationship between special courts and truth commissions, could be especially noteworthy given that Africa is still today the scene of some of the world's worst conflicts. This has in turn led to the large-scale commission of atrocity crimes against numerous African victims of those armed conflicts. The wave of brutal pre- and post-election violence, which gripped several countries on the continent over the past few years, from Ivory Coast to Nigeria, Gabon, Central Africa Republic, Kenya, Zimbabwe, Burundi, the Democratic Republic of the Congo and South Sudan, all underscore the possible significance of the present research. All the more so given the commensurately increased civil society calls for the establishment of institutions similar to the SCSL to mete out accountability to the perpetrators of crimes condemned under international law. In some of the instances, such as the South Sudan, the SCSL blue print was used as the model to guide the agreement and the statute of the Hybrid Court for South Sudan.

1.5 METHODOLOGY

An academic researcher could approach a study of the SCSL's legal legacy or contributions to the development of international law in multiple ways. These include through a historical, political science, anthropological or legal lens, using the doctrinal methodology of a single discipline or through a combination of one or more of these as part of an overarching interdisciplinary evaluation. The purpose of this study is to analyze the SCSL and its contributions from a legal perspective. In particular, as stated above, I will examine the core judicial contributions of the Tribunal to the interpretation, clarification and application of international penal law in relation to the discrete but important topics highlighted in the preceding section. This work will thereby seek to join those of other scholars who have done similar doctrinal assessments of the contributions of the various ad hoc tribunals to the maturation of international criminal law.[55]

---

[55] *See*, in this regard, the works of Mugwanya, van den Herik and Njikam cited in *supra* notes 33 and 43.

As to methodology, this work will engage in a descriptive, prescriptive and comparative analysis of the related jurisprudence of the ICTY, ICTR and the ICC as well as the associated secondary literature in international criminal, humanitarian and human rights law. Descriptively, I hope to identify and critically analyze the lesser known areas where the SCSL jurisprudence, that is the trial and appeals judgments and interlocutory decisions, made, or failed to make, useful additions to international criminal law in relation to the specific topics under scrutiny. This work will attempt to show how the SCSL interpreted its statute, sometimes creatively and in line with established international law jurisprudence, and sometimes not so creatively.

The prescriptive and comparative methodologies should help to locate some of the lessons that may already be gleaned from the work and legacy of the SCSL. How well did the SCSL do in bringing the law forward on the issue of personal jurisdiction over persons deemed to bear greatest responsibility? Did it advance our understanding of the law and policy concerning the prosecution of the crime against humanity of forced marriage, the war crime of conscription and enlistment of children under fifteen, or the immunity of sitting heads of third states accused of international crimes? What about the customary international law implications of a nationally conferred amnesty on the prosecution of international crimes before an independent international criminal court? Lastly, based on the Sierra Leone experience, can special criminal tribunals and truth commissions coexist and complement each other without undermining each other's mandates? To what extent did the judicial approach on these core issues comport with the SCSL's statute and the judicial practice in other ad hoc courts?

To address these research questions, I will take as a starting point the traditional primary and secondary sources of international law set out in Article 38 of the Statute of the International Court of Justice, that is, treaties, customary law, general principles of law, and as subsidiary means for determination of rules of law, judicial decisions as well as the teachings of the most qualified publicists. In this context, the UN-Sierra Leone Agreement which established the Tribunal, the Statute of the SCSL (SCSL Statute), an annex to that binding treaty, its Rules of Procedure and Evidence as well as its jurisprudence will serve as principal sources. Comparisons will be made, as necessary, with the relevant instruments, jurisprudence and practice of the ICTY and ICTR.

Since the goal is to discern the judicial contributions on these important topics, the analysis must necessarily rely on the Court's case law especially the Appeals Chamber's interlocutory decisions which often constituted the final disposition of the issues. I take as a working assumption that judges, in applying the law, help to shape the development of that law. When they do so, I further assume that they can leave a legacy, which could be measured in terms of the quality of the legal reasoning and how well used the decisions are in relevant future cases. The analysis also draws, as necessary, on the writings of scholars which – along with judicial decisions – form part of Article 38(1)(d) of the ICJ Statute.

I approach the various topics from a comparative perspective, reflecting whenever possible, the judicial thinking on the same or similar questions in the ICTY and ICTR. The centrality of case law for an international criminal law analysis like that carried out here admittedly goes beyond its traditional status as a mere secondary means for the determination of law under Article 38(1)(d) of the ICJ Statute. But this may well be inevitable in that it tracks the general experience of domestic systems before the periods of codification of criminal law. In the end, as is the case of international law of which it is but a subset, judicial decisions seem to play a crucial function in the development of the emerging system of global penal law. This is especially so given the general reluctance of states to give up control over criminal law matters, which they often perceive as both a function and an attribute, of their sovereignty. It is also a reflection of the "dynamic and unconventional way in which international criminal law has developed in recent years."[56]

In addition to its constitutive instruments, judicial decisions and the writings of scholars, I also consider key UN documents, for example Resolution 1315(2000), which was adopted by the Security Council and authorized the Secretary-General to negotiate with the Sierra Leonean government to establish the Court. I evaluate prior and contemporaneous official UN reports on the conflict situation in Sierra Leone and the various attempts to address the threat that it posed to the maintenance of international peace and security. These will include the seminal Report of the UN Secretary-General on the Establishment of a special court, which constitutes the unofficial *travaux préparatoires* of the SCSL. The Tribunal's annual reports, verbatim records of the UN deliberations relating to the accountability question in Sierra Leone, reports on the human rights situation in the country at the time, and other documents will sometimes be relevant sources. These sources are all detailed in the extensive bibliography attached to this work for ease of reference.

Besides the correspondence between the UN and the GoSL, as published in documents of the former, I could not find in the public record the Sierra Leone government position on some of the issues relating to the negotiations of the SCSL Statute. Yet, as a formal equal partner of the UN in the SCSL project, it would have been insightful to examine the Sierra Leone government's own position on some of the key issues. Sierra Leone, being the jurisdiction that requested the tribunal in the first place, no doubt had its own views on some of the issues as developed both before and during the negotiations between the two sides. How then to fill the gap giving a national perspective on the process?

I drew on the best substitutes available: The memoirs and other writings of the key officials, in particular the Sierra Leonean President Ahmad Tejan Kabbah, who initiated the process of establishment of the SCSL with his request for UN support to

---

[56]   van den Herik, *supra* note 33, at 9.

create the tribunal. I also draw on the revelations of Solomon Berewa, the Attorney-General and Minister of Justice and later Vice-President of Sierra Leone. Berewa headed the Sierra Leonean delegation which negotiated with UN counterparts the treaty that eventually formed the basis for the SCSL. Prior public and policy statements by those officials should additionally help identify the government or national position on some of the issues. This approach, and reference to those hitherto unmined sources, should help bring forth Sierra Leonean perspectives to bear on the legal questions under discussion including those that might have been formed before the establishment of the tribunal. The combination of materials assist to illuminate the extent to which the Court can be said to have fulfilled the expectations of both its national and international founders.

This book will also draw on the secondary literature on the SCSL, including the writings of publicists and reports by non-governmental organizations. The insights gleaned from these works will be situated within the broader backdrop of public international law, including the law of the UN Charter, regional and universal international human rights law norms, principles of international humanitarian law, and international treaty law. Taken together, these should aid us in better understanding the state of affairs prevailing before the advent of the SCSL. They will also inform my attempt to identify and distinguish what the Court's bench added to the law and practice of contemporary ad hoc international penal tribunals.

1.6 CONTRIBUTION TO LEGAL SCHOLARSHIP

This book aims to make an original contribution to the advancement of international legal scholarship. At a general level, it seeks to articulate the place of the SCSL's judicial legacy in the post–Cold War international criminal law landscape. That landscape was not a barren one. Rather, because of the judicial fertility of the prior ad hoc tribunals and the extensive body of legal rules and principles that they developed, applied and refined, I evaluate what the SCSL possessed in its legal toolkit to resolve thorny legal questions and ask how well it used what it had to contribute to the solidification of those norms.

Assuming that it is possible to already trace the SCSL's main legal legacy, even if only in a *preliminary* fashion given that legacies are dynamic and tend to also evolve over time, I argue that the Court's establishment and subsequent practice made useful contributions to the growth of international criminal law. Focusing in particular on the SCSL approach to the selected aspects of its case law, I argue that the judges assisted in clarifying some key legal issues for international criminal law. At a purely technical level, the decisions of SCSL judges are not binding on other courts. Nonetheless, to the extent that persuasive reasoning was developed on these issues by the SCSL, I maintain that they will – and have already – facilitated the work of other tribunals and therefore arguably made valuable additions to international criminal law. Though its jurisprudence reflected some shortcomings, which will also be discussed throughout this work, it can be said with considerable authority that the Sierra Leone Tribunal joined the ICTY and ICTR in advancing the cause of justice for atrocity crimes through the development of a solid body of case law on a range of topics with wider global significance. Those topics will naturally be of interest to others well beyond Sierra Leone.

Overall, the key contribution that this book makes is demonstrating that by virtue of its *practice*, especially through the interpretation and application of certain aspects of its jurisprudence, the SCSL bequeathed an important jurisprudential legacy to international law. First, on the concern over the scope of *greatest responsibility personal jurisdiction*, the book demonstrates that the phrase (though apparently simple in its formulation) proved hard to apply in practice. The ambiguity stemmed from its possible divergent interpretations, including whether the language was intended as a jurisdictional requirement that prosecutors had to prove beyond reasonable doubt and whether it was meant to reflect only leadership criteria or also to accommodate the gravity and scale of the crimes.

By analyzing the judicial rulings on this question, the present study advocates the need for more careful framing of personal jurisdiction in future ad hoc international criminal courts and recommends against the use of the greatest responsibility terminology whenever possible. That said, the idea that such tribunals could have a limited mandate focusing on a limited class of persons may politically be unavoidable. Thus, if there is a desire to refer to greatest responsibility, this ought to be reflected in policy documents but might lead to unnecessary legal headaches if included in the *jurisdictional provisions* of the relevant founding documents such as the statutes of future courts. The use of the phase could be better avoided in constitutive instruments. If the tactic of avoidance to include in the founding instruments is not realistic, say due to a preference to include such limiting language by the law-giving states or international organization concerned, the preferred method of interpreting such a jurisdictional clause is elucidated based on the experiences of the Sierra Leone Tribunal.

Second, as regards *forced marriage as a crime against humanity* and the *war crime of child recruitment*, I demonstrate that the SCSL was confronted with novel issues of how also to confront egregious crimes perpetrated against vulnerable groups. The efforts to investigate, charge and prosecute such conduct, which became associated with the Sierra Leone conflict, were undoubtedly laudable. The prosecutors relied on existing criminal prohibitions. They also, controversially, sought to expand the reach of the law to encompass conduct deemed so egregious that it warranted the introduction of a new crime against humanity into the lexicon of international criminal law. While the case law in relation to the former revealed divisions amongst the judges, and as between the prosecution and the trial chambers, the same was not true when it comes to the latter. The latter, to some extent, benefited from the relative clarity of the war crime of child recruitment which was not a judicial innovation. In any case, with the ICC precedent in hand including an elements of crimes document which fleshed it out, there could be greater agreement on the contours or elements of this war crime. The two sets of decisions, in respect of forced marriage as a crime against humanity and child recruitment as a war crime, have already proved influential in ICC and ECCC case law and should help to guide future international criminal prosecutions that follow the SCSL in order to provide for greater justice for the victims of such crimes.

Third, on the often controversial international legal issue of immunity, this work finds significance in the SCSL ruling that customary international law does not admit of any exceptions from prosecution for incumbent head of states for serious international crimes. I show that, though sometimes sharply criticized by commentators for allegedly misusing and misapplying ICJ precedent, the core added value of the *Taylor* immunity decision seems to have been overlooked. That is, the Appeals Chamber's determination that the classical rationale for immunity which is justified on the basis of the need to maintain serene relations between equal sovereigns at the *horizontal* level, is – or rather should be – of little relevance in *vertical* relationships such as those between states and international penal courts partly created by the UN in the exercise of its primary mandate to ensure international peace and security.

The jurisprudential promise of this line of legal reasoning as a way to limit immunities – which would otherwise operate to procedurally block prosecutions for atrocity crimes before such courts – should be explored by other tribunals such as the ICC. The ICC, which has had challenges in applying the law of immunity, has already benefited from use of the *Taylor* precedent in several cases involving Malawi and Jordan. The most recent ruling, given by the Appeals Chamber of the ICC in May 2019, has been met with some criticism by some commentators. But that same decision seems to have been embraced by other scholars. Either way, the judgment of the highest court in the ICC takes up and reinforces the *Taylor* precedent which it also found to be reflective of customary international law. The decision on immunity, though not perhaps as settled an area as one might expect, adds to a line of authority proclaiming the absence of immunity from arrest and prosecution for serious international crimes under customary international law. It in many ways dates back to the seminal Nuremberg Trials and the subsequent formulation of the Nuremberg Principles by the UN International Law Commission.

As to the SCSL jurisprudence denying legal effect to a blanket domestic amnesty in respect of international crimes, this book contends that the judges may have reached the right legal result but that their legal reasoning seemed somewhat complicated. They concluded that a qualified domestic amnesty does not per se seem prohibited in relation to international crimes. They also found that a norm against blanket amnesties for international crimes may be crystallizing. Still, the court conceded that the use of conditional amnesties as a way of settling bitter conflicts may in some cases be unavoidable. The contribution of the SCSL in this regard, as will be seen, is at least threefold: First, towards solidifying the norm that no such amnesties are available when it comes to universally condemned international crimes. Amnesties may not be illegal, but to the extent that they are legal, their scope must be understood to be rather narrow.

Second, the decision of one jurisdiction such as that of Sierra Leone to confer an amnesty for all crimes including the core international ones is not necessarily binding on other sovereigns. Other sovereigns would continue to retain the jurisdiction to investigate and prosecute the offenders should they wish to do so. This raises a question about the actual effectiveness of domestic amnesties for international crimes.

Third, as a direct lesson of the Sierra Leone experience, amnesties cannot operate to bar criminal prosecutions for international crimes before future international penal courts. Wherever used, amnesties could henceforth be deemed illegitimate at the UN level, assuming the latter's practice does not change and is not challenged by the Member States. With the passage of time, such a practice could in the future come to form the firm basis of a claim of illegality under customary international law. The SCSL amnesty rulings appear to have added a healthy sized cup in the bucket of water accumulating against amnesties for core international crimes.

Turning to the potentially tenuous relationship between, on the one hand, truth and reconciliation mechanisms, and on the other hand ad hoc criminal courts, this book adds to our understanding of the challenges that arise in such tandem situations. Sierra Leone offers a negative lesson in the sense of what not to do, rather than a positive lesson of what to do. The case study suggests that, to avoid future problems, it might have been better to clarify upfront how the two institutions with their inherently tense mandates should relate to each other. This should have occurred before or during their creation, with the issue thoroughly discussed by the State (Sierra Leone) and the international organization (UN) concerned. But failing that, the entities created could work to frame the expectations as between themselves through the conclusion of a memorandum of understanding between the two institutions. I find that only in this way would such entities complement, instead of compete, with each other.

A further original contribution of this chapter of the book is in demonstrating that, contrary to the contentions of the TRC and some of the leading commentators on the issue to date, the SCSL was always intended to have priority if the two bodies clashed during the discharge of their disparate institutional functions. The way they were created, and official government policy statements which had been misunderstood to say the opposite of what they did actually intended, are used as basis to add this insight to the literature on the Sierra Leone TRC-SCSL transitional justice experiment. Ultimately, of course, a reading that tried to portray the institutions as in harmony with each other is to be preferred over one that takes the two institutions as antagonistic or in competition with each other. That, however, is a normative question of policy; not a legal position.

Taken together, the chapters in this book advance the present knowledge on some of the largely unexplored and largely misunderstood topics pertaining to the SCSL and its judicial contributions to the wider system of international criminal law.

1.7 ORGANIZATION OF THE CHAPTERS

This book is divided into eleven substantive chapters. Chapter 1, which serves as the Introduction, sets out the background and purpose of this book, discusses the aims of the research and why it is significant, the methodology that it uses, and describes the anticipated contribution to the international law literature.

Chapter 2 provides the background necessary to understanding the SCSL's mandate. It briefly discusses the origins of the Sierra Leonean conflict. I show how widespread killing, rape and acts of sexual violence, particularly against women and young girls, mass amputations, use of child soldiers, acts of terrorism against civilians, including the burning of entire towns and villages, and the attacks on United Nations peacekeepers, became the signatures associated with the Sierra Leone conflict. I show that the shocking atrocities perpetrated on innocent civilians is what ultimately led to the successful calls by the victims and their supporters, locally and internationally, for the investigation and prosecutions of those presumed responsible.

In Chapter 3, I consider the controversial circumstances giving rise to the establishment of the SCSL. I demonstrate that the Sierra Leonean government decision to prosecute was a result of the breakdown of a hastily put together peace agreement between the authorities and the rebels. That had been provoked by an official stance, which had initially prioritized non-prosecution and amnesty for the sake of securing the peace, but eventually led it to reverse itself and instead request international help to establish a credible special tribunal. The thrust was to punish the authors of the conflict as well as their collaborators. This part is also a case study demonstrating the difficult choices that government officials in conflict-ridden states are sometimes forced by circumstances to make. The short-term desire for peace, and the long-term imperative of accountability and justice, appear to clash in Sierra Leone – as it has in so many other historical and contemporary conflicts.

Having set the context of the conflict and the creation of the tribunal, and turning more to the substance, Chapter 4 then moves to a discussion of the legal competence of the SCSL over persons (*ratione personae* jurisdiction), the mixed local and international crimes that it could prosecute (*ratione materiae* jurisdiction), the geographic space over which it could exercise its authority (*ratione loci* jurisdiction), as well as the limited time period (*ratione temporis* jurisdiction) within its scope. I situate the Court in the wider context of the prior international criminal courts that preceded it with particular reference to the ICTY and ICTR. I demonstrate that the main prosecution objective set for the SCSL was ultimately driven more by pragmatics than principle. This is reflected in the fact that it was specifically designed to deliver a limited quantity of justice through the prosecutions of a handful of persons rather than all those who may have committed international crimes.

In turning to the core of the original analysis offered by this work, in Chapter 5, I evaluate the SCSL's key contributions on the personal jurisdiction over persons "bearing greatest responsibility," a concept that presently seems vogue in international criminal discourse. Drawing on an earlier work, a key finding of this chapter is that, despite the initial disagreement amongst the judges of the Court regarding the best way to construe "greatest responsibility," that is to say whether as a *guideline* or as a *jurisdictional threshold*, the determination that it should be treated as guidance enabling the prosecution of what I call "killer-perpetrators" along with those in the "political-military leaders" category is a useful approach to the future application of this type of personal jurisdiction in international criminal courts. This is a thoughtful judicial contribution of the SCSL to the work of other courts, as already evidenced by the case law of the Cambodia Tribunal.

The treatment of gendered crimes continues to be a challenge for international criminal tribunals, which have been sometimes criticized for their indifference to the plight of women and girls who so often bear the brunt of conflicts. In Chapter 6, I examine the SCSL's landmark contribution to the law of crimes against humanity, focusing in particular, on the novel crime of forced marriages as an "other" inhumane act. The crime was designed to take into account the gendered nature of the armed conflict in Sierra Leone but takes place against the backdrop of the need to also ensure that the fair trial rights of suspects and accused persons are respected.

Chapter 7 turns to another core crime, the war crime prohibiting the recruitment and use of children under the age of fifteen for the purposes of using them to participate actively in hostilities. This crime, first prosecuted in Sierra Leone, gained in global importance when it was included in the Rome Statute of the International Criminal Court in 1998 and invoked in the first case before the ICC. This chapter ultimately shows the influence of the SCSL in road testing the application of this crime.

The issue of immunities from prosecution for sitting heads of state continues to be one of the most challenging for international criminal lawyers. Immunities, because of their nature, raise questions about whether this body of law can adhere to the traditional principle of equality of all persons before the law in light of the gravity of international crimes. The problem is compounded since removal of immunities appear to challenge age-old notions of sovereignty, which limit the assertion of jurisdiction by the courts of one state over the officials of another state, largely for the sake of maintaining stable international relations. I analyze the SCSL's interaction with and treatment of the controversial law of head of state immunity in Chapter 8. I use the trial of former Liberian president Taylor, who was indicted by the SCSL while in office, to critically assess the Appeals Chamber's conclusion that he was not entitled to any immunity from prosecution in light of the ICJ's firm position on customary international law immunities.

Essentially, the Appeals Chamber ruled that personal immunity was irrelevant to proceedings carried out by an international criminal court established with the support of the international community – at least where such a community is represented by the UN. It is significant that such involvement appeared to undermine traditional conceptions of sovereignty of the state and may offer the safeguards to constrain potentially troubling unilateral actions by one state against the leader of another state. This finding should inform the development of future case law on the immunity of serving heads of third states in respect of other high-profile presidents and heads of government charged with international crimes.

Amnesties are well-known alternatives to criminal prosecutions, and as a historical matter, were widely used as incentives to help a given society move on from a difficult political past. They continue to be popular, as a policy option, among some war tormented countries. Among the most recent examples is Colombia. The question which arises, in this age of individual criminal responsibility, is whether blanket amnesties can be considered compatible with the present trend of international criminal prosecutions and the rights of victims to receive at least a limited measure of justice in atrocity situations.

Chapter 9 studies Sierra Leone's initial conferral of a generous or rather over generous amnesty on all the combatants that perpetrated international crimes during the war, and the ensuing legal debate whether the subsequent unilateral withdrawal of that measure barred the SCSL prosecutions. I demonstrate that, while normatively the Tribunal apparently reached the right conclusion that there was nothing in its statute that prevented the SCSL from trying the specific suspects before it for their alleged crimes, the full potential of this decision was not taken advantage of to clarify the development of future jurisprudence on the interface between amnesties and the prosecution of war crimes, crimes against humanity and other serious international humanitarian law violations. At the same time, the SCSL case law has been invoked in other regional human rights courts and in international expert bodies, including treaty bodies and the International Law Commission. It has thus formed part of the global debate on the question of amnesties for international crimes and maybe reflective of an increasing intolerance towards their continued application.

In Chapter 10, I step back and examine the criminal trials carried out by the SCSL against the backdrop of its concurrent operation, for a period of eighteen months, with the TRC. The two institutions were traditionally not used simultaneously in other post-conflict situations. They operated alongside each other as a result of special circumstances instead of by deliberate design. I study the practical issues that arose in that context. This included whether the two institutions could share information and the implications of any such collaboration for the integrity of their individual processes as well as the achievement of their core mandates.

The book demonstrates that the concurrent existence of a truth-seeking institution rooted in an amnesty to all perpetrators of mass atrocities during a vicious conflict contradicted the goals of criminal accountability and thereby threatened to undermine the work of the SCSL. The failure of the founders to specify how the two institutions should cooperate in their work, and which of the two bodies, if any, should have primacy in the event of a clash of their separate functions led to tensions in one of the earliest judicial examinations of such relationships. The lessons derived from the analysis should add to our knowledge of the risks stemming from such situations. It also identifies some mistakes that can be avoided in future transitional justice situations and should therefore inform future transitional justice practice.

Finally, Chapter 11 of the book summarizes the key arguments. It provides a synopsis of the main conclusions derived from each of the previous chapters. On the whole, while conceding that its jurisprudence was sometimes lacking, on balance, I argue that by its mere existence and judicial practice, the SCSL made some important judicial contributions to the development of international criminal law. Many of its contributions are already proving to be influential to the work of other national and international courts. The evidence indicates it is likely that this trend will continue.

2

The Sierra Leone Conflict

2.1 INTRODUCTION

In the last decade of the twentieth century, which had been quite bloody with several deadly conflicts, Sierra Leone, a relatively small country in West Africa just about the size of Austria in Europe and the American State of South Carolina, became the scene of one of the "greatest human tragedies"[1] in modern history. The Sierra Leone war, which officially started on March 23, 1991 and ended on January 18, 2002, gained notoriety around the world for its brutality and the commission of some of the worst atrocities against civilians ever witnessed in a contemporary conflict.[2] The conflict, which was characterized by widespread killings, mass amputations, abductions of women and children, recruitment and use of children as combatants, rape, sexual violence against mostly women and underage girls (including their taking as "bush wives"), arson, pillage, looting and burning, is estimated to have resulted in the deaths of between fifty and seventy thousand people.[3] It also led to the displacement of about 2.6 million of the country's population of 5 million, the maiming of thousands of others, and the wanton destruction of private and public property. These included schools, government buildings, police stations and other public infrastructure that has since taken many years to rebuild.

Sierra Leone, which was a former British colony first established as a trading post in the sixteenth century, is comprised of seventeen ethnic groups, each with its own

---

[1] A WITNESS TO TRUTH: REPORT OF THE SIERRA LEONE TRUTH AND RECONCILIATION COMMISSION 97, ¶ 1 (2004) (hereinafter SIERRA LEONE TRC REPORT).

[2] Several books offer important accounts on the history of the Sierra Leone conflict. *See, e.g.*, LANSANA GBERIE, A DIRTY WAR IN WEST AFRICA: THE RUF AND THE DESTRUCTION OF SIERRA LEONE (2005); DAVID KEEN, CONFLICT AND COLLUSION IN SIERRA LEONE (2005); PETER PENFOLD, ATROCITIES, DIAMONDS AND DIPLOMACY: THE INSIDE STORY OF THE CONFLICT IN SIERRA LEONE (2012). An official account, comprising several volumes, was produced by the Sierra Leone Truth and Reconciliation Commission in 2004. Most of the material in this introduction is drawn from the TRC REPORT. A helpful and detailed summary of the origins of the conflict in the context of the trials at the SCSL can also be found in the various judgments of the Tribunal. *See*, for instance, Prosecutor v. Taylor, Case No. SCSL-03-01-T, Judgment, ¶¶ 18–70, (May 18, 2012) (hereinafter Taylor Trial Judgment).

[3] UNDP, Evaluation of UNDP Assistance to Conflict Affected Countries-Human Security: Case Study Sierra Leone, UN Development Program Evaluations Office, at 7 (2006).

distinctive language and culture. The Mende (31 percent) and Temne (35 percent) are the two largest groups, making up about 66 percent of the population. The former occupies most of the southern part of the territory, centered around the cities of Bo and Kenema. The latter group is based primarily in the north, especially around the town of Makeni. Other groups include the Limba (8 percent) from the north and the Kono (5 percent), who occupy parts of the diamond-rich east.

Administratively, at the time of the war, Sierra Leone was divided into three provinces: Northern, Southern, and Eastern in addition to the Western Area. Freetown, which is the nation's capital, was founded as a haven for repatriated slaves from Great Britain and North America. The latter included Nova Scotia, following the American War of Independence; Freetown remains a port-city and the seat of the central government. Though Sierra Leone has been blessed with rich diamond deposits, first discovered in the 1930s, as well as many other minerals such as gold, aluminum, bauxite and iron ore, as well as fishery resources, the majority of the population subsists on agriculture with farming as a primary occupation. The country, both before and after the war, has repeatedly ranked at or towards the bottom of global human development indices as one of the poorest in the world. With the outbreak of the deadly Ebola virus that turned into an epidemic that resulted in the loss of many lives in 2014, Sierra Leone, which is still struggling to stabilize politically and to recover from the deleterious effects of a traumatic conflict-filled decade, has seen its otherwise growing economy contract sharply.

2.2 THE PURPOSE AND STRUCTURE OF THIS CHAPTER

This chapter will provide a brief rather than a comprehensive overview of the circumstances that are widely believed to have given rise to the outbreak of war in Sierra Leone. This discussion seems justified because it is important to understand the wider historical and political context against which we will be embarking upon an assessment of the main legal legacy of the Special Court for Sierra Leone (SCSL), which is the primary focus of this book, to international criminal law. Of course, the SCSL, as explained in Chapter 1 and as will be further discussed in the next chapter, was set up as a partnership between Sierra Leonean authorities and the United Nations. It was tasked with the responsibility to investigate and prosecute those most responsible for the gross international and humanitarian law violations committed during the country's notorious conflict.

Structurally, the next section of this chapter discusses the precursors to the conflict. The first subsection considers the origins of the war, while the second reflects on the country's transition from military to democratic rule at roughly the midway point of the war. Thereafter, I briefly evaluate the various attempts of the elected government of President Ahmed Tejan Kabbah to negotiate peace, first at Abidjan, Ivory Coast in November 1996, and later, at Lomé, Togo in July 1999. The main goal of those negotiations was to bring an end to the brutal conflict.

But there were hitches along the way because of the collapse of aspects of those two peace accords. I therefore take up the government's apparent policy shift from conferring a blanket amnesty on all wartime combatants, in return for peace, to actively seeking their prosecution before an internationally supported tribunal that became known as the SCSL. Due to its topical significance, not just for Sierra Leone but also many other contemporary conflicts, I will return to closely analyze the controversy over the amnesty provision in Chapter 9 of this book. The final subsection summarizes the key points and foreshadows the next chapter discussing the wider context of the ad hoc penal tribunal's establishment in Freetown in 2002.

2.3 ANTECEDENTS TO THE OUTBREAK OF CONFLICT IN SIERRA LEONE

The tragedy of the Sierra Leonean conflict and that country's recent association with mass atrocities, "blood diamonds," and the prosecutions of international crimes through the SCSL, is that Sierra Leone was previously considered a haven of political stability and a center of higher learning in West Africa. Sierra Leone, which along with Ghana, Nigeria, and The Gambia were the four British colonies in West Africa, secured political independence from Britain on April 27, 1961. Self-government was followed by what seemed to be an auspicious start for democracy with the first peaceful transfer of power to an elected opposition party in an independent African State in 1967.[4] However, the British legacy of a Westminster style democracy proved to have little longevity as the country quickly degenerated down the path of instability with a spate of military coups and countercoups.[5] Ultimately, the civilian All People's Congress (APC) party formed a stable government around 1970.

Unfortunately, the APC regime, under the stewardship of then-president Siaka P. Stevens, stifled democracy by transforming itself into a despotic one-party regime and sustaining its stranglehold on the country through massive corruption, nepotism, plunder of public assets and exacerbation of ethnic, regional and rural–urban cleavages.[6] In the decade between 1980 and early 1990, bad governance, economic decay, corruption, intolerance for dissent and the shrinking of the democratic space, among other factors, had created sufficient malaise for the outbreak of conflict in the country.[7] A motley group comprised of a mix of former university student activists and unemployed youth, led by some disgruntled former army officers with political ambitions such as the Revolutionary United Front (RUF) Leader Foday Sankoh, emerged after a while with the purported goal of launching a people's revolution.

---

[4] JOHN R. CARTWRIGHT, POLITICS IN SIERRA LEONE 1947–1967 (1970).
[5] SIERRA LEONE TRC REPORT, *supra* note 1, at Executive Summary, vol. 2, ch. 1 at 3.
[6] *Id.* at 6.
[7] *Id.* at 3–12.

The apparent goal was to forcibly remove the APC Government and to restore real democracy and good governance to Sierra Leone.

2.4 THE OUTBREAK OF CONFLICT IN SIERRA LEONE

On March 23, 1991, a group of an estimated forty to sixty armed men invaded Bomaru Village in Kailahun District, eastern Sierra Leone near the Liberian border. The attack, in which only two of thirteen casualties were combatants, turned out to be one of the first salvoes of the murderous RUF rebels allegedly led by one Sankoh, a retired infantryman from the Sierra Leone Army (SLA), whose apparent goal was to overthrow the then-government under President Joseph Saidu Momoh. Sankoh had an axe to grind. He had been previously dishonorably discharged from the army after being arrested, tried, convicted and sentenced to a seven-year jail term for his involvement in a failed 1971 military coup. He had fled the country after his release, joining a group of West African revolutionaries trained in Libya, at the Mathaba Alimia – a military and ideological outfit that promoted Pan-Africanism and Libyan President Muamar Gaddafi's brand of socialism. In late February 1991, Sankoh had issued an ultimatum to the Momoh Government, insisting that the president resign within ninety days or else face a revolt. The Bomaru attack occurred before the three-month deadline expired, perhaps after Sankoh realized that no one in Freetown was taking him seriously.

In a few weeks, the rebels, with human, material, logistical and other support from Charles Taylor of the National Patriotic Front of Liberia (NPFL),[8] who helped to train at Camp Naama in neighboring Liberia the bulk of the RUF fighters that launched the first attacks into Sierra Leone known as the Vanguards, increased the intensity and frequency of their attacks. The ill-equipped SLA, which had more experience putting down peaceful pro-democracy student demonstrations than fighting a war, proved unable to contain the unrelenting hit-and-run guerrilla attacks. In a few months, most of Kailahun District in the east and Pujehun District in the south, both not far from the Liberian border, had fallen under rebel control. The RUF spread westwards, setting up bases, and training and using captured civilians to grow their numbers. Given the SLA's inability to combat the war, and the lack of leadership among the Freetown government elite, it was only a matter of time before the war would spread to all parts of the country – with devastating consequences for the local population.

---

[8]   Taylor started a guerrilla war in Liberia in 1989 similar to that led by Sankoh in Sierra Leone. He served as Liberia's president from 1997 to 2003. His trial is discussed, *infra*, at Chapters 4 and 8. On the need for accountability for the wartime atrocities in Liberia, *see* Charles Jalloh & Alhagi Marong, *Ending Impunity: The Case for War Crimes Trials in Liberia*, 2 Afr. J. Legal Stud. 53 (2005) (arguing for the expansion of the SCSL's jurisdiction to try those bearing greatest responsibility for serious international crimes committed during the Liberian conflict).

President Momoh seemingly lacked a coherent strategy to deal with the nation's security even as his largely undisciplined and inexperienced army continued to suffer terrible losses from the ragtag RUF and the Liberian fighters from the NPFL. The rebels, as they experienced initial military setbacks, resorted to more guerrilla style hit-and-run tactics aimed at instilling fear in their enemy as well as in the local civilian population. The rebels' strategy of terrorizing and then abducting civilians, drugging and enlisting children to fight, burning and looting villages and raping young girls and women, developed in the early days of the war, would later become the tragic images associated with the Sierra Leone conflict by those in other parts of the world.

With the army having lost confidence in their commander-in-chief, Momoh was ousted from power in April 1992 by a group of mutinying soldiers led by a twenty-seven-year-old Captain Valentine Strasser, an army paymaster with no political experience. They took over the reins of state in a coup and formed a junta regime styling itself the National Provisional Ruling Council (NPRC). Although very popular at the beginning, especially among urban youth and university students, the NPRC suspended the national constitution, and thereafter, ruled the country by decree. The RUF perceived the NPRC as the culmination of their struggle to end the APC's one-party rule. But Strasser, as well as his former deputy (Julius M. Bio)[9] who later overthrew him in a palace coup in January 1996, refused to negotiate with them. Instead, they tried but failed to decisively end the conflict by launching crushing military offensives against the RUF and its forces.

Partly because of deep mistrust of the national army, who locals aptly labeled "sobels" (a coinage from the words *soldier* and *rebels* used to describe the phenomena of soldiers by day and rebels by night), the government turned to hiring mercenaries, first from Nepal and afterward South Africa, to help fight the war in return for generous diamond concessions. The presence of foreign fighters, especially the battle-hardened Executive Outcomes from the days of apartheid and the war with UNITA in Angola, initially offered some respite to the government forces. They routed the RUF in various areas, and in the account of some, proved to be a major factor in forcing the rebels to strategically take up the government's invitation to conclude a cease-fire and peace agreement. However, reliance on mercenaries was ultimately only a Band-Aid rather than a permanent solution. It only temporarily enabled the government to continue its sovereign control of the mineral-rich mining areas in the east and south of Sierra Leone.

---

[9] Interestingly, in the presidential contest in Sierra Leone held on Nov. 17, 2012, Bio, who had long resigned from the army, was the lead opposition Sierra Leone People's Party candidate. He ran against incumbent president Ernest Bai Koroma. Koroma won a second term with 58.7 percent while Bio secured up to 37.4 percent of the vote. *See* NATIONAL ELECTORAL COMMISSION, STATEMENT FROM NEC CHAIRPERSON ON THE CONDUCT AND RESULT OF THE PRESIDENTIAL ELECTIONS, (Dec. 4, 2012), www.nec-sierraleone.org/index_files/STATEMENT%20%20FROM%20NEC%20CHAIRPERSON%20(press%20district).pdf. Since then, Bio has become president of Sierra Leone following peaceful democratic elections after Koroma's two terms.

2.5 DEMOCRATIC ELECTIONS AND EXCHANGING PEACE FOR TRUTH AND RECONCILIATION

Under pressure from war-weary Sierra Leoneans clamoring to participate in their country's governance through the ballot box, the NPRC junta eventually restored constitutional rule. Long-anticipated democratic elections were finally conducted in 1996. The Sierra Leone People's Party (SLPP) candidate Ahmad Tejan Kabbah, a former UN bureaucrat who had returned home to enter the contest, won the elections. President Kabbah, who ran on a powerful campaign that he would swiftly end the war (music to the ears of the war-weary population), immediately entered into negotiations with the RUF. To entice them to the bargaining table, he offered them an amnesty from prosecution and agreed to the establishment of a National Unity and Reconciliation Commission (NURC). He concluded a peace accord with the RUF in Ivory Coast on November 30, 1996. The Abidjan Accord[10] contained, among others, important provisions calling for termination of the hostilities on both sides, disarmament and reintegration of combatants into society, and removal of the Executive Outcomes foreign mercenaries from the country within three to six months. In return for the peace, and their participation in the political process, the government promised an amnesty under which it undertook to ensure that no judicial or other official action would be taken against the members of the RUF for the crimes perpetrated by them up to the date of signature of the agreement.[11]

Nevertheless, as there did not appear to be good faith on the rebel side to transform itself into a political movement with all the rights, privileges and duties recognized under Sierra Leonean law, the Abidjan Accord failed: hostilities resumed, and yet another military coup took place on May 25, 1997, this time by a group of seventeen disgruntled and underpaid junior officers calling themselves the Armed Forces Revolutionary Council (AFRC). They were, among other things, unhappy with the government's support for local militias and felt the professional army – the SLA – had been sidelined. President Kabbah fled to neighboring Guinea where he essentially set up a government-in-exile in the capital Conakry. The AFRC coupists, who released Major Johnny Paul Koroma who was in jail at the time, installed themselves as the new regime, declared martial law, and invited Sankoh and the RUF leadership to share power. Sankoh, though in Nigeria where he had been arrested and placed under house arrest allegedly for weapons violations, accepted the invitation and was appointed deputy. The RUF fighters and

---

[10]   See Peace Agreement between the Government of the Republic of Sierra Leone and the Revolutionary United Front of Sierra Leone, UN Doc. S/1996/1034 (Nov. 30, 1996) (hereinafter Abidjan Accord), *reprinted in* CONSOLIDATED LEGAL TEXTS FOR THE SPECIAL COURT FOR SIERRA LEONE 545–556 (Charles Jalloh ed. 2007).

[11]   See id. at arts. 1, 2, 12, 14. For a thoughtful analysis arguing that the peace deals signed by the government were illegal both under Sierra Leonean Constitutional and international law, *see* JEREMEY I. LEVITT, ILLEGAL PEACE IN AFRICA: AN INQUIRY INTO THE LEGALITY OF POWER SHARING WITH WARLORDS, REBELS, AND JUNTA (2012).

commanders came out of the bush and joined the government in Freetown. All political parties were banned.

But the uneasy AFRC–RUF coalition, which was comprised of two sets of former enemies (the government's mutinying army, on the one hand, and the rebels on the other), had little long-term common interests and failed to gain international recognition. Both sides publicly claimed that they had only joined forces in order to restore peace and stability. A massive and unprecedented campaign of civil disobedience from Sierra Leoneans simply fed up with the war effectively shut down the country for periods at a time. As the army was no longer loyal, the desperate Kabbah government in exile in Conkary designated a civilian militia made of traditional hunters, the Civil Defense Forces (CDF) led by Sam Hinga Norman, Kabbah's deputy defense minister, to help fight the rebels. The CDF was comprised of volunteer fighters who were given the responsibility to protect their communities. Attempts were made to reach an accord under which the AFRC–RUF would transfer power back to the civilian government, but this too failed. The military option was to prove decisive.

With strong regional backing, especially from the regional Economic Community of West African States (ECOWAS), Kabbah was reinstated to power after ten months on March 10, 1998. ECOWAS forces, which were committed to restoring the democratically elected government, had launched a major offensive against the AFRC–RUF coalition in February 1998. Kabbah triumphantly returned to Freetown, where in a controversial decision, several individuals involved in unseating him from power were promptly subjected to court martial trials and executed. Again, based on his belief that the war could only be ended through negotiated political settlement and combined with pressure from external powers, President Kabbah resumed discussions with the RUF. In July 1999, a militarily weakened Kabbah government concluded the comprehensive Lomé Peace Agreement with the RUF in the hope of ending the conflict once and for all.[12] The Lomé package, reflecting the weaknesses of a government teetering on the brink of collapse, tried to placate the rebels through a form of power oversharing. These included offering four deputy minister positions, four key minister positions, and even the *status* of vice-presidency of Sierra Leone to the leader of the RUF Sankoh.[13] The adamant civilian government was to later justify this measure essentially using a two-pronged necessity argument: (1) that the population had demanded the end of the war, at whatever cost; and (2) consequent upon that, the RUF would not have laid down their weapons absent such a guarantee. Both positions appeared to be supported by some evidence.

---

[12] *See* Peace Agreement between the Government of Sierra Leone and the Revolutionary United Front, UN Doc. S/1999/777 (July 7, 1999) (hereinafter Lomé Accord), *reprinted in* CONSOLIDATED LEGAL TEXTS FOR THE SPECIAL COURT FOR SIERRA LEONE 563–84 (Charles Jalloh ed. 2007).

[13] *See id.*, Lomé Accord art. 5.

In any event, in perhaps the worst strategic blunder that could have been made by a Sierra Leonean government dependent on minerals for core revenue, President Kabbah agreed to create a commission that would be solely responsible for overseeing the exploitation of the country's immense gold, diamond and other strategic mineral resource wealth.[14] He ceded the chairmanship of that board to Sankoh, the RUF rebel leader, who could now lawfully take what he previously had to plunder. It was like making the bank robber the guard and turning over to him the keys to the safe where all the money was kept. The parties also agreed to disarmament, rehabilitation and reintegration of the former combatants into society.[15] The United Nations and ECOWAS undertook to serve as the "moral guarantors" of the peace through the subsequent deployment of peacekeepers to monitor the parties' implementation of the agreement.

Significantly, to avoid any type of criminal accountability for the crimes that had been committed up to that point of the conflict, the parties broadened the terms of the failed Abidjan Accord from November 1996. To placate the critics, who had argued against such a move, they provided for the establishment of a Truth and Reconciliation Commission (TRC) to purportedly "address impunity, break the cycle of violence, provide a forum for both victims and the perpetrators of human rights violations to tell their story" about the war and to promote national healing.[16] In a controversial move, especially within Sierra Leone, President Kabbah capitulated to the RUF demands and expanded the amnesty concession first included in Article 14 of the Abidjan Accord to cover *all the combatants* who had fought in the war.

However, even the blanket amnesty granting Sankoh personally and all other combatants and collaborators "absolute and free pardon and reprieve"[17] in respect of all their actions between the start of the war and the conclusion of the Lomé Peace Agreement proved insufficient to restore peace to Sierra Leone. The UN Special Representative at the talks entered what has been sometimes described as a "reservation" to the amnesty clause, in which he stated the international community's "understanding" that the amnesty would not apply in respect of international crimes. This decision was to later give the SCSL, which had been established after the rebels reneged on the agreement, the legal basis upon which to rule against the defendants' arguments that they could not be prosecuted because the Tribunal lacked jurisdiction over them. The judicial ruling on whether international law recognized such a blanket amnesty clause, or whether it did not, will be analyzed in depth in Chapter 9 of this book.

Around this time, even though the Sierra Leonean war had largely been ignored by most mainstream Western media up to that point, the sensational stories of

[14]   See Lomé Accord, *supra* note 12, at art. 7.
[15]   See *id.* at art. 16.
[16]   See *id.* at art. 6, § 2 and art. 26.
[17]   See *id.* at art. 9.

human savagery to fellow humans going on in the West African nation had started generating external interest. The publicity efforts were led by local and international civil society advocacy groups, with Sierra Leonean women's groups fed up with the war taking the lead in several mass public protests in Freetown. Human Rights Watch and Amnesty International led the international naming and shaming efforts with a series of widely disseminated and shocking reports.[18] The demobilization, reintegration and rehabilitation programs for the combatants soon began to run into difficulties, and it became evident that some factions of the RUF were bent on undermining the peace. They were not sufficiently invested in winning the peace as much as they were in the continuation of war to voluntarily lay down their weapons.

2.6 FROM FORGIVE AND FORGET TO RETRIBUTION AND CRIMINAL PROSECUTIONS

The Kabbah Government, which had refused to seriously pursue any criminal accountability options, appeared to undergo a significant change of heart when, in May 2000, over 500 UN peacekeepers were disarmed and held hostage by renegade rebel commanders. This embarrassing incident occurred in the northern province of Sierra Leone. A second turn of events that angered the governmental leadership occurred when hundreds of peaceful protesters who had marched on Sankoh's residence in Freetown to insist on rebel compliance with the terms of the peace accord were caught in a shootout by his security detail. Over twenty unarmed protesters were killed.

The taking of UN peacekeepers hostage and the killing of some of them, as well as the murder of protesters, were the proverbial straws that broke the camel's back for the Kabbah Administration. They were increasingly frustrated with and embarrassed by the continued recalcitrance of the RUF. Sankoh, it had become evident, wielded only nominal influence over his key battlefield commanders. Placing faith in him for a negotiated end of the conflict made them look naïve. The whole effort seemed to be futile.

Indeed, following the cold-blooded murder of the peaceful demonstrators at his house in the West End of Freetown, Sankoh was arrested by Sierra Leonean authorities. He was thereafter detained at an undisclosed location. Just the following month, in early June 2000, President Kabbah formally declared that his government could no longer tolerate further RUF violations of the key terms in the Lomé Peace Agreement.[19] Consequently, given the repeated violations of the agreement

---

[18] *See, e.g.*, Human Rights Watch, *Sierra Leone: Getting Away with Murder, Mutilation, Rape*, Vol. 11, No. 3A (July 1999) (documenting, inter alia, shocking victim testimony of RUF atrocities, and calling for the international community to oppose the blanket amnesty for all combatants and accountability for crimes under Sierra Leonean and international law).

[19] CHARLES JALLOH, THE SIERRA LEONE SPECIAL COURT AND ITS LEGACY: THE IMPACT FOR AFRICA AND INTERNATIONAL CRIMINAL LAW 9 (Charles Jalloh ed., 2014).

combined with renewed pressure from the local and international civil society to repudiate the amnesty and establish some type of prosecution mechanism to pursue the worst offenders, President Kabbah turned to the United Nations to ask for assistance to create a credible special court to try the worst offenders.

2.7 CONCLUSION

This chapter has briefly described the origins and key features of the Sierra Leone conflict. Drawing on authoritative sources, it has discussed the main actors in the conflict, all of whose role will be relevant to the later discussion of the various charges issued by the Tribunal and the trials later carried out by the SCSL. To recap, the lead faction was the RUF on the one hand, which had started a rebellion aimed at unseating the APC government, and the Sierra Leone Army on the other. The former enjoyed the initial support of the NPFL from neighboring Liberia, which served as their staging post for the initial incursion into eastern Sierra Leone in March 1991. The RUF would later part company with some members of the NPFL. It would eventually form a coalition with the mutinying ex-soldiers from the AFRC, around the halfway point of the war, to briefly govern Sierra Leone before the ragtag coalition was ousted from power.

For their part, the government forces, that is the SLA, received operational support from West African peacekeepers as part of the Economic Community Military Observer Group (ECOMOG) contingent deployed to help restore peace to Sierra Leone. As mentioned earlier, the government had at one point hired South African and Nepalese mercenaries, and after those groups departed, the government under President Kabbah (who had won democratic elections in 1996) supported a locally established paramilitary group known as the CDF. The Kabbah Administration's goal of returning Sierra Leone to normalcy after a bloody few years would eventually lead to controversial grants of a blanket amnesty to combatants in 1996 which was expanded even further in the 1999 accord. These purported to absolve all the actors in the conflict of all responsibility. But the two peace deals had to be terminated, and following some troubling incidents, the local authorities requested international intervention to establish a credible special criminal tribunal that would prosecute its former enemies and their collaborators for some of the atrocities that they had committed during the war. The next chapter examines the detailed circumstances surrounding the establishment of the SCSL.

3

The Establishment of the Special Court for Sierra Leone

3.1 INTRODUCTION

At the time the United Nations (UN) got involved with the establishment of the Special Court for Sierra Leone (SCSL), it could draw from the experiences it had developed when creating the first ad hoc tribunals in 1993 and 1994. The UN first became involved with the creation of such courts after the Balkan Conflict, which resulted in the establishment of the International Criminal Tribunal for the Former Yugoslavia (ICTY). The ICTY was created by the Security Council on May 25, 1993, when it adopted Resolution 827 to address serious violations of international humanitarian law arising from the conflict in the former Yugoslavia.[1] Before the ICTY's establishment, the Security Council had asked the UN Secretary General, in October 1992, to convene an impartial expert commission to investigate the commission of international crimes and to collect credible evidence of atrocities.[2] The inquiry determined that grave breaches of international humanitarian law had been committed in the territory of the former Yugoslavia, including murder, "ethnic cleansing," rape, pillage, destruction of property and arbitrary arrests.[3]

But there was no blueprint for the UN to use in creating the first ad hoc international criminal tribunal. Prior to the ICTY's creation, the only major international effort to establish such a court had been the Allies' decision to prosecute the Nazi leadership during World War II through the Nuremberg International Military Tribunal (IMT), and the similar mechanism used in Tokyo, to try Japanese leaders in the IMT for the Far East (IMTFE).[4] The IMT model, in addition to expert studies, State suggestions,

---

[1] S.C. Res. 827, ¶ 2 (May 25, 1993).
[2] VIRGINIA MORRIS & MICHAEL P. SCHARF, AN INSIDER'S GUIDE TO THE INTERNATIONAL CRIMINAL TRIBUNAL FOR THE FORMER YUGOSLAVIA 26 (1995) [hereinafter ICTY INSIDER'S GUIDE].
[3] Id. at 28.
[4] See Agreement for the Prosecution and Punishment of the Major War Criminals of the European Axis, Aug. 8, 1945, 59 Stat. 1586, 82 U.N.T.C. 279; Charter of the International Military Tribunal, Aug. 8, 1945, 59 Stat. 1544, 82 U.N.T.S. 279; International Military Tribunal for the Far East Special Proclamation: Establishment of an International Military Tribunal for the Far East, Jan. 10, 1946, T. I.A.S. No. 1589; Charter for the International Military Tribunal for the Far East, Jan. 19, 1946, T.I.A.S. No. 1589.

individual and NGO comments, as well as formulations found in several international instruments, served as the main inspiration for the ICTY Statute taking into account modern developments.[5] However, when designing the ICTY, the Secretary-General did not follow the traditional route of creating such a court through a treaty. The Secretary-General justified his approach, first on the basis that such a process would require considerable time to resolve the details of the instrument, and second, it would be difficult to secure the necessary agreements and ratifications for entry into force. Instead, in a stroke of legal innovation that had not yet been invoked up to that point and which therefore seemed like a radical idea, the Secretary-General proposed that the ICTY be created by decision of the Security Council.[6] The Secretary-General claimed this would be legally justified as well as legitimate.[7] The Secretary-General also stated it would be consistent with the object and purpose of the resolution as an enforcement measure, and crucially, would have the effect of being legally binding on all UN Member States pursuant to Chapter VII of the UN Charter.

One year after the ICTY was created, the UN established the second ad hoc tribunal: the International Criminal Tribunal for Rwanda (ICTR).[8] The ICTR's mandate was to prosecute those responsible for the 1994 genocide in the East African Nation of Rwanda, in which an estimated half a million to a million people were killed. The Council followed the same multistep process for the ICTR as it had done for the ICTY by first establishing an ad hoc international commission.[9] The Commission of Experts recommended amending the ICTY Statute and extending its jurisdiction to cover the crimes committed in Rwanda.[10] But, for several legal and practical reasons, the Council deviated from that recommendation. Instead, drawing from the ICTY precedent, the Security Council wisely created a standalone court with the adoption of Resolution 955 on November 8, 1994. Forging a legal path for the second ad hoc international tribunal was relatively smoother. Not only had Rwanda requested the Court, the UN had learned from its recent experience creating the ICTY. There was, simply put, no need to reinvent the wheel.

Even though they had some differences, the ICTY and the ICTR were substantially similar. The former was precedent for the latter. Both were United Nations Security Council (UNSC) creatures and therefore subsidiary organs of the United Nations.[11] Both were legally rooted in Chapter VII of the UN Charter. Additionally, both were

[5]   ICTY INSIDER'S GUIDE, *supra* note 2, at 33.
[6]   *Id.* at 42.
[7]   *Id.* at 43.
[8]   S.C. Res. 955 (Nov. 8, 1994).
[9]   GEORGE W. MUGWANYA, THE CRIME OF GENOCIDE IN INTERNATIONAL LAW: APPRAISING THE CONTRIBUTION OF THE UN TRIBUNAL FOR RWANDA 54 (2007).
[10] U.N. Secretary-General, Preliminary Report of the Independent Commission of Experts Established in Accordance with Security Council Resolution 935, U.N. Doc. S/1994/1125 (Oct. 4 1994); see also Lyal Sunga, *The Commission of Experts on Rwanda and the Creation of the International Criminal Tribunal for Rwanda*, 16 HUM. RTS. L. J. 121 (1995).
[11] The UNSC can create subsidiary bodies. These then become part of the UN, including its financial responsibility. That said, it is possible that agreement could have been reached to create the court by

funded from the UN's regular budget. Indeed, for the early period of their lifespans, the two tribunals were legally conjoined in at least three other ways.

First, they shared a common prosecutor.[12] Second, they formally shared a common group of Appeals Chamber judges, although each was considered legally distinct.[13] The idea of a shared appellate judicial chamber had been crafted in order to ensure the continued development and application of a coherent body of international criminal law. The former only changed about nine years later, on September 15, 2003, when the ICTR got its own separate Prosecutor.[14] An individual Prosecutor was appointed to lead the ICTR. This would help address the perception that the latter tribunal had not benefited sufficiently from the attention of a distant European prosecutor based in The Hague and that the ICTR based in Africa was essentially a poor second cousin of the ICTY. Although the ICTR now had its own Prosecutor, the two tribunals nonetheless still shared an Appeals Chamber until the Tribunal closed down on December 1, 2015 and transformed into a residual mechanism.

Finally, the ICTY Rules formed the basis for those of the ICTR under Article 14 of the ICTR Statute.[15] Today, as the two Chapter VII courts have completed their work and shut down, they maintain a joint residual mechanism including a single joint prosecutor, president and a common roster of judges as well as an appellate chamber.[16] The Security Council established the International Residual

way of treaty. But since the Government of Rwanda objected to several features of the tribunal, this course of action might not have been fruitful.

[12] *Supra* note 8, at art. 15 § 3 of the ICTR Statute states:

> The Prosecutor of the International Tribunal for the Former Yugoslavia shall also serve as the Prosecutor of the International Tribunal for Rwanda. He or she shall have additional staff, including an additional Deputy Prosecutor, to assist with prosecutions before the International Tribunal for Rwanda. The Secretary-General on the recommendation of the Prosecutor shall appoint such staff.

[13] *Supra* note 8, at art. 12 § 2 of the ICTR Statute provided:

> The members of the Appeals Chamber of the International Tribunal for the Prosecution of Persons Responsible for Serious Violations of International Law Committed in the Territory of the Former Yugoslavia since 1991 (hereinafter referred to as "the International Tribunal for the Former Yugoslavia") shall also serve as the members of the Appeals Chamber of the International Tribunal for Rwanda.

[14] In Security Council Resolution 1503 (2003), the Council called on the ICTY to adopt a Completion Strategy. In the same resolution, it also amended Article 15 of the Statute of the ICTR, to create an independent prosecutor that is appointed by the Council upon nomination by the Secretary-General. See S.C. Res. 1503 (Aug. 28, 2003).

[15] *Supra* note 8, at art. 14, of the ICTR Statute, provided that:

> The Judges of the International Tribunal for Rwanda shall adopt, for the purpose of proceedings before the International Tribunal for Rwanda, the Rules of Procedure and Evidence for the conduct of the pre-trial phase of the proceedings, trials and appeals, the admission of evidence, the protection of victims and witnesses and other appropriate matters of the International Tribunal for the former Yugoslavia with such changes as they deem necessary.

[16] See S.C. Res. 1966 (Dec. 22, 2010) (wherein the Council created a Mechanism for International Criminal Tribunals to handle residual activities for the ICTY/ICTR).

Mechanism for Criminal Tribunals, following the completion of the respective mandates of the ICTY and ICTR, to carry on some essential functions such as the completion of the remaining cases and the review of sentences. The UN tribunals and their processes have, in essence, come full circle. Moving from being one, to becoming two separate bodies, and towards the end of their formal mandates, reuniting into a single International Residual Mechanism for Criminal Tribunals.

The SCSL was the UN's next major international justice project. As the third ad hoc international criminal tribunal, the Sierra Leone government followed the footsteps of the Rwandese government and actively requested a tribunal be created. Being the third ad hoc tribunal created, the legal framework of the SCSL benefited tremendously from the existence of the ICTY and the ICTR. The ICTR, as the Africa-based court and more recent of the two ad hocs addressing an internal armed conflict, supplied the basic template for the SCSL. The SCSL, was different in legal nature as it was based on a bilateral agreement between the UN and one of its Member States. The SCSL Statute also reflected some legal developments brought about by the Rome Statute of the International Criminal Court. The latter instrument was adopted in July 1998 following months of negotiations in a diplomatic conference. The Rome Statue was the legal basis for the establishment of the world's first and only permanent international criminal tribunal which was mandated to prosecute genocide, crimes against humanity and war crimes. Although the Rome Statute was not in force by the time the SCSL Statute was finalized in January 2000, as that entry into force only occurred on July 1, 2002, the SCSL Statute benefited from it by, for instance, borrowing some crimes that States had agreed to in 1998.[17]

The point is that the UN and Sierra Leone did not have to start from scratch when devising the fundamental structure of the ad hoc court that they wanted to create both at a substantive and structural level. The Court was also perhaps created in comparatively less controversial circumstances of Sierra Leone vis-à-vis the complex dynamics for the States of the former Yugoslavia and Rwanda. As the parties (that is, the UN and the Government of Sierra Leone) were both keen to establish the tribunal, they could return to the more traditional international law route to creating such a court through consensual treaty basis. In fact, Sierra Leone was the champion for creating a tribunal. This can be compared to Rwanda, which initially was enthused about such a court but was so dissatisfied with the elements of it agreed in the Security Council that it voted against its establishment. For instance, Rwanda opposed the short temporal jurisdiction of the ICTR, which was limited to 1994, the proposed location of the ICTR outside Rwandan territory (in the neighboring State

---

[17]   The inclusion of child recruitment and the prosecution of crimes against UN peacekeepers could be attributed to both the specific facts of what occurred in Sierra Leone but benefited, albeit with some differences, from the precedents contained in the Rome Statute. Complementarity, a cornerstone of the ICC Statute, was also included in the SCSL Statute in relation to prosecutions of peacekeepers. See Micaela Frulli, *The Special Court for Sierra Leone: Some Preliminary Comments*, 11 EUR. J. INT'L L. 857 (2000).

of Tanzania) and the absence of the death penalty as a possible punishment for those eventually convicted. In the end, in Sierra Leone, unlike the case of Rwanda, there was no need for a Security Council imposition of an international court using Chapter VII of the United Nations Charter.

Interestingly, in Sierra Leone's scenario, the national authorities advocated for a Chapter VII court because of their concern about improving the effectiveness of the future tribunal. The idea of having a court that would be able to legally require the cooperation of all states in its work was attractive to President Kabbah. The idea of a mandatory international legal basis, which would flow from the Security Council creation of the Sierra Leone tribunal under Chapter VII, appeared to gain some type of endorsement from the Secretary-General since that would make the court a subsidiary organ. Nonetheless, it failed to garner the requisite support from the Security Council. Some of the Security Council's key permanent members seemed concerned about the implications of pursuing that track. This included the financial implications of creating yet another subsidiary body that would then be the financial responsibility of the UN. They were not too excited with the prospect of being asked to carry the major financial burden required for an international tribunal, which would additionally require state contributions based on assessments reflecting a state's ability to pay.

On the other hand, even though there was some benefit of following a beaten path, the SCSL was established at a time when some of the perceived short-comings of the Chapter VII ad hoc tribunal model had begun to preoccupy some of the UN Member States; especially those holding permanent seats in the Security Council. Prominent among these concerns were that, as the now late Italian jurist Antonio Cassese summed up, the trials were perceived as too costly, took too long and in any event, such courts were thought to no longer be necessary because of the existence of the permanent International Criminal Court (ICC).[18] For this reason, the so-called "tribunal fatigue"[19] in the Security Council meant that the SCSL did not meet the kind of openness and flexibility that some States were willing to give the two prior tribunals. This meant that some States, such as the United Kingdom of Great Britain and Northern Ireland, seemed committed to avoid recreating another ICTR or ICTY. State pushback against having another new Chapter VII ad hoc tribunal for Sierra Leone demonstrates that each of these UN-supported tribunals is a product of its time. Each should be judged on its merits, given the legal, political and historical circumstances of its establishment and the practical imperatives driving decision-making within the halls of the United Nations.

---

[18]   Antonio Cassese, *Report on the Special Court for Sierra Leone*, ¶ 12 (Dec. 12, 2006).
[19]   David Scheffer, US Ambassador at Large for War Crimes Issues, *Address at the New England School of Law: Challenges Confronting International Justice* (Jan. 14, 1998).

3.2 THE PURPOSE AND STRUCTURE OF THIS CHAPTER

Drawing on both the drafting history and the Court's case law, this chapter provides an overview of the establishment of the SCSL. The first part begins with a discussion of the type of "credible special court" that the government of Sierra Leone sought to have when it initiated the processes leading up to the creation of the ad hoc tribunal. This will then be followed by an assessment of the compromise that the West African country, in a seemingly weak bargaining position, was able to eventually reach with the United Nations and its key decision-makers. A final section makes concluding observations and anticipates the subsequent focus on the SCSL's subject matter, personal, temporal and territorial jurisdiction as well as its organization. Chapters 4 and 5 will take up and develop these topics.

3.3 THE COMPETING VISIONS OF A "SPECIAL COURT FOR SIERRA LEONE"

3.3.1 *President Kabbah's Ambitious Vision for a "Special Court"*

On June 12, 2000, Sierra Leonean President Ahmed Tejan Kabbah wrote what must by now be an infamous letter to the President of the Security Council. The purpose of the correspondence, on behalf of his government and the people of Sierra Leone, was to seek UN support to establish a "special court for Sierra Leone" to bring to "credible justice those members of the Revolutionary United Front (RUF) and their accomplices responsible for committing crimes against the people of Sierra Leone and for the taking of United Nations peacekeepers as hostages."[20] In that letter, President Kabbah described the need for a new court that would seek to achieve two principal objectives. First, to bring justice; and second, to help ensure "lasting peace" to his country and the West Africa subregion.[21] He advocated for a "strong and credible court" that would prosecute those "most responsible" as well as the leaders of the rebel RUF and their accomplices who had planned and executed a brutal decade-long civil war in which ordinary civilians were routinely targeted.[22]

In making the case for international support, the Sierra Leonean leader primarily grounded his arguments in his country's experience with a brutal civil war. He explained that, in the course of nearly ten years of war, the RUF had committed many atrocities against civilians. These included the indiscriminate murder, amputations, abductions, abuse of civilian girls and use of women as sex slaves. This, to

---

[20] Letter from Alhaji Ahmad Tejan Kabbah, President of the Republic of Sierra Leone to the President of the Security Council (June 12, 2000) (annex to Letter dated Aug. 9, 2000 from Ibrahim M. Kamara, Ambassador and Permanent Representative of Sierra Leone to the United Nations addressed to the President of the Security Council, U.N. Doc. S/2000/786 (Aug. 10, 2000) [hereinafter Kabbah Letter to U.N.S.C.].

[21] *Id.* at 2.

[22] *Id.* at 2, § 5 of Enclosure.

him, amply demonstrated why the RUF's reign of terror in his country had led to one of the worst civil conflicts in history. His government's prior dealings with the rebels over the failed 1999 Lomé Peace Agreement, in which he had even "conceded to the granting of total amnesty to the RUF leadership and its members in respect of all the acts of terrorism committed by them"[23] up to the signature of that agreement, confirmed that it was only by bringing their leaders to justice that peace, national reconciliation and democracy would be restored to Sierra Leone. The implication of this request was that the government's main purpose was to secure international assistance to prosecute its adversaries rather than all those who might have perpetrated atrocity crimes. These were principally presumed to be the RUF leaders, and their supporters, with whom the President had become frustrated, due to their repeated broken promises to end Sierra Leone's first and only conflict since independence in April 1961.

In his second principal justification for requesting UN support, President Kabbah sought to explain why his desire for accountability was not just about a small country in West Africa known as Sierra Leone. Rather, it was also about the international community interest being engaged in several ways. He, in this regard, first cited precedents situating the Sierra Leone case within broader developments elsewhere in the world, observing in particular that the creation of a special tribunal would be consistent with prior UN efforts to prosecute international crimes in respect of the conflicts in the former Yugoslavia and Rwanda. By resolving to set up such a court for Sierra Leone, he argued, the international community would be helping bring to justice those who had attacked ordinary Sierra Leoneans as well as the UN peace-keepers sent to their aid. He recalled, in relation to the latter, that the rebels had at one point abducted over 500 Blue Helmets, seized their weapons and uniforms, and even murdered some of them.[24] This argument made a direct connection between the conflict and the work of the UN.

President Kabbah also emphasized several other issues. To him, the magnitude and types of offenses that the RUF leadership and their supporters had perpetrated in Sierra Leone were necessarily "of concern to all persons in the world, as they greatly diminish[ed] respect for international law and the most basic of human rights."[25] This idea builds on the notions that seem to permeate international criminal law in which the victims of heinous crimes are not just presumed to be the direct victims, but also others further away whose conscience is shocked by the commission of crimes condemned by the international community.

Sierra Leone was also unequivocal that it was willing to prosecute the crimes that had occurred on its territory. However, but for international support, the country would simply be unable to timeously dispense credible justice on behalf of the victims.[26] It lacked the resources, expertise and domestic legislation necessary to

---

[23]   *Id.* at 2.
[24]   *Id.* at 2.
[25]   *Id.*
[26]   *Id.*

prosecute the gross human rights violations committed by the RUF fighters and their collaborators.[27] This was particularly so given the country's largely decimated legal and judicial infrastructure, which had been one of the casualties of the war, as well as the widespread nature and extent of the crimes.[28] He further advocated that the "special needs and requirements of the Sierra Leonean situation" be factored into consideration, but expressed a preference for an international tribunal created under the "Security Council's authority."[29] This, in his conception, would give it strong enforcement powers, including the ability to require all states to cooperate with its investigations, arrests, extradition and enforcement of sentences.[30] His ultimate dream was for a "court that [would] meet international standards for the trial of criminal cases while at the same time having a mandate to administer a blend of international and domestic Sierra Leonean law on Sierra Leonean soil."[31]

Overall, President Kabbah's vision appeared to envisage a unique model of a full-fledged Chapter VII international penal court but one that also left some space for the inclusion of some strong national elements. This would include location in the territory of Sierra Leone, use of national law in its statute and the power to appoint key officials, including judges and prosecutors. The Attorney-General of Sierra Leone was to be a co-chief prosecutor, representing the interests of the country, a model that would be similar to that later agreed by the UN in relation to the Cambodia Tribunal. Whereas the international prosecutor would be the co-chief prosecutor essentially representing the international community, especially in relation to the internationally condemned crimes that had been committed against the UN peacekeepers.

3.3.2 *The Secretary-General's Assessment and the Emergence of an Alternative Model*

The Secretary-General promptly acted on President Kabbah's formal request for UN support. First, he took up Sierra Leone's invitation to dispatch a needs assessment mission to Freetown.[32] A senior UN legal officer, from the Office of Legal Affairs, immediately travelled to Sierra Leone to gather more information.[33] Her role was to also evaluate and report back on the needs and capacity of the domestic criminal justice system.[34] As relayed by the Secretary-General, in his subsequent report, the UN lawyer had discussions with a broad set of stakeholders in Sierra Leone. Besides

---

[27] *Id.* at 3.
[28] Kabbah Letter to U.N.S.C. *supra* note 20.
[29] *Id.* at § 1 of Enclosure.
[30] *Id.* at § 5 of Enclosure.
[31] *Id.* at § 3.
[32] *Id.* at § 1 of Enclosure.
[33] U.N. Secretary-General, *Fifth Report of the Secretary General of the Situation in Sierra Leone*, ¶ 9, U. N. Doc. S/1998/486 (June 9, 1998).
[34] *Id.*

the individuals comprising the government, judiciary, police and prison authorities, she also met with persons drawn from local NGOs as well as other representatives of local civil society.[35]

The report was frank about the status of the local justice system. It confirmed President Kabbah's contention that there was lack of national capacity to prosecute. It further affirmed that, of what was there in the domestic legal system, it was "understaffed and underfunded."[36] That being said, even though President Kabbah's letter had expressed a desire for a UN created tribunal, some of the professionals in the Sierra Leonean justice sector seemed to contradict the government's preferred position. They, in meetings with the UN staff, suggested that the local criminal justice venue was "capable of producing a fair trial."[37]

At the same time, the legal professionals admitted some of the more notable challenges facing the local justice sector in a way that confirmed President Kabbah's claim. For example, even those that favored holding national trials conceded that due to low salaries, there were very few judges on the bench, and prosecutors would require substantial assistance in terms of expertise to investigate and prosecute the types of international crimes that would fall within the Court's jurisdiction. The same concern did not apply to defense counsel of whom there will be enough experienced attorneys in the private criminal law bar to represent the accused.[38] The other members of the legal profession that were consulted also made known their "clear preference"[39] for a Sierra Leonean court with strong international components in all its organs. In other words, they felt that the country needed international support to carry out prosecutions within the national justice system. They opined that three elements would be critical, especially keeping in mind the context of a country emerging from conflict: funding, equipment and legal expertise. This conception would bring the tribunal idea closer to a nationalized hybrid court that would essentially play a key role in rebuilding the capacity of the national justice system. It would be embedded within the national courts of Sierra Leone, much as would be later established by another African State in the case of the War Crimes Division within the Ugandan High Court.

From the perspective of the Kabbah government, the security of the eventual court, its premises, equipment, personnel, and the accused, were the principal concerns.[40] That said, several additional issues were identified by the UN Office of Legal Affairs as crucial to resolution of whatever would be later agreed upon. These related to the subject matter jurisdiction for war crimes, crimes against humanity, other serious violations of international humanitarian law and genocide.

---

[35]   *Id.* at ¶ 10.
[36]   *Id.* at ¶ 11.
[37]   *Id.* at ¶ 11.
[38]   *Id.*
[39]   *Id.* at ¶ 9.
[40]   *Id.* at ¶ 10.

The first three crimes reflected the reality of the war. The consideration of the latter offense was later dropped because no evidence of genocidal acts emerged from the facts of the Sierra Leone conflict. At the same time, due perhaps in part to natural nationalistic reasons, Sierra Leone also wanted to include offenses drawn from its own domestic law within the material jurisdiction of the SCSL. With the types of crimes to be included within the subject matter jurisdiction settled, the outstanding issues were the personal jurisdiction of the Court (which was to exclusively focus on either those "most responsible" or those "bearing greatest responsibility"), as well as the temporal jurisdiction. Another concern was the appropriate form of sentence, and whether this could include possible use of the death penalty (which the Secretary-General rejected because he felt it would be a non-starter for many UN Member States) and the issue of the status of the amnesty (discussed briefly in Chapter 2 and in detail in Chapter 8 of this work) that had been granted to the rebels in July 1999 to the extent of its legality under international law.[41]

Given the delicate nature of the issue, certain aspects of the government's vision for the special court were very clear. However, Kabbah's letter to the UN was somewhat vague on the government's view regarding the legal validity of the previously granted amnesty. Did it cover pre-Lomé as well as post-Lomé offenses? In his speeches to Parliament, contemporaneous with the request for UN support for the establishment a special tribunal, the President basically maintained that the government would pick and choose which aspects of the accord it would implement.[42] This approach allowed the government to insist that both sides abide by the ceasefire, and to continue to put in place the other institutional mechanisms that had been part of the Lomé arrangement to find a way forward out of the brutal conflict. At the same time, as regards the blanket amnesty, the official position was different. The rebels' failures to abide by its terms implied that they had forfeited their amnesty which had been conferred conditioned on the termination of the hostilities. The aspects relating to power sharing as well as rehabilitation, demobilization and reconstruction of the country would remain intact and continued to attract compliance.

3.3.3 *The Security Council's Preference for a Treaty-Based International Court*

Besides sending a fact finder to Sierra Leone, the UN Secretary-General forwarded the government's request to the Security Council. Drawing on the initial framework proposed by President Kabbah, as attached to his letter, the Council reacted positively. Although it did not invoke its Chapter VII authority, as Sierra Leone had urged it to do and as it had done for the ICTY and ICTR in 1993 and 1994

---

[41] Kabbah Letter to U.N.S.C., *supra* note 20.
[42] His Excellency the President Dr. Ahmad Tejan Kabbah, Address at the Start of Public Hearings of the Truth and Reconciliation Commission, Freetown (Apr. 14, 2003).

respectively, the Security Council did adopt Resolution 1315 on August 14, 2000. In that resolution, it mainly requested Secretary-General Annan to negotiate an agreement with the national government "to create an independent special court consistent with this resolution."[43] In that same decision, the Council also drew on aspects of the Kabbah proposal to set out the basic parameters it envisaged for the Court.[44] The resolution reflected several underlying purposes, some of which remained central to the SCSL's mission throughout its existence.

First, the preamble to the resolution affirmed the deep desire of the Security Council and the Sierra Leonean government to ensure the prosecution of those who had committed serious crimes in the country in accordance with "international standards of justice, fairness and due process of law."[45] Paragraph 6 of the preamble emphasized the importance of compliance with international humanitarian law, and stressed the need to uphold the principle of individual criminal responsibility for those who violate its norms.[46] President Kabbah's goal of "bringing justice"[47] and ending impunity was underscored by the Security Council's determination to "exert every effort"[48] to bring those individuals responsible for such heinous crimes to justice. The language of the resolution in this respect is similar to the ICTY and ICTR resolutions.

Second, the resolution recalled the parties' conviction that, in the particular circumstances of Sierra Leone, a credible system of justice and accountability will not only help end impunity for the grave offences that had been committed there, but would also contribute to the "process of national reconciliation" and "to the restoration and maintenance of peace."[49] Promoting reconciliation and restoring peace thus became at least one of the hortatory goals of the SCSL – even though national criminal trials appear unlikely, even in the best of times, to advance reconciliation or peace.[50]

Paragraph 11 of the preamble to Resolution 1315 highlighted the "negative impact of the security situation on the administration of justice in Sierra Leone and the pressing need for international cooperation to assist in strengthening the judicial system of Sierra Leone."[51] The next section acknowledged the important contribution that qualified persons from West African States, the Commonwealth, the UN

---

43 S.C. Res. 1315, ¶ 1 (Aug. 14, 2000) [hereinafter S.C. Res. 1315].

44 *Id.*

45 *Id.* at pmbl. ¶ 6.

46 *Id.*

47 Kabbah Letter to U.N.S.C., *supra* note 20, at 2; See, for this same discussion, Charles Chernor Jalloh, *Special Court for Sierra Leone: Achieving Justice?*, 32 Mich. J. Int'l L. 395, 413 (2011) and Charles Chernor Jalloh, *The Law and Politics of the Charles Taylor Case*, 43 Denv. J. Int'l L. & Pol. 229, 246–247 (2015) [hereinafter jointly Jalloh].

48 S.C. Res. 1315, *supra* note 43, at pmbl. ¶ 6; Jalloh, *supra* note 47.

49 S.C. Res. 1315, *supra* note 43, at pmbl. ¶¶ 2, 7.

50 Mirjan Damaska, *What Is the Point of International Criminal Justice*, 83 Chi.-Kent. L. Rev. 329, 331–32 (2008).

51 S.C. Res. 1315, *supra* note 43, at ¶ 11; see also Jalloh, *supra* note 47.

and other international organizations can make in expediting that process as well as to the challenge of "bringing justice and reconciliation to Sierra Leone and the region."[52]

President Kabbah had requested a tribunal created under the "Security Council's authority."[53] This would give it strong enforcement powers, including the ability to require all UN Member States to cooperate with it.[54] That request was rejected. Still, the Security Council reiterated, in the final preambular paragraph of Resolution 1315 using Chapter VII type language, that the Sierra Leone situation "continues to constitute a threat to international peace and security in the region."[55] This, however, was not a decision to act under the most robust enforcement power in this particular resolution. It was a reference back to an earlier decision in which the same Security Council had invoked Chapter VII to declare that the situation in Sierra Leone constituted a threat to international peace and security.

The parties sought to achieve all the above objectives expressed in the preamble through the establishment of a new, efficient and lean ad hoc tribunal. While President Kabbah's request and the subsequent consultations with relevant stakeholders in Sierra Leone revealed a local predilection for a national court with strong international components and support in all its organs (an argument that apparently won British support), the UN instead preferred an international court with strong national elements.[56] This was partly because of concerns about the state of the local judicial system and the feeling that making the tribunal part of the national criminal justice machinery implied that the death penalty could apply for those convicted.[57] Despite these major differences, between the two sides, Sierra Leonean and UN officials quickly reached an agreement on the core aspects of the SCSL. This was within a relatively short period compared to other tribunals; indeed, it took the Secretary-General much longer to negotiate the parameters of the Cambodia Tribunal.[58] In fact, the main negotiations, which were conducted in September 2000, were concluded in less than a week. Though, consistent with diplomatic negotiations, it is clear that much of the technical legwork had been done in advance before the formal negotiations actually began.[59]

Matters were more complicated when it came to the positions of two countries on the Security Council most interested in supporting criminal accountability in Sierra Leone. The United States, which early on endorsed the idea of trials for the crimes

---

[52]   S.C. Res. 1315, *supra* note 43, at ¶ 12.
[53]   Kabbah Letter to U.N.S.C., *supra* note 20, at § 1.
[54]   *Id.* at § 4 of Enclosure.
[55]   S.C. Res. 1315, *supra* note 43, at pmbl. ¶ 13; see also Jalloh, *supra* note 47.
[56]   *Fifth Report of the Secretary General of the Situation in Sierra Leone, supra* note 33, at ¶ 9.
[57]   *Id.* at ¶ 10 (noting that the UN and many of its Member States would oppose a legal process involving application of the death penalty).
[58]   Craig Etcheson, *Politics of Genocide Justice in Cambodia,* in INTERNATIONALIZED CRIMINAL COURTS: SIERRA LEONE, EAST TIMOR, KOSOVO, AND CAMBODIA 181–205 (Cesare P.R. Romano et al., eds., 2004).
[59]   U.N. Secretary General, Report of the UN Secretary-General on the Establishment of a Special Court for Sierra Leone, ¶ 56, U.N. Doc. S/2000/915 (Oct. 4, 2000) [hereinafter U.N.S.G. Report].

committed and has been a key player in the development of the modern field of international criminal law, reportedly took the view that a Chapter VII international tribunal was the best option.[60] Key Sierra Leonean officials, including the President and his Attorney-General, had conceded that there was no national capacity to prosecute.[61] This seemed to bolster the US view. At the same time, the Americans wished to have some local elements including input and staff hiring to make it more attractive to Sierra Leone. Some US government officials were skeptical that the national authorities could prosecute the crimes given the lack of capacity in the local courts, the lack of security in the country and the possibility that there might not be fair trials for the defendants.[62]

In light of this, as reported by David Scheffer, the then US ambassador at large for war crimes, Washington officials even considered the option of expanding the ICTR's jurisdiction. But that was thought to be politically unworkable for several reasons.[63] A different proposal later emerged that envisaged a regional criminal court for West Africa that would sit in Sierra Leone, and if need be, outside of it including in the Malian capital Bamako if the security situation demanded it.[64] The US would later return to the idea of an international court along the lines of the ICTY and ICTR.

On the other hand, the United Kingdom, which is the former colonial power in Sierra Leone, was initially reluctant to have a special court. Instead, it hoped to bolster international support for the domestic courts to enable trials within the local criminal courts. It also opposed the idea of a Chapter VII international tribunal, due to the cost implications, but warmed up to the idea of a special criminal prosecution regime possibly because of fear of political embarrassment about not having done enough to prevent the 1994 Rwandan Genocide. The United Kingdom did not reportedly want its opposition to be perceived as a reflection of bias and yet another Western indifference to an African country's plight. All the more so given the strong intervention it had helped to lead, within the framework of NATO, in respect of the Kosovo conflict.[65]

---

[60] DAVID SCHEFFER, ALL THE MISSING SOULS: A PERSONAL HISTORY OF THE WAR CRIMES TRIBUNALS 322 (2013).

[61] SOLOMON BEREWA, A NEW PERSPECTIVE ON GOVERNANCE, LEADERSHIP, CONFLICT AND NATION BUILDING IN SIERRA LEONE 176 (2011).

[62] *Id.*

[63] It was felt that Rwanda's government would oppose the move; that Burundi, which had unsuccessfully sought expansion of the ICTR's jurisdiction would not take kindly to being trumped by Sierra Leone; that the ICTR might not administratively handle addition of a new situation; and finally, the expansion could prove to be a non-starter for Freetown and the major countries that had donated peacekeepers.

[64] Scheffer, *supra* note 60, at 33.

[65] Peter Penfold, *International Community Expectations of the Special Court for Sierra Leone*, in THE SIERRA LEONE SPECIAL COURT AND ITS LEGACY: THE IMPACT FOR AFRICA AND INTERNATIONAL CRIMINAL LAW 62 (Charles C. Jalloh, ed., 2014).

But the United Kingdom was at the same time worried about having another full-fledged international penal tribunal that could give rise to allegations of corruption and incompetence, which had already occurred only a few years before in relation to the ICTR. Neither were British authorities happy to take away the focus from the establishment of the ICC.[66] If the ICC could not be used, as was the case since the Rome Statute had not yet entered into force, the British government favored for Sierra Leonean courts to prosecute those responsible for the crimes. It is reported that they also liked the idea that the Security Council would get out of the business of creating more ad hoc tribunals.[67]

The UK Foreign Office's other argument was that the Commonwealth, not the UN, should give the assistance needed to avoid a tribunal becoming caught in the UN's bureaucratic snarls.[68] Ralph Zacklin, a British national who also worked in the UN Secretariat as Deputy Legal Counsel, also urged only domestic trials. Any problems with the local justice system would be addressed with US, UN and international support.[69] Interestingly, the United Kingdom's view seemed more consistent with the wishes of the local Bar, which apparently preferred trials within the national court system. On the other hand, the US view was more consistent with that of the Kabbah government. For the UN to conclude an agreement would require compromise on these competing visions, to find a middle ground. The text of paragraph 11 of Resolution 1315 (2000) thus appeared to nod to the British concerns. In the same vein, it ultimately centered on the creation of a special ad hoc international court with a limited personal and temporal jurisdiction. We will return to a detailed analysis of the SCSL's jurisdictional competence in the next Chapter of this work.

In sum, the legal framework of the SCSL was determined by several factors. First, the views of Sierra Leone, which honed in on the idea of having a robust Chapter VII tribunal along lines similar to the ICTY and ICTR. Second, the views of the United Nations. In the latter, there were differing ideas on what would be the best option as between the Secretary-General, on the one hand, and the Security Council, on the other hand. Within the latter organ, where the key decisions were made, the US was more favorable to a full international criminal tribunal anchored in Chapter VII while the UK favored domestic trials within the national courts of Sierra Leone both for reasons of cost and efficiency. The result of a hybrid international tribunal, with national and international elements, was in the final analysis the compromise between the main actors who helped to shape the legal framework of the Tribunal.

---

[66] Mark Tran, *US-UK split halts bid for Sierra Leone war crimes court*, THE GUARDIAN (July 19, 2000), www.theguardian.com/world/2000/jul/19/sierraleone.

[67] *Id.*

[68] *Id.*

[69] Scheffer, *supra* note 60, at 326.

3.4 THE COMPROMISE: A *SUI GENERIS* INTERNATIONAL TRIBUNAL JURISDICTION

The final version of the bilateral agreement, to which was annexed the statute for the special court, was subsequently signed by representatives of the UN and the Government of Sierra Leone in Freetown, Sierra Leone, on January 16, 2002.[70] It was a compromise between the Sierra Leonean, British and American positions setting out the legal framework for a mixed ad hoc international court, featuring both local and international elements, while attempting to account for some of the experiences of the ad hoc ICTY and ICTR. The constitutive instruments did not situate the Court within Sierra Leone's national justice system but outside of it; nor did it envisage or create the Tribunal as a subsidiary body of the Security Council based in a Chapter VII resolution with all the legal and fiscal implications that would flow from that for the UN and its more wealthy Member States. The Court, rather than being a subsidiary body of the UN, would be an independent international organization that would be financed by donations from States.

The statute, an annex to the UN-Sierra Leone agreement, elaborated many novel features that were intended to reflect the specificities of the country's conflict and the brutal nature of the crimes perpetrated.[71] The constitutive instruments establishing the SCSL formally entered into force on April 12, 2002, when Sierra Leone and the UN had each fulfilled their respective formalities for their implementation.[72]

There are six major institutional features, that Chapter 1 already alluded to, which can be highlighted from a study of the Court's founding instruments. First, the

---

[70] See Agreement between the United Nations and the Government of Sierra Leone on the Establishment of a Special Court for Sierra Leone, 2178 U.N.T.S. 137 (Jan. 16, 2002) [hereinafter U.N.-Sierra Leone Agreement], reprinted in CONSOLIDATED LEGAL TEXTS 7–17 (Charles Jalloh ed., 2007).

[71] U.N.S.G. Report, *supra* note 59, at ¶ 11; for more on the widely hailed features of the SCSL, see Charles C. Jalloh, *The Contribution of the Special Court for Sierra Leone to the Development of International Law*, 15 AFR. J. INT'L & COMP. L. 165, 175–76 (2007) [hereinafter *The Contribution of the SCSL*]. See generally Micaela Frulli, *The Special Court for Sierra Leone: Some Preliminary Comments*, 11 EUR. J. INT'L. L. 857 (2000); Robert Cryer, *A "Special Court" for Sierra Leone*, 50 INT'L & COMP. L.Q. 435 (2001); Suzannah Linton, *Cambodia, East Timor and Sierra Leone: Experiments in International Justice*, 12 CRIM. L. F. 185 (2001); Avril McDonald, *Sierra Leone's Shoestring Special Court*, 84 INT'L REV. RED. CROSS. 121 (2002); Stuart Beresford & A. S. Muller, *The Special Court for Sierra Leone: An Initial Comment*, 14 LEIDEN J. INT'L L. 635 (2001); Melron C. Nicol-Wilson, *Accountability for Human Rights Abuses: The United Nations' Special Court for Sierra Leone*, AUSTL INT'L L. J. 159 (2001); Celina Schocken, *The Special Court for Sierra Leone: Overview and Recommendations*, 20 BERKELEY J. OF INT'L L. 436 (2002); John Cerone, *The Special Court for Sierra Leone: Establishing a New Approach to International Criminal Justice*, 8 ILSA J. INT'L & COMP. L. 379 (2002); Nicole Fritz & Alison Smith, *Current Apathy for Coming Anarchy: Building the Special Court for Sierra Leone*, 25 FORDHAM INT'L L. J. 391 (2001).

[72] U.N.-Sierra Leone Agreement, *supra* note 70, at art. 21 (providing for entry into force after both parties notified each other that the legal requirements for entry into force have been complied with). Sierra Leone passed the Special Court (Ratification) Act 2002, Supplement to the Sierra Leone Gazette vol. CXXX No. 2, Mar. 7, 2002.

SCSL, in contrast to the ICTY and ICTR, was established pursuant to a bilateral treaty[73] between the UN and Sierra Leonean authorities. This made the Court the first international criminal tribunal to be created by a treaty between the UN and one of its Member States. On the other hand, the ICTY and ICTR were created by the Security Council as subsidiary organs of the UN using Chapter VII resolutions.[74] These were thus enforcement measures intended to restore international peace and security to the former Yugoslavia and Rwanda respectively under Articles 39,[75] 42[76] and 29[77] of the UN Charter. While Chapter VII resolutions are coercive in the sense of imposing binding legal obligations on all UN members, the SCSL consensual bilateral treaty approach offered a practical alternative to the use of such exceptional powers where the affected state is willing to prosecute serious international law violations but is unable to do so for some reason, as in, for example, Burundi.[78] By serving as a functional model of such international penal courts, the SCSL furnished an example that the UN and the concerned state(s) could resort to in order to create and structure such courts and minimize institutional design flaws stemming from prior mistakes. This was the approach later taken from the Sierra Leone example in the context of Lebanon's request for UN support for a special court to prosecute those involved in the assassination of Prime Minister Rafiq Hariri.

Second, the SCSL had a mixed subject matter jurisdiction permitting the Prosecutor to invoke either or both international and Sierra Leonean law to prosecute offenders. This aspect of the Court, which will be further discussed in Chapter 4, is one of its more legally significant deviations from the ICTY and ICTR models. Indeed, while various national courts have been "internationalized" in Kosovo, Bosnia, East Timor and Cambodia thereby permitting them to exercise jurisdiction over specific international crimes, the SCSL was the first international criminal tribunal empowered to try a limited group of persons bearing the "greatest responsibility" for national offences alongside offences under international law. It was an

---

[73]   The treaty-based nature of the SCSL is comparable to that of the ICC, which is also based on a treaty, albeit a multilateral one. Before these modern international criminal courts, the Nuremberg Tribunal was also set up via a multilateral treaty. A plan to establish a tribunal, in 1919, was incorporated into the Versailles Treaty but that tribunal never came to fruition.

[74]   While the option of establishing the ICTY through a multilateral treaty was considered, it was discarded for a number of pragmatic reasons.

[75]   The Security Council shall determine the existence of any threat to the peace, breach of the peace, or act of aggression and shall make recommendations, or decide what measures shall be taken in accordance with articles 41 and 42, to maintain or restore international peace and security.

[76]   Art. 42: "Should the Security Council consider that measures provided for in Article 41 would be inadequate or have proved to be inadequate, it may take such action by air, sea, or land forces as may be necessary to maintain or restore international peace and security. Such action may include demonstrations, blockade, and other operations by air, sea, or land forces of Members of the United Nations."

[77]   It provides: "The Security Council may establish such subsidiary organs as it deems necessary for the performance of its functions."

[78]   Based on a request from Burundi, the UN is currently negotiating the establishment of a special tribunal for that country.

important symbolic feature of the Court for the Sierra Leonean government, and for UN Member States, it was a signal of what could be described as a turn to justice on the cheap. The "greatest responsibility" jurisdiction of the SCSL, which has since taken on a popularity of its own among international criminal lawyers, in practice raised some legal controversies among tribunal lawyers and judges. Those controversies are discussed in Chapter 5 of this book.

Third, and particularly significant, the SCSL was the first modern ad hoc international criminal court to be located in the country where the crimes being prosecuted occurred. Though there were concerns about security due to the ongoing hostilities, for obvious reasons, Sierra Leone thought this was an important element of the SCSL that would allow the people of the country to observe the trials first hand. It was also significant to end the pattern of modern international criminal tribunals such as the ICTY being based in The Netherlands and the ICTR in Tanzania. Establishing the SCSL in the *locus criminis* – the place where the crimes were committed – contrasted favorably to the ICTY and ICTR which were later criticized because of their location in The Hague and Arusha respectively, far away from the communities in the former Yugoslavia and Rwanda in whose name they were actually rendering justice. Indeed, today, barring exceptional circumstances such as active hostilities, it seems settled based on various studies tracking popular attitudes towards the ICTY and ICTR that placing an international criminal court away from the affected country limits or undermines its contribution to post-conflict healing and reconciliation.[79]

On the other hand, locating international criminal courts in the current or former scene of the conflict carries inherent risks because the wounds of war are so raw and memories of atrocity so vivid that they could easily be reopened and manipulated by disgruntled belligerents. This could potentially endanger witnesses and victims' families, especially in circumstances where fighting had not fully ceased at the time of establishment of the Tribunal.[80] The SCSL thus had initial concerns about security. These concerns led the Court to develop a contingency plan to sit elsewhere in West Africa, or further afield, should that prove to be necessary.[81] Once indictees were arrested, these security concerns played out in practice. This was especially the case following the indictment of the popular former Sierra Leonean deputy defense minister, Sam Hinga Norman, who was considered by parts of the local population to be a hero for defending the nation. These security concerns remained throughout the life of the SCSL. They were later invoked as the main justification for the controversial transfer of the SCSL's star indictee, former Liberian president Charles Taylor, to The Hague for his trial.

---

[79] U.N. Secretary-General, *The Rule of Law and Transitional Justice in Conflict and Post Conflict Societies*, ¶ 44, U.N. Doc. S/2004/616 (Aug. 23, 2004).
[80] RAMA MANI, SEEKING JUSTICE IN THE SHADOWS OF WAR (2002).
[81] U.N.-Sierra Leone Agreement, *supra* note 70, at ¶ 2.

As Justice Geoffrey Robertson of the SCSL's Appeals Chamber noted in the First Annual Report of the Court to the UN, "a war crimes court in a war torn country so soon after the war's end carries obvious risks, especially for its personnel."[82] Nevertheless, many would now agree that locating an international criminal court *in situ* has fundamental advantages because it eases prosecutorial investigations, and facilitates the collection of evidence and the identification and presentation of witnesses. It also reduces the cost of prosecution, and ultimately, assists in securing justice for the victims and their families who can witness their former tormentors facing justice.[83] This seemed to work in Sierra Leone. That said, the security conditions in different post conflict situations will differ and it seems hard to have a one-size-fits-all solution. Nonetheless, these types of practical and other legitimacy gains would seem to help outweigh any presumed disadvantages of placing such courts in the country where the crimes occurred. Provided, of course, the security situation permits it. Bolstering the security in the country might, on balance, still be better than moving the trials away from the victim communities.

Fourth, as subsidiary organs created by the Security Council, the ICTY and ICTR received funding from the regular UN budget. The basis is Article 17 of the UN Charter which empowers the General Assembly to consider and approve the budget of the organization, and importantly, to ensure that the expenses of the organization are borne by the members as apportioned by it.[84] By contrast, the SCSL relied on funding from Member State being willing and interested to voluntarily fund or support the Court.[85] This mode of financing international justice initiatives introduced for the first time by the UN and Sierra Leone was firmly opposed by President Kabbah. This funding method was also strongly opposed by the UN Secretary-General who presciently characterized it as "neither viable nor sustainable" because of its inherently unstable nature. Nonetheless, the Secretary-General's alternative suggestion to instead use "assessed contributions" was also rejected.[86] Regrettably, the fundraising difficulties experienced by the SCSL even before it began operations confirmed the UNSG's worst fears.[87] The financial challenges lasted throughout the Tribunal's lifetime. They neared crisis portions at various moments, resulting in occasional reliance on subvention grants from the UN. This funding insecurity prevailed until formal closure of the SCSL's doors in December 2013. It has become a similar challenge for the residual tribunal that replaced the SCSL.

[82] Geoffrey Robertson (President of the Special Court for Sierra Leone), *First Annual Report of the President of the Special Court for Sierra Leone, Foreword* (Dec. 2, 2002 to Dec. 1, 2003), www.rscsl.org /Documents/AnRpt1.pdf.

[83] *Id.*

[84] See ICTY Statute, *supra* note 1, at art. 32; ICTR Statute, *supra* note 8, at art. 30.

[85] U.N.-Sierra Leone Agreement, *supra* note 70, at art. 6.

[86] U.N.S.G. Report, *supra* note 59, at ¶ 70.

[87] U.N. Secretary-General, *The Rule of Law and Transitional Justice in Conflict and Post Conflict Societies*, ¶ 44, U.N. Doc. S/2004/616 (Aug. 23, 2004).

The fifth institutional feature that can be discerned from the Court's founding instruments is that its non-judicial activities were to be managed by a group of states sitting on an oversight committee.[88] Established by Article 7 of the UN-Sierra Leone Agreement, the aptly named "Management Committee" was comprised of major donors mandated to "provide advice and policy direction on all non-judicial aspects" of the Tribunal's work. This supervisory mechanism would later raise concerns in some quarters about the actual and perceived independence and accountability of the SCSL to third-party states, especially but not exclusively, in relation to operational matters.[89] The fear was that the oversight body could be abused in order to influence the judicial aspects of the Tribunal's work. Although, this concern might have been theoretically legitimate, in the practice during the SCSL's operations, no evidence publicly emerged of political interference in the work of the SCSL. This type of third-party engagement and support for the SCSL helped ensure that real-time resolutions of administrative and fiscal difficulties were not encumbered or subjected to the bureaucratic and political processes of the UN or the vagaries of General Assembly politics.[90]

In any event, because the Court's major donors could track its work closely by sitting on such a committee, it seemed to have encouraged their continuous engagement with the anti-impunity campaign long after the media cameras were gone and long after the crisis had been struck from the top of the Security Council's priority list. Indeed, Canada, a Commonwealth country and one of the donors, served as chair of the Management Committee throughout the existence of the SCSL. This enabled it to be a champion of the SCSL, periodically assisting in building the political and diplomatic support required for compliance with the Tribunal's funding and other requests for state cooperation. It appeared to have even been a way to increase the chances that donors and the international community would maintain funding and other forms of cooperation for such ad hoc courts through to completion. Notably, the UN has replicated this model, despite the apparent legal challenges raised in the Sierra Leone situation, in the Special Tribunal for Lebanon (STL) which also has an SCSL-inspired "Management Committee" comprised of third-party countries. Whether the STL's own equivalent

---

[88] For more on this, see Phakiso Mochochoko & Giorgia Tortora, *The Management Committee for the Special Court for Sierra Leone*, in INTERNATIONALIZED CRIMINAL COURTS, *supra* note 58, at 141–56 (Romano et al., eds.).

[89] See Prosecutor v. Norman, Case No. SCSL-2004-14-AR72-E, Preliminary Motion Based on Lack of Jurisdiction (Judicial Independence), (June 14, 2004). Norman filed a motion challenging the independence and fairness of the proceedings before the SCSL because of its funding arrangement and the oversight of the Management Committee. The Appeals Chamber held (1) that the funding arrangements were not such as to lead to bias in the Court's determination of the matters before it and (2) that the Management Committee has no reason to seek to influence the outcome of the cases before the SCSL.

[90] Though it could be argued that politicking within the UN has been merely replaced by politicking within the Management Committee with the bigger donors having a greater influence.

body, which interestingly also had similar membership to that of the Sierra Leone Court, was more effective remains to be seen.

Sixth, the Sierra Leonean government, unlike the governments of Rwanda and the former Yugoslavia, actively participated in the founding of SCSL and appointing its officials. This included selection of some of its judges[91] and the deputy prosecutor.[92] This may be contrasted with the ICTY and ICTR, whose judges and Prosecutor were selected by the UN General Assembly and the Security Council respectively.[93] Strong host country involvement in making high level appointments seems to have had the effect of enhancing local participation at all levels in the work of the Tribunal. Nationals bring to bear available local expertise, languages, history and nuances of a particular conflict that could easily be missed by internationals. Local experts can serve as a bridge between such courts and the community by bringing back stories to friends and relatives about the legal process even as they learn about, and contribute to, the application of international standards of justice. This was one of President Kabbah's soft objectives when he proposed a co-national prosecutor for the SCSL. He did not succeed in securing support for the idea in the UN but won the concession of appointing a deputy prosecutor.

In practice, if we set aside the provisions in the founding Statute, a local prose-cutor was only proposed several years into the SCSL trials. Even the government's own initial appointments to the deputy prosecutor post were of non-Sierra Leoneans, raising questions about the actual benefits of this aspect of the hybridity. Yet, later on, the government did put forward a Sierra Leonean deputy prosecutor. In relation to the judges, Sierra Leoneans were appointed early on. In retrospect, from the earliest days, greater participation of Sierra Leoneans at the more senior levels would likely have boosted achievement of the Court's short-term objective of holding context-sensitive trials. One wonders whether a senior Sierra Leonean deputy prosecutor, present when the initial indictments were being considered, might have not opposed some of the persons selected for indictment by the SCSL. At the same time, if that had been the case and the information became publicly known, the question would have been asked whether the prosecutor's omission of certain indictees from their list was for political reasons. In any case, the presence of a deputy might have also helped to shore up the long-term objectives of leaving a cadre of qualified attorneys on the ground in Sierra Leone. This is particularly so if

---

91 Sierra Leone appointed four out of eleven of the Court's judges; only two of those four it appointed are Sierra Leonean. See U.N.- Sierra Leone Agreement, *supra* note 70, at art. 2, and art. 12 SCSL Statute. Although one would hope that the local government would not abuse this appointment power, keeping in mind the need for the independence and impartiality of the judges. See WILLIAM A. SCHABAS, THE UN INTERNATIONAL CRIMINAL TRIBUNALS 508 (2006).

92 To the dismay of many, for unclear reasons, the Kabbah government did not appoint a Sierra Leonean to the deputy prosecutor position until towards the end of the Tribunal's life. See U.N.-Sierra Leone Agreement *supra* note 70, at art. 3; S.C. Res. 1315 *supra* note 42, at 15 § 4.

93 ICTY Statute, *supra* note 1, at art. 13 bis, 13 ter, 16 § 4; ICTR Statute *supra* note 8, at art. 12 bis and 12 ter, 15 § 4.

the national lawyers with experience in the prosecution and defense of international crimes remained in the country after the trials would be completed. This experience, with the appointment of some key officials and inclusion of nationals, seems to have served somewhat as a precedent for the STL. With the benefit of hindsight, though still better than nothing compared to the ICTY/ICTR model, it might not have borne as much fruit as some in Sierra Leone may have initially hoped for in relation to the SCSL.

On the whole, it appears self-evident that the bulk of the institutional innovations in the founding instruments of the Court were impelled by the need to address the peculiar aspects of the Sierra Leonean conflict, the negotiating demands of the national authorities, and what the UN, especially its Security Council, was willing to support. This suggests that different factors will have to be weighed when setting up ad hoc tribunals for other post-conflict situations. That said, the solutions developed by the UN and Sierra Leone to tackle various concerns nevertheless introduced new elements to the international criminal tribunal equation. These arguably collectively constitute a useful addition to international criminal practice. The experiences of the SCSL may be particularly valuable given the similarities between modern conflicts and the reality that, today, it seems highly unlikely that the UN would establish full-fledged international criminal tribunals like the ICTY and ICTR in the future. Among other reasons, there seems to be a sense that such courts are generally expensive and generally slow, meaning that there might not be the type of political will to make Security Council agreement on such major international justice projects possible.[94]

It is remarkable that, in the context of the more recent discussions of the establishment of a Hybrid Court for South Sudan, the SCSL agreement and statute were the templates used by the drafters of the legal instruments for that court. The expert group convened by the African Union's Office of the Legal counsel basically replicated the Sierra Leone model when drafting the legal instruments of the court. This demonstrates the SCSL's continued relevance and influence on questions of accountability for conflicts on the continent. Before then, following the post-election violence in Kenya in December 2008, public discussions about the establishment of a Special Tribunal for Kenya demonstrated reliance by that country's parliament on the SCSL precedent.

3.5 CONCLUSION

This chapter has provided a detailed background on the establishment of the SCSL. It explained the genesis of the Court in a proposal originating from President Kabbah of Sierra Leone. His plea, in the name of the people and government of his country, was for UN support towards the establishment of a credible court that

---

[94] Cassese, *supra* note 18, at ¶ 12.

would prosecute those responsible for the crimes committed during the Sierra Leone conflict. The appeal did not necessarily stem from a deep commitment to the idea of accountability for atrocity crimes or a principled commitment to the enforcement of international humanitarian law. The Kabbah Government was – at least initially – not apparently keen to prosecute the rebel leaders whose actions had caused mayhem in Sierra Leone.

To the contrary, like the stark choice often faced by political leaders in other conflicts, the Sierra Leonean president was even willing to confer an unconditional amnesty on the perpetrators of the violence. In place of criminal prosecutions, the Kabbah Administration had acceded to the creation of a national truth commission. Ending the war was, perhaps understandably, the number one priority. The calculus of the government was similar to that made by many other governments faced with similar dilemmas in situations of conflict and transition. Amnesty was perceived as the hard but inevitable short-term price to pay in order to secure Sierra Leone's long-term future. The government's change of heart only occurred after the rebels violated the key terms of the Lomé Accord; foremost amongst these was violation of the cease-fire and killing of innocents, including some UN peacekeepers in May 2000. This led to the Kabbah decision to instead request international support to establish a special tribunal to investigate and prosecute the worst offenders.

While President Kabbah's case for an international court was strong, and ultimately successful, the present chapter has demonstrated that the challenge was that the Security Council was not open to creating another ad hoc international penal tribunal for Sierra Leone along the same lines as the ICTY and ICTR . Experience had shown that such tribunals could last for years and cost in the billions of dollars. Instead, as will be discussed in the next chapter in relation to the jurisdiction and organization of the SCSL, the Security Council preferred a court with a more circumscribed mandate over a handful of leaders deemed to bear the greatest responsibility. This consideration eventually shaped the model of the special court that was later established to investigate and prosecute the atrocity crimes in Sierra Leone. It also resulted in a limited time frame that in effect meant the exclusion of about half of the atrocities in the decade-long war. Pragmatics, not principle, won out. The UN even sought an informal three-year window in which it hoped the SCSL would complete all its cases. That timeline did not come to pass, as the Tribunal took over a decade to complete all its trials. In the end, the rest of the Court's no-frills jurisdiction and its slim organization ought to be understood as a reflection of the overarching concern to keep costs down to a minimum.

This analysis of the origins and creation of the SCSL leads to at least two preliminary conclusions. First, as we have seen, the idea that the international community represented by the UN could work with a willing but battle-weary state to prosecute grave international crimes committed during a brutal conflict originated in Freetown, Sierra Leone's capital. Nonetheless, though the country won some concessions including use of its domestic law in the founding statute and the power to appoint some of the principal officials, the government did not get all the things on its wish list. The resulting compromise was a relatively inexpensive court with a narrowly framed jurisdiction. The SCSL's very creation thus reflected the tension between the increasingly powerful notion that at least some justice must be rendered for the victims of heinous international crimes, and what politically was deemed acceptable to the wealthier UN Member States who would be asked to pay for it. This wider context should always be kept in mind in any assessments of the success, and failures, of the SCSL, and perhaps even more significantly, the limits of internationally supported justice more broadly.

Second, as the foregoing discussion and any cursory examination of the founding instruments of the SCSL will confirm, the primary mandate was the task to prosecute, in fair trials, a small number of persons deemed most culpable for the atrocities committed against the people of Sierra Leone and the attacks on UN peacekeepers. The SCSL was mandated to hand down cost-effective justice. Nothing more. Nothing less. But, as with the exaggerated statements that were often made in the context of discussions of the prior ICTY and ICTR, it was also thought that the SCSL would help achieve many other secondary goals. This, rather ambitiously, included assisting to rebuild the capacity of the national justice system and helping to restore the rule of law and even peace and national reconciliation. Such grand expectations were never realistic objectives to foist on a criminal court in the first place, let alone a shoestring donations-funded entity that would later struggle throughout its lifespan to meet the most basic of its operational expenses. Their net effect was to generate high international and local expectations, whether fairly or unfairly, against which the shoe string court that was first road tested in Sierra Leone is often judged.

A key preliminary lesson from this discussion of the mixed international-national SCSL model may be that there can be a partnership between the local and international authorities to dispense some justice. But, for this to work given the extraordinary circumstances in which post-conflict countries may find themselves in, the international community of states should stand ready to help fund the accountability effort. After all, the international community interest in having a stable world and in the enforcement of its legal prohibitions through the prosecution of atrocity crimes condemned by international law is also engaged.

Ultimately, the more support that can be offered by the UN, as perhaps the best representative of that "international community," the more accountability there will be for the victims of such crimes. A country like Sierra Leone seeking to transition from war to peace may see the light and seek to do what is right to abide by its international legal obligations to prosecute the perpetrators of international crimes. The reality, however, is that such countries, torn apart by conflict, are unlikely to have the national legal capacity and other infrastructure and funding to do so. This wider backdrop of artificial practical and political limits of international justice should be kept in mind as we turn to a discussion of the jurisdiction, organization and trials of the SCSL in the next chapter.

4

The Special Court's Jurisdiction, Organization, and Trials

4.1 INTRODUCTION

It is axiomatic that the competence of the Special Court for Sierra Leone (SCSL) must be determined by reference to its constitutive instruments, in this case, the bilateral treaty concluded between the United Nations and the Government of Sierra Leone in January 2002 and its annexed Statute of the Special Court for Sierra Leone.[1] Both entered into force in April 2002.[2] The SCSL, by its mere treaty basis, already differed from the International Criminal Tribunals for the former Yugoslavia and Rwanda (ICTY, ICTR) in that it was neither a subsidiary organ of the United Nations imposed by a Security Council resolution nor a domestic criminal court of Sierra Leone.[3] The SCSL, as the previous chapter explained, was thus an unprecedented international penal court of mixed jurisdiction and composition.

4.2 THE PURPOSE AND STRUCTURE OF THIS CHAPTER

Structurally, the first part of this chapter draws on the founding instruments to examine the SCSL's legal competence, in particular what lawyers refers to as the subject matter, personal, territorial and temporal jurisdiction. Next, I discuss the organizational structure of the Tribunal, before summarizing the main trials carried out by the SCSL. The analysis focuses on the core cases involving suspects accused of serious international crimes. For that reason, I do not consider incidental cases concerning witness tampering and contempt of court or others stemming from the

---

[1] Agreement between the United Nations and the Government of Sierra Leone on the Establishment of a Special Court for Sierra Leone (Jan. 16, 2002) [hereinafter U.N.-Sierra Leone Agreement] 2178 U.N. T.S. 38342. Annexed to the U.N.-Sierra Leone Agreement was the Statute of the Special Court for Sierra Leone [hereinafter SCSL Statute].

[2] Herman von Hebel, *Foreword, in* Consolidated Legal Texts for the Special Court for Sierra Leone xi (Charles C. Jalloh ed., 2007).

[3] See U.N. Secretary-General, *Report of the UN Secretary-General on the Establishment of a Special Court for Sierra Leone,* ¶ 9 U.N. Docs. S/2000/915 (Oct. 4, 2000) [hereinafter Report on SCSL Establishment].

Court's exercise of its inherent jurisdiction. A final section offers preliminary conclusions.

4.3 THE JURISDICTION OF THE SPECIAL COURT FOR SIERRA LEONE

4.3.1 *Subject Matter Jurisdiction*

There were two considerations that informed the framing of the SCSL's subject matter or *ratione materiae* jurisdiction.[4] First, the offenses aimed to reflect the specificities of the Sierra Leonean conflict, the brutal nature of the crimes committed, as well as the youth of those persons presumed responsible for them.[5] Thus, the crimes selected for inclusion in the material jurisdiction anticipated the most common practices of the rebels and other combatants during the war. These included mass killings, extrajudicial executions, widespread mutilation of various limbs of the body, sexual violence (especially against girls and women), sexual slavery, abduction of thousands of children and adults, forced labor and forced recruitment into armed groups, looting and setting fire to entire towns and villages.

Second, the Secretary-General also recognized, as he had done in respect of the ICTY and the ICTR, that the principle of legality and the prohibition on the retrospective application of criminal legislation had to be upheld. Therefore, he only endorsed the use of crimes that he felt bore the characteristics of customary international law at the time that they were carried out, meaning that they would constitute codification of existing legal norms, rather than forms of progressive development of international criminal law.[6]

The Court's subject matter jurisdiction, as proposed in Resolution 1315, covered two broad categories of crimes: (1) crimes under international law and (2) offenses under Sierra Leonean law. Both categories were later included in the founding statute, although in practice the prosecution only relied on the former during the trials, thereby rendering the second category superfluous. The Tribunal's international subject matter jurisdiction entailed crimes against humanity, violations of Common Article 3 to the Geneva Conventions and of Additional Protocol II (that is, war crimes) and the residual catchall of other serious violations of international humanitarian law. The international crimes were defined at Articles 2, 3 and 4 of the SCSL Statute, whereas Article 5 governed the crimes under Sierra Leonean law. Even though initially mentioned in one of his reports, there was no evidence that the fighting factions in Sierra Leone targeted, whether wholly or partly, any of the protected national, ethnical, racial or religious groups within the meaning of the Genocide

---

[4]   Report on SCSL Establishment, *supra* note 3, at ¶ 11.
[5]   The issue of what to do with the alleged young criminals is discussed further below. See *id.* at ¶¶ 32–38 .
[6]   Report on SCSL Establishment, *supra* note 3, at ¶ 12.

Convention.[7] There were, for sure, some tensions and even a regional national character to the Sierra Leone conflict which for a long period remained in the east and south of the country. There was an ethnic dimension to the violence. But the crimes committed did not rise to the level of special or specific intent to annihilate a group that would be required for the conduct to rise to the level of a genocide. In contrast to the ICTR, where genocide was the main crime prosecuted, and the ICTY where it was sometimes invoked, that "crime of crimes"[8] was sensibly excluded from the Sierra Leone Court's subject matter jurisdiction. In fact, it was not even included in the Security Council resolution which recommended three international crimes for inclusion in the material jurisdiction.

With respect to the three enumerated international crimes, the crimes against humanity were patterned on those of the ICTY (Article 5) and ICTR (Article 3), which were in turn, traceable to the Nuremberg International Military Tribunal (Article 6). The ICTY crimes against humanity definition required a connection to armed conflict, while the ICTR required discriminatory national, political, ethnic, racial or religious grounds. The SCSL definition did not require either and is arguably more consistent with customary international law, which does not require the so-called conflict nexus or discriminatory grounds for the purpose of proving crimes against humanity. Thus, crimes against humanity, as defined in Article 2 of the SCSL Statute, prohibited widespread or systematic attacks against any civilian population. The underlying list of prosecutable acts generally followed that which was contained in the ICTY and ICTR statutes and included murder, extermination, enslavement, deportation, imprisonment, torture, rape, sexual slavery, enforced prostitution, forced pregnancy or any other form of sexual violence, persecution on political, racial, ethnic or religious grounds and other inhumane acts.

The Court's later interpretation of crimes against humanity generally followed the jurisprudence of the Chapter VII tribunals with an emphasis on that of the ICTR. The latter made sense given the greater similarity between the SCSL and ICTR Statute vis-à-vis that of the ICTY. At the same time, one would be remiss not to highlight the fact that the SCSL statute and jurisprudence went further in clarifying key aspects of crimes against humanity in relation to, for instance, the addition of rape, sexual slavery, enforced prostitution, forced pregnancy and any other form of sexual violence (Article 2(g)) borrowed from Article 7 of the Rome Statute to the International Criminal Court (ICC) and in relation to the meaning of "attack directed against any civilian population." As will be discussed further in Chapter 6, the Court also jurisprudentially added to the law when it recognized the novel crime against humanity of forced marriage to address a gendered feature of the Sierra Leonean conflict as part of the residual "other inhumane acts" category of crimes against humanity.

---

[7] SCSL Statute, *supra* note 1, at art. 3 §1.

[8] Prosecutor v. Kambanda, Case No. ICTR 97–23-S, Judgment and Sentence, ¶ 16 (Sept. 4, 1998).

The second offense, that is violations of Article 3 Common to the Geneva Conventions and of Additional Protocol II, was prohibited by Article 3 of the SCSL Statute. These included violence to life, health and physical or mental well-being of persons, especially murder and cruel treatment such as torture, mutilation or any form of corporal punishment; collective punishments; hostage taking; acts of terrorism; outrages upon personal dignity specifically humiliating and degrading treatment, rape, enforced prostitution and any form of indecent assault; pillage; the passing of sentences and carrying out of executions without previous judgment affording due judicial guarantees; and threats to commit any of these acts. Violations of common Article 3 had long been considered customary international law and were generally similar to those covering internal armed conflicts in the Rome Statute.

Serious violations of international humanitarian law, listed in Article 4 of the SCSL Statute, entailed intentionally direct attacks against the civilian population as such or against individuals not partaking in the hostilities; intentionally directing attacks against personnel, installations, material, units or vehicles involved in a humanitarian or peacekeeping mission in circumstances where they are entitled to the protection given to civilians or civilian objects under the international law of armed conflict; and conscripting or enlisting children under the age of fifteen into armed forces or groups or using them to participate actively in hostilities. The aspects relating to conscription of children and the prohibition of attacks against peacekeepers were newer crimes inspired both by the facts of the Sierra Leone conflict and their specifications in the Rome Statute. The prosecution of those crimes, for the first time in international law by the Sierra Leonean Tribunal, would later lead to other useful judicial contributions to the development of international criminal law that were picked up by the ICC in its seminal first case involving Thomas Lubanga. These contributions have been addressed by others elsewhere, but in relation to the war crime of child recruitment, is also the subject matter of Chapter 7 of this book.[9]

Turning to the crimes under national law, which the Prosecutor did not ultimately use to charge anyone throughout the Court's existence, these were included in the statute on two main grounds. First, according to the Secretary-General, it was felt that the Sierra Leonean crimes ought to be included as gap fillers to cater for two situations:

---

[9] *See*, in this regard, Noah Novogrodsky, *Litigating Child Recruitment Before the Special Court for Sierra Leone*, 7 SAN DIEGO INT'L L. J. 421, 422–26 (2006); Alison Smith, *Child Recruitment and the Special Court for Sierra Leone*, 4 J. INT'L CRIM. JUST. 1141 (2004); Mohamed Bangura, *Prosecuting the Crime of Attack on Peacekeepers: A Prosecutor's Challenge*, 23 LEIDEN J. INT'L L. 165 (2010); Alhagi B. M. Marong, *Fleshing Out the Contours of the Crime of Attacks against United Nations Peacekeepers – The Contribution of the Special Court for Sierra Leone*, *in* THE SIERRA LEONE SPECIAL COURT AND ITS LEGACY: THE IMPACT FOR AFRICA AND INTERNATIONAL CRIMINAL LAW (Charles C. Jalloh ed., 2014). For the impact of the SCSL's jurisprudence on the interpretation of the war crime of child recruitment in the ICC's Lubanga Judgment, *see* Cecile Aptel, *Unpunished Crimes: The Special Court for Sierra Leone and Children*, *in* THE SIERRA LEONE SPECIAL COURT AND ITS LEGACY: THE IMPACT FOR AFRICA AND INTERNATIONAL CRIMINAL LAW (Charles C. Jalloh ed., 2014).

(1) where a specific situation or an aspect of it was considered to be unregulated; or (2) where it was indeed regulated but *inadequately* so under the relevant international law.[10] Two domestic offenses were judged to fit this criterion. But, as there was no parsing out of their separate rationales, we are left to guess which of these two categories they fell into. The first, offenses relating to the sexual abuse of minors, focused on three specific circumstances of crimes against the person that would constitute what is more commonly now referred to as "statutory rape" in some jurisdictions. The second focused on crimes against property, more specifically, the burning or destruction of private homes, and public buildings as well as other dwellings. These offenses covered conduct that frequently took place in the course of the Sierra Leone conflict. Both of these crimes, as codified in the SCSL Statute, drew from local laws that Sierra Leone had inherited from nineteenth- and twentieth-century England during the colonial period.[11]

The second reason for including local (that is Sierra Leonean) offenses in the Court's subject matter jurisdiction was more symbolic. In his initial letter requesting UN support, President Kabbah argued that the Tribunal should employ Sierra Leonean criminal law and procedure. The Special Court was to be endowed with jurisdiction over the "grave" domestic criminal offences. He argued that this would help foster (1) a sense of local (that is national) ownership of and identification with the Court and its processes; (2) that it would allow greater flexibility to the Prosecutor who could pick and choose which of national and or international offences to charge suspects with; and finally, (3) would permit them to cast a wider net to ensure that the leaders responsible for the atrocities do not escape punishment.[12] These factors, President Kabbah concluded, "roots the process in Sierra Leone and makes it uniquely Sierra Leonean."[13]

William Schabas has suggested that the inclusion of domestic crimes in the SCSL's jurisdiction *ratione materiae* was one of the "bizarre concessions" to the Sierra Leone government which, in his view, "really had no place in international justice."[14] It is unclear whether his concern was with the use of national offenses as

---

[10]   SCSL Statute, *supra* note 1, at art. 3 §19.

[11]   This point is well taken. But Schabas' characterization of both crimes as reflecting nineteenth-century English law may be a bit exaggerated. Whereas the Malicious Damage Act was indeed from 1861, therefore fitting that description, the second set of offenses relating to abuse of girls under the Prevention of Cruelty to Children Act stems from 1926 and therefore are more properly described as twentieth-century crimes. *See* William A. Schabas, *Foreword, in* THE SIERRA LEONE SPECIAL COURT AND ITS LEGACY: THE IMPACT FOR AFRICA AND INTERNATIONAL CRIMINAL LAW at xxv (Charles C. Jalloh, ed., 2014).

[12]   Letter from Alhaji Ahmad Tejan Kabbah, President of the Republic of Sierra Leone to the President of the Security Council, at Enclosure, U.N. Doc. S/2000/786 (June 12, 2000) (annex to Letter dated Aug. 9, 2000 from Ibrahim M. Kamara, Ambassador and Permanent Representative of Sierra Leone to the United Nations addressed to the President of the Security Council) [hereinafter Kabbah Letter to U.N.S.C.].

[13]   *Id.* at § 3 of Enclosure.

[14]   *See* Schabas, *Foreword, supra* note 11, at xxv.

such, or whether the critique related to dissatisfaction with the types or even the definitions of the municipal crimes which reflected the "the archaic language of nineteenth-century England."[15] The first concern, if that explains his objection, would not be a strong one for at least two reasons. First, as a partner in a negotiation process with the UN, Sierra Leone as a sovereign state is the natural forum for the prosecution of the crimes that occurred during the war. As such, it was fully entitled to insist on the use of applicable domestic offenses in the statute it was negotiating with the United Nations to create the SCSL. This is particularly so where it had advanced good legal and other practical reasons for taking such a position. Those positions seemed aimed at advancing the overall success of the process. It may also be that any sovereign state would, in such circumstances, insist on the use of its domestic legislation where those laws had been egregiously violated. The case perhaps becomes even stronger if the local statutes would have formed the basis of its own prosecutions had such trials taken place within its national courts. One is therefore hard pressed to understand the thrust of Schabas' concern on this particular issue.

Second, there is at least one ad hoc international penal court whose entire subject matter jurisdiction relies purely on domestic offenses in its statute rather than a mix of national and international crimes. The Special Tribunal for Lebanon (STL), although created five years after the SCSL, only exercises *ratione materiae* jurisdiction over common crimes under Lebanese Law.[16] The use of crimes against humanity in the STL Statute was initially considered, during the negotiations of the founding instruments, but the UN did not adopt it for various complex reasons. No other international crime was deemed sufficiently applicable. The domestic law of Lebanon, as the law of the relevant jurisdiction, became the gap filler. In the SCSL setting, it was not a choice of either international law or national law; a bit of both was used.

Certainly, the definitions of the offenses concerning the abuse of girls in the Prevention of Cruelty to Children Act, 1926 and those relating to wanton destruction of property under the Malicious Damage Act, 1861 smack of a different time period. In fact, and Schabas is right on this, they harken back to British Law which Sierra Leone had inherited when it was still an English colony. It may also be surprising that, even as such laws have since been updated in the United Kingdom, the older superseded versions continue to apply in Sierra Leone. Unfortunately, this is not a problem unique to Sierra Leone. It is a general issue with numerous outdated laws that were "received" during colonial times and that continue to be found and applied in the statute books of other African and other Commonwealth countries. These are legal legacies of colonialism found in all parts of the world.

---

[15] *Id.* at xxv.

[16] Statute of the Special Tribunal for Lebanon, annexure to S.C. Res. 1757 (May 30, 2007); *See also* U.N. Secretary-General, *Report of the U.N. Secretary-General on Establishment of a Special Tribunal for Lebanon*, U.N. Doc. S/2006/893 (Nov. 15, 2006).

That said, beyond concerns with offenses defined in archaic language, Schabas seemed troubled with including such offenses in the SCSL's subject matter jurisdiction. All the more so if they were judged to potentially help make the Tribunal more effective in addressing what the founders considered potential gaps in the law, laws that would, in any event, be ordinarily applicable to govern the situation had the country prosecuted the crimes using its own domestic laws without any UN assistance. It is interesting, in this regard, that Sierra Leone – even though a party to the 1949 Geneva Conventions – had not incorporated any of the prohibitions found in those international instruments into its national penal codes before the war started in March 1991. The Parliament only passed the Geneva Conventions Act on August 21, 2012, basically just a year before the conclusion of the SCSL trials.

Admittedly, and it is unclear what the official reasons were, the SCSL Prosecutor did not later use any of these local offenses when framing charges against the suspects. All the indictments charged only the international crimes. It is not publicly known why. One plausible explanation could be that the prosecution did not find evidence that any of the conduct that they charged the suspects with was either unregulated or inadequately regulated under international law – as the Secretary-General (and Sierra Leone) appeared to have concluded during the negotiations of the SCSL Statute.[17] On the other hand, recall that we are now able to benefit from hindsight. During the negotiations of the founding instruments, the appearance of the existence of gaps might have been clear even though the prosecution could, presumably following more thorough investigations, later choose to avoid Sierra Leonean law when it sought charges against the suspects. The decision not to use the local criminal law might also have little to do with the initial rationale offered for their inclusion.

Be that as it may, the abuse of young girls under the age of thirteen, or statutory rape in many jurisdictions, falls within the material jurisdiction of Article 2 (g) (crimes against humanity of rape) as well as rape as an outrage upon personal dignity contrary to Common Article 3 to the Geneva Conventions and of Additional Protocol II. Related prohibited conduct could also be captured by charging sexual slavery, enforced prostitution, forced pregnancy and any other form of sexual violence as well as enforced prostitution and any form of indecent assault. On the other hand, that the prosecution went ahead during the Freetown cases to innovate a whole new crime against humanity of forced marriage within the residual category of other inhumane acts suggests that there was cogent evidence that there were unique aspects of the Sierra Leone conflict that had not been adequately regulated under international law. As to the wanton destruction of property, some of the prohibited conduct could be covered by Article 3 of the Statute as acts of terrorism. In fact, the trial judgments would later extensively refer to arson, looting and burning

---

[17]   SCSL Statute, *supra* note 1, at art. 3.

of villages, all of which were common features of perpetrator activities during the conflict.

Another, and perhaps the better reason for setting aside the domestic crimes, could be that there was concern that using Sierra Leonean law, as we shall see in Chapter 9 in more detail, would potentially allow defendant claims to immunity from prosecution arising from the amnesty that the national authorities had offered all combatants in the 1999 Lomé peace accord. Under the amnesty arrangement, the government promised to shield all combatants from any legal action against them. To the extent that this undertaking was made, and is presumed valid as a consequence, it would potentially only apply in relation to Sierra Leonean law. This concern about being bogged down with the implications of using national law might best explain the Prosecutor's decision not to charge the suspects with the municipal crimes included in the SCSL Statute. This is an important point because even the disclaimer entered by the UN special representative that the international community does not recognize the conferral of immunity was later found to have applied only in respect of the *international* crimes instead of those under *national law* as well. The Sierra Leonean President had taken the view that the Revolutionary United Front (RUF) had repudiated their side of the bargain. He insisted that government would thus select which elements of the bargain would continue to benefit the rebels.[18] The Prosecutor would have also noted that Sierra Leone did subsequently request international support to establish the court. In doing so, the government repudiated the amnesty promised to all the combatants albeit, at least arguably, in relation only to the international crimes. It would logically follow that by charging only those crimes contained in the SCSL Statute pertaining to international law, as opposed to the domestic Sierra Leonean offenses as well, the prosecution would circumvent the legal and moral difficulties that would otherwise have arisen for contestations of the continued validity of the Kabbah amnesty as a bar to prosecution.

Further, another concern could have been that the first limb of crimes under Article 5 appears discriminatory in the sense that it would have permitted prosecutors to charge rape of underage minor girls but not necessarily the same in respect of boys who were also minors. Yet, there was evidence, certainly during the SCSL trials and presumably also in the lead up to the drawing up of indictments, that the rape and sexual violence visited upon the victims in the Sierra Leone conflict did not necessarily spare boys even if the bulk of the burden disproportionately affected girls.

Finally, because the Office of the Prosecutor was predominantly staffed by internationals (especially at the senior levels), it might have been less comfortable for them to use unfamiliar Sierra Leonean law instead of the presumably more familiar international law. A general issue in this regard, which was especially

---

[18]   President Ahmad Tejan Kabbah, Address Opening of The Fourth Session of The First Parliament of The Second Republic (June 16, 2000).

exacerbated by the war, would have been the lack of access to reliable case reporters of Sierra Leonean law in the country's national courts. Sierra Leonean procedural rules would also apply to the Sierra Leonean crimes, much as the international rules of procedure would apply to the international crimes.

Yet, rather interestingly, one of the oft-touted features of the SCSL was the supposed hybridity in terms of the subject matter jurisdiction. That hybrid nature of the Court was reflected in the formal use of Sierra Leonean law and the appointment of some of its principal officials. Be that as it may, even more cynically, it could be argued that the inclusion of Sierra Leonean crimes in the Tribunal Statute was intended as mere lip service to assuage the nationalistic demands of the Sierra Leone Government and as a way of bringing about agreement with the UN. It is possible that the lack of access to Sierra Leonean law, lack of adequate reporting on domestic criminal cases and even international prosecutor's unfamiliarity with the domestic legal order of Sierra Leone could have played a role in their decision to stay closer to the relatively more familiar terrain of international criminal and international humanitarian law.

4.3.2 *Personal Jurisdiction*

The UN-Sierra Leone Agreement, to which the Statute of the SCSL was an annex, defined the Court's *ratione personae* jurisdiction . Article 1(1) of the Statute provided, in relevant part, that the Special Court:

> shall, except as provided in subparagraph (2), have the power to prosecute persons who bear the greatest responsibility for serious violations of international humanitarian law and Sierra Leonean law committed in the territory of Sierra Leone since November 30, 1996, including those leaders who, in committing such crimes, have threatened the establishment of and implementation of the peace process in Sierra Leone.[19]

By its plain text, this provision sets out the jurisdiction of the SCSL over "persons" and emphasized those among them deemed to bear greatest responsibility. It further clarifies the focus to be those leaders who, in the course of committing crimes under international and Sierra Leonean law, had imperiled the establishment and implementation of the Sierra Leonean peace process.

During the negotiations of the SCSL Statute, there was serious debate regarding which way to formulate the personal jurisdiction provision. And, very importantly, the scope of its reach. For example, whether such reach should entail jurisdiction over underage persons especially juvenile child soldiers; and whether or not an

---

[19]   Statute of the Special Court for Sierra Leone, 16 January 2002, Annex to the Agreement between the United Nations and the Government of Sierra Leone on the Establishment of a Special Court for Sierra Leone, 2178 U.N.T.S. 137 at Art. 2. Art. 2 (3) also provided a problematic carve out from the Court's jurisdiction, as discussed further below.

exception ought to be carved out for any potential crimes that might have been committed by peacekeepers. With respect to framing the personal jurisdiction provision, President Kabbah's letter, which had an annex containing a suggested framework for the future court, had endorsed a personal jurisdiction over a limited group of persons. He assumed that this would more likely garner international support for the establishment of a special court, stating that the mandate "could be designed to be narrow in order to prosecute the *most responsible* violators and the leadership of the [RUF]."[20] This was expected to make the SCSL's work quicker by limiting its jurisdiction to a small number of persons.

At the same time, it would more likely help the future court achieve the task of rendering justice because it would help break the "command structure of the criminal organization"[21] (that is, the RUF) behind the violence. The President's explicit focus on the enemies of his government is notable, and it would seem, was deliberately selected.[22] It stands to reason that Sierra Leone did not at the time of the request appear to envisage that any other actors, such as its own armed forces and the government supported militia, would be prosecuted in the Tribunal.

On the other hand, this focus on the RUF can plausibly be read as an attempt by the national authorities to effectively shield their own forces from accountability before the eventual penal court. This would explain why they would refer only the crimes of the other side despite some evidence of the atrocities committed by government forces. This, of course, is not unheard of in international criminal law – as we have amply seen in the International Criminal Court's experience with the referral by the Ugandan Government of its enemy Lord's Resistance Army to the ICC for investigation and possible prosecution. Since the Sierra Leone military was partly disloyal, and Kabbah's government itself prosecuted some of its low-level mutinying members for domestic offenses, this argument would seem fair only if we assumed that he would have been inclined to protect the civilians turned paramilitary forces. The civilians, who organized themselves into self-defense units under the umbrella of Civil Defense Forces, were widely perceived as heroes. They were admired for standing up to the murderous RUF rebels forces. Nonetheless, in the course of doing so with great zeal, they are also said to have committed excesses of their own.

In any event, Security Council Resolution 1315 (2000), which had authorized the Secretary-General to enter into negotiations with the Sierra Leonean government to establish the Court, reformulated Kabbah's "most responsible" jurisdiction *ratione personae* proposal by recommending instead that the special court "should have personal jurisdiction over persons who bear the greatest responsibility for the

[20] Kabbah Letter to U.N.S.C., *supra* note 12, at 4 (emphasis added).
[21] *Id.* at 4.
[22] See William A. Schabas, *A Synergistic Relationship: The Sierra Leone Truth and Reconciliation Commission and the Special Court for Sierra Leone*, in Truth Commissions and Courts: The Tension Between Criminal Justice and the Search for Truth (William Schabas et al. eds., 2004.

commission of the crimes."[23] This was to include "those leaders who, in committing such crimes, have threatened the establishment of and implementation of the peace process in Sierra Leone."[24] Their explicit goal, driven by concerns about creating another costly ad hoc tribunal monster that would be impossible to shut down, was to limit the number of individuals that the SCSL would eventually prosecute. Conversely, although it appears that this language actually originated from President Kabbah's letter, the Secretary-General expressed a preference to use the phrasing "persons most responsible" – an arguably wider formulation.[25] The Secretary-General's view was that his alternative phraseology was more general, and more accurate in capturing the focus on the leadership or authority positions of the accused as well as more precise in emphasizing the gravity, seriousness or scale of the crimes. The Secretary-General lost on the point when the Security Council expressed a preference for the "greatest responsibility" language.

But there was also a measure of ambiguity about the actual meaning of greatest responsibility personal jurisdiction. This was not settled at the negotiation stage. The issue of how exactly greatest responsibility should be interpreted later generated considerable controversy among SCSL jurists as to the actual purpose of the language. There were further questions, which sharply divided the prosecution and defense lawyers as well as the judges, regarding whether the formulation created an evidential threshold that the prosecution must fulfill or some type of guideline or threshold for the exercise of prosecutorial discretion. This topic will be taken up in-depth in Chapter 5.

Briefly, because we will examine this issue in greater detail later, only a few observations need at this stage be made about the SCSL's personal jurisdiction. Compared to its equivalents in the statutes of other international or internationalized criminal tribunals since World War II to now, the SCSL's jurisdiction was highly circumscribed. At the Nuremberg Tribunal, Article 6 specified that the International Military Tribunals (IMT) "shall have the power to try and *punish persons*," (emphasis added) whether as individuals or as members of organizations, who committed certain crimes. In its provision, at Article 5, the Tokyo Tribunal also had the power "to try and punish Far Eastern war criminals who as individuals or as members of organizations are charged with offenses."[26] In identical provisions in the more recent ICTY and ICTR Statutes adopted in 1993 and 1994 respectively, Articles 1 specified that each "shall have the power to prosecute *persons responsible*" (emphasis added) for the commission of the international crimes within their jurisdiction.[27]

---

[23]   S.C. Res. 1315, ¶ 2 (Aug. 14, 2000).

[24]   *Id.* at ¶ 3.

[25]   Report on SCSL Establishment, *supra* note 3, at ¶¶ 29–31.

[26]   The same jurisdiction "for the trial of those persons charged individually, or as members of organizations, or in both capacities, with offenses which include crimes against peace." *See Special Proclamation – Establishment of an IMT, in* DOCUMENTS ON THE TOKYO INTERNATIONAL MILITARY TRIBUNAL: CHARTER INDICTMENT AND JUDGMENTS 5 (Neil Boister & Robert Cryer eds., 2008).

[27]   See Statute of the International Tribunal for the Prosecution of Persons Responsible for Serious Violations of International Humanitarian Law Committed in the Territory of the Former Yugoslavia

A similar formulation was used in the Statute of the Special Tribunal for Lebanon. Article 1 of the latter confers "jurisdiction over *persons responsible*."[28] Along the same lines, in the Rome Statute, which is not an ad hoc but a permanent tribunal, the personal jurisdiction clause endows it with the relatively broader authority to exercise its jurisdiction "over *persons*"[29] who have committed various crimes of concern to the international community as a whole. The latter is significant for its exclusion of the greatest responsibility language. This is because the ICC was generally anticipated to cover leaders or other similarly situated persons involved with the crimes in its States Parties that have proved unwilling or unable to investigate and prosecute them.

Upon first blush, at least formally, the above ways of framing those courts' personal jurisdiction was wider. They certainly could investigate and reach a broad range of possible suspects, giving a wide margin to prosecutors for the exercise of discretion in selecting whom to prosecute. But there are some subtleties found either in the same provisions cited above or elsewhere in the constitutive instruments or policy documents of those tribunals that tended to also narrow down the reach of those courts. In the Nuremberg and Tokyo Tribunals, for example, the limitations were to "persons acting in the interests of the Axis countries" and the "war criminals of the Far East" respectively. It was implied that those not from the mentioned regions would not fall within those courts' jurisdictions.[30] The personal jurisdiction clause was, in other words, reframed by the limited *territorial* reach of those courts. Nevertheless, whether in relation to those other statutory aspects or through the actual practice of those tribunals, the end result was that the SCSL still had a more severely limited *ratione personae* jurisdiction compared to its sister courts.

There is another issue relating to the type of "persons" that can be tried before the Court. In the ICTY and ICTR Statutes, Articles 6 and 5 provided, respectively, for jurisdiction "over natural persons."[31] As Larissa van den Herik observed in the context of her study on the ICTR, but which point can also be broadened in relation to the ICTY as well, this meant that states or international organizations could not be prosecuted before those courts.[32] Neither, for that matter, could legal persons such as

---

since 1991 ("ICTY Statute"), U.N. Doc. S/25704 at 36, annex (1993) and S/25704/Add.1 (1993), adopted by Security Council on 25 May 1993, U.N. Doc. S/RES/827 (1993) and Statute of the International Tribunal for Rwanda ("ICTR Statute"), adopted by S.C. Res. 955, U.N. SCOR, 49th Sess., 3453d mtg. at 3, U.N. Doc. S/RES/955 (1994), 33 I.L.M. 1598, 1600 (1994).

[28] *See* Statute of the Special Tribunal for Lebanon, *supra* note 16 (emphasis added).

[29] Rome Statute of the International Criminal Court, 2187 U.N.T.S. 90, *entered into force* July 1, 2002 at art. 1 [hereinafter Rome Statute] (emphasis added).

[30] Of course, in terms of the territorial jurisdiction, this was confined to Sierra Leone. This meant that crimes that related to the same war, but which might have occurred on the border or in Liberian or Guinean territory were excluded. This is significant given the porous borders between the countries and the fact that there were incidents of atrocities committed in neighboring states.

[31] *See* Arts. 5 and 6 of the ICTY and ICTR Statutes, *supra* note 27.

[32] L. J. VAN DEN HERIK, THE CONTRIBUTION OF THE RWANDA TRIBUNAL TO THE DEVELOPMENT OF INTERNATIONAL LAW 72 (2005).

private companies or paramilitary forces or other organizational units of the countries in the former Yugoslavia or Rwanda. This stands in sharp contrast to the IMTs, since they did not only have jurisdiction over individuals but they also had power to reach corporate bodies – several of which were qualified as criminal bodies for the purposes of reaching their members (though this was not prosecution of those legal persons as such).

In the SCSL Statute, unlike those of the ICTY and ICTR, there was no limitation of the personal jurisdiction to "natural persons."[33] This seemed to imply that there was nothing in principle that could stop the SCSL Prosecutor from prosecuting corporate persons involved with atrocities in Sierra Leone. The Secretary-General's report provided no explanation for this difference in language when the ICTR Statute had been the precedent used for Sierra Leone. This has led to some speculation that this could have reflected an interest in leaving the door open to corporate responsibility in Sierra Leone's blood diamond-driven conflict or even wider concern with the increased role of financial actors in modern conflict.[34] That said, as normatively desirable as the lifting of that limitation might have been from a policy perspective, there is no credible evidence that this explains the final decision on how best to frame the SCSL's personal jurisdiction at the Security Council.

In comparison to the SCSL, the Lebanon Tribunal's own limitation was not to personal jurisdiction as such. But to the persons deemed responsible for the attack of February 14, 2005, which resulted in the demise of Lebanese Prime Minister Rafiq Hariri, and in the death or injury of other persons that were present at the time. With respect to the Rome Statute, the Court has a limited power to exercise its jurisdiction "over persons for the most serious crimes of international concern."[35] The ICC was also to be complementary to "national criminal jurisdictions,"[36] meaning in a substantive sense that its powers could not be triggered except if as per Article 18 and 19, the admissibility requirements of inaction, unwillingness or inability to prosecute are fulfilled. Importantly, the gravity threshold would also have to be fulfilled before the Prosecutor could assert her authority to prosecute. The leaders and those at the top of the command structure will properly fall within the ICC's remit, in this burden-sharing model, while those at or towards the bottom of the hierarchy would be left to the national criminal courts of the States Parties.

In the Extraordinary Chambers in the Courts of Cambodia (ECCC), another ad hoc court whose instrument was negotiated around the same time as that of the Sierra Leone court, the personal jurisdiction provision was more restricted. It in fact was similar to that of the SCSL. The ECCC was mandated to bring to trial "senior

---

[33]   *Compare* S.C. Res. 827, art. 6 (May 25, 1993) (establishing the ICTY) and S.C. Res. 955, art. 5 (Nov. 8, 1994) (establishing the ICTR) *with* S.C. Res. 1315 (Aug. 14, 2000) (authorizing the negotiation of the treaty that would eventually establish the SCSL).

[34]   WILLIAM A. SCHABAS, THE UN INTERNATIONAL CRIMINAL TRIBUNALS 139 (2006).

[35]   Art. 1 Rome Statute].

[36]   *See id.* at arts. 1 (the court), 17 (complementarity) and 18 (admissibility).

leaders of Democratic Kampuchea" and those who were *"most responsible"* for the crimes and serious violations of Cambodian and international law.[37] This brought that court closer in personal jurisdiction to that exercised by the SCSL. The ECCC's own legal challenges purporting to unearth the meaning of the second half of that phrase, which was raised by the defense, will also be briefly considered in Chapter 5. The SCSL jurisprudence proved to be influential in shaping the ECCC's ruling on the same topic.

Turning now to the controversial issue during the UN-Sierra Leone negotiations of whether the SCSL's personal jurisdiction should cover child soldiers, the starting point was that the ICTY and the ICTR did not contain any such explicit provisions focusing on the responsibility of child soldiers. It is commonplace that young persons participated in the commission of atrocities in both the Balkans and Rwanda. But this does not appear to have been to the degree that this was a signature associated with those conflicts, as was the case in Sierra Leone. Article 7 of the SCSL Statute contained one of the two exceptions that served to narrow the court's personal jurisdiction by fixing a minimum age for prosecution. It provided that the tribunal shall not have jurisdiction over any person who was under the age of fifteen at the time of the alleged commission of the crime.[38] The possibility was left that there could be prosecution of a person whose prohibited conduct was carried out between fifteen and eighteen. The clear emphasis was on ensuring that any such person be treated with dignity and a sense of self-worth, taking into account his youth and the need to rehabilitate and reintegrate him into society. The latter was more consistent with international human rights standards, especially concerning the rights of the child.

The types of measures available, in the event a juvenile was prosecuted, would largely be non-punitive. It was envisaged to entail, among others, the use of community service orders, counseling, foster care, correctional, educational and vocational training programs and placement in approved schools. Partly to assuage concern that there could be prosecution of underage children, the Secretary-General had also added a provision in the SCSL Statute explicitly directing the Prosecutor to ensure that child rehabilitation programs are not placed at risk, and where appropriate, he was to have resort to alternative truth and reconciliation mechanisms that may be available.[39]

---

[37] Law on the Establishment of the Extraordinary Chambers in the Courts of Cambodia for the Prosecution of Crimes Committed during the Period of Democratic Kampuchea, art. 1 (NS/RKM/ 1004/006), Oct. 27, 2004 (emphasis added).

[38] Two points are worthy of note. International human rights law requires a minimum age of criminal responsibility, *see* the Convention on the Rights of the Child art. 40(3) (a), Nov. 20, 1989, 1577 U.N.T.S. 3. National jurisdictions vary widely on the age of criminal responsibility. Most recognize ages under eighteen. In Sierra Leone, as with many other common law jurisdictions, criminal liability starts as early as seven – the same standard that applies in the United Kingdom. In the ICC, specifically art. 26 of the Rome Statute, the permanent criminal court excludes jurisdiction over any person who was under the age of eighteen at the time of the alleged commission of a prosecutable offense.

[39] SCSL Statute, *supra* note 1, at app. II, art. 15(5).

It has been reported that it was the Sierra Leonean Government which insisted on including the above provisions contemplating the prosecution of children under the SCSL Statute.[40] The justification was that Sierra Leoneans would disapprove of any criminal accountability process that excluded up-front the possibility of trying child soldiers whom many thought had been particularly vicious in the course of their commission of crimes during the war.[41] On the other hand, the Secretary-General, the United Nations Children's Fund and some international human rights and local NGOs claimed that many of those same children had been transformed from victims into perpetrators by others. They point to circumstances of duress where some children had been psychologically and physically abused by the adults, who effectively used them to commit heinous crimes.[42] This latter argument seems to hold some merit. At the same time, it is possible that it might have failed to account for the fact that there were many willing and even enthusiastic youthful participants in the Sierra Leone war. Some of them became notorious for the viciousness with which they carried out horrific acts against innocents. Be that as it may, though this could be subject to some criticism, the issue became moot in the practice of the SCSL because the Prosecutor actually exercised his discretion not to seek charges against any child soldiers. There was also a legitimate question whether the jurisdiction over child soldiers was appropriate given that children might not have easily fallen within the high threshold of those bearing "greatest responsibility," except if that phrase was understood as not capturing only those holding leadership positions instead of also the gravity of the crimes committed.[43]

The final controversial point about the SCSL's personal jurisdiction, because it will not be examined later, is the additional carve out from the Court's jurisdiction.[44] Here, the Court also stands apart from the ICTY, ICTR, ECCC and the STL. None had any exemptions to personal jurisdiction in its statute. In accordance with Article 1(2) of the SCSL Statute,

> [a]ny transgressions by peacekeepers and related personnel present in Sierra Leone pursuant to the Status of Mission Agreement between the United Nations and the Government of Sierra Leone or agreements between Sierra Leone and other Governments or regional organizations, or, in the absence of such agreements, provided that the peacekeeping operations were undertaken with the consent of the

---

[40] Report on SCSL Establishment, *supra* note 3, at ¶ 35.

[41] *Id.* at ¶ 36.

[42] *Id.* at ¶ 32.

[43] Prosecutor v. Brima, Case No. SCSL-04-16-T, Judgment, ¶ 658, (June 20, 2007) [hereinafter AFRC Trial Judgment].

[44] This provision appears to have been without precedent in the international criminal law context, even though such is common in Status of Forces Agreements. However, in the UNSC referrals of the Sudan and Libya Situations to the ICC, its substantive content has been carried forward in other contexts. For example, similar controversial language purporting to exclude from the jurisdiction of the Court the nationals of non-party states contributing to the peacekeeping missions can be seen in the Sudan and Libya Situations. *See* S.C. Res. 1593, ¶ 6 (Mar. 31, 2005); S.C. Res. 1970 (Feb. 26, 2011).

Government of Sierra Leone, shall be within the primary jurisdiction of the sending state.

The thrust of this provision was to cover not only peacekeepers, but also related personnel (presumably including private contractors). It essentially ensured, despite the use of the less politically loaded but still problematic term ("transgressions" over "crimes"), that their home states would have primary jurisdiction over any offenses that they might have committed. This exception from jurisdiction, which is common in Status of Forces Agreements, can be criticized on principle. There was also some credible evidence which emerged later on during the SCSL trials suggesting alleged war crimes and other humanitarian law violations were committed by West African peacekeepers operating in Sierra Leone under the umbrella of the Economic Community of West African States Military Observer Group (ECOMOG). That evidence, which suggests that there was good reason for the States with troops that had been deployed in Sierra Leone to have this preference, indicates that there was at least some concern about possible legal exposure for some of the peacekeepers. The information was notably also consistent with the later findings of the Sierra Leone Truth and Reconciliation Commission, even though the incidents documented in their report seemed relatively minor when compared to the atrocities committed by those eventually prosecuted by the Tribunal from the RUF, Armed Forces Revolutionary Council (AFRC) and the Civil Defense Forces (CDF) factions.[45]

This paragraph is to be read, in light of Article 1(3) of the SCSL Statute, which also provided, in the only ad hoc international court outside of the ICC, a complementarity clause. It stated that, "[i]n the event the sending State is unwilling or unable genuinely to carry out an investigation or prosecution, the Court may, if authorized by the Security Council on the proposal of any State, exercise jurisdiction over such persons."[46] The notion of complementarity, which is of course the central organizing principle in the Rome Statute, presupposes a duty on the part of states to prosecute the crimes within the permanent court's jurisdiction. The major differences between that regime and the one anticipated for Sierra Leone were the three level legal hurdles that had to be cleared before any such prosecutions could be initiated. These required that (1) there be a proposal from a willing state; (2) the sending state was to have been (a) unwilling or (b) unable genuinely to investigate or prosecute; and (3) the Security Council permit or authorize both the state and the Court to exercise such jurisdiction. In the end, the SCSL could have, but did not, proceed to exercise such jurisdiction over any person where the sending state was unwilling or unable genuinely to do so. Besides the question of gravity, these legal qualifiers in Article 1 of the SCSL Statute placed an extremely high threshold requiring that the Court be first authorized by the Security Council to assert

---

[45] TRUTH AND RECONCILIATION COMMISSION OF SOUTH AFRICA REPORT (2001).
[46] *See* SCSL Statute, *supra* note 1, at art. 1.

jurisdiction over such a person upon the request of a willing state. This, as one might reasonably expect, did not occur. Ultimately, the present author could not find any evidence that there were any prosecutions of any peacekeepers for violations of the law of armed conflict or international criminal law in Sierra Leone or in their home states.

4.3.3 *Temporal Jurisdiction*

After the personal jurisdiction, which will be revisited in Chapter 5 along with its possible interpretive implications for other international criminal courts, the second most controversial element of the SCSL's jurisdiction related to the time period of the conflict that would be covered for the purposes of the investigations and prosecutions. Here, compared to the jurisdictional debate over greatest responsibility which split the Security Council and the Secretary-General into two opposite camps, the disagreement came from Sierra Leone instead of within the UN itself. As included in the Statute, Article 1 gave the Court competence to pursue those bearing greatest responsibility for serious international and national crimes committed "since November 30 1996." In this respect, the SCSL was similar to the ICTY, which had a start ("beginning January 1, 1991") but not an end date for its jurisdiction. The conflicts in both countries were ongoing at the time. The ICTR on the other hand had both a start and end date to its jurisdiction ("between January 1, 1994 and December 31, 1994").

Prima facie, international law does not impose a limit on the temporal competence of an international tribunal since there is no statute of limitation for the prosecution of international crimes such as war crimes or crimes against humanity.[47] So, the choice of having an open-ended jurisdiction going forward from a particular start date for the ICTY and a closed and limited one for the ICTR and the SCSL must be explained by political, economic or other factors. As George Mugwanya has rightly argued, in the case of the ICTR, the choice of temporal jurisdiction was "arbitrary and not based on any international law rule."[48] In fact, the Rwandan Government was dissatisfied with the narrow scope of that temporal jurisdiction. While on the one hand the Council wished to have a time-bound international tribunal, Rwanda's powerful argument was that the jurisdiction should date back to the formal beginning of the conflict between Hutus and Tutsis in October 1990. Several incidents that had apparently been trial runs for genocide had also occurred, between 1990 and 1994, all of which would have fallen within the ICTR's legal competence. Conspiracy to commit acts that were genocidal in nature

---

[47] *See* Convention on Non-Applicability of Statutory Limitations to War Crimes and Crimes Against Humanity, Nov. 11, 1970, 754 U.N.T.S. 73.

[48] For a similar argument problematizing temporal restrictions to the ICTR's jurisdiction, *see* GEORGE MUGWANYA, THE CRIME OF GENOCIDE IN INTERNATIONAL LAW: APPRAISING THE CONTRIBUTION OF THE UN TRIBUNAL FOR RWANDA 54 (2007).

seemed to have occurred before 1994, and by implication, would either be excluded or very difficult to prove. This issue of the time frame of the tribunal, alongside its location outside the country and the lack of use of the death penalty, were among the reasons why the government in Kigali eventually voted against the creation of the ICTR.

In the Sierra Leone context, matters of temporal jurisdiction seemed relatively less political. But they were still controversial. The same conclusion may not necessarily be reached that the choice of temporal reach for the SCSL was arbitrary. Arbitrary implies a decision taken without sound reasoning. There was in fact some reasoning offered to justify the limited SCSL jurisdiction. Indeed, according to the Secretary-General's report, various considerations were taken into account. Three main ones guided the parties' selection of an appropriate start date for the Court's jurisdiction: the desire to have (1) a reasonably limited time frame be covered in order to avoid overburdening the Court's Prosecutor; (2) a beginning date corresponding to an event or a new phase in the conflict which does not have any political connotations; and (3) encompassing the most serious crimes committed by persons of all the parties to the conflict in all parts of Sierra Leone.

The war had started on March 23, 1991, as explained in Chapter 2 of this work. The Attorney-General and Minister of Justice, Solomon Berewa, who was the lead negotiator for the government of Sierra Leone felt that the temporal jurisdiction over the crimes should start then. This would seem to be the natural default given that it represents the beginning of the conflict. One might have thought that there would be no issue of an end date, as it would have been prudent for both parties to not select an end date given that the conflict in the country was ongoing at the time of the UN-Sierra Leone negotiations. In a thoughtful proposal, however, Sierra Leonean Justice Minister Berewa proposed July 7, 1999 (the date of the signing of the final peace accord) as the cutoff date for the jurisdiction.[49] This seemed like a good proposal intended to connect Sierra Leone's two separate transitional justice mechanisms by making the SCSL's jurisdiction, in his words, "co-terminus with that of the TRC."[50] This would have been a crucial decision, given the tension that later arose between the two institutions, partly because of the overlap between the SCSL and the TRC time frame that is analyzed in Chapter 10 of this book. Still, Attorney-General Berewa would later acquiesce to the UN's logic that since the conflict was continuing, in various parts of Sierra Leone, the temporal scope of the tribunal's

---

[49]   It may be noted that S.C. Res 1315 did not specify a start or end date for jurisdiction. The Security Council requested, in paragraph 7, that the Secretary-General "address the question of the temporal jurisdiction." Perhaps reading the mood was not right for an expansive tribunal, he proposed to limit the jurisdiction.

[50]   It is not entirely clear whether Sierra Leone pressed for this during the early part of the negotiations or whether that decision came later. Berewa noted that Sierra Leone's request was made on Mar. 20, 2001, but that the UN indicated it preferred to retain the Nov. 30, 1996 commencement date. *See* Solomon E. Berewa, *Addressing Impunity using Divergent Approaches: The Truth and Reconciliation Commission and the Special Court, in* Truth and Reconciliation in Sierra Leone 178 (1999).

jurisdiction was better left open-ended.[51] This made sense. From the UN perspective, this had been the same approach used in the circumstances of the former Yugoslavia where, much as in the West African country, a war was ongoing at the time of creation of the tribunal. However, this meant that the overlap of jurisdiction between the Truth and Reconciliation Commission (TRC) and the SCSL was never addressed. The former was not necessarily limited in the start date of its historical assessment of the reasons for the outbreak of conflict in Sierra Leone.

From the UN's perspective on the start date of the SCSL's jurisdiction, "reaching back to 1991"[52] was out of the question, for practical reasons of not *overburdening* the Tribunal. The language of overburdening was a euphemism for giving limited justice in light of the positions of some Security Council members that they would not fund an ICTY-ICTR style international penal tribunal for Sierra Leone. Thus, the Attorney-General's proposed start date coincident with the beginning of the war was only briefly considered. It was ultimately rejected, albeit over Sierra Leone's strong objections, as a possible opening date for the SCSL's prosecutions.[53] Three other alternative dates were thereafter briefly floated. November 30, 1996, which was the eventual date chosen, coincided with the conclusion of the first comprehensive peace agreement between the Kabbah Government and the RUF. The agreement had collapsed not long afterwards. The Secretary-General's position was that this would put the conflict in perspective without necessarily going back to the start of hostilities in March 1991. It would also, at the same time, account for the most serious offenses committed during the war.[54]

The second date considered, May 30, 1997, coincided with the coup d'état which drove the democratically-elected Kabbah government to exile in neighboring Conakry, Guinea. AFRC-RUF coalition forces carried out widespread violations during this period. But this incident had political connotations. It was correctly felt that Sierra Leoneans might not appreciate the implication that the international community was more interested in punishing the coupists than those who had committed some of the worst atrocities against them before and after that period.[55]

Finally, the January 6, 1999 option was in many ways the culmination of the war and rebel military attacks on the Sierra Leonean capital Freetown. It marked one of the largest single incidents of widespread and systematic attacks against unarmed civilians, both in terms of scale and the heinous nature of the conduct such as killings, rape of women and girls, burning, looting and other reprehensible conduct. Selecting the three weeks when the rebels controlled Freetown, the country's largest urban center, would appear to ignore the many crimes committed in rural Sierra

[51] Report on SCSL Establishment, *supra* note 3, at ¶ 28.
[52] *Id.* at ¶ 25.
[53] U.N. Secretary-General, *Eleventh Report of the Secretary-General on the United Nations Mission in Sierra Leone*, ¶ 48, U.N. Doc. S/2001/857 (June 14, 2001).
[54] Report on SCSL Establishment, *supra* note 3, at ¶ 27.
[55] *Id.*

Leone. This would fuel arguments about selectivity in the type of justice rendered for the atrocities during the war. It would effectively have meant writing out the first eight years of the gruesome war (which largely affected rural Sierra Leoneans), something that would have been very problematic given that the majority of the country's population lived in rural areas.

In the end, although a compromise of November 30, 1996 seemed to be the preferred way to delimit the start of the Tribunal's temporal jurisdiction, Sierra Leonean civil society and even the government regretted that the trials at the SCSL did not coincide with the opening of the war. Significantly, Attorney-General Berewa – who later became the Vice-President of Sierra Leone – has since argued that the SCSL failed to address the issue of justice and impunity fully due to this temporal limitation.[56] In his view, the rule of law was not applied fully in so far as the Court's truncated jurisdiction meant that war crimes (and this writer would add *other* international crimes) that occurred in Sierra Leone were only partially and selectively prosecuted.[57] Berewa blamed the "rather severe limitation"[58] placed on the Court's personal and temporal jurisdictions as the main culprit for this.

Abdul Tejan-Cole, a Sierra Leonean lawyer, observed even before the Statute of the SCSL was adopted, the effect of the November 1996 start date of jurisdiction was a conferral of a de facto amnesty or pardon for international criminal acts committed in Sierra Leone for the period between March 23, 1991 and November 29, 1996.[59] He took exception to the temporal exclusion on other additional grounds, with which this writer concurs: (1) that this limited the successful prosecution of some accused thereby prospectively imposing a difficult and exacting burden of proof for prosecutors and creating an impunity gap; and (2) sent a message of preferential treatment for Freetownians compared to their compatriots in other parts of the country. The latter had borne the worst of the war during the early part of the conflict.[60]

Before finalizing agreement on the November 1996 start of the SCSL jurisdiction, the parties had to also resolve the question of possible legal validity of the sweeping amnesty that had been granted by the Kabbah government to the combatants involved with the conflict. If that amnesty was deemed to be valid, the Tribunal's jurisdiction would only come into effect for crimes committed after the date of its signature in Togo on July 7, 1999. If found to be invalid, the temporal jurisdiction

---

[56] Solomon E. Berewa, A New Perspective On Governance, Leadership, Conflict and Nation Building in Sierra Leone 185 (2011) (observing that the SCSL "failed to address the issue of justice and impunity fully, or apply the rule of law to its full extent in relation to the war crimes committed during the conflict").

[57] *Id.*

[58] *Id.*

[59] Abdul Tejan-Cole, *The Special Court for Sierra Leone: Conceptual Concerns and Alternatives*, 1 Afr. Hum. Rts. L. J. 107 (2001).

[60] *Id.*

could theoretically date back to the pre-amnesty period. So, while this author considers the legal debate raised about the status of the amnesty later on in this book, it might be be noted that a good question that the Attorney-General avoided is the extent to which some of these failures of the SCSL could be attributed to the national authorities rather than the UN itself.

The position that the government had taken with respect to the Lomé amnesty, which it essentially determined had been invalidated upon the request for the UN help to create a criminal court, makes it obvious that Sierra Leone could well have also undertaken its own prosecutions of international crimes committed in the country. Indeed, in all the other contemporary conflicts where ad hoc international criminal tribunals have been established, there have been concomitant national prosecutions. In the countries and the region of the former Yugoslavia, numerous prosecutions have taken place, albeit with the help of the ICTY. The same has been true with respect to Rwanda, both in the East African country and by other states further afield such as Belgium and Canada. The latter countries have invoked universal jurisdiction. However, as William Schabas has observed, this pattern of apportioning liability to perpetrators of atrocities using national courts has been nearly entirely absent in Sierra Leone.[61]

It can be argued that the lack of national prosecutions was justified because Sierra Leone had promised amnesty to the RUF and all other combatants. But the amnesty would only have applied to the national crimes. Indeed, due to the fact that the government explicitly declared the amnesty void, there would have been nothing to prevent the national prosecutors from charging offenders using war crimes, crimes against humanity and other serious violations of international law as the basis for their domestic prosecutions. This conclusion is reinforced by the fact that the local courts in Sierra Leone had in any event also dismissed the challenges mounted in the high court against the government's repudiation of the amnesty by the suspects before the SCSL. The national courts adopted the same stance as the SCSL that Sierra Leonean authorities were not competent to amnesty international crimes. With those rulings, the purported obstacles to the domestic trials were effectively removed.

4.3.4 *Territorial Jurisdiction*

Article 1 of the SCSL Statute sets out the geographic scope of the Tribunal's jurisdiction *ratione loci*. Much like the ICTY, but unlike the ICTR, the reach of the Court extended only to the "territory of Sierra Leone." In the statutes of the Chapter VII tribunals, the term "territory" reflects how that term is understood in general international law as covering their land surface, airspace and territorial

---

[61] Although an attempt was made to prosecute a handful of people. *See* Schabas, *Foreword, supra* note 11, at xxvii.

waters (although the latter did not apply to Rwanda as a landlocked state). There was no such definition of what constituted Sierra Leonean "territory." In any case, in the absence of a specific definition, it can reasonably be presumed that the same international law definition of territory would govern. Thus, acts on the land surface, in the airspace and territorial waters of Sierra Leone, would have the necessary nexus to the war. There does not appear to have been allegations of widespread atrocities committed from the airspace and the territorial waters of Sierra Leone. It may be that this point would only have been relevant had the allegedly indiscriminate bombing of Freetown, which was carried out by ECOMOG forces on land and sea, not being excluded from the SCSL's jurisdiction.

In one sense, although no substantial controversy arose in relation to the question of territory, the clarification of what territory was covered might have been a reasonable one to contemplate. The reason is that, at various times of the conflict, the rebels – not the central government – exercised effective control over parts of Sierra Leone. This was sometimes the case for long periods of time. The question is whether the government's loss of territory to the rebels would have forestalled its jurisdictional authority over such spaces, especially when those might have been forcibly seized during hostilities. In any event, as of the creation of the Tribunal, it was likely obvious that jurisdiction extended to any acts forming any part of Sierra Leonean territory even if occupied by the RUF and AFRC fighters.

In the ICTR, the geographic jurisdiction of the Tribunal was also extended to cover crimes, which might have occurred in the territory of neighboring states. All the more so because certain Hutu militia groups had simply continued carrying out their attacks against Tutsis in the refugee camps of the countries neighboring Rwanda. Thus, the expanded jurisdictional reach was consistent with the desire to not only end the genocide, which was ongoing with many Hutu extremists having escaped from Rwanda, but also as a way to help restore peace to Rwanda. The connector was a requirement that the crimes must have been carried out by Rwandan citizens and be linked to the conflict in Rwanda. These jurisdictional linkages were deemed necessary to ensure that the attacks by Hutu extremists of Tutsis in the refugee camps in places such as Tanzania and the Democratic Republic of the Congo could also be prosecuted. It is unclear the extent to which ICTR prosecutors pursued crimes committed in neighboring states, considering the massive scale of the atrocities actually committed *within* Rwanda. This was probably due to problems with investigations. It also seems that the ICTR might have had run-ins with some of the countries in the region which proved to be opposed to the extension of its jurisdictional reach into their territories.

It does not appear, based on the available record, that the question of extending the SCSL's jurisdiction to cover Sierra Leoneans who carried out such acts in neighboring states, such as Liberia and Guinea, was discussed. However, a review of the Security Council's own statements and resolutions, the Court's judgments and the findings of the TRC showed that there are ample links between the Sierra

Leonean and Liberian conflicts.[62] Those connections were deep and enduring and lasted several years. Many were widely reported on. Indeed, some might argue that the conflicts in each of Sierra Leone and Liberia, and at some point Guinea, fed off of or were mirrors of the other. Among other things, there were apparently close personal links between the rebel leadership, especially Foday Sankoh and Charles Taylor, who assisted each other to wage war in Sierra Leone and Liberia.[63] The names of other prominent rebels, from other countries like the Gambia, Senegal and Burkina Faso, widened the geographic spread of the criminal enterprise responsible for the atrocities in Sierra Leone well beyond the Mano River Union countries into the wider West Africa. In some ways, these were just different sites of one massive conflict. The involvement of forces from other states did not seem to have provoked a question of how to classify the Sierra Leone conflict from the point of view of international humanitarian law. It was simply assumed to have been an internal armed conflict – a proposition that could be contestable.

Against this backdrop, given the interconnected nature of the wars and even the similarity of the means and methods of warfare deployed by the parties, it might have been more appropriate to make provision for the extension of jurisdiction to acts carried out by nationals of Sierra Leone (and possibly others from neighboring states) in the SCSL Statute. The rebels are known to have deliberately attacked various towns and villages in Guinea. And, in reacting to rebel activities, militant groups fighting Taylor and others staged operations from Guinea, Liberia and even Sierra Leone into the sovereign territory of Liberia. Considering that no tribunals were created to prosecute those responsible for such crimes, those too could have been covered by the SCSL jurisdiction.[64] A reason for ignoring these might have been the concern on the part of some Security Council members that there be a limited reach to whatever tribunal was created so that it would complete its work within the three years initially envisaged. But this was a political and practical choice, it was not a legal choice, and it appears to have left impunity intact in relation to some of the more serious international crimes committed during the fighting in those other West African States in the decade of the 1990s to the 2000s.

By way of preliminary conclusion about the crimes, persons, time frame and territory over which the SCSL was entrusted with authority to prosecute, the preceding sections have shown that both the UN and the Government of Sierra Leone appeared to be guided by the overall desire to ensure the prosecution of some of those most responsible for some of the atrocities carried out during the conflict. This was consistent with the view, as the Security Council had expressed in

---

[62] *See* Prosecutor v. Taylor, Case No. SCSL-03-01-T, Sentencing Judgment, (May 30, 2012); Prosecutor v. Sesay, Case No. SCSL-04-15-T, Judgment, (Mar. 2, 2009); Prosecutor v. Brima, Case No. SCSL-04-16-T, Judgment, (June 20, 2007).

[63] Prosecutor v. Taylor, Case No. SCSL-03-01-T, Judgment, (May 30, 2012).

[64] Charles C. Jalloh & Alhagi Marong, *Ending Impunity: The Case for War Crimes Trials in Liberia*, 1 AFR. J. LEGAL STUD. 53 (2005).

Resolution 1315 of August 14, 2000, that some of those who committed or authorized serious human rights violations are individually criminally responsible and that they should be subject to trial in accordance with international standards of justice, fairness and due process of law. It was also a way, using the example of Sierra Leone, to put in place a national-international system of accountability that is credible to pursue the perpetrators of the very serious crimes. The hope was that this would help to end the culture of impunity in Sierra Leone and contribute to the process of national reconciliation.

But, as the analysis in this and in the previous chapter demonstrates, the high rhetoric about addressing accountability to all those suspected of crimes against innocents which characterized the debate during the establishment of the SCSL was ultimately bogged down in practical and legal considerations. The former may be said to have won out over the latter. The end result was the extremely circumscribed substantive jurisdiction for the SCSL. This came in the form of the limitation to prosecute those bearing greatest responsibility for crimes that occurred during a short time frame amounting only to the latter half of a conflict in which many atrocities had been committed. It covered only a handful of offenses committed within the territory of Sierra Leone. This despite the many violations that were related to the war, but which had occurred in neighboring states. In other words, the problem of selectivity of justice permeated nearly all the aspects of the SCSL's jurisdiction. And despite the reference to other ambitious goals, largely as a way of nodding to the Sierra Leonean government's wishes, the conclusion must be that the SCSL was only tooled to dispense only a limited quantity of *symbolic justice* for the victims of the atrocities witnessed during the Sierra Leone conflict.[65]

4.4 THE ORGANIZATION OF THE SPECIAL COURT FOR SIERRA LEONE

To appreciate the organizational structure of the Tribunal requires analysis of both the UN-Sierra Leone Agreement and the SCSL Statute. The SCSL, as an ad hoc tribunal that did not form either part of the Sierra Leonean legal system or the United Nations, was conceptualized as a sort of self-contained entity. It therefore had three main organs, to wit: Chambers (two trial and one appeals); the Office of the Prosecutor; and the Registry. The structure of the SCSL basically mirrored that of the Chapter VII Tribunals. Because those others lacked the fourth quasi-organ, the Defense Office, such an office was also missing in the Tribunal's statute. Thus, in the SCSL, while the first three organs were formally created by statute, the latter consequently had to be established by the judges in their Rules of Procedure and Evidence. The Defense Office became one of the more important institutional

---

[65] *See* Charles C. Jalloh, *Conclusion, in* THE SIERRA LEONE SPECIAL COURT AND ITS LEGACY: THE IMPACT FOR AFRICA AND INTERNATIONAL CRIMINAL LAW 771 (Charles C. Jalloh ed., 2014).

innovations of the SCSL. It formed the basis for the establishment of a similar office in the Special Tribunal for Lebanon, where it was also elevated to the status of a full organ. This part of the chapter briefly examines the formal organs included in the Statute that comprised the SCSL, starting with the Chambers. Thereafter, we will examine the role of the judicially created Defense Office, which was a subunit of the Registry.

4.4.1 *The Chambers*

At its founding, the SCSL was comprised of a Trial Chamber and an Appeals Chamber. During the negotiations the parties considered the feasibility of incorporating *two* separate trial chambers, but instead of creating one from the get-go, decided to sequence the two. The reason was largely financial. Upon the establishment of the Court, Trial Chamber I was created. About six months after the date of commencement of the Court, Trial Chamber II was opened. This decision, which reflected the lack of money and the donations-based funding structure, was a mistake. It prolonged the ultimate time frame of the Tribunal's life. It is apparent, in retrospect, that it would have been more efficient to set up the two trial chambers from day one.

Each Trial Chamber was comprised of three judges. Whereas in the ICTY and the ICTR all three were appointed by the United Nations, with no formal role for the former Yugoslavia and the Rwandese governments, in the SCSL the appointments were shared with the national authorities. This involvement reflects the consensual and hybrid nature of the SCSL. The parties were to consult with each other and cooperate on ensuring the best judicial selections.[66] Two of the three members of each trial chamber were to be judges appointed by the UN Secretary-General from a pool nominated by UN Member States. This assured an international majority. Sierra Leone was to appoint the third judge. The Statute provided a sort of preference for nominees from the countries of the Economic Community of West African States (ECOWAS) as well as the Commonwealth[67] (Article 2(2) of the UN-Sierra Leone Agreement). Sierra Leone had advocated for this priority, which made sense, given the similarity of its legal culture to those of its neighbors in the West Africa sub-region. In principle, the ECOWAS States totaled fifteen. But, only four other countries in the region (that is Cameroon, Gambia, Ghana, Nigeria), shared British origins for their legal system as Sierra Leone (with Liberia sharing in Anglo-American law as well). Some attention was paid to this aspect of the judicial selection.

Trial Chamber I was comprised of Judges Pierre Boutet (Canada), Benjamin Itoe (Cameroon) and Bankole Thompson (Sierra Leone). They were sworn in

---

[66] U.N.-Sierra Leone Agreement, *supra* note 1, at art. 2(3).
[67] *Id.* at art. 2(2).

2002. Trial Chamber II had on its bench Teresa Doherty (Northern Ireland), Julia Sebutinde (Uganda) and Richard Lussick (Fiji and Samoa), all of whom were sworn in 2005. The initial appointments were for three years, reflecting the expected time span of the SCSL. The judges were eligible for reappointment, and they all were renewed periodically until the completion of their cases.

Five judges served in the Appeals Chamber. Of those, two were to be appointed by Sierra Leone while the Secretary-General named the other three. This was not terribly different from the Trial Chamber, where the national authority also appoints the minority of the judges, with a 2–1 split in the positions. The Trial and Appeals Chamber judges in each of the chambers elects a Presiding Judge, whose role it is to conduct the proceedings in the Chamber s/he serves. The presiding judge of the Appeals Chamber doubled as the President of the Tribunal.

The Sierra Leone government's request for support for the establishment of a special court mooted the idea of a common court of appeals that would be shared with the ICTY and ICTR.[68] In Resolution 1315 (2000), the Security Council was open to the idea and in fact asked the Secretary-General to formally consider the "advisability, feasibility, and appropriateness of an appeals chamber in the special court or of sharing the Appeals Chamber of the [ICTY/R] or *other effective options.*"[69] In his report, the Secretary-General seemed to reinterpret this task to mean as only requiring him to do the former (that is, examining the feasibility of the SCSL either having its own appeals court or sharing one with the ad hoc courts). He did not consider other options, a possibility that the last part of the sentence seemed to leave open. His report, as well as the Security Council resolution for that matter, was silent as to what the third option might have been (that is, it seemingly failed to consider other likely effective options). There might have been other effective options. For instance, given the context of a national/international partnership to create the SCSL, the possibility of using the Sierra Leonean Supreme Court as the final court of appeal might have also been explored. This, of course, will have required amendment to the domestic legislation.

In any case, focusing on the question of a single versus unified appeals chamber, Annan explained that the creation of separate tribunals not anchored in either a national legal system or an international court implied that "the inclusion of the Appeals Chamber within the same Court" was the "obvious choice."[70] This is what he then recommended for two reasons. Those being reasons that were informed by the consultations he undertook with the ICTY President. First, in his view, establishing a common appellate chamber with the

---

[68]   Kabbah Letter to U.N.S.C., *supra* note 12, at annexure ¶ 6 (stating that "the court of appeals for Rwanda and for the former Yugoslavia based in The Hague could be used as the court of appeals for the special court for Sierra Leone.").

[69]   S.C. Res. 1315, *supra* note 22, at ¶ 7 (emphasis added).

[70]   Report on SCSL Establishment, *supra* note 3, at ¶ 39.

distinctive Chapter VII Tribunals on the one hand and the treaty-based SCSL on the other was both legally unsound and practically cumbersome,[71] legally unsound because of the problems arising from mixing distinctive sources of law. Practically, it would mean that in addition to a Hague to Arusha circuit, the ICTY and ICTR judges would have to travel to Freetown to mix with different judges from a third separate tribunal. The fact that funds for the SCSL Appeals Chamber would have to be paid out of the UN budget, in this arrangement, irrespective of which way the SCSL would be financed, could all potentially have imposed high administrative and financial costs.[72]

Second, Annan argued that, as a theoretical matter, the use of a common appeals chamber to promote harmony in the interpretation and application of the relevant law could be helpful. However, in his view, a simpler alternative would be to require the Appeals Chamber to be (1) "guided" by the ICTY and ICTR decisions (as found in Article 20(3) of the Statute) and (2) providing that the ICTR Rules obtaining at the time would apply, *mutatis mutandis*, to the SCSL legal proceedings.[73] The safety valve was that the latter could still be amended by the judges, and if those proved inadequate, they could be guided as appropriate by Sierra Leonean criminal procedure. In the end, Annan's conclusion was that a single Appeals Chamber for all the three courts could either lead to delay beyond acceptable human rights standards pending hearing of appeals from either or all jurisdictions, or even worse, lead to a collapse of the entire appeals system given the dramatic increase in workload for the judges.[74] The outcome would be untenable for the ICTY/ICTR as well as the SCSL, which especially if it had the similar number of cases, would have been an ineffectual appeals system. These arguments settled the issue. Still, it is not entirely clear whether the Secretary-General also considered an enlargement of the appeals bench to accommodate the new tribunal. That would have been a way to mitigate the concern about overburdening the appellate chamber. The Security Council, in any case, never reopened the issue. The result was that while the Chapter VII courts in essence shared a common appeals chamber, the SCSL had its own freestanding appeals court but was linked to them through the guidance provided by their decisions. Even in the absence of such a provision, in the SCSL Statute, it is difficult to see how the SCSL judges might have avoided examining the ICTY and ICTR case law for non-binding but authoritative guidance in their own decisions.

With respect to qualifications for judicial posts on the SCSL bench, the judges were under the statute required to be "be persons of high moral character, impartiality, and integrity who possess the qualifications required in their respective

---

[71]   *Id.* at ¶ 40.
[72]   *Id.* at ¶ 63.
[73]   *Id.* at ¶ 20.
[74]   *Id.* at ¶¶ 41, 46.

countries for appointment to the highest judicial offices."[75] Key considerations for their qualifications accounted for experience in judging in international law, including international humanitarian law and criminal law. The judges were to be independent when carrying out their duties and were prohibited from accepting or seeking instructions from any government or any other sources. This is all standard protocol for international judges.

A question about the independence and impartiality of the SCSL judges was later raised by Defense Counsel during the trials.[76] In a preliminary motion, in the *CDF* case, the defendants argued that the funding structure of the Court through donations by interested states and the oversight by a management committee comprised of donor states deprived the judges of the necessary guarantees of independence and impartiality because of the likelihood of political interference. The Appeals Chamber described the motion as almost in "bad taste."[77] To them, the applicant's logic was far-fetched. The funding structure could not reasonably lead to denial of a fair hearing. They explained that the judges were on fixed three-year contracts, and that though subject to reappointment, the Court was duty bound to pay those salaries. There was therefore no way that salaries could be used to curry favor in a particular case or be manipulated to obtain certain results. The judges seemed to have reached the right decision.

But this issue, which goes to the issue of the legitimacy of the Tribunal, may not seem as self-evident as their strident though understandable decision implied. This was because it was not just about whether there were in fact attempts to influence the judges, but *perceptions* of the likelihood of such possible influence. Indeed, at least one prominent commentator has suggested that the funding structure of the SCSL was such that it permitted the wealthier contributing states to keep the Court on the "drip feed" – perhaps as a way to better influence "decisions and the behavior of the Court."[78] This claim is speculative, and although it is obvious that such information would not easily be in the public domain, there was no evidence to indicate any state sought to corrupt the judges in return for a favorable decision in a particular case.

The Appeals Chamber was variously comprised, and towards the end of the last half of the SCSL trials, had the following judges who served until completion of all its work: Renate Winter (Austria), Emmanuel Ayoola (Nigeria), Leone) and Shireen Fisher (USA) were the three appointed by the UN while George King (Sierra Leone) and Jon Kamanda (Sierra Leone) served as Sierra Leone's two appointees.

---

[75] SCSL Statute, *supra* note 1, at appendix II, art. 13.
[76] Prosecutor v. Norman, Case No. SCSL-2004-14-AR72 (E), Decision on Preliminary Motion Based on Lack of Jurisdiction (Judicial Independence), (Mar. 13, 2004).
[77] *Id.* at ¶41.
[78] See Schabas, *Foreword*, *supra* note 11, at xxvi–xxvii.

4.4.2 *The Prosecution*

In his initial letter to the United Nations, in which he sought assistance for the creation of a special court, President Kabbah proposed two alternative structures for the prosecutorial organ. The first would enable the Attorney General of Sierra Leone to serve as the "chief" prosecutor of the future court.[79] This would permit the government "to play a lead role in the prosecution while receiving international assistance and expertise."[80] In the second (and alternative) model, the Attorney-General would be the "co-chief" prosecutor of the Court. Under this latter approach, the "international community" will be represented much like it is presently in the Cambodia Tribunal. Interestingly, this would be only in relation to the "international crimes committed against the peacekeepers."[81] Presumably, the reason for this was that the government felt that the remaining international crimes were crimes against the Sierra Leonean people as well. Whatever the model chosen, the two prosecutors would lead a combined team of national and international prosecutors and investigators to pursue investigations within and outside the country for the "crimes committed against Sierra Leone."[82] The latter element was later retained. Nonetheless, the idea of a Sierra Leonean prosecutor assisted by an international one or a co-prosecuting authority did not in the end make its way into the design in the final statute.

The then US Ambassador at large for war crimes David Scheffer, in his memoirs, has explained that Sierra Leonean Attorney-General Berewa had "boldly suggested" that he wanted to be co-prosecutor during the negotiations for the SCSL.[83] This was an interesting statement. It might be borne of Scheffer's feeling that this was a self-interested proposal. But, as a matter of principle under national practice, it is not as unusual as Scheffer made it out to be given that the country's attorney-general is ultimately typically responsible for prosecutions of crimes in the domestic system (with the Director of Public Prosecutions – a relic of British practice – working underneath him albeit quasi-independently). The involvement of a national prosecutor is also, as we have seen, something that we have seen in the Cambodia Tribunal context. However the ECCC model has come under serious question for its effectiveness. There are many rumors about battles between the national and international co-prosecutors over even the most minor decisions, let alone major ones. It is therefore possible that Scheffer's concerns in the context of the SCSL were based on his awareness of the limitations that have emerged from the ECCC model. Unlike the judicial chambers, where the parties considered but after investigation rejected the idea of joining the SCSL Appeals Chamber with the ICTR Appeals

---

[79]   Kabbah Letter to UNSC, *supra* note 12, at § 7 of Enclosure.

[80]   *Id.*

[81]   *Id.*

[82]   *Id.* at 2.

[83]   David J. Scheffer, All the Missing Souls: A Personal History of the War Crimes Tribunals 323 (2013).

Chamber, there did not appear to be any official consideration of the idea of having a joint prosecutor for all three international tribunals. This is likely because the ICTY and ICTY had experience with the idea of a shared prosecutor, a model that ultimately did not work well and led to the separation of the two positions with each of the two courts having its own independent prosecutor.

The better model ultimately chosen was to have an independent prosecutor within the independent SCSL. The Secretary-General appointed the Prosecutor for a three-year term following consultations with the Sierra Leonean authorities. The Prosecutor was charged with the responsibility to investigate and prosecute those who bore greatest responsibility for the crimes committed and was eligible for reappointment. Regarding qualifications, he was to be a person of high moral character and an attorney with extensive experience in the conduct of investigations and prosecutions of criminal cases. The Prosecutor, whose office collects evidence and conducts investigations, including interviews with suspects, victims and witnesses, was at all times to act independently under Article 15(1) of the Statute "as a separate organ of the Special Court" and could not therefore "seek or receive instructions from any Government or from any other source."

But the hitherto discussed idea of some national involvement in the prosecutorial organ was not repudiated entirely. The Prosecutor was to be assisted by a Deputy Prosecutor who was to be appointed by the Government after consultations with the Secretary-General and the Prosecutor. The qualifications for the Deputy Prosecutor were the same as those for the substantive prosecutor. They were both to be assisted by such Sierra Leonean and international staff as may be required to perform the functions assigned to their office effectively and efficiently.

The first Prosecutor, David Crane (USA), was appointed on April 17, 2002. His deputy was Sir Desmond da Silva (UK). After Crane's departure, da Silva became prosecutor effective July 2005 and was replaced by Christopher Staker (Australia) who became Acting Prosecutor for the last half of 2006. Thereafter, the first Deputy Prosecutor from Sierra Leone Joseph Kamara was appointed. In the subsequent step, Stephen Rapp (USA), formerly chief of prosecutions in the ICTR, was appointed the SCSL Prosecutor with Kamara acting as his deputy. Following Rapp's departure, Brenda Hollis (USA), a Senior Trial Attorney in the *Charles Taylor* trial, became the Prosecutor. Some local lawyers apparently campaigned for preference to be given to hiring a Sierra Leonean Prosecutor. Kamara's ascension to the position of Acting Prosecutor had raised the expectations in the local bar, which had long been distant from the SCSL, that there was a serious chance that a national prosecutor would now finally be appointed. This would essentially be for symbolic reasons as the Tribunal was well into its last trial. This turned out not to be the case, apparently because some of the external supporters overseeing the SCSL in its Management Committee did not agree with the Sierra Leonean government's express desire for such an appointment. Hollis was reappointed as Prosecutor for the Residual Special Court for Sierra Leone (RSCSL) in December 2013. In October 2019, she was replaced by another

American Prosecutor, James Johnson. Essentially, from the earliest through to the final days, the position of chief prosecutor was occupied by a US or UK national. This perhaps is a form of acknowledgement of the status of the US and the UK as two of the biggest supporters of the SCSL. Sierra Leone's desire to symbolically bring the RSCSL home by nominating a national as Prosecutor for first the SCSL, and then the RSCSL, is yet to yield a positive result.

In terms of its own internal functioning, the Office of the Prosecutor was later organized into several subunits. Besides the Deputy Prosecutor's Office, there were three sections: Investigations, Administration and Prosecution. The Investigation Section was further broken down into three units, consisting of an Investigation Team, Intelligence Tracking Team and a Crime Scene Investigation Unit. In the Prosecution Section, which was the one to which most of the lawyers belonged, were the Trial Section, the Legal Advisory Group and the Team Legal Advisors Unit.

4.4.3 *Registry*

The Registry of the SCSL, as with those for the ICTY and ICTR, was an independent organ responsible for administrative issues. Under Article 4 of the UN-Sierra Leone Agreement, the Registrar was a staff member of the United Nations. The Secretary-General appointed him for a three-year term, after consultations with Sierra Leone. As head of the Registry, his primary responsibility was to service the Chambers and the Office of the Prosecutor and the Defense. He was to recruit all tribunal staff and manage the financial and staff resources of the Tribunal.

Under the Statute, the Registry was mandated to set up a Victims and Witnesses Unit.[84] But, as the largest administrative body, it also had several other units. These included an Office of the Deputy Registrar and Public Affairs and Outreach Sections as well as a Court Management Unit and Detention Facility. Falling underneath the Deputy Registrar were several subunits such as Administrative Support, Finance, Personnel, Procurement and Clinic. The Integrated Support Services arm of the Tribunal had Communications, Information Technology, Security, General Services (Facility Management, Transport, Contracting Services).[85]

The Registrar, although a lead administrator, was not ultimately the head of administrative matters for the Court as a whole. That function, at least in principle, rested in the President of the Tribunal. The Registrar technically worked under the authority of the President, who for that reason, also had powers of independent administrative review over certain of the Registrar's decision.[86] Some of the additional functions of the Registry were fleshed out in the Rules of Procedure and

---

[84] U.N.-Sierra Leone Agreement, *supra* note 1, at §16(4).

[85] Geoffrey Robertson (President of the Special Court for Sierra Leone), *First Annual Report of The President of the Special Court for Sierra Leone* (Dec. 1, 2002 to Dec. 1, 2003), www.rscsl.org /Documents/AnRpt1.pdf.

[86] UN-Sierra Leone Agreement, *supra* note 1, at art. 16.

Evidence – as is the case in the ICTY/ICTR.[87] Under Rule 33 of the SCSL Rules, for instance, the Registrar was to serve as the main channel of communication in the Tribunal. He was also permitted to make oral and written representations to Chambers on any issues arising from specific cases, which could affect his ability to discharge his duties, including implementing judicial decisions. The Registrar could also adopt and amend rules of detention, which were to be consistent with the fundamental human rights guarantees enjoyed by the accused, especially the presumption of innocence. He could also issue practice directives in relation to any matters within his ordinary competence.

The first registrar, Robin Vincent (UK), was appointed in April 2002. He was later replaced by Lovemore Munlo (Malawi), the Deputy Registrar of the ICTR, who was in turn replaced by Herman von Hebel (Netherlands), who had come to be his deputy. Following von Hebel's departure, the first Sierra Leonean, Binta Mansaray, became deputy registrar, assuming the position of Acting Registrar before later seeking and obtaining appointment to the substantive position. She held the job to the conclusion of the Tribunal. Later, following the closure of the SCSL, she took up the same post in the Residual Special Court for Sierra Leone, a position that she still holds at the time of this writing.

4.4.4 *Defense Office*

The SCSL, like other ad hoc international criminal courts, did not in its Statute specify which organ ought to be primarily responsible for ensuring the protection of the rights of suspects, the accused and the defense more generally.[88] In fact, it was only on the eve of the arrests that the Management Committee and the Plenary of Judges, realizing the limitations inherent in asking the Registrar – an otherwise neutral administrator – to fulfill this protective role, decided to create the Defense Office. The President of the Court, Justice Robertson, had flagged the issue and proposed a framework for a public defender system that was specific to the Court.[89] His proposal garnered support but was modified. Rule 45 of the Rules of Procedure and Evidence directed the Registrar "to establish, maintain and develop a Defense

---

[87]   *Id.*

[88]   SCSL Statute, *supra* note 1, at art. 17 (referring to each of the rights using some variation of the phrase "The accused shall" without specifying duties of any organs of the Court to protect these rights); Prosecutor v. Brima, Case No. SCSL-2004-16-AR73, Decision on Brima-Kamara Defence Appeal Motion Against Trial Chamber II Majority Decision on Extremely Urgent Confidential Joint Motion for the Re-Appointment of Kevin Metzger and Wilbert Harris as Lead Counsel for Alex Tamba Brima and Brima Bazzy Kamara, ¶¶ 82, 84, (Dec. 8, 2005) (inferring that according to the Statute, no organ carries the responsibility for ensuring the rights of the Accused, but rather it must be "a common duty shared by the three organs") [hereinafter Prosecutor v. Brima, Decision on Re-Appointment]. *See*, for a similar discussion of the role of the Defense Office in prior works, Charles C. Jalloh, *The Special Tribunal for Lebanon: A Defense Perspective*, 47 VAND. J. TRANS. L. 765 (2015), at 437–44.

[89]   *See* Jalloh, *supra* note 88, at 437–44, for the discussion of the origins of the Defense Office proposal.

Office, for the purpose of ensuring the rights of suspects and accused" persons before the Court.[90]

Part of the motivation for the entire scheme was to ensure that the accused would not be arraigned before the SCSL without some provision for them to be represented by defense counsel. The other imperative was the overarching concern with reducing costs, in light of the limited budget and prohibitive legal fees associated with providing legal aid in the ICTY and ICTR. Rule 45(B) therefore envisaged an office that had mixed functions, which reflected these mixed objectives. It was asked to fulfill those functions by providing, among other things, initial legal advice, and assistance through duty counsel situated within a reasonable proximity of the detention facility; legal assistance as ordered by the Court if the accused does not have sufficient means; and adequate facilities for counsel in the preparation of the defense.

The first Principal Defender was Simone Monasebian (USA). After her departure, she was replaced by Vincent Nmehielle (Nigeria), followed by Elizabeth Nahamya (Uganda) and a Sierra Leonean lawyer who had been duty counsel in the CDF case, Claire Carlton-Hanciles. The latter held office until closure of the SCSL in December 2013. She has been replaced by Ibrahim Yilla, another Sierra Leonean, who today serves as Principal Defender of the Residual Special Court for Sierra Leone.

By around March 2003, when the first five accused were transferred to the SCSL's custody, the Defense Office had already begun to carry out its main responsibilities. It offered initial legal advice and representation to the accused, developed a list of counsel, from which it appointed generally competent counsel to the various indictees. Even after counsel was assigned, the lawyers in the office continued to assist the defense counsel generally by monitoring the progress of the trials; providing some legal research assistance; and arguing matters of common interest. It also sought to create working relationships with governments and NGOs to address defense concerns.[91]

The unprecedented and innovative Defense Office was initially conceived of as an independent subunit within the Registry. But, in practice, it lacked the necessary autonomy to actually fulfill its immense potential. It was envisaged, at least by some key court officials including the first president Justice Robertson, that the office could eventually become its own independent entity.[92] Still, efforts by Simone Monasebian to convince the parties to make amendments to the instruments of the Court to achieve this conception of an independent office proved futile. These

[90] Special Court for Sierra Leone Rules of Procedure and Evidence, Rule 45 (Mar. 7, 2003), http://hrlibrary.umn.edu//instree/SCSL/Rules-of-proced-SCSL.pdf.

[91] Vincent O. Nmehielle, *Position Paper on the Independence of the Office of the Principal Defender at the Special Court for Sierra Leone* 2 (Submitted to the Management Committee of the SCSL by Principal Defender) (on file with the author).

[92] See Prosecutor v. Brima, *supra* note 86.

efforts were resuscitated by Vincent Nmehielle, the second Principal Defender and his staff, including the present writer, but those too were unsuccessful.

In advocating the interests of the accused, the Defense Office, which has been heralded as an important innovation in the practice of international courts, took responsibility for crucial detention issues, which had the potential to impact defendant participation in hearings and court processes, and therefore, their fair trial rights. The office also represented defense interests in the plenary meetings of the Court's judges, wherein rule changes were adopted, sometimes at the behest of the Prosecutor.[93] Similarly, it played a role in outreach to Sierra Leoneans by helping to educate them about the presumption of innocence and the right to a fair trial. In a country that was still reeling from the trauma and devastating impact of a savage war, this was important given the popular perception that the accused were guilty before they were even tried.[94]

While the foregoing discussion mainly captures the Defense Office's conception of its role, even during its heyday, this assessment was the subject of some controversy.[95] The Court and some assigned counsel questioned the usefulness of the office, especially as conflicts arose between it and defense lawyers over issues of representation of the accused.[96] The office also struggled to keep costs down, within the provision of the legal services contract (which was based on a fixed, lump sum system). Somewhat ironically, it made enemies with defense counsel in the process, as it sought to administer a modest budget that is probably the lowest ever allocated for the cost of legal aid for accused persons in any of the four UN affiliated ad hoc international criminal tribunals.

As the SCSL completed all its trials, the Defense had played an important role putting in place a good legal aid defense system for the Tribunal. The office was also vital in preserving the rights of Taylor in that important trial of the first former African head of state. It sought to become a fourth organ of the tribunal. But, in the end, it was unable to fulfill its self-declared vision of becoming recognized as the "fourth pillar" of the Court.[97] Its dependence on the Registrar also limited its role and affected its ability to provide adequate facilities for counsel in the preparation of the defense in the *AFRC*, *CDF* and *RUF* trials.[98] These challenges, as well as the wider and significant modeling role played by the SCSL's Defense Office for the

---

[93] *Id.*

[94] John R. W. D. Jones et al., *The Special Court for Sierra Leone: A Defense Perspective*, 2 J. INT'L. CRIM. JUST. 211, 215 (2004) (stating "[i]t is a sad fact that many of the persons detained at the Special Court's facility in Bonthe are '*presumed guilty*' by popular opinion. This has to be reversed if they are to receive fair trials").

[95] For a scathing critique that was strongly contested by the Defense Office, *see* Alison Thompson & Michelle Staggs, *The Defense Office at the Special Court for Sierra Leone: A Critical Perspective*, at 27, WAR CRIMES STUD. CTR. UNIV. CAL. BERKLEY (2007).

[96] *Id.* at 40–41 (*citing to* Prosecutor v. Sesay, Case No. SCSL-04-15-T, Written Reasons for the Decision on Application by Counsel for the Third Accused to Withdraw from the Case (June 19, 2006)).

[97] Transcript of Record, Prosecutor v. Sesay, Case No. SCSL-2004-15-T, 39-40 (Mar. 28, 2006).

[98] *See* Antonio Cassese, *Report on the Special Court for Sierra Leone*, ¶ 136 (Dec. 12, 2006).

STL, have been discussed elsewhere as contributions to international criminal practice. I will not pursue those arguments here -for space reasons.[99]

Overall, in terms of its organization, the preceding analysis brings us to a point where we can now make two concluding observations about the structure of the SCSL. First, the tripartite structure of chambers, prosecution and registrar organs reflected in the UN-Sierra Leone Agreement and in the SCSL Statute is consistent with the model that we have seen deployed for other ad hoc international criminal tribunals both before and after the Tribunal was created. These are for a court of law that would be principally focused on ensuring that it would undertake fair trials of a small group of persons accused of the serious international crimes over which it had jurisdiction. The differences between the SCSL and its predecessors related to the manner of appointment of key officials. The Sierra Leone case allowed the national authorities involvement in selecting a minority of key officials including the Deputy Prosecutor and some of the judges of the trial and appeals chambers. This was a significant enhancement compared to the non-formal participation of the affected states in the ICTY and ICTR contexts.

On the other hand, the SCSL model did not go as far as the Cambodia Tribunal model. In the ECCC, the local authorities effectively insisted on a rough parity between the domestic and international roles in a variety of the settings. This would have be attractive to national jurisdictions, giving them greater say in affairs relating to their justice problems. The flip side of that is that the latter feature did seemingly create problems for that ad hoc court, reportedly leading to deadlock in some instances. Viewed against that backdrop, it could be argued that the SCSL model, which was a bit more mixed but weighted in favor of the international community, suggests that it was possible to better calibrate the imperatives of national sovereignty and the international community interest. These were all done in a manner that could ensure some independence and some impartiality of the institution and its processes.

The second observation is that the most interesting feature of the SCSL was not any of the conventional organs seen in its founding instruments, but rather the Defense Office, which was a judicial innovation under the Rules of Procedure and Evidence. The office offers a contrast to the otherwise valid criticisms of judicial procedural lawmaking that scholars have observed in the ad hoc international penal tribunal context.[100] That novelty in the SCSL helped to ensure that there was greater equality of arms between the prosecution and the defense. It also gave a greater institutional voice for the independent defense counsel who were not staff members

99 Charles C. Jalloh, *The Contribution of the Special Court for Sierra Leone to the Development of International Law*, 15 AFR. J. INT'L & COMP. L. 165, 175–76 (2007); Jalloh, *supra* note 88.

100 *See*, for a thoughtful example of how the tribunals might lack transparency in rule making and even themselves violate international human rights standards, Göran Sluiter, *Procedural Lawmaking at the International Criminal Tribunals, in* JUDICIAL CREATIVITY AT THE INTERNATIONAL CRIMINAL TRIBUNALS 315–31 (Shane Darcy & Joseph Powderly eds., 2011).

but privately contracted counsel representing the suspects and accused persons before the Court. The SCSL Defense Office model thus elevated the stature of what might be the weakest institutional link in the international criminal justice system, which relates to the rights of the defense and defendants in the trials, and later on influenced the creation of defense office arms in other settings including in permanent and regional criminal courts. It has inspired the establishment of similar offices in the Special Tribunal for Lebanon as well as the African Court of Justice and Human and Peoples' Rights, both of which explicitly relied on the SCSL model in fashioning the framework to guide the establishment of its defense offices. The dedicated Defense Office at the SCSL also played a role in developing unprecedented codes of conduct and other ancillary instruments to govern the ethics of practicing counsel appearing in these courts. The codes were for all lawyers, including those from other organs. This too was an important contribution that seems to have inspired similar practices in other international criminal courts.

4.5 THE TRIALS CONDUCTED BY THE SPECIAL COURT FOR SIERRA LEONE

4.5.1 *The SCSL Indictments*

As the SCSL only completed a handful of trials, due largely to the lack of political will to bankroll another expensive ad hoc tribunal and the narrowly framed jurisdiction discussed earlier in this chapter, this last section of this Chapter will offer a short summary of its nine completed cases and their final verdicts and sentences. This subsection is primarily for the benefit of the non-specialist readers, although it could be a useful refresher for international criminal law specialists as well.

By about December 2002, about eight months after its instruments entered into force, the UN Secretary-General was putting in place arrangements for the SCSL through appointment of its key officials such as the Prosecutor and Registrar who then subsequently took up their functions in Freetown. With record speed for such ad hoc courts, only a few months after his arrival in 2003, Prosecutor Crane had carried out some investigations and unveiled applications for thirteen indictments. These were largely for military and political leaders drawn from the three main warring factions involved with the Sierra Leone armed conflict.[101] These suspects

---

[101]   Several additional indictments were issued by the Court for RUF Leader Foday Sankoh, one of his alleged field commanders Sam Bockarie (aka "Mosquito"), and AFRC junta leader Major Johnny Paul Koroma who served as president for just over a year. These will not be discussed here because both Sankoh's and Bockarie's Indictments were withdrawn, following their confirmed deaths. However, as Major Koroma is missing, his Indictment remains valid. He is the only remaining fugitive from the SCSL. Although there was evidence alleging that he was dead presented during the Taylor Trial in The Hague, because it was deemed inconclusive, provision has been made in the Statute of the Residual Special Court for Sierra Leone for Koroma's trial should he surface at some point in the future.

comprised the mutinying elements of the national army known as the Armed Forces Revolutionary Council, the Civil Defense Forces militia and the Revolutionary United Front rebels.

Remarkably, most of the indictments were executed without difficulty. The SCSL could mostly avoid the notorious cooperation nightmares that dogged other international criminal tribunals since most of the indictees were nearly all present in Sierra Leone.[102] It, of course, helped that the government was a direct partner in the justice process and was willing and able to deploy its police force and army to implement the Tribunal's judicially approved arrest warrants. Below, I brief review each of the SCSL's main international crimes trials.

4.5.2 *The* RUF, AFRC *and* CDF *Cases*

The *RUF* and *CDF* cases were heard by Trial Chamber I, while the *AFRC* and later the *Taylor* case, were entrusted to Trial Chamber II. In the first of the *SCSL* cases to conclude were three AFRC commanders, namely Alex Tamba Brima, Brima Bazzy Kamara and Santigie Borbor Kanu. All three men had held leadership positions in the Sierra Leone government after leading a coup d'état which unseated President Kabbah, who fled into exile, in 1997. Between March 7, 2003, and September 16, 2003, Brima, Kamara and Kanu were separately indicted on seventeen counts of war crimes, crimes against humanity and other serious violations of international humanitarian law. About a year later, their separate indictments were amended, and the charges reduced to three counts. At the Prosecution's request, the Trial Chamber ordered the joint trials of the three men on February 18, 2005. A consolidated Indictment, containing fourteen counts, was later approved. The trial opened in Freetown a year later (on March 7, 2005), and eight months later, the Prosecution case concluded. On June 5, 2006, the defense case opened and closed around the end of October 2006, after the Accused had called eighty-seven witnesses. The final oral arguments were heard in Freetown during the first week of December 2006. On June 20, 2007, the Judges of Trial Chamber II found all three men guilty of eleven out of fourteen counts of war crimes, crimes against humanity and other serious violations of international humanitarian law. The three were sentenced on July 19, 2007 to prison terms of fifty years each for Brima and Kanu and forty-five years for Kamara. The Appeals Chamber upheld all the sentences on February 22, 2008.

Besides the *AFRC* cases, the SCSL completed the joint trials of six others from the CDF and RUF groups respectively. Whereas Sam Hinga Norman, a former Deputy

---

[102]   For a helpful discussion of the various horizontal and vertical models of cooperation and how the SCSL compares to the ad hoc Chapter VII courts, *see* Göran Sluiter, *The Legal Assistance to Internationalized Criminal Courts and Tribunals, in* INTERNATIONALIZED CRIMINAL COURTS: SIERRA LEONE, EAST TIMOR, KOSOVO, AND CAMBODIA 10 (Cesare Romano et al. eds., 2004); and the difficulties that the ICC has encountered, Göran Sluiter, *The Surrender of War Criminals to the International Criminal Court*, 25 LO. L.A. INT'L. & COMP. L. REV. 605 (2003).

Defense Minister in Sierra Leone, was indicted on March 7, 2003, his CDF compatriots Moinina Fofana and Allieu Kondewa were indicted just over three months later on June 26, 2003. The first accused Norman was the "National Coordinator" of the paramilitary CDF, while Fofana – the second accused – was the "Director of War," and the third accused Kondewa, the "High Priest." The Trial Chamber granted the Prosecution's request for a joint trial of the three leaders, described as the "Holy Trinity," on February 28, 2004 and approved a consolidated Indictment not long afterward. The CDF trial opened on June 3, 2004, and on July 14, 2005, the Prosecution closed its case. Final arguments did not take place until the end of November 2006. This was due to disposition of the motion for judgment of acquittal and the alternating schedule of this same group of Judges, who were during the intervals also adjudicating the RUF case.

On August 2, 2007, the Trial Chamber rendered the Court's second trial judgment, finding in respect to Fofana and Kondewa that each was guilty of four counts in the Indictment. The two men were convicted by a majority comprised of a Canadian and Cameroonian judge. In an interesting but controversial twist, especially outside Sierra Leone, the lone Sierra Leonean judge on the bench refused to convict. He would have acquitted the defendants because of necessity and the role that they were playing in the restoration of democracy to the country. On October 9, 2007, Fofana was sentenced to six years while Kondewa received eight years. However, on appeal, the Appeals Chamber modified some of the grounds for the convictions. But in perhaps the most significant part of their May 28, 2008 judgment, at least for the defendants, the appeals judges increased the sentences for Fofana to fifteen years while Kondewa was awarded twenty years.

In the meantime, in the period between the close of the CDF case and rendering of trial judgment on August 2, 2007, Norman - the third accused in the CDF case – had died in a hospital in Senegal where he had been taken for medical treatment. In May 2007, the Chamber terminated the proceedings against him. This was a strange turn of events, given the unpopularity of the Norman prosecution amongst some Sierra Leoneans who until this day remain divided on its propriety.

In the RUF group of cases, Issa Sesay and Morris Kallon, the first and second accused respectively, were indicted on March 7, 2003 on seventeen counts for war crimes, crimes against humanity and other serious violations of international humanitarian law. Sesay was Interim RUF Leader and he and Kallon were commanders. One count was later added to the Indictment. A third accused was Augustine Gbao. The latter was indicted on April 16, 2003. On March 5, 2004, the Trial Chamber ordered the joint trials of all three suspects. The RUF case started on July 5, 2004, with seventy-five witnesses testifying for the Prosecution, while eighty-five appeared for the Defense. The parties made closing submissions to the trial court on August 5, 2008.

The Trial Chamber rendered its verdict on February 25, 2009 holding that Sesay and Kallon were guilty on sixteen of the eighteen counts in the Indictment. Gbao, for his part, was found guilty on fourteen counts including for his role in abducting UN peacekeepers as hostages in May 2000. Sesay was sentenced to fifty-two years, Kallon was awarded forty years, while Gbao was condemned to twenty-five years. On October 26, 2009, the Appeals Chamber overturned Gbao's conviction on one of the counts but otherwise generally upheld the other Trial Chamber findings in respect of him and the other RUF commanders, including the sentences.

4.5.3 *The Trial of Former Liberian President Taylor*

Charles Taylor, former Liberian president and Sankoh associate, was the only non-Sierra Leonean to be indicted by the Prosecutor. An initial seventeen-count Indictment was issued for Taylor on March 7, 2003 for war crimes, crimes against humanity and other serious international humanitarian law violations. The indictment was sealed. The world learned about it on June 4, 2003, when the Prosecution hastily announced its existence. They sought to have Taylor arrested in Ghana where he was attending peace talks – as discussed in Chapter 8 of this work. It took several years, and much diplomatic wrangling between West African and other states, but Taylor was eventually arrested and transferred to the custody of the SCSL on March 29, 2006. Some concerns were then expressed about the security conditions in Liberia and Sierra Leone, both of which were emerging from the shadows of devastating armed conflicts. It was speculated that Taylor still had supporters capable of engaging in violence and destabilization of the two countries. Thus, in one of the most controversial decisions to ever be taken by the Court, Taylor was transferred to The Hague on June 30, 2006.[103] This was after the UN Security Council gave its imprimatur to the decision and Dutch authorities had indicated a willingness to allow his trial to be conducted on their territory. A precondition was Taylor not stay in the country after the completion of his trial.

A month before the trial opened, on May 29, 2007, his seventeen-count indictment was reduced to eleven counts. The *Taylor* trial formally opened on June 4, 2007. However, because the Accused fired his legal team and insisted that he would represent himself because of inadequate time and resources allocated to his provisionally assigned counsel, the case was delayed for the evidentiary phase until January 2008. In the meantime, the Trial Chamber appointed the present writer as duty counsel for the defendant, pending the appointment of permanent defense counsel. The Defense Office had found and appointed replacement counsel from the British Bar in August 2007. But they needed a few months to read into the case file. Once the trial got underway, in the early part of 2008, the *Taylor* trial largely continued without significant interruptions until towards the completion of the case. Taylor, for his part, took the stand and testified in his own defense for several

---

[103]   For the controversies surrounding the arrest and trial of Taylor including the issue of change of venue, *see* Charles C. Jalloh, *The Law and Politics of the Charles Taylor Case*, 43 DENV. J. INT'L. L. & POL'Y 229 (2015). See chapter 8 for an in-depth discussion of the Taylor trial.

months. Closing arguments were heard on February 8, 2011. Final briefs were turned in a month later.

The Trial Chamber issued its judgment on April 26, 2012. Taylor was convicted on all eleven counts as an aider and abettor and a planner of war crimes, crimes against humanity and other serious humanitarian law violations committed by his RUF subordinates in Sierra Leone. On May 30, 2012, he was sentenced to fifty years' imprisonment. He appealed his conviction. Appeals hearings were conducted in The Hague in January 2013. The final appeals judgment was rendered in September 2013, upholding nearly all the convictions, thereby marking the milestone end of the last and most important SCSL trial.

The eight AFRC, CDF and RUF convicts were serving their jail terms at a maximum-security prison near the Rwandan capital, Kigali, under an enforcement of sentence agreement between the government of Rwanda and the SCSL. They were transferred there in October 2009. Fofana was released, after completing two-thirds of his sentence, back to Sierra Leone in fall 2015 and became the first convict to successfully complete his sentence on 28 May 2018. Kondewa, his co-accused, received early conditional release on 9 July 2018. In contrast, Taylor, whose appeal was denied in September 2013 by the SCSL appellate chamber, is serving his jail term in Great Britain. Taylor's plea to be sent to Rwanda or another part of Africa for his imprisonment was denied by the Appeals Chamber as recently as 2015. Alex Tamba Brima, from the AFRC trial group, died of illness at a hospital in Rwanda on 9 June 2016. His body was repatriated to Sierra Leone where he was buried. The results of the inquest surrounding the circumstances of his illness and his death has not been made public. The remaining convicts will be eligible for early release, once they serve most of their sentences.

Consistent with the UN Security Council-mandated Completion Strategy, the SCSL wound down its main operations at the seat of the Court in Freetown in December 2013. Even though it was the last to be created of the three ad hoc international criminal courts for the former Yugoslavia, Rwanda and Sierra Leone, and leaving aside the East Timor trials because of their different legal basis, the SCSL became the first of the modern ad hoc international criminal tribunals to accomplish its statutory mandate. It has since been succeeded by the Residual Special Court for Sierra Leone. The RSCSL was established by the UN and the Government of Sierra Leone, and today, it formally sits in The Hague with a branch office in Freetown

4.6 CONCLUSION

This chapter has analyzed the jurisdiction, organization and trials of the SCSL. It has demonstrated how, though the SCSL emanated from a proposal by President Kabbah of Sierra Leone, his plea for international (in particular UN) support for the prosecution of those presumed responsible for crimes committed in his country only secured qualified commitment. The Security Council was happy to support the idea but seemed not really interested in creating another full-fledged *international tribunal* for Sierra Leone along the lines of the ICTY and ICTR.

For these types of reasons, as alluded to earlier in this chapter and as will be developed further in the next chapter, the Security Council chose to create a court with a severely restricted personal jurisdiction over a small number of persons bearing greatest responsibility. This shaped the model of the final tribunal that was used to prosecute some of the international crimes committed in Sierra Leone. As a result, because its jurisdiction started after November 1996, this meant that less than half of the atrocities committed during a decade-long war were prosecuted. The use of national law, alongside the international crimes, apparently assuaged sovereignty concerns but proved to have limited practical value in the end. The temporal and territorial reach of the SCSL was also explicitly designed for a limited number of trials focused on those holding leadership positions. It was such practical realities that gave rise to the unrealistic expectation that the SCSL would complete its trials that subsequently occurred in the *AFRC, CDF, RUF* and *Taylor* cases within a three-year period instead of the actual eleven-year time frame that it actually took to complete them.

The SCSL has been widely lauded for indicting all the sides in the Sierra Leone conflict. It is said to have avoided "victor's justice," which since at least the Nuremberg IMT and continuing through to the ICTR, has haunted the international criminal law field. In this narrative, which eschews prosecution of one side of a conflict in favor of prosecuting all the sides, the ghosts of Nuremberg may have found welcome in The Hague and Arusha. But not in Freetown.

In the SCSL, alongside the rebels, the leaders from the government's mutinying army as well as the paramilitary forces created and financed by President Kabbah and his government were all indicted and prosecuted. This remarkably occurred without leading to any serious pushback from the national authorities, which continued to cooperate fully with the Tribunal, even as they explicitly rejected domestic political pressures to interfere in the SCSL's yeoman's work for some justice. This equality of treatment of all the sides to the conflict can be lauded for opening a new chapter for international criminal tribunals.

On the other hand, though equal justice in principle has great merits, it could be argued that blindly seeking indictments against "all sides" of a conflict can also be problematic. And, in the context of Sierra Leone, legitimate questions have been asked especially among Sierra Leonean commentators about the implications of undertaking apparently *equal prosecutions* in circumstances where the majority of the crimes were found to have been committed by the RUF and its members. The specter that equal justice may be seen as negative as victor's justice might have been hard to imagine, in the aftermath of Nuremberg, but seems to be a reality in Sierra Leone today. In such circumstances, does prosecuting their leading figures alongside others distort perceptions of who was responsible for the main atrocities committed during the conflict? Finally, there remains today the further question whether the justice rendered by the SCSL, though important, is *sufficient justice*. All the more so given the widespread nature of the international crimes committed during the war, the duration of the conflict, and the heinous means and methods used against the numerous innocent victims of the Sierra Leonean conflict.

5

"Greatest Responsibility" Personal Jurisdiction

5.1 INTRODUCTION

As discussed in the previous chapter, in addition to its near unique subject matter jurisdiction which reflected a mix of international and domestic crimes, one of the most distinctive features of the jurisdiction of the Special Court for Sierra Leone (SCSL) related to its personal jurisdiction (*ratione personae*). Article 1(1) of the UN-Sierra Leone Agreement,[1] and its annexed statute, defined the Court's *ratione personae* jurisdiction – that is, the "power to bring a person into its adjudicative process."[2] It gave the SCSL competence, in relevant part, in the following terms: "to prosecute persons who bear the *greatest responsibility* for serious violations of international humanitarian law and Sierra Leonean law . . . including those leaders who, in committing such crimes, have threatened the establishment of and implementation of the peace process in Sierra Leone."[3]

This chapter will examine the greatest responsibility personal jurisdiction in greater detail. The reason is that this way of framing this aspect of an ad hoc tribunal's jurisdiction was unique to the SCSL. In fact, no other international court had used the same "greatest responsibility" formulation before. It thereby generated considerable controversy during the SCSL trials about its intended meaning and scope of application. Perhaps even more significantly, however, this specification of *ratione personae* jurisdiction has since been widely embraced both in international criminal law circles and by states. It seems to now be consistently

---

[1] Agreement between the United Nations and the Government of Sierra Leone on the Establishment of a Special Court for Sierra Leone, Jan. 16, 2002, 2178 U.N.T.S. 138 [hereinafter UN-Sierra Leone Agreement]; Annexed to the UN-Sierra Leone Agreement was the Statute of the Special Court for Sierra Leone [hereinafter SCSL Statute].

[2] *Ratione Personae Jurisdiction*, BLACK'S LAW DICTIONARY 930 (9th ed. 2009).

[3] U.N.-Sierra Leone Agreement, *supra* note 1 (emphasis added), at art. 1 provides as follows:

"(1) There is hereby established a Special Court for Sierra Leone to prosecute persons who bear the greatest responsibility for serious violations of international humanitarian law and Sierra Leonean law committed in the territory of Sierra Leone since 30 November 1996.

(2) The Special Court shall function in accordance with the Statute of the Special Court for Sierra Leone. The Statute is annexed to this Agreement and forms an integral part thereof."

invoked in debates about the jurisdictional reach of international penal courts including at the permanent International Criminal Court (ICC). The judicial interpretations of the concept of greatest responsibility developed by the judges in Freetown may thus hold valuable lessons for that ongoing deliberation. Depending on the interpretive choice made, it could mean the difference between someone being prosecuted, and someone not being prosecuted. The analysis offered might therefore be useful to the ICC and other ad hoc special criminal tribunals. As such, it constitutes the first example in the series of topics that will be studied by this book, wherein the SCSL made a contribution that left a legal legacy for the development of international criminal law. Indeed, in the context of the Extraordinary Chambers in the Courts of Cambodia (ECCC) as well as the relatively more recent 2008–09 post-election violence in the Special Tribunal for Kenya (STK), the legislation proposed contained either a similar standard (persons most responsible) or exactly the same standard (greatest responsibility personal jurisdiction). As it is possible that such formulations will be used in future courts established to prosecute a limited number of persons in other post-conflict situations, the judicial discussion of the interpretive options available in the first court to use the formulation is highly warranted.

5.2   THE PURPOSE AND STRUCTURE OF THIS CHAPTER

There was no aspect of the SCSL's jurisdiction that was more controversial than the idea that it should prosecute only those persons bearing "the greatest responsibility" for what happened in Sierra Leone during the second half of that country's notoriously brutal conflict. Indeed, the idea of greatest responsibility had been controversial from the moment the UN Security Council (UNSC) proposed the phrase to the UN Secretary-General (UNSG) as a way to define the SCSL's personal jurisdiction in the resolution requesting him to negotiate with the Sierra Leonean government to establish the Court.[4] Several factors explain why this qualified personal jurisdiction was contentious, which in turn, make this understudied question worthy of further inquiry.

First, while both the UN-Sierra Leone Agreement and the SCSL Statute included the phrase, neither specified what it meant.[5] Yet, both instruments gave prominence to the idea as each mentioned the phrase at least twice: first, in the personal jurisdiction provision in Article 1(1),[6] and second, in the clause setting out the powers of the Prosecutor in Article 15 of the Statute.[7] Although the framers had included these two provisions to underscore the Court's narrow jurisdiction, and to

---

[4]   *See* S.C. Res. 1315, ¶ 3 (Aug. 14, 2000); *see also* U.N. Secretary-General, *Report of the Secretary-General on the Establishment of a Special Court for Sierra Leone*, ¶¶ 29–31, U.N. Doc. S/2000/915 (Oct. 4, 2000) [hereinafter Report on the SCSL Establishment].

[5]   Charles C. Jalloh, *Special Court for Sierra Leone: Achieving Justice?*, 32 MICH. J. INT'L L. 395, 413 (2011).

[6]   SCSL Statute, *supra* note 1, at art. 1 § 1; U.N.-Sierra Leone Agreement, *supra* note 1, at art. 1.

[7]   SCSL Statute, *supra* note 1, at art. 15 § 1.

ensure that the prosecutions would stay within the strict boundaries that they had demarcated, Article 1 and Article 15, when taken separately but also when considered together, sent two apparently contradictory messages.

When taken separately, the provision in Article 1 suggested, at least to the defense counsel, that the greatest responsibility phrase established a jurisdictional requirement that the Prosecution must fulfill.[8] A failure to do so meant that the Defense could challenge the non-compliance before the judges. If successful, in this view, the defendants would not be prosecutable by the Tribunal. Article 15 was a different type of provision with the heading "the prosecutor," whose powers it sets out in five succinct paragraphs. In essence, in relevant part, it provided that the prosecution shall be responsible for the investigation and prosecution of persons who bear the greatest responsibility and affirmed that the prosecution shall act independently as a separate organ and not seek or receive instructions from any government or from any other source.

Taken together, Article 1 and Article 15 led to a debate about the mandate and function of the Prosecutor, in particular, the extent and limits of his discretion in deciding whom to prosecute. Effectively, the defendants sought to take advantage of the vagueness of the greatest responsibility language in both provisions. They thus sought to further curb the scope of the prosecutorial power by suggesting that the Prosecutor had acted beyond his competence in seeking to prosecute them instead of others.[9] The problem is that the Prosecution's fight to keep its turf tended to exaggerate the broad scope of its authority and further masked the real nature of greatest responsibility jurisdiction.

Second, although the UNSC, the UNSG and Sierra Leone purportedly agreed on the meaning of "greatest responsibility" in an exchange of letters during the negotiations of the Court's founding instruments,[10] that correspondence masked key disagreements. It ultimately left a measure of ambiguity regarding the actual purpose, and perhaps more importantly, the implications of the phrase.[11] So, once the Tribunal was established and became operational, it would only be a matter of time for the issue to boil to the surface and for the judges to be asked to rule on the subject.

Third, starting with the International Military Tribunal at Nuremberg (IMT or Nuremberg Tribunal) through to the ad hoc ICTY and ICTR and the permanent ICC, the thrust of international criminal law has been to focus

[8] Jalloh, *supra* note 5, at 414–15.
[9] *See* discussion *infra* Section 5.5.3.
[10] President of the Security Council, Letter dated Jan. 31, 2001 from the President of the Security Council to the Secretary-General, ¶ 1, U.N. Doc. S/2001/95 (Jan. 31, 2001) [hereinafter Letter dated Jan. 31, 2001 from Pres. of S.C.].
[11] Yet, undoubtedly aware of the controversies that haunted this phrase in Sierra Leone, the draft statute for the Special Tribunal for Kenya, which failed to obtain sufficient support in that country's Parliament, at least attempted to provide a definition. *See* Special Tribunal for Kenya Bill (2009) pt. 1 § 2 (Kenya).

on prosecuting the top leaders and architects of mass atrocities.[12] However, this was the first time that the language delimiting the prosecution of only those bearing *greatest responsibility* was introduced into the statute of an ad hoc international penal tribunal.[13] On one level, this could be argued to be an innovation in the SCSL. The reality is that, as this chapter will show, the vague greatest responsibility phrase was more of an explicit limitation on the Court's jurisdiction in terms of the number of people that it was mandated to eventually prosecute.[14]

While the SCSL's work has now reached completion, with the issuance of the last appeals judgment in the case involving former Liberian President Charles Taylor in 2013,[15] consideration of the nature and scope of greatest responsibility personal jurisdiction is important for a proper assessment of the jurisprudential legacy of the Court. This seems crucial because it might offer useful lessons for future formulations of personal jurisdiction in other international criminal tribunals. Indeed, while both the ICTY and ICTR were endowed with personal jurisdiction to investigate and prosecute "persons responsible," since the establishment of the SCSL, it appears that the "greatest responsibility" threshold has become the informal gold standard for the framing of *ratione personae* jurisdiction in contemporary international criminal tribunals.

Surprisingly, although a decade-long controversy persisted over the meaning of greatest responsibility at the Court, the question of what exactly the phrase means and the benchmark, if any, that the prosecutors in ad hoc international criminal courts should use to select those persons most deserving of prosecution inside their own courtroom (as opposed to domestic ones) seems to have escaped the attention of legal scholars.[16] Perhaps the general feeling outside the Defense Bar at the SCSL was that resolving this question would not change the outcome in the concrete cases brought by the Prosecution, or that, as David Cohen has argued, this type of narrow personal jurisdiction essentially relieved the Court of the burden of deciding whether to prosecute any middle- or lower-ranking perpetrators.[17] Or it may be

---

[12] *See* discussion *infra* Section 5.5.2.

[13] *See* SCSL Statute, *supra* note 1, at art. 1 § 1.

[14] In fact, the President of the Special Court later presented the uniquely structured personal jurisdiction as an "innovation in the structure of international courts and tribunals." Geoffrey Robertson (President of the Special Court for Sierra Leone), *First Annual Report of the President of the Special Court for Sierra Leone* (Dec. 2, 2002–Dec. 1, 2003), www.rscsl.org/Documents/AnRpt1.pdf.

[15] Oral hearing of the appeal commenced at 10:00 a.m. on Jan. 22, 2013. Prosecutor v. Taylor, Case No. SCSL-03-01-A, Decision on Urgent Motion for Reconsideration or Review of "Scheduling Order" (Dec. 5, 2012); Jennifer Easterday, Trial Charles Taylor, INT'L JUST. MONITOR, *Parties in Taylor Trial Make Appeals Submissions* (Jan. 22, 2013) www.charlestaylortrial.org/2013/01/22/parties-in-taylor-trial-make-appeals-submissions/.

[16] Although a Westlaw TP-ALL database search of the phrase "those who bear the greatest responsibility" returned approximately 120 results, only one English Language article seems to have taken up the issue. *See* Sean Morrison, *Extraordinary Language in the Courts of Cambodia: Interpreting the Limiting Language and Personal Jurisdiction of the Cambodian Tribunal*, 37 CAP. U. L. REV. 583, 610–14 (2009).

[17] David Cohen, *"Hybrid" Justice in East Timor, Sierra Leone, and Cambodia: "Lessons Learned" and Prospects for the Future*, 43 STAN. J. INT'L L. 1, 11 (2007) (discussing the creation of the SCSL).

that, as William Schabas has rightly suggested, academic lawyers recognized greatest responsibility as a rather vacuous concept that said more about donor generosity in the first court which would be funded entirely by donations from states than something with "any autonomous legal meaning."[18]

Yet, the practical dangers of glossing over "greatest responsibility" jurisdiction will remain for time- and resource-constrained international criminal tribunals. The SCSL's attempt to grasp this principle appears to, therefore, have wider significance for other penal courts tasked with a similar mandate. This is all the more so because states increasingly resort to the greatest responsibility formula popularized by the Court. They reflect the attitude that the expensive work of international penal courts should generally be limited to trials of only a handful of top leaders, instead of contemplating a large number of perpetrators including lower-ranked suspects.[19]

It is against this backdrop that this chapter, which forms part of this book's study of the less prominent jurisprudential contributions of the SCSL in key areas, will attempt to unpack the meaning of "greatest responsibility" personal jurisdiction. My principal aims are twofold. First, to determine and expose how that phrase was developed, interpreted and road tested for the first time in international criminal law at the SCSL. Essentially, even as the Court introduced this phrase to the international law lexicon and tried to give it a positive spin, I will examine whether the SCSL judges advanced our understanding of this type of narrow way of framing personal jurisdiction, and, if so, how and if not, why not.

Second, the chapter will situate the SCSL's experience within the broader normative evolution of international criminal justice. The idea is to identify, to the extent possible, the types of lessons that could be gleaned for future courts created with an expressly limited mandate of bringing only the architects of the core crimes to justice.

Finally, besides the moral hazards inherent in effectively conferring impunity on some perpetrators through their non-prosecution, while prosecuting a few others, it is important to determine whether the SCSL devised a principled approach to greatest responsibility. This would at least serve as a starting point for considerations of who should be the targets for internationally supported prosecutions from among a mass of perpetrators in other situation countries in Africa and other parts of the world.

Overall, while contending that the UN, in particular the UNSC, made some difficult jurisdictional choices that ultimately resulted in the SCSL conducting only a limited number of prosecutions compared to the ICTY and the ICTR, I will show that the Court's jurisprudence on this question has offered international criminal justice a useful point of departure regarding how to determine who it is that may be said to bear *greatest responsibility* for the purposes of prosecution in an international

---

[18]   William A. Schabas, *Genocide Trials and Gacaca Courts*, 3 J. Int'l Crim. Just. 879, 882 (2005).
[19]   See *infra* notes 75–79 and accompanying text.

criminal court. The main takeaway is that such prosecutions should be presumed to reflect both those in leadership/authority position and the gravity/scale of the crimes carried out by the more wicked perpetrators.

Structurally, the chapter is organized as follows. The next part develops the theme in the preceding paragraph. It explains why this topic deserves a chapter in this book. To situate the novelty of this phraseology from the SCSL, it appears necessary to examine how personal jurisdiction was framed by the prior international tribunals that preceded the Sierra Leone Tribunal. For this reason, the second part provides a brief overview of the way personal jurisdiction was expressed in the statutes of international criminal courts from the watershed Nuremberg International Military Tribunal through to the modern UN-supported tribunals. This section of the chapter will attempt to show that the focus of the SCSL's predecessors was generally to punish only a limited number of persons in high-ranking leadership positions and those whose conduct was so beyond the pale that they were deemed to deserve international condemnation. This tendency to emphasize the so-called big fish, instead of small fish, has generally continued with the modern ad hocs – as exemplified by the International Criminal Tribunal for the former Yugoslavia (ICTY) and the International Criminal Tribunal for Rwanda (ICTR). And, because of various factors including concerns about cost and speed, it reached its apex by the time the SCSL was formally established.

In the third part, I examine the strong disagreements regarding the meaning of "greatest responsibility," which, driven by the challenges made by some defense counsel, arose between the judges of two separate trial chambers at the SCSL. I will demonstrate that Trial Chamber I correctly determined that greatest responsibility as expressed in the SCSL Statute was intended to be both a jurisdictional require-ment and a guideline for the exercise of prosecutorial discretion, whereas Trial Chamber II incorrectly interpreted it as a guideline for the exercise of prosecutorial discretion. Although the Appeals Chamber weighed in to endorse what I argue was the wrong position, thereby limiting the overall value of the Court's case law on this topic, there was sufficient common ground among the majority of the SCSL judges. We can therefore discern a clear jurisprudential path holding that the greatest responsibility phrase should be understood to include both those in leadership and high-ranking positions as well as their cruel underlings whose outrageous conduct merited international, instead of domestic, investigation, prosecution and punishment.

The fourth and fifth parts of the chapter use classic treaty interpretation rules in an attempt to locate the meaning of the ambiguous phrase "to prosecute persons who bear the greatest responsibility." I explore the ordinary text, object and purpose of the SCSL Statute and the drafting history of that provision as well as the Tribunal's practice. In this regard, I assess the extent to which the solution proffered by the appeals court judges was consistent, or inconsistent, with the stated intention behind Article 1. I submit that had the Appeals Chamber adopted a different reading of the law, it would still have been able to dispense justice – contrary to what it implied in its judgment – and in that way, would likely have made a better contribution to the Court's jurisprudential legacy on greatest responsibility for the still developing international criminal justice system.

The final part summarizes the key arguments and draws preliminary conclusions. At a normative level, I advocate for broader and thus more inclusive grants of personal jurisdiction for future ad hoc international criminal tribunals. This would mean a return to the traditional formula of granting jurisdiction over persons responsible rather than those bearing greatest responsibility or those most responsible. However, given the reality that this preference might not match the narrower approach seemingly preferred by cost-conscious states as we see in the ECCC in Cambodia and the STK in Kenya, I propose alternate ways treaty drafters might alleviate some of the challenges inherent in employing the greatest responsibility standard as the statutory mandate for the investigation and prosecution of some of the world's worst crimes.

5.3 EVOLUTION OF PERSONAL JURISDICTION IN INTERNATIONAL PENAL LAW

5.3.1 *The Nuremberg and Tokyo Tribunals' Limited Personal Jurisdiction*

Although unique in its statutory terminology, the SCSL is not alone in having a restricted personal jurisdiction.[20] In fact, there is a discernible trend to limit international tribunal prosecutions to a handful of political and military leaders deemed most responsible for the widespread violence.[21] This doctrinal attitude dates back to the origins of modern international criminal law, even if it was not as explicit.[22] It seems predicated on the pragmatic recognition that individual accountability at the international level, when compared to domestic legal systems, can only be meted out swiftly and efficiently in relation to a handful of key perpetrators. Thus, by circumscribing the scope of international trials in the hope of deterring the top brass, rather than all of them together with the rank and file, international penal law also carves out an informal division of labor between national and international criminal jurisdictions.

---

[20] *See generally* Morrison, *supra* note 16, at 605–15 (discussing the limiting language in personal jurisdiction statutes of ad hoc and hybrid tribunals, as well as the manner in which that language has been interpreted).

[21] *Id.* at 588.

[22] *See* Charter of the International Military Tribunal art. 6, Aug. 8, 1945, 59 Stat. 1544, 82 U.N.T.S. 279 [hereinafter IMT Charter]; *see also* Memorandum to President Roosevelt from the Secretaries of State and War and Attorney General, § III (Jan. 22, 1945) (on file with Yale Law School) (noting that the "outstanding offenders are, of course, those leaders of the Nazi Party and German Reich who since January 30, 1933, have been in control of formulating and executing Nazi policies").

One way it increasingly does this is to devise institutional mechanisms to ensure that the planners, leaders and others responsible for fomenting heinous international crimes are prosecuted at the international level wherever the relevant national jurisdictions are unable or unwilling to prosecute.[23] States may, of course, be unable or unwilling to pursue the leaders, but at the same time may still be willing or be capable to prosecute the rank and file. This de facto arrangement anticipates that the middle- and lower-ranking suspects would be investigated and prosecuted in domestic courts so that there is no impunity gap.[24] This general approach finds expression in the prior personal jurisdiction clauses of international criminal courts and in their practice.[25]

Article 1 of the IMT Charter, which was important as the first attempt to prosecute persons in an international tribunal, declared as its purpose "the just and prompt trial and punishment of the *major* war criminals of the European Axis."[26] Under the heading "Jurisdiction and General Principles," Article 6 specified that the tribunal "shall have the power to try and punish persons who . . . whether as individuals or as members of organizations, committed . . . crimes against peace[,] . . . war crimes[,] . . . [and] crimes against humanity."[27] In a provision that seems to be more about the modes of participation in international crimes than about personal jurisdiction as such, Article 6 spelled out the types of individuals that were envisaged to fall within the personal jurisdiction as those "[l]eaders, organisers, instigators and accomplices participating in the formulation or execution of a common plan or conspiracy to commit any of the foregoing crimes" and, moreover, placed responsibility on these individuals "for all acts performed by any persons in execution of such plan."[28] The Tokyo Tribunal essentially reflected an identical position in Articles 1 and 5 of its statute,[29] although its geographic focus was on the "major war criminals in the Far East,"[30] whereas the IMT addressed those who masterminded the atrocities committed in the European war theatre.[31]

Though there might be some legitimate criticisms of those tribunals as "victor's justice,"[32] it is undisputed that as part of their achievements, they did prosecute and

---

[23]   *See, e.g.*, Off. of the Prosecutor, *Prosecutorial Strategy 2009–2012*, ¶ 19, (Feb. 1, 2010); Off. of the Prosecutor, *Report on Prosecutorial Strategy*, pt. II (Sept. 14, 2006).

[24]   Off. of the Prosecutor, *Prosecutorial Strategy 2009–2012*, ¶ 19, (Feb. 1, 2010); Off. of the Prosecutor, *Report on the Prosecutorial Strategy*, pt. II § a (Sept. 14, 2006).

[25]   *See* SCSL Statute, *supra* note 1, at art. 1 § 1; Agreement Between the United Nations and the Royal Government of Cambodia Concerning the Prosecution Under Cambodian Law of Crimes Committed During the Period of Democratic Kampuchea, U.N.-Cambodia, art. 1, June 6, 2003, 2329 U.N.T.S. 117 [hereinafter U.N.-Cambodia Agreement]; U.N.-Sierra Leone Agreement, *supra* note 1, at art. 1 § 1; Morrison, *supra* note 16, at 587–88.

[26]   IMT Charter, *supra* note 22, at art. 1 (emphasis added).

[27]   *Id.*, at art. 6.

[28]   *Id.*

[29]   *Id.* at arts. 1–6; *cf.* International Military Tribunal for the Far East arts. 1–5, Jan. 19, 1946, T.I.A.S. No. 1589 [hereinafter IMTFE Charter].

[30]   *Id.* at art. 1.

[31]   IMT Charter, *supra* note 22, at art. 1.

[32]   William A. Schabas, *Victor's Justice: Selecting "Situations" at the International Criminal Court*, 43 J. Marshall L. Rev. 535, 537 (2010) (quoting Prosecutor v. Tadic, Case No. IT-94-1-T, Decision on

convict high-ranking government officials associated with the German and Japanese wartime regimes. In the Nuremberg Tribunal, these ranged from Herman Goering, the "Successor Designate"[33] to Herr Adolf Hitler, to the commander-in-chief of the Germany Navy, Admiral Karl Doenitz, who later replaced the *Fuehrer* after he committed suicide, and to a number of other highly-ranked military and civilian officials.[34] Those prosecutions of the "major" war criminals set the stage for the subsequent American and other Allied national prosecutions of World War II offenses within their respective zones of occupation under Control Council Law 10.[35] Even in the setting of allied country prosecutions, it was, at least initially, mainly senior military officers who were tried.[36] These officers spanned from lieutenant colonels to majors, captains, and generals, as exemplified by, for instance, the *United States v. Pohl* case.[37]

Similarly, at the International Military Tribunal for the Far East (IMTFE), twenty-eight of the eighty initially detained "Class A war criminals" were prosecuted, eighteen of whom were military officers.[38] United States Army General Douglas McArthur effectively shielded Japanese Emperor Hirohito from prosecution.[39] This shows the selectivity of international criminal law goes back to its very beginnings. In any event, the list of others put on trial at the IMTFE included four former Japanese premiers, six generals, several former ministers, going through ranking ambassadors, and other important advisers on matters of state.[40]

This brief summary appears sufficient to confirm that, although not employing the "greatest responsibility" language to frame the contours of their personal jurisdiction, from the genesis of international criminal law, the focus of cases in the ad hoc international courts created by states has not been to prosecute everyone who might have committed a crime. Rather, the objective has been to prosecute a smaller number of leaders, architects, and planners of the mass atrocities, the "major" war

---

Prosecutor's Motion Requesting Protective Measures for Victims and Witnesses, ¶ 21 (Int'l Crim. Trib. for the Former Yugoslavia Aug. 10, 1995).

[33] *Id.*; International Military Tribunal, Indictment, app. A, *reprinted in* 1 TRIAL OF THE MAJOR WAR CRIMINALS BEFORE THE INTERNATIONAL MILITARY TRIBUNAL 27 (1945) [hereinafter IMT, *Indictment*, app. A].

[34] *Id.*

[35] Nuremberg Trials Final Report, appendix D art. III (Dec. 20, 1945), http://avalon.law.yale.edu/imt/imt10.asp.

[36] *See Id.* at art. 2; IMT, *Indictment*, app. A, *supra* note 33.

[37] United States v. Pohl, Indictment of the International Military Tribunal, Trials of the War Criminals Before the Nuremberg Military Tribunals Under Control Council Law No. 10, vol. 5 (Jan. 13, 1947).

[38] United States v. Araki, Indictment of the International Military Tribunal for the Far East, app. E (1946), *reprinted in* DOCUMENTS ON THE TOKYO INTERNATIONAL MILITARY TRIBUNAL: CHARTER, INDICTMENT, AND JUDGMENTS 63–69 (Neil Boister & Robert Cryer eds., 2008) [hereinafter *Araki* Indictment]; *see also* TIMOTHY P. MAGA, JUDGMENT AT TOKYO: THE JAPANESE WAR CRIMES TRIALS 2 (2001) (noting that the eighty indicted men classified as "Class A war criminal suspects" including, "war ministers, former generals, economic and financial leaders, an imperial advisor, an admiral, and a colonel . . . were accused of plotting and carrying out a war of conquest; murdering, maiming, and ill-treating civilians and prisoners of war; plunder; rape; and 'other barbaric cruelties'").

[39] HERBERT P. BIX, HIROHITO AND THE MAKING OF MODERN JAPAN 587 (2000).

[40] *Araki* Indictment, *supra* note 38, at appendix E.

criminals of the European and Asian theatres. The text also apparently contemplated the inclusion of instigators, organizers, accomplices and others. It was a pick and choose approach to criminal accountability that sought to define in a narrow manner who shall be prosecutable for atrocity crimes

As with national criminal law, the assumption seems to be that this will deter specific individuals as well as others generally who might otherwise emulate them in their repugnant conduct. Indeed, the persons tried, both at Nuremberg and at Tokyo, were those who largely held important political and military posts in the government hierarchy. For the most part, these were not direct perpetrators, but people who used, or rather abused, their positions of authority to order, instigate or encourage subordinates, accomplices and others to commit reprehensible crimes. The convicted perpetrators were deemed more culpable than their junior partners and enforcers who actually implemented their orders.[41] In any event, in the other instances where the actual perpetrators of the crimes were prosecuted through national-level prosecutions, the gravity, brutality and scale of their crimes generally served as ample justification for their investigation, prosecution, and punishment.

5.3.2 *Modern International Tribunals Also Possess Limited Personal Jurisdiction*

The ICTY and ICTR Statutes adopted similar ways of defining their personal jurisdictions as the IMT and IMTFE immediately after World War II. The context of their establishment suggested that they were also created largely to bring the top perpetrators of international crimes to justice. Perhaps reflecting what may have been the golden age of international criminal justice, and its perceived high potential to assist in solving the intractable problems of impunity in post-conflict situations, in their respective jurisdictional provisions, the constitutive documents of the UN twin tribunals both provided in their Article 1 that they "shall have the power to *prosecute persons responsible* for serious violations of international humanitarian law."[42] This was notably distinct from the formulation used in the later Sierra Leone court conferring "the power to prosecute persons who bear the greatest responsibility" for the serious international humanitarian and Sierra Leonean law violations that took place in the context of that country's conflict.[43]

---

[41] *See generally* IMT, *Indictment, supra* note 33, at appendix A (referring to misuse of high-ranking positions, personal influence and intimate connections in the statement of responsibility for individuals indicted).

[42] U.N. Secretary-General, *Report of the Secretary-General Pursuant to Paragraph 2 of Security Council Resolution 808*, U.N. Doc. S/25704 (May 3, 1993) (emphasis added); S.C. Res. 955, art. 1 (Nov. 8, 1994); *Id.* at arts. 5, 6; Articles 6 and 5 of the ICTY and ICTR Statutes, respectively, clarify that the jurisdiction of the Tribunal only applies to natural persons; Under Articles 15 § 1 and 16 § 1, the Prosecutor's role is to prosecute "persons responsible" for the serious violations of IHL committed in the former Yugoslavia; S.C. Res. 955, art. 15 § 1 (Nov. 8, 1994) and S.C. Res. 808, art. 16 § 1 (Feb. 22, 1993) established the Tribunals would prosecute "persons responsible."

[43] *See* SCSL Statute, *supra* note 1, at art. 1.

It is true that in the resolutions preceding the creation of the ICTY and ICTR, the UNSC repeatedly emphasized its determination to bring to justice *all those persons* responsible for the commission of international crimes.[44] But those decisions should be understood in context. They were taken at a time when the international community was faced with bitter and ongoing conflicts characterized by atrocity crimes and a climate of ongoing hostilities in which stopping the further commission of heinous offenses was an obvious international policy goal.[45] They were thus worded in a way that exaggeratingly suggested that more than a limited group of perpetrators would be prosecuted and punished by each of those institutions. This emphasis made sense given the clear deterrence goal, espoused for the tribunals, and the stated desire to warn others to desist from engaging in criminal behavior.

The reality proved to be slightly different and more complicated, however, although far more than the IMT and IMTFE, the UN tribunals have also succeeded in prosecuting a seemingly large part of the middle management of the atrocities in the former Yugoslavia and Rwanda respectively. Sometimes, for various pragmatic reasons, such as the need to show concrete results in the early days, those ad hoc tribunals even ended up with prosecutions of otherwise insignificant perpetrators, such as Dusko Tadic and Jean-Paul Akayesu, who were not necessarily the most culpable persons in the grand scheme of things – at least when it comes to their official or leadership ranks. Leadership, however, does not have to depend on official rank or position; it can be both de facto or de jure. In this example, both men were closer to the bottom of the official hierarchy, more akin to the foot soldiers who carried out the orders that came from above, than those who drafted them. In other words, even though those perpetrators were important, they were ultimately relatively minor players in the context of the wider conflict; they were certainly not the brains behind the massive offenses committed in the tragic Balkans and African conflicts during the early 1990s.

The problem is that the initial enthusiasm for international criminal justice, which coincided with the end of the Cold War and a new era of East–West cooperation in the Council, did not last. In the intervening years between the creation of the ICTY and ICTR tribunals in 1993 and 1994,[46] and the SCSL in 2002,[47] there had been much discussion among the powerful countries (especially the United States) about the viability of the ad hoc Chapter VII tribunal model.[48] The so-called "[t]ribunal fatigue,"[49] driven primarily by concerns about the slow

---

[44] S.C. Res. 827, ¶ 2 (May 25, 1993); S.C. Res. 955, ¶ 1 (Nov. 8, 1994).

[45] *Id.*

[46] *Id.*

[47] U.N.-Sierra Leone Agreement, *supra* note 1, at art. 1 § 1, § 23.

[48] David J. Scheffer, All The Missing Souls: A Personal History of the War Crimes Tribunals (2012).

[49] David J. Scheffer, Ambassador at Large for War Crime Issues, Challenges Confronting International Justice Issues, Address before the New England School of Law (Jan. 14, 1998), *in* 4 New Eng. J. Int'l & Comp. L. 1 (1998).

pace of the international trials and the spiraling costs of those UN courts,[50] is said to have taken hold in the UNSC and the United States government in particular.[51] It was therefore a deliberate choice, in a move to what some might have perceived to be a more financially viable and a more politically acceptable model, to limit the jurisdiction of future courts, such as the SCSL, to prosecuting only a handful of persons in leadership or authority positions deemed to bear greatest responsibility for the serious international humanitarian law violations committed during the West African nation's brutal war.

Interestingly, although the phrasing of the personal jurisdiction clause that granted the SCSL authority was a departure from the equivalent personal jurisdiction language in the statutes for the UN Chapter VII tribunals,[52] the ICTY and ICTR, in their respective Rules of Procedure and Evidence,[53] jurisprudence[54] and Completion Strategies,[55] now use similar language expressing the greatest responsibility limitation. Those rules and policies served as directives to those tribunals to guide the judicial exercise of discretion towards the cases involving senior leaders and other persons deemed to be among those most responsible. As states expressed pragmatic concerns about their viability, they essentially in practice co-opted the preferred greatest responsibility language to signal that they were also aware of the need for limitations of their caseload and cost-cutting and other related measures. The ad hoc tribunals thus seem to have adjusted, willingly or unwillingly, to the political environment in which they functioned. This makes sense given the criticism of their cost and generally slow pace of trials. Indeed, as the tribunals came under increased pressure from the Council to wrap up their work, the Prosecutors have pragmatically had to make a policy choice to identify the top layer deemed most responsible and most appropriate for trial within their jurisdiction.[56] They could justify this position by arguing that they had no choice but to leave it to the

---

[50]   Morrison, *supra* note 16, at 587–88; Sean D. Murphy, *Contemporary Practice of the United States Relating to International Law*, 94(2) AM. J. INT'L L. 482, 483 (2002); Sean D. Murphy, *State Department Views on the Future of War Crimes Tribunals*, 96(2) AM. J. INT'L L. 482, 483 (2002).

[51]   Scheffer, *supra* note 49.

[52]   *Compare* SCSL Statute, *supra* note 1, at art. 1 § 1 ("greatest responsibility"), *with* S.C. Res. 955, art 1 (Nov. 8, 1994) and S.C. Res. 827, art. 2 (May 25, 1993) ("persons responsible").

[53]   International Tribunal for the Former Yugoslavia, Rules of Procedure and Evidence, Rule 11 *bis*, 28, U.N. Doc. IT/32/Rev. 45 (Dec. 8, 2010); International Tribunal for Rwanda, Rules of Procedure and Evidence, U.N. Doc. ITR/3/REV.1 (June 29, 1995).

[54]   Prosecutor v. Luckic, Case No. IT-98-32/1-PT, Decision on the Referral of Case Pursuant to Rule 11 *bis* with Confidential Annex A and Annex B, ¶¶ 28, 30 (Int'l Crim. Trib. for the Former Yugoslavia Apr. 5, 2007); Prosecutor v. Todović, Case No. IT-97-25/1-AR11*bis*.1, Decision on Savo Todović's Appeal Against Decision on Referral under Rule 11 *bis*, ¶¶ 19–22 (Int'l Crim. Trib. for the Former Yugoslavia Sept. 4, 2006).

[55]   S.C. Res. 1503 (Aug. 28, 2003); U.N. Secretary-General, Letter dated Oct. 3, 2003 from the Secretary-General addressed to the President of the Security Council, p. 6, U.N. Doc. S/2003/946 (Oct. 6, 2003) (providing the Completion Strategy for the International Criminal Tribunal for Rwanda).

[56]   Sean D. Murphy, *State Department Views on the Future of War Crimes Tribunals*, 96(2) AM. J. INT'L L. 482, 483 (2002) (explaining US encouragement of the ad hoc tribunal completion strategies); Pierre-Richard Prosper & Michael A. Newton, *The Bush Administration View of International*

territorial states or other willing national jurisdictions to pursue the remainder of the fugitives, either through independently initiated prosecutions of lower-ranked suspects or voluntary acceptance of transferred cases of the alleged middle-level perpetrators to national courts.[57] The point is that, in the result, the guidance in the rules and other tribunal policies were not jurisdictional requirements the failure to comply with which would result in a decision not to proceed with the cases.

In the other ad hoc criminal court negotiated by the UN with one of its Member States around the same time period as the SCSL, the ECCC, the international community as represented by the UN adopted a similarly worded jurisdictional provision to the language of greatest responsibility.[58] The framing of personal jurisdiction sought to encompass "senior leaders of Democratic Kampuchea and those who were most responsible." This lends further credence to the idea of tribunal exhaustion at the level of some UN Member States, although an additional set of considerations were admittedly also at play in explaining the limited competence of the ECCC for the Cambodia context. These included a government that might not necessarily have been acting in good faith, when compared to the Sierra Leone negotiations with the UN, which demonstrated strong national–political will to deal with accountability for the international crimes experienced during the conflict. Be that as it may, Article 1 of the ECCC Law empowered it to prosecute the *"senior leaders* of Democratic Kampuchea and those who were *most responsible* for the crimes."[59] Much like the Sierra Leone court, which was also territorially and temporally confined in its ability to prosecute compared to the ICTY and ICTR, the Cambodia Tribunal was intended to carry out only a limited number of prosecutions of senior persons along with those apparently deemed to possess the greatest level of individual responsibility for committing heinous offenses.[60] Both tribunals' jurisdiction clauses therefore reflect the fiscally conservative spirit informing the late 1990s ad hoc court models.

In a similar vein, although having a distinctive multilateral treaty basis, Article 1 of the Rome Statute of the permanent ICC defines the competence of the global penal court as the power to "exercise its jurisdiction over *persons* for the most serious crimes of international concern."[61] There is plainly no explicit limitation on the

---

Accountability, 36 NEW ENG. L. REV. 891, 897 (2002) (analyzing the US support for the greatest responsibility limitation).

[57] Prosper & Newton, *supra* note 56, at 896–97.

[58] Law on the Establishment of the Extraordinary Chambers in the Courts of Cambodia for the Prosecution of Crimes Committed during the Period of Democratic Kampuchea, (NS/RKM/1004/006), Oct. 27, 2004.

[59] *Id.* at art. 1 (emphasis added); U.N.-Cambodian Agreement, *supra* note 25, at art. 1.

[60] *Id.*; Even though it is expected to only prosecute a handful of people, Article (1) of the Statute of the Lebanon Tribunal has, perhaps as a reflection of a lesson learned by the Secretary-General about the controversies of greatest responsibility, returned to use of the phrase "to prosecute persons responsible." See S.C. Res. 1757, annex, art. 1 (May 30, 2007).

[61] Rome Statute of the International Criminal Court art. 1, July 17, 1998, 2187 U.N.T.S. 3 (emphasis added).

ICC's personal jurisdiction. Indeed, in contrast to the ad hoc courts, it appears that many states were clearly interested in having a broader personal jurisdiction for the permanent international tribunal than a narrower one.[62] On the other hand, the concern about the way to delimit jurisdiction in a very narrow way was less of an issue in the ICC's context since various restrictions had already been inserted into the permanent court's statutory framework through several carefully negotiated substantive provisions that gave the first bite at the apple of investigation and prosecution to willing and able states. The Rome Statute preamble was thus unequivocal that the effective prosecution of the grave crimes within the ICC's competence was primarily the duty of all states, and that their effective prosecution will only be ensured if measures are taken at the national level and by enhancing international cooperation.

However, rather interestingly for the argument advanced in this chapter, the ICC Prosecutor has in her policy papers, strategy documents and emerging practice interpreted this reference to personal jurisdiction as mandating a focus only on those "who bear the greatest responsibility."[63] Put differently, though not textually required to endorse and follow the greatest responsibility standard in the Rome Statute, the principal official deciding on the scope of the ICC's investigations has adopted this same threshold. It is arguable that this is the pragmatic position since it would simply be impossible for a distant international court to supplant the work of national jurisdictions in the many atrocity situations around the world on any given day. The use of greatest responsibility also has an expressive function. It signals to states that the permanent Court too will play its part to limit its costs while at the same time endorsing the prevailing belief in the necessity of limiting the possible situations that could come within the permanent court's jurisdiction.

To recap key points, this foregoing review suggests that, as states and tribunal authorities have developed more experience designing, interacting with and/or managing international criminal tribunals, they increasingly seem to prefer to confer a relatively narrow type of personal jurisdiction – at least when it comes to the more prominent, situation-specific ad hoc international criminal courts. In the ICC, which has a broad jurisdiction in relation to 123 States Parties currently, this

---

[62] *Id.* at pmbl, art 1.

[63] *See* ICC-OTP, *Paper on Some Policy Issues Before the Office of the Prosecutor* 7 (Sept. 2003), www.icc-cpi.int/nr/rdonlyres/1fa7c4c6-de5f-42b7-8b25-60aa962ed8b6/143594/030905_policy_paper.pdf (stating that the Office of the Prosecutor will "focus its investigative and prosecutorial efforts and resources on those who bear the greatest responsibility, such as the leaders of the State or organization allegedly responsible for those crimes" (emphasis omitted)); *see also* Off. of the Prosecutor, *Prosecutorial Strategy 2009–2012*, ¶ 19, (Feb. 1, 2010) ("In accordance with this statutory scheme, the Office consolidated a policy of focused investigations and prosecutions, meaning it will investigate and prosecute those who bear the greatest responsibility for the most serious crimes, based on the evidence that emerges in the course of an investigation." (Emphasis omitted)); Off. of the Prosecutor, *Report on Prosecutorial Strategy*, ¶ 2(b) (Sept. 14, 2006); Luis Moreno-Ocampo, *The International Criminal Court: Seeking Global Justice*, 40 CASE W. RES. J. INT'L L. 215, 221 (2008) (stating that "[m]y role is to prosecute those bearing the greatest responsibility for the most serious crimes").

captures the SCSL trend in terms of demarcating who can be prosecuted in specific situation countries. From the point of view of States Parties, much of this concern is ultimately about controlling costs and keeping international justice on the cheap.

This wider international environment helps to explain why the UN, and in particular the Council, introduced and insisted on the "greatest responsibility" personal jurisdiction contained in the SCSL Statute. The reasonable inference is that it was all about the money, the need for which was being balanced against the Nuremberg norm that persons must be prosecuted when they engage in the commission of international crimes. This took the form in this context that, at least some persons, ought to be prosecuted for the international crimes committed during the latter half of the Sierra Leonean conflict. If this is correct, it suggests reasons to be cautious in celebrating the addition of this phrase into our vocabulary because of what it apparently implies. To me, the phrase effectively signals a reduced political will amongst states to ensure the broadest possible investigations and prosecutions of perpetrators of serious international offenses that reach beneath the top layer to uncover others, perhaps of a lesser rank, who should also be held accountable for mass atrocity crimes. But it may be countered that settling on a more realistic phraseology for personal jurisdiction, in a world of limited budgets and rampant atrocity crimes, is part of the necessary evolution of international criminal tribunals. Such jurisdiction can also be seen as a way to indirectly manage the currently high expectations about what these courts can realistically contribute in societies torn apart by brutal conflict.

At the end of the day, more than any other factor, the UNSC's decision to limit the jurisdiction of the SCSL to those with greatest responsibility was driven by pragmatic, political, economic, and other *realpolitik* considerations. This in turn affected the mandate that the Court was given – essentially, to investigate and prosecute a handful of persons in leadership positions based on a strict personal, temporal and territorial jurisdiction,[64] which would help to ensure, it was hoped at the time, that all the trials would be completed within three years.[65] The circumstances of the emergence of greatest responsibility standard set the stage for the showdown that would later occur during the SCSL trials.

---

[64] *See* SCSL Statute, *supra* note 1, at art. 1 § 1.

[65] As I have argued elsewhere, the number of persons that it was expected would be prosecuted by the SCSL reportedly totaled between two to three dozen. Unfortunately, the Tribunal, partly because of this constrained greatest responsibility mandate and a conservative prosecutorial interpretation of that language, only successfully completed about nine cases. For a court that operated for over ten years, this meant that the tribunal averaged less than one case per year. *See* Charles Chernor Jalloh, *Special Court for Sierra Leone: Achieving Justice?*, 32 MICH. J. INT'L L. 395, 413, 420-22 (2011) (criticizing the "extremely small number of trials" ultimately carried out).

5.4 JUDICIAL CONTROVERSIES ABOUT GREATEST RESPONSIBILITY

5.4.1 *Approaches to Interpretation of Greatest Responsibility*

Once the SCSL indictments were issued and the suspects arrested, some of the defense counsel at the SCSL immediately filed preliminary motions asking the judges to clarify the exact scope of Article 1(1) of the SCSL Statute, which is entitled "Competence of the Special Court."[66] As the provision is key to the original analysis advanced by this chapter, and was reproduced in essentially the same form in Article 1(1) of the UN-Sierra Leone Agreement, it is worth setting out in full, as follows:

> The Special Court shall, except as provided in subparagraph (2), have the power *to prosecute persons who bear the greatest responsibility* for serious violations of international humanitarian law and Sierra Leonean law committed in the territory of Sierra Leone since November 30, 1996, including those leaders who, in committing such crimes, have threatened the establishment of and implementation of the peace process in Sierra Leone.[67]

In construing this clause, honing in for now on the italicized portion, we can discern at least *three* plausible interpretations.[68]

The first is that Article 1(1) authorized the prosecution of the persons deemed most responsible or most culpable for the serious crimes perpetrated in Sierra Leone. On this view, a key criterion for selection could be the rank or position held by the persons in this category and whether they were the movers and shakers behind the conflict and the widespread commission of the crimes. This interpretation, which as we shall see later the Prosecution seemed to prefer,[69] would emphasize the leadership status of the suspect and whether the suspect had the capacity to impact the general course of events over the years of the war, but failed to prevent or punish the wrongful conduct of the perpetrators. The thrust would effectively be on the top political and/or military leaders who committed, planned, instigated, ordered or otherwise aided and abetted the heinous international crimes that were perpetrated by the combatants under their command, control and supervision. For convenience, in this chapter, we may call this the *political military leader category*.

A second interpretation implied by the greatest responsibility language in the above clause was that the Prosecutor could scour the lower rank and file of the

---

[66] SCSL Statute, *supra* note 1, at art. 1; *see, e.g.*, Prosecutor v. Norman, Case No. SCSL-04-14-PT, Decision on the Preliminary Defense Motion on the Lack of Personal Jurisdiction Filed on Behalf of Accused Fofana, ¶¶ 1–2 (Mar. 3, 2004).

[67] SCSL Statute, *supra* note 1, at art. 1 § 1 (emphasis added); *see* U.N.-Sierra Leone Agreement, *supra* note 1, at art. 1.

[68] Further on in this chapter, I will examine the second part of that phrase reading as follows: including whose leaders who, in committing such crimes, have threatened the establishment of and implementation of the peace process in Sierra Leone.

[69] *See* discussion *infra* Section 5.5.3.

thousands of persons who perpetrated the various crimes within the SCSL's jurisdiction and select from among them those who did not necessarily hold high-ranking positions in the military or political structures of the various parties to the conflict. Instead, she would choose those who were most cruel and most notorious for the brutality and depravity of their crimes. In other words, the jurisdiction mentioned in Article 1(1) could be read as a directive to pursue the worst persons, killers or ordinary combatants whose criminal acts caused the most harm, to the most victims, in the most brutal manner during the period within the SCSL's limited temporal jurisdiction. We can refer to this group of prospective suspects bearing greatest responsibility as the *killer perpetrator category*. Irrespective of which of the two preceding categories a particular defendant falls into, it is likely that he would argue that he fell outside the jurisdiction of the Court because he was merely a foot soldier, rather than a political or military leader, and vice versa.

But many criminal lawyers might perhaps agree more with the third plausible interpretation of the first part of Article 1(1). In this view, asserting that the Tribunal has power to prosecute those bearing greatest responsibility would indicate that individuals from either, or better yet, both the political military leadership and the killer perpetrator categories are prosecutable. The latter interpretation of Article 1(1) and its drafting history,[70] as well as the SCSL's practice, seems to confirm that the last is ultimately the better way to construe the greatest responsibility personal jurisdiction – at least from a prosecutorial, and certainly an interest-of-justice, perspective.

The simplicity with which these three optional interpretations of Article 1(1) of the SCSL Statute are identified here belies the fierce discord among the judges of Trial Chambers I and II on how best to construe this phrase during the Sierra Leone trials. It also masks the fact that the Prosecution faced a steady stream of challenges from the Defense, throughout some of the trials, claiming that a particular accused should not be prosecuted because that person was not among those envisaged to fall within the *greatest responsibility* competence of the Tribunal. Indeed, so much time and energy was wasted by lawyers and judges debating the meaning of greatest responsibility that it might even have had a chilling effect on the Prosecutor's decision not to pursue additional suspects for the crimes apparently committed in Sierra Leone. The former SCSL Chief Prosecutor Stephen Rapp has confirmed that this was a major concern, pointing out that the prosecuting attorneys lived for a while in fear that the judges could reject a case on the basis that the suspect was not one of those bearing the greatest responsibility.[71]

Nonetheless, despite curiously reaching divergent legal conclusions as to whether Article 1(1) was a jurisdictional requirement (Trial Chamber I)[72] or a mere guideline

---

[70] See discussion *supra* Section 5.4.2.
[71] See Stephen J. Rapp, *The Challenge of Choice in the Investigation and Prosecution of International Crimes in Post-Conflict Sierra Leone*, in THE SIERRA LEONE SPECIAL COURT AND ITS LEGACY: THE IMPACT FOR AFRICA AND INTERNATIONAL CRIMINAL LAW 23–37 (Charles C. Jalloh ed., 2014).
[72] Prosecutor v. Norman, Case No. SCSL-04-14-PT, Decision on the Preliminary Defense Motion on the Lack of Personal Jurisdiction Filed on Behalf of Accused Fofana, ¶ 27 (Mar. 3, 2004).

for prosecutorial strategy (Trial Chamber II),[73] the SCSL judges were in general agreement that the phrase mandating the prosecution of those bearing greatest responsibility contained in the statute implicitly included what I have here characterized as the political-military leadership and killer perpetrator categories.[74] This seems to suggest that this is the more reasonable interpretation of the phrase. Put differently, even though the phrase "greatest responsibility" was highly divisive when debated before and in the course of the Freetown trials,[75] a key lesson from the SCSL case law is that the greatest responsibility phrase should, as a prima facie matter, be interpreted as a broad jurisdictional grant. A form that is capable of covering both different types of actors and different types of conduct in a given armed conflict.[76] This reading would be consistent with the definition of greatest responsibility that would be later offered in the context of the proposal to establish a STK:

> "persons bearing the greatest responsibility" means a person or persons who were knowingly responsible for any or all of the following acts: planning, instigating, inciting, funding, ordering or providing other logistics which directly or indirectly facilitated the commission of crimes falling within the jurisdiction of the Tribunal; in determining whether a person or persons falls within this category, the Tribunal shall have regard to factors including the leadership role or level of authority or decision making power or influence of the person concerned and the gravity, severity, seriousness or scale of the crime committed.[77]

Clearly, the drafters of the STK statute reflected an awareness of the doubts in the SCSL over the meaning of the greatest responsibility phrase. Thus, their definition of it encompassed both persons said to be responsible by fiat of their high or leadership rank and those whose conduct was so grave, severe, and serious that it warranted prosecution. That said, as this chapter will show shortly, a review of the relevant SCSL case law demonstrates that there was in the analysis a conflation of several important questions that muddied the greatest responsibility waters even further. For analytical purposes, these questions could be broken down into the following sub-issues: (1) whether the phrase to prosecute persons bearing greatest responsibility established a jurisdictional threshold or was a type of guidance for the Prosecutor's determination of whom to prosecute; (2) if so, the timing or stage of the criminal proceedings at which an accused should raise the objection that the Tribunal lacks authority to try him because he did not bear greatest

---

73   Prosecutor v. Brima, Case No. SCSL-04-16-T, Judgment, ¶ 653 (July 20, 2007).
74   *Compare* Prosecutor v. Norman, Case No. SCSL-04-14-PT, Decision on the Preliminary Defense Motion on the Lack of Personal Jurisdiction Filed on Behalf of Accused Fofana, ¶¶ 23–27 (Mar. 3, 2004), *with* Prosecutor v. Brima, Case No. SCSL-04-16-T, Decision on Defense Motion for Judgment of Acquittal Pursuant to Rule 98, ¶¶ 30–34 (Mar. 31, 2006).
75   *See, e.g., Brima*, Case No. SCSL-04-16-T, Decision on Defense Motion, ¶¶ 28–29.
76   *Id.* ¶¶ 34–35.
77   Special Tribunal for Kenya Bill (2009), § 2 (Kenya).

responsibility; (3) the evidentiary burden that the Defense would have to discharge if they chose to raise the issue (and the nature of the Prosecution's burden to counter it); (4) the role of the evidence and judges in the assessment of greatest responsibility considering the separation of the judicial from the prosecutorial functions in the SCSL; and, finally, (5) the consequences of positive or negative findings on jurisdiction for the defendant, the Prosecutor and the Tribunal itself. We turn next to an analysis of the first of these five issues.

5.4.2 *Greatest Responsibility As a Jurisdictional Requirement*

In the first defense motion to raise the argument that the SCSL was not entitled to try a particular defendant because it lacked the legal capacity to do so, the assigned defense counsel for Moinina Fofana[78] filed a preliminary jurisdictional challenge before Trial Chamber I on November 17, 2003.[79] The counsel submitted that the Court did not have personal jurisdiction over Fofana because the suspect fell outside the category of persons who bore "the greatest responsibility" for the alleged serious international humanitarian law violations contained in his indictment.[80]

The Defense asserted that the personal jurisdiction discussed in Article 1(1) of the Tribunal Statute could be interpreted in only one of two ways.[81] First, it could be taken as a reference to the leaders of the parties or states bearing the greatest responsibility for the Sierra Leonean armed conflict, including those who had threatened the establishment and implementation of the peace process.[82] Second, and alternatively, it could be seen as a way of referring to those individuals responsible for most of the crimes committed during the armed conflict.[83] According to the Defense, neither Fofana's

---

[78] Moinina Fofana held the rank as the National Director of War of the CDF, the armed state-supported militia faction involved in the Sierra Leone conflict. *See* Prosecutor v. Norman, Case No. SCSL-04-14-PT, Decision on the Preliminary Defense Motion on the Lack of Personal Jurisdiction Filed on Behalf of Accused Fofana, ¶ 42 (Mar. 3, 2004); Prosecutor v. Fofana, Case No. SCSL-2003-11-PT, Preliminary Defense Motion on the Lack of Personal Jurisdiction, ¶ 14 (Nov. 17, 2003).

[79] Prosecutor v. Fofana, Case No. SCSL-2003-11-PT, Preliminary Defense Motion on the Lack of Person Jurisdiction (Nov. 17, 2003).

[80] *Id.* ¶ 2; Rule 72B provides:

> Preliminary motions by the accused are (i) objections based on lack of jurisdiction; (ii) objections based on defects in the form of the indictment; (iii) applications for severance of crimes joined in one indictment Rule 49, or for separate trials under Rule 82(B); (iv) objections based on the denial of request for assignment of counsel; or (v) objections based on abuse of process.
>
> Special Court for Sierra Leone Rules of Procedure and Evidence (Mar. 7, 2003). The Rules further provide that "[o]bjections based on lack of jurisdiction or to the form of the indictment, including an amended indictment, shall be raised by a party in one motion only, unless otherwise allowed by the Trial Chamber."

> *Id.* at 72C.

[81] Prosecutor v. Norman, Case No. SCSL-04-14-PT, Decision on the Preliminary Defense Motion on the Lack of Personal Jurisdiction Filed on Behalf of Accused Fofana, ¶ 2 (Mar. 3, 2004).

[82] *Id.* at ¶ 2(a).

[83] *Id.* at ¶ 2(b).

indictment nor the subsequent prosecution disclosure supported the view that the suspect belonged to the latter class of persons.[84] Indeed, under neither interpretation could he be deemed among those bearing greatest responsibility. It followed that he was not properly within the Court's personal jurisdiction.

The Prosecution responded that the documents forming the context for the establishment of the SCSL amply showed that the question whether a particular person is one of those who bore the greatest responsibility was a matter of prosecutorial discretion based on the evidence collected during the investigations.[85] To justify judicial review of the exercise of that discretion, the defendant needed to demonstrate that the Prosecutor unlawfully exercised his power or acted based on improper or impermissible discriminatory motives.[86] The Accused had failed to adduce any proof establishing such intentions.[87] According to the Prosecution, although defense counsel had suggested that Fofana was associated with the Civil Defense Forces (CDF) militia that was known more for its work in attempting to restore peace in Sierra Leone, rather than the commission of international crimes, this was not substantiation that he might not ultimately be found guilty after the conclusion of the trial as among those bearing greatest responsibility.[88] Fofana was, in any event, a leader fitting that description since he had been the second in command of the CDF organization, as had been alleged in his indictment.[89]

In their unanimous ruling, the three judges of Trial Chamber I reviewed the drafting history of the provision and correspondence between the UN Secretary-General and the Council discussing "greatest responsibility" and the former's proposed alternative to use those "most responsible"[90] instead. The judges rightly pointed out that the UNSC's preference was to limit the jurisdiction of the SCSL primarily to the prosecution of those who had played a leadership role.[91] But the UNSG had insisted that the greatest responsibility clause should not be taken to imply that personal jurisdiction would be limited only to the political and military leaders.[92] The UNSG had clarified that it would also extend to others considered to be so on the basis of the scale or severity of their crimes.[93] After this review, Trial Chamber I unanimously concluded that "the issue of personal jurisdiction is a jurisdictional

---

[84] *Id.* at ¶ 2.

[85] *Id.* at ¶ 5; *see also* Prosecutor v. Fofana, Case No. SCSL-2003-11-PT, Prosecution Response to the Defense Preliminary Motion on Lack of Personal Jurisdiction, ¶ 6 (Nov. 26, 2003).

[86] *Id.* at ¶¶ 12–14.

[87] Prosecutor v. Norman, Case No. SCSL-04-14-PT, Decision on the Preliminary Defense Motion on the Lack of Personal Jurisdiction Filed on Behalf of Accused Fofana, ¶ 7 (Mar. 3, 2004).

[88] *Id.* at ¶ 8.

[89] *Id.* at ¶ 10.

[90] *Id.* at ¶ 40.

[91] *Id.*

[92] U.N. Secretary-General, Letter dated Jan. 12, 2001 from the Secretary-General addressed to the President of the Security Council, ¶ 2, U.N. Doc. S/2001/40 (Jan. 12, 2001) [hereinafter Letter dated Jan. 12, 2001 from Secretary-General].

[93] *Id.* at ¶¶ 2–3.

requirement, and while it does of course guide the prosecutorial strategy, it does not exclusively articulate prosecutorial discretion, as the prosecution has submitted."[94]

Having essentially determined that Article 1(1) established a jurisdictional threshold, which the Prosecution ought to show it could fulfill, the judges ruled that the Prosecution had discharged that burden in the context of that particular case.[95] They were satisfied that Fofana *appeared* to fall within the court's personal jurisdiction because there was sufficient prima facie evidence tending to show that he held a leadership position as the number two person in the CDF – one of the main parties in Sierra Leone's armed conflict.[96] They underscored, however, that whether or not he could be found to be among those actually holding greatest responsibility is a factual and "an evidentiary matter to be determined at the trial stage."[97] The Chamber clarified that, at the stage of the Defense's preliminary motion, it was merely concerned with basic allegations whether he can be said *to appear to* bear greatest responsibility.[98] The Trial Chamber therefore correctly underscored that it was not, in reaching that finding, pronouncing on Fofana's ultimate guilt or innocence. The latter assessment would only be adjudged after the conclusion of his trial and consideration of all the evidence.[99]

In its judgment on the merits, which followed several years later, Trial Chamber I reiterated its initial holding that Article 1(1) created a jurisdictional requirement.[100] However, although the judges had (at the preliminary motions stage) deferred the question of whether in *actuality* Fofana could be one of those bearing greatest responsibility until the end of the trial (because such assessment could only follow after hearing all the evidence against the Accused), they appeared to somewhat sidestep the issue. The judges simply stated that the personal jurisdiction requirement did not constitute a legal or material ingredient of the crimes since greatest responsibility was only a jurisdictional question which had been previously determined.[101] It followed that, to secure a conviction, the Prosecutor would not have to prove as a material element beyond a reasonable doubt that Fofana was one of those *in fact* bearing greatest responsibility.[102] Put differently, at the judgment stage when it reviewed the evidence and found Fofana actually guilty, the Trial Chamber implied that it had accepted the Prosecutor's conclusion that the defendant was one of those that bore greatest responsibility for the events and crimes in Sierra Leone. This suggested that the judges saw the assessment of whether personal jurisdiction existed

---

[94] Prosecutor v. Norman, Case No. SCSL-04-14-PT, Decision on the Preliminary Defense Motion on the Lack of Personal Jurisdiction Filed on Behalf of Accused Fofana, ¶ 27 (Mar. 3, 2004).

[95] *Id.* at ¶ 45.

[96] *Id.* at ¶ 42.

[97] *Id.* at ¶ 44.

[98] *Id.*

[99] *Id.* at ¶ 47.

[100] Prosecutor v. Fofana, Case No. SCSL-04-14-T, Judgment, ¶¶ 91–92 (Aug. 2, 2007).

[101] *Id.*

[102] *Id.*

to try Fofana as being only a relevant question for consideration at the indictment review stage on a prima facie basis to believe standard, as opposed to a matter to be put to prosecutorial proof *beyond a reasonable doubt* during or at the completion of the trial.

Two other observations seem pertinent to highlight about Trial Chamber I's useful analysis of the greatest responsibility formulation in Article 1(1). First, the Chamber helpfully clarified that the statutory clause should essentially be understood as expressing two separate, if closely related, ideas. To begin with, the phrase confirmed that the prosecution of persons who bear the greatest responsibility constituted a personal jurisdictional requirement before the Court and that it is the Prosecutor's function in carrying out the mandate that is then prescribed in Article 15.[103] This demonstrated that the Prosecution must establish that a particular suspect fulfilled this criterion by tendering evidence, assessed at the low reasonable basis to believe indictment review threshold, that the person was a *leader* (whether military or political) *appearing* to be one of those bearing greatest responsibility. If the Prosecution meets that burden – which would not be difficult because the threshold is very low – of having reasonable grounds to believe that the suspect in question committed the crime charged, then the Chamber can properly try the defendant. Conversely, if the Prosecution failed to prove even a prima facie case existed against the suspect, showing that the Court has jurisdiction over him covering particular crimes on a given territory during an appropriate time period, then the Chamber would have to dismiss the case. The Court's logic was likely that the suspect did not need to endure an unnecessary trial when the SCSL lacked the basic personal, temporal and subject matter jurisdiction to try him. This seems sensible as there would be no point in subjecting the suspect to the hassle of an unnecessary trial when the Tribunal actually lacked the personal jurisdiction to commit him to trial.

A related point is that, unlike the first part of Article 1(1) of the SCSL Statute, Trial Chamber I implied that the second part of the same sentence, "including those leaders who, in committing such crimes, have threatened the establishment of and implementation of the peace process in Sierra Leone[,]" was not an element of the crime.[104] Rather, it was intended to guide the Prosecutor in his determination of his strategy regarding whom to prosecute.[105] The judges illustrated that the practical focus of who the Tribunal ought to investigate and try, from the perspective of the Security Council during the negotiations, were the important political and military leaders;[106] whereas, from Secretary-General Annan's perspective, it would include

---

[103] Prosecutor v. Norman, Case No. SCSL-04-14-PT, Decision on the Preliminary Defense Motion on the Lack of Personal Jurisdiction Filed on Behalf of Accused Fofana, ¶¶ 21, 26, 27 (Mar. 3, 2004).

[104] *Id.* at ¶ 38.

[105] *Id.* at ¶¶ 24–25, 27.

[106] *Id.* at ¶¶ 22–25.

the top leaders plus anyone else that was found to be among those who carried out the worst of the crimes perpetrated in Sierra Leone.[107]

Second, Trial Chamber I essentially confirmed the interpretation that the phrase those "who bear the greatest responsibility" was sufficiently flexible phraseology to capture all those (1) who held high-ranking positions and (2) those whose crimes were so cruel that they would be among the worst perpetrators of the crimes during the Sierra Leone Civil War.[108] The caveat, of course, was that the judges unanimously, and correctly in my view, held that the UNSC's stated preference for the "greatest responsibility" language signaled that the leadership role of the suspect should be the *primary criterion* with the severity of a crime and its massive nature bearing only secondary importance to the decision as to whom to charge and prosecute.[109]

Overall, when assessed using the language of the three-part interpretive scheme suggested above, the Trial Chamber I judges concluded that Fofana fell within the *political military leader* category instead of the killer perpetrator category, the former being the main element that presumably led the Prosecutor to indict him. In fact, in its judgment on the merits, Trial Chamber I found that Fofana was one of the top three men in the so-called Holy Trinity of the CDF organization.[110] It underscored, much like the founders of the SCSL did during the negotiations of the constitutive founding instruments, that greatest responsibility should, at least partly, be understood as a reflection of rank or position of the suspect in the organization(s) that perpetrated the crimes within the subject matter jurisdiction of the international tribunal. This did not however preclude the trials of others, whose responsibility may be based not on their leadership status but their cruelty. These deductions, therefore, seem to be helpful clarifications to the jurisprudence and eventual literature on the scope of personal jurisdiction in international criminal courts.

5.4.3 Greatest Responsibility As Guideline for Prosecutorial Discretion

The *Armed Forces Revolutionary Council* (AFRC) case, which Trial Chamber II judges heard, involved three mutinying soldiers from the Sierra Leone Army who organized a coup d'état that unseated the democratically elected Kabbah government in 1997.[111] Once they assumed power, the three suspects directed others within their command and control to commit some of the most brutal acts witnessed during the Sierra Leone conflict.[112] Unlike the *Fofana* case, none of the three defense teams in the AFRC joint trial filed preliminary challenges objecting to the Court's

---

[107]   Letter dated Jan. 12, 2001 from Secretary-General, *supra* note 92, at ¶ 2.
[108]   *See* Prosecutor v. Norman, Case No. SCSL-04-14-PT, Decision on the Preliminary Defense Motion on the Lack of Personal Jurisdiction Filed on Behalf of Accused Fofana, ¶ 39 (Mar. 3, 2004).
[109]   *Id.* at ¶ 40.
[110]   *See id.* at ¶¶ 38–40.
[111]   Prosecutor v. Brima, Case No. SCSL-04-16-T, Judgment, ¶¶ 4, 316, 432, 507 (June 20, 2007).
[112]   *See, e.g., id.* at ¶¶ 233–39.

assertion of personal jurisdiction over their clients during the limited twenty-one day period following the release of the prosecution disclosure under the SCSL Rules of Procedure and Evidence.[113] It is unclear whether this was just an oversight or a deliberate defense strategy. However, at the halfway point of the trial when the Prosecution had rested its case-in-chief, the defendants addressed the issue as part of their no case to answer or motion for judgment of acquittal submissions.[114] This procedural step of the trial allows a defendant to request the court to dismiss all the charges against him, and if successful, dispenses with the requirement that he advance his own defense.

As part of this, the accused Brima contended that the reference in Article 1(1) and 15 of the SCSL Statute *to persons who bear the greatest responsibility* was a "limitation on the Court's jurisdiction as to which persons may or may not be prosecuted and creates an evidentiary burden to be satisfied by the Prosecution."[115] According to the Defense, the Prosecutor had not discharged his burden because its witnesses instead showed that other more prominent military leaders higher in rank, not their accused clients who were only *lower-ranked non-commissioned officers*, bore greatest responsibility for the offenses perpetrated in Sierra Leone.[116] In its response, the Prosecution advanced a two-pronged response. First, there was no jurisdictional threshold that had to be met under Article 1(1). Second, the question of whether an accused is among those who bears greatest responsibility ought to only be determined after the conclusion of the trial.[117] Alternatively, and in any event, based on the evidence presented up to that point in the case, a reasonable trier of fact could find the Accused to fall within the Court's personal jurisdiction.[118]

In its judgment, Trial Chamber II reviewed the documents discussing the history of the personal jurisdiction provision, and in particular, it examined two letters exchanged between the UNSG and the Council in 2001.[119] The Chamber observed that in the January 12, 2001 letter, the UNSC rejected Annan's preferred "most responsible" personal jurisdiction language in favor of retaining its own "greatest responsibility formulation."[120] The Secretary-General had insisted on clarifying that the greatest responsibility wording should not be taken to mean that the Court's personal jurisdiction was limited to "political and military leaders" only, a position which the Council subsequently appeared to approve in its January 31, 2001 reply.[121]

---

[113]   Prosecutor v. Norman, Case No. SCSL-04-14-PT, Decision on the Preliminary Defense Motion on the Lack of Personal Jurisdiction Filed on Behalf of Accused Fofana, ¶ 27 (Mar. 3, 2004).

[114]   Prosecutor v. Brima, Case No. SCSL-04-16-T, Joint Legal Part Defense Motion for Judgment of Acquittal under Rule 98, ¶¶ 1–2 (Dec. 13, 2005).

[115]   Prosecutor v. Brima, Case No. SCSL-04-16-T, Decision on Defense Motion for Judgment of Acquittal Pursuant to Rule 98, ¶ 28 (Mar. 31, 2006).

[116]   *Id.*

[117]   *Id.* at ¶ 29.

[118]   *Id.*

[119]   *Id.* at ¶¶ 32–33.

[120]   *Id.* at ¶ 32.

[121]   *Id.* at ¶¶ 33–34.

This SCSL chamber found that "greatest responsibility" jurisdiction in Article 1(1) *"solely purports to streamline the focus of prosecutorial strategy."*[122] The judges then went on to observe that the phrase, understood in its ordinary sense, was meant to include, at a minimum, two groups of perpetrators, at the top of which were the political and military leaders of the parties to the conflict.[123] They emphasized, nevertheless, that the broad language used in the clause implied that an even wider range of individuals, presumably including ordinary combatants whose conduct might have been very egregious, were all potentially prosecutable before the Court.[124]

It seems apparent but perhaps surprising that, in reaching two divergent conclusions, the two sets of three judges in each of the SCSL trial chambers examined the same drafting history and historical documents. While all six judges essentially agreed on the importance of those documents and relied on the analysis contained therein, each chamber's legal reasoning towards its respective conclusions differed.[125] The natural next question is, why? Two reasons seem to stand out.

First, it would appear that the Trial Chamber II judges did not extract in their entirety the drafting history of Article 1(1) and the subsequent correspondence between Secretary-General Annan and the UNSC. After the Secretary-General's January 12, 2001 letter proposing that the Council switch from its preferred, but apparently narrower, "greatest responsibility" formulation to his alternative and purportedly wider "most responsible" standard for personal jurisdiction, he conceded that, in rejecting his alternative proposal, the Council was thus "limiting the focus of the Special Court to those who played a leadership role."[126] He pled, however, that the phrase should not be construed to "mean that the personal jurisdiction is limited to the political and military leaders only."[127] Indeed, in his view, this determination in a concrete case would initially have to be made by the Prosecutor and, ultimately, by the Court itself. The President of the Council, in a somewhat ambiguous subsequent reply, stated that the UNSC shared in the Secretary-General's "analysis of the importance and role of the phrase 'persons who bear the greatest responsibility.'"[128] This can be seen as an endorsement of the idea that greatest responsibility was to be construed broadly to include what I have called the political military leader category as well as the killer perpetrator category.

[122] Prosecutor v. Brima, Case No. SCSL-04-16-T, Joint Legal Part Defense Motion for Judgment of Acquittal under Rule 98, ¶¶ 653 (Dec. 13, 2005) (emphasis added).

[123] *Id.* at ¶¶ 34–35.

[124] *See id.* at ¶ 35.

[125] *Compare Id.* at ¶¶ 32–34, *with* Prosecutor v. Norman, Case No. SCSL-04-14-PT, Decision on the Preliminary Defense Motion on the Lack of Personal Jurisdiction Filed on Behalf of Accused Fofana, ¶¶ 22–25 (Mar. 3, 2004).

[126] Letter dated Jan. 12, 2001 from Secretary-General, *supra* note 92, at ¶ 2; *see also* Report on SCSL Establishment, *supra* note 4, at ¶¶ 30–31.

[127] Letter dated Jan. 12, 2001 from Secretary-General, *supra* note 92, at ¶ 2.

[128] Letter dated Jan. 31, 2001 from Pres. of S.C., *supra* note 10, at ¶ 1.

Second, Trial Chamber I introduced a nuance when it reached the conclusion that greatest responsibility was both a jurisdictional requirement in Article 1(1) and also a description of the prosecutorial duty as fleshed out in Article 15. This group of judges emphasized the second part of the January 12, 2001 letter from the Secretary-General to the Council, in which it accepted that the particular reference made in the second sentence of Article 1(1) would then explicitly encompass "those leaders who, in committing such crimes, have threatened the establishment of and implementation of the peace process in Sierra Leone."[129] This links both the first and second parts of the phrase and in fact underscores what greatest responsibility was supposed to be. Secretary-General Annan, for his part, understood the second sentence to serve as "guidance to the Prosecutor in determining his or her prosecutorial strategy."[130] The UNSC, in a subsequent reply to him, also endorsed the Annan clarification that the words in the second sentence of Article 1(1), following the comma, were intended as a type of guideline to frame the prosecutorial strategy.[131] This gave credence to the later Trial Chamber I position that the effect of that preference for the greatest responsibility, instead of the people most responsible language, meant that leadership, instead of severity of the crime, ought to be the primary consideration when determining which suspect to prosecute.[132]

In other words, even though the two trial chambers used two different routes to the promised land of interpreting this phrase and Trial Chamber I felt that leadership, as a criterion, was to have primacy over severity of conduct, the judges from both chambers were on essentially the same page that greatest responsibility as phrased in the Statute meant that both political military leaders as well as killer-perpetrators could be prosecuted. They had effectively reached the same outcome, but using different analytical routes. The difference is that Trial Chamber I correctly distinguished between the first sentence of Article 1(1) (which it read as outlining the personal jurisdiction) and the second sentence of the same clause (which put in place the criteria – later explicitly developed in Article 15 – that would serve to guide or circumscribe prosecutorial discretion towards a particular class of individual obstructionists towards the peace).[133]

Whereas, for its part, Trial Chamber II interpreted the second part of the phrase in Article 1(1) as being subsumed by the first and reasoned that both elements, taken as one, did not establish a jurisdictional requirement, but rather, functioned as additional guidance for the Prosecutor's strategy.[134] To the latter group of judges then, Article 1(1) was not so much a jurisdictional clause as much as it was a guidance

---

129   Prosecutor v. Norman, Case No. SCSL-04-14-PT, Decision on the Preliminary Defense Motion on the Lack of Personal Jurisdiction Filed on Behalf of Accused Fofana, ¶¶ 38, 40 (Mar. 3, 2004).

130   Letter dated Jan. 31, 2001 from Pres. of S.C., *supra* note 10, at ¶ 1.

131   *Id.*

132   Prosecutor v. Norman, Case No. SCSL-04-14-PT, Decision on the Preliminary Defense Motion on the Lack of Personal Jurisdiction Filed on Behalf of Accused Fofana, ¶¶ 39–40 (Mar. 3, 2004).

133   *Id.*

134   Prosecutor v. Brima, Case No. SCSL-04-16-T, Judgment, ¶ 653 (June 20, 2007).

clause. However, the Trial Chamber II reasoning appears hard to reconcile with the fact that the rest of the elements in Article 1(1) of the Statute explicitly referred to matters of (geographic, territorial and temporal) jurisdiction only. Their decision in the *AFRC* trial also failed to confront the question why the same "greatest responsibility" language separately found its way into Article 15, which stated the functions of the Prosecutor. One way of possibly reconciling the Trial Chamber II ruling would be to say that the judges saw the provision enumerating the prosecutorial power (Article 15) as doing the same job as the clause explaining the Tribunal's jurisdictional competence (Article 1(1)). Under this reading, both articles point the Prosecutor to make the choice of whom to pursue from those in leadership roles as well as those in lower ranks because they could prove to bear "greatest responsibility" for the crimes perpetrated in Sierra Leone.

As we will see presently, when the Appeals Chamber confronted this same greatest responsibility conundrum, it adopted lock-stock-and-barrel the Trial Chamber II reasoning that greatest responsibility, as worded in Article 1(1) of the SCSL Statute, was solely a guideline to the Prosecutor for the exercise of his discretion instead of a jurisdictional requirement. It is submitted that this conclusion, which effectively endorsed the faulty prosecution and Trial Chamber II reasoning, was not necessarily borne out by the *travaux préparatoires*[135] of the SCSL's founding instruments. The demonstration of the latter is one of the key added values of this contribution to the literature.

5.4.4 *The Appeals Chamber Rules Greatest Responsibility Is Guidance*

Because the two trial chambers of the Court had fiercely disagreed on the interpretation of "greatest responsibility" in separate decisions, it naturally fell to the Appeals Chamber as the highest court in the SCSL to break the tie and furnish an authoritative interpretation of the clause once and for all. Santigie Borbor Kanu, the third defendant in the *Brima* trial, raised greatest responsibility as his first ground in the appeal of his conviction and sentence. He claimed that the trial court erred when it failed to establish that it had proper jurisdiction over him pursuant to Article 1(1).[136] In assessing his plea, the Appeals Chamber first distinguished separation of power issues relating to the competence of the Court, its organizational structure and the role of the Prosecutor as set out in the SCSL Statute vis-à-vis the judicial chambers from issues pertaining to jurisdiction.[137]

To begin, it assessed the role of the Prosecutor set out in Article 15.[138] The Chamber then observed that, flowing from that rule, the Prosecutor is mandated

---

[135] *See* Prosecutor v. Norman, Case No. SCSL-04-14-PT, Decision on the Preliminary Defense Motion on the Lack of Personal Jurisdiction Filed on Behalf of Accused Fofana, ¶ 40 (Mar. 3, 2004).

[136] Prosecutor v. Brima, Case No. SCSL-2004-16-A, Kanu's Submissions to Grounds of Appeal, ¶¶ 1.1–.30 (Sept. 13, 2007).

[137] Prosecutor v. Brima, Case No. SCSL-2004-16-A, Judgment, ¶¶ 280–81 (Feb. 22, 2008).

[138] *Id.*

to act as "a separate organ" and is therefore barred from seeking or receiving instructions from any government or from any other source.[139] Accordingly, the Appeals Chamber concluded, "[i]t is evident that it is the Prosecutor who has the responsibility and competence to determine who are to be prosecuted as a result of investigation undertaken by him."[140] It is then up to the chambers, as the adjudicative organ, to "try such persons who the prosecutor has consequently brought before it as persons who bear the greatest responsibility."[141] Put more succinctly, the decision as to whether someone bears greatest responsibility is made by the Prosecutor, during his investigations, and is not one for the judges whose sole function it is to adjudicate the individual cases brought before them. It was implied that it is not for them to inquire into the correctness of that determination, given the separate roles of each of the two entities.

This position seems correct because it demarcates the sharp division of responsibilities between the prosecutorial and judicial organs of the Court. But it does not take us that far in answering the core of the greatest responsibility question. For example, Trial Chamber II had similarly reasoned that, because of the separation of the prosecutorial and judicial roles in the Tribunal's founding instrument, Article 15 of the Statute implied that even the exercise of prosecutorial discretion in bringing a case against a particular accused was not reviewable by the court.[142] Rather interestingly, this was a broader finding than even the Prosecutor would have expected. In fact, he had conceded in the briefing process, both at trial and during the appeal, that a discretionary decision in choosing whom to prosecute is reviewable by the judges if exercised in a manifestly unreasonable manner, for instance, by violating the rights of the accused through abuse of process or exercising the power for impermissible or discriminatory motives.[143]

However, with respect, there appear to be errors in the judicial reasoning. Both the Appeals Chamber and Trial Chamber II's interpretation of Article 1(1), as a whole, was that the language delineated the outer boundaries of how far the Prosecutor can go when exercising her discretion. There are obvious difficulties with this conclusion, which the judges did not address in either the trial or appellate decisions. Among other issues, this stance ignores why a traditional jurisdictional provision setting out the competence of an ad hoc international criminal court would be adopted by the framers of a statute only to be reduced to a simple guideline for prosecutorial policy at a later time. This position also goes against the grain of national criminal practice where, at least in common law adversarial systems,

---

[139]   *Id.* at ¶ 280 (emphasis omitted).
[140]   *Id.* at ¶ 281.
[141]   *Id.*
[142]   Prosecutor v. Brima, Case No. SCSL-04-16-T, Judgment, ¶ 654 (June 20, 2007).
[143]   *Id.* at ¶ 643; Prosecutor v. Brima, Case No. SCSL-04-16-T, Decision on Defense Motion for Judgment of Acquittal Pursuant to Rule 98, ¶ 29 (Mar. 31, 2006); Prosecutor v. Norman, Case No. SCSL-04-14-PT, Decision on the Preliminary Defense Motion on the Lack of Personal Jurisdiction Filed on Behalf of Accused Fofana, ¶ 7 (Mar. 3, 2004).

prosecutorial independence is respected but the bad exercise of prosecutorial discretion makes it vulnerable to judicial review under certain circumstances.

A related concern in the SCSL specific context is that the judges did not speak to the obvious link between Article 1(1), which usually enumerates the personal jurisdiction of the Tribunal, with Article 15(1), which defined the power of the Prosecutor, when it provided that he or she shall be responsible for the investigation and prosecution of persons who bear the greatest responsibility for the crimes committed in Sierra Leone after November 30, 1996. In other words, why would the drafters adopt Article 15(1) if Article 1(1) serves essentially the same purpose? Conversely, why would they include Article 1(1) if Article 15(1) sufficiently described both the Court's jurisdiction and the mandate of the Prosecutor? The answer is that they adopted each of these separate provisions because each played a distinctive role in the statute: The former setting out the scope of the jurisdiction of the Tribunal, and the latter, expressly outlining the functions (and limitations) imposed on the Prosecutor and her exercise of her power.

In Kanu's appeal, the Prosecution had further argued that the Appeals Chamber should not hold the phrase "persons who bear the greatest responsibility" as a test criterion or a distinct jurisdictional threshold.[144] To do so, according to the Prosecution, would lead to an "absurd interpretation"[145] requiring a factual determination at the pre-trial stage that there is no person who has been indicted who bears greater responsibility than the particular accused when it would be impossible to determine the precise scope of criminal liability before the trial concludes. Yet, at the same time, it would be "unworkable to suggest that this determination should be made by the Trial or Appeals Chamber at the end of the trial."[146] By analogy to Article 1 of the ICTY and ICTR Statutes, which provide for prosecution of "persons responsible," the Prosecution submitted that construing "greatest responsibility" as a jurisdictional requirement would imply that those other tribunals could prosecute only those who are actually guilty.[147]

Adopting this line of argument, the Appeals Chamber, in a crucial statement that betrayed the real concern underpinning their conclusion, ruled as follows:

> [I]t is inconceivable that after a long and expensive trial the Trial Chamber could conclude that although the commission of serious crimes has been established beyond reasonable doubt against the accused, the indictment ought to be struck out on the ground that it has not been proved that the accused was not one of those who bore the greatest responsibility.[148]

---

[144]   Prosecutor v. Brima, Case No. SCSL-2004-16-A, Kanu's Submissions to Grounds of Appeal, ¶¶ 274–75 (Sept. 13, 2007).

[145]   *Id.* at ¶ 274.

[146]   *Id.*

[147]   *Id.*

[148]   *Id.* at ¶ 283.

The Appeals Chamber, like Trial Chamber II that first accepted this prosecution argument, should have queried this submission. For one thing, the argument assumes that a determination that greatest responsibility was a personal jurisdiction requirement implied that the judges had to find at the pre-trial stage, in violation of the presumption of innocence and before even hearing any evidence, that there was no other person that bore greater responsibility than the particular accused before the Court. For another thing, without referring to the prosecution evidence, it implied that the case would not necessarily have been proved beyond a reasonable doubt. Both these propositions seem untenable.

To begin with, as the Trial Chamber I judges held in their *Fofana* preliminary decision, an assessment of whether someone can be said to bear greatest responsibility should be handled differently by evaluating, during the indictment review stage, whether the prosecution had made out a prima facie case that a particular suspect *appears to be* one of the individuals bearing greatest responsibility for what happened in a particular armed conflict.[149] If there is some minimal evidence supporting the prosecution's case, then the trial would proceed, much like it would with respect to the other jurisdictional criteria that had to be met, for example, persuading the judges that the suspect appears to have committed crimes within the jurisdiction of the SCSL.[150] Another possibility is for the greatest responsibility issue to be considered at the Rule 98 (no case to answer) stage, when the judges would have heard all the evidence from the prosecution. They could then decide, on the standard reflecting that stage of the process, if there was substantial evidence that – if believed – would support the charges in the indictment such as to put the defendant to answer the Prosecution case made up to that point of the trial.

But, even more fundamentally, the Appeals Chamber, in endorsing the Prosecutor's argument, did not distinguish the situation of the SCSL from that of the ICTY and the ICTR. Yet, the UN twin tribunals were differently situated vis-à-vis the SCSL for several reasons. First and most importantly, the personal jurisdiction provision at issue is simply framed differently. Second, the debate that arose in the Court did not arise in the UN twin tribunals as a consequence of the wider formulation of their jurisdiction compared to the narrower one of the SCSL. The latter was not only saddled with explicit limitations on its jurisdiction, it was also saddled with specific directives narrowing down the powers of the Prosecutor. In other words, it seems like a false analogy to treat as equal the circumscribed Sierra Leone Tribunal jurisdiction and the broader jurisdiction clauses of the Yugoslav and Rwanda Tribunals.

Be that as it may, the crucial question arises whether the drafting history of the Statute of the SCSL reflected the position taken by the Appeals Chamber and Trial Chamber II. In the next part of this chapter, I will argue that the Appeals Chamber

---

[149] Prosecutor v. Fofana, Case No. SCSL-04-14-T, Judgment, ¶¶ 91–92 (Aug. 2, 2007).
[150] Prosecutor v. Norman, Case No. SCSL-04-14-PT, Decision on the Preliminary Defense Motion on the Lack of Personal Jurisdiction Filed on Behalf of Accused Fofana, ¶¶ 28–45 (Mar. 3, 2004).

misconstrued Article 1 of the Statute. I submit that, clouded by its concern for the practicalities of finding differently on the personal jurisdiction provision for the concrete cases before them, the appeals court misinterpreted the provision. I will contend that Trial Chamber I, which methodically reviewed the greatest responsibility formula with closer and more complete reference to the drafting history, more accurately reflected the intention of the drafters of the SCSL Statute. For clarity, that intention was that Article 1(1) would establish the personal jurisdiction of the Court, while Article 15(1) would further circumscribe the discretion of the Prosecutor to pursue only a limited class of suspects deemed to bear greatest responsibility.

Ultimately, as I will hopefully convincingly demonstrate, despite their various differences, the overall and helpful conclusion to draw from the Sierra Leone court case law appears to be that the greatest responsibility language was sufficiently broad to ensure that the Tribunal could prosecute individuals from both the political-leader and the killer-perpetrator groups. That much agreement existed between all of the judges, even if their reasoning towards that conclusion differed.

5.5 THE PLAIN MEANING OF "GREATEST RESPONSIBILITY"

The drafting history of Article 1(1) in the Statute of the SCSL supports my contention that at least part of the provision was initially intended as a jurisdictional requirement, while another part of the provision was intended as a sort of red line not to cross. An examination of the ordinary textual meaning of the provisions, in accordance with Article 31 of the Vienna Convention on the Law of Treaties demonstrates this theory. Article 31, in relevant part, provides that:

1. A treaty shall be interpreted in good faith in accordance with the *ordinary meaning* to be given to the terms of the treaty in their context and in the light of its object and purpose.
2. The context for the purpose of the interpretation of a treaty shall comprise, in addition to the text, including its preamble and annexes
    (a) any agreement relating to the treaty which was made between all the parties in connexion with the conclusion of the treaty;
    (b) any instrument which was made by one or more parties in connexion with the conclusion of the treaty and accepted by the other parties as an instrument related to the treaty.

    . . . .

4. A special meaning shall be given to a term if it is established that the parties so intended.[151]

---

[151] Vienna Convention on the Law of Treaties art. 31, May 23, 1969, 1155 U.N.T.S. 331 [hereinafter Vienna Convention] (emphasis added).

As the agreement between the UN and the Sierra Leone government constitutes a bilateral treaty,[152] Article 31 of the Vienna Convention on the Law of Treaties (VCLT) is applicable.[153] The Statute of the Tribunal, which of course contains the identical provision on personal jurisdiction, is an annex to the UN-Sierra Leone Agreement and therefore forms an integral part of the treaty.[154] The ordinary meaning of the phrase "to prosecute persons who bear the greatest responsibility" in Article 1(1) of those two instruments can therefore be read in light of the context. Consideration must also be given to the preamble, object and purpose of the provision and the statute; as well as the Court's intended role to ensure accountability for international crimes committed in Sierra Leone. Furthermore, any special meaning accorded to the term by the founders of the SCSL will also be accounted for in light of the Tribunal's practice.

5.5.1 *The Ordinary Meaning of "Persons Who Bear the Greatest Responsibility"*

Let us examine, using a standard English dictionary, each of the terms in the phrase "to prosecute persons who bear the greatest responsibility." The *Oxford English Dictionary* defines "person" in various ways. For our purposes the most relevant is the following: "an individual human being; a man, woman or child"; and, as used in a technical legal sense, as "[a] human being (natural person) or body corporate or corporation (artificial person), having rights and duties recognized by the law."[155] It is clear from even the ordinary dictionary meaning that the term "person" refers most likely to a natural person. So far, all the SCSL prosecutions have related to natural persons, although there is nothing to foreclose trials of legal persons. That said, in the context of this particular chapter, this issue does not appear to have a major bearing on the argument so it need not detain us.

The noun "who" is used "[a]s the ordinary interrogative pronoun, in the nominative singular or plural, used of a person or persons: corresponding to *what* of things."[156] More specifically, it is "[a]s compound relative in the nominative in general or indefinite sense: Any one that . . . ."[157]

The term "bear," which is the root word for "bearing," means "to carry; to sustain; to thrust, press; to bring forth."[158] Bearing is therefore "the action of carrying or conveying" or "[t]he carrying of oneself (with reference to the manner); carriage, deportment; behaviour, demeanour."[159]

---

[152]   Report on the SCSL Establishment, *supra* note 4, at ¶ 9.
[153]   Vienna Convention, *supra* note 151, at art. 1. I use the VCLT as it essentially sets out the same standard as can be found in the equivalent 1986 Vienna Convention that governs treaties between States and international organizations (which is not yet in force at the time of this writing).
[154]   SCSL Statute, *supra* note 1, at art. 1 § 1; U.N.-Sierra Leone Agreement, *supra* note 1, at art. 1.
[155]   *Person*, OXFORD ENGLISH DICTIONARY (2nd ed., 1989) (emphasis omitted).
[156]   *Who*, OXFORD ENGLISH DICTIONARY (2nd ed., 1989).
[157]   *Id.* at 289.
[158]   *Bear*, OXFORD ENGLISH DICTIONARY (2nd ed., 1989).
[159]   *Id.* at 26.

Of course, "the" is a definite article. As used in Article 1(1) of the SCSL Statute outlining personal jurisdiction, it modifies or rather particularizes the superlative "greatest" as a way of connoting that about which the Tribunal *is* or *should be most concerned*. It thus essentially captures the notion of individuals who belong to a class or group of persons bearing relatively greater responsibility, although, admittedly, the idea of those with which it should be most concerned does not necessarily imply exclusivity.

"Greatest" is, of course, the "superlative of great in various senses."[160] As used ordinarily, "the greatest" is a reference to "[t]hat which is great; great things, aspects, qualities, etc. collectively; also, great quantity, large amount."[161] When used to describe persons who bear the qualities of "being great," the *Oxford English Dictionary* clarifies that it is an allusion to persons "[e]minent by reason of birth, rank, wealth, power, or position; of high social or official position; of eminent rank or place."[162] Greatest is, more helpfully in our context, an additional way of denoting "conditions, actions, or occurrences; with reference to degree or extent . . . . [and of] things, actions, [or] events . . . [o]f more than ordinary importance, weight, or distinction; important, weighty; distinguished, prominent; famous, renowned."[163]

As to "responsibility," it is defined as "[t]he state or fact of being responsible. . . *for*. . . [a] charge, trust, or duty, for which one is responsible."[164]

From the above, we can distill from the ordinary dictionary meaning of each of the words when combined together and viewed in their context, that the phrase "persons who bear the greatest responsibility" is a description of two separate but not entirely distinct ideas. First, it describes a person of high rank, position or power who carries out certain actions and brings forth events or conditions of more than ordinary importance. It also describes a person who, given the core object of establishing the SCSL as an independent tribunal that would administer credible justice, should be investigated and prosecuted for his crimes.

Second, and flowing from these definitions, we can also discern that the ordinary meaning of the phrase is also a reference to the degree or amount of something or event that a person engages upon as part of a certain type of behavior – in this case, the commission of crimes during the course of the Sierra Leone conflict. Individual criminal liability was rightly deemed necessary for those actions or events. It also reveals the state or fact of being in charge of or of having a duty or obligation towards a person or thing, which was then breached by those persons. A reference to the drafting history will demonstrate that these two ordinary definitions of the personal jurisdiction provision were also expressed during the negotiations of the agreement creating the SCSL.

---

[160]   *Greatest*, Oxford English Dictionary (2d ed., 1989).
[161]   *Id.* at 800 (footnote omitted).
[162]   *Id.* at 797.
[163]   *Id.* (formatting omitted).
[164]   *Responsibility*, Oxford English Dictionary (2d ed., 1989).

As argued previously, and as will be further detailed in the next part, focusing specifically on the drafting history, the category of persons over which the Court was to have jurisdiction was always going to be limited due to the fear of another expensive ad hoc court that never shuts down. The Council's preference was evidently that the leadership role or command authority of a suspect should be the principal criterion for the application of the greatest responsibility formulation.[165] Whereas, the Secretary-General's view was that the gravity, scale or massive nature of the crime should also be taken into account, if not be the main consideration, in the exercise of personal jurisdiction.[166] Bear in mind that although the former seemingly endorsed the juxtaposition of these two separate ideas, according to Trial Chamber I, the Council ultimately saw the scale or gravity of a particular crime as being of secondary, instead of primary, importance vis-à-vis the leadership or functional positions held by the suspects.[167]

5.5.2 *The Drafting History of "Persons Who Bear Greatest Responsibility"*

Under Article 31(2) of the VCLT, in addition to the preamble and annexes, the context for a treaty is additionally comprised of any subsequent agreements relating to the treaty made between all the parties in connection with the conclusion of the treaty.[168] No such subsequent agreements seem to have been concluded. Nonetheless, the four paragraphs of the preamble to the UN-Sierra Leone Agreement refer to Council Resolution 1315, adopted on August 14, 2000, in which the Council expressed deep concern at the very serious crimes committed within the "territory of Sierra Leone against the people of Sierra Leone and United Nations and associated personnel and at the prevailing situation of impunity."[169] It therefore asked the Secretary-General to negotiate an agreement with the Sierra Leone government to "create an independent special court to prosecute persons who bear the greatest responsibility" for the commission of the serious international and Sierra Leonean law violations committed.[170]

The same language contained in the resolution was reiterated verbatim in Article 1(1) of the SCSL Statute, which prescribed the competence of the Court and delimited its core jurisdictional components.[171] In the Statute, as opposed to Agreement, however,

---

[165]   President of the Security Council, *Letter dated Dec. 22, 2000 from the President of the Security Council addressed to the Secretary-General*, ¶ 1, U.N. Doc. S/2000/1234 (Dec. 22, 2000) [hereinafter Letter dated Dec. 22, 2000 from Pres. of S.C.].

[166]   *See* Report on the SCSL Establishment, *supra* note 4, at ¶ 30.

[167]   Prosecutor v. Norman, Case No. SCSL-04-14-PT, Decision on the Preliminary Defense Motion on the Lack of Personal Jurisdiction Filed on Behalf of Accused Fofana, ¶ 40 (Mar. 3, 2004).

[168]   Vienna Convention, *supra* note 151, at art. 31(2).

[169]   U.N.-Sierra Leone Agreement, *supra* note 1, at pmbl.

[170]   U.N.-Sierra Leone Agreement, *supra* note 1, at pmbl.

[171]   SCSL Statute, *supra* note 1, at art. 1 § 1.

a clarification was added to the effect of "including those leaders who, in committing such crimes, have threatened the establishment of and implementation of the peace process in Sierra Leone."[172] Besides the text of those two instruments, the *travaux préparatoires*[173] reveal a subsequent discussion between, on the one hand, internal organs of the UN (the Council and the Secretary-General), and on the other hand, the UN as a single entity vis-à-vis the other party (Sierra Leone).

In Resolution 1315, the UNSC directed the Secretary-General that the personal jurisdiction of the Tribunal shall cover only "persons who bear the greatest responsibility for the commission of crimes" in Sierra Leone.[174] As the Secretary-General later tried to explain, the Council intended that phrase to mean two things, which also appear to coincide with the ordinary dictionary meaning discerned in the previous section.[175]

In his Report to the Council explaining the steps he had taken to implement Resolution 1315, the Secretary-General suggested that an alternative phrase, "persons most responsible," replace "greatest responsibility."[176] Annan rationalized this suggestion as follows:

> While those "most responsible" obviously include the political or military leadership, others in command authority down the chain of command may also be regarded "most responsible" judging by the severity of the crime or its massive scale. "Most responsible" therefore, denotes either a leadership or authority position of the accused, and a sense of the gravity, seriousness or massive scale of the crime. It must be seen, however, not as a test criterion or a distinct jurisdictional threshold, but as guidance to the Prosecutor in the adoption of a prosecution strategy and in making decisions to prosecute in individual cases.[177]

However, the Council did not endorse that proposal because, for one thing, it implicitly disagreed that the phrase "those most responsible" was broader than the phrase those "bearing greatest responsibility."[178] The President of the Council, in a December 22, 2000 letter, rejected the Secretary-General's proposed modification to the personal jurisdiction provision.[179] The UNSC reiterated its preference contained in Resolution 1315 that jurisdiction should extend to only those in the leadership category who bear the greatest responsibility for the commission of crimes under national and international law.[180] The President put it as follows: "The

---

[172] *Compare* SCSL Statute, *supra* note 1, at art. 1 § 1, with U.N.-Sierra Leone Agreement, *supra* note 1, at art. 1 § 1.

[173] *See supra* note 140 and accompanying text.

[174] S.C. Res. 1315, ¶ 3 (Aug. 14, 2000).

[175] Report on the SCSL Establishment, *supra* note 4, at ¶ 30; *see also* Letter dated Jan. 12, 2001 from Secretary-General, *supra* note 92, at ¶¶ 2–3.

[176] Report on the SCSL Establishment, *supra* note 4, at ¶¶ 29–31.

[177] *Id.* at ¶ 30.

[178] *See* Letter dated Dec. 22, 2000 from Pres. of S.C., *supra* note 165.

[179] *Id.*

[180] *Id.* at ¶ 1; *see* S.C. Res. 1315, ¶ 3 (Aug. 14, 2000)

members of the Security Council believe that, by thus limiting the focus of the Special Court to those who played a leadership role, the simpler and more general formulations suggested in the appended draft will be appropriate."[181] It seems apparent enough, then, that the Council's main interest was to hone in on those holding a leadership role, as both the judges of Trial Chamber I have also since confirmed. Essentially the same interpretation was adopted and can be substantiated by reference to the Prosecutor's practice of charging only those in the leadership of the AFRC, CDF and RUF organizations along with former Liberian President Charles Taylor.

In the Secretary-General's response to the President of the UNSC, which followed about three weeks later (January 12, 2001), Annan canvassed the difference between the two positions.[182] He then tried to reframe his argument to again reassert the relevance of the gravity, scale and severity of the crimes – a point he had initially made when he suggested that "the term 'most responsible' would not necessarily exclude children between 15 and 18 years of age" from possible responsibility for crimes within the SCSL jurisdiction.[183] The question surrounding the responsibility of child soldiers, who had been some of the most notorious perpetrators of atrocities during the war, was one of the thorniest issues for the Sierra Leonean negotiators.[184] So the Secretary-General effectively used that issue as a trump card to emphasize why the gravity of the crimes is a vital consideration in addition to the functional (leadership) position held by the suspect.

He wrote in his report, as follows: "While it is inconceivable that children could be in a political or military leadership position (although in Sierra Leone the rank of 'Brigadier' was often granted to children as young as 11 years), the gravity and seriousness of the crimes they have allegedly committed would allow for their inclusion within the jurisdiction of the Court."[185] With the benefit of hindsight, we know that the evidence that later came out of the trials only partially supported this contention. However, the foregoing extract does indicate that at least one of the main negotiators, the UNSG, intended the gravity of the conduct to be a crucial element of greatest responsibility personal jurisdiction. The above accepts that the Council's purpose in framing jurisdiction this way was to limit the prosecutorial investigations to those in leadership or authority positions. Going by the reasoning of Trial Chamber I, which discerned this singular thrust that leadership was or should be the determinative criterion for prosecutorial decisions, the massive nature of the crime could and should also be taken into account – albeit as a secondary factor. If this deduction is correct, it would permit the prosecution of either, or both, of the lower-ranked perpetrators in addition to leaders in the same jurisdiction.

[181]   Letter dated Dec. 22, 2000 from Pres. of S.C., *supra* note 165, at ¶ 1.
[182]   Letter dated Jan. 12, 2001 from Secretary-General, *supra* note 92, at ¶¶ 1–2.
[183]   Report on the SCSL Establishment, *supra* note 4, at ¶ 31.
[184]   *Id.* at ¶ 34.
[185]   *Id.* at ¶ 31.

In fact, in the same report, one might also recall, Secretary-General Annan had claimed that the wording of Article 1(1) of the draft statute, as the Council had proposed it, did "not mean [to limit] personal jurisdiction . . . to the political and military leaders only."[186] Almost as a tiebreaker in case the powers that be in the UNSC continued to disagree with him, he observed that the determination of the meaning of the term "persons who bear the greatest responsibility in any given case falls initially to the Prosecutor, and ultimately to the SLSC itself."[187] This seems obvious in the sense that part of the initial determination of whom to prosecute falls within prosecutorial discretion.

Using this language, the Secretary-General adopted a negotiating tactic in an attempt to have his way, although he did not later clarify whether his position that the "most responsible" language should not require proof beyond a reasonable doubt,[188] which was ultimately rejected,[189] was also equally applicable to the "greatest responsibility" formulation. It reasonably could be read as being equally applicable. We might thus speculate as to the omission. One explanation is that he left some ambiguity on the point in the hope that it would help bolster his reading, which invoked Sierra Leone's concerns as well, to caution the UNSC that it would be up to the Prosecutor and judiciary to settle on the final position as to what greatest responsibility jurisdiction ultimately entailed. Essentially, it is an argument that says to the Council the limits of how much it could realistically expect from the Statute, considering that the Court could independently diverge from that expectation. He also, by framing things in this way, sent a message to the future Prosecutor that s/he still enjoyed a measure of discretion, despite the apparent prescriptive greatest responsibility language contained in the Agreement and Statute. If this analysis is correct, it would seem that great weight can therefore be attached to the Tribunal's practice in line with that Annan position as well as the VCLT principles.

It is this context that informs the Secretary-General's letter, which then stated, with explicit reference to the second half of Article 1(1):

> Among those who bear the greatest responsibility for the crimes falling within the jurisdiction of the Special Court, particular mention is made of "those leaders who, in committing such crimes, have threatened the establishment of and implementation of the peace process in Sierra Leone." *It is my understanding that, following from paragraph 2 above, the words "those leaders who. . . threaten the establishment of and implementation of the peace process" do not describe an element of the crime but*

---

[186]   Letter dated Jan. 12, 2001 from Secretary-General, *supra* note 92, at ¶ 2.

[187]   *Id.* (internal quotation marks omitted).

[188]   *See* U.N. Secretary-General, *Letter dated July 12, 2001 from the Secretary-General addressed to the President of the Security Council*, U.N. Doc. S/2001/693 (July 12, 2001) [hereinafter Letter dated July 12, 2001 from Secretary-General] (indicating acceptance of the agreement by the parties with no subsequent mention of the "most responsible" and "greatest responsibility" language).

[189]   *See* SCSL Statute, *supra* note 1, at art. 1 § 1 (containing the language "persons who bear the greatest responsibly"); U.N.-Sierra Leone Agreement, *supra* note 1, at art. 1 § 1 (containing the language "persons who bear the greatest responsibility").

rather provide guidance to the prosecutor in determining his or her prosecutorial strategy. Consequently, the commission of any of the statutory crimes without necessarily threatening the establishment and implementation of the peace process would not detract from the international criminal responsibility otherwise entailed for the accused.[190]

The President of the Council's response to the Secretary-General appeared to endorse Annan's preferred ways of interpreting Article 1(1) in the following terms: "The members of the Council share your analysis of the *importance* and *role* of the phrase 'persons who bear the greatest responsibility[.'] The members of the Council, moreover, share your view that the words beginning with 'those leaders who . . .' are intended as guidance to the Prosecutor in determining his or her prosecutorial strategy."[191] This language was vague in that the reference to the "importance" and "role" of Article 1(1) provision does not entirely specify whether the UNSC felt that the personal jurisdiction phrase is (1) limited to leaders alone, or (2) not necessarily limited to leaders alone because it will include those whose actions were so grave that they merited prosecutions (even if they did not functionally hold high-ranking positions). As to the second sentence of the clause, and arguably by implication not the first sentence, it appears evident that the Council agreed with Annan that Article 1(1) does constitute a guideline for the Prosecutor's exercise of his or her discretion without necessarily serving as a legal ingredient or legal requirement of the crimes that ought to be proven beyond a reasonable doubt.

Thus, consistent with the finding of this chapter as shown in Part 5.3, Article 1(1) offered two separate meanings: The first part of the sentence being a personal jurisdictional threshold; and the second part, especially when read together with Article 15(1) outlining the powers of the Prosecutor, establishing a limitation for the prosecutorial application of her discretion without necessarily foreclosing the extension of the jurisdiction to the political leaders and the killer perpetrators.

In his last publicly available letter on the greatest responsibility issue, dated July 12, 2001, Annan notified the Council that the exchange of letters led to modifications of the text in both the draft UN-Sierra Leone Agreement and the Statute annexed to it.[192] As this back and forth communication had been an internal conversation between two UN organs, he confirmed that "[t]he Government of Sierra Leone was consulted on these changes and by letter of February 9, 2001 to the Legal Counsel expressed its willingness to accept the texts."[193] This fact, therefore, made the communication a subsequent agreement among all the parties in connection with the conclusion of the treaty in the Article 31(2) VCLT sense.

In *Fofana*, Trial Chamber I, after meticulously reviewing this drafting history, had also ruled that the "agreed text resulted in the adoption of the phrase" on personal

---

[190]   Letter dated Jan. 12, 2001 from Secretary-General, *supra* note 92, at ¶ 3 (emphasis added).
[191]   Letter dated Jan. 31, 2001 from Pres. of S.C., *supra* note 10, at ¶ 1 (emphasis added).
[192]   Letter dated Letter dated July 12, 2001 from Secretary-General, *supra* note 188.
[193]   *Id.*

jurisdiction as articulated in Article 1(1) of the Statute with the specific duties of the Prosecutor in that regard prescribed in accordance with Article 15(1).[194] It was on this basis that the Chamber concluded that "the issue of personal jurisdiction is a jurisdictional requirement, and while it does of course guide the prosecutorial strategy, it does not exclusively articulate prosecutorial discretion, as the Prosecution has submitted."[195]

Upon closer examination, it appears clear that Trial Chamber I believed, correctly in my view, that personal jurisdiction created a jurisdictional threshold. However, the nuance in the language is that this group of judges did not say that "greatest responsibility" was a jurisdictional requirement in the entirety of the provision. Rather, they felt that the *"issue* of personal jurisdiction" (emphasis added) also contained language purporting to guide the Prosecutor on how she should use her power. It follows that it is correct that Article 1(1) was neither exclusively jurisdictional nor exclusively directed at demarcating the contours of prosecutorial discretion. In contrast, Trial Chamber II, for its part, was critical of the judicial colleagues in the other chamber and explicitly determined that the "greatest responsibility" did not create a jurisdictional requirement because it only limited to a small category the number of persons that were to be prosecuted.[196] Significantly, the above reading that the two ideas were encompassed in the same phrase, as well as in that clause enumerating the Prosecutor's duties, appears to be confirmed by the contents of the July 12, 2001 letter to the Council, in which the Secretary-General explained as follows: "Members of the Council reiterated their understanding that, without prejudice to the independence of the prosecutor, the *personal jurisdiction* of the Special Court *remains limited to the few who bear the greatest responsibility* for the crimes committed."[197] In the Cambodia Tribunal, which has the closest personal jurisdiction wording to that of the Sierra Leone court, an identical concern arose as to the meaning of Article 1(1) of the ECCC Law, which provided for the trial of "senior leaders of Democratic Kampuchea and those who were most responsible for the crimes."[198] This phrase is in one way an improvement on what was used in Sierra Leone in the sense that the first part of it specifically identifies senior leaders while the second part mentions those most responsible. In that way, the ECCC approach apparently adequately addresses the policy concerns of Secretary-General Annan in the Sierra Leone situation: That the leaders, architects or planners of the mass crimes as well as their followers responsible for grave crimes should all as a prima facie matter be deemed prosecutable.[199] The legal framework must be clear and

---

[194] Prosecutor v. Norman, Case No. SCSL-04-14-PT, Decision on the Preliminary Defense Motion on the Lack of Personal Jurisdiction Filed on Behalf of Accused Fofana, ¶ 26 (Mar. 3, 2004).

[195] *Id.* at ¶ 27.

[196] *See* Prosecutor v. Brima, Case No. SCSL-04-16-T, Judgment, ¶ 653 (June 20, 2007).

[197] Letter dated July 12, 2001 from Secretary-General, *supra* note 188 (emphasis added).

[198] U.N.-Cambodia Agreement, *supra* note 25; *see also* G.A. Res. 57/228, ¶ 1 (May 13, 2003) (approving draft of ECCC Agreement).

[199] Report on the SCSL Establishment, *supra* note 4, at ¶¶ 29–30.

accommodating, but the Prosecutor should ultimately make the final choice. The Cambodia formulation also reflects the general purpose behind internationally supported criminal prosecutions which, as we saw in our historical review starting with the Nuremberg Tribunal, had always aimed to ensure the prosecution of leaders and perpetrators of grave crimes are brought to justice.

The only difficulty is that even the ECCC phrase is still somewhat ambiguous. The second part of the sentence, speaking to those most responsible, suggests a focus on the persons to be tried for the depravity or severity of their acts. Unsurprisingly, taking a cue from the developments respecting their brethren at the SCSL, the defense counsel litigated that issue arguing, at the close of the first trial, that the Cambodia Tribunal lacked jurisdiction over the first defendant Duch.[200] The Chamber, drawing on the logic of the Sierra Leone Court, determined that the accused, as a senior leader, fell within its personal jurisdiction as one of those most responsible.[201] That conclusion was unsuccessfully challenged on appeal with the judges adopting a stance similar to the one we saw by the SCSL.[202] Importantly, in that and several other decisions from the ECCC, explicit reference was made to the SCSL case law to confirm the correct nature of the interpretation given by the judges. On the other hand, partly because of the nature of the jurisdiction, some Cambodian co-investigating judges did find that the formulation of most responsible constituted a jurisdictional threshold which had not been met and thus refused to proceed with cases against the defendants.[203]

5.6 CONCLUSION

In taking up previously uncharted terrain, outside the confines of the debates in the trials in Sierra Leone, this chapter hopes to have shown that it is imperative for the creators of international criminal tribunals to properly delineate their personal jurisdiction. The greatest responsibility formula used at the SCSL, which has been the object of close analysis, was politically convenient for the Council. For one thing, it was keen to establish a cheap and time limited ad hoc court that would prosecute only a handful of persons in Sierra Leone. But, as I have demonstrated through this contribution, without further specificity, such general statements of personal jurisdiction in practice raise serious issues of interpretation and application in concrete cases. Vagueness, it seems, is hardly a positive in a criminal tribunal instrument.

---

[200]   Prosecutor v. Duch, Case No. 001/18-07-2007/ECCC/TC, Judgment, ¶ 14 (July 26, 2010).
[201]   *Id.* ¶ 24–25.
[202]   Prosecutor v. Duch, Case No. 001/18-07-2007-ECCC/SC, Appeal Judgment, ¶ 79 (Feb. 3, 2012).
[203]   Press Release, Extraordinary Chambers in the Courts of Cambodia, Co-Investigating Judges Issue Two Separate Closing Orders in the Case Against Meas Muth, www.eccc.gov.kh/en/articles/co-investigating-judges-issue-two-separate-closing-orders-case-against-meas-muth.

With respect to the contributions and lessons learned from Sierra Leone, it may well be too early to draw final conclusions. Nevertheless, based on the foregoing analysis, the following tentative observations may still be offered regarding the case law that the SCSL has bequeathed us on this particular issue. First, the type of "greatest responsibility" clause found in Article 1(1) of the SCSL Statute setting should be avoided at all cost. Failing that, if such language needs to be used, it is important to at least attempt to define what the phrase means to say that a court shall prosecute those bearing greatest responsibility. There is helpful precedent, in this area, as this is in fact what the draft statute of the Special Tribunal for Kenya attempted to do. Again, in that instance, the same logic of focusing on leaders in positions of authority and influence as well as those most vicious in committing the crimes was already evident in the relatively more precise definition that was offered.[204] The drafters of that clause clearly knew of the SCSL experience, since they attempted to resolve some of the thorny issues that led to much ink being spilled by counsel and judges during the Sierra Leone Tribunal's decade-long life. Regrettably, because the Kenya hybrid tribunal never saw the light of day, as the bill failed to obtain sufficient support for passage into law in the Kenyan Parliament,[205] there was a missed opportunity to see whether that relatively clearer phrase would have fared better during the trials of the suspects allegedly responsible for the post-election violence which rocked that country in December 2007.

Second, future ad hoc tribunal statutes should explicitly state whether such a phrase is or is not a jurisdictional requirement that must be proved beyond a reasonable doubt as an element of the crime. It seems obvious that it should not be treated as a jurisdictional requirement, because it would otherwise make prosecutions of concrete cases both procedurally cumbersome and difficult. This is the lesson of the Sierra Leone Court, which struggled throughout its trials to repeatedly make the simple point to defendants and their defense counsel that the focus of prosecution of persons in leadership positions did not mean that those of lower rank, in effective control, could not also simultaneously or alternatively be pursued by an international court with "greatest responsibility language" as the center of its personal jurisdiction. Instead, as we have seen, attempts to judicially settle the issue led to

---

[204]   Special Tribunal for Kenya Bill, *supra* note 11 (emphasis added). The Bill offers the following definition:

> "[P]ersons bearing the greatest responsibility" means a person or persons who were knowingly responsible for any or all of the following acts: planning, instigating, inciting, funding, ordering or providing other logistics which directly or indirectly facilitated the commission of crimes falling within the jurisdiction of the Tribunal; *in determining whether a person or persons falls within this category, the Tribunal shall have regard to factors including the leadership role or level of authority or decision making power or influence of the person concerned and the gravity, severity, seriousness or scale of the crime committed.*

[205]   *Kenya: Quorum Stops the Bill on the Establishment of the Special Tribunal to Try Violence*, AFRICAN PRESS INT'L (Feb. 6, 2009).

more challenges, in different cases, at different stages of the trial process (pre-trial, trial and appeal).

Third, and closely related to the second point, if greatest responsibility is to be used to delineate the boundaries of the power that the Tribunal prosecutors enjoy, that purpose should be stated explicitly. Although it seems unlikely, if there is another purpose for employing such language going beyond limiting prosecutorial wiggle room, that purpose too would ideally be stated. Indeed, it may be wise to include a provision discussing the relationship and link between the personal jurisdiction article and the limitations to the prosecutorial mandate. This would help to avoid unnecessary hurdles during trials of the suspects and arguments that the prosecution lacks the power to make choices as to whom to prosecute from among a wide range of potential perpetrators. The obviousness of that position did not make the task of the SCSL prosecutors any less challenging. At the least, these points and intersections should be discussed in the founding documents and a clear position taken to guide the later interpreters of the text.

Fourth, though not discussed in this chapter per se, to put the matter beyond any doubt, consideration should also be given to clarifying that the judges possess *ex proprio motu*[206] power to review whether the prosecution has fulfilled the personal jurisdiction and other requirements when making a prima facie case. It is the duty of the judges to ensure fair trials that respect the rights of the accused take place in a given criminal case. It is therefore not enough for them to abdicate this function of deciding who falls within the jurisdiction solely to the prosecution, as one chamber effectively did at the SCSL, by holding that the judges were not empowered to review the choices made by the prosecutorial organ. This wrongly implied that the chamber was simply there to rubber stamp the prosecutorial *allegations* in an indictment that someone is among those bearing greatest responsibility for the atrocities committed during a particular conflict.

Fifth, the drafters of statutes, especially at the United Nations Office of Legal Affairs, should explicitly consider stating the consequences of a finding that personal jurisdictional requirements had either been fulfilled or not. What standard should apply to determine that it had been fulfilled, and at what stages of the trials? If the threshold is not fulfilled, what should happen? Would the tribunal have to release the defendant, and if so, should this be with or without prejudice to the prosecution? Given the Sierra Leone experience, it may also be helpful to indicate whether any such determinations require factual assessments of evidence or are purely legal questions to be considered by the judges even before the Prosecution calls any witnesses. If factual assessments are required, then the stage of the trial at which the point should be considered should be delineated keeping in mind the appropriate standard of proof. If it is a legal assessment, that too should guide how the claims can be made, using what evidentiary burden, before reaching the legal conclusion.

---

[206] *Of one's own accord*, BLACK'S LAW DICTIONARY (9th ed., 2009).

These fundamental concerns need some answers. While they cannot always be addressed in the statute, as a practical matter, they could form part of the drafting history of the relevant tribunal's instruments.

Finally, while this chapter has observed that the ICC Prosecutor has adopted the "greatest responsibility" standard to guide her prosecutorial policy, it may be worth noting that the concern about personal jurisdiction does not arise there in the same way as it did at the SCSL. Although the structure and content of the Rome Statute makes this rather difficult, it may be only a matter of time for a creative defendant to argue that he should not be prosecuted because he is not among those bearing greatest responsibility for what happened in a given conflict. Fortunately, the phrase "greatest responsibility," though widely used in ICC prosecutorial practice, is not included in the ICC Statute in the same way it was in the founding document of the SCSL. Its use in the permanent tribunal is therefore purely a function of prosecutorial policy, which, although logical, could also be changed at any time without requiring any amendments to the Rome Statute. Interestingly, though this will not be pursued here, the use of a gravity threshold, in the ICC Statute, might well provoke similar types of concerns as greatest responsibility. In any event if we return to greatest responsibility, a function of prosecutorial policy, defendants should not be able to rely on the phrase to mount a jurisdictional challenge, at least one that would cause the same type of difficulties for the Court as occurred in Sierra Leone. If a defendant did, it would presumably be relatively easy for the pre-trial or trial chambers to resolve the issue on the ground that the prosecutorial policy is mere policy, rather than a statutory requirement. Such clarity would undoubtedly benefit from the important judicial contribution and legacy of the SCSL on this important question of greatest responsibility personal jurisdiction in international criminal law.

6

Forced Marriage As a Crime Against Humanity

6.1 INTRODUCTION

In times of civil war and conflict, women and children are often the most victimized. The women and girls living in Sierra Leone during the conflict were no exception. A 2002 study conducted by Physicians for Human Rights estimated that, during the conflict, between 50,000 to 64,000 women and girls experienced war-related sexual violence.[1] Sexual violence against women can take various forms including rape, sexual slavery, enforced prostitution, and forced pregnancy.[2] Historically, the commission of crimes targeting women such as rape in conflicts have been generally treated as inevitable or trivialized. This notwithstanding some national instruments, such as the Instructions of the Government of Armies of the United States during the American civil war in 1863, which prohibited rape by soldiers under penalty of death or such other severe punishment as may seem adequate for the gravity of the offense. During the maiden effort to prosecute persons for international crimes in the immediate aftermath of World War II, rape was entered into the language of record during the Nuremberg Trials though nowhere mentioned in the Nuremberg Indictment or Judgment.[3]

The gendered crimes prevalent in historical and contemporary conflicts have only recently been acknowledged as international crimes, such as crimes against humanity and war crimes, prosecutable in international tribunals like the International Tribunal for the Former Yugoslavia (ICTY), the International Criminal Tribunal for Rwanda (ICTR) and the Special Court for Sierra Leone (SCSL). But there has been some progress shedding even more light on the phenomenon. In this regard, it is notable that, in 2005, the United Nations General Assembly in the World Summit

---

[1] Physicians for Human Rights, *War-Related Sexual Violence in Sierra Leone*, at 3–4 (2002).
[2] Agreement between the United Nations and the Government of Sierra Leone on the establishment of a Special Court for Sierra Leone, Jan. 16, 2002, 2178 U.N.T.S. 137 [hereinafter UN-Sierra Leone Agreement] Annexed to the U.N.-Sierra Leone Agreement was the Statute of the Special Court for Sierra Leone [hereinafter SCSL Statute].
[3] Beth Van Schaack, *Engendering Genocide: The Akayesu Case Before the International Criminal Tribunal for Rwanda*, SANTA CLARA LAW DIGITAL COMMONS, 14 (2008).

Outcome[4] condemned all forms of violence against women and girls, during and after conflicts, and resolved to end impunity in relation to them. In 2008, the United Nations Security Council also unanimously adopted Resolution 1820, recognizing for the first time, sexual violence as a tactic of warfare and importantly also as a serious threat to international peace and security.[5]

The recent acknowledgment by the international community in international criminal tribunals recognizing and prosecuting gender-based violence crimes has been strongly driven by the contributions of national and international women's rights advocacy groups. In 2010, the UN established the United Nations Office of the Special Representative of the Secretary-General on Sexual Violence in Conflict (SRSG-SVC). The establishment of this office was a significant development in the fight against impunity for conflict-related sexual violence, as it strengthens the UN efforts in this area. The UN Secretary-General, in his 2019 report on conflict-related sexual violence, stated that since 2010 there has been a paradigm shift in the world's understanding of the crime of sexual violence in conflict.[6] This demonstrated that the international community has begun to embrace the concept of conflict-related sexual violence and move away from the traditional regard that sexual violence was a reproductive health or a development issue.[7]

This recognition has not come without decades of frequent criticism towards the operation of the international legal system and its largely male organizational and normative structure. The recognition of gender-based crimes has come after a long period in which men primarily dominated the international legal field. A gender critique started to emerge in reaction to the International Bill of Rights,[8] enacted after World War II.[9] An earlier gender critique arose at the historic San Francisco Conference of August 1945, when the United Nations Charter was finalized, signed, and adopted. Out of the 850 delegates that were present for that historic occasion, only eight were reported to be women. Ironically, it was the United Nations Charter which recognized the principle that human rights and fundamental freedoms should be enjoyed by everyone without distinction as to sex;[10] marking a decisive break with the longstanding position of women as lacking in full legal and civil capacity. Despite the promise of their full recognition in the United Nations Charter,[11] from the

---

[4] G.A. Res. 60/1, 2005 World Summit Outcome (Sept. 16, 2005).

[5] S.C. Res. 1820 (June 19, 2008); STEPHEN SHUTE & S. L. HURLEY, ON HUMAN RIGHTS: THE OXFORD AMNESTY LECTURES 85 (1993).

[6] U.N. Secretary-General, *Conflict related sexual violence*, ¶ 2, U.N. Doc. S/2019/280 (Mar. 29, 2019).

[7] U.N. Secretary-General, *Report of the Secretary-General on the implementation of Security Council resolutions 1820 (2008) and 1888 (2009)*, ¶ 6, U.N. Doc. A/65/592*-S/2010/604* (Nov. 24, 2010).

[8] G.A. Res. 217 (III) A, (Dec. 10, 1948) [hereinafter Universal Declaration of Human Rights]; International Covenant on Civil and Political Rights, Dec. 16, 1966, 999 U.N.T.S. 171; International Covenant on Economic, Social and Cultural Rights, Dec. 16, 1966, 993 U.N.T.S. 3.

[9] Marie-Bénédicte Dembour, *Critiques [in] International Human Rights Law*, in INTERNATIONAL HUMAN RIGHTS LAW 41 (Daniel Moeckli et al. eds., 3d ed. 2017).

[10] U.N. Charter art. 1, ¶ 3.

[11] U.N. Charter art. 1, ¶ 3; Universal Declaration of Human Rights, *supra* note 8, at art. 1.

standpoint of the development of international criminal law, the notion of criminal responsibility continued to be at risk of bypassing the concerns and interests of women.

Sexual violence impacting women has typically been invisible to international criminal law, which is why the relatively recent recognition of gender-based crimes is significant. Feminist legal scholars, for example Charlesworth, Chinkin, and Wright, among many others, have challenged both the structures of international lawmaking and the substantive content of the rules of international law, generally criticizing the pretense of gender equality.[12] An important feature of the gender critique of international law is the often referred to 'paradox of feminism', depicting the question of whether women's rights are best recognized and protected through general norms that treat women the same as men, or through specific norms applicable only to women.[13] The paradox is aimed at forcing us to ask hard questions about how women's inclusion as full subjects of the universal regime of international law can be achieved.

The efforts that have been made thus far to raise awareness of and the need to address the general marginalization of women have been successful in several respects. In the work of the international tribunals, a greater awareness of the gendered dimension to conflict has led to the investigation and prosecution of cases that also address liability to the perpetrators of sexual violence on women. The willingness of prosecutors to address such hitherto unnoticed crimes is exemplified by the jurisprudence of the SCSL concerning the novel crime of "forced marriage" as a crime against humanity. The notion of forced marriage, as part of the "other inhumane acts" category of crimes against humanity, can be assessed against whether it constitutes a jurisprudential contribution of the tribunal to the development of international criminal law. The issue of forced marriage, which generated much controversy within the tribunal during the trials, will be the focus of the present chapter.

6.2 THE PURPOSE AND STRUCTURE OF THIS CHAPTER

This chapter aims to provide an analysis of the *Armed Forces Revolutionary Council* (AFRC), *Revolutionary United Front* (RUF), *Civil Defense Forces* (CDF), and *Taylor* cases at the SCSL, and the implication of their judgments on future cases and tribunals in relation to the crime against humanity of forced marriage as part of the residual category of "other inhumane acts" criminalized under Article 2(i) of the Statute of the SCSL. In the main, I aim to demonstrate that the SCSL has made important contributions to addressing the gendered nature of some crimes witnessed in Sierra Leone by focusing on acts of sexual violence and other practices targeting

[12] Hilary Charlesworth, Christine Chinkin, & Shelley Wright, *Feminist Approaches to International Law*, 85 Am. J. Int'l L. 615, 615 (1991).

[13] Hilary Charlesworth, *Not Waiving but Drowning – Gender Mainstreaming and Human Rights*, 18 Harv. Hum. Rts J. 1, 2 (2005).

women; but that the process of doing so was characterized by confusion in the manner in which the (a) crime of "forced marriage" as a crime against humanity was charged by the Prosecution and its relationship to already existing crimes found in the SCSL Statute; (b) how the trial chamber judges addressed it with one chamber rejecting the charges (in the *CDF* case) with another accepting them (in the *AFRC* and *RUF* cases); (c) how the issues and disagreements of the trial level judges were resolved by the Appeals Chamber as the authoritative body to interpret the law of the SCSL; and lastly, (d) the inherent limits/risks that arise when judges consciously attempt, even if for morally compelling reasons, to develop the law if not legislate from the bench. The latter could prove to be problematic as judges enter into new territory to ensure victims were provided justice while also being mandated to ensure that the rights of the Accused to a fair trial under Article 17 of the SCSL Statute and under international human rights treaties were not violated.

The chapter will proceed as follows. Section 6.3 of this chapter will begin by discussing the wider context addressing prior efforts to prosecute gender crimes in the ad hoc international criminal tribunals. I then turn to the historical background of marriage under Sierra Leone law and international law and a brief discussion on the use and sexual abuse of women during the Sierra Leone conflict. Section 6.4 will discuss the *AFRC, RUF, CDF,* and *Taylor* cases and the Prosecution's shift to charging "forced marriage" and the subsequent opposition expressed by the Defense through objections to the "forced marriage" Indictments. Section 6.5 will address the key legal issues that arose in relation to the charges of "forced marriage" in comparison to acts of sexual violence and sexual slavery, and how those elements contributed to the Court's holding that "forced marriage" constituted a crime against humanity under the residual category of "Other Inhumane Acts." This section will also analyze the implications of the *AFRC* case on subsequent international jurisprudence in the International Criminal Court (ICC), ICTY, ICTR, and Extraordinary Chambers in the Courts of Cambodia (ECCC) cases. Section 6.6 concludes.

6.3 BACKGROUND

To properly understand and appreciate the landmark cases of the SCSL, on forced marriage as a crime against humanity, three preceding cases which in a way paved the way for the SCSL judgment must first be reviewed.

First, the case of *Akayesu* at the ICTR.[14] Akayesu was the mayor of the Taba Commune in Rwanda. He gave orders which helped facilitate the atrocities that occurred in Taba during the genocide in Rwanda in 1994.[15] At the time of the Indictment, the ICTR Prosecutor estimated Akayesu contributed to the murder of at least 2,000 individuals within the Taba Commune between April and June 1994.[16]

---

[14] Prosecutor v. Akayesu, Case No. ICTR-96-4-I, Judgment (Sept. 2, 1998).

[15] Van Schaack, *supra* note 3, at 1.

[16] *Id.* at 5.

Although now known as one of the leading cases for the prosecution of sexual violence in the time of conflict, it might come as a surprise that the initial Indictment of Akayesu did not include allegations of sexual violence. The element of sexual violence arose almost accidently when a witness was testifying about the violence that occurred in the Taba Commune and off-handedly mentioned that her then six-year old daughter had been raped by three men.[17]

In response to this admission by the witness, nearly forty NGOs rallied to submit an *amicus brief* to the Trial Chamber petitioning for a thorough investigation into sexual violence crimes conducted during the Rwanda Genocide.[18] Subsequently, the Prosecution determined through an independent investigation, that it would request the Trial Chamber to allow for an amended Indictment to include crimes of sexual violence perpetrated against displaced civilian Tutsi women and girls who were seeking refuge at the bureau communal in Taba.[19] The Prosecution added the multiple acts of sexual violence which affected the victims' physical and psychological health as "a predicate act of genocide, although it had not expressly sought, or received, leave to do so."[20] The day after the Indictment was amended, by decision of the Trial Chamber, to include charges under Article 3(g) (rape as a crime against humanity), Article 3(i)(other inhumane acts as crimes against humanity), and Article 4(e)(outrages upon personal dignity, in particular humiliating and degrading treatment, rape, enforced prostitution, and any form of indecent assault) of the ICTR Statute, the Prosecution brought its first witness to testify regarding the sexual violence encountered by Tutsi women at the Taba Commune. This testimony of the Prosecution's six witnesses described attacks of rape, gang rape, and murder. The Accused was aware of or was a witness to such incidents.[21] The Defense argued that the charges of sexual violence had been brought as a result of public pressure. They claimed that the charges were unsupported by credible evidence. They brought witnesses who alternatively claimed that the Accused did not take part in the attacks, had no control over the attacks, and could not stop the crimes from occurring.[22]

The Trial Chamber ultimately found Akayesu guilty of rape under the category of crimes against humanity of "Other Inhumane Acts" as well as "outrages upon personal dignity" and "serious mental or bodily harm."[23] The Trial Chamber also simultaneously produced the first definition of rape and sexual violence which would be used in future cases to progress the prosecution of some gender-based crimes in conflicts.[24] In justifying the holding, the Chamber ruled that rape "could constitute genocide as '[s]exual violence was a step in the process of destruction of

---

[17] *Id.* at 7.
[18] *Id.* at 8.
[19] *Id.* at 11; Prosecutor v. Akayesu, Case No. ICTR-96-4-I, Amended Indictment (June 17, 1997).
[20] Prosecutor v. Akayesu, Case No. ICTR-96-4-I, Amended Indictment (June 17, 1997).
[21] Van Schaack, *supra* note 3, at 12.
[22] *Id.* at 13.
[23] *Id.* at 20.
[24] *Id.* at 20.

the Tutsi group – destruction of the spirit, of the will to live, and of life itself."[25] This case was the first major step in the progressive development of the recognition and prosecution of gender-based crimes, which would lay the groundwork for additional cases to follow.

The second case which contributed to the progressive development of the prosecution of gender-based crimes is *Delalic* at the ICTY.[26] The Trial Chamber indicted Zejnil Delalic, Zdravko Mucic (Pavo), and Hazim Delic, Esad Landzo (Zenga) on forty-nine counts of various international crimes.[27] Most significantly, in this case, the Accused were charged with the war crime of rape as a form of torture in violation of Article 3(1)(a) of the Geneva Convention.[28] The Prosecution argued that the Trial Chamber should apply the standard given in the 1984 Convention against Torture and other Cruel, Inhuman, or Degrading Treatment of Punishment, as this definition required the application of the broader customary international law instead of the narrow definition found in the Fourth Geneva Convention.[29] The Prosecution aimed for the latter definition as it established that the crime of torture could be found in more scenarios than those in which the intent of torture was solely to elicit information.[30] The Prosecution further argued that the issue of rape as torture in Yugoslavia was used on a mass scale with the purpose of "punishing victims and/or intimidating community" and it was not used to exclusively illicit information.[31]

The Defense responded that the application of customary international law definition of torture was not widespread practice and should be construed narrowly, as the expansion of such a definition would violate the rights of the Accused under the principle *nullum crimen sine lege*.[32] The Defense further argued that the definition should not be expanded to include the crime of rape as torture as the "prohibited purpose" was already established and should be interpreted in favor of the Accused.[33]

The Trial Chamber held that, although an internationally condemned act, there was a limited attempt to articulate the exact definition of the crime of torture.[34] The Trial Chamber found that the definition of torture presented by the Prosecution did constitute customary international law.[35] The Trial Chamber further established that there were two elements of torture: (1) a level of severity and (2) a prohibited

---

[25]   *Id.* at 21.
[26]   Prosecutor v. Delalic, Case No. IT-96-21-T, Judgment, ¶495 (Int'l Crim. Trib. for the Former Yugoslavia Nov. 16, 1988).
[27]   *Id.* at ¶ 2.
[28]   *Id.* at ¶ 440.
[29]   *Id.*
[30]   *Id.* at ¶ 447.
[31]   *Id.* at ¶ 448.
[32]   *Id.* at ¶ 449.
[33]   *Id.* at ¶ 451.
[34]   *Id.* at ¶ 455.
[35]   *Id.*

purpose.[36] While establishing these elements the Trial Chamber made a substantial point in the prosecution of rape as torture:

> A fundamental distinction regarding the purpose for which torture is inflicted is that between a "prohibited purpose" and one which is purely private. The rationale behind this distinction is that the prohibition on torture is not concerned with private conduct, which is ordinarily sanctioned under national law. In particular, rape and other sexual assaults have often been labelled as "private", thus precluding them from being punished under national or international law. However, such conduct could meet the purposive requirements of torture as, during armed conflicts, the purposive elements of intimidation, coercion, punishment or discrimination can often be integral components of behavior, thus bringing the relevant conduct within the definition.[37]

The Trial Chamber reasoned that the definition of rape established in the *Akayesu*[38] judgment was in fact the correct definition to be used in these proceedings. Further, the Trial Chamber analyzed the definition of rape in light of recent international practice at the Inter-American Court of Human Rights, which acknowledged that rape not only had physical consequences for victims but also created psychological and social consequences.[39] The Trial Chamber ultimately held "the rape of any person to be a despicable act which strikes at the very core of human dignity and physical integrity"[40] and that the act of rape by an official or by "acquiescence of an official" could, during times of armed conflict, "involve punishment, coercion, discrimination or intimidation," which amount to the crime of rape or other sexual violence as torture.[41]

The third major case that contributed to the SCSL judgments is the *Kunarac* case, which was also heard at the ICTY, under which it was recognized that the crime of rape could amount to a crime against humanity and also expanded the definition of rape and consent. There were multiple charges against the three Accused including torture as a war crime, and significantly, rape as a crime against humanity.[42] When first assessing if the crime of rape amounted to a crime against humanity the Trial Chamber examined the definitions of rape in *Furundizija*.[43] The Trial Chamber agreed with the definition

---

[36]   *Id.* at ¶ 470.

[37]   *Id.* at ¶ 471.

[38]   Prosecutor v. Akayesu, Case No. ICTR-96-4-I, Judgment (Sept. 2, 1998).

[39]   Prosecutor v. Delalic, Case No. IT-96-21-T, Judgment, ¶ 486 (Int'l Crim. Trib. for the Former Yugoslavia Nov. 16, 1988).

[40]   *Id.* at ¶ 495.

[41]   *Id.* at ¶¶ 494–96.

[42]   Prosecutor v. Kunarac, Case No. IT-96-23-PT, Amended Indictment (Int'l Crim. Trib. for the Former Yugoslavia Nov. 8, 1999).

[43]   Prosecutor v. Furundžija, Case No. IT-95-17/1-T, Judgment, ¶ 185 (Int'l Crim. Trib. for the Former Yugoslavia Dec. 10, 1998) (finding that the *actus reus* of the crime of rape are "(i) the sexual penetration, however slight: (a) of the vagina or anus of the victim by the penis or the perpetrator or any other object used by the perpetrator; or (b) of the mouth of the victim by the penis of the perpetrator; (ii) by coercion or force of threat of force against the victim or a third person.'");

of rape provided in *Furundizija*, and also expanded the requirement by noting that "[c]onsent for this purpose must be consent given voluntarily, as a result of the victim's free will, assessed in the context of the surrounding circumstance."[44] The Trial Chamber also held that the *mens rea* for the crime was the "intention to effect this sexual penetration, and the knowledge that it occurs without the consent of the victim."[45] This new expansive definition of rape would be used in future cases at both the trial chambers and in other ad hoc tribunals.[46] All the above cases, by spotlighting gendered crimes, laid a foundation which would later allow the AFRC Appeals Chamber to determine that the conduct labelled as "forced marriage" which was prevalent in Sierra Leone during the war amounted to a crime against humanity.

6.3.1 *Marriage under Sierra Leonean and International Law*

Marriage is a complex social institution. The rules that regulate it may differ, depending on the context. National and international law may apply, and in some cases, have substantial overlap. Norms that may apply in peacetime, as in arranged marriages, may be manipulated for the sake of expediency. Those must be distinguished from those that apply during wartime. In Sierra Leone, there are eighteen ethnic groups whose different history, cultural, and religious practices have resulted in a pluralistic legal system.[47] The Sierra Leonean legal system constitutes of three coexisting systems of law: general law, Islamic law, and customary law.[48] Thus, marriage law has to be examined from the standpoint of either legal regime, depending on the ethnic group to which the person belongs. The majority of the population are governed by customary law pertaining to their particular group, or by Islamic law, while the common law, which was inherited from the United Kingdom, is primarily applied in Freetown – the largest city in the country and also the country's capital and official seat of government.[49]

Under the general legal system, the Christian Marriage Act[50] and the Civil Marriage Act[51] are governing marriage laws. In both the Civil and Christian

Prosecutor v. Kunarac, Case No. IT-96–23-PT, Judgment, ¶¶ 437–438 (Int'l Crim. Trib. for the Former Yugoslavia Feb. 22, 2001).

44 Prosecutor v. Kunarac, Case No. IT-96–23-PT, Judgment, ¶ 460 (Int'l Crim. Trib. for the Former Yugoslavia Feb. 22, 2001).

45 *Id.*

46 Patricia Viseur Sellers, *The Prosecution of Sexual Violence in Conflict: The Importance of Human Rights as Means of Interpretation*, at 21, www.un.org/ruleoflaw/files/Paper_Prosecution_of_Sexual_Violence[1].pdf.

47 Human Rights Watch, *"We'll Kill You If You Cry" Sexual Violence in the Sierra Leone Conflict*, Vol. 15, No. 1 (A) (Jan. 2003).

48 Ida E. P. Lisk & Bernadette L. Williams, *Marriage and Divorce Regulation and Recognition in Sierra Leone*, 29 FAM. L. Q. 655, 665 (1995).

49 *Id.*

50 Christian Marriage Act 1907, ch. 96 (Sierra Leone).

51 Civil Marriage Act 1910, ch. 97 (Sierra Leone).

Marriage Acts, monogamous marriages are provided for, and mutual consent of the husband and wife is required.[52] Islamic law has also been recognized by statute in Sierra Leone in relation to marriage, inheritance, and divorce among Muslims and marriage under Islamic Law is governed under the Mohammedan Marriage Act.[53] For all civil purposes, the marriages which are valid under the Islamic law are recognized and provided registration as a means of proof of marriage. The Mohammedan Act does not provide much for the regulation of Islamic marriages and no consent requirement is mentioned in the Act. Under Islamic law, a husband is permitted to have up to four wives. Customary law refers to laws governing the various ethnic groups in the country and does not provide uniform rules or procedures governing marriage, which hence vary from one ethnic group to another. Tribal councils of elders and chiefs generally apply customary law in local courts.[54] Some general notes can however be made.

Traditionally, for a valid customary law marriage, both the parties and their families must have expressed consent along with other marriage formalities.[55] Customary law traditionally contemplates for the woman to hold an inferior status in relation to the husband which will vary depending on contextual and cultural circumstances. A valid marriage under customary law generally results in the transference of the rights to the domestic, procreative, and sexual services of a women from her family, to her becoming husband and his family. Furthermore, customary law recognizes polygamy and a common feature of customary law marriage is the requirement of a bridal price from the groom's family to the prospective bride's family.[56] The entering into every Sierra Leonean marriage, regardless of the legal regime, is carried out with the fulfillment of certain ceremonies and rituals relating to the marriage, manifesting the required ceremonial passage for the marriage's validation.

Under national law, the Child Rights Act 2007, which was enacted into law several years after the end of the conflict, requires that the minimum age of marriage of whatever kind shall be eighteen years.[57] To the contrary, the Customary Marriage and Divorce Act 2009,[58] allows customary marriages with persons under eighteen years old with parental consent. No minimum age in regard to this exception is stated in the Customary Marriage and Divorce Act 2009. By 2030, Sierra Leone has committed to eliminate child, early, and forced traditional marriage in line with target 5.3 of the Sustainable Development Goals.[59]

---

[52] Christian Marriage Act 1907, ch. 96, § 6(2)(b) (Sierra Leone).
[53] The Mohammedan Marriage Act 1960, ch. 96 (Sierra Leone).
[54] Pamela O. Davies, *Marriage, Divorce and Inheritance Laws in Sierra Leone and Their Discriminatory Effects on Women*, 12 Hum. Rts. Brief 17, 18 (2005).
[55] Lisk & Williams, *supra* note 48, at 661.
[56] *Id.* at 660; Davies, *supra* note 54, at 19.
[57] The Child Rights Act 2007, art. 34(1) (Sierra Leone).
[58] The Customary Marriage and Divorce Act 2009, art. 2(2) (Sierra Leone).
[59] Ministry of Finance and Economic Development, Adaptation of the Goals in Sierra Leone Progress Report, at 30 (2016), https://sustainabledevelopment.un.org/content/documents/10720sierraleone.pdf.

Under international law, marriage law is closely connected to the right to family, which is understood to be "the natural and fundamental group unit of society and is entitled to protection by society and the State," pursuant to article 16(3) Universal Declaration of Human Rights (UDHR).[60] Family life is recognized as a fundamental right in international law, enunciated in major international instruments and conventions, such as the International Covenant on Civil and Political Rights[61] and in the International Covenant on Economic, Social and Cultural Rights.[62] These provisions of international law relating to marriage, forming part of the global bill of rights, are joined by the Convention on the Elimination of All Forms of Discrimination against Women[63] and the Convention on Consent to Marriage, Minimum Age for Marriage and Registration of Marriages.[64] The family and the right to marriage is granted broad protection by international law which dictates the right to marriage without discrimination and with the distinct requirement of the free and full consent. Forced marriage violates the independently recognized basic right to consensually marry and establish a family[65] and international and regional instruments forbid discrimination on the basis of sex in the implementation of the right to marriage and explicitly expresses the requirement of consent.

In this regard, Article 10(1) of the International Covenant on Economic, Social and Cultural Rights states that "[t]he States Parties to the present Covenant recognize that ... Marriage must be entered into with the free consent of the intending spouses."[66]

Article 23(3) of the International Covenant on Civil and Political Rights states that: "... No marriage shall be entered into without the free and full consent of the intending spouses."[67]

The regional convention, the African Charter on Human and People's Rights, recognizes various rights relating to the family. It provides in Article 18 that:

1. The family shall be the natural unit and basis of society. It shall be protected by the State which shall take care of its physical health and moral.

---

[60] Universal Declaration of Human Rights, *supra* note 8, at art. 16 (3).
[61] International Covenant on Civil and Political Rights art. 10, Dec. 16, 1966, 999 U.N.T.S. 171.
[62] International Covenant on Economic, Social and Cultural Rights, Dec. 16, 1966, 993 U.N.T.S. 3.
[63] Convention on the Elimination of All Forms of Discrimination against Women, Dec. 18, 1979, 1249 U.N.T.S. 13.
[64] Convention on Consent to Marriage, Minimum Age of Marriage and Registration of Marriages, Nov. 7, 1962, 521 U.N.T.S. 231.
[65] International Covenant on Civil and Political Rights art. 23, Dec. 16, 1966, 999 U.N.T.S. 171; Universal Declaration on Human Rights, *supra* note 8, at art. 16; Convention on the Elimination of All Forms of Discrimination against Women art. 16, Dec. 18, 1979, 1249 U.N.T.S. 13.
[66] International Covenant on Economic, Social and Cultural Rights art. 10(1), Dec. 16, 1966, 993 U.N. T.S. 3.
[67] International Covenant on Civil and Political Rights art. 23(3), Dec. 16, 1966, 999 U.N.T.S. 171.

2. The State shall have the duty to assist the family which is the custodian of morals and traditional values recognized by the community.
3. The State shall ensure the elimination of every discrimination against women and also ensure the protection of the rights of the woman and the child as stipulated in international declarations and conventions.
4. The aged and the disabled shall also have the right to special measures of protection in keeping with their physical or moral needs.

The Protocol to the African Charter on Human and Peoples' Rights on the Rights of Women in Africa expands upon women's right to marry, including the right not to be married without their full and free consent to do so in Article 6, albeit at the minimum age of eighteen, with the right to register under national law in order to secure legal recognition, as well as the right – like for husbands – to have a nationality or to acquire it through marriage both for herself and her children as well as to acquire and hold property. Sierra Leone is a party to all the major universal human rights and regional instruments. Some of these instruments, such as most aspects of the Universal Declaration of Human Rights, are considered part of customary international law and will be binding as such. Many of the same rights are enshrined in the Sierra Leone Constitution and reflected in a number of cases in other national legislation. It would flow from the brief review above that, under international human rights and Sierra Leonean law, the rules of marriage require consent for one person to take another person as a spouse. The same is true of the cultural practice of arranged marriage, which though often ceremonial and distinct from the legal requirements, relies on the consent of the two concerned families. In the tradition of just about all Sierra Leonean ethnic groups, a marriage would only take place if the parties concerned first give their consent either directly or indirectly through their families. Thus, as the next section of this chapter will show, the experiences that women had during the war constituted an aberration, a betrayal of the traditional rules or formalities of marriage in Sierra Leone. The type of conduct prosecuted by the SCSL, with women forced to marry men, goes well beyond what tradition allowed and is in fact criminal under both national and international law.

6.3.2 *Sexually Using and Abusing Women during the Sierra Leone Conflict*

In this section, I provide a brief discussion regarding the sexual abuse of women during the Sierra Leone conflict. That said, it should be noted that the brief background is not likely to exhaustively cover the sociocultural and historical context in which the events of the civil war in Sierra Leone unfolded. Some of the general historical context has been discussed in an earlier chapter of this book.

Below, only a brief summary of certain relevant highlights that relate to this chapter are provided.

In April 1961, Sierra Leone, a former British colony, became an independent State within the Commonwealth. After its independence and for most of the three next decades, Sierra Leone was governed by the All People's Congress (APC) which established a one-party State in 1978. Despite its rich natural resources, especially diamonds, gold, and bauxite, Sierra Leone experienced economic decline during the 1980s as a result of corruption and nepotism under the APC regime.[68] Frustration with government corruption and fiscal mismanagement led to the formation of the RUF which aimed to overthrow the APC. The difficulties in the country were compounded in March 1991 when the armed fighters of the RUF attacked Sierra Leone from Liberia, triggering the civil war that was to last ten years.[69] The civil war was complex, featuring a number of armed groups which formed alliances with each other and also experienced internal divisions and fracturing.[70]

During the conflict, widely thought to be one of the worst in Africa in recent memory, egregious crimes against civilians took place. There is reliable evidence that rape and other forms of sexual violence were rampant throughout the civil war.[71] Disturbing reports of incidents by both rebel forces and government troops revealed the common occurrence of widespread rape and abduction of women and girls, subjecting them to repeated acts of rape and other forms of sexual violence and sexual slavery.[72] The Truth and Reconciliation Commission (TRC) of Sierra Leone, which was established as part of the peace arrangement concluded in July 1999 that helped to bring the war to an end, found that perpetrators singled out women and children for some of the most brutal violations of human rights recorded in any conflict pointing out that some of the victims were as young as ten years old.[73] Other human rights violations included other forms of sexual violence, killings, forced pregnancy, enforced sterilization, slave labor, amputations, torture, trafficking, mutilations, and forced cannibalism.[74]

---

[68] Prosecutor v. Taylor, Case No. SCSL-03-01-T-1283, Judgment, ¶ 20 (May 18, 2012).

[69] BRITANNICA ACADEMIC ENCYCLOPEDIA, "SIERRA LEONE", academic-eb-com.ludwig.lub.lu.se/levels/col legiate/article/Sierra-Leone/110795.

[70] Prosecutor v. Taylor, Case No. SCSL-03-01-T-1283, Judgment, ¶ 19 (May 18, 2012).

[71] SIERRA LEONE TRUTH & RECONCILIATION REPORT, WITNESS TO TRUTH: REPORT OF THE SIERRA LEONE TRUTH & RECONCILIATION COMMISSION (vol. 2, 2004).

[72] BRITANNICA ACADEMIC ENCYCLOPEDIA, "SIERRA LEONE", academic-eb-com.ludwig.lub.lu.se/levels/col legiate/article/Sierra-Leone/110795.

[73] SIERRA LEONE TRUTH & RECONCILIATION REPORT, WITNESS TO TRUTH: REPORT OF THE SIERRA LEONE TRUTH & RECONCILIATION COMMISSION ¶¶ 503–04 (vol. 2, 2004).

[74] *Id.* at ¶ 497.

In the *AFRC* case, the SCSL Trial Chamber II heard expert testimony in 2005 from Mrs Zainab Bangura and Dr Dorte Thorsen on the issue of forced marriage.[75] In the *AFRC* Trial, the expert evidence that was used to assist the Trial Chamber in its understanding and characterization of "forced marriage" in Sierra Leone, stated in their description of West African traditional marriages that girls and young women are commonly coerced into arranged marriage by the bride and groom's kin and "seniors."[76] According to the Thorsen report, the practice is not universal, and men and women also marry a person of their own choice.[77] The reports explained that arranged marriages entail the involvement and agreement of the families and seniors of the prospective bride and groom, in particular the approval of the family of the female spouse, as well as the fulfillment of certain ceremonies and rituals relating to the marriage.[78]

Distinct from the well-established cultural tradition of arranged marriage during times of peace was a separate phenomenon constituting the forceful abduction and holding of women and girls in captivity. The latter phenomenon, which became common during the civil war, were forced marriages under which women and girls, without consent or choice, would be taken as so-called "bush wives" or "rebel wives." Importantly, both experts made clear distinctions between the practices described as arranged or traditional marriages, and the forced marriages that had taken place in the course of the conflict.[79] So did the judges. Justice Sebutinde, in her concurring opinion in the *AFRC* Trial Judgment, emphasized the difference between arranged marriages the violations of which could constitute breach of human rights law and the engagement in the egregious type of conduct that is *criminal* in nature and would attract the individual criminal responsibility of the perpetrator. The latter was being alleged as the phenomenon of "forced marriage," described as "the forceful abduction and holding in captivity of women and girls ('bush wives') against their will, for purposes of sexual gratification of their 'bush husbands' and for gender-specific forms of labor including cooking cleaning, washing clothes (conjugal duties)."[80] However, as discussed in the next part, the phenomenon of "forced marriage" as charged in the indictment came to be handled differently in the separate cases heard before the SCSL.

---

[75]   Prosecutor v. Brima, Case No. SCSL-04-16-T, Prosecution Filing of Expert Report Pursuant to Rule 94(*bis*) and Decision on Prosecution Request for Leave to Call an Additional Expert Witness (Aug. 8, 2005); Prosecutor v. Brima, Case No. SCSL-2004-16-T, Joint Defence Disclosure of Expert Report on Forced Marriages by Dr. Dorte Thorsen (Aug. 21, 2006).

[76]   Prosecutor v. Brima, Case No. SCSL-2004-16-T, Joint Defence Disclosure of Expert Report on Forced Marriages by Dr. Dorte Thorsen (Aug. 21, 2006).

[77]   Prosecutor v. Brima, Case No. SCSL-04-16-T, Partly Dissenting Opinion of Justice Doherty on Counts 7 (Sexual Slavery) and 8 (Forced Marriages), ¶ 25 (June 20, 2007).

[78]   *Id.* at ¶ 26.

[79]   *Id.* at ¶ 36.

[80]   Prosecutor v. Brima, Case No. SCSL-04-16-T, Concurring Opinion of Justice Sebutinde, ¶ 12 (June 20, 2007).

6.4 THE PROSECUTION'S EFFORTS TO CHARGE FORCED MARRIAGE AS A CRIME AGAINST HUMANITY AND THE DEFENSE CHALLENGES TO THE INDICTMENTS

6.4.1 *The* AFRC *Case*

On 20 June 2007, the SCSL Trial Chamber provided one of the most substantial rulings on "forced marriage" to date. Although the finding concerning "forced marriage" as an "other inhumane act" of crimes against humanity would be later reversed at the Appeals Chamber, the holding of the Trial Chamber provides an inside look as to the initial view of the SCSL on this gender-based crime. The case *Prosecutor v. Brima*[81] (AFRC case) was a joint trial of Alex Tamba Brima, Brima Bazzy Kamara, and Santigie Borbor Kanu for multiple counts of war crimes, crimes against humanity, and other serious violations of international humanitarian law. Among the multitude of international crimes committed during the Sierra Leone conflict was the first charge of "forced marriage" as a crime against humanity under Article 2(i) "Other Inhumane Acts."[82]

The first hurdle of this charge of "forced marriage" was faced when the Prosecution attempted to amend the indictment to include the crime of forced marriage as a crime against humanity. This crime was not known to international criminal law. In the request to amend the indictment, the Prosecution sought to justify its decision to develop this new crime and amend the indictment by acknowledging the difficulties and complexities of the case and the charge.[83] The Prosecution asserted that this did not violate the principle of equality of arms as the Defense would now benefit from a full-view of the acts, and the Prosecution would benefit from the Accused being indicted for the totality of the crimes committed.[84] The Prosecution recalled the precedent set in the case of *Akayesu*, which allowed for an amended indictment to be completed during trial and even at a later point once the trial was ongoing.[85]

The Defense rebutted with two main arguments. First, the Defense argued that allowing this amendment was not supported by customary international law since the crime alleged could not be found in the Statute of the SCSL, the ICC Statute, or the Geneva Conventions.[86] Further alongside this argument, the Defense argued alternatively that even if the crime of forced marriage was found in customary international law, it could not be added. This was because of the principle of legality

---

[81] Prosecutor v. Brima, Case No. SCSL-04-16-T, Judgment, (June 20, 2007).

[82] *Id.* at ¶ 6.

[83] Prosecutor v. Kanu, Case No. SCSL-04-15-PT, Request for Leave to Amend the Indictment, ¶ 2 (Feb. 9, 2004).

[84] *Id.* at ¶ 24.

[85] *Id.* at ¶ 27.

[86] Prosecution v. Kanu, Case No. SCSL-2004-16-PT, Defense Response to Prosecution's Request for Leave to Amend the Indictment (Feb. 17, 2004).

under which any addition of such charge would violate the rights of the Accused.[87] Second, the Defense argued that the amendment was not compliant with the rules of specificity as laid out by the ICTY Trial Chamber in *Kovacevic* and *Kupreski*.[88]

In response to the Defense's initial argument the Prosecution further explained that the crime of forced marriage amounted to a crime against humanity under the residual category of "Other Inhumane Acts."[89] The Prosecution emphasized the importance of this residual category "Other Inhumane Acts," which was purposefully created to encompass a series of criminal acts not specifically enumerated in the Statute with the purpose of ensuring unforeseen crimes against humanity are not committed without accountability.[90] It was suggested that the amendment was justified both in law and on the evidence since it would better reflect the culpability of the Accused, there had been no undue delay in bring forth the amendment, and the filing of the amendment would not prejudice the rights of the Accused. Continuing, the Prosecution asserted that the charge of "forced marriage" did not violate the principle of specificity because the evidence presented with the charge of "forced marriage" had already been disclosed and no new factual allegations were being added, that would unequally impact the Defense.

The Trial Chamber, in accepting the request to amend the indictment, ultimately held in favor of the Prosecution relying on the precedent set by the ICTR Appeals Chamber in the *Karemera*[91] judgment. The Trial Chamber also examined other ICTR and national case law and emphasized that it had to be satisfied that the timing of the amendment would not prejudice the defendants' rights to a fair and expeditious trial. In justifying its decision, the majority of the trial chamber judges explained that the principle of equality of arms had not been violated and the proposed amendment had been made in the overall interests of justice rather than to advantage the Prosecution. There was no breach of the rights of the Accused, to add the count regarding forced marriage. The requested addition was merely "a kindred offence" to those gender offences which were presented in the initial indictment, and therefore, would not need a new defense investigation to uncover facts and further delay the proceedings.[92] Although the majority found in favor of the amended indictment, Judge Thompson dissented and stressed the importance of the rights of the Accused, responsibility of professional due diligence on the part of the Prosecution, the importance of ensuring that there was no undue delay, and the eight-month time gap from when the initial indictment had been filed, the discovery of the facts that would support the charge and the filing of the application to amend the indictment.[93]

[87]   *Id.*

[88]   *Id.* at ¶¶ 5–7.

[89]   *Id.* at ¶ 5.

[90]   *Id.* at ¶ 12.

[91]   Prosecutor v. Karemera, Case No. ICTR-98-44-T, Judgment and Sentence (Feb. 2, 2012).

[92]   *Id.* at ¶ 52.

[93]   Prosecutor v. Brima, Case No. SCSL-04-16-PT, Dissenting Opinion of Judge Bankole Thompson, Presiding Judge of the Trial Chamber on Prosecution's Motion for Leave to Amend Indictment

With the Amended Indictment approved, by the majority of the Trial Chamber, the case continued to trial. At Trial, the Prosecution submitted that the acts of "forced marriage" constitutes: "words or other conduct intended to confer a status of marriage by force or threat of force or coercion, such as that caused by fear or violence, duress, detention, psychological oppression or abuse of power against the victim, or by taking advantage of a coercive environment, with the intent of conferring the status of marriage."[94] With this allegation the Prosecution also emphasized that the charge of "forced marriage" was, although similar to the crime of sexual slavery, nonetheless substantially different as it required victims to not only be forced to commit sexual acts, but also conform to societal norms and requirements of a "wife."[95] It was important for the Prosecution to establish that this was a distinct crime and violation which amounts to its own distinct conduct, which although not defined can be included in the category of "Other Inhumane Acts," thereby meeting the requirements of customary international law.[96]

The Trial Chamber, in the consideration of this new crime, found that in order for the crime to amount to a crime against humanity under the residual category of "Other Inhumane Acts" the crime must not be otherwise subsumed by other crimes in Article 2 of the SCSL Statute under an alternative crime.[97] Although there had been during the addition of the initial charge by the Prosecution prima facie evidence of a non-sexual crime at the initial motion for acquittal stage, with the benefit of the whole evidence in the case at the end of the trial, the Trial Chamber was not convinced that the Prosecution evidence could establish the elements of a non-sexual crime of "forced marriage" different than that of sexual slavery. As sexual slavery, which was defined in Article 2(g) of the Statute could not be independently established, the crime could not be charged as a crime against humanity under the residual category of "Other Inhumane Acts." The Trial Chamber found that the crime of "sexual slavery" was a specific form of slavery which was part of customary international law and that slavery for the purpose of sexual abuse amounts to *jus cogens* in the same way as slavery for the purpose of physical labor.[98] The Trial Chamber further explained the elements of sexual slavery, in addition to the contextual requirements of crimes against humanity in Article 2 of the SCSL Statute, were that:

1. The perpetrator exercised any or all of the powers attaching to the right of ownership over one or more persons, such as by purchasing, selling, lending or bartering such a person or persons, or by imposing on them a similar deprivation of liberty.

Against Accused Alex Tamba Brima, Brima Bazzy Kamara and Santigie Borbor Kanu, ¶ 12 (May 6, 2004).
[94] Prosecutor v. Brima, Case No. SCSL-04-16-T, Judgment, ¶ 701 (June 20, 2007).
[95] *Id.*
[96] *Id.*
[97] *Id.* at ¶ 703.
[98] *Id.* at ¶ 705.

2. The perpetrator caused such person or persons to engage in one or more acts of sexual nature;

3. The perpetrator committed such conduct intending to engage in the act of sexual slavery or in the reasonable knowledge that it was likely to occur.[99]

The Trial Chamber reasoned that the crimes alleged by the Prosecution, although egregious, were not distinguishable from those of sexual slavery as any marriage was bogus and the conduct committed within the confines of the "marriage" were that of sexual slavery and not an independent crime.[100] The Trial Chamber made this determination based on the fact that the victims did not claim that they had suffered any distinct trauma from being a "wife," and even if they had, it would have not been a sufficient amount of trauma of the gravity similar in nature to the acts constituting crimes against humanity as defined under Article 2, paragraphs (a) to (h), of the SCSL Statute.[101] Therefore, with these considerations, the Trial Chamber ruled that the alleged crime of "forced marriage" was not distinct from sexual slavery. The totality of the evidence that the Prosecution had submitted was subsumed by that crime, and as a consequence, there was no gap in the law that would necessitate a separate crime against humanity of forced marriage as another inhumane act. In order to avoid duplicity, the evidence of sexual slavery would be considered in the separate count 9 concerning sexual slavery.[102]

Justice Doherty dissented from the majority, finding on the basis of the evidence before her, that the act of forced marriage is of similar gravity and nature to the other prohibited crimes against humanity and that the act caused serious bodily or mental harm. She found the reasons of her colleagues rejecting the count as duplicitous too formalistic, and that the crime of "forced marriage" contained sufficient gravity to meet the requirements of a crime against humanity under Article 2(i).[103] Doherty, when distinguishing the crimes (forced marriage, on the one hand, and sexual slavery on the other), recalled the societal implications that were imposed on women who were forced in to these marriages, and how this decision was not one based on choice but rather were a means for survival. It bore consequences in terms of forced pregnancy, miscarriages, and sexual health issues such as becoming HIV positive.[104] Justice Doherty also recalled statements by the Prosecution's witness which established that, even post-conflict, the affected women continually suffered from those crimes[105] including stigmatization from their communities. They were

---

[99]   *Id.* at ¶ 708.

[100]   *Id.* at ¶ 710.

[101]   *Id.*

[102]   *Id.* at ¶ 713.

[103]   Prosecutor v. Brima, Case No. SCSL-04-16-T, Partly Dissenting Opinion of Justice Doherty on Counts 7 (Sexual Slavery) and 8 (Forced Marriages), ¶ 15 (June 20, 2007).

[104]   *Id.* at ¶ 30.

[105]   *Id.* at ¶ 30.

stereotyped as prone to "rebel behavior" based on their former forced conjugal associations, and in some cases, women were rejected from communities and/or families.[106] The judge considered that the women who were subjected to "forced marriage" were subjected to more than sexual violence as the crime of sexual slavery would entail, as they were also obligated to carry the status of "wife" and perform household tasks for their "husbands" such as carrying their supplies, cooking for them, and other obligations typical of traditional marriages.[107] In her view, the status was forced through violence or by coercion or through threats and included acts of rape and a forced conjugal association which made the conduct distinguishable from the phenomenon of sexual slavery.

The Prosecution appealed the dismissal of the charge of forced marriage as a crime against humanity.[108] The Appeals Chamber found that the Trial Chamber did err as a matter of law in holding that the list in Article 2(g) was exhaustive and that other crimes which have a sexual and gendered component could not be charged under Article 2(i) "Other Inhumane Acts" as crimes against humanity.[109] The Appeals Chamber engaged in a detailed discussion of the nature of the crime of "forced marriage" in which it emphasized the subsequent trauma suffered by victims. It also noted the residual nature of the other inhumane acts which aimed to punish criminal conduct not specifically recognized as a crime against humanity, but which are of comparable gravity to the enumerated crimes. The prohibition is inclusive and recognized in a large number of international legal instruments and constituted customary international law. The judges noted that a wide variety of criminal acts, including crimes of a sexual nature, had been recognized and stressed that the determination must be made on a case by case basis.

Several factors including the nature of the act or omission, the context, and the personal circumstances of the victims had to be considered, requiring that the category not be too restrictively interpreted. Forced marriage, in the view of the appellate judges, could be distinguished on several grounds from the crime of sexual slavery. The Appeals Chamber thus rejected the finding that forced marriage is subsumed by sexual slavery. In this regard, while there were certain elements between the two crimes that overlapped, there were at least two important distinctions between the crimes which would result in the reasonable conclusion that forced marriage is not predominantly a sexual crime. On the question whether forced marriage would satisfy the elements of "other inhumane acts" as a crime against humanity, the Appeals Chamber agreed with the Prosecution that this requirement expressed in Article 2(i) of the SCSL Statute constituted part of customary international law. But, even after providing some insight into the nature of the crime, the Appeals Chamber ultimately did not decide to enter "fresh

---

[106] *Id.* at ¶ 33.
[107] *Id.* at ¶ 49.
[108] Prosecutor v. Brima, Case No. SCSL-2004-16-A, Judgment (Feb. 22, 2008).
[109] *Id.* at ¶ 187.

convictions" on these charges.[110] The judges considered that it was sufficient, in the context of the *AFRC* case, to only recognize and attach opprobrium to the conduct to reflect societal disapproval of the forceful abduction and use of women would incur criminal responsibility under international law.

The holding in the *AFRC* case can be appreciated for its strong analysis in understanding that the principle of legality, though important, should not be a means by which a perpetrator of certain types of conduct could escape justice. The judgment, by recognizing the existence of the crime without applying it to the particular persons before the court, sought to strike a balance between the need to develop the law of crimes against humanity to better condemn certain egregious conduct while at the same time ensuring its compatibility with fair trial rights under human rights law. Indeed, it can be argued that the form of recognition helped bring the crime of "forced marriage" in closer alignment with the spirit underlying many human rights instruments such as Article 16 of the Universal Declaration on Human Rights,[111] Article 23(3) of the International Covenant on Civil and Political Rights,[112] and Article 16 of the Convention on the Elimination of All Forms of Discrimination against Women.[113] The AFRC case developed an understanding of "forced marriage" and the sexual and non-sexual elements of such crimes will likely be used in the future to help ensure that perpetrators of such atrocities are properly recognized for their acts and do not evade justice based on the lack of a prosecutorial crime available.

6.4.2 *The* RUF *Case*

The second pillar of the SCSL judgment on "forced marriage" was developed from the judgment of the case of the *Prosecutor v. Sesay, Kallon, and Gbao (RUF* case).[114] The defendants were among the leaders of the RUF movement during the Sierra Leone conflict.[115] One of the many charges against the Accused include the charge of "forced marriage" as a crime against humanity, though like in the *AFRC* case, the Prosecution's initial indictment did not contain that allegation.[116] Rather, the Prosecutor requested the amendment to the indictment on 20 February 2006 – that is, after the defendants had been arraigned on the prior charges to which they

---

[110]   Valerie Oosterveld, *Evaluating the Special Court for Sierra Leone's Gender Jurisprudence, in* THE SIERRA LEONE SPECIAL COURT AND ITS LEGACY: THE IMPACT FOR AFRICAN AND INTERNATIONAL CRIMINAL LAW 234–59 (Charles Chernor Jalloh ed., 2013).

[111]   Universal Declaration of Human Rights, *supra* note 8, at art. 16.

[112]   International Covenant on Civil and Political Rights art. 23(3), Dec. 16, 1966, 999 U.N.T.S 171.

[113]   Convention on the Elimination of All Forms of Discrimination Against Women art. 16, Dec. 18, 1979, 1249 U.N.T.S. 13; Micaela Frulli, *Advancing International Criminal Law: The Special Court for Sierra Leone Recognizes Forced Marriage as a "New" Crime against Humanity*, 6 J. INT'L CRIM. JUST. 1033, 1039 (2008).

[114]   Prosecutor v. Sesay, Case No. SCSL-04-15-T, Judgment (Mar. 2, 2009).

[115]   *Id.* at ¶ 4.

[116]   *Id.* at ¶ 465.

had pled not guilty.[117] The Prosecution requested this revision on the basis that there had been no undue delay in the filing and that the new charges would better reflect the full culpability of the Accused and thus be in the interest of justice.[118] Reliance was placed on the ICTR precedent in *Karemera*,[119] which had held that the prosecutorial amendments to an indictment must be made without undue delay lest the rights of the Accused be violated.[120] The Prosecution recalled that the ICTR Appeals Chamber in the *Karemera* judgment had determined that amendments could even better support the presentation of a defense as it could serve to narrow the scope of the allegations against the Accused.[121] The Defense contested the existence of forced marriage as a crime against humanity under international law. They argued that the charge should have been added in the original indictment and that the Prosecution had not provided an adequate explanation as to why that had not been done.[122] The Defense additionally pleaded that the failure of the Prosecution to amend the indictment in a timely manner violated the principle of promptness and undue delay and would jeopardize the preparation of the defense case for which investigations were already underway.[123] The Prosecution retorted that the addition of the charges were based on the same factual circumstances as for the counts related to the acts of sexual violence and that there was therefore no prejudice to the Defense stemming from the additional charges.[124]

Considering the arguments of both parties, the Trial Chamber permitted the Prosecution to amend the indictment.[125] In its justification for the decision, the Trial Chamber explained that the crucial question turned on the timing and specifically whether permission of the amendment would affect the fair and expeditious trial of the defendant. The Prosecution had filed the amendment within a timely manner and therefore did not breach the doctrine of equality of arms.[126] The majority further explained that the Prosecution still bore the burden to demonstrate guilt "beyond all reasonable doubt"[127] as stipulated in the relevant provisions of the SCSL Statute. It pointed out that its decision was consistent with other tribunals' case law, such as *Prosecutor v. Alfred Musema*,[128] where a similar amendment to an indictment had

---

[117]   Prosecutor v. Sesay, Case No. SCSL-2004-15-PT, Request for Leave to Amend the Indictment (Feb. 9, 2004).

[118]   *Id.* at ¶ 4.

[119]   Prosecutor v. Karemera, Case No. ICTR-98-44-T, Judgment and Sentence (Feb. 2, 2012).

[120]   *Id.* at ¶ 15.

[121]   *Id.* at ¶ 18.

[122]   Prosecutor v. Sesay, Case No. SCSL-2004-16-PT, Defence Response to Prosecution's Application to Amend the Indictment, ¶ 14 (Feb. 19, 2004).

[123]   *Id.* at ¶ 13.

[124]   Prosecutor v. Sesay, Case No. SCSL-2004-15-PT, Consolidated Reply to Defence (Sesay and Gbao) Response to Prosecution's "Request for Leave to Amend the Indictment", ¶¶ 4–9 (Feb. 24, 2004).

[125]   Prosecution v. Sesay, Case No. SCSL-04-15-PT, Decision on Prosecution Request for Leave to Amend the Indictment, ¶ 14 (May 6, 2004).

[126]   *Id.* at ¶ 27.

[127]   *Id.* at ¶ 29.

[128]   Prosecutor v. Musema, Case No. ICTR-96-13-T, Judgment and Sentence (Jan. 27, 2000).

been permitted since it was only technical and not considered to be prejudicial to the rights of the Accused.[129] Lastly, and in any event, the Trial Chamber reasoned that the addition of this "new charge" did not violate the rights of the Accused as the factual basis surrounding this charge had already been disclosed to the Defense.[130]

Judge Thompson dissented using reasoning similar to that articulated in his dissenting opinion in the *AFRC* case. According to the Sierra Leonean judge, the amendment of the indictment had not been fully justified and would have prejudicial effects upon the right of the Accused to a fair and expeditious trial. He observed, among other things, that it had taken the Prosecution eight months from the discovery of the evidence alleging gender crimes to the date of the motion seeking leave to amend the indictment.[131]

During the trial, witness testimony provided by the Prosecution established during multiple occasions fighters kidnapped and abducted women and girls from their villages or from along the side of the road to forcibly become "wives" to rebel fighters.[132] In these forced marriages, women were obligated to provide domestic services to the fighters such as cooking and housework, and were also simultaneously subject to sexual violence to fulfill the sexual needs of their captors.[133] Forcing these women to be subjected not only to sexual violence was mentally and physically traumatic. The impact of this was perhaps most appropriately described by the testimony of a woman in which she recalled telling her eleven year old daughter, who had been raped, to "be patient because 'this is war' and there was nothing that women could do about it."[134] Another witness testified to the fact that these forced conjugal associations meant they had no option but to become bush wives, as they had no leverage to negotiate and "could not escape for fear of being killed."[135]

Based on evidence, the Trial Chamber found that the RUF captured women and girls and claimed them as their "wives," which established the *actus reus* of the crime of "forced marriage."[136] The Trial Chamber also held that the conjugal association which was created through the "forced marriage" created a long-lasting stigmatization of the women and girls which made it difficult for reintegration.[137] The Trial Chamber also held that the *mens rea* of the crime was met as the actions of the "husbands" were conducted in a manner in which perpetrators were aware of the gravity of the mental and physical harm inflicted from their actions.[138] Therefore,

---

[129]   *Id.* at ¶ 56.

[130]   *Id.* at ¶ 44.

[131]   Prosecutor v. Sesay, Case No. SCSL-04-15-PT, Decision on Prosecution Request for Leave to Amend the Indictment: Dissenting Opinion of Judge Bankole Thompson, ¶ 13 (May 6, 2004).

[132]   Prosecutor v. Sesay, Case No. SCSL-04-15-T, Judgment, ¶¶ 1154–55 (Mar. 2, 2009).

[133]   *Id.* at ¶ 1155.

[134]   *Id.* at ¶ 1213.

[135]   *Id.* at ¶¶ 1410–12.

[136]   *Id.* at ¶ 1294.

[137]   *Id.* at ¶ 1295.

[138]   *Id.* at ¶ 1296.

the Trial Chamber held that the rebels committed acts of "forced marriage" as a crime against humanity.[139]

The Trial Chamber also found that the crime of "forced marriage" along with rape and sexual slavery amounted to "Outrages on Personal Dignity."[140] The Trial Chamber also determined that the practice of "forced marriage" and sexual slavery was used while knowing the stigmatization it created, and that it was used with the intent to spread terror among civilians.[141] Additionally, that the use of these practices of rape, sexual slavery, "forced marriage," and other outrages on personal dignity were committed with the intent to terrorize a community of civilians rising to the level of an act of terror.[142] Finally, the Trial Chamber held that "forced marriage" could be charged distinctly and alongside rape and sexual slavery and was not "subsumed" under those crimes.[143]

The holding in the *RUF* case substantially contributed in acknowledging that the crime of "forced marriage" occurred on a large scale. It seemed to confirm that they were not just other acts of violence towards women during war, but instead held that the act of forced marriage was a "pattern of conduct" of the RUF.[144] This recognition also helped emphasize that the impact of the "forced marriage" title had on women included a long-lasting stigmatization. That made it a unique crime which did not constitute just sexual enslavement, but also a crime against humanity under the category of "Other Inhumane Acts."[145] The Trial Chamber acknowledged that this practice had been used to instill fear while acting with the knowledge that this would cause psychological and physical harm to victims.[146] This recognition of the impact that gender-based crimes has on victims' physical and psychological health can be used in the future to maintain the emphasis of the impact on women of gender-based crimes.

6.4.3 *The* CDF *Case*

The third pillar is the SCSL judgment in the *CDF* case. In 2007, three leading members of the CDF were put on trial for a variety of violations of war crimes, crimes against humanity, and international humanitarian law.[147] The Accused consisted of Samuel Hinga Norman (known as the "National Coordinator"), Moinina Fofana (known as the "Director of War"), and Allieu Kondewa (known as the "High Priest").[148] The prosecution of these three high ranking individuals

---

[139] *Id.* at ¶¶ 1297, 1473.
[140] *Id.* at ¶ 1298.
[141] *Id.* at ¶ 1351.
[142] *Id.* at ¶ 1352.
[143] *Id.* at ¶¶ 2306–07.
[144] *Id.* at ¶ 248.
[145] *Id.*
[146] *Id.*
[147] Prosecutor v. Fofana, Case No. SCSL-04-15-T, Judgment, ¶ 3 (Aug. 2, 2007).
[148] *Id.* at ¶ 1.

became known as the "CDF Trial."[149] But, prior to the judgment being rendered against the Accused, Norman died in hospital. The Trial Chamber could thus not issue a final judgment on his guilt or innocence.[150]

This case has been recognized for the Prosecution's attempt to amend the indictment to include crimes of sexual violence.[151] The Prosecution requested the Indictment be amended to include "'Rape, a crime against humanity', 'Sexual Slavery and other form of sexual violence, a crime against humanity', '"Other Inhumane Acts," as crimes against humanity (forced marriages)' and 'Outrages upon personal dignity, a violation of article 3 common to the Geneva Conventions and of Additional Protocol II.'"[152] The Prosecution made several arguments to justify the motion requesting leave to amend the indictment.[153]

The Defense argued that there had been undue delay by the Prosecution and contested the addition of new charges.[154] The Defense further argued that the need to prepare for these new charges would unnecessarily delay the Accused's trial in violation of the rights of the Accused under Article 17(4) of the Statute of the Special Court,[155] and further submitted that the Prosecution would possess an unfair tactical advantage if the amendment were to be granted.[156] The Defense relied on the rights of the Accused defined in the Statute which provided, inter alia, that:

> In the determination of any charge against the accused pursuant to the present statute, he or she shall be entitled to the following minimum guarantees in full equality:
>
> (a) To be informed promptly and in detail in a language which he or she understand of the nature and cause of the charge against him or her;
> (b) To have adequate time and facilities for the preparation of his or her defence;
> (c) To be tried without undue delay.[157]

The Trial Chamber explained that the motion for amendment was governed by Rule 50 which read:

---

[149]   *Id.*

[150]   *Id.* at ¶ 15.

[151]   Prosecutor v. Fofana, Case No. SCSL-04-15-T, Majority Decision on the Prosecution's Application for Leave to File an Interlocutory Appeal Against the Decision on the Prosecution's Request for Leave to Amend the Indictment Against Samuel Hinga Norma, Moinina Fofana and Allieu Kondewa (Aug. 2, 2004); Prosecutor v. Fofana, Case No. SCSL-04-15-T, Decision on Prosecution Request for Leave to Amend the Indictment (May 20, 2004).

[152]   Prosecutor v. Fofana, Case No. SCSL-04-15-T, Decision on Prosecution Request for Leave to Amend the Indictment, ¶ 10 (May 20, 2004).

[153]   *Id.* at ¶ 10 (c).

[154]   *Id.* at ¶ 11.

[155]   *Id.* at ¶ 16.

[156]   *Id.* at ¶ 11.

[157]   *Id.* at ¶ 27.

(A) The Prosecutor may amend an indictment, without prior leave, at any time before its approval, but thereafter, until the initial appearance of the accused pursuant to Rule 61, only with leave of the Designated Judge who reviewed it but, in exceptional circumstances, by leave of another Judge. At or after such initial appearance, an amendment of an indictment may only be made by leave granted by a Trial Chamber pursuant to Rule 73. If leave to amend is granted, Rule 47(G) and Rule 52 apply to the amended indictment.

(B) If the amended indictment includes new charges and the accused has already made his initial appearance in accordance with Rule 61:
   (i) A further appearance shall be held as soon as practicable to enable the accused to enter a plea on the new charges;
   (ii) Within seven days from such appearance, the Prosecutor shall disclose all materials envisaged in Rule 66(A)(i) pertaining to the new charges;
   (iii) The accused shall have a further period of ten days from the date of such disclosure by the Prosecutor in which to file preliminary motions pursuant to Rule 72 and relating to the new charges.[158]

With these two rules in mind, the Trial Chamber found merit in the argument that it was the responsibility of the Chamber to ensure that there was an "equality of arms" between the Defense and Prosecution and that any motion granted would not place either party at a disadvantage.[159] Following this line of reasoning, the Trial Chamber found that the strategy of the Prosecution in light of the arguments of judicial economy were not sufficient to overrule the rights of the Accused to a "fair and expeditious trial" and the right to a trial without "undue delay." The judges determined that the Prosecution was in breach of the ingredient of timeliness as required by the Statute as would any such order emanating from their granting the motion. Here, a differently constituted trial chamber, unlike their colleagues from the *AFRC* and *RUF* Trial Chambers, rejected the Prosecution's requested amendment to the indictment to, inter alia, add the forced marriage count.

In Judge Boutet's dissent, he stated that he would have allowed the amendment and recalled the obligation of the Prosecutor to ensure the rights of the Accused. Laying out a timeline of events, Judge Boutet demonstrated that the decision of joinder was rendered on January 28, 2004 and that the motion to amend the Indictment was filed on February 9, 2004.[160] Judge Boutet argued that the deciding factor in this case was whether the Prosecution had provided this information "without undue delay" which ultimately amounted to a matter of "timeliness" in

---

[158] *Id.* at ¶ 28.
[159] *Id.* at ¶ 36.
[160] Prosecutor v. Fofana, Case No. SCSL-04-14-PT, Dissenting Opinion of Judge Pierre Boutet on the Decision on Prosecution Request for Leave to Amend the Indictment, ¶ 6 (May 31, 2004).

submission.[161] To determine the meaning of this term "without undue delay" he drew on the Appeals Chamber decisions of *Bizimungu*[162] and *Kovacevic*.[163] He found that an amendment is appropriate at the point in time in which the Prosecutor "has what he [or she] considers to be sufficient, credible evidence that can be used and is relevant to what he [or she] is alleging that he [or she] should proceed to bring an Indictment."[164]

Further, Judge Boutet explained that the Prosecution must be in possession of the evidence and hold a reasonably certain belief that the evidence was sufficient for a conviction.[165] With this, he also acknowledged there could be difficulty in locating witnesses for gender-based crimes.[166] The dissent observed that, due to the "nature of the offences," victims can often be reluctant to discuss these matters as women may be shamed, socially ostracized, or suffer retribution from reporting. Others might be fearful of having their families and communities know what happened to them, and the hesitation to relive the trauma during testimony.[167] Thus, in Judge Boutet's view, the Prosecution did not possess the necessary information to properly add the sexual crimes charges, and at the point in which the Prosecution did later verify evidence and secure witnesses to the point of a "reasonable certainty of conviction" could be obtained, the Prosecution was correct in filing a request for amendment as it did and was not seeking an unfair advantage in doing so.[168]

Upon the Trial Chambers denial for amendment the Prosecution requested leave to appeal the trial chamber decision in order to "prosecute to the 'full extent of the law,'" and further urged that "the high profile nature of gender based crimes under international law constitutes another exceptional circumstance."[169] The Prosecution even suggested that the evidence and material on sexual violence and gender-based crimes could be left for the end of the trial so the Defense would have more than adequate time to prepare.[170] In their response, the Defense, in response to the Prosecution, argued that the case of the CDF suspects was substantially different from the *AFRC* and *RUF* cases; thus, the need to amend was unnecessary, the request

---

[161]   *Id.* at ¶ 8.

[162]   *Id.* at ¶ 10; Prosecutor v. Bizimungu, Case No. ICTR-99-50-AR50, Decision on Prosecutor's Interlocutory Appeal Against Trial Chamber II Decision of 6 October 2003 Denying Leave to File Amended Indictment (Feb. 12, 2004).

[163]   Prosecutor v. Karemera, Case No. ICTR-98-44-AR-73, Decision on Prosecutor's Interlocutory Appeal against Trial Chamber III Decision of 8 October 2003 Denying Leave to File an Amended Indictment, ¶¶ 10–11 (Dec. 12, 2003).

[164]   *Id.* at ¶ 24.

[165]   *Id.* at ¶ 25.

[166]   *Id.* at ¶ 26.

[167]   *Id.* at ¶¶ 26–27.

[168]   *Id.* at ¶¶ 35–37.

[169]   *Id.* at ¶ 3.

[170]   *Id.* at ¶ 8.

to amend was untimely filed, and any injustice faced by the victims of these crimes did not amount to an "irreparable prejudice" as alleged by the Prosecution.[171]

The Prosecution's request for an interlocutory appeal was denied by the Trial Chamber. In the second attempt to the Appeals Chamber, the Prosecution did not argue for the Appeals Chamber to reverse the judgment and remand for a full trial, but rather, asked the Appeals Chamber to determine for future reference that the trial court should have allowed to amend the indictment and to collect evidence on the charges of sexual violence under the residual category of "Other Inhumane Acts."[172] The majority of the Appeals Chamber denied this request, finding it "an unnecessary exercise,"[173] with Justice Winter in dissent.

Justice Winter found that the failure of the majority to rule of the merits of the case was a "miscarriage of justice" and the decision of the Trial Chamber amounted to an error of law.[174] She held that the investigation into gender-based offenses was conducted within a reasonable time frame, and in light of the difficulties in locating witnesses and evidence for these crimes, the decision of the Prosecution to wait until adequate evidence had been verified was appropriate.[175] Judge Winter also found justification in the argument of judicial economy on behalf of the Prosecution.[176] She further found merit in the Defense argument that the rights of the Accused must be protected, but did not find that the rights of the Accused would have been violated had there been an amendment to the indictment.[177]

Judge Winter reasoned that although both parties were held to the principle of "equality of arms" the obligation imposed on the Defense was not the same obligation faced by the Prosecution.[178] The Prosecution has the burden of collecting enough evidence to demonstrate what it believes to be (1) sufficient for conviction and (2) compliant with the standard of beyond a reasonable doubt, which in this case, took the Prosecution nearly a year to complete. Whereas, for their part, the Defense held the obligation "to show that the threshold of proof beyond a reasonable doubt was not proved."[179] Justice Winter also recalled that the Trial Chamber could have produced an alternative solution instead of a blanket denial of the charges, for instance, not allowing the Prosecution to present new evidence after a certain point.[180] But, with the decision of a blanket denial of the amendment, the Trial Chamber had impeded the SCSL's ability to fulfill its Statute by failing to prosecute the gender-based offenses and facilitate justice against the alleged perpetrators of

[171]   *Id.* at ¶ 11.
[172]   Prosecutor v. Fofana, Case No. SCSL-04-14-PT, Judgment, ¶¶ 425–28 (Aug. 2, 2007).
[173]   Prosecutor v. Fofana, Case No. SCSL-04-14-A, Judgment, ¶ 427 (May 28, 2008).
[174]   Prosecutor v. Fofana, Case No. SCSL-04-14-A, Partially Dissenting Opinion of Honourable Justice Renate Winter, ¶ 65 (May 28, 2008).
[175]   *Id.* at ¶ 80.
[176]   *Id.* at ¶ 81.
[177]   *Id.* at ¶ 83.
[178]   *Id.* at ¶ 84.
[179]   *Id.*
[180]   *Id.*

such atrocities.[181] It also denied victims the right to justice of having their crimes and abuses heard in the SCSL which had been created to address such human rights violations and with the view to being provided a remedy.[182]

Although the *CDF* Trial and Appeals Chambers did not accept the arguments on forced marriage, the cases do provide some useful authority. There were substantial considerations in both the dissents of Judge Boutet at the Trial Chamber and Judge Winter in the Appeals Chamber. Those could prove to be useful for future prosecutions, especially in regard to the possibility of amending indictments to include gender-based crimes. The *CDF* case could be seen as a lack of acknowledgment, or perhaps even, silence on the importance of gender-based crimes.[183] The decision by the Trial Chamber and Appeals Chamber could be seen as regressive in the struggle for justice for victims of gender-based crimes. After the decision, two researchers conducted a study on the impact that this denial had on the victim-witnesses.[184] The research concluded that the "active silencing" of victims resulted in a "negative psychological impact" on victims.[185]

6.4.4 *The* Taylor *Case*

The *Taylor* case was the fourth and final case heard by the SCSL. Therefore, the judgment benefitted from the previous legal analysis undertaken in the former cases, which allowed it to confirm, expand, and clarify international criminal law on gender-based crimes.[186] Charles Taylor, like the other suspects arraigned before the SCSL, had been charged for war crimes, crimes against humanity, and other serious violations of international humanitarian law. The Accused was the President of Liberia from August 1997 to August 2003, when he resigned from office due to the political pressure following the unsealing of his Indictment and Warrant of Arrest on 4 June 2003 by the Special Court.[187] As President of Liberia, and as leader of the National Patriotic Front of Liberia, the Accused was alleged to have acted in concert with members of the rebel groups such as RUF, AFRC, and the AFRC/RUF Junta in Sierra Leone, terrorizing the civilian population in Sierra Leone including murder, sexual violence, physical violence, illegal recruitment of child soldiers, burning of civilian homes, and forced labor.[188]

After the initial Indictment was amended twice, Taylor was officially charged on eleven counts on March 29, 2007, out of which three counts were regarded as sexual

---

[181] *Id.* at ¶ 85.
[182] *Id.* at ¶ 86.
[183] Oosterveld, *supra* note 110, at 257.
[184] *Id.* at 258.
[185] *Id.*
[186] Valerie Oosterveld, *Gender and the Charles Taylor Case at the Special Court for Sierra Leone*, 19 WM & MARY J. WOMEN & L. 7, 10 (2012).
[187] *Id.* at 9.
[188] *Id.* at 12–13.

violence crimes.[189] Two counts charged Taylor with crimes against humanity pursuant to Article 2(g) SCSL Statute: Rape and sexual slavery; and one count charged outrages upon personal dignity, a violation of article 3 common to the Geneva Conventions and Additional Protocol II, pursuant to Article 3(e) SCSL Statute.[190]

The Trial Chamber considered a number of preliminary issues in its written judgment, some of which related to sexual violence.[191] The Defense raised several fair trial issues in addition to the submission that the prosecution of Taylor had been selective in nature.[192] One of the fair trial issues that was raised by the Defense in relation to the Indictment was the concern regarding the absence of evidence relating to specific locations in Sierra Leone,[193] particularly in the case of offenses of a continuous nature, such as sexual slavery.[194] In consideration of this issue, the Trial Chamber, in accordance with the AFRC Trial Judgment, held that the prolonged nature of these crimes, especially in the context of the Sierra Leone conflict where the perpetrators often were on the move, may make pleading particular locations sometimes impracticable. A significant amount of evidence had been provided in respect of each of these crimes, and additionally that in the interest of justice, the pleadings of these counts in the Indictment would be permissible despite the Prosecution having not pleaded specific locations of every single alleged crime.[195]

On April 26, 2012, after several years of hearings, Trial Chamber I rendered the final judgment over the alleged acts committed by the former Liberian President. It can be further noted, as discussed in Chapter 8 of this book, that the *Taylor* case was the first involving a former Head of State by a modern international criminal tribunal with regard to crimes carried out in another State.[196] The Trial Chamber unanimously found Taylor responsible under Article 6(1) of the SCSL Statute[197] for aiding and abetting the commission of the crimes set forth in Counts 1 to 11 of the Indictment, including the crimes against humanity of rape and sexual slavery and the war crime of outrages upon personal dignity.[198]

The Trial Chamber's decision to allow sexual slavery charges in spite of the lack of a specific location allowed for a significant gender-related development in the *Taylor* case in the court's consideration of sexual slavery and, as part of that discussion,

---

[189] *Id.*
[190] *Id.* at 19; Prosecutor v. Taylor, Case No. SCSL-03-01-T-PT, Prosecution's Second Amended Indictment, (May 29, 2007).
[191] Prosecutor v. Taylor, Case No. SCSL-03-01-T-PT, Prosecution's Second Amendment, (May 29, 2007).
[192] *Id.*
[193] *Id.* at ¶ 112.
[194] *Id.* at ¶ 118.
[195] *Id.* at ¶ 119.
[196] Prosecutor v. Taylor, Case No. SCSL-03-01-T-1283, Judgment, ¶ 70 (May 18, 2012).
[197] *Id.* at ¶ 6994; SCSL Statute, *supra* note 2.
[198] Prosecutor v. Taylor, Case No. SCSL-03-01-T-1283, Judgment, ¶ 6971 (May 18, 2012).

"forced marriage" or conjugal slavery.[199] Unlike in the *AFRC* and the *RUF* cases, the Accused was not charged with "forced marriage" as an other inhumane act of crimes against humanity, but the Prosecutor did introduce evidence of the "bush wife" phenomenon to support the sexual slavery charges.[200]

In the *Taylor* judgment, which was written by the same group of judges as in the *AFRC* case, sexual slavery was defined as:

> The perpetrator exercised any or all of the powers attaching to the right of ownership over one or more persons, such as by purchasing, selling, lending or bartering such a person or persons, or by imposing on them a similar deprivation of liberty.
>
> The perpetrator caused such person or persons to engage in one or more acts of a sexual nature;
>
> The perpetrator intended to engage in the act of sexual slavery or acted with the reasonable knowledge that this was likely to occur.[201]

The Trial Chamber discussed the linkages between sexual slavery and "forced marriage" in the former *AFRC* and *RUF* judgments. In these cases, the Prosecutor had covered the "bush wife" phenomenon by charging the crime of "forced marriage" under the crime against humanity of "Other Inhumane Acts."[202] A majority of the *AFRC* Trial Chamber did not accept this categorization and found that forced marriages was completely subsumed within the crime against humanity of sexual slavery. However, as mentioned above, the Appeals Chamber agreed with the Prosecutor's contention that "forced marriage" was correctly classified under the crime against humanity of "Other Inhumane Acts."[203]

As the "bush wife" phenomenon was introduced by the Prosecutor as evidence of "forced marriage," albeit as proof of sexual slavery, the Trial Chamber expressed its views on "forced marriage."[204] According to the Trial Chamber, the term "forced marriage" was a misnomer for the forced conjugal association that was imposed on women and girls in the circumstances of armed conflict, as there was no actual marriage.[205] As the term "forced marriage" was meant to capture both sexual slavery and forced labor in the form of domestic work such as cleaning and cooking, it proposed the term "conjugal slavery" instead, noting that conjugal relations involve both sexual and non-sexual acts.[206] These forced acts, both sexual and non-sexual acts, should fall within the definition of conjugal slavery which the Trial Chamber described as a form of

---

[199]   Oosterveld, *supra* note 186, at 15.
[200]   SCSL Statute, *supra* note 2, at art. 2(g); Prosecutor v. Taylor, Case No. SCSL-03-01-T, Judgment, ¶ 422 (May 18, 2012).
[201]   Prosecutor v. Taylor, Case No. SCSL-03-01-T, Judgment, ¶ 418 (May 18, 2012).
[202]   Prosecutor v. Sesay, Case No. SCSL-04-15-T, Judgment, ¶¶ 152, 164 (Mar. 2, 2009); Prosecutor v. Brima, Case No. SCSL-2004-16-A, Separate Concurring Opinion of the Hon. Justice Sebutinde Appended to Judgment Pursuant to Rule 88(c), ¶¶ 13-18 (June 20, 2007).
[203]   Prosecutor v. Brima, Case No. SCSL-2004-16-A, Judgment, (Feb. 22, 2008).
[204]   Prosecutor v. Taylor, Case No. SCSL-03-01-T, Judgment, ¶¶ 422, 424, 1101 (May 18, 2012).
[205]   *Id.* at ¶ 425.
[206]   *Id.* at ¶¶ 427-29.

enslavement wherein "the perpetrator exercised the powers attaching to the right of ownership over their 'bush wives; and imposed on them a deprivation of liberty, causing them to engage in sexual acts as well as other acts."[207] The view of the Trial Chamber was not to conceptualize a new crime, establishing additional elements, but merely to capture two different forms of enslavement under one heading.[208]

By splitting the classification of what had previously been termed "forced marriage" into evidence of the existing crimes of sexual slavery and enslavement, thus satisfying *nullum crimen sine lege*, the Trial Chamber satisfied the critique that the name (forced marriage) refers to marriage while still no marriage, as defined by international human rights law or domestic Sierra Leonean law, was involved.[209] Furthermore, the Trial Chamber also avoided the categorization of the "bush wife" phenomenon as a purely or mainly sexual crime, as it has both sexual and non-sexual components.[210] The *Taylor* case recognized that enslavement through forced labor can be a gendered crime. It drew attention to the fact that the category of gender-based crimes contains much more than just crimes of sexual violence by, for example, being forced into highly gendered labor roles.[211]

The Trial Chamber in the *Taylor* judgment added helpful detail to the different forms of sexual slavery and "forced marriage" and could thereby be said to have taken another step forward in international jurisprudence on gender crimes. The judgment helped to further confirm the definition of the crime of sexual slavery and also ensured that it would be understood as a continuing crime, reflecting the reality of the victims' lives.[212] The significance of the *Taylor* case has raised key questions in proposing international criminal law to turn away from "forced marriage" and turn to conjugal slavery, a combination of gendered forms of forced labor and sexual violence through enslavement.[213]

6.5 KEY LEGAL ISSUES IN THE SPECIAL COURT FOR SIERRA LEONE CASE LAW

6.5.1 *Distinction between Forced Marriage and Other Offences of a Sexual Nature*

"Forced marriage" as a crime is distinctly different from other offenses of a sexual nature, because although victims are subjected to rape, forced pregnancy,

---

[207]   *Id.* at ¶ 427.
[208]   *Id.* at ¶¶ 429–30.
[209]   Oosterveld, *supra* note 186, at 21.
[210]   *Id.*
[211]   Prosecutor v. Taylor, Case No. SCSL-03-01-T, Judgment, ¶¶ 1697–1699 (May 18, 2012) (as "bush wives," they fetched water, pounded rice, harvested palm oil, cooked meals, carried loads, looked for food, cleaned houses, fished, planted seeds, and weeded).
[212]   Oosterveld, *supra* note 186, at 33.
[213]   *Id.*

miscarriages, and sexual health related issues the crime itself also has non-sexual components as part of the act.[214]

6.5.2 *Distinction between Forced Marriage and Sexual Slavery*

The crime of "forced marriage" is also distinct from the crime of sexual slavery. The AFRC Trial Chamber found that the requirement of sexual slavery for a Crime Against Humanity under Article 2(g) of the Statute were:

(1) The perpetrator exercised any or all of the powers attaching to the right of ownership over one or more person, such as by purchasing, selling, lending or bartending such a person or persons, or by imposing on them a similar deprivation of liberty.

(2) The perpetrator caused such person or persons to engage in one or more acts of a sexual nature;

(3) The perpetrator committed such conduct intending to engage in the act of sexual slavery or in the reasonable knowledge that it was likely to occur.

The Trial Chamber held that this crime was not distinctly different from "forced marriage" as in cases of "forced marriage" women were deemed the property of their "husband" even though no money was exchanged. And further that the conditions in which victims felt there was no options to flee or escape meant that victims could then be entrapped in conditions of enslavement.[215]

   Although the Trial Chamber held that the crime of "forced marriage" was not distinctly different from sexual slavery because the "husbands" were exhibiting "ownership" and control over the "wives," Justice Doherty found differently in the dissent. Justice Doherty distinguished the crimes of sexual slavery and "forced marriage" and established that the title of "wife" did not only give victims the protection from rape, but rather also "stigmatized them as 'rebel wives' or 'bush wives.'"[216] Further Justice Doherty found that the crime of "forced marriage" met the *mens rea* and *actus reus* of an "Other Inhumane Act." Justice Doherty recalled that the crime of sexual slavery focuses on the acts and possession which occurs,[217] unlike the crime of "Other Inhumane Act," which focuses on the mental and moral suffering of the victims. For the crime of "Other Inhumane Act" to be committed the Trial Chamber must find as in *Akayesu*[218] that:

[The Crime] may also be non-violent in nature, like imposing a system of apartheid, which is declared a crime against humanity in article 1 of the Apartheid Convention

---

[214]   Prosecutor v. Brima, Case No. SCSL-04-16-T, Partly Dissenting Opinion of Justice Doherty on Count 7 (Sexual Slavery) and 8 (Forced Marriages), (June 20, 2007).

[215]   Prosecutor v. Brima, Case No. SCSL-04-16-T, Judgment, ¶ 709 (June 20, 2007).

[216]   Prosecutor v. Brima, Case No. SCSL-04-16-T, Partly Dissenting Opinion of Justice Doherty on Count 7 (Sexual Slavery) and Count 8 (Forced Marriages), ¶ 50 (June 20, 2007).

[217]   *Id.* at ¶ 52.

[218]   Prosecutor v. Akayesu, Case No. ICTR-96-4-T, Judgment, (Sept. 2, 1998).

of 1973, or exerting pressure on the population to act in a particular manner, may come under the purview of an attack if orchestrated on a massive scale or in a systematic manner.

The crime of "forced marriage" fits into this category as victims of "forced marriage" are forced into these conjugal associations with their perpetrators "by threat or physical force arising from the perpetrator's words or other conduct."[219] The AFRC Appeals Chamber established that although the two crimes may possess similar characteristics the crimes themselves were not the same. The AFRC Appeals Chamber held that the crime of "forced marriage" required the victims to (1) by force or threat of force to become part of a "forced conjugal association" with another person resulting in great suffering, or serious physical or mental injury on the part of the victim and (2) required the victim to be in an "exclusive" association between "husband" and "wife" which held disciplinary measure for violation of such exclusivity.[220]

Comparatively, in the *Taylor* case, even though the Accused was not charged with "forced marriage" as an inhumane act of crimes against humanity, the Prosecutor introduced evidence of the "bush wife" phenomenon to support the sexual slavery charges which allowed the judges to further develop the jurisprudence on "forced marriage" and sexual slavery.[221] First, the Trial Chamber confirmed the definition of the crime of sexual slavery[222] (as described in the AFRC Trial Chamber) and further ensured that it would be understood as a continuing crime.[223] Second, the Chamber proposed the term "conjugal slavery," instead of "forced marriage," to capture both the sexual slavery and the gendered forms of forced labor and forced associations imposed on women in circumstances of armed conflict.[224]

6.5.3 *Whether Forced Marriage Satisfies the Elements of "Other Inhumane Acts" of Crime against Humanity*

According to Justice Doherty, in many national legislations and international instruments, "forced marriage" was established as a violation of general customary law.[225] In the final deliberations, Justice Doherty held that marriage was a relationship of consent and that the crime of "forced marriage" was completed when a victim was "forced in to a relationship of a conjugal nature with the perpetrator thereby subsuming the victim's will and undermining the victim's

---

[219] Prosecutor v. Brima, Case No. SCSL-04-16-T, Partly Dissenting Opinion of Justice Doherty on Counts 7 (Sexual Slavery) and Count 8 (Forced Marriages), ¶ 53 (June 20, 2007).

[220] *Id.*

[221] Prosecutor v. Taylor, Case No. SCSL-03-01-T, Judgment, ¶ 422 (May 18, 2012) (*see* Count 5: Sexual Slavery, art. 2(g) of the Special Court for Sierra Leone Statute).

[222] Prosecutor v. Taylor, Case No. SCSL-03-01-T, Judgment, ¶ 418 (May 18, 2012).

[223] Oosterveld, *supra* note 186, at 33.

[224] *Id.* at 22.

[225] *Id.* at ¶¶ 58–68.

exercise of the right to self-determination."[226] She also correctly noted that the crime of "forced marriage" placed more reliance on the impact of "mental and moral suffering of the victim" and did not require elements of physical violence, although elements of physical violence could be used to further demonstrate the lack of consent on behalf of the victim.[227]

In the *AFRC* Appeal, the Chamber held that for an act to be considered a crime against humanity in the residual category of "Other Inhumane Act," the Prosecution must demonstrate the act or omission meets the requirement of Article 2(i) Crime:

> (i) inflict great suffering, or serious injury to body or to mental or physical health;
>
> (ii) are sufficiently similar in gravity to the acts referred to in article 2(a) to 2(h) of the Statute and
>
> (iii) the perpetrator was aware of the factual circumstances that established the character of the gravity of the act.

The Appeals Chamber also reiterated that all crimes against humanity must also meet the general chapeau requirements of widespread or systematic attacks against a civilian population.[228] The Appeals Chamber found that the victims were subjected to crimes which amounted to the similar level of gravity to the predetermined crimes against humanity of enslavement, imprisonment, torture, rape, sexual slavery, and sexual violence.[229] Further the Trial Chamber believed that the acts of the perpetrators were conducted with such knowledge that their conduct would inflict "serious suffering or physical, mental or psychological injury to the victims."[230] And although the crime was perpetrated in conjunction with other crimes such as abduction, imprisonment, sexual slavery, and rape, the crime met the distinct requirement of a crime against humanity enough to be prosecuted under the category of "Other Inhumane Acts." Distinctly from the *AFRC* Appeals Judgment a definition for "forced marriage" was derived: "a perpetrator compelling a person by force or threat of force, through the words or conduct of the perpetrator or those associated with him, into a forced conjugal association with another person resulting in great suffering, or serious physical or mental injury on the part of the victim."[231]

The *RUF* Trial Chamber later clearly established that the *actus reus* for the crime of "forced marriage" occurred when the "rebels captured women and 'took them as their wife'" and forced them into conjugal association.[232] The *RUF* Trial Chamber

[226] *Id.* at ¶ 69.

[227] *Id.* at ¶ 70.

[228] ROBERT DUBLER SC & MATTHEW KALYK, CRIMES AGAINST HUMANITY UNDER CUSTOMARY INTERNATIONAL LAW AND THE ICC: THE CHAPEAU ELEMENTS 639 (2018) (a Crime against humanity must be an (1) attack, (2) directed against, (3) any civilian, (4) population, (5) widespread or systematic, (6) the policy element, and (7) meet the requisite *mens rea*).

[229] Prosecutor v. Brima, Case No. SCSL-2004-16-A, Judgment, ¶ 200 (Feb. 22, 2008).

[230] *Id.* at ¶ 201.

[231] Oosterveld, *supra* note 186, at 66.

[232] Prosecutor v. Sesay, Case No. SCSL-04-15-T, Judgment, ¶ 1296 (Mar. 2, 2009).

also explained that the *mens rea* for the crime was met when the perpetrators act with the knowledge that their action would inflict "grave suffering and serious injury to the physical and mental health of the victims, and that the perpetrators were aware of the gravity of their actions."[233]

6.5.4 *Impact of the Special Court for Sierra Leone Jurisprudence on the Work of Other Tribunals*

Much attention has been focused on the considerations and judgments made by the SCSL on "forced marriage" to the international criminal law's gender lexicon along with the Court's nuanced understanding of how gender-based crimes intersect with other crimes, thereby allowing a deeper understanding of the complexity of victimization during conflict.[234] The Trial Chamber in the *Taylor* judgment, the last one handed down by the SCSL, summed up conjugal slavery as a distinctive form of sexual slavery with additional non-sexual elements such as forced labor. The label of conjugal slavery as set out in the *Taylor* case has not received traction in the jurisprudence of contemporary international criminal courts and tribunals.[235] Factual situations surrounding forced conjugal association have arisen in other cases that have come before the ICC and other international criminal tribunals such as the ECCC, which seems to have given rise to a somewhat unsettled jurisprudence in the legal characterization of forced conjugal association.

The ECCC charged defendants in Case 002/02 with "forced marriage" as a distinct crime against humanity of "forced marriage" as "Other Inhumane Acts." It thereby followed the definition set out by the SCSL Appeals Chamber in the *AFRC* case.[236] Some factual differences are, however, apparent comparing the incidents of "forced marriage" in Sierra Leone and those in Cambodia. In the Cambodia context, both men and women could be viewed as the victims of the crime against humanity of forced marriage.[237] The Closing Order issued in 2010 by the investigative judges of the Cambodia Tribunal indicated that the Khmer Rouge would perform official group ceremonies, forcing twenty to thirty couples at a time with the threat of execution to marry partners.[238] This is another contextual difference between the "forced marriage" incidents in Cambodia compared to those recorded in conflicts in Africa such as in Sierra

---

[233]   *Id.*

[234]   Oosterveld, *supra* note 110.

[235]   Annie Bunting & Izevbuwa Kehinde Ikhimiukor, *The Expressive Nature of Law: What We Learn from Conjugal Slavery to Forced Marriage in International Criminal Law*, 18 INT'L CRIM. L. R. 331, 345 (2018).

[236]   Prosecutor v. Nuon, Case No. 002/19-09-2007-ECCC-OCIJ /No: D427, Closing Order, ¶¶ 1442–47 (Sept. 10, 2010).

[237]   *Id.* at ¶ 842.

[238]   *Id.*

Leone, where in the latter, there were no actual ceremonies validating the forced unions.[239]

The ICC has conflated the practice of forced conjugal association as crime against humanity in *Prosecutor v Germain Katanga (Katanga* case),[240] and most recently in the *Prosecutor v Dominic Ongwen (Ongwen* case),[241] where in the latter, the Pre-Trial Chamber confirmed the charges in March 2016 and opened the trial on December 6, 2016.[242]

The first time that charges of sexual violence were part of the Indictment in the ICC was the case against the Congolese militia leader, Germain Katanga. In the *Katanga* case, the Pre-Trial Chamber seemed to agree with the SCSL Trial Chamber (AFRC) and conflated "forced marriage" with sexual slavery. When considering a charge of sexual slavery, the Chamber held that sexual slavery "also encompassed situations where women and girls are forced into 'marriage', domestic servitude or other forced labor involving compulsory sexual activity, including rape, by their captors."[243]

The latest stage in the evolutionary process of defining and categorizing "forced marriage" was reached by the Pre-Trial Chamber of the ICC in its decision of March 23, 2016 confirming the charges against Dominic Ongwen. Ongwen is accused of seventy counts of war crimes and crimes against humanity allegedly committed in Uganda, including crimes against humanity of "Other Inhumane Acts" within the meaning of Article 7(1)(k) of the Rome Statute, in the form of "forced marriage."[244] According to the Pre-Trial Chamber, the central element of "forced marriage" is the imposition of "marriage" on the victim, that is the imposition, regardless of the will of the victim, of duties that are associated with marriage, as well as of a social status of the perpetrator's "wife."[245] It noted that the element of exclusivity of the forced conjugal union imposed on the victim is the characteristic aspect of "forced marriage" and is an element which is absent from any other crime with which Dominic Ongwen is charged.[246] It furthermore relied on the SCSL jurisprudence from the AFRC Appeal Judgment: "As held by the SCSL, unlike sexual slavery, 'forced marriage' implies a relationship of exclusivity between the

---

[239]   Bunting & Ikhimiukor, *supra* note 235, at 331.

[240]   Prosecutor v. Katanga, Case No. ICC-01/04-01/07, Decision on the Confirmation of Charges, ¶ 431 (Sept. 30, 2008).

[241]   Prosecutor v. Ongwen, Case No. ICC-02/04-01/15, Decision on the confirmation of charges against Dominic Ongwen (Mar. 23, 2016).

[242]   Press Release, International Criminal Court, Ongwen trial opens at International Criminal Court, ICC-CPI-20161206-PR1262 (Dec. 6, 2016).

[243]   Prosecutor v. Katanga, Case No. ICC-01/04-01/07, Decision on the confirmation of charges, ¶ 431 (Sept. 30, 2008).

[244]   Prosecutor v. Ongwen, Case No. ICC-02/04-01/15, Decision on the confirmation of charges against Dominic Ongwen, ¶ 88 (Mar. 23, 2016).

[245]   *Id.* at ¶ 93.

[246]   *Id.*

'husband' and 'wife', which could lead to disciplinary consequences for breach of this exclusive arrangement and, therefore, is 'not predominantly a sexual crime'."[247]

The Pre-Trial Chamber determined that the interest protected by the characterization of "forced marriage" as "Other Inhumane Acts" is the independently recognized basic right to consensually marry and establish a family, as enshrined in international human rights instruments, which differ from the other values underlying the crime of sexual slavery (physical and sexual integrity).[248] The Pre-Trial Chamber concluded that the conduct of "forced marriage" constitutes the crime of "crimes against humanity of 'Other Inhumane Acts'" and distinguished it from sexual slavery and other crimes against humanity.[249] With the *Ongwen* case, which is ongoing as of writing, the ICC will likely have the ability to influence and shape the direction of future prosecutions of forced conjugal associations before it and possibly other criminal jurisdictions.[250] The *Ongwen* case presents an opportunity for the ICC to bring greater clarity to the crimes against humanity of other inhumane acts in relation to the element of forced marriage. It will be interesting to see how the ICC Trial and Appeals Chamber rules on this question and the implications for the development of this jurisprudence for the future treatment of such crimes in international criminal law.

6.6 CONCLUSION

In summary, two strands of the SCSL jurisprudence have emerged from the three cases in which the SCSL addressed forced marriage.[251] The first strand emerged from the *AFRC* case and the *RUF* case and the second from the *Taylor* case. The *AFRC* Appeal Chamber, in a reversal of the Trial Chamber's decision, characterized forced marriage as a distinct crime of "Other Inhumane Acts" of crimes against humanity, as it later affirmed in the *RUF* case. The second strand emerged from the *Taylor* case, which first of all termed the forced marriages as "conjugal slavery,"[252] then used the phenomenon as proof of the sexual slavery count, and then finally advanced the crime in such a way that it clarified that this kind of enslavement captured both sexual slavery and forced labor.[253]

The groundbreaking cases at the SCSL in the *AFRC*, *RUF*, and *Taylor* judgments have all provided some important progress in the legal recognition of gender-based crimes. The SCSL has built on the work of the ICTY and ICTR to contribute to the global development of norms that recognize the place of gendered phenomenon in

---

[247] *Id.*; Prosecutor v. Brima, Case No. SCSL-2004-16-A, Judgment, ¶ 195 (Feb. 22, 2008).

[248] Prosecutor v. Ongwen, Case No. ICC-02/04-01/15, Decision on the confirmation of charges against Dominic Ongwen, ¶ 94 (Mar. 23, 2016).

[249] *Id.* at ¶ 95.

[250] Bunting & Ikhimiukor, *supra* note 235, at 353.

[251] *Id.*

[252] Prosecutor v. Taylor, Case No. SCSL-03-01-T-1283, Judgment, ¶ 427 (May 18, 2012).

[253] *Id.*

contemporary armed conflicts. In this regard, although progress in this area as in other areas of international law seems incremental, the SCSL can indeed rightly be lauded as the first international penal tribunal to formally recognize the crime of "forced marriage" as a crime against humanity. As violence targeting or impacting women typically has been overlooked by the international criminal law community, which can be somewhat attributed to the historical absence of women in formulating international law and by the continued inequality faced by women in many parts of the world, it is now more important than ever to ensure that the international community is aware of the substance and importance of these rulings in order to secure the future of prosecutions of gender-based crimes. The manner in which the SCSL judges of the trial and appeals chamber addressed these issues can, at the end of the day, be said to have made a valuable contribution by giving express international legal condemnation to certain egregious conduct that was carried out largely by men against women and girls during the brutal civil war in Sierra Leone.

7

Child Recruitment As a War Crime

7.1 INTRODUCTION

Children have been a part of armed conflicts for as long as wars have occurred. They are primarily victims, but in some cases, they are also perpetrators. In 1995, a seminal study commissioned by the United Nations found that thirty intrastate conflicts were raging in different parts of the world.[1] Millions of children were affected. Many were raped, maimed or exposed to hunger, disease or deprivation. Many others had been abducted, denied humanitarian assistance, or even worse, killed. The seminal Machel Report highlighted that children were usually the primary victims of armed conflict. It also documented one of the most alarming trends of modern warfare in all different regions of the world: The conscription and use of children (mostly boys, but also girls) as "soldiers" in combat.[2] The report also highlighted children's role in performing combat support functions for fighting forces as cooks, porters, messengers, and spies, whether for government armies or rebel forces and militia groups. The trend continues to the present day.

The Sierra Leone conflict, like the closely interlinked one in neighboring Liberia, was widely associated with the phenomenon of abducting and using "child soldiers."[3] Partly for that reason, and the shocking nature of some of the acts carried out by the youthful combatants, it generated considerable attention from the international community. Many children were abducted, forced to fight for their abductors, and if they resisted, they were compelled to kill or to be killed.[4] Children were often drugged, forced to work for their captors, raped, and exposed to drugs and other forms of physical violence and abuse.[5]

---

[1] U.N. Secretary-General, *Promotion and Protection of the Rights of Children: Impact of Armed Conflict on Children*, U.N. Doc. A/51/306 (Aug. 26, 1996).
[2] UNICEF, *Impact of Armed Conflict on Children: Wars Against Children*, https://static.unicef.org /graca/.
[3] Child Soldiers International, *Child Soldiers Global Report 2004 – Sierra Leone* (2004).
[4] *Id.*
[5] *Id.*

Girls aged between ten and fourteen years were especially targeted. Indeed, even before the war ended, it was reported that just about all the parties to the Sierra Leone conflict had pursued a policy of deliberate targeting of children.[6] The different leadership of the warring parties, especially the Revolutionary United Front (RUF) rebels, were found to have instituted and implemented an organized system for the conscription, training, and use of children in the hostilities. The vulnerability of children was exploited to advance the goals of the adults and their fighting forces. Some children and youth, with little or no other prospects in life, joined the cause for economic or other complex reasons.[7] This included to protect their families, acquire social or political power, or for ideological reasons.[8] This situation provoked sometimes heated debates whether those children could voluntarily join fighting forces or can give informed consent for their activities.

Unsurprisingly, given the prominent role which made them among the most feared by local Sierra Leoneans during the war, how to address the problem of "child soldiers" preoccupied national and international policy-makers as they sought a way to end the brutal conflict. A human-rights driven child protection model was adopted. It was predicated on the idea of disarmament, demobilization, and reintegration of the combatants back into society. This was matched by provision for the punishment of the adults who recruited and used the children during the war. Both these elements, which were the focus in Sierra Leone, tracked the efforts and approach of the international community to develop global norms aimed at condemning this abhorrent practice. Such efforts included the criminalization of the forcible recruitment and use of children under the age of fifteen for the purpose of using them to participate actively in hostilities.

Though international humanitarian law has been a key feature of international law for several centuries, the development of a body of international criminal law purporting to hold individuals criminally liable for certain international crimes, such as war crimes and crimes against humanity, was a largely mid-twentieth century affair. There were earlier efforts, such as the Commission on the Authors of Responsibility for the War which followed in the immediate aftermath of World War I in 1919.[9] But, as is well known among international lawyers, the watershed was the establishment of the International Military Tribunal at Nuremberg in 1945. Within that broader context, the development of the legal prohibitions of enlisting, conscripting, and using children under the age of fifteen to participate actively in hostilities as a war crime condemned by international law is even more recent in so far as it was largely taking place within the last decade of that same century. Before

---

[6] *Id.*

[7] *Id.*

[8] *Id.*

[9] Commission on the Responsibility of the Authors of the War and on Enforcement of Penalties, *Report Presented to the Preliminary Peace Conference*, 14 Am. J. Int'l L. 95 (1920).

then, and to varying degrees, international law frowned upon the practice but did not impose criminal responsibility on the perpetrators.

7.2 PURPOSE AND STRUCTURE OF THIS CHAPTER

In a significant legal development, the prohibition of child recruitment as a war crime in both international and non-international armed conflicts was enshrined as Article 8(c)(vii) of the Rome Statute of the International Criminal Court (ICC).[10] The Rome Statute, which was adopted in July 1998 and entered into force in July 2002, in turn formed the basis for the inclusion of the war crime in the Special Court for Sierra Leone (SCSL). The SCSL Statute contained Article 4(c), which was largely identical to the provision in the Rome Statute, when the bilateral treaty between the United Nations and the Government of Sierra Leone was signed in January 2002.[11] It entered into force in April 2002, and within short order, a number of indictments were issued and suspects arrested for, among other things, the war crime of conscripting or enlisting children under the age of fifteen years into armed forces or groups or using them to participate actively in hostilities.

This means that the *application* of that novel body of law, to a first set of concrete cases, is yet more novel. This is because, by dint of the peculiarities of the child soldier driven conflict and the inclusion of the crime within its subject matter jurisdiction, the SCSL became the first international criminal tribunal to actually charge and successfully prosecute suspects with this war crime. The trial and appellate judges of the SCSL therefore became the first to adjudicate that war crime. The potential significance of the SCSL interpretation and application of that crime to concrete cases increased when the ICC Prosecutor, invoking the horrific impact of the child soldier phenomenon and figures such as 30,000 underage children in the Democratic Republic of the Congo, relied on the same war crime of child recruitment in the ICC's historic first case involving Congolese warlord Thomas Lubanga Dyilo.[12] The prosecution's press release asserted that children are being trained to be machines of war, and that turning children into such machines, jeopardizes humankind's future and expressed his resolve to work to put an end to such crimes. In the course of that case, from beginning through to end, the legal findings of the SCSL became a key point of reference for the prosecution and defense cases and ultimately the findings of the ICC Chambers from the pre-trial, trial, and appeals chambers.

This chapter examines the legacy of the SCSL concerning the prohibition of the recruitment and use of children under fifteen into armed forces or groups or using

---

[10] Rome Statute of the International Criminal Court art. 8(c)(vii), 2187 U.N.T.S. 3 (1998) [hereinafter Rome Statute].

[11] Statute of the Special Court for Sierra Leone art. 4(c) (2002) [hereinafter SCSL Statute].

[12] Prosecutor v. Dyilo, ICC-01/04-01/06-2842, Judgment pursuant to Article 74 of the Statute (Mar. 14, 2012).

them to participate actively in hostilities as a war crime under customary international law. The chapter proceeds as follows. First, to contextualize the subsequent discussion, I will briefly explain the key role of children in the Sierra Leone conflict. I then address how the problem of child soldiers was addressed by the parties to the conflict in the final peace accord which initially contemplated only a truth and reconciliation commission. I then briefly explore how that vision was affected with the shift to a criminal prosecution mechanism through the creation of the SCSL. Thereafter, I examine two defendants' interlocutory challenge to the jurisdiction of the SCSL and the important ruling of the Appeals Chamber finding that the war crime was also a crime under customary international law. In the next part, I examine how that SCSL interpretation has informed the ICC's application of that crime in relation to the conduct (*actus reus*) and mental elements (*mens rea*) of the crime in its own case law. This would assist in assessing the influence, if any, of the SCSL case law on the world's only permanent international criminal tribunal with regards to the prosecution of this crime.

Overall, though critical of some of the reasoning, the chapter argues that the SCSL's understanding and treatment of the child soldier phenomenon as a war crime constitutes a useful contribution to the development of modern international criminal law. This amounts to an important legacy for the future, which having helped to shape the ICC's adjudication of the crime through clarification of certain aspects of the crime, will likely resonate well beyond the four corners of Sierra Leone and Africa to help address a particularly vicious feature of modern non-state actor driven armed conflicts which continues to this day. In my view, this amounts to a useful legal legacy that contributes to the development of modern international criminal justice.

7.3 CHILDREN IN THE SIERRA LEONE CONFLICT

7.3.1 *Child Poverty As a Breeding Ground for Child Recruitment in Sierra Leone*

At the time of the Sierra Leone conflict, the best population estimates suggested that the country was comprised of 4.5 million people.[13] Of those, over half of the population were said to be boys and girls under the age of nineteen with the majority of the population being on the more youthful side. The conflict had a major impact on the largest part of the population: children. Their rights were systematically violated. Abductions, forced recruitment by armed factions, sexual slavery, rape, amputations, mutilation, displacement, and torture became common.[14] This showed a level of cruelty in Sierra Leonean society in ways that had not been

---

[13]   World Peace Foundation, *Mass Atrocity Endings, Sierra Leone* (2015).

[14]   Child Soldiers Int'l, *Child Soldiers Global Report 2004 – Sierra Leone* (2004).

experienced before. Although accurate statistics of the number of children asso-ciated with the conflict, whether as child soldiers or others in more support roles may not ever be fully known, there are some credible estimates to give a sense of the scale of the problem.[15]

On the lower side, it was estimated that about 5,000 boys and girls under the age of eighteen were used as fighters during the war. On the high side, according to other estimates, the figure ranged from 6,000 (United Nations International Children's Emergency Fund – UNICEF) to 10,000 (United Nations Assistance Mission in Sierra Leone – UNAMSIL), or even as many as 20,000 children involved with the war. The discrepancies can probably be explained by the different criteria used to arrive at the numbers. In any case, after the war ended, about 6,774 children registered for the disarmament, demobilization, and reintegration program, accord-ing to Sierra Leone's National Committee for Demobilization, Disarmament and Reintegration. It may be assumed that not all combatants participated in the disarmament program, since a gendered reading of who was a child soldier as opposed to camp followers may have led to undercounting of girls who had partici-pated as combatants. Also, girls that had been abducted or feared stigmatization did not participate in the program. This reality implies that the official estimates ended up in the middle of the extremes of the numbers offered by the two UN agencies (UNICEF and UNAMSIL).

There may remain some doubts about the exact statistics. But based on the available evidence, ultimately, three points about children and the Sierra Leone conflict would seem to be uncontroversial. First, children played a substantial role in the conflict, as was later confirmed by both the Truth and Reconciliation Commission (TRC) and the Special Court for Sierra Leone (SCSL).[16] Second, and tied directly to that first point, there was widespread use of children by all the warring parties, though the extent of this differed from group to group. This is to be expected given the non-state actor driven nature of the conflict. According to some reports, as many as half of the RUF's fighting force were children,[17] meaning that they were of significant importance to the RUF as an organization. Indeed, without a formal recruitment track, the RUF relied heavily on abducted children and its practice of "training and using children for military purposes demonstrated a consistent pattern of conduct"[18] that dated back to the beginning of the war in 1991. Whereas children were also part of the Civil Defense Forces (CDF) fighting forces, as well as the Armed Forces Revolutionary Council (AFRC), and to a lower extent, the Republic of Sierra Leone Armed Forces. These actions of the parties to

[15] A. B. Zack-Williams, *Child Soldiers in the Civil War in Sierra Leone*, 28 Rev. Afr. Pol. Econ. 73 (2001) (estimating that roughly 10,000–14,000 children fought between 1991 and 2002).

[16] Prosecutor v. Sesay, Case No. SCSL-04-15-T, Judgment, ¶ 1614 (Mar. 2, 2009) [hereinafter RUF Trial Judgment].

[17] Jan Goodwin, *Sierra Leone Is No Place To Be Young*, N.Y. Times, Feb. 14, 1999, § 6 at 48.

[18] RUF Trial Judgment, *supra* note 16, at ¶¶ 1615–16.

the conflict contradicted the general prohibition against involving children in fighting.

Third, and in consequence, the role of children in the Sierra Leone war posed a key challenge on how to address the plight of children in a post-conflict dispensation. This invites consideration of their position in pre- and post-conflict dispensation of the country. Several explanations have been offered to explain the situation of children that made them vulnerable for involvement in the war. First, according to the Truth and Reconciliation Commission, educational opportunities were not equitably distributed.[19] Corruption, bad governance, and other factors ensured elites and those in urban areas were more likely to access education.[20] By the time the conflict started, 88.75 percent of all girls and 69.3 percent of boys had enrolled in school.[21] It is also estimated that less than half (that is, 45 percent) of all children of school-going age entered primary schools. Of those, only 9 percent entered secondary schools and a bare 1 percent made it through to tertiary level institutions.[22] Indeed, according to the TRC, the RUF claimed that a major impetus for their starting of the war was the failure of the government to offer free education to all children in the country.

A second factor was more social and cultural. Though Sierra Leone is not unique in this respect, and instead reflected a pattern found across Africa and in other parts of the world, children are wards of their adult parents and others who make decisions for them. This means that, when combined with their exclusion from decision-making and the culture that they are to be seen but not necessarily heard, a level of disgruntlement is found to have existed. A gendered aspect of this is that in some parts of the country, girls are not given opportunities to attend school, are often married off early, and in many cases, suffer from adverse cultural practices such as genital mutilation. In already dire circumstances, in relative terms, the boys fared better than girls in most ethnic groups.

Third, the economic decline that Sierra Leone suffered in the two decades leading up to the war meant that the health and economic status of the most vulnerable in society suffered tremendously. Sierra Leone fell to the bottom of the Human Development Index, which among other things, measures child mortality. The latter increased significantly.[23] Already bad conditions in health and nutrition were exacerbated with more of the children that survived having to fend for themselves. Many youth did not have access to education, had to work and lacked access to basic social programs.

---

[19] Sierra Leone Truth and Reconciliation Comm'n, *Children and the Armed Conflict in Sierra Leone*, in Witness to Truth: Final Report of the TRC (vol. 3B, ch. 4) (2004).

[20] *Id.*

[21] *Id.*

[22] *Id.*

[23] U.N.D.P., *Human Development Reports: Sierra Leone*, http://hdr.undp.org/en/countries/pro files/SLE.

In the end, the situation of children in Sierra Leone as it related to education, health, and their involvement in the economy gave rise to a high level of dissatisfaction amongst Sierra Leonean youth. Many became disenchanted. Successive governments failed to address the issue. With hope lost, combined with marginalization and exclusion from society and lack of employment or any meaningful life prospects, the ground was fertile for many of them to take up arms. They became that much more vulnerable to recruitment and manipulation by adults. According to the TRC, many of those who voluntarily joined the RUF explained that the poor social and economic conditions in the country gave them little choice but to join the rebels.[24]

7.3.2 *The Place of Children in Early Efforts to Make Peace in Sierra Leone*

Whatever the reasons, and there are many, children did play a substantial role in the Sierra Leone conflict – as victims as well as perpetrators. Their plight therefore had to be considered in any serious effort to bring the war to an end. It took time for the warring parties to recognize this. Before the conclusion of the comprehensive Lomé Peace Agreement in July 1999,[25] several earlier attempts were made to end the war in Sierra Leone. The first major peace agreement, the Abidjan Accord signed by the RUF and the Government of Sierra Leone on November 30, 1996, was concluded by the government and the rebels. The agreement did not explicitly address the plight of child soldiers. It did so only implicitly.[26] The majority of the twenty-eight clauses were general in nature and focused on laying out a framework for a ceasefire, and after the ceasefire, the disarmament, demobilization, and the reintegration of combatants.[27] This reflected the preoccupation with the cessation of the hostilities. Children were not mentioned anywhere in the agreement except in relation to the call for the improvement of educational services to enable "all children of primary and junior-secondary school age" to receive "free and compulsory schooling."[28]

The peace accord also contemplated that there would be opportunity for "the youth" and "all Sierra Leoneans" to receive affordable quality education.[29] This provision could be seen as confirmation of the RUF view that the lack of education for children was a key malaise that contributed to the start of the war in the first place. Significantly, and this clause also confirms the TRC's finding regarding rebel concern about the high level of youth unemployment, the agreement also called for government to "provide job opportunities in a systematic and sustainable way for the

---

[24] Sierra Leone Truth and Reconciliation Comm'n, *supra* note 19.
[25] Lomé Peace Agreement between the Government of Sierra Leone and the Revolutionary United Front of Sierra Leone, U.N. Doc. S/1999/77 (July 7, 1999) [hereinafter Lomé Peace Agreement].
[26] *Id.*
[27] *Id.*
[28] *Id.*
[29] *Id.*

people, especially the youth." In a way, between education to address child illiteracy and a demand for employment to include youth, this provision might be one to have expected since future job opportunities would also redound to the benefit of the RUF's former combatants themselves.

Once the Abidjan Accord collapsed, which occurred not long after it was signed, another peace plan was concluded. The Conakry Peace Plan was agreed under the auspices of the Economic Community of West African States (ECOWAS), which was to support its implementation.[30] It contained a six month timetable and again only spoke to the needs of child soldiers implicitly by providing for either job training or alternative employment and the provision of scholarships/grants for further education.[31] It was envisaged that access to education at all levels would be made available to all demobilized persons. Ex-combatants were to be provided with assistance that would facilitate their reintegration into their communities. ECOWAS and the international community were to provide appropriate assistance towards achievement of those objectives. This recognized the limited capacity that the Sierra Leonean government would have had at that time.

In sum, both the Abidjan and Conakry accords contemplated what was required to bring about a cease fire, to disarm, demobilize, and reintegrate combatants back into society. They did not address the needs of children as such. Nonetheless, the presence of children in large numbers amongst the warring parties implied that they would be beneficiaries of certain socioeconomic programs. This necessarily included disarmament, but also the provision of educational and employment opportunities. Up to this point, as conceived by the warring parties, children generally and child soldiers in particular were not as central to the post-conflict dispensation.

7.3.3 *Children and the War in the First Comprehensive Peace Agreement*

The seeming lack of substantial attention to the child soldier problem all changed with the negotiation of the first comprehensive peace agreement between the RUF and the Sierra Leonean government. This made that accord the first peace agreement to explicitly contemplate the role of child combatants. After various averments, the tenth preambular paragraph explicitly recognized "the imperative that the children of Sierra Leone, especially those affected by armed conflict, in view of their vulnerability, are entitled to special care and the protection of their inherent right to life, survival and development, in accordance with the provisions of the International Convention on the Rights of the Child."[32] The human rights approach is evident in this paragraph when it indicated that children are entitled to "special care." Their fundamental right to "life, survival and development" also deserved

---

[30]   Conakry Peace Plan, U.N. Doc. S/1997/824 (Oct. 23, 1997).
[31]   *Id.*
[32]   Lomé Peace Agreement, *supra* note 25.

protection.[33] The explicit link was then made to international human rights law, citing to the most widely ratified UN human rights treaty, which deals with the rights of children generally. Sierra Leone was by then already a party, as it acceded to it on June 1990. In contrast, the Abidjan and Conakry accords both omitted a mention to children in the preamble or recognition of the need for children to have special status or protection. The word child/children appeared once in the former of these agreements in one substantive provision but not at all in the latter.

But more important than the preamble, Article XXX, which is found in Part V of the Lomé Peace Agreement, specifically addressed the issue of "child combatants."[34] This substantive article aimed to help achieve the ambition of the agreement stated as follows:

> The Government shall accord particular attention to the issue of child soldiers. It shall, accordingly, mobilize resources, both within the country and from the International Community, and especially through the Office of the UN Special Representative for Children in Armed Conflict, UNICEF and other agencies, to address the special needs of these children in the existing disarmament, demobilization and reintegration processes.[35]

This provision marked a step forward compared to the previous agreements. However, in the main, it purported to address the situation of "child combatants" in a largely narrow sense. This is because it focused only on changing the combatant status of the children. This is clear from the principal obligation it imposed on the authorities, which was that the government (1) shall pay special regard to the situation of child soldiers; and, (2) "accordingly," carry responsibility to "mobilize" the resources needed to disarm, demobilize, and reintegrate the children. Whereas the first and second sentences of the paragraph could have been read as establishing independent duties, the use of the "accordingly," makes clear that there was one major duty which was to address the special needs of children through their disarmament, demobilization, and reintegration into society. In doing so, it was contemplated that the government will use its own resources but also rely on external partners such as the named UN agencies especially UNICEF to meet those goals.

Two final points can be noted. First, the only addressee of the obligation is the government, implying that there was no corresponding duty on the part of the other parties to the conflict, most notably, the RUF. Second, the parties could have provided for more specific language such as contemplating the possibility for economic, psychological, social, or other forms of support for children. The latter only appeared to be the case in respect of the undertaking of the government to provide free compulsory education for the first nine years of schooling (Article

[33] *Id.*
[34] *Id.*
[35] *Id.*

XXXI). The same provision also required the government to provide free primary healthcare throughout Sierra Leone. Despite these limitations, however, the very fact of inclusion of the ideas contained in the agreement helped to move the plight of child combatants and children more generally into the center instead of leaving them in the periphery.

7.4 THE SHIFT IN DEALING WITH CHILD SOLDIERS IN THE SCSL

Once Sierra Leonean authorities shifted to a criminal prosecution model to address the aftermath of the war, instead of the initial amnesty/forgive and forget policy discussed in Chapters 9 and 10 of this book, the government and the international community unsurprisingly continued their focus on addressing the issue of child soldiers. Their place was also a matter of concern when the SCSL was going to be established. In this context, the UN, as represented by the Secretary-General, noted that the potential prosecution of children for war crimes and crimes against humanity committed throughout the war presented a difficult moral dilemma.[36] The dilemma arose as a function of the differing perspectives of Sierra Leonean authorities, and the local population, on the one hand; and on the other hand, the views of the UN and the international community. Unsurprisingly, in the former category, people who had suffered directly the atrocities of the war demanded that child soldiers also be held criminally accountable in the SCSL. Whereas the UN, and its human rights agencies as well as other NGOs, held the opposite stance. The Secretary-General understood the magnitude of the issue, especially after the visit of his representatives to Sierra Leone. Indeed, he argued that although Sierra Leoneans might perceive children as among those who have committed the worst crimes against them, children were to be regarded "first and foremost as victims."[37] This child protection and human rights approach informed the framework that would be eventually agreed.

The Secretary-General also emphasized that, more than in any other conflict where children have been used as soldiers, in Sierra Leone, the children deserved special treatment, all the more so given the circumstances under which children had been initially abducted, forcibly recruited, sexually abused, enslaved as well as trained to kill, maim, and burn, often while under the influence of drugs. This view, which effectively challenged the arguably more complex view of the role of children in the Sierra Leone war, prioritized the international over the local perspective and stressed the psychological and physical abuse and duress which

---

[36] See U.N. Secretary General, *Report of the Secretary-General on the Establishment of a Special Court for Sierra Leone,* ¶ 36, U.N. Doc. S/2000/915 (Oct. 4, 2000); *see also* Ilene Cohn, *The Protection of Children and the Quest for Truth and Justice,* 55 J. INT'L AFF. 1, 12 (2001).

[37] Alette Smeulers, Barbara Hola, & Tom van den Berg, *Sixty-Five Years of International Criminal Justice: The Facts and Figures, in* THE REALITIES OF INTERNATIONAL CRIMINAL JUSTICE 32 (2003).

had transformed children from victims into perpetrators. This led to two important policies in relation to the treatment of children that would be later written into the SCSL Statute.

First, in the negotiations of the legal framework for the tribunal, the emphasis was to establish a mechanism to pursue the adults who had stolen the livelihoods of the children. In this regard, the subject matter competence of the tribunal reflected this in its composition of crimes under international law as well as Sierra Leonean law. The material jurisdiction honed in on the worst of the practices, including criminalizing the abduction of thousands of children. In so doing, and in recognition of the principle of legality and in particular *nullum crimen sine lege* and the prohibition on retroactive criminal legislation, the Secretary-General elected to only include crimes that were considered to have the character of customary international law at the time they were committed. In this regard, and as discussed in Chapter 3, in relation to the international crimes, crimes against humanity, war crimes, and other serious violations of international humanitarian law were included in the statute. The prohibition of the abduction and forced recruitment of children under the age of fifteen years into armed forces or groups for the purpose of using them to participate actively in hostilities was included in Article 4(c) of the SCSL Statute and was the linchpin of the form of protective mechanism sought for children. The international criminal prohibition was then matched also by the inclusion of *domestic crimes* to cover situations or aspects of them that were considered to be either unregulated or inadequately regulated under international law. Though with hindsight we know that these provisions were not in fact subsequently used, as initially contemplated, it was interesting that the two sets of crimes covered two features of the war that were widely known: (1) the abuse of underage girls; and (2) arson. These prohibitions, drawn from national legislation, were ultimately included as the prohibitions contained in Article 5 of the SCSL Statute addressing Sierra Leonean law.

The second element of this policy on child soldiers concerned the individual criminal responsibility of children. It was clear to the Secretary-General, from his consultations with Sierra Leonean authorities and civil society, that views were divided on the question of prosecuting children for their conduct during the war. The government and the local civil society clearly preferred a process of judicial accountability for child combatants presumed responsible for the crimes falling within the SCSL's jurisdiction. This camp suggested that sparing the children would mean that the process of criminal accountability risked being seen as a failure. On the other hand, in the second camp, were those in the international civil society and the UN itself who objected to such prosecutions. The fear was that the rehabilitation program for children would be placed at risk.

Given these divergent views, the Secretary-General sought to strike a balance between the two sets of interests. For that reason, he noted that the language of persons bearing greatest responsibility would not necessarily exclude children who may have committed such crimes. This would have reassured Sierra Leonean authorities that criminal responsibility could follow for any children deemed to be among those most responsible for the atrocious crimes committed against civilians. Nonetheless, invoking international instruments, language was added in the SCSL Statute providing for the creation of a juvenile chamber. Juveniles were to be treated with dignity and provided a separate trial process from that of adults. They were to be released, rather than kept in remand, pending their trial. Punishment was also set to be different. There was to be diversion of the children, should they be convicted, into alternative mechanisms for rehabilitation rather than imprisonment. It was felt that this struck an appropriate balance between the competing interests. In the end, the choice whether to proceed on this path lay both with the Security Council, and if it approved the proposal that persons under the age of eighteen be eligible for prosecutions, ultimately would be the responsibility of the SCSL's Prosecutor. The Prosecutor would later announce a policy that he would focus on addressing the responsibility of adults rather than the children that they recruited.

7.5 THE SCSL APPEALS CHAMBER AND THE WAR CRIME OF CHILD RECRUITMENT AS A CRIME UNDER CUSTOMARY INTERNATIONAL LAW

7.5.1 *Norman's Preliminary Motion*

Making good on his promise to pursue cases against adults that recruited children, on March 7, 2003, the SCSL Prosecutor issued an indictment for Samuel Hinga Norman. Norman, who was a deputy minister, was accused of eight counts of war crimes, crimes against humanity, and other serious violations of international humanitarian law that he allegedly committed from November 30, 1996.[38] To the surprise of many Sierra Leoneans, in what proved to be a highly controversial trial, he was arrested at his office in Freetown a week later and handed over to the SCSL. Following his initial appearance, at which he pleaded not guilty in the town of Bonthe, Norman's counsel filed a preliminary motion challenging the court's jurisdiction to try him, in part, on the basis that he had been charged with a crime that was not recognized under customary international law.

Norman argued in his June 26, 2003 motion, which was later joined by another accused, Moinina Fofana, that the SCSL had no jurisdiction to try him under Article 4(c) of the SCSL Statute as charged in count 8 of the indictment. According to the defense submission, at all times relevant to the indictment, customary international law had not established a prohibition of the recruitment of children under fifteen into armed forces or groups or using them to participate

---

[38] Prosecutor v. Norman, Case No. SCSL-2004-14-AR72(e), Decision on Preliminary Motion Based on Lack of Jurisdiction (May 31, 2004).

actively in hostilities. Consequently, although under Article 4(c) incorporated a provision creating an obligation for states to refrain from recruiting children as soldiers, the relevant treaties had not criminalized such activity. It followed that the laying of that charge constituted a violation of the principle *nullum crimen sine lege* since recruiting children was not a crime known to international law. The SCSL prosecution of any crime within its own material jurisdiction will only be possible, in light of the principle of legality, if the conduct it seeks to punish was criminal under customary international law during the period in which the alleged crime took place.

On the other hand, according to the Prosecution response, the crime of child recruitment was already part of customary international law at the time the alleged offence took place. There was sufficient state practice demonstrating the existence of such a norm of international law. This was because some states had made the practice of recruiting children to fight illegal under their domestic laws. Such national legislation was backed up by subsequent international conventions which prohibited child recruitment. In this regard, child recruitment had been included in the Rome Statute, which codified existing customary international law. As a secondary argument, the prosecution claimed that established jurisprudence from other tribunals indicated that individual criminal responsibility may arise for a person even where not specified by treaty. In any event, the *nullum crimen sine lege* principle should be applied flexibly since the acts in issue are universally deemed abhorrent.

The trial judges determined that Norman's motion raised a serious issue relating to jurisdiction. Thus, under the mandatory and controversial provision in Rule 72(E) of the Rules of Procedure and Evidence of the SCSL, the motion was referred to the Appeals Chamber. Following the submissions of the parties, and amici, all of which will be discussed in detail momentarily, the majority of the SCSL Appeals Chamber dismissed the defense motion on May 31, 2004.[39] It determined that the recruitment of children below fifteen did in fact constitute a crime that had "crystallised" under customary international law before the start of the temporal jurisdiction of the SCSL on November 30, 1996.

The significance of this ruling stems from two features. First, it enabled the SCSL Appeals Chamber to opine on the open question whether the war crime of child recruitment had matured or passed into customary international law. That issue had been a matter of debate among states during the negotiations of the Rome Statute and was also contentious between key UN organs as evidenced by the views, on the one part, of the Secretary-General, and on the other part, the Security Council. The second reason why the decision seems important is that, having incorporated the standards contained in the Rome Statute and now become the first court to have

---

[39] Prosecutor v. Norman, Case No. SCSL-2004-14-AR72(e), Decision on Preliminary Motion Based on Lack of Jurisdiction (May 31, 2004).

a case that relies partly on its provisions, it fell to the judges of the SCSL to study the crime further and to discern its elements. The elements would later become relevant in discussions of the crime during the first trial at the ICC in The Hague.

7.5.2 *The Appeals Chamber's Majority Ruling*

In addressing the defense motion, concerning the question whether the prohibition contained in Article 4(c) of the Statute of the SCSL codified a customary international law rule making it a war crime to recruit children for the purposes of using them in hostilities at the time of the alleged acts in November 1996, the Appeals Chamber considered two sources of international law set out in Article 38(1) of the Statute of the International Court of Justice. [40] First, the Appeals Chamber examined whether or not there were "international conventions, whether general or particular, establishing rules especially recognized by the contesting states." Second, the majority thereafter considered whether there was "international custom, as evidence of a general practice accepted as law." For analytical purposes, it is worth reviewing the findings of the Court in relation to each of these important aspects.

7.5.2.1 Child Recruitment in International Treaty Law

With regard to the first element, the Appeals Chamber did not consider it "necessary to elaborate on this point in great detail." The reason being that the Defense, although more specifically the Fofana Defense team, did not "dispute the fact that international humanitarian law is violated by the recruitment of children." Here, the majority considered the Fourth Geneva Convention, Additional Protocols I and II, and the Convention on the Rights of the Child. Perhaps, because of this view that one of the parties had conceded the point, the Appeals Chamber did not spend much time analyzing the prohibition of child recruitment under international treaty law. But the deeper problem is that the various instruments cited did not per se prohibit the recruitment of children as a matter of treaty law. Yet, in what appears to be a two-part reasoning, the majority of the Appeals Chamber implied that the prohibition of the war crime had occurred as of November 1996 under both treaty and customary law.

With regard to the Fourth Geneva Convention concerning the protection of civilian persons and populations in times of war, which at the time had been endorsed by 187 States including Sierra Leone which ratified it 1965, the majority of the Appeals Chamber referenced Articles 14 and 24. The former clause provided that, during peacetime as well as after the outbreak of hostilities, the parties to the Convention may establish, in their own territories, or if necessary in occupied areas,

---

[40]   Article 38(1)(b) of the ICJ Statute provides that the Court, whose function is to decide in accordance with international law such disputes as are submitted to it, shall apply international custom, as evidence of a general practice as law.

hospitals, and safety zones and localities "so organized as to protect the effects of war, wounded, sick and aged persons, children under fifteen" as well as expectant mothers as well as mothers of children under seven years. Article 24, for its part, obligated parties to the conflict to "take the necessary measures to ensure that children under fifteen, who are orphaned or are separated from their families as a result of the war, are not left to their own resources and that the exercise of their religion and their education are facilitated in all circumstances." Additionally, by virtue of Article 51 of the Fourth Geneva Convention, an occupying power "may not compel protected persons to serve in its armed or auxiliary forces." Moreover, it is prohibited to use pressure or propaganda to secure voluntary enlistment.

It is clear that the provisions of the Geneva Convention mentioned here establish a duty, for the parties to the conflict, to protect children under fifteen from war's harmful effects. By their own terms, however, these provisions do no more than impose a general duty on the Contracting States. The vulnerable class of children, that is those under fifteen, and further who are orphaned or not with their parents as a consequence of the war, are not to be left on their own without any assistance.

As Justice Robertson noted in his dissenting opinion in *Norman*, the Geneva Convention "identified 'children under fifteen' as a class which required a special protection in war, along with other vulnerable categories identified by Article 14 – the sick and wounded, the aged, expectant mothers and mothers of children under seven."[41] Additionally, the general duty imposed is on the occupying power, rather than "on any other state or non-state actor." Furthermore, "it is not enforceable and is not part of the 'grave breaches' regime of the Geneva Convention."[42]

In its commentary on the article, the International Committee of the Red Cross (ICRC) has further explained that the application of the article "must be governed by the degree of development of the physical and mental faculties of the persons concerned."[43] According to the terms of Article 50, occupying powers must, with the cooperation of the national and local authorities, facilitate the proper working of children's institutions. This provides not only a negative duty on the occupying authorities to avoid interfering with the activities of the institutions, but also a positive duty to support the institutions. As stated in the ICRC commentary, "[t]his provision assures the continuity in the educational and charitable work of establishments referred to and is of the first importance, since it takes effect at a point in children's lives when the general disorganization consequent upon war might otherwise do irreparable harm to their physical and mental development."

Turning to Additional Protocols I and II to the 1949 Geneva Conventions, both of which were ratified by Sierra Leone in 1986 (that is ten years before the contested

---

[41] Prosecutor v. Norman, Case No. SCSL-04-14-AR72, Judgment: Dissenting Opinion of Justice Robertson, ¶ 24 (May 31, 2004) [hereinafter Dissenting Opinion of Justice Robertson].

[42] *Id.* at ¶ 25.

[43] International Committee of the Red Cross, Convention (IV) relative to the Protection of Civilian Persons in Time of War: Commentary of 1958 (Aug. 12, 1949).

dates) and which apply to international and non-international armed conflicts respectively, the Appeals Chamber found as relevant Articles 77 and 4. The first of these, Article 77, addressed specifically the "protection of children." It mandates that the parties to the conflict "shall take all feasible measures in order that children who have not attained the age of fifteen years do not take a direct part in hostilities, and in particular, they shall refrain from recruiting them into their armed forces." The provision also concerns children who are between fifteen and eighteen years, requiring that if they are recruited, the parties will give priority to those that are oldest. Though this clause is important, in view of the SCSL finding that the Sierra Leone conflict was not international in nature, it is hard to see the direct relevance of this provision to the discussion. The more pertinent provision, found in Article 4 of Additional Protocol II which applies to non-international armed conflicts, makes clear that children are to be provided with the care and aid that they require, and in particular, that those of them that had not "attained the age of fifteen years shall neither be recruited in the armed forces or groups nor allowed to take part in hostilities."

The last instrument, relied upon by the majority decision, was the Convention on the Rights of the Child (CRC). It entered into force on September 2, 1990. Sierra Leone became party that same day through ratification. In this regard, the majority of the Appeals Chamber confirmed, the CRC mandated states to ensure respect for the norms of the law of armed conflict by taking appropriate measures. The general obligation, contained in Article 4, requires all States Parties to "undertake all appropriate, legislative, administrative, and other measures for the implementation of the rights recognized in the present convention." All States Parties were to take "all feasible measures" to ensure that persons who have not attained the age of fifteen do not take a direct part in hostilities. The remainder of the provision, recalling the duty of states to ensure international humanitarian law, essentially reproduced the content of the Geneva Convention and Additional Protocol I.

A number of observations can be made about this part of the majority decision. First, it seems that the Appeals Chamber confused the issues. It invoked Article 38(1) of the International Court of Justice (ICJ Statute). In then embarking upon the path to analyze it, in a methodical way, it appeared to rule that international instruments such as those it cited indicate that the criminalization of the prohibition of child recruitment had occurred under international treaty law. This is evident in the language used. In its decision, having set out the various treaties that generally prohibited the recruitment of children into armed forces, the majority indicated that "prior to November 1996, the prohibition of child recruitment had *also* crystallised as customary international law." (Emphasis added). This despite that the majority decision's initial suggestion that it was highlighting "the key words of the relevant international documents" "in order to set the stage for the analysis required by the issues raised in the Preliminary Motion."

Second, as a matter of the reasoning behind the Appeals Chamber position, one will have to agree with Judge Robertson's dissent. He observed, correctly in my view, that all the provisions from the Geneva Convention and the Additional Protocols relied upon by the majority are relevant. However, the Protocol is "directed only to parties to the conflict and relates to involving children in front-line hostilities."[44] The duty spelled out in Protocol 1 to "take all feasible measures" means to do what is practicable in the circumstances – it does not imply a duty to legislate for a new crime.[45] Justice Robertson discusses additional international and regional instruments to reach his conclusion that these instruments do not significantly add to the Convention before November 1996. Furthermore, he indicates that "Sierra Leone acknowledged in its report to the Committee on the Rights of the Child that there was no minimum age for the recruitment of persons into the armed forces 'except provision in the Geneva Convention that children [under] fifteen years should not be conscripted into the army.'"[46] Justice Robertson goes on to explain that as far as local legislation is concerned, Norman could not "have understood there to be any criminal law against enlisting children who volunteered to serve in militias." Justice Robertson ultimately argues that the rule against enlistment of child soldiers had not passed beyond a mere general rule of international humanitarian law.[47]

7.5.2.2 Child Recruitment under Customary International Law

The majority, when considering international custom, as evidence of a general practice accepted by law established that "[t]he formation of custom requires both state practice and a sense of pre-existing obligation (opinio iuris)."[48] Regarding state practice, the Appeals Chamber cites to the 185 States, including Sierra Leone, which were parties to the Geneva Conventions prior to 1996, and proceeds to state that the provisions of those conventions were widely recognized as customary law.[49] In addition, 133 States, including Sierra Leone, had ratified Additional Protocol II before 1995. In relying on this number, the Chamber concludes that many of the provisions of Additional Protocol II, including the fundamental guarantees, were widely accepted as customary international law by 1996.[50] Furthermore, the judges highlight that all but six States had ratified the Convention on the Rights of the Child by 1996. The huge acceptance, the chamber states, indicates that the provisions of the CRC became international customary law almost at the time of the entry into force of the Convention.[51]

---

[44]   Dissenting Opinion of Justice Robertson, *supra* note 40, at ¶ 26.
[45]   *Id.*
[46]   *Id.* at ¶ 31.
[47]   *Id.*
[48]   Prosecutor v. Norman, Case No. SCSL-2004-14-AR72(e), Decision on Preliminary Motion Based on Lack of Jurisdiction, ¶ 17 (May 31, 2004).
[49]   *Id.* at ¶ 18.
[50]   *Id.*
[51]   *Id.* at ¶ 16.

Accordingly, the chamber reasoned that the widespread recognition and acceptance of the norm prohibiting child recruitment in Additional Protocol II and the
CRC proves that the conventional norm entered customary international law much
before 1996.[52] In addition, the majority cites the African Charter on the Rights and
Welfare of the Child, which reiterates the prohibition of child recruitment.[53] The
chamber also mentions that since the mid-1980s, states as well as non-state entities
began committing themselves to preventing the use of child soldiers and to ending
the use of already recruited soldiers.[54]

Trial Chamber II, in their later judgment in the *CDF* case, confirmed the status
of customary international law of the crime of conscripting or enlisting children
under the age of fifteen years into armed forces or using them to participate actively
in hostilities. The Trial Chamber II referred to the ruling of the Appeals Chamber,
which as mentioned above found that, prior to November 1996, the crime had
"crystallized" as customary law, regardless of whether the crime was committed in
internal or international conflict. This decision creates an important precedent in
international criminal jurisprudence applicable by other tribunals such as the
ICC to perhaps exceptionally consider charges against individuals for the crime of
child recruitment and the use of children that took place prior to the adoption of
the Rome Statute in 1998.[55]

7.6 THE LONE DISSENT BY JUSTICE ROBERTSON

The majority in the *Norman* case concluded that the crime of conscripting or
enlisting children under the age of fifteen as soldiers existed as a customary international law crime at least by 1996, even before that act was criminalized in treaty
law. However, Justice Robertson's dissent was much more measured. As he indicated in his dissent, the majority could cite no evidence of widespread state practice
as of that time. Justice Robertson concluded that although the law prohibits states
from forcibly enlisting child soldiers (as a breach of Common Article 3 of the
Geneva Conventions), the crime of non-forcible enlistment for those under the
age of fifteen, which is an offense in the SCSL, was not recognizable under
international criminal law as of 1996. According to Justice Robertson's dissent, the
crime of non-forcible enlistment of child soldiers became a war crime only in 1998
when it was incorporated into the Rome Statute.[56]

---

[52]   *Id.* at ¶ 20.
[53]   *Id.* at ¶ 21.
[54]   *Id.* at ¶ 23.
[55]   Pilar Villanueva Sainz-Pardo, *Is Child Recruitment as a War Crime Part of Customary International
       Law*, 12 Int'l J. Hum. Rts. 555 (2008).
[56]   Jose E. Alvarez, *The Main Functions of International Adjudication, in* The Impact of International
       Organizations on International Law 301 (2017).

7.7 THE ACTUS REUS OF THE WAR CRIME OF CHILD RECRUITMENT

7.7.1 *The Use, Conscription, and Enlistment of Child Soldiers at the SCSL*

The case law stemming from the SCSL provides unique insight into the war crime of child recruitment. The case *Prosecutor v. Alex Tamba Brima, Brima Bazzy Kamara and Santigie Borbor Kanu*[57] (AFRC case) was the first instance that an international tribunal was faced with the task of adjudicating this crime. Although some people expected the war crime of child recruitment to be easy, it proved challenging. Nonetheless, the judgment of this case provided the world with the first convictions regarding the crime. The indictment in the AFRC case read as follows: "at all times relevant to this Indictment, throughout the Republic of Sierra Leone, AFRC/RUF routinely conscripted, enlisted and/or used boys and girls under the age of 15 to participate in active hostilities. Many of these children were first abducted, then trained in AFRC/RUF camps in various locations throughout the country, and thereafter used as fighters."[58] In its 630-page trial judgment, the SCSL found all three defendants guilty on eleven counts of war crimes and crimes against humanity. The Trial Chamber ruled that Brima had ordered each soldier to provide military training to young boys between the ages of ten and twelve years old, therefore determining that the necessary elements of recruitment of child soldiers had been sufficiently proven.[59] Kanu was found guilty of planning the abduction of children. These children were later forced to commit atrocities and carry goods.[60] Kamara was similarly found guilty of planning the abduction and use of child soldiers in the Bombali District and the Western area.[61]

In this case, conscription was defined as including "acts of coercion, such as abductions and forced recruitment by an armed group against children committed for the purpose of using them to participate actively in hostilities."[62] The Trial Chamber defined enlistment as "accepting and enrolling individuals when they volunteer to join an armed force or group." The Trial Chamber went on to explain that enlistment is a voluntary act, and the child's consent is therefore not a valid defense.[63] Finally, in the AFRC case, the Special Court provided a broad definition of the "use" element by stating the following:

[57] Prosecutor v. Brima, Case No. SCSL-03-06-PT-088, SCSL-03-06-PT-088-II, Decision and order on Prosecution motions for joinder (Jan. 28, 2004).

[58] Prosecutor v. Brima, Case No. SCSL-04-16-PT-006, Indictment, ¶ 65 (Feb. 5, 2004).

[59] Transcript of Judgment Hearing, Prosecutor v. Brima, Case No. SCSL-04-16-T, ¶¶ 14–15 (June 20, 2007).

[60] *Id.* at ¶ 31.

[61] *Id.* at ¶ 15.

[62] Prosecutor v. Brima, Case No. SCSL-04-16-T, Judgment, ¶ 734 (July 20, 2007) [hereinafter AFRC Trial Judgment].

[63] *Id.* at 735.

an armed force requires logistical support to maintain its operations. Any labour or support that gives effect to, or helps maintain, operations in a conflict constitutes active participation. Hence carting loads for the fighting faction, finding and or acquiring food, ammunition or equipment, acting as decoys, carrying messages, making trails or finding routes, manning checkpoints or acting as human shields are some examples of active participation as much as actual fighting and combat.[64]

The next case from the SCSL dealing with the crime was not as "straightforward" – for lack of a better term – as the *AFRC* case. In *Prosecutor v. Moinina Fofana and Allieu Kondewa* (*CDF* case), it was suggested that "conscription represented an aggravated form of enlistment."[65] The Trial Chamber in this case followed the AFRC Trial Judgment and rejected the distinction between "voluntary and forced enlistment."[66] Additionally, in the *CDF* case, the Trial Chamber recognized that "forced enlistment" represented a form of the crime.[67] Although the Trial Chamber set out the specific elements of enlisting and using children under the age of fifteen, the Appeals Chamber interpreted the Trial Chamber's definition as being too narrow and broadened it by stating that enlistment includes "any conduct accepting the child as part of the militia."[68] The Appeals Chamber established that there must be two elements present for enlistment to take place. First, there must be a "nexus between the act of the accused and the child joining the armed force or group."[69] Second, there must be "knowledge on the part of the accused that the child is under the age of 15 years and that he or she may be trained for combat."[70]

7.7.2 *International Criminal Court*

7.7.2.1 The Existence of Armed Forces and Armed Groups

The Rome Statute does not define the concepts of armed conflict, armed forces, or armed groups. This is not unusual as many other treaties of international law, including the Geneva Conventions of 1949 and the Additional Protocols thereto, do not include such specific definitions.[71]

In its *Lubanga* Judgment, Trial Chamber I relied on the jurisprudence of the International Criminal Tribunal for the former Yugoslavia (ICTY). According to the ICTY Appeals Chamber, "an armed conflict exists whenever there is a resort to

---

[64]   *Id.* at 737.
[65]   Prosecutor v. Fofana, Case No. SCSL-04-14-T, Judgment, ¶ 192 (Aug. 2, 2007) [hereinafter CDF Judgment].
[66]   JULIE MCBRIDE, THE WAR CRIME OF CHILD SOLDIER RECRUITMENT 128 (2014).
[67]   *Id.*
[68]   Prosecutor v. Fofana, Case No. SCSL-04-14-A, Appeals Chamber, Judgment, ¶ 144 (May 28, 2008) [hereinafter CDF Appeal Judgment].
[69]   *Id.* at ¶ 141.
[70]   *Id.*
[71]   Anthony Cullen, *The Characterization of Armed Conflict in the Jurisprudence of the ICC*, *in* THE LAW AND PRACTICE OF THE INTERNATIONAL CRIMINAL COURT 765 (2015).

armed force between States or protracted armed violence between governmental authorities and organized armed groups or between such groups within a State."[72] Other tribunals, such as the International Criminal Tribunal for Rwanda (ICTR), have also defined the term armed conflict. For example, the ICTR stated that, "the term, armed conflict in itself suggests the existence of hostilities between armed forces organized to a greater or lesser extent."[73]

Turning back to the focus of this section, in the *Lubanga* case, the Trial Chamber of the ICC clarified that control over territory is not required.[74] For non-international armed conflict, the parties engaged must simply possess a "minimum level of organization and the hostilities must reach a certain threshold of intensity."[75] Additionally, the "level of organization required for a group to qualify as an armed group" does not require command over territory either. The ICC specified the factors required to determine if a body was an organized armed group. The Court stated that the following non-exhaustive list of factors is potentially relevant: "the force or group's internal hierarchy, the command structure and rules, the extent to which military equipment, including firearms, are available, the force or group's ability to plan military operations and put them into effect; and the extent, seriousness, and intensity of any military involvement. None of these factors are individually determinative."[76]

7.7.2.2 Active Participation in Hostilities

Article 77(2) of Additional Protocol I uses the phrase "direct participation in hostilities" to distinguish between indirect and direct participation in international conflict. However, the Rome Statute has moved away from this distinction. Unlike the SCSL, the ICC refrains from "listing specific activities as falling within the ambit of 'active participation'."[77] Thus, the ICC's preferred methodology is to proceed on a "case by case basis to determine whether an essential support function has been fulfilled by a given child in a given case."[78]

Under international humanitarian law, "direct participation" relates to the protection of civilians from being legitimately targeted during hostilities. Direct participation is synonymous with active participation under international humanitarian

---

[72] T. L. Akinmuwagun & M. Vormbaum, *in* Africa and the International Criminal Court 150 (Gerhard Werle, Lovell Fernandez, & Moritz Vormbaum eds., 2014). *See also* Prosecutor v. Tadić, Case No. IT-94-1-T, Judgment, ¶ 70 (Int'l Crim. Trib. for the Former Yugoslavia).

[73] T.L. Akinmuwagun and M. Vormbaum, *supra* note 72, at 150. *See also* Prosecutor v. Akayesu, Case No. ICTR-96-4-I, Judgment, ¶ 260 (Sept. 2, 1998).

[74] Prosecutor v. Dyilo, ICC-01/04-01/06-2842, Trial Judgment, ¶ 536 (Mar. 14, 2012).

[75] Cullen, *supra* note 71, at 769.

[76] Prosecutor v. Dyilo, ICC-01/04-01/06-2842, Judgment pursuant to Article 74 of the Statute, ¶ 537 (Mar. 14, 2012).

[77] McBride, *supra* note 66, at 119.

[78] *Id.*; *See also* Prosecutor v. Dyilo, ICC-01/04-01/06-2842, Judgment pursuant to Article 74 of the Statute, ¶ 628 (Mar. 14, 2012).

law. However, the ICC has interpreted the phrase "participate actively in hostilities" broadly for the purposes of Article 8. In the *Lubanga* decision, the Trial Chamber "juxtaposed 'participate actively in hostilities' in Article 8(2)(e)(vii) of the Rome Statute with 'direct participation' in Article 77(2) of Additional Protocol I."[79] In that case, the Chamber concluded that the children were used to participate actively in hostilities by the Union des Patriotes Congolais (UPC) and the Force Patriotique pour la libération du Congo (FPLC), because they had participated in combat, worked as bodyguards and escorts of UPC and FPLC main staff and commanders, and had been part of a special unit of approximately forty-five child soldiers. The court also considered the role of girls, who were assigned domestic household tasks, such as cooking, in addition to their combat, patrol, and bodyguard duties.[80]

7.7.2.3 The *Mens Rea* of the Crime of Child Recruitment

Regarding the examination of *mens rea*, Article 30 of the Rome Statute, under "[m]ental element," states, "unless otherwise provided, a person shall be criminally responsible and liable for punishment for a crime within the jurisdiction of the Court only if the material elements are committed with intent and knowledge."[81] In relation to child recruitment, Article 8(2)(e)(vii) of the Statute prohibits "[c]onscripting or enlisting children under the age of fifteen years into armed forces or groups or using them to participate actively in hostilities." Here, the Article lacks any indication whether the default *mens rea* provided in Article 30 applies. However, although a *mens rea* element is not "otherwise provided" in the Rome Statute, the Statute's supplementary Elements of Crimes contains a provision on *mens rea*. Article 8(2)(e)(vii) provides, "[t]he perpetrator knew or should have known that such person or persons were under the age of 15 years."[82] This creates two competing criteria, where the Elements of Crime prescribes a *mens rea* that deviates from the *mens rea* established in Article 30, and where the *mens rea* element can only be found in the Rome Statute itself.

The SCSL incorporated the negligent liability standard into its analysis of *mens rea* in relation to child recruitment. The SCSL felt that the Rome Statute may be seen as reflecting customary international law, and therefore, established that the elements for the crime of child recruitment "are elaborated in

---

79 Joshua Yuvaraj, *When Does a Child "Participate Actively in Hostilities" under the Rome Statute? Protecting Children from Use in Hostilities after Lubanga*, 32 Utrecht J. of Int'l and Euro. L. 69, 78 (2016).

80 *Id.*

81 Rome Statute, *supra* note 10, at art. 30(1).

82 Preparatory Comm'n for the Int'l Crim. Court, Finalized draft text of the Elements of Crimes, art. 8(2)(b)(xxvi) element 3, U.N. Doc. PCNICC/2000/1/Add.2 (Nov. 2, 2000).

the Elements of Crimes adopted in 2000."[83] The *Norman* case marks a clear *mens rea* for the crime of child recruitment. In *Norman*, the court stated, "[b]oth the Elements of Crimes formulated in connection with the Rome Statute and the legislation of a large population of the world community specified the elements of the crime."[84] The SCSL's determination of *mens rea* marks a critical development for the crime of child recruitment. It was a thoughtful choice, since the definition of the crime in the SCSL Statute was inspired by the definition from the Rome Statute.

The ICC's Pre-Trial Chamber has sought to resolve the discrepancy between the two *mens rea* standards and concluded that *mens rea* is established if the accused "is aware of the risk that the objective elements of the crime may result from his or her actions or omissions and accepts such an outcome by reconciling himself or herself with it or consenting to it." The defense in the *Lubanga* trial judgment argued that the prosecution must prove that the accused had the relevant level of intent and knowledge when carrying out the material elements of the crime.[85] The defense further argued that an accused can only be considered to have the requisite intention if he meant to engage in the conduct and, as to consequences, he either meant to cause them or was aware that they would occur in the ordinary course of events.[86] Moreover, the defense argued that the prosecution must prove that the accused had the relevant level of intent and knowledge when carrying out the material elements of the crime (Article 30(1) of the Statute).[87]

The Trial Chamber concluded "the accused meant to conscript, enlist or use children under the age of 15 to participate actively in hostilities or he was aware that by implementing the common plan these consequences [would] occur in the ordinary course of events." The defense, in the *Lubanga* trial judgment, challenged the approach of the Pre-Trial Chamber on the *mens rea* element stating that the concept of *dolus eventualis*, an "indirect intention" that arises when the possibility of a certain consequence is appreciated by the accused, but he or she proceeds with reckless disregard as to whether it will occur, does not form any part of Article 30.[88] As stated, the trial judgment avoided the issue of negligence. However, the analysis of the Pre-Trial Chamber marks a development for the *mens rea* for this crime under international law. The Trial Chamber ultimately avoided the issue of the negligence provided by the Elements of Crimes, choosing not to rule in the abstract.

---

[83] Prosecutor v. Norman, Case No. SCSL-2004-14-AR72(e), Decision on Preliminary Motion Based on Lack of Jurisdiction (Child Recruitment), ¶ 32 (May 31, 2004).

[84] *Id.* at ¶ 40.

[85] Prosecutor v. Dyilo, ICC-01/04-01/06, Trial Judgment, ¶ 956 (Mar. 14, 2012).

[86] *Id.* at ¶ 953.

[87] *Id.* at ¶ 956.

[88] *Id.* at ¶ 957.

7.8 THE CONTRIBUTION OF THE SCSL CASE LAW TO THE ICC DEBATE ON THE CRIME TO INTERNATIONAL LAW

7.8.1 *The* Lubanga *Case*

The President of the Democratic Republic of the Congo (DRC) referred the situation of his country to the ICC in March 2004. From the prosecution investigation, there arose the case of Thomas Lubanga Dyilo. Two years after, in 2006, Pre-Trial Chamber I issued an arrest warrant for Lubanga for committing, as co-perpetrator, the war crime of enlisting and conscripting children under the age of fifteen and using them to participate in hostilities as members of the armed group FPLC. One month later, in March 2006, Lubanga was transferred to the ICC and the charges against him were confirmed in January of 2007. His trial began on January 26, 2009 and culminated in Trial Chamber I delivering its verdict on March 14, 2012.

By 2001, the time of President Kabila's assassination, the DRC was ravaged by conflict. The conflicts were both economically and ethnically motivated. Eventually, armed conflict broke out and the UPC was created with Lubanga serving as its President. He was also Commander-in-Chief of the armed wing of the FPLC.

Lubanga was convicted of recruiting child soldiers. The crime of enlisting and conscripting children under the age of fifteen into the FPLC and using them to participate actively in hostilities in the context of an international armed conflict is punishable under Article 8(2)(b)(xxvi) of the Rome Statute.[89] The crime of enlisting and conscripting children under the age of fifteen into the FPLC and using them to participate actively in hostilities in the context of an armed conflict not of an international character is punishable under Article 8(2)(e)(vii) of the Rome Statute. It was a significant first case for the ICC which relied solely on this crime. The debate about Lubanga's alleged criminal responsibility, throughout the trial, was carried out against the backdrop for the SCSL interpretation of that crime. It can therefore be seen to have made a substantial contribution to the understanding and application of this new crime.

7.8.2 *The* Ongwen *Case*

The *Lubanga* case is not the sole case at the ICC dealing with the war crime of child recruitment. The charge of this crime is included in the arrest warrants issued in the case of *Prosecutor v. Joseph Kony, Okot Odhiambo and Dominic Ongwen*.[90] Dominic Ongwen's arrest warrants includes counts of crimes against humanity

---

[89] Claudia Morini, *First Victims then Perpetrators: Child Soldiers and International Law*, 3 ANUARIO COLOMBIANO DE DERECHO INTERNACIONAL 187, 198 (2010).

[90] Prosecutor v. Kony, ICC-02/04-01/05-57, Arrest Warrant (July 9, 2005).

and counts of war crimes, including attacks against civilian population; murder and attempted murder; rape; sexual slavery; forced marriage; torture; cruel treatment of civilian and other inhumane acts; enslavement; outrage upon personal dignity; conscription and use of children under the age of fifteen to participate actively in hostilities; pillaging; destruction of property; and persecution allegedly committed in northern Uganda.[91] It is further alleged that from at least July 1, 2002 until December 31, 2005, Dominic Ongwen, Joseph Kony, and the other Sinia Brigade commanders were part of a common plan to abduct women and girls in northern Uganda that were then used as forced wives and sex slaves, tortured, raped, and made to serve as domestic help; and to conscript and use children under the age of fifteen to participate actively in hostilities in the Lord's Resistance Army (LRA).

Undoubtedly, the facts of the *Ongwen* case are interesting. The LRA abducted Ongwen when he was just ten years old. He has been fighting with the group since then, which is one of the many aspects that makes this case so intriguing. A question that has been posited by many authors and legal professionals on the subject is whether Ongwen can be held liable. As some authors have noted, "[h]is early victimization created the conditions under which he committed serious crimes and also the conditions under which he became one of the leaders of the Lord's Resistance Army."[92] A second question that adds to the complexity of the case deals with Ongwen's age. Only crimes that occurred after 2002 may be prosecuted according to the terms of the ICC's mandate. However, by that time, Ongwen was already an adult. "Therefore, the case does not directly illustrate a situation where an individual is being prosecuted for crimes committed when he was a child."[93] The case opened before Trial Chamber IX on December 6, 2016 at the ICC.

In his appeal against Trial Chamber IX's Decision on Defence Motions Alleging Defects in the Confirmation Decision, Ongwen raised four grounds of appeal. First, he argued that the Trial Chamber incorrectly exercised its discretion, in the decision granting leave to appeal, by mischaracterizing the issues in the Decision on Defence Motions Alleging Defects in the Confirmation Decision of March 7, 2019 (Impugned Decision). Under the second and fourth grounds, he challenged the Trial Chamber's interpretation of the applicable law, in particular rule 134 of the Rules, arguing that the Trial Chamber erred when it found that the alleged defects in the Confirmation decision fell under rule 134(2) of the Rules, rather than 134(3). Under the third ground of appeal, raised in the alternative, Ongwen argued that the Trial Chamber incorrectly exercised its discretion by refusing to grant leave under rule 134(2).

---

[91]   *Id.*

[92]   Fanny Leveau, *Liability of Child Soldiers Under International Criminal Law*, 4 OSGOODE HALL REV. L. & POL'Y, 36, 59 (2013).

[93]   *Id.*

On July 17, 2019, the Appeals Chamber issued its judgment on Ongwen's appeal. The Appeals Chamber found that the Trial Chamber did not err in its interpretation of rule 134 of the Rules and in holding that rule 134(2), rather than rule 134(3), is applicable to the present case.[94] This case will continue to unfold before our eyes and merits careful consideration due to its complexity. It will be interesting to await the outcome given that, in this case, the accused himself is alleged to have been recruited as a child soldier.

The crime of child recruitment continues to be relevant. In fact, the DRC case *Prosecutor v. Germain Katanga and Mathieu Ngudjolo Chui*,[95] was before the ICC and one of the charges related to the crime of child enlistment, conscription, or use. Katanga and Ngudjolo Chui were opponents of Lubanga's UPC. Katanga and Njudjolo Chui allied their two militias to battle the UPC.

The Trial Chamber found that there "were children within the Ngiti militia and among the combatants who were in Bogoro on the day of the attack. However, [it also] concluded that the evidence presented in support of the Katanga's guilt did not satisfy [] the beyond reasonable doubt"[96] burden of proof. Katanga was sentenced to twelve years' imprisonment for other crimes, including one count of crimes against humanity (murder) and four counts of war crimes (murder, attacking a civilian population, destruction of property, and pillaging).[97]

7.9 CONCLUSION

This chapter has examined the SCSL's jurisprudence on the war crime of child recruitment. Like the previous chapter, which examined the crime of forced marriage as a crime against humanity, this chapter has sought to explain the significance of the case law of the SCSL as the first international criminal tribunal to successfully invoke this crime. As the first tribunal presented with the opportunity of adjudicating this crime, the Court's jurisprudence is highly relevant and may be said to constitute a significant contribution to the development of modern international criminal law. Evidence of this can be found in the use of its interpretation and application of the same crime at the ICC. The ICC has determined, building on the SCSL case law, that the crime can be committed in three ways, namely enlistment, forced enlistment, or conscription, or by using a child to participate in armed conflict. Additionally, as the chapter has shown, convicting perpetrators of the crime is not a "straightforward" task and requires a cautious and rigorous consideration of the crime's elements. Finally, although the chapter has

---

[94] Prosecutor v. Ongwen, ICC-02/04-01/15-1562, Judgment (July 17, 2019).
[95] Prosecutor v. Katanga, ICC-01/04-01/07, Judgment (Mar. 7, 2014). The cases were severed on Nov. 21, 2012.
[96] *Id.*
[97] *Id.*

shown that the decisions of the tribunal are not binding on the ICC, it does supply the ICC with a persuasive framework to follow as precedent. The ICC's use of that framework in some of its cases, including the *Lubanga* trial, stands as an early testament of the jurisprudential legacy and impact of the SCSL with respect to the war crime of child recruitment in international criminal law.

8

Head of State Immunity

8.1 INTRODUCTION

The Special Court for Sierra Leone (SCSL) indictment of Liberian President Charles Taylor on March 3, 2003 was highly controversial partly because of his status as a serving head of state. Although all international criminal tribunals since the Nuremberg Trials have adjudicated the criminal responsibility of high-level state officials, Taylor was the first *sitting* African president to be charged and successfully tried in adversarial proceedings for the commission of international crimes by a modern international penal court. The case against Taylor followed the indictment of the President of the Federal Republic of Yugoslavia (FRY), Slobodan Milošević, by the International Criminal Tribunal for the former Yugoslavia (ICTY) on May 24, 1999. Milošević was the Head of State of the FRY from July 15, 1997 to October 6, 2000, and thus, incumbent president when he was indicted. Taylor followed in his footsteps, becoming only the second serving president to be confronted with an international prosecution by an international criminal tribunal while still in office.

Both the *Milošević* and *Taylor* cases were politically and legally significant. Politically, the SCSL indictment and arrest warrant against President Taylor may have influenced his early departure from power in August 2003. Similarly, the ICTY's decision to indict President Milošević appears to have contributed to his subsequent defeat in Yugoslavia's September 2000 general elections. Legally, although the very first attempt in 1919 to prosecute a former head of state against German Kaiser Wilhelm II was stillborn, the growing pattern of investigation, indictment, and prosecution of several current or former heads of state by modern international tribunals including the permanent International Criminal Court (ICC) would suggest that the concept of immunity is dead and that international criminal law has truly come of age.[1] Such a conclusion would appear justified given the giant strides that the international community has taken towards the

---

[1] *See, e.g.*, Prosecutor v. Al Bashir, Case No. ICC-02/05-01, Decision on the Prosecution's Application for a Warrant of Arrest against Omar Hassan Ahmad Al Bashir (Mar. 4, 2009); v. Al Bashir,

establishment of the principle of individual criminal responsibility at the international level for even those holding the highest government office since World War II.[2]

However, rather than prematurely announce the death of immunity, it may be more accurate to assert that immunity is ill, or perhaps even terminally ill. Among the reasons is that, traditionally, international law has recognized the inviolability of incumbent heads of state and of government as an outcrop of the sovereignty of the state that they represented. Indeed, much as in the ICTY indictment of President Milošević (whose trial was in fact never completed due to the untimely passing of the defendant), the SCSL's charges against President Taylor threw two diametrically opposite international legal principles into conflict: the age-old idea of equality of all sovereigns which implies immunity from criminal and civil jurisdiction before foreign courts, and the largely post–World War II human-rights driven notion that all persons who commit certain international crimes are investigable and prosecutable, irrespective of their official rank or status.

Today, the tension between the imperatives of state sovereignty and the demands of individual accountability for gross human rights violations is exemplified by the ongoing debates concerning whether heads of state such as President Omar Al Bashir of Sudan should have been arrested by Chad, Malawi, South Africa, or Jordan and surrendered to the ICC in order that they may answer allegations of involvement with crimes against humanity and genocide.[3] Indeed, as three judges of the International Court of Justice (ICJ) aptly put it in the infamous immunity case between the Democratic Republic of Congo (DRC) and Belgium, one of the key

---

ICC-02/05–01/09, Second Decision on the Prosecution's Application for a Warrant of Arrest (July 12, 2010); Prosecutor v. Milošević, Case No. IT-99–37, Decision on Review of the Indictment and Application for Consequential Orders (Int'l Crim. Trib. for the Former Yugoslavia May 24, 1999); Prosecutor v. Kambanda, Case No. ICTR-97–23-S, Judgment and Sentence (Sept. 4, 1998); Prosecutor v. Gbagbo, ICC-02/11–01/11, Decision on the Prosecutor's Application Pursuant to Article 58 for a warrant of arrest against Laurent Koudou Gbagbo (Nov. 30, 2011).

[2] Since the Nuremberg Trials, various international penal tribunals have attempted to or actually tried several persons holding the status of incumbent or former head of state or government: Karl Doenitz (Germany), Slobodan Milosevic (Federal Republic of the Yugoslavia), Kambanda (Rwanda), and Charles Taylor (Liberia). At the International Criminal Court, there have been cases initiated against Laurent Gbagbo (Ivory Coast), Uhuru Kenyatta (Kenya), Pierre Bemba (Congo), Muamar Gaddafi (Libya), and Omar Al Bashir (Sudan). Similar attempts have been made, albeit sometimes successfully, at the national level though not always for international crimes such as the cases involving Alberto Fujimori (Peru), Saddam Hussein (Iraq), Hosni Mubarak (Egypt), and Pinochet Urgarte (Chile). For a thoughtful analysis of this trend, see PROSECUTING HEADS OF STATE (Ellen Lutz & Caitlin Reiger, eds., 2009).

[3] See, for a discussion of the main legal questions that arise, Dapo Akande, *The Legal Nature of Security Council Referrals to the ICC and its Impact on Al Bashir's Immunities*, 7 J. INT'L. CRIM. JUST. 333 (2009); Paola Gaeta, *Does President Al Bashir Enjoy Immunity from Arrest?*, 7 J. INT'L. CRIM. JUST. 315 (2009); Erika de Wet, *The Implications of President Al-Bashir's Visit to South Africa for International and Domestic Law*, 13 J. INT'L. CRIM. JUST. 1049 (2015); Dire Tladi, *The Duty on South Africa to Arrest and Surrender President Al-Bashir under South African and International Law*, 13 J. INT'L. CRIM. JUST. 1027 (2015).

challenges for modern international law is "to provide for stability of international relations and effective international intercourse while at the same time guaranteeing respect for human rights."[4] As they observed, "[t]he difficult task" for international law is to contribute the necessary stability to the international legal order "by a means other than the impunity of those responsible for major human rights violations."[5] Ultimately, the interests of the international community to prevent and stop impunity for perpetrators of serious atrocities, on the one hand, and the necessity of allowing states to act freely on the interstate level without undue interference in their conduct of international relations, on the other, implies that a delicate "balance . . . must be struck between two sets of functions which are both valued by the international community."[6]

8.2   PURPOSE AND STRUCTURE OF THIS CHAPTER

The previous chapter of this book has considered the main SCSL jurisprudence on the war crime of child recruitment. This chapter turns to the questions of immunity, and considers the significance of the *Taylor* case, "the jewel in the crown of the SCSL,"[7] to the advancement of the concept of individual criminal responsibility under international law. The primary focus here is not on the process and policy challenges of trying Taylor, which the present author has dealt with elsewhere, but rather the doctrine of head of state immunity.[8] More specifically, and consistent with the wider goal of this book, my purpose is to discern the contributions, if any, that the SCSL's approach to its sole head of state trial might have made to our understanding of the present status of immunity under international law. This thrust seems justified because, although the ICTY indicted Yugoslav President Milošević four years before the SCSL charged Liberian President Taylor and six years before the International Criminal Tribunal for Rwanda (ICTR) prosecuted the deposed Rwandese Interim Government Prime Minister Jean Kambanda,[9] Taylor was the first serving president to mount a legal challenge to his indictment and arrest warrant on the basis that he was entitled to immunity under customary international law because of his privileged status as a sitting head of state. This in turn required the SCSL to consider and rule on whether Taylor's immunity shielded him from prosecution.

---

[4]   Arrest Warrant of 11 April 2000 (Dem. Rep. Congo v. Belg.), Judgment, 2002 ICJ Rep. 3, ¶ 5 (Feb. 14) (*See* Joint Separate Opinion of Judges Higgins, Kooijmans, and Buergenthal).

[5]   *Id.*

[6]   *Id.* at ¶ 75.

[7]   Charles C. Jalloh, *The Law and Politics of the Charles Taylor Case*, 43 Denv. J. Int'l L. & Pol'y, 229 (2015) [hereinafter Jalloh, *Law and Politics of the Taylor Case*].

[8]   *Id.; See also* Charles C. Jalloh, *Charles Taylor, in* Cambridge Companion to International Criminal Law 312 (William A. Schabas ed., 2016).

[9]   Prosecutor v. Kambanda, Case No. ICTR-97-23-S, Indictment (Oct. 28, 1997); *see also* Prosecutor v. Kambanda, Case No. ICTR 97-23-S, Judgment and Sentence (Sept. 4, 1998); Prosecutor v. Kambanda, Case No. ICTR 97-23-A, Judgment (Oct. 19, 2000).

As we shall see presently, the Appeals Chamber rejected Taylor's assertion of immunity before the SCSL thereby removing any legal obstacles to his later prosecution. It reasoned that immunity, which applied as between states in their relations with each other and is predicated on notions of sovereign equality, has no bearing on international crimes proceedings carried out by an international criminal court discharging a mandate entrusted to it by the international community. Nonetheless, by relying heavily on a much criticized ICJ opinion instead of advancing a fresh approach, the SCSL might have missed a good opportunity to add significantly to contemporary debates about the place of an international crimes exception in the prosecution of serving presidents for core international crimes before international courts. Nonetheless, on balance, this chapter will argue that, as the first international penal court to grapple with the application of the normatively troubling ICJ case law in this area, the *Taylor* immunity ruling has made a constructive contribution to the development of the *law* and *practice* respecting head of state indictment and prosecution in international criminal courts. The precedent set has already, and will likely continue, to impact on the debate on this important principle in other judicial fora including at the ICC.

The chapter is structured as follows. First, I open with a brief discussion of who Taylor is and explain how he got involved with the Sierra Leone conflict. This explains why he attracted the interest of the Tribunal's prosecutors, as the only non-Sierra Leonean that was indicted and eventually tried by the SCSL. Second, I then briefly recall the state of immunity law before Taylor, as espoused by the ICJ in the *Arrest Warrant* case, and highlight two of the fundamental ambiguities that the World Court left unresolved. It was these open questions that the SCSL valiantly tried to resolve in its application of the ICJ dictum to the fact pattern that the *Taylor* case presented.

Third, I closely analyze the *Taylor* Defense motion and the Appeals Chamber decision on his immunity. I then consider the scholarly reaction to the decision while offering my own assessment of it. Here, I suggest that one of the best arguments against the recognition of immunities for sitting and former heads of state and government charged with core international crimes before certain types of international tribunals is the customary international law approach first applied in a major international trial in a concrete case by the SCSL judges in the *Taylor* case.

In the last part, I summarize my main arguments on the head of state immunity issue. I then anticipate the next chapter of this work which considers the controversy over whether Sierra Leone could confer a blanket amnesty on all combatants that perpetrated atrocities despite evidence of their commission of war crimes, crimes against humanity and other serious violations of international humanitarian law. The topics of immunity and amnesty are, of course, related. Both implicate sovereignty and each could, if accepted and deployed, serve as a procedural bar to prevent or stop a criminal prosecution. They stand as two potential sources of exceptions to the rule requiring accountability. It will be submitted that the SCSL practice in respect of each of these topics amount to a useful contribution to international law.

8.3 THE SCSL AND CHARLES TAYLOR'S ROLE IN THE SIERRA LEONE CONFLICT

8.3.1 *The Rise of Charles Taylor*

Born in the small town of Arthington, Montserrado County, in north western Liberia on January 28, 1948, Taylor by his own account came from a modest background.[10] He hailed from a large family, the third of eleven children, born to a mother who was a former servant and a father who was a Baptist school teacher.[11] He began his early career following in the footsteps of his father as a teacher,[12] although he quickly became an accountant, receiving an associate degree in accounting in 1974 and a bachelor's degree in economics in Massachusetts in 1976.[13] In the eight years between his arrival in the United States in 1972, and his return to Liberia in 1980, Taylor and several of his Liberian compatriots founded the Union of Liberian Associations in the Americas (ULAA).[14] The apparent goal of the ULAA, which exists to this day, is to help bring about peaceful and democratic change in Liberia.[15]

Taylor returned to Liberia in January 1980, at the invitation of then President William Tolbert.[16] His arrival coincided with the successful coup d'état by Master Sergeant Samuel Kanyon Doe just four months later.[17] He then joined the Doe government as a Director General of the General Services Administration and Deputy Minister of Commerce.[18] About three years later, Taylor abandoned that junior cabinet post after the Doe regime charged him with embezzlement of public funds.[19] He fled to the United States where he was arrested in June 1984, following an extradition request by Liberian authorities.[20] He was held, pending return to his native country, until November 1985, when he allegedly escaped from prison and returned to West Africa.[21] Taylor next surfaced in West Africa where he and several

---

[10]   Prosecutor v. Taylor, Case No. SCSL-03–01-T, Judgment, ¶¶ 23, 25 (May 18, 2012); Prosecutor v. Taylor, Case No. SCSL-03–01-A, Judgment (Sept. 26, 2013). Note that this subsection of this chapter draws on earlier work discussing the *Taylor* Trial. See, in this regard, Jalloh, *Law and Politics of the Taylor Case, supra* note 7, at 229, 237–57.

[11]   *Id.*; Transcript of Record, Prosecutor v. Taylor, Case No. SCSL-03–01-T, at 24357–59 (July 14, 2009).

[12]   Prosecutor v. Taylor, Case No. SCSL-03–01-T, Judgment, ¶ 4 (May 18, 2012).

[13]   *Id.*

[14]   *Id.* at ¶ 5.

[15]   *Id.* The ULAA website can be found here: http://ulaalib.org/.

[16]   *See id.* at ¶ 6; Transcript of Record, Prosecutor v. Taylor, Case No. SCSL-03–01-T, at 24384–85 (July 14, 2009).

[17]   Prosecutor v. Taylor, Case No. SCSL-03–01-T, Judgment, ¶ 6 (May 18, 2012).

[18]   *Id.*

[19]   *Id.*

[20]   *Id.*

[21]   *Id.* at ¶¶ 6–7.

others founded the National Patriotic Front of Liberia (NPFL) in Côte d'Ivoire shortly thereafter.[22] The NPFL operatives subsequently took up military training in Libya in 1987.[23] With the launch of a military attack from the Ivorian side of the border into the town of Butoa in Liberia on December 24 , 1989, Taylor and approximately one hundred so-called "special forces," set off a civil war that would eventually engulf Liberia and several countries including Sierra Leone, Guinea, and later on Côte d'Ivoire.[24]

Within a few months, Taylor and his fighters marched from the Liberia-Côte d'Ivoire border to the capital Monrovia, recruiting many anti-Doe activists to the NPFL.[25] In the meantime, in the Liberian regions of the country that the NPFL forces captured, he and his followers established the National Patriotic Reconstruction Assembly government.[26] He served as head of that government until 1996, when the first Liberian civil war ended with the conclusion of the Abuja Accord in 1996, and democratic elections were subsequently held.[27] Taylor, running as the National Patriotic Party candidate in July 1997, won the presidential elections reportedly with 75 percent of the vote and two-thirds of the seats in the legislature.[28] The official vote count was never formally released.[29] According to the Liberian Truth and Reconciliation Commission, in an important study, Taylor's "authoritarian" rule was marked by "poor governance, administrative malfeasances, corruption, intimidation and intolerance of opposition, threats, torture, terroristic acts," and routine extrajudicial and summary executions.[30] This would later give rise to Liberia's second war. The conflict only ended after Taylor, who never successfully transitioned from warlord to chief of state, was forced to step aside on August 11, 2003.

8.3.2 *The Fall of Charles Taylor*

Ironically, Taylor did not fall from grace because of his conduct fomenting and leading a brutal civil war in his native Liberia. Instead, it was his meddling in Sierra Leonean affairs that ultimately led to his downfall. That involvement originated from his association with Revolutionary United Front (RUF) Leader Foday Sankoh, whom he apparently met in guerrilla training camps in Libya. They agreed to help each other's projects to take over Liberia and Sierra Leone respectively.[31] Indeed,

---

[22]   *Id.* at ¶¶ 7, 22.
[23]   *Id.* at ¶ 7.
[24]   *Id.* at 24603–08.
[25]   TRUTH & RECONCILIATION COMM'N, REPUBLIC OF LIBER., CONSOLIDATED FINAL REPORT 151–58 (2009) [hereinafter LIBERIAN TRC REPORT].
[26]   *Id.* at 157.
[27]   Prosecutor v. Taylor, Case No. SCSL-03–01-T, Judgment, ¶ 8 (May 18, 2012).
[28]   LIBERIAN TRC REPORT, *supra* note 25, at 164.
[29]   *Id.*
[30]   *Id.*, at 167.
[31]   SIERRA LEONE TRUTH & RECONCILIATION REPORT, WITNESS TO TRUTH: REPORT OF THE SIERRA LEONE TRUTH & RECONCILIATION COMMISSION, 3A (2004) [hereinafter SL TRC REPORT].

according to the Sierra Leone Truth and Reconciliation Commission, when Taylor's forces first invaded Liberia in December 1989, the NPFL included many Sierra Leonean fighters in its ranks.[32] Sankoh, who was one of them, was a key commando.[33] He assisted in planning and carrying out attacks against strategic Liberian government military positions.[34] He thus put his Libyan guerilla training to use in anticipation of his war in Sierra Leone.[35] Sankoh would bank on Taylor to return the favor not long afterwards. As a part of this, he shared with the NPFL a captured Armed Forces of Liberia military base, Camp Naama, to train around three hundred RUF fighters known as Vanguards.[36] The Vanguards later played a pivotal role in the Sierra Leone conflict. Notorious figures thought to bear greatest responsibility like Sam Bockarie, Issa Sesay, Morris Kallon, and Augustine Gbao were Vanguards, all of whom – along with Sankoh and Taylor – were later indicted by the SCSL.[37]

Similarly, on March 23, 1991, a group of between forty and sixty fighters attacked the remote village of Bomaru in the Kailahun District in eastern Sierra Leone near the Liberian border – as discussed in greater detail in Chapter 2. The bulk of the attackers were drawn from the NPFL.[38] The Sierra Leonean authorities, under then President Joseph S. Momoh, attributed responsibility for the invasion solely to Taylor and the NPFL.[39] The Momoh government, which had permitted the Economic Community of West African States (ECOWAS) fighter jets to bomb NPFL positions in Liberia from the Lungi International Airport near Freetown, the Sierra Leonean capital, ignored the RUF for a long time before it formally recognized it as an independent force to reckon with.[40]

To President Momoh, the RUF was in effect the Sierra Leonean wing of the NPFL.[41] For Taylor, the military and political alliance with the RUF helped to not only achieve tactical goals such as fighting common enemies in Sierra Leone, including dissident Liberian groups such as United Liberation Movement of

---

[32] *Id.* at 94–95.
[33] *Id.* at 100.
[34] *Id.*
[35] *Id.* at 101.
[36] Prosecutor v. Taylor, Case No. SCSL-03–01-T, Judgment (May 18, 2012); SL TRC REPORT, *supra* note 31, at 101–02.
[37] *See* the list of cases in Prosecutor v. Sesay Special Court for Sierra Leone: Residual Special Court for Sierra Leone, www.rscsl.org/RUF.html.
[38] SL TRC REPORT, *supra* note 31, at ¶¶ 112, 120–21; Prosecutor v. Taylor, Case No. SCSL-03–01-T, Judgment, ¶ 2378 (May 18, 2012) (concluding the "[t]he evidence unequivocally establishes that NPFL soldiers constituted the large majority of the invasion force on Sierra Leone").
[39] Prosecutor v. Taylor, Case No. SCSL-03–01-T, Judgment, ¶ 27 (May 18, 2012).
[40] SL TRC REPORT, *supra* note 31, at ¶ 40; Prosecutor v. Taylor, Case No. SCSL-03–01-T, Judgment, ¶¶ 41, 45, 113 (May 18, 2012). This seems to have justified, in Taylor's mind, retaliation against Sierra Leone in addition to the fact that the government supported and armed Liberian dissidents to form groups to fight against the NPFL.
[41] *See* MICHAEL S. KARGBO, BRITISH FOREIGN POLICY AND THE CONFLICT IN SIERRA LEONE, 1991–2001, 20–21 (Peter Lang AG ed., 2006).

Liberia for Democracy that had organized against him with the Sierra Leone government's help,[42] but it also enabled him to exploit the country's diamonds for private gain.[43] The RUF, which often captured territory and mined diamonds and other minerals with forced civilian labor, exchanged its precious stones for arms primarily through Monrovia.[44] Liberia, which was not a country particularly well-known for diamonds, saw a remarkable increase in its official diamond exports.[45] Those exports appear to have since suffered a dramatic drop. In its heyday, much of the profits from the lucrative diamond trade allegedly went to Taylor.[46] By the time he became president, he reportedly extended his influence into several areas of the Liberian private sector including exploitation of natural resources such as timber.[47] As of the end of the 1990s, Monrovia had reportedly become a haven for many other illicit activities in the West Africa subregion involving drug, gun, and diamond runners. The Liberian capital became their home base as they could rely on a friendly government that patronized them or looked the other way.[48]

During the early part of the Sierra Leone conflict, until the Liberian fighters and the RUF rebels fell out and turned on each other, the NPFL forces reportedly carried out much of the atrocities against civilians in Sierra Leone.[49] Indeed, though the actual figure might never be known, it is estimated that up to 1,600 of the 2,000 fighters comprising the initial invasion force into Sierra Leone from Liberia were NPFL rebels.[50] Together with their RUF collaborators and a smaller cadre of combatants from Burkina Faso, Ivory Coast, and The Gambia, they used shocking tactics of terror in prosecuting the war. They not only murdered and raped, but also amputated civilians,

---

[42] *See* Prosecutor v. Taylor, Case No. SCSL-03-01-T, Judgment, ¶¶ 30–31, 33–34 (May 18, 2012).

[43] *See* JANNA LIPMAN, CHARLES TAYLOR'S CRIMINAL NETWORK: EXPLOITING DIAMONDS AND CHILDREN (Louise Shelley ed., 2009); *See generally* Iryna Marchuk, *Confronting Blood Diamonds in Sierra Leone: The Trial of Charles Taylor*, 4 YALE J. INT'L AFF. 87, 87–89 (2009).

[44] *See* IAN SMILLIE ET AL., THE HEART OF THE MATTER- SIERRA LEONE, DIAMONDS AND HUMAN SECURITY 6, 47 (2000). *See generally* U.N.S.C., *Report of the Panel of Experts Appointed Pursuant to Security Council Resolution 1306, Paragraph 19, in Relation to Sierra Leone*, U.N. DOC. S/2000/1195 (Dec. 20, 2000).

[45] SMILLIE, *supra* note 44, at 48. *See also* Mersie Ejigu, *Post Conflict Liberia: Environmental Security as a Strategy for Sustainable Peace and Development* (Foundation for Environmental Security and Sustainability, Working Paper No. 3, 2006). *See generally* David Pratt M.P., Nepean-Carleton (Special Envoy to Sierra Leone), *Sierra Leone: The Forgotten Crisis Rep. to the Minister of Foreign Affairs, the Honourable Lloyd Axworthy, P.C.* (Apr. 23, 1999).

[46] SMILLIE, *supra* note 44, at 48.

[47] GLOBAL WITNESS, TIMBER, TAYLOR, SOLDIER, SPY: HOW LIBERIA'S UNCONTROLLED RESOURCE EXPLOITATION, CHARLES TAYLOR'S MANIPULATION AND THE RE-RECRUITMENT OF EX-COMBATANTS ARE THREATENING REGIONAL PEACE 6, 12 (2005) (submitted to the U.N. Security Council).

[48] Abdul Tejan-Cole, *A Big Man in a Small Cell: Charles Taylor and the Special Court for Sierra Leone*, in PROSECUTING HEADS OF STATE 205, 209 (Ellen L. Lutz & Caitlin Reiger eds., 2009). For another perspective, see *Charles C. Jalloh, Charles Taylor*, in CAMBRIDGE COMPANION TO INTERNATIONAL CRIMINAL LAW 312–32 (William A. Schabas, ed., 2016).

[49] SL TRC REPORT, *supra* note 31, at ¶¶ 239–42. *See also* Prosecutor v. Taylor, Case No. SCSL-03-01-T, Judgment, ¶¶ 32 (May 18, 2012).

[50] SL TRC REPORT, *supra* note 31, at 120.

including babies as young as six months old.[51] With Taylor's human, material, and other logistical support, and the successive Sierra Leonean government's inept handling of the war, the rebels quickly captured much territory in the two geographic areas that they fought in eastern and southern Sierra Leone.[52] Soon, although their fortunes changed sometimes, the RUF had the upper hand.

As discussed in more detail in Chapter 2, setting out the context and nature of the Sierra Leone conflict, the RUF and NPFL fighters also burned villages and looted property.[53] The catalogue of their hair-raising horrors included alleged acts of cannibalism, decapitation of civilians, forced enlistment and drugging of children to fight, the use of human entrails at check points, and the slitting open of pregnant women to settle bets on the sex of the fetus.[54] The war was formally declared over in January 2002. At that point, it was estimated that approximately 75,000 people had been killed, thousands more victimized, and hundreds of thousands more displaced.[55] Even the belated comer to the Sierra Leone conflict, the UN Security Council, passed several Chapter VII resolutions deploring Liberia's active support of rebel groups in neighboring countries especially the RUF. It also determined in several presidential statements as well as in other resolutions that Taylor's involvement with the Sierra Leonean rebels, and provision of safe haven and a transit point for the diamonds, weapons and drugs smuggled to fuel the conflict, constituted a threat to international peace and security in the region and thereafter imposed sanctions on Liberia.[56] This would partly later lead the UN Security Council to declare Liberia under Taylor as a threat to international peace and security and to subsequently impose sanctions on the country which were only lifted many years later.

---

[51] Catherine E. Bolten, *The Memories They Want. Autobiography in the Chaos of Sierra Leone*, 44 ETHNOLOGIE FRANCAISE 429, 430 (2014).

[52] *See Chronology of Sierra Leone: How Diamonds Fuelled the Conflict*, AFR. CONFIDENTIAL (Apr. 1998), www.africa-confidential.com/special-report/id/4/Chronology_of_Sierra_Leone.

[53] Jamie O'Connell, *Here Interest Meets Humanity: How to End the War and Support Reconstruction in Liberia, and the Case for Modest American Leadership*, 17 HARV. HUM. RTS. J. 207, 213 (2004).

[54] *See id.* at 214.

[55] J. Andrew Grant, *Salone's Sorrow: The Ominous Legacy of Diamonds in Sierra Leone, in* RESOURCE POLITICS IN SUB-SAHARAN AFRICA 251, 252 (Matthias Basedau & Andreas Mehler eds., 2005). Statistics are hard to come by, and of what there is, there is conflicting information. A leading American human rights NGO has estimated the total number of deaths at 50,000 while the number of displaced was put at one million. *See* Human Rights Watch, *Sierra Leone: Getting Away with Murder, Mutilation, Rape*, Vol. 11, No. 3(A) (July 1999). A U.N. Report estimated 70,000. *See also* U.N.D.P., Evaluation of UNDP Assistance to Conflict Affected Countries-Human Security: Case Study Sierra Leone, U.N. Development Program Evaluations Office (2006). The present writer opted for the 70,000 figure in the U.N. report in Charles C. Jalloh, *Assessing the Legacy of the Special Court for Sierra Leone, in* THE SIERRA LEONE SPECIAL COURT AND ITS LEGACY: THE IMPACT FOR AFRICA AND INTERNATIONAL CRIMINAL LAW 5, 1–19 (Charles C. Jalloh ed., 2014).

[56] S.C. Res. 1343, ¶ 2, 5–6 (Mar. 7, 2001).

8.3.3 *The SCSL Indictment of Taylor and the Delayed*
Arrest

The SCSL was endowed under Articles 1 to 4 of its Statute with the required competence in terms of subject matter, territorial, personal, and temporal jurisdiction to prosecute any persons – including leaders – deemed to bear greatest responsibility for crimes against humanity, war crimes, and other serious violations of international humanitarian law committed in Sierra Leone after November 30, 1996. This included in particular, as discussed extensively in Chapters 3 and 5 of this book, those among them deemed to bear the greatest responsibility for threatening or interfering with the success of the peace process. There was therefore no legal question as to whether the SCSL possessed the power under its founding statute to potentially exercise jurisdiction over Taylor for crimes committed within Sierra Leone. Indeed, given his widely reported role in the Sierra Leone conflict, many observers were not surprised to later learn that, on March 7, 2003, at the SCSL prosecution's request, Judge Bankole Thompson had approved a seventeen count indictment of Taylor.[57] The indictment, which was one of several that had been issued against high-ranking persons in the rebel and government forces, was accompanied by an arrest warrant and request for the suspect's arrest and transfer.[58] The documents were placed under seal. On June 12, 2003, the Chamber formally granted a request unsealing them.[59]

Taylor's indictment was first made public by the SCSL prosecution on June 4, 2003, about eight days before written judicial permission was received to do so.[60] He had travelled to Accra, Ghana to attend peace talks that had been convened in the hope of ending the brutal civil war prevailing in Liberia at the time.[61] The SCSL Prosecutor, David Crane, arranged for the indictment to be hand-delivered to the Ghanaian High Commission in Freetown as well as transmitted directly to the Foreign Ministry in Accra.[62] Crane requested the Ghanaian authorities to arrest

---

[57] Prosecutor v. Taylor, Case No. SCSL-2003–01-I, Indictment, ¶¶ 32–59 (Mar. 7, 2003); Prosecutor v. Taylor, Case No. SCSL-2003–01-I, Decision Approving the Indictment and Order for Non-Disclosure (Mar. 7, 2003).

[58] Prosecutor v. Taylor, Case No. SCSL-2003–01-I, Order for the Disclosure of the Indictment, the Warrant of Arrest and Order for Transfer and Detention and the Decision Approving the Indictment and Order for Non-Disclosure (June 12, 2003).

[59] *Id.*

[60] Clarence Roy-Macaulay, *Sierra Leone Court Indicts Liberia Leader*, GUARDIAN (June 4, 2003), www .globalpolicy.org/component/content/article/163/29115.html (quoting Prosecutor David Crane). For analysis of the legal implications of the release of the Taylor indictment, accounting for his status as incumbent president, *see* Cesare Romano & André Nollkaemper, *The Arrest Warrant Against the Liberian President Charles Taylor*, 8 AM. SOC'Y INT'L L INSIGHTS 16 (2003).

[61] Abdoulaye W. Dukulé, *West Africa: Taylor at Accra Peace Talks: "Honourable Exit or Extended Mandate?"*, ALLAFRICA (June 4, 2003), http://allafrica.com/stories/200306040021.html.

[62] James L. Miglin, *From Immunity to Impunity: Charles Taylor and the Special Court for Sierra Leone*, 16 DALHOUSIE J. LEGAL STUD. 21, 26 (2007).

Taylor and transfer him into the custody of the SCSL.[63] He also issued a press release announcing the indictment.[64]

The suspect and other West African leaders learned that he had been indicted by the SCSL for his role in the Sierra Leonean conflict. President John Kufuor of Ghana, the chair of the ECOWAS at the time, apparently felt betrayed by his international community partners for springing a surprise on his government when peace negotiations had made great progress – something that might have angered him even more given the disclosure that "finding an exit strategy for Charles Taylor to vacate the Presidency of Liberia" was even on the summit agenda.[65] Rather than arresting Taylor, as the SCSL Prosecutor requested, an apparently embarrassed Ghanaian President Kufuor gave Taylor his presidential aircraft to fly him home to Liberia.[66] The peace talks continued in Taylor's absence. The Accra Ceasefire Agreement, which paved the way for a cessation of hostilities and anticipated negotiations of a final peace settlement in Liberia that excluded Taylor, was later signed by the Liberian Government under Taylor and two other armed factions that were fighting his forces on the outskirts of Monrovia on June 17, 2003.[67] For various reasons, including the military and political pressure on him and perhaps even the indictment which he had been promised would be rendered "moot,"[68] Taylor agreed to resign from the Presidency of Liberia several months later on August 11, 2003.[69] He took up residence in Nigeria, believing that by keeping his word to exit the political scene under African Union and ECOWAS-led political arrangements as per the

---

[63] *See* Davan Maharaji, *Liberian President is Sought on War Crimes Indictment*, L.A. TIMES (June 5, 2003), http://articles.latimes.com/2003/jun/05/world/fg-indict5.

[64] Press Release, Special Court for Sierra Leone the Office of the Prosecutor, Statement of David M. Crane Chief Prosecutor (June 5, 2003) www.rscsl.org/Documents/Press/OTP/prosecutor-060503 .pdf [hereinafter Press Release of David M. Crane's Statement]. *See also* Prosecutor v. Taylor, Case No. SCSL-2003-01-I, Order for the Disclosure of the Indictment, the Warrant of Arrest and Order for Transfer and Detention and the Decision Approving the Indictment and Order for Non-Disclosure, (June 12, 2003).

[65] SOLOMON E. BEREWA, A NEW PERSPECTIVE ON GOVERNANCE, LEADERSHIP, CONFLICT AND NATIONAL BUILDING IN SIERRA LEONE 181–82 (2011); PRISCILLA HAYNER, NEGOTIATING PEACE IN LIBERIA: PRESERVING THE POSSIBILITY FOR JUSTICE 8 (2007), www.ictj.org/sites/default/files/ICTJ-Liberia-Negotiating-Peace -2007-English_0.pdf; Kathy Ward, *Might v. Right: Charles Taylor and the Sierra Leone Special Court*, 11 HUM. RTS. BRIEF 8, 8 (2003).

[66] Miglin, *supra* note 62, at 26–27.

[67] Permanent Rep. of Ghana to the U.N., Letter dated June 18, 2003 from the Permanent Rep. of Ghana to the United Nations addressed to the President of the Security Council, U.N. Doc. S/2003/657 (June 18, 2003).

[68] Transcript of Record, Prosecutor v. Taylor, SCSL-03-01-T, at 31505 (Nov. 10, 2009) [hereinafter Transcript of Record – Nov. 10, 2009].

[69] The Accra Comprehensive Peace Agreement was signed just days later, on June 18, 2003, bringing an end to Liberia's fifteen-year civil war. *See* LIBERIAN TRC REPORT, *supra* note 25, at 169. See also the annexure to *supra* note 67, for the official copy of the signed agreement forwarded to the Security Council.

Accra negotiations, he would be spared prosecution at the SCSL.[70] He would subsequently express dismay that he had been duped.[71]

The Nigerian government, under President Olusegun Obasanjo, which for a long period insisted that it would not violate the compromise reached with Taylor given the implications for future peacemaking in Africa, later indicated that it was amenable to turning him over.[72] On March 29, 2006, after much political back and forth with the SCSL and pressure from various governments such as that of the United States and human rights groups in Nigeria and elsewhere, the new Liberian government of President Ellen Johnson Sirleaf formally requested that Taylor be extradited home to Liberia. The man, who just a day before had allegedly disappeared from his Calabar villa and had been declared a fugitive from justice, was suddenly "found" and detained at a remote border outpost near the Nigerian border with Cameroon. Taylor would later claim that he was in fact under the escort of Nigerian military personnel that had been assigned as his security detail by the host government. He was flown on a military plane to Monrovia.[73] On the tarmac at Robertsfield International Airport in Monrovia, Taylor was turned over to Liberian authorities. He was thereafter formally arrested by UN peacekeepers who had been so mandated by the Security Council in a Chapter VII resolution. Taylor, accompanied by a couple of lawyers from the UN Mission in Liberia to ensure his fair treatment, was flown to Freetown on a UN helicopter where he was in turn transferred into the custody of the SCSL.[74]

The first indictment against Taylor charged him with individual criminal responsibility, pursuant to Articles 6(1) and 6(3) of the SCSL Statute, for providing various types of support to the RUF in its bid to destabilize Sierra Leone and in order to gain access to the country's diamonds.[75] Under Article 6(1), the prosecution alleged that Taylor, by his acts or omissions, planned, instigated, ordered, committed, aided and abetted, or otherwise participated with Sankoh in a common plan involving the crimes charged in eighteen counts.[76] They also alleged that he had engaged in a joint criminal enterprise with the RUF by providing financial support, military training, personnel, arms, ammunition, and other forms of support and

---

[70] Transcript of Record – Nov. 10, 2009, *supra* note 68.

[71] *Id.*

[72] *See* Federal Government of Nigeria, Statement, Former President Charles Taylor to be transferred to the custody of the Government of Liberia (Mar. 25, 2006).

[73] Transcript of Record – Nov. 10, 2009, *supra* note 68, at 31521–22.

[74] *Id.*

[75] Agreement between the United Nations and the Government of Sierra Leone on the Establishment of a Special Court for Sierra Leone, U.N.-Sierra Leone, Jan. 16, 2002, 2178 U.N.T.S. 137 [hereinafter U.N.-Sierra Leone Agreement]. Annexed to the UN-Sierra Leone Agreement was the Statute of the Special Court for Sierra Leone [hereinafter SCSL Statute]. These instruments are included in the appendix.

[76] *Id.* art. 6(1); Prosecutor v. Taylor, Case No. SCSL-2003-01-I, Indictment, ¶ 26 (Mar. 7, 2003); Prosecutor v. Taylor, Case No. SCSL-2003-01-I, Decision Approving the Indictment and Order for Non-Disclosure (Mar. 7, 2003).

encouragement to them. In addition to, or in the alternative, pursuant to Article 6(3), the prosecution claimed that Taylor was criminally responsible as a superior for the crimes contained in the indictment.[77] In their view, Taylor knew, or had reason to know, that his subordinates in the RUF and the AFRC/RUF coalition were about to carry out the crimes, or had done so, but that he failed to take the necessary measures to prevent the acts or to punish the perpetrators as required under the law of armed conflict and international criminal law.[78]

Taylor's indictment was amended twice, first on March 16, 2006 (before he was arrested and transferred to the custody of the SCSL), and on May 29, 2007, just days before his trial was set to begin in The Hague where his case was controversially transferred.[79] The final version on which he was ultimately tried alleged three international crimes and eleven counts.[80] In five counts he was charged with *crimes against humanity*, punishable under Article 2 of the SCSL Statute, namely: murder (Count 2); rape (Count 4); sexual slavery (Count 5); other inhumane acts (Count 8); and enslavement (Count 10).[81] Five other counts charged what are typically referred to as *war crimes*, or in more technical jargon, violations of Common Article 3 and Additional Protocol II of the Geneva Conventions, which are punishable under Article 3 of the SCSL Statute,[82] namely: acts of terrorism (Count 1); violence to life, health and physical or mental well-being of persons, in particular murder (Count 3); outrages upon personal dignity (Count 6); violence to life, health and physical or mental wellbeing of persons, in particular cruel treatment (Count 7); and pillage (Count 11).[83] Finally, the last count in the Taylor indictment alleged that he had carried out *other serious violations of international humanitarian law*, punishable under Article 4 of the SCSL Statute, and in particular, by conscripting or enlisting children under the

---

[77] SCSL Statute, *supra* note 75, art. 6(3);); Prosecutor v. Taylor, Case No. SCSL-2003–01-I, Indictment, ¶ 27 (Mar. 7, 2003).

[78] Prosecutor v. Taylor, Case No. SCSL-2003–01-I, Indictment, ¶ 27 (Mar. 7, 2003).

[79] Prosecutor v. Taylor, Case No. SCSL-2003–01-I, Decision on Prosecution's Application to Amend Indictment and on Approval of Amended Indictment (Mar. 16, 2006); Prosecutor v. Taylor, Case No. SCSL-2003–01-I, Decision on Prosecution Motion Requesting Leave to Amend Indictment (May 25, 2007).

[80] Prosecutor v. Taylor, Case No. SCSL-2003–01-I, Prosecution's Second Amended Indictment (May 29, 2007).

[81] SCSL Statute, *supra* note 75, at art. 2; Prosecutor v. Taylor, Case No. SCSL-2003–01-I, Decision on Prosecution's Application to Amend Indictment and on Approval of Amended Indictment, (Mar. 16, 2006); Prosecutor v. Taylor, Case No. SCSL-2003–01-I, Decision on Prosecution Motion Requesting Leave to Amend Indictment (May 25, 2007).

[82] Geneva Convention for the Amelioration of the Condition of the Wounded and Sick in Armed Forces in the Field, art. 3, Aug. 12, 1949, 75 U.N.T.S. 31; Protocol II Additional to the Geneva Conventions of Aug. 12, 1949 Relating to the Protection of Victims of Non-International Armed Conflicts art. 3, June 8, 1977, 1125 U.N.T.S. 609; SCSL Statute, *supra* note 75, at art. 3.

[83] Prosecutor v. Taylor, Case No. SCSL-2003-01-I, Decision on Prosecution's Application to Amend Indictment and on Approval of Amended Indictment (Mar. 16, 2006); Prosecutor v. Taylor, Case No. SCSL-2003-01-I, Decision on Prosecution Motion Requesting Leave to Amend Indictment (May 25, 2007).

age of fifteen years into armed forces or groups or using them to participate actively in hostilities (Count 9).[84] Notably, as with all the other indictees before the SCSL, none of the charged crimes invoked any of the Sierra Leonean offenses codified in Article 5 of the SCSL Statute.[85]

The indictment, alleging that Taylor was among those most responsible for the crimes committed during the war, covered the entire Sierra Leonean territory. These included five of the country's largest districts as well as the capital Freetown. Thus, the SCSL had seemingly complied with the personal and territorial jurisdiction requirements of Article 1(1) of its Statute, which provided that the tribunal's jurisdiction was delimited to those bearing greatest responsibility for the crimes "committed in the territory of Sierra Leone." With respect to temporal jurisdiction, Taylor's crimes allegedly began with the SCSL's assumption of jurisdiction on November 30, 1996 until the end of hostilities on January 18, 2002.[86] This established that *ratione temporis* jurisdiction also existed. Notwithstanding the limitation on temporal jurisdiction, however, some of the evidence later adduced during Taylor's trial included acts dating as far back as the beginning of the war in 1991. This provided helpful context and is consistent with the practice of other ad hoc tribunals. Though he was ultimately convicted, the Trial Chamber did not use any of the pre-November 1996 evidence for the purposes of convicting him.[87]

It seems noteworthy that Taylor formally assumed power in Liberia on August 2, 1997, and resigned on August 23, 2003, just over six years later. Some of the conduct for which he was charged and later convicted occurred just before he became president. But much of it took place during his presidency, which largely coincided with the period of the SCSL's jurisdiction. It was interesting that the various versions of his indictments averred that he was at all relevant times the leader of the NPFL and/or Liberia's President. Further, that because of those positions and his

---

[84] SCSL Statute, *supra* note 75, art. 4; Prosecutor v. Taylor, Case No. SCSL-2003-01-I, Decision on Prosecution's Application to Amend Indictment and on Approval of Amended Indictment (Mar. 16, 2006); Prosecutor v. Taylor, Case No. SCSL-2003-01-I, Decision on Prosecution Motion Requesting Leave to Amend Indictment (May 25, 2007).

[85] Prosecutor v. Taylor, Case No. SCSL-2003-01-I, Decision on Prosecution's Application to Amend Indictment and on Approval of Amended Indictment (Mar. 16, 2006); Prosecutor v. Taylor, Case No. SCSL-2003-01-I, Decision on Prosecution Motion Requesting Leave to Amend Indictment (May 25, 2007).

[86] Prosecutor v. Taylor, Case No. SCSL-2003-01-I, Prosecution's Second Amended Indictment (May 29, 2007).

[87] Under the jurisprudence of the ad hoc international tribunals, a trial chamber may convict an accused only when all the elements of the crime required to establish guilt are established as having occurred within the temporal jurisdiction of the court. Nonetheless, in important exceptions with some potential for abuse, the judges may rely on evidence that falls outside the court's temporal timeframe in order to (1) clarify a given context, (2) establish by inference the elements of criminal conduct occurred during the material period, or 3) to show a deliberate pattern of conduct. See, for the leading case on the matter, Prosecutor v. Nahimana, Case No. ICTR-99-52-A, Judgment, ¶¶ 313–15 (Nov. 28, 2007). For the discussion of these exceptions in relation to the evidentiary evaluation in the Taylor trial, *see* Prosecutor v. Taylor, Case No. SCSL-03-01-T, Judgment, ¶¶ 99–105 (May 18, 2012).

relationships with Sankoh and other militia commanders in Sierra Leone, he had both the authority and the means to participate in planning and aiding and abetting the crimes committed.[88]

It appears that there was prima facie evidence that Taylor was involved in the Sierra Leonean conflict as a collaborator/supporter of the RUF. Thus, as a legal matter, the SCSL also had power under international law to *exercise* jurisdiction over him when he was indicted in 2003. The controversial question, which this chapter will focus on, is whether immunity law as it existed at the time of the indictment precluded the SCSL from *asserting* that jurisdiction given that Liberia was not party to the agreement establishing the Tribunal and the fact that Taylor was a sitting president. Before addressing that and other related issues, it seems helpful to discuss the doctrine and rationale for immunity law as articulated by the ICJ. This will in turn help contextualize the debates which subsequently dogged the *Taylor* case at the SCSL and the Appeals Chamber's attempts to help clarify them.

8.4 THE LAW OF HEAD OF STATE IMMUNITY BEFORE TAYLOR

Much has been written, and will continue to be written, about the controversial and evolving area of head of state immunity under customary international law and its compatibility, or lack thereof, with the emerging principle of individual criminal responsibility for core crimes in international criminal law. One cannot therefore purport to offer a comprehensive overview in a chapter of this kind. That would, in any event, be unnecessary for our more limited purposes. It suffices to highlight a few important things that focus on the relationship between immunities for senior government officials and their interaction with criminal prosecution for atrocity crimes in international penal tribunals. To put the issue of scope to rest, the discussion here is narrow and must necessarily be so because it does not address the existence or applicability of immunities in the course of *civil* proceedings. Nor does it take up broader questions about *state immunity*, or for that matter, the immunities of high officials under the domestic laws of the concerned state (that is, the Republic of Liberia) in the context of the SCSL prosecution of Taylor. Neither am I concerned with other types of immunities, under treaty or customary international law, in relation to *diplomatic* or *consular* officials or state officials on special missions or other such circumstances because these issues simply did not come up before the Sierra Leone Tribunal and are in any event covered by the relevant conventions.[89]

---

[88] *See*, Prosecutor v. Taylor, Case No. SCSL-2003-01-I, Indictment, ¶¶ 22, 26, 29 (Mar. 7, 2003); *See also*, *e.g.*, Prosecutor v. Taylor, Case No. SCSL-03-01-T, Judgment, ¶ 3112 (May 18, 2012) (noting Taylor's role in decision to take the diamond-rich town of Kono on the way to Freetown).

[89] For an excellent discussion of the distinct topics of State immunity, as well as Diplomatic and Consular immunities, *see* Ian Brownlie, Principles of Public International Law 323–67 (7th ed., 2008); For a short redux on immunity pertaining to serving and former heads of state and other senior government officials in criminal proceedings, see Malcolm N. Shaw, International Law 735–42 (6th

To begin with, the doctrine of head of state immunity is traceable to the concept of sovereignty and the felt need for one sovereign to confidently send envoys to another sovereign without fear that criminal or civil jurisdiction could be used as a pretext to harass her representatives.[90] Immunities predated but were substantially bolstered by the advent of the "Westphalian conception of international relations"[91] under which all states were considered sovereign and deemed to be coequals. Today, immunities for state officials from criminal jurisdiction are frequently divided into two main categories, each of which is discussed separately below, with both sharing a similar set of overarching goals.[92] These are *functional* immunity and *personal* immunity.[93]

According to the International Law Commission (ILC) Special Rapporteur, immunities, as a general matter and irrespective of classification, seek "to ensure respect for the principle of the sovereign equality of States, prevent interference in their internal affairs and facilitate the maintenance of stable international relations by ensuring that the officials and representatives of States can carry out their functions without external difficulties or impediments."[94] Increasingly, in a twentieth-century development that appears to be driven mostly by the normative pull of human rights and other community values, treaties, and institutions, traditionally deferential attitudes towards immunities as well as the sovereignty basis upon which they rest have come under fire. To some, this implies that immunities do not, or rather should no longer, be given a privileged place in international affairs,[95] at least, whenever they would obstruct the prosecution of those who perpetrate heinous international offenses, which by their very nature, tend to be committed either by or at the behest or toleration of the state and its organs or high officials. The largely post–World War II push for the

---

ed., 2008). A leading treatise on the subject of state immunities can be found in HAZEL FOX AND PHILIPPA WEBB, THE LAW OF STATE IMMUNITY (3d ed., 2013). The ICJ has recently ruled on the question of State immunity in respect of civil proceedings in a decision that rebuked the attempt to create an exception for sovereign immunity to permit claims against the concerned State for the gross human rights violations committed by its armed forces during World War II. *See,* in this regard, Jurisdictional Immunities of the State (Ger. v. It., Greece Intervening), Judgment, 2012 ICJ Rep. 95, ¶ 99 (Feb. 3).

90 ROBERT CRYER ET AL., AN INTRODUCTION TO INTERNATIONAL CRIMINAL LAW AND PROCEDURE 540 (3d ed., 2014).

91 M. C. BASSIOUNI, INTRODUCTION TO INTERNATIONAL CRIMINAL LAW 73 (2nd rev. ed., 2012).

92 It has been argued that immunity *ratione personae* should be divided into two categories, immunity attaching to an *office or status* and immunity attaching *to official acts,* to facilitate better understanding and clearer demarcation of the immunity's purpose and role. *See,* Dapo Akande & Sangeeta Shah, *Immunities of State Officials, International Crimes, and Foreign Domestic Courts,* 21 EUR. J. INT'L L. 815 (2010).

93 For a detailed distinction between functional and personal immunities, *see* CRYER ET AL., *supra* note 90, at 542–43. Judicial discussion of the distinction on the facts of a concrete case may be found in Certain Questions of Mutual Assistance in Criminal Matters, (Djib. v. Fr.) Judgment, 2008 I.C.J. Rep. 177, ¶¶ 187–89 (June 4).

94 Concepcion Escobar Hernandez (Special Rapporteur on the Immunity of State officials from foreign criminal jurisdiction), *Second Rep. on the Immunity of State Officials from foreign criminal jurisdiction,* U.N. Doc. A/CN.4/661 (Apr. 4, 2013) [hereinafter ILC SR Report on Immunities].

95 ANTONIO CASSESE, INTERNATIONAL CRIMINAL LAW 308, 311–12 (2008).

retrenchment of immunity in relation to individuals for certain conduct prohibited under international law is somewhat similar to the movement and evolution concerning state immunity in civil matters. State or sovereign immunity was for a long time initially treated as absolute. But, partly as a reflection of the changing mores and priorities of international society in the twentieth century and the involvement of the modern state in the private/commercial sphere, it is no longer considered so. In fact, international law now accepts a restricted theory of immunity based on a distinction between acts *jure imperii* and acts *jure gestionis*. A similar type of shift seems to be taking place in respect of criminal matters.

8.4.1 *Immunity Attaching to Official State Acts or Immunity* Ratione Materiae

Under customary international law, functional immunity (*immunity ratione materiae*) broadly attaches to shield *official acts or conduct* executed on behalf of a state from scrutiny in foreign courts. As the ILC Special Rapporteur has helpfully summarized, immunity *ratione materiae* has the following characteristics: "(a) It is granted to all State officials; (b) It is granted only in respect of acts that can be characterized as 'official acts' or 'acts performed in the exercise of official functions'; (c) It is not time-limited since immunity *ratione materiae* continues even after the person who enjoys such immunity has left office."[96] This type of immunity attaches to a large set of officials – that is to say, all who execute state functions and are uncontroversial when it comes to their applicability to the person of the head of state or the head of government. The same views have been confirmed by the ICJ, as well as by states and scholars, as discussed further in Section 8.6 below.[97]

Under this general international law doctrine, Taylor, as Head of State of Liberia, would ordinarily be entitled to functional immunity before foreign (national) courts such as those of Sierra Leone for official acts carried out in the exercise of his duties as Head of State. His official acts, whatever those may be, are entitled to protection because they are deemed to be the official acts of the Republic of Liberia. It would seem doubtful, however, whether the commission of international crimes should be considered official rather than private acts. In any event, on this logic of attribution of the acts of a leader to his state, Taylor could not be held criminally responsible for such conduct before a foreign domestic court, even after he has vacated the presidency of that state. The main rationale for this substantive protection seems to be twofold and straightforward: first, the need to ensure the stability of international affairs and necessity of state officials being able to carry out their duties without any let or hindrance; and second, the fact that allowing the domestic courts of one state (Sierra Leone) to adjudicate the official acts of the most senior officials of

---

[96]   ILC SR Report on Immunities, *supra* note 94, at ¶ 50.

[97]   See Arrest Warrant of 11 April 2000 (Dem. Rep. Congo v. Belg.), Judgment, 2002 ICJ Rep. 3, ¶¶ 53–54 (Feb. 14).

another state (Liberia) would violate the principle of sovereign equality between the two states.

Of course, the equality of all sovereign states is now enshrined as one of the fundamental principles of the Charter of the United Nations at Article 2(1) and is widely considered to be part of customary international law. This foundational principle, according to the ICJ, must be read together with the notion that each state possesses sovereignty over its own territory including the jurisdiction over events and persons within its territory.[98] It follows therefore that exceptions to the immunity of the state, which perforce flows to include its officials, is a form of departure from the notion of sovereign equality.

A further difficulty that justifies the existence of immunities exists. Subjecting the official acts of a foreign state (Liberia) to the domestic law of another state (Sierra Leone) would elevate the law of the latter (Sierra Leone) over that of the former (Liberia). Through either lens, an equal would be seeking to exercise authority over another equal. That would make no sense. This idea is said to be captured in the oft-repeated Latin maxim *par in parem non habet imperium* (among equals none has dominium). Worse, and this is equally significant, it could easily lead to unnecessary tensions if not outright disputes between states.

Put differently, under the functional immunity doctrine that applies to a large set of state officials carrying out official state functions, State A (Sierra Leone) could not bring criminal proceedings against an official from State B (Liberia). To do so would mean that the former is doing indirectly what it is not permitted to do directly, that is to say, to sit in judgment over the conduct of another state. It would interfere with the performance of official functions and may even create chaos in interstate relations. As one commentator has suggested in a thoughtful article, this type of immunity serves a dual role that is both substantive and procedural: substantive, in the sense that it becomes a defense to liability which the official can plead because it imputes his conduct to his state;[99] procedural because it puts in place a jurisdictional hurdle that prevents a foreign court from using a pretext to indirectly scrutinize or control the acts of the foreign state by initiating criminal proceedings against the official who carried out the act.[100]

Though the point is not entirely free of doubt, there seems to be two significant exceptions associated with functional immunity.[101] First, this type of immunity only covers the conduct of a former or serving official that was an official act of a state. Thus, criminal actions that are carried out in a *private* capacity are still subject, at least in principle, to prosecution.[102] The second limitation is that immunity *ratione*

---

[98] Jurisdictional Immunities of the State (Ger. v. It., Greece Intervening), Judgment, 2012 ICJ Rep. 95, ¶ 123 (Feb. 3).

[99] Dapo Akande & Sangeeta Shah, *Immunities of State Officials, International Crimes, and Foreign Domestic Courts*, 21 EUR. J. INT'L L. 815, 826 (2010).

[100] *Id.* at 827.

[101] See CRYER ET AL., *supra* note 90, at 549–52.

[102] *Id.*

materiae is said to be rejected where the person is charged with certain international crimes such as genocide, war crimes, and crimes against humanity.[103] A key justification to sustain the latter proposition, which apparently reflects present customary international law, is that acts that could be characterized as international offenses including the so-called core crimes and torture cannot be considered official acts of a state. This view appears to have received some judicial endorsement in the significant *Pinochet* precedent and had found much earlier endorsement by the ILC and UN Member States over six decades ago as well as in the more recent ICTY case law.[104] In this regard, it was interesting that in the *Taylor* case, the prosecutors suggested that he acted in his official instead of private capacity when in fact the conduct alleged in the indictment was said to be tied to an alleged desire to secure diamonds for private accumulation.[105] During the trial, after his guilt was determined, he was adjudged to have abused his official position as Head of State. The trial court then took this abuse of office into account as an aggravating factor in apportioning his sentence.[106]

8.4.2 *Immunity Attaching to an Office or Status or Immunity* Ratione Personae

Immunity *ratione personae*, also often described as personal immunity, is simultaneously broader in scope and more circumscribed in application. Whereas functional immunity is limited to "official acts," immunity *ratione personae* encompasses both personal and official acts. The application of this immunity, however, is only available to prominent officials, usually thought to be limited to the so-called "troika"[107] of *head of state*, *head of government*, and *foreign ministers*, and ceases when the actor leaves office. Accordingly, in the view of the ILC SR, immunity

---

[103] *Id.*

[104] *See* G.A. Res. 95(I) Affirmation of the Principles of International Law Recognized by the Charter of the Nurnberg Tribunal (Dec. 11, 1946); Principles of International Law Recognized in the Charter of the Nurnberg Tribunal and in the Judgment of the Tribunal, *Report of the International Law Commission*, U.N. Doc. A/CN.4/21 (1950), *reprinted in* [1950] 2 Y.B. Int'l L. Comm'n 274–378, U. N. Doc. A/CN.4/SER.A/1950/Add.1; R v. Bow Street Metropolitan Stipendary Magistrate, ex parte Pinochet Ugarte (No. 2) 1999 1 All ER 577 HL and (No. 3) 1999 2 All ER 97 (especially the opinions of Lords Browne-Wilkinson and Hutton); and CASSESE, *supra* note 95, at 311–12. For further commentary, on international crimes not being the type of official conduct that should benefit from functional immunity, *see* Christine Chinkin, *United Kingdom House of Lords: Regina v. Bow Street Stipendary Magistrate, Ex Parte Pinochet Ugarte*, 93 AM. J. INT'L L. 703 (1999). The finding was made that there is no exception for core international crimes even while carried out in an official capacity in Prosecutor v. Blaskic, Case No. IT-95-14, Judgment on the Request of the Republic of Croatia for Review of the Decision of Trial Chamber II of 18 July 1997, ¶ 41 (Int'l Crim. Trib. for the Former Yugoslavia Oct. 29, 1997); and reiterated in Prosecutor v. Furundžija, Case No. IT-95-17/1-T, Judgment, ¶ 140 (Int'l Crim. Trib. for the Former Yugoslavia Dec. 10, 1998).

[105] *See* Romano & Nollkaemper, *supra* note 60, at 16 (asking the question whether acts so motivated could be considered something else other than official acts).

[106] Prosecutor v. Taylor, Case No. SCSL-2003-01-I, Sentencing Judgment, ¶¶ 29, 97 (May 30, 2012).

[107] *See* Int'l Law Comm'n, Rep on the Work of its Fifty-First Session, U.N. Doc. A/54/10 (2011).

ratione personae, which is absolute in character and temporally limited in use, has essentially the following characteristics:

> (a) It is granted only to certain State officials who play a prominent role in that State and who, by virtue of their functions, represent it in international relations automatically under the rules of international law; (b) It applies to all acts, whether private or official, that are performed by the representatives of a State; (c) It is clearly temporary in nature and is limited to the term of office of the person who enjoys immunity.[108]

Because these types of immunities are meant to promote international relations by helping to avoid "a foreign state either infringing sovereign prerogatives of states or interfering with the official functions of a state agent under the pretext of dealing with an exclusively private act,"[109] these officials enjoy absolute immunity and inviolability.[110] Thus, an official is immune from prosecution even for clearly illegal personal acts for the duration of his tenure. On his first day as a private citizen, however, he can no longer enjoy immunity from prosecution in a foreign state. In fact, assuming all other jurisdictional requirements are established, he may be subject to foreign criminal processes for those acts. The ICJ would, along these lines, permit the courts of other states to prosecute acts committed *before* or *after* the period of service in office and in respect of acts committed *during* that service period in a private capacity.[111] This appears to leave open the prospect that acts carried out in violation of international law in relation to core crimes are potentially prosecutable, assuming those are not construed as falling within the ambit of purely official acts. Again, in the Taylor context, an attempt to secure Sierra Leonean diamonds for private gain would likely fall outside the realm of official acts.

At the same time, in contrast to functional immunity, there is no exception for personal immunities permitting the arrest and trial of the holder of one of the protected offices, whether before national or international courts.[112] The case law and state practice bears this out and apparently pays no regard to the nature or gravity of the crimes.[113] Even in circumstances where the person is alleged to have committed international crimes, certain personal immunities will still continue to be available. In this scheme, the only way to defeat immunity *ratione personae* is through *consent* or *waiver* of the concerned state. This classical doctrinal attitude, which basically prioritizes the smooth conduct of international relations between states, fails to account fully for the increasingly popular modern view that all persons

---

[108]   ILC SR Report on Immunities, *supra* note 94 at ¶ 50.

[109]   CASSESE, *supra* note 95.

[110]   Arrest Warrant of 11 April 2000 (Dem. Rep. Congo v. Belg.), Judgment, 2002 ICJ Rep. 3 (Feb. 14).

[111]   *Id.* at 25–26.

[112]   *Id.* at 3, 20.

[113]   CRYER ET AL., *supra* note 90, at 552 (discussing how, even if Pinochet had been a sitting head of state at the time of the British proceedings, the House of Lords determined that his immunity would have been personal and absolute irrespective of the nature of the charge).

irrespective of their status must be morally and legally accountable for their actions. In a different context, in relation to the work of the ILC on the topic of immunity of state officials from foreign criminal jurisdiction, I have expressed some concern that the argument about instability caused in international relations as a result of removing immunity fails also to take into account the instability that results when those responsible for carrying out heinous international crimes are shielded from prosecution. All the more so in circumstances where those actions might have led to the (ongoing) perpetration of odious offenses condemned by international law.

Overall, regardless of which of the two categories of immunity are under discussion, it is widely understood that the purpose of immunities is not to shield the individual from criminal prosecution as such but rather to preserve the interest of one state vis-à-vis that of another state while promoting cooperation and helping to avoid friction between equal sovereigns.[114] Thus, international law carves out for special preservation the *conduct* carried out as part of a person's official duties and establishes a protective shield around it, even after the person has vacated the office. That is the essence of the functional immunity doctrine.

Conversely, for personal immunities, the *person* enjoys the protection of the law albeit only to the extent s/he occupies the official position which justifies the grant of the immunity in the first place. There is consequently some overlap between the two forms of immunity. In effect, an official can enjoy personal immunity, as a result of his or her position, and at the same time, any official acts he carries out could be shielded by functional immunity. The essential difference is that the latter immunity (*ratione materiae*), which is not tied to his status, would survive his departure from office because it protects his conduct whereas the former (*ratione personae*) which protects the person would not.

We may conclude from the above review that the conventional rationale for head of state immunity centers on the need to facilitate cooperative state-to-state interaction. These immunities are intended to redound to the benefit of the state not the official. That is why it is the same entity (that is, the state) that is holder of the right and that can waive it if it deems fit.[115] If this assumption is correct, a key question that arises is whether the justification for immunities, which are primarily rules aimed at facilitating equal interstate relationships on the horizontal level, make any sense in scenarios where we essentially have vertical relationships such as those arising between states and international penal tribunals.[116] The SCSL answer to this question, which is an important addition to the present immunity debate including at the ICC, is that international courts reflecting the collective interests of states may rank in hierarchy above those of individual states. They possess the attributes that make the logic that underpin immunities *inapplicable* in their relations inter se. Thus, one

---

[114] *See id.* at 542–43 (where the authors summarize the similarities and dissimilarities for these two types of immunity).

[115] *See id.* at 542–43, 545–46.

[116] CASSESE, *supra* note 95, at 312.

of the main contributions of the SCSL Appeals Chamber decision in *Taylor* is the determination that the classical justification for immunities does not, or more normatively, *should not* encumber prosecutions for international offenses before international criminal courts.

In this regard, despite some of the political complaints we have seen in relation to the work of the ICC in Africa for example,[117] there seems to be limited empirical evidence that the independent judiciaries in such tribunals can be successfully manipulated to hamper a state's ability to conduct its foreign affairs with other states through a frivolous prosecution. On the other hand, it can be argued that the state practice, national legislation, and other evidence such as the decisions of international and national courts are clear that there is – at least at present – no customary law exception to head of state immunity for international crimes. That much was repeated in a recent decision of the Supreme Court of Appeal of South Africa and in some academic writings.[118]

8.5 STATUS OF PERSONAL IMMUNITY UNDER CUSTOMARY INTERNATIONAL LAW

The ICJ handed down a "most unfortunate"[119] judgment on customary international law immunities in the *Case Concerning the Arrest Warrant of 11 April 2000 (Democratic Republic of Congo v. Belgium)(Yerodia)*.[120] *Yerodia*, which was cited by everyone involved in the proceedings at the SCSL and today remains the backbone of the World Court's view of immunity in the context of criminal proceedings, basically supplied the legal edifice for the *Taylor* immunity controversy.[121] The same decision also, perhaps unsurprisingly, shaped the final outcome and ultimately the contributions of the SCSL to the international criminal law jurisprudence on head of state immunity.

Although as a threshold matter, ICJ judgments are binding only on the parties in relation to the particular dispute[122] and the ICJ was not among those to which the SCSL Appeals Chamber was formally directed by its statute for guidance,[123] it is

---

[117] Charles C. Jalloh, *Regionalizing International Criminal Law?*, 9 INT'L CRIM. LAW REV. 445 (2009).

[118] The Minister of Justice and Constitutional Development v. The Southern African Litigation Center 2016, (17) SA (CC) at 3 ¶¶ 66–75 (S. Afr.); Roger O'Keefe, *An "International Crime" Exception to the Immunity of State Officials from Foreign Criminal Jurisdiction: Not Currently, Not Likely*, 109 AM. J. INT'L. L. UNBOUND 168 (2015).

[119] Alain Pellet, *Response to Koh and Buchwald's Article: Don Quixote and Sancho Panza Tilt at Windmills*, 109(3) AM. J. INT'L. L. 557, 564 (2015).

[120] Arrest Warrant of 11 April 2000 (Dem. Rep. Congo v. Belg.), Judgment, 2002 ICJ Rep. 3, 3 (Feb. 14).

[121] It is that fact which led one author to characterize the *Taylor* case as "The Arrest Warrant Case Continued." *See* Sarah M. H. Nouwen, *The Special Court for Sierra Leone and the Immunity of Taylor: The Arrest Warrant Case Continued*, 18 LEIDEN J. INT'L. L. 645 (2005).

[122] Statute of the International Court of Justice art. 59, June 26, 1945, 33 U.N.T.S. 933 [hereinafter ICJ Statute].

[123] SCSL Statute, *supra* note 75, at art. 20(3).

undeniable that the ruling of the UN's only principal judicial organ carries great weight. The core elements of that dispute warrant a brief discussion. For one thing, the ICJ resolved the case under customary international law since there was no applicable treaty regulating the specific immunities of foreign ministers. For another, the SCSL, as an international criminal court, would be bound to apply such a source of law even though the ICJ's pronouncements on the question could have also been distinguished as *obiter*.[124] Nevertheless, despite the cool reception that *Yerodia* has received from scholars and a significant change to the composition of its bench, the ICJ has – albeit over the strong objections of some of its members – in two more relatively recent judgments reiterated its deferential attitude towards both sovereign immunity and the immunity of high state officials in respect of both civil and criminal proceedings.[125] The ICJ, even while being criticized by some of its judges, seems to have continued maintaining that position.

Briefly, the relevant facts of *Yerodia* are these. On April 11, 2000, a Belgian magistrate issued an arrest warrant for the then Congolese Minister of Foreign Affairs Abdoulaye Yerodia Ndombasi alleging his commission of war crimes and crimes against humanity.[126] The warrant, which was based on a Belgian law domesticating the 1949 Geneva Conventions and their 1977 Additional Protocols, was transmitted to the DRC and circulated internationally via INTERPOL.[127] Congo initiated proceedings at the ICJ, on October 17, 2000, asserting inter alia that the mere issuance and circulation of the arrest warrant violated international law which prohibits the courts of one state from exercising their authority in another state as well as the principles of sovereign equality and the absolute immunity enjoyed by incumbent foreign ministers for official acts.[128]

Belgium objected to Congo's application on several grounds.[129] These included that, while serving foreign ministers enjoyed immunity from criminal jurisdiction before the courts of a foreign state, such immunity applied only to official acts instead of the private acts in respect of which Yerodia had been charged. In any event, since he was no longer incumbent foreign minister by the time of the

---

[124] It can be noted here that although the tribunal statute only mandated that the SCSL Appeals Chamber be "guided" by decisions of the Appeals Chamber of the ICTY and ICTR, under the Rules of Procedure and Evidence of the SCSL, it is confirmed that the Court was in essence required to follow the sources of law found in Art. 38 of the Statute of the International Court of Justice. In relevant part, it is clarified that the applicable law of the SCSL includes, as appropriate, other treaties and principles and rules of customary international law as well as general principles of law derived from national legal systems. *See* Arts. 20(3) of the SCSL Statute and Rule 73bis of the RPE (note latter was adopted after *Taylor* in 2004).

[125] Jurisdictional Immunities of the State (Ger. v. It., Greece Intervening), Judgment, 2012 ICJ Rep. 95, 141 ¶¶ 93-95 (Feb. 3); Certain Questions of Mutual Assistance in Criminal Matters, (Djib. v. Fr.) Judgment, 2008 I.C.J. Rep. 177, ¶¶ 170–71 (June 4).

[126] Arrest Warrant of 11 April 2000 (Dem. Rep. Congo v. Belg.), Judgment, 2002 ICJ Rep. 3, ¶ 13 (Feb. 14).

[127] *Id.* at ¶ 14.

[128] *Id.* at ¶ 17.

[129] *Id.* at ¶¶ 24, 29, 33, 37, 41.

proceedings, any objection based on his official immunities was moot.[130] The latter Belgian argument essentially challenged Yerodia's possible entitlement to *ratione personae* immunity because he was no longer in office and would have been sufficient ground also in the later *Taylor* case to also deny him immunities.[131]

In a contested judgment both in relation to its methodology used and the ultimate conclusion, starting with the separate opinions of some of the concurring judges, the ICJ ruled in favor of Congo. It determined that, under customary international law, "it was firmly established that, as diplomatic and consular agents, certain holders of high ranking office in a State, *such as* the Head of State, Head of Government and Minister for Foreign Affairs, enjoy immunities from jurisdiction in other States, both civil and criminal."[132] The Court emphasized that the underlying purpose of personal immunities was to ensure the smooth conduct of interstate relations. Thus, according to the judges, "the immunities accorded to Ministers of Foreign Affairs are not granted for their personal benefit, but to ensure the effective performance of their functions on behalf of their respective States."[133] Though at a technical level the ICJ was addressing the position of a foreign minister, it did not limit the scope of its ruling to exclude heads of state or government. In any event, the immunities discussed would apply even more so to more senior officials like sitting presidents – as the Court has since confirmed specifically in relation to heads of state in *Djibouti v. France*.[134]

The judges focused on the essential role of foreign ministers who must travel internationally to carry out their responsibilities. The Minister "occupies a position such that, like the Head of State or the Head of Government, he or she is recognized under international law as representative of the State solely by virtue of his or her office."[135] In service to this important ambassadorial function, the ICJ underscored that a foreign minister "throughout the duration of his or her office, he or she when abroad enjoys full immunity from criminal jurisdiction and inviolability."[136]

Moreover, in terms of the unacceptability of impediments to the exercise of his functions, there was no distinction between official or private acts or official or private visits, or between acts performed during or before assumption of the office. The consequences were also deemed to be equally serious whether the minister was charged in absentia or arrested when present on the territory of the arresting state. All these norms flowed from the fact that any attempt to exercise criminal, or for that

---

[130] *Id.* at ¶¶ 24–25; 29–30.
[131] *Id.* at ¶¶ 49–50.
[132] *Id.* at ¶ 51 (emphasis added).
[133] *Id.* at ¶ 53.
[134] Certain Questions of Mutual Assistance in Criminal Matters, (Djib. v. Fr.) Judgment, 2008 I.C.J. Rep. 177, ¶¶ 170–71 (June 4) (where the ICJ reiterated that a head of state enjoys full immunity from criminal jurisdiction and inviolability which allows him to be free from any constraining acts of authority by the courts of another state).
[135] Arrest Warrant of 11 April 2000 (Dem. Rep. Congo v. Belg.), Judgment, 2002 ICJ Rep. 3, ¶ 53 (Feb. 14).
[136] *Id.* at ¶ 54.

matter civil or any other type of jurisdiction by a foreign court over the person of the foreign minister, would hinder her ability to carry out her functions as lead diplomat of the state on the international plane.[137]

As to Belgium's claim that there was in essence an international crimes exception to the absolute personal immunity enjoyed by incumbent foreign ministers, at least when it comes to *core* international crimes, the ICJ again disagreed – a position that the Court has since reiterated and which continues to find support in the subsequent decisions of various national and international courts.[138] The judges could not discern in the state practice or the statutes or decisions of national or international courts any rule that customary international law permitted any exemption for war crimes or crimes against humanity to the absolute immunity and inviolability of foreign ministers before foreign national courts.[139] Such immunities protect persons against the exercise of any act of authority of another state. Nonetheless, in a seeming acknowledgement of the difficulties of its position as a matter of the present *lex lata*,[140] the Court emphasized that its ruling does not imply that such personalities "enjoy *impunity* in respect of any crimes they might have committed, irrespective of their gravity."[141] Indeed, immunity from criminal jurisdiction, which is only a procedural bar, does not imply absence of criminal responsibility which is a separate question of substantive law.[142]

Even more significantly for our purposes, after laying down the general rule emphasizing the absolute immunities of foreign ministers (which would also apply to heads of state such as Taylor), the majority of the Court enumerated the four exceptions that would permit the prosecution of a *serving* or *former* foreign

---

[137]   *Id.* at ¶ 55.

[138]   *See* the recent judgments of the World Court in the cases involving Djibouti v. France and Italy v. Germany; Certain Questions of Mutual Assistance in Criminal Matters, (Djib. v. Fr.) Judgment, 2008 I.C.J. Rep. 177 (June 4); Interpretation of the Agreement of Mar. 25, 1951 between the WHO and Egypt, Advisory Opinion, 1980 I.C.J. Rep. 80 (May 28). For academic commentary analyzing these decisions and concluding that immunities will continue to remain available because these rulings are supported by the practices of states, *see* O'Keefe, *supra* note 118.

[139]   Arrest Warrant of 11 April 2000 (Dem. Rep. Congo v. Belg.), Judgment, 2002 ICJ Rep. 3, ¶ 58 (Feb. 14).

[140]   The ICJ's position seems correct as a matter of existing law and seems to be supported by a wealth of state practice and jurisprudence, all of which has unequivocally upheld personal immunities regardless of the nature of the charges. That said, on a more normative level in terms of where the law *ought to go*, the significant argument put forth by Antonio Cassese pointed out with reference to the purposes of international law that (1) the ICJ did not make the lifting of immunity before international courts conditional upon the implicit or explicit withdrawal of such immunity in the relevant tribunal's statute to the extent that it possessed jurisdiction over the international crime that the state official is charged with; (2) that the rationale for foreign state officials being entitled to stand on personal immunities before national tribunals does not apply to international criminal tribunals; and finally, (3) that the current trend of international law is to widen the net of accountability by making those engaged in heinous crimes accountable. *See* CASSESE, *supra* note 95, at 312.

[141]   Arrest Warrant of 11 April 2000 (Dem. Rep. Congo v. Belg.), Judgment, 2002 ICJ Rep. 3, ¶ 60 (Feb. 14) (emphasis added).

[142]   *Id.*

minister in a *domestic court* (although some of the concurring judges rightly felt less sanguine about them). First, such officials may be prosecuted in their *home countries* in accordance with their respective countries' domestic laws.[143] Of course, in the context of the SCSL case against Taylor, this exemption was simply inapplicable. His home state (Liberia) which he ran at the time of his SCSL indictment did not issue an arrest warrant or seek to try Taylor for acts he might have committed during the civil war there. Nor, more importantly, did it claim universal jurisdiction under customary international law or invoke applicable treaties to pursue him for the war crimes for which he was later charged and convicted in Sierra Leone. This should not come as a surprise, despite that Taylor's Liberia had come under serious scrutiny and even been sanctioned by the UN Security Council for providing personnel, ammunition, safe passage, and various types of other support to the RUF which in turn helped to fuel the war and the commission of atrocities in Sierra Leone. This implies that this domestic prosecution option is limited, and in reality, will be hard to find much practice supporting it. Many states simply prefer not to be involved in prosecuting the former leaders of other states within their national courts. Exceptions are rare to find, and as an example of the type of advocacy that it might take to accomplish such a result, one can cite to the recent trial of the former president of Chad, Hissène Habré, on allegations of torture and war crimes in a special chamber of the courts of Senegal.[144] Indeed, the examples of Taylor and Habré indicate that it is unrealistic when taken in the broader context, to expect that a leader will be tried by the domestic courts of his own country unless there is a change of government.

Second, according to *Yerodia*, because these immunities are based on the coequal status of sovereigns, the state which the official represents or has represented may waive the immunity.[145] One might easily imagine a situation, like that of former Chadian president Hisséne Habré in which the home country is as displeased with the actions of the official as the foreign jurisdiction. This tends to happen after a change of government. Unsurprisingly, in that example, Habré could no longer claim to be entitled to personal immunities, as Chad had waived any such rights he may have to functional immunities to permit a foreign prosecution before a special chamber of the Senegalese courts to go forward.[146] In other words, states are *permitted*, but not *required*, by international law to invoke immunities in favor of their officials. Here was an example of the exercise of a waiver to allow a prosecution. It might have been possible only because a former enemy had unseated Habré and had an interest in his political demise.

---

[143] *Id.* at ¶ 61.

[144] See Questions relating to the Obligation to Prosecute or Extradite (Belg. v. Sen.), Judgment, 2012 I.C. J. Rep. 422, ¶ 27 (July 20).

[145] Arrest Warrant of 11 April 2000 (Dem. Rep. Congo v. Belg.), Judgment, 2002 ICJ Rep. 3, ¶ 61 (Feb. 14).

[146] Human Rights Watch, Press Release, *Chad Lifts Immunity of Ex-Dictator: Green Light to Prosecute Hissène Habré in Belgium* (Dec. 5, 2002), www.hrw.org/news/2002/12/05/chad-lifts-immunity-ex-dictator.

This exception would, at first blush, seem to be unhelpful in the Taylor context. This is because Sierra Leone, as a State, did not seek to prosecute Taylor as a president using its *domestic* courts for which a waiver might be sought. Rather, as already noted above, he was indicted by the SCSL which is an independent international court that operated in the sphere of international law and was not part of the Sierra Leonean domestic judicial system. Thus, Sierra Leone did not and could not request a waiver of his immunity in order to try him before its national courts. Had it tried to obtain a waiver, when Taylor was in power in Liberia, this request would obviously have been futile. It might have been more likely obtainable from the successor government of President Ellen Johnson Sirleaf with whom Taylor fell out.

Of course, even in relation to an international penal tribunal like the SCSL, it might have still been possible to seek a waiver of Taylor's immunities. That would have required Liberia to insist that he still enjoyed them, which was never the case. Nonetheless, it is interesting that although Nigeria did not indict Taylor but gave him some type of safe haven after he resigned from the presidency on August 11, 2003, the subsequent democratically elected President of Liberia did request, on March 5, 2006, that Nigeria extradite him home to Liberia. That request from Johnson Sirleaf, which enabled his arrest and transfer to the SCSL, could be seen as a waiver of any residual immunities Taylor might have enjoyed through Liberia under international law.[147]

Third, all the *personal immunities* enjoyed in the courts of other states under international law "cease" to apply to a foreign minister or head of state once he leaves the office, at least with respect to "acts committed prior or subsequent to his or her period in office, as well as in respect of acts committed during that period of office in a private capacity."[148] This means that, provided it has jurisdiction under international law, another state could try him. Importantly, at the time of his SCSL indictment on June 3, 2003, Taylor was still president of Liberia. It had been widely rumored, in the month before, that he was willing to relinquish power for the sake of restoring peace to Liberia.[149] The very next day, after the opening of the peace talks in Ghana's capital Accra, he made a public declaration in which he indicated acceptance not to be part of a future political arrangement in Liberia. He subsequently resigned from the presidency in August 2003. This would appear to suggest, on the ICJ dictum, that Taylor enjoyed absolute personal immunities and inviolability at the time of the indictment which were violated by the SCSL.

But that conclusion, contrary to the views of some commentators, could also be incorrect.[150] This is because this third exception would only be available if Taylor

---

[147]   S.C. Res. 1638, ¶ 1 (Nov. 11, 2005).
[148]   Arrest Warrant of 11 April 2000 (Dem. Rep. Congo v. Belg.), Judgment, 2002 ICJ Rep. 3, ¶ 61 (Feb. 14).
[149]   Jalloh, *Law and Politics of the Taylor Case, supra* note 7, at 251.
[150]   *See, e.g.*, Vanesa Klingberg, *(Former) Heads of State before International(ized) Criminal Courts: The Case of Charles Taylor before the Special Court for Sierra Leone*, 46 GERMAN Y.B. INT'L L. 537, 552 (2004).

had been indicted by a domestic (Sierra Leonean) instead of an international penal court (like the SCSL). It is undisputed that the ICJ in *Yerodia* was addressing a situation wherein the courts of one state were seeking to indict an apparently immune senior ministerial official from another state. It was not a scenario where an international tribunal, established with the support of the Security Council, was purporting to do so.[151] Indeed, the Taylor Defense motion at the SCSL was predicated largely on the significant and basically faulty *premise* that the Tribunal was a Sierra Leonean instead of an international penal court. The success of the entire immunity challenge therefore hinged on the classification of the tribunal as domestic, instead of international, whereas it could have likely made a stronger case focusing on Liberia's lack of express consent to the agreement creating the SCSL. Under the latter line of argumentation, as we shall see below, the lack of consent would ride on the absence of a waiver of Taylor's personal immunities which in fact benefitted the State (Liberia) rather than the person holding the office (Taylor). That would be an argument of treaty law rather than the legal nature of the SCSL.

As we saw earlier, absent the removal of the personal immunities by consent of Liberia, there would have to be some other legal basis for the removal of the immunity in the constitutive instruments of the Tribunal or on the basis of a binding Chapter VII decision of the Security Council. That is, assuming that the mere fact of UNSC involvement in creating the SCSL to prosecute international crimes, was not by itself sufficient to give legal imprimatur to the Tribunal's attempt to prosecute. Failing that, the conclusion might seem inescapable that, barring an additional justification being found say on the ground that there was an international crimes exception to immunity for international crimes under *customary international law*, the SCSL violated Taylor's personal immunities at the time of the issuance of his indictment. This is because he occupied the ultimate position as Head of State of Liberia and could not be brought within the processes of the Court.

The fourth and last ICJ exception was certainly the most relevant to the subsequent dispute whether Taylor enjoyed immunity before the SCSL at the time of the disclosure of his arrest warrant and indictment in June 2003. In this regard, in *Yerodia*, the ICJ had explained that "an incumbent or former Minister for Foreign Affairs may be subject to criminal proceedings before certain international criminal courts, where they have jurisdiction."[152] The Court then listed as "examples" the ad hoc ICTY and ICTR (noting their establishment by the UNSC under Chapter VII) and the ICC (which was treaty based and contained an explicit disavowal of any substantive immunities under Article 27(2) of the Rome Statute).

---

[151] *See* Arrest Warrant of 11 April 2000 (Dem. Rep. Congo v. Belg.), Judgment, 2002 ICJ Rep. 3, ¶ 58 (Feb. 14) (where the court removed any ambiguity that it found that "these rules likewise do not enable it to conclude that any such an exception exists in customary international law in regard to national courts").

[152] *Id.* (emphasis added).

Preliminarily, we can observe that the SCSL was not among the examples of an international criminal tribunal that the ICJ cited. The Taylor Defense read something into this. And tried to make the most of it. But this omission should not be surprising. The reason is simple. As noted in Chapter 2, the UN and Sierra Leone signed the treaty to create the SCSL in January 2002. That was only a month before the ICJ rendered the *Yerodia* Judgment. Meaning that there would have been discussions and negotiations of the SCSL's instruments during the period of deliberations over *Arrest Warrant*. Still, at that stage in which the pleadings of the parties were already before the ICJ and oral hearings had been completed, there would have been no formal conclusions of the negotiating process between the Sierra Leonean and UN authorities. The SCSL idea was, at that point, speculative at best.

On top of that, on its plain terms, the treaty establishing the SCSL would require formalities to be completed before it would enter into force.[153] That was going to need time. To make matters worse, on the part of the Government of Sierra Leone, it was not automatic because parliamentary approval was required. The formalities were completed but only about four months later,[154] when the Statute entered into force in April 2002. While the process proved to be relatively quick and smooth, it was not something that could have been predicted or taken for granted at the outset. By the same token, the ICJ did not reference any of the other so-called "hybrid" courts such as those for East Timor or Cambodia among the examples in its judgment – even if for no other reason than to distinguish them from the truly international criminal tribunals. In other words, the SCSL was not alone in not being mentioned. That it was not is not, in and of itself, as significant as the Taylor Defense lawyers tried to make it.

The ICJ did refer to the ICTR and ICTY and the "future International Criminal Court."[155] But the former two were well established having been created by the Security Council in 1993 and 1994 respectively. The ICC, at that point, had fifty-four of the sixty States Parties[156] required for the Rome Statute – a multilateral treaty – to enter into force and was only going to be dependent upon the passage of time. Notably, all three were "examples" that the term "international criminal courts" "includes"; thus, from the use of these words, this was obviously not meant to be an exhaustive list. That much was evident from the plain language ("examples," "includes"), as the Court would have otherwise likely then chosen to refer to "all" international tribunals. Consequently, the omission to mention the SCSL from an illustrative list could therefore hardly be deemed determinative.

---

[153] U.N.-Sierra Leone Agreement, *supra* note 75.

[154] Prosecutor v. Kallon, Case Nos. SCSL-2003-14-PT; SCSL-15-PT; SCSL-16-PT, Decision on Constitutionality and lack of Jurisdiction, ¶¶ 44–46, 60 (Mar. 13, 2004).

[155] *See* Arrest Warrant of 11 April 2000 (Dem. Rep. Congo v. Belg.), Judgment, 2002 ICJ Rep. 3, ¶ 61 (Feb. 14).

[156] *See* U.N.T.S., Rome Statute of the International Criminal Court, https://treaties.un.org/Pages/ViewDetails.aspx?src=TREATY&mtdsg_no=XVIII-10&chapter=18&lang=en (showing chronology of ratifications).

Still, especially when taken alongside the presence of various Sierra Leonean features in its statute, the non-inclusion of the SCSL among the elite list of established international penal tribunals seemingly exposed the international legal nature of the SCSL as doubtful.[157] If the distinction between national and international courts was significant for the purposes of determining whether immunities were applicable, as the ICJ had ruled, then it was near inevitable that Taylor's lawyers would question whether the SCSL, with its by then still unique bilateral treaty basis and involvement of a national government in its creation, was capable of removing the immunities of Liberia's then sitting president.

8.5.1 *The Ambiguities of the ICJ Ruling in the* Arrest Warrant *Case*

Because of the nature of customary international law, which classically requires both state practice and *opinio juris* to confirm the existence of a binding international legal rule, and the fact that the immunity of sitting heads of state, heads of government, and foreign ministers are not codified in a particular treaty, the ICJ's statement in *Yerodia* was significant for attempting to clarify the state of modern immunity law. However, as important as it might have been, the Judgment left a number of fundamental questions unresolved. In the next subsections, I will highlight two of these, as they might help explain some of the confusion in the *Taylor* case. This approach enables us to subsequently identify the added value of the SCSL's contributions to the evolving law on immunity as articulated by contemporary international criminal tribunals.

8.5.2 *The Ambiguity of "Certain International Criminal Courts ... "*

First, in its brief discussion of the last exemption under which it is permissible to try foreign ministers and heads of state or government, the ICJ did not specify what features or characteristics a penal court must possess in order to fall within the four corners of the "certain international criminal courts" exception. Put differently, upon determining that immunities may not be opposable before *certain international penal courts*, the question that naturally follows is how we are supposed to distinguish between a national court, before which immunities can be pleaded, and an international court, where such immunities are *not* available and thus cannot be pleaded. The ICJ judges did not proffer an answer.

Nor did they clarify what they meant, in this context, by ordinary but apparently important terms such as "certain," which according to the *Oxford English Dictionary* (originates from the Latin word *certus* which translates as "settled, sure") means "[e]stablished as a truth or fact to be absolutely received, depended,

---

[157] U.N. Secretary-General, *The Report of the Secretary-General on the establishment of a Special Court for Sierra Leone*, ¶ 9, U.N. Doc. S/2000/915 (Oct. 4, 2000).

or relied upon; not to be doubted, disputed, or called in question."[158] Of course, viewed in perspective, "certain" was evidently intended as a qualifier. The implication is that to assess whether a "certain" court will qualify to be among those where immunities are not applicable, further analysis of the legal basis of the tribunal including the form by which it was established, such as whether under domestic or international law, the powers it has in relation to the removal of immunities and the substantive law which it applies will be required. This caveat seems captured by the other dictionary meaning of the term as a reference to "some but not all," without any further specification of the relevant determinative criteria. These doubts raised by the terminology arguably implied that they wanted to leave the question open. As to the "international" part of the phrase in the ICJ's pronouncement, in ordinary English usage, it would primarily mean something "existing, occurring, or carried on between two or more nations"[159] or secondarily "agreed by all or many nations" or "used by people of many nations."[160]

Taking these terms together, based on their plain meaning, it was unclear whether what we would be looking for under this part of the *Yerodia* exceptions is simply an agreement between two or more states which would be what is required for a treaty under international law or something that is agreed by *some* or *many* states or agreed by *all* states. The phrase *certain international criminal courts* seem straightforward enough in the abstract, but upon further consideration in practice, may actually be ambiguous. The subsequent step of the determination can only be inferred and would mandate a review of the legal basis of the tribunal and the authority conferred on it.

In other words, what would ordinarily even come across as plain English begs immediate questions in the context of complex cases such as Taylor's. The SCSL assumed this ordinary dictionary meaning of international is what matters for the purposes of removing immunities. That is why, as I explain further below, the Appeals Chamber apparently went about explaining the involvement of many states and the international community in the creation of the tribunal. This seems like helpful analysis because, by its very nature, the involvement of other states in the creation of the SCSL changes to an extent the nature and quality of the acts at issue. By this, I mean that it was not just one state coming together with another state and acting in bad faith to create a special tribunal to pursue goals that the national courts of those two states are unable to accomplish.

But even so, if we accept this to be the relevant inquiry, new questions will then arise. For example, does it matter how many states come together to create the international tribunal? What is the magic number of states, if any, that will need to be involved in an "inter-national" court for it to become sufficiently "international" such as to displace the immunities of a sitting president? Would, as the ordinary

---

[158]   *Certain*, OXFORD ENGLISH DICTIONARY (2015).
[159]   *Id.*
[160]   *Id.*

dictionary meaning of the term suggests, a bilateral or trilateral treaty be sufficient to nullify customary law immunities? What about a multilateral treaty between four or more states? What about 10 states, or 15, 20, 80, or 100, 193 or more? These are all interesting questions that may raise relevant considerations. The essence of those will be whether the entity created is a result of unilateralism on the part of the sovereigns of one or two states against another equal sovereign, which cannot be said to be the case in the SCSL *Taylor* example. It will also depend on which states are parties to the instrument and whether the relevant tribunal statute removes the immunities. If immunity is removed, by the parties in respect of which the court will be applied, then the immunities may not be available not so much because of the involvement of other states but because of the consensual element that effectively serves as the waiver by the sovereigns of their rights under customary international law. The additional safeguard is the truly international nature of the process in the sense that the driver of those processes also matters in the sense that actions taken by states within the multilateral framework of the UN, for instance, would presumably carry greater presumption of good faith action by those involved with creating the tribunal. In my view, although it will be incorrect to impute – as the SCSL did – the decision to negotiate the agreement with the Sierra Leone government to all Member States of the UN when the organization enjoys a separate legal personality from its Member States, the nature of the UN organization and its large number of states would more likely make the international court under discussion capable of derogating from immunities.

On the other hand, notice that so far we have spoken about *states agreeing* on the establishment of an international criminal tribunal. But can the party creating the international tribunal extend beyond just states to international organizations, comprised of states that are also recognized legal personalities under international law? If so, does an agreement to create such a court by a state, or a group of states and say the United Nations or the African Union and or the European Union, give it the prerequisites to be considered an international criminal court for the purposes of denying the applicability of customary international law immunities for serving presidents accused of international crimes? And does it matter what international organization is behind the establishment of the tribunal and the nature of that organization's mandate? Indeed, the involvement of the UN, especially its Security Council, whether acting within or outside Chapter VII authority in the performance of its responsibilities to ensure the maintenance of international peace and security puts a new spin to the possible removal of immunity since such actions could not be construed as the illegitimate unilateral acts of a single troublesome state.

The ICJ did not address these types of questions. Rather, as Judges Higgins, Kooijmans, and Buergenthal pointed out in their separate opinion, the Court bypassed the discussion of jurisdiction and focused on immunity, thereby giving the impression that immunity has some intrinsic value. Whereas, in reality, it was an "exception to a normative rule that would otherwise apply."[161] Though, in fairness to the majority of the World Court, the consideration of the kinds of questions above might not have been required for the purposes of deciding on the particular dispute between DRC and Belgium and whether the courts of the former can implead the highest officials of the latter. The judges did, implicitly, give some loose guidance when they alluded to the ICTY and ICTR. They noted that the Security Council created those two ad hoc courts, based on its Chapter VII powers in the UN Charter. The judges stopped there without spelling out the full legal implications, perhaps because they felt that this would be obvious to international lawyers.

Yet, a relevant consideration was perhaps implied that those ad hoc courts were thus legally binding measures on all UN Member States. And, in consequence, that immunities which are removed by their respective statutes made them unavailable in relation to the indicted persons despite the official rank of the suspect. Surely, this makes sense, since it cannot be the case that a court like the SCSL, created partly by the UN, would be treated for all intents and purposes as equivalent to the national courts of a single state like Belgium which were deemed incapable of removing immunities. The frailties of the Taylor decision on some of these aspects suggest that some ICJ attention to these issues could have been helpful to the SCSL and other judges that will be seized with the question of presidential immunity for a serving president.

The ICJ, elsewhere in *Yerodia*, had adverted to the distinctive basis of the existing tribunals. But it could have also explained that the rules rendering immunity irrelevant to prosecutions before those tribunals, as expressed in Articles 7(2) and 6(2) of the ICTY and ICTR Statutes respectively, were not substantive defenses as such. Rather, they operated only as procedural bars in respect of the jurisdiction before those particular courts. Their thrust was that the official position of any accused persons before them, whether as heads of state or responsible government officials, did not relieve such persons of criminal responsibility nor could they serve as basis to mitigate their punishment. Those tribunal provisions were themselves traceable to Articles 6 and 7 of the Tokyo and Nuremberg Tribunals.[162] Yet, their substance – at least in respect of the removal of immunities as blocks to prosecutions – had received widespread endorsement as declarative of customary international law by the UN General Assembly in a 1946 resolution and by the ILC in 1950.[163]

A plausible argument could thus have been made that, as Belgium submitted, those clauses amounted to evidence that customary international law sanctions the removal of immunities as procedural obstacles to prosecutions for war crimes,

---

[161] *See* Arrest Warrant of 11 April 2000 (Dem. Rep. Congo v. Belg.), Judgment, 2002 ICJ Rep. 3, ¶ 74 (Feb. 14) (Joint Separate Opinion of Judges Higgins, Kooijmans, and Buergenthal).

[162] Charter of the International Military Tribunal, Aug. 8, 1945, 59 Stat. 1544, 82 U.N.T.S. 279; Charter of the International Military Tribunal for the Far East, Jan. 19, 1946, T.I.A.S. No. 1589.

[163] G.A. Res. 177 (II) (Nov. 21, 1947); ILC SR Report on Immunities, *supra* note 94.

crimes against humanity, and genocide irrespective whether before a national or international court. The SCSL did reach this analysis to make this finding. Thus, one of its normative contributions is the broader holding vis-à-vis the ICJ position that *customary* international law does not allow for immunities for trials before special international courts established with the support of the UN to prosecute serious international crimes.

In addition to the UN tribunals, the ICJ evidently determined that the ICC, a multilateral treaty-based body, also fits its criteria for an international court. Here, the judges specifically cited Article 27(2) of the Rome Statute, which provided that "immunities or special procedural rules which may attach to the official capacity of a person, whether under national or international law, shall not bar the Court from exercising its jurisdiction over such person."

Again, beyond reference to that provision, they did not further elaborate what made the ICC the type of international penal court that was entitled to ignore the immunity of a sitting head of state. Indeed, the involvement of the Security Council, whether acting within or outside Chapter VII authority, in the performance of its responsibilities to ensure the maintenance of international peace and security adds a new dimension to the judicial argument justifying the removal of Taylor's immunity since that is not the unilateral act of a state.

Importantly, the ICJ did not differentiate between a tribunal created by treaty, as in the ICC, or the ICTY and ICTR which were by fiat of a Security Council Chapter VII resolution. On closer consideration, it would be clear that the UN courts, in contrast to the former, had no direct memberships by states because they were not created by treaties but via binding Security Council resolutions. The feature common to them was that there was in each category some type of state consent to the tribunal: Either direct as in the ICC context, or indirect, as in the case of the UN tribunals through the UN Charter. Another element was that each of their statutes provided for non-recognition of immunity. And, finally, each of them addressed the scourge of international crimes with strong international, especially UN, involvement in their creation.

To sum up the analysis on the first part of the ICJ's *certain international criminal courts* conundrum, there were open questions stemming from the limited guidance from *Yerodia* on what legal basis makes an international tribunal one before which immunities will not shield a sitting president from prosecution and one before which they could (as the language of *certain* suggested). The ICJ's silence on these questions engendered the prospect for confusion and may be hard to explain. One possibility could be because, in many situations (with the exception of so-called "hybrid courts"), it maybe that it is probably generally easy to draw a firm line between a *national* court and an *international* court. Moreover, and this is about judicial economy, there was no dispute between the Congo and Belgium as to whether the courts of the latter were municipal courts.

8.5.3 *The Ambiguity of " ... Where They Have Jurisdiction"*

The second fundamental question after *Yerodia*, which proved to be important in the SCSL's *Taylor* decision, turned on the qualifier in the second part of the ICJ pronouncement that an incumbent or former foreign minister, and *a fortiori* head of state, may be subject to criminal proceedings before certain international criminal courts *"where they have jurisdiction."*[164] Of course, jurisdiction, which in its narrowest formulation is a reference to the power of a properly constituted court to exercise certain authority, logically comes before immunity as a procedural bar or exception to that jurisdiction can be pleaded. Indeed, the question whether a court possesses *jurisdiction* or *competence* is distinct from the question whether it will choose to *exercise* that jurisdiction or competence. The jurisdiction or competence will speak to elements such as the types of persons, subject matter, territory, and time frame covered. All of those components, in the context of treaty-based tribunals like the SCSL or the ICC, are necessarily based on the consent of the state whose leader would be subject to the authority of the international tribunal. Consent, of course, flows from sovereignty and is ordinarily required as a matter of international law before a state can be bound by a given rule.

The implication of all this is that, at the SCSL, which was created by a *bilateral treaty* between the UN and the Government of Sierra Leone, a *threshold* or *preliminary* question was whether – before the SCSL could even establish itself as an international criminal court for the purposes of deciding on immunities – it had first to determine it had jurisdiction over Taylor who was the then president of Liberia. That was not in issue in relation to person, the crimes, territory, or temporal jurisdiction of the SCSL. All of those were fulfilled. The real issue is that Liberia, being a third party to the instrument that created the SCSL, was not technically bound by the Agreement between the UN and the Sierra Leone Government because of the fundamental rule of treaty law that *pacta tertiis nec nocent nec prosunt* (a treaty binds the parties and only the parties to it). In effect, as one commentator has suggested, the ICJ position that international immunities may not be pleaded before certain international penal tribunals must be read as subject to two further conditions: First, provided that the instruments creating those tribunals expressly or implicitly removed the relevant immunity, and second, that the home state of the official concerned is bound by the instrument eliminating the immunity.[165] On this view, it would logically follow that "a senior serving state official entitled to immunity *ratione personae* (for example, a head of state) is entitled to such immunity before an international tribunal that the state concerned has not consented to."[166]

---

[164] Arrest Warrant of 11 April 2000 (Dem. Rep. Congo v. Belg.), Judgment, 2002 ICJ Rep. 3, ¶ 61 (Feb. 14) (emphasis added).

[165] Dapo Akande, *International law Immunities and the International Criminal Court*, 98 AM. J. INT'L L. 420 (2004).

[166] *Id.*

It follows that one of the oversights in the SCSL Appeals Chamber decision on Taylor was that it carefully attended to the first part of the ICJ dictum in *Yerodia* on the international legal nature of the SCSL (that is, "certain international criminal courts ... ") but failed to address the second half of this essentially two-prong requirement (that is, "where they have jurisdiction"). It broadly addressed the former when it explained the basis of its jurisdiction, but it left out the latter which had established a precondition. It will be demonstrated that while the present writer and many other commentators are in agreement that the SCSL reached the right conclusion that it was an international court, thereby fulfilling the first part of the *Yerodia* international criminal courts exception test, it only implicitly rather than explicitly showed the legal basis upon which its jurisdiction or authority over Taylor was predicated or fulfilled. Essentially, the Appeals Chamber somewhat glossed over the important issue of Liberia's third party status to the bilateral treaty that had created the SCSL. That was the heart of the matter, and the sort of resolution it proffered though adequate to justify the conclusion that it could try Taylor since he was no longer head of state at the time of his trial, could have been better. We return to this issue in the next section after first examining defense counsel's detailed submissions challenging the propriety of the SCSL indictment of Taylor.

8.6 THE SCSL AND PRESIDENT TAYLOR'S IMMUNITY

8.6.1 *The* Taylor *Defense Challenge to Jurisdiction*

On July 23, 2003, President Taylor, as an individual, and jointly with the Republic of Liberia, filed a motion before the SCSL seeking to quash the indictment and order approving a warrant for his arrest.[167] The Trial Chamber referred the question to the Appeals Chamber pursuant to Rule 72E of the Rules of Procedure.[168] In the same referral decision, the trial court struck out the joint part of the claim with the Liberian government. The judges ruled, perhaps erroneously given that immunities ordinarily belong to the state rather than the person, that Liberia did not have any

---

[167] Prosecutor v. Taylor, Case No. SCSL-03-01-I-024, applicants motion made under protest and without waiving of immunity accorded to a Head of State President Charles Ghankay Taylor requesting that the Trial Chamber do quash the said approved indictment of 7th March 2003 of Judge Bankole Thompson and that she aforesaid purported Warrant of Arrest and Order for transfer and detention of the same date issued by Judge Bankole Thompson of the Special Court for Sierra Leone, and all other consequential and related ORDER(S) granted thereafter by either the said Judge Bankole Thompson OR Judge Pierre Boutet on 12th June 2003 against the person of the said President Charles Ghankay Taylor be declared null and void, invalid at their inception and that they be accordingly cancelled and/OR set aside as a matter of Law, (July 23, 2003) [hereinafter Taylor, Motion to Quash Indictment based on Immunity].

[168] Rule 72(E) provides: "Preliminary motions made in the Trial Chamber prior to the Prosecutor's opening statement which raise a serious issue relating to jurisdiction shall be referred to a bench of at least three Appeals Chamber Judges, where they will proceed to a determination as soon as practicable."

standing to initiate such a motion or to join it as a party since the indictment was
personal to Taylor as the accused person, not to Liberia as a State.[169] This ruling
meant that only Taylor's motion was ripe for the referral and later decision by the
Appeals Chamber comprised only of three of its five judges.

To begin with, the Defense argued based on *Yerodia* that the indictment was
a violation of customary international law because President Taylor enjoyed absolute
immunity from criminal prosecution due to his status as a *serving* head of state.[170]
They further argued that the principle of sovereign equality of states prohibits the
courts of Sierra Leone from exercising its authority on the territory of Liberia.[171]
Furthermore, in their view, even the mere issuance and attempt to serve the indictment and arrest warrant to Ghana when Taylor was on official business there
prejudiced his ability to carry out his functions as Liberia's head of state.[172] These
were precisely the type of circumstances that immunities were intended to help avoid.

The Defense launched a frontal attack on the SCSL's status as an international
court, an unsurprising strategy given the significance of the national versus international court distinction that *Yerodia* apparently turned on. Though it accepted that
Security Council Resolution 1315 authorized the Secretary-General to negotiate an
agreement with Sierra Leone, the Defense motion claimed that the SCSL – unlike
the ICTY, ICTR, and the ICC – had the "character of a bi-lateral cooperation
agreement between the Government of Sierra Leone and the United Nations in
which the United Nations promised technical and other *assistance* to the *domestic*
legal process of Sierra Leone."[173] As a corollary to this domestic character, the SCSL
was created not by the Security Council or even the United Nations more broadly,
but by Sierra Leone through the Special Court Agreement 2002 (Ratification) Act
No. 9 of 2002. To their credit, defense counsel accepted that exceptions to personal
immunity can derive from other rules of international law such as Security Council
resolutions. However, since the SCSL lacked the Chapter VII powers which were
necessary for it to abrogate customary international immunities, its judicial orders
were akin to those of a domestic (that is, Sierra Leonean) court.[174]

The Prosecution response on July 28, 2003 made several procedural and substantive arguments. The first was that the Government of Liberia was not a party to the
processes before the SCSL, and that therefore, its views on immunity are irrelevant
and should thus be excluded.[175] In any event, the Taylor motion was premature and

---

[169]   Prosecutor v. Taylor, Case No. SCSL-2003-01-I, Order Pursuant to Rule 72(E) Defence Motion to
        Quash the Indictment and to Declare the Warrant of Arrest and all Other Consequential Orders
        Null and Void (Sept. 19, 2003).
[170]   Taylor, Motion to Quash Indictment based on Immunity, *supra* note 167, at ¶ 3.
[171]   *Id.*
[172]   *Id.* at ¶ 4.
[173]   *Id.* at ¶ 5 (emphasis added).
[174]   Taylor, Motion to Quash Indictment based on Immunity, *supra* note 167, at 6.
[175]   Prosecutor v. Taylor, Case No. SCSL-2003-01-PT, Prosecution Response to Defence Motion to
        Quash the Indictment Against Charles Ghankay Taylor, ¶ 3 (July 28, 2003).

not a true preliminary objection "based on the lack of jurisdiction" because "[i]n cases where jurisdictional immunities apply, a court *has* jurisdiction, but is barred from *exercising* that jurisdiction."[176] An applicant like Taylor who had not yet appeared to enter his plea could not at the same time avail himself of the processes of the Tribunal to mount such a challenge.[177] He lacked any standing to do so.

Addressing the substance of Taylor's argument, the Prosecution refuted the classification of the SCSL as a national court of Sierra Leone, saying that it "exists and functions in the sphere of international law. The judicial power that it exercises is not the judicial power of the Republic of Sierra Leone."[178] They attempted to distinguish the *Yerodia* ruling. They argued that while relevant, it concerned only the application of immunities from "the jurisdiction of the courts of *another State*,"[179] which was not the case in relation to the *Taylor* case since the SCSL was an international criminal tribunal. Furthermore, and in any event under that ICJ ruling, customary international law allowed international criminal courts such as the SCSL to indict serving heads of state. The Statute, by fiat of Article 6(2), had rendered official capacity irrelevant to prosecutions and endowed the Tribunal with the required competencies to try all persons including even a sitting president.[180]

At the same time, much as observed above, the Prosecution conceded one of the key ambiguities of *Yerodia* to the effect that it "did not expressly articulate the criteria for determining whether an international court is one before which Head of State immunity will not apply."[181] Nonetheless, in their view, the determinative issue was not whether the Security Council had endowed the tribunal in question with Chapter VII powers.[182] The ICC's rejection of immunities amply demonstrated that such powers may be exercised by treaty-based courts which did not explicitly find their legal roots in the UN Charter. In any event, the SCSL was not created under Sierra Leonean law. Rather, it was created by the international community at large through the UN Secretary General, who himself was acting at the request of the Security Council. Accordingly, in the Prosecution submission, the "Special Court is necessarily ... exercising the judicial power of the international community."[183] Further, the trial of former Rwandan Prime Minister Kambanda at the ICTR and former Yugoslav President Milošević at the ICTY amply showed that the recognized exceptions to immunities in *Yerodia* allowed the SCSL to prosecute suspects like Taylor who was charged with international crimes. Finally,

---

[176] *Id.* at ¶ 5 (emphasis added).

[177] *Id.* at ¶ 8.

[178] *Id.* at ¶ 15.

[179] Arrest Warrant of 11 April 2000 (Dem. Rep. Congo v. Belg.), Judgment, 2002 ICJ Rep. 3, ¶ 61 (Feb. 14) (emphasis added).

[180] SCSL Statute, *supra* note 75, at art. 6(2).

[181] Prosecutor v. Taylor, Case No. SCSL-2003-01-PT, Prosecution Response to Defence Motion to Quash the Indictment Against Charles Ghankay Taylor, ¶ 18 (July 28, 2003).

[182] *Id.* at ¶ 17.

[183] *Id.* at ¶ 18.

as to the final defense contention about the rights of sovereigns, the mere service of the indictment could not have violated the sovereignty of Ghana.[184]

The Appeals Chamber appointed *amici curiae* to assist in its consideration of the motion: Professors Diane Orentlicher[185] and Phillipe Sands.[186] It also granted an NGO, the African Bar Association's request to make submissions.[187] Although somewhat differing in their approaches to the question, in essence, all three submitted briefs arguing that Taylor enjoyed no immunity before the SCSL with respect to the grave crimes for which he had been charged. Professor Sands, in a four-part submission expressing similar views to those of Professor Orentlicher, opined that

> [i]nternational practise and a majority of academic commentary supports the view that [] an international criminal court or tribunal (whether or not is has been established under Chapter VII of the UN Charter) may exercise jurisdiction over a serving head of state and that such person is not entitled to claim immunity under customary international law in respect of international crimes.[188]

Further, he argued that the similarity of the SCSL's jurisdiction *ratione materiae* and *ratione personae* to that of the ICTR, the ICTY, and the ICC left him "no reason to conclude that the Special Court should be treated as anything other than an international tribunal or court."[189]

Professor Orentlicher also concurred that the SCSL was an international court within the meaning of *Yerodia*.[190] She accepted that its creation was not rooted in a binding Chapter VII resolution, as was the case for the ICTY and ICTR, but nevertheless found that "Chapter VII is not a *sine qua non* for obligations to arise from Security Council action."[191] Through this argument, she hinted at an important idea that later found its way into the final decision in a slightly expanded form when she concluded "that there [was] nothing in the Agreement or the Statute (or in their context) to preclude the Special Court from seeking to exercise jurisdiction over offences committed on the territory of Sierra Leone by the Head of State of Liberia [.]"[192] As an international, instead of a domestic court, the SCSL could validly exercise its jurisdiction over both incumbent and former heads of state in accordance with its statute and customary international law.[193] In a nutshell, under

---

[184] *Id.*, at ¶ 19.

[185] Prosecutor v. Taylor, SCSL-03-01-I, Submission of the Amicus Curiae on Head of State Immunity in the Case of the Prosecutor v. Taylor, (Oct. 23, 2003) [hereinafter Orentlicher Amicus Brief].

[186] Prosecutor v. Taylor, SCSL-03-01-I, Submission of the Amicus Curiae on Head of State Immunity (Oct. 23, 2003) [hereinafter Sands Amicus Brief].

[187] Prosecutor v. Taylor, SCSL-2003-01-AR72(E), Decision on Application by the African Bar Association for Leave to File *Amicus Curiae* Brief, (Nov. 20, 2003).

[188] Sands Amicus Brief, *supra* note 186, at ¶ 76.

[189] *Id.*

[190] Orentlicher Amicus Brief, *supra* note 185, at 9–20.

[191] *Id.* at ¶ 75.

[192] *Id.* at ¶ 87.

[193] *Id.* at ¶ 26.

this view, Taylor was not entitled to any procedural immunities barring the SCSL's exercise of jurisdiction nor any substantive immunities that would shield his official conduct from tribunal scrutiny.

The African Bar Association, represented by then Secretary-General Femi Falana, a Nigerian Attorney, also added observations on several issues one of which pertained to immunity.[194] Falana cited various cases and the Rome Statute of the International Criminal Court and concluded, much like the other *amici*, that "notwithstanding his status as a former Head of State of the Republic of Liberia," Taylor lacked any immunity from prosecution for the international crimes he and his cohorts had allegedly committed in Sierra Leone.[195]

On May 31, 2004, after additional rounds of oral and written submissions by the parties on largely the same points outlined above, the SCSL rendered its decision. As further analyzed in depth in the next sections, the Appeals Chamber, after disposing of several procedural issues, ruled that the SCSL, as an international criminal tribunal, was entitled to exercise jurisdiction over Taylor despite his purported entitlement to customary international law immunities at the time of his indictment.[196] In effect, the SCSL was an international criminal tribunal exercising an international mandate over international crimes.[197] The Tribunal, being international, therefore fell within one of the four exceptions that the ICJ had identified.[198] As a consequence, although no longer a president entitled to *ratione personae* immunity after having left office by the time of delivery of its decision, Taylor's official status as a serving president when the criminal proceedings were initiated could not foreclose his prosecution.[199] Thus, Taylor's case was properly within the SCSL's jurisdiction.[200]

---

[194] Prosecutor v. Taylor, Case No. SCSL-03-01-I, Amicus Brief on Objections filed by Mr. Charles Taylor and Other Suspects (Nov. 28, 2003) [hereinafter Falana Amicus Brief].

[195] *Id.* at ¶ 4.09.

[196] Prosecutor v. Taylor, Case No. SCSL-03-01-A, Appeals Chamber, Decision on Immunity from Jurisdiction (May 31, 2004). *See* Charles Jalloh, *Immunity from Prosecution for International Crimes: The Case of Charles Taylor at the Special Court for Sierra Leone*, 8 AM. SOC'Y INT'L L. INSIGHT 21 (2004).

[197] Prosecutor v. Taylor, Case No. SCSL-03-01-A, Appeals Chamber, Decision on Immunity from Jurisdiction, ¶ 38 (May 31, 2004).

[198] *Id.* at ¶ 50.

[199] *Id.* at ¶¶ 47, 59.

[200] *Id.* at ¶ 53. *See also* Nouwen, *supra* note 121, at 645, 651; *contra* Miglin, *supra* note 62; Micaela Frulli, *Piercing the Veil of Head of State Immunity: The Taylor Trial and Beyond, in* THE SIERRA LEONE SPECIAL COURT AND ITS LEGACY: THE IMPACT FOR AFRICA AND INTERNATIONAL CRIMINAL LAW 325–39 (Charles C. Jalloh ed., 2014). *See generally* Annie Gell, *Lessons from the Trial of Charles Taylor at the Special Court for Sierra Leone, in* THE SIERRA LEONE SPECIAL COURT AND ITS LEGACY: THE IMPACT FOR AFRICA AND INTERNATIONAL CRIMINAL LAW 642–62 (Charles C Jalloh ed., 2014) (providing a post-trial completion analysis).

8.6.2 *Is the SCSL An International Tribunal within*
the Meaning of Yerodia?

In ruling on the *Taylor* motion, which because of the way the parties had pleaded the issue turned primarily on whether the SCSL was an international criminal court which was legally capable of removing immunities, the Appeals Chamber basically offered two principal justifications for its decision. The first part of the decision attempted to explain and substantiate the international origins of the SCSL. In so doing, instead of clarifying the *legal foundation* of the ad hoc tribunal as rooted in international law and drawing conclusions on the consequences flowing therefrom, the judges described the *international features* of the SCSL. Their apparent goal was to show that, rather than being a creature of Sierra Leonean law which would be incapable of abrogating immunities as per *Yerodia*, the SCSL was a truly international penal tribunal which could under its statute and customary international law ignore Taylor's immunities. The Court suggested that, based on a consideration of the conventional rationale for immunities, the critical factor enabling an international court to remove immunities was *international community* involvement in creating it. Here the judges seemed to rely on the earlier discussed meaning of "international" to show how wide the "international" support for the tribunal was. Thus, they sought to establish how principal UN organs had played important roles in creating the SCSL. The judges assumed they could deny Taylor's claim because they were discharging an international community mandate rather than pursuing the parochial mandate and interests of a single state like Sierra Leone. Though not an argument without difficulties, this could be an original contribution to the way we could approach the acceptability, or lack of it, in relation to immunities. Let's take each of the Court's main arguments in turn.

8.6.3 *The "International Community" Involvement*
in Creating the SCSL

In the first part of its decision, the Appeals Chamber examined the legal basis of the SCSL before addressing the question whether the Court was an international tribunal.[201] It correctly observed that the issues raised by Taylor's motion were dependent on the legal nature of the SCSL.[202] The judges explained that the SCSL was established through the bilateral treaty concluded between the UN and the Government of Sierra Leone and charged it with prosecuting the various crimes committed in the territory of Sierra Leone. They went on to highlight the international involvement in creating the tribunal, especially the role of the Security Council and the Secretary-General.

---

[201] Prosecutor v. Taylor, Case No. SCSL-03-01-A, Appeals Chamber, Decision on Immunity from Jurisdiction, ¶¶ 34–36 (May 31, 2004).
[202] *Id.* at ¶ 49.

These factors are important in separating the situations in which the international community might choose to accept the adoption of an instrument in which is included the potential removal of the immunities of a sitting president on charges of involvement with international crimes. The argument seems implied that the interests of the international community, in the maintenance of international peace and security and in the enforcement of international law, must in some situations give way to the parochial interests of a single state. This is so especially where that state of which the person is leader is itself a source of insecurity and the commission of international crimes against the nationals of another state.

If this argument is plausible, in its *Taylor* ruling, the Appeals Chamber could have gone further to observe that the SCSL was not only created via treaty under international law, but that it also possessed all the characteristics of a classical international organization which enabled it to operate in the realm of international law. This included independent international legal personality which permitted it to enter into agreements with other legal persons governed by international law. It also had a mandate to prosecute international crimes broadly similar to that of the ICTY, the ICTR, and the ICC, including rules providing that no person before the court can plead immunity as a procedural bar to trial. The majority of the judges and principals were appointed by the Secretary-General. It was financed by voluntary contributions of many states, and also assisted by a management committee comprised of several states from all parts of the world. The Appeals Chamber might have also explained that, though the bilateral treaty had been domesticated by the Sierra Leonean Government and enabled the country's participation in appointment of key officials, those aspects were not sufficient to deprive the SCSL of its international legal character or to transform it into a municipal court of Sierra Leone. In fact, both the UN-Sierra Leone treaty and Sierra Leone's implementing legislation had made clear the autonomous legal nature of the SCSL rather than considering it an integral part of the domestic judiciary of Sierra Leone.

Second, the Appeals Chamber clarified that while the SCSL was rooted in a treaty and therefore differed from the ICTY and ICTR which were created directly by Chapter VII resolutions of the Security Council, that agreement had been entered into pursuant to UNSC Resolution 1315.[203] The Security Council was acting within its wide general competence to address threats to peace and security in the UN Charter when it adopted that resolution and initiated the establishment of the SCSL. The UNSC participation in creating the tribunal was consistent with the general purposes of the UN as outlined in Article 1 of the Charter, but also in line with its specific powers under Article 41, which provided inter alia that it "may decide what measures not involving the use of armed force are to be employed to give effect to its decisions."[204]

---

[203] *Id.* at ¶ 37.
[204] U.N. Charter art. 41.

In Resolution 1315, the Security Council had reiterated that the situation in Sierra Leone constituted a threat to international peace and security in the region. This essentially placed the country and the crimes committed there on the pedestal of serious matters of global concern. The *"international community,"*[205] which phrase was undefined but appeared to have been used as a synonym to refer to the Security Council and the UN as a representative of that community of states, had exclusive authority in Article 39 to "determine the existence of any threat to the peace."[206] That body had further stated its clear intention in the same resolution to "exert every effort" to bring to justice the persons who had committed or authorized the perpetration of serious international humanitarian law violations in Sierra Leone *"in accordance with international standards of justice, fairness and due process of law."*[207] The judges rightly reasoned that, in executing its duties to address threats to peace, the Security Council acts on behalf of all UN members as per Article 24(1) of the UN Charter.[208] The treaty was "thus an agreement between all members of the United Nations and Sierra Leone"[209] and an "expression of the will of the international community."[210] The SCSL had been "established to fulfil an *international mandate* and is part of the machinery of *international justice*."[211] A special court created in such circumstances was "truly international."[212] This could be verified by reference to the numerous indicia of its status as an international criminal

---

[205]   The SCSL Appeals Chamber did not define the meaning of the phrase "international community." But, as used by the judges, could be taken to be a reference to the United Nations as a representative of all states in the "international community as a whole." The latter notion has been used in various treaties and featured in famous cases and therefore appears to have autonomous legal meaning. Whereas the same expression can be found in the Vienna Convention on the Law of Treaties art. 53, May 23, 1969, 1155 U.N.T.S. 331, the terminology of "international community" is frequently used in treaties and other international instruments including G.A. Res. 56/83 (Jan. 28, 2002) (adopting the Draft Articles on Responsibility of States for internationally wrongful acts); Convention on the Prevention and Punishment of Crimes Against Internationally Protected Persons, including Diplomatic Agents pmbl. ¶ 3, Dec. 14, 1973, 1035 U.N.T.S. 167; International Convention Against the Taking of Hostages pmbl. ¶ 4, Dec. 17, 1979, 1316 U.N.T.S. 205; International Convention for the Suppression of Terrorist Bombings pmbl. ¶ 10, Dec. 15, 1997, 2149 U.N.T.S. 256; G.A. Res. 52/164 (Jan. 9, 1998); Rome Statute of the International Criminal Court pmbl. ¶ 9, July 17, 1998, 2187 U.N.T.S. 3. See also the famous dictum, articulating this concept of international community in relation to obligations *erga omnes*, in ICJ, Barcelona Traction, Light and Power Company, Limited (Belg. v. Spain), Judgment, 1970 I.C.J. Rep. 3, 32 ¶¶ 32–33 (Feb. 5); and JAMES CRAWFORD, THE INTERNATIONAL LAW COMMISSION'S ARTICLES ON STATE RESPONSIBILITY: INTRODUCTION, TEXT AND COMMENTARIES 184–85, 279 (2002).

[206]   U.N. Charter art. 39.

[207]   *See* S.C. Res. 1315, pmbl. ¶ 6 (Aug. 14, 2000).

[208]   U.N. Charter art. 24(1) provides "In order to ensure prompt and effective action by the United Nations, its Members confer on the Security Council primary responsibility for the maintenance of international peace and security, and agree that in carrying out its duties under this responsibility the Security Council acts on their behalf."

[209]   Prosecutor v. Taylor, Case No. SCSL-03-01-A, Appeals Chamber, Decision on Immunity from Jurisdiction, ¶ 38 (May 31, 2004).

[210]   *Id.*

[211]   *Id.* at ¶ 39 (emphasis added).

[212]   *Id.* at ¶ 38.

court in its constitutive documents.[213] From the perspective of public international law, some of the arguments advanced by the Appeals Chamber holding that the creation of the SCSL constituted a treaty between all UN members and Sierra Leone are highly problematic because they contradict existing law. They also give unlimited license for judicial lawmaking, all in the name of acting in the interests of an amorphous and somewhat ill-defined international community. The soundness of these arguments is critiqued below.

Having reached the conclusion affirming the SCSL's international credentials using the imprimatur of UN involvement with its creation, the Appeals Chamber then considered in the second part of its analysis whether *customary international law immunities* would be unavailable to Taylor before the Court. Their goal was to determine whether their statute, which had removed immunities, could otherwise be incompatible with peremptory norms of general international law. Here, they compared Article 6(2) of the SCSL Statute, which provided that "[t]he official position of any accused persons, whether as Head of State or Government or as a responsible Government official, shall not relieve such a person of criminal responsibility nor mitigate punishment," with Articles 6(2) and 7(2) of the ICTR and ICTY Statutes and 27(2) of the ICC Statute, and found them all to be substantially the same.[214] These modern expressions of this principle dated as far back as to Article 7 of the Charter of the Nuremberg International Military Tribunal.[215] The IMT Judgment interpreting that provision had been subsequently endorsed, and thus had been firmly established as customary international law by the General Assembly and the ILC in 1947 and 1950 respectively.[216] These arguments would appear to support the SCSL Appeals Chamber assertion that there was in fact a customary international law exception to the invocation of immunities at least in relation to the prosecution of certain egregious international crimes before certain internationally created criminal courts.[217]

As the first international criminal tribunal to apply *Yerodia* to a concrete case, the SCSL judges attempted to explain why immunities would have been deemed irrelevant before international criminal tribunals. Here is where they were most original. The Appeals Chamber advanced two separate arguments why the ICJ might have distinguished between national and international courts for the purposes of removal of immunities. In the first step, after conceding that the ICJ reasoning was not entirely clear, the judges postulated that this might well relate to the classical rationale upon which immunity was based.[218] Thus, the SCSL appellate chamber mentioned the principle *par in parem non habet imperium*, under which as noted

[213]   *Id.* at ¶ 42.
[214]   *Id.* at ¶¶ 43–46.
[215]   *Id.* at ¶ 47.
[216]   *Id.*
[217]   *Id.* at ¶ 50.
[218]   *Id.* at ¶ 51.

above at the opening of this chapter, "one sovereign state does not adjudicate on the conduct of another state."[219] They asserted that this notion, which was rooted in the concept of sovereign equality of states, is basically irrelevant to international criminal courts which are not organs of states but instead "derive their mandate from the international community."[220] This position has been criticized by some scholars apparently for misstating the theoretical basis for *ratione personae* immunities.[221] Yet, as Harmen van der Wilt has more convincingly argued, this reaction might have failed to account for the ultimate thrust underpinning the Taylor Immunity Decision.[222] In this view, the rationale for that type of immunity (*ratione personae*) is not all necessarily that distinctive from the one for immunities *ratione materiae*. This would thus imply, assuming this contention is correct, some erosion of a state's sovereignty can be expected in the course of giving effect to the norms of international criminal law and the principle of individual criminal responsibility which is presently under development.

Furthermore, by introducing the idea that future courts should question bare assertions of immunity by examining the underlying purposes of having the rule in the first place, at least in trials for international crimes condemned by international law before internationally constituted courts, it can be argued that the SCSL made a helpful contribution to the corpus of emerging jurisprudence on head of state immunity. On the other hand, a strong counterargument can be made from the perspective of general international law, namely that to accept such a judicial finding as a useful advance in immunity law amounts to acceptance of the judicial usurpation of the traditional lawmaking functions of states that is the basis of the consensual system of international law. All the more so because the SCSL judges reached this conclusion without thorough analysis of the implications of their ruling and in the absence of strong evidence of consistent state practice in support of their position endorsing the removal of immunities. Yet, in fairness to the SCSL, it did point to state practice since Nuremberg highlighting the unavailability of immunities in respect of at least certain trials pertaining to international crimes before international courts.

In fact, though the ICJ in *Yerodia* did not squarely address the question about the availability of an international crimes exception in an international court not endorsed by a particular state for a leader of that state, it can be argued that there

---

[219]   *Id.*

[220]   *Id.*

[221]   *See* CRYER ET AL., *supra* note 90, at 563 (arguing that while the outcome in the *Taylor* case supports the conclusion that there was no immunity, the reasoning towards that conclusion is problematic. Among the reasons to be skeptical, in this argument, the *Taylor* decision was rooted in the idea that one state cannot adjudicate the conduct of another state which serves as the rationale for functional immunities rather than personal immunity, which exists to protect international relations by prohibiting undue interference with high officials without the sending state's consent).

[222]   *See* Harmen van der Wilt, *The Continuing Story of the International Criminal Court and Personal Immunities* (2016) (Amsterdam Law School Research Paper No. 2015-48) (on file with Amsterdam Center for International Law, University of Amsterdam).

is some support as evidenced by the provisions of the instruments of the various ad hoc international penal courts contemplated during the twentieth century. Thus, Article 227 of the Versailles Treaty in 1919, Article 7 of the Nuremberg Charter in 1945, Articles 7 and 6 of the ICTY and ICTR Statutes in 1993 and 1994 respectively, Article 27 of the Rome Statute of the ICC in 1998, and Article 6(2) of the Statute of the SCSL itself all expressly deemed *irrelevant* the official status of a suspect as a sitting head of state to block a prosecution. In fact, recalling our discussion about the classic justification for immunity as well as the functional necessity arguments of the ICJ when justifying its protection of Yerodia's immunities, it can be seen that the immunity from arrest and inviolability for heads of state and senior officials all stem from the need to ensure the integrity of officials from abuse of process by foreign jurisdictions as well as the desire to foster the smooth conduct of international affairs. To avoid using legal mechanism as a pretext to attack the foreign sovereign interest, certain classes of officials enjoy immunity from any civil or criminal violation in foreign national courts at the domestic level – despite the nature or gravity of the alleged crime or harm in issue.

As the Appeals Chamber emphasized, the rationale for the maintenance of immunities sits uncomfortably alongside the admittedly emerging notion that there ought to be individual criminal culpability at least for those most responsible persons (including leaders) who mastermind the commission of international crimes. Normatively, and as recognized as far back as the Nuremberg Trials, it would be illogical for international law to prohibit heinous crimes such as war crimes and crimes against humanity and at the same time permit those who carry out those heinous offenses to shield themselves behind immunity to procedurally prevent their own prosecutions before international criminal tribunals established to enforce those prohibitions.[223] International penal courts, at least those whose creation attract substantial international community involvement, arguably act above the narrow self-interests of a particular sovereign in favor of those of the collective peace of all states as a whole. Such tribunals are not political organs of states, but independent judicial entities with a specific mandate to prosecute specific crimes condemned under international law.

Such tribunals also generally guarantee fairness and impartiality, both in terms of the selection of their principal officials such as prosecutors and judges, and act in

---

[223] Prosecutor v. Taylor, Case No. SCSL-03-01-A, Appeals Chamber, Decision on Immunity from Jurisdiction, ¶ 51 (May 31, 2004). *See*, in this regard, Judgment of the International Military Tribunal at Nuremberg, *reprinted in* 41 AM. J. INT'L L. 172, 221 (1947) (holding that "[t]he principle of international law which, under certain circumstances, protects the representatives of a State cannot be applied to acts which are condemned as criminal by international law. The authors of these acts cannot shelter themselves behind their official position in order to be freed from punishment ... individuals have duties which transcend the national obligations of obedience imposed by the individual State. He who violates the laws of war cannot obtain immunity while acting in pursuance of the authority of the State, if the State in authorizing action moves outside of its competence under international law.")

accordance with the due process requirements of international human rights law. The fair trial guarantees of such courts are of course the types of rights often missing in the national courts of many conflict or post-conflict states where international crimes tend to be rampant because of lack of rule of law or the existence of broken justice systems. These courts, and I am here thinking of the ICC with its present 123 States Parties, pursue the international mandate and assist through limited prosecutions of leaders to repress the odious conduct that is itself defined as criminal under international law. The fact is that they, like the SCSL, are created within the framework of a collective body such as that of the UN and this must be relevant to help to engender their legitimacy. This is so even where the UN's and the community of states' interest might coincide with the desires of one state such as Sierra Leone.

All these notions might undermine the justification for the maintenance of these immunities before international tribunals. This might therefore be an important contribution of the SCSL, if admittedly *de lege ferenda*, especially given the ICJ's apparent nod to sovereignty in *Yerodia* and other immunity cases since then. The fact that the SCSL Appeals Chamber position is normatively the preferable stance takes on new significance when we consider the traditional reluctance of states to prosecute international crimes committed in foreign lands in their national courts using universal jurisdiction.[224]

A second reason that the SCSL judges offered for differentiating their treatment of immunities in national and international criminal courts drew on the submissions of one of the *amici*.[225] This was that, rather than being based on unilateral judgment, states considered that the collective judgment of the international community of states within the UN system would serve as an adequate safety valve to neutralize the destabilizing effect of potentially controversial action by one sovereign against another's leader.[226] The judges seemed to have made this finding to underscore their central point that the SCSL was not created by Sierra Leone to exercise the competence of that state, which the defense painted as arrogating for itself power that it did not have over Liberia's head of state. Rather, the SCSL's existence represented the collective will and interests of the international community as a whole – as manifested through UN involvement and support for its creation. This seems like a sound rationale that exposes the weak underbelly of some of the justifications for immunity from prosecution for international crimes.

---

[224] For the controversies that erupt in the few instances that they do, *see* Harmen van der Wilt, *Universal Jurisdiction under Attack: An Assessment of African Misgivings towards International Criminal Justice as Administered by Western States*, 9 J. INT'L. CRIM. JUST. 1043 (2011); Charles C. Jalloh, *Universal Jurisdiction, Universal Prescription? A Preliminary Assessment of the African Union Perspective on Universal Jurisdiction*, 21 CRIM. L. FORUM. 1 (2010).

[225] Orentlicher Brief, *supra* note 185, at 15.

[226] Prosecutor v. Taylor, Case No. SCSL-03-01-A, Appeals Chamber, Decision on Immunity from Jurisdiction, ¶ 51 (May 31, 2004).

In this regard, one has to keep in mind the trend of international human rights law whereby immunity is increasingly seen as incompatible with the commission of certain types of international crimes, the judges concluded that Article 6(2) of the SCSL Statute did not conflict with peremptory norms (though the latter argument has since been cast into doubt by the ICJ itself).[227] In the final analysis, in their view, "the principle seems now established that the sovereign equality of states does not prevent a Head of State from being prosecuted before an international criminal tribunal or court."[228] Accordingly, in their judgment, Taylor's official position as incumbent president at the time of initiation of the SCSL proceedings against him would not bar his prosecution.[229]

In sum, the Appeals Chamber has furnished a two-pronged argument that could, and indeed has since been used by judges in other tribunals such as the ICC, to hold that immunities should not prevent prosecutions of even those at the highest levels of power in the state – at least when it comes to international penal courts established with the significant involvement of the international community.[230] It erred when it adjudged the international legal status of the tribunal by reference to the international community involvement in its creation. The latter was a new justification for the removal of immunities. But, at a policy if not legal level, even that rationale should not be dismissed without further scrutiny. In fact, it may not be a bad argument. The reason is that international involvement in the creation of such courts enhances the prospects for greater avoidance of political manipulation of judicial processes such as those that the Congo claimed against Belgium at the ICJ.[231] This helps to stem the tendency towards self-help which could generate friction among states.

In fora such as the UN, the involvement of many states, as happened in the creation of the SCSL, can virtually be guaranteed. This is not insignificant. The essentially global membership of the UN and the principles of equitable geographic representation in just about all its main activities permits universal participation than might otherwise be ordinarily impossible. Having linked denial of immunity to the key collective security organization in the world, it may be that there might be ways to address the concern of those who would object to the removal of immunities in such circumstances as Taylor found himself because of fear of abuse of the sovereignty of weaker states. In other words, we may already have some of the required safeguards emanating from the type of collective deliberation that flows from collective UN action in the fight against impunity. It may also be relevant that the principal organs, such as the Security Council and the General Assembly, are in

---

[227] *Id.* at ¶ 53.
[228] *Id.* at ¶ 52.
[229] *Id.* at ¶ 59.
[230] *Id.* at ¶¶ 37–42.
[231] *See, e.g.*, Arrest Warrant of 11 April 2000 (Dem. Rep. Congo v. Belg.), Judgment, 2002 ICJ Rep. 3, ¶ 47 (Feb. 14).

this regard also holders of a power that states themselves have delegated to them to ensure the maintenance of international peace and security.[232]

On the other hand, some commentators would reject this line of argument on the basis that the immunities (especially of the functional variety) are conferred "to prevent foreign states from unduly interfering in the affairs of other states and from exercising judicial jurisdiction over another state in circumstances where it has not consented."[233] In this view, as has been argued, "it makes little difference whether the foreign states seek to exercise this judicial jurisdiction unilaterally or through some collective body that the state concerned has not consented to."[234] Furthermore, "[t]o suggest that immunity is nonexistent before an international tribunal that has not been consented to by the relevant state is to allow subversion of the policy underpinning international law immunities."[235]

I generally agree with some of the significant concerns that Akande and other scholars have raised. Nonetheless, I do not believe it undermines the ultimate value of the SCSL contribution to the development of the policy and practice underpinning immunity. Indeed, the reasonable scenario he postulated about in the above quote was not in fact in issue at the SCSL. The reason is that this was simply not a case of Sierra Leone unduly coming together with, say, neighboring Guinea or Nigeria, to interfere in the domestic affairs or foreign relations of Liberia by creating a special court that then seeks to besmirch Taylor by entangling him in spurious criminal proceedings. Rather, it was a case of Sierra Leone and the UN creating an international court, which acts independently of its creators, and in the exercise of that mandate guarantees fairness and impartiality to all persons when it exercises its jurisdiction to prosecute the international crimes committed within Sierra Leone. It was that entity, whose independent prosecution, which then found sufficient evidence to implicate Taylor for helping foment war and atrocity crimes.

To take it a bit further, Liberia and not just Sierra Leone, is also a member of the UN. Both states consented to being involved with that collective security organization. Both states have delegated powers to the Security Council the power to decide, on their behalf, threats to international peace and security and act thereon. Both countries had not asserted that, in the exercise of its powers, the UNSC cannot take explicit or implicit decisions for the sake of maintaining the peace that can then becoming binding upon them under the UN Charter. Viewed in this light, it seems fundamental but has largely been ignored by academics that the Security Council

[232] By the same token, mere involvement of the UN might not suffice to address the *perception* that the deck is stacked against less influential states, whether those are from Africa or other parts of the world. Again, the complaints by African States regarding the present allegedly biased trajectory of international justice (which can also be understood as a pushback against the dominance of Western States in international institutions) cuts against the argument here. Nonetheless, the actual factors explaining those objections are highly complex.
[233] Akande, *supra* note 165, at 417.
[234] *Id.* at 417.
[235] *Id.*

had, even before it helped to create the SCSL, in fact deemed Liberia and Taylor to be major enablers of the Sierra Leonean conflict through their illegal support for the RUF. The members of the latter included widely known committers of atrocity crimes in Sierra Leone. It was for that reason that the Security Council had warned Liberia to halt its support for the RUF as this would help the destabilization of the subregion. It is for the same reason that Liberia and all states were encouraged (not required) to cooperate fully with the Court. Put differently, the SCSL immunity scenario was far from the ugly specter of a handful of two or three sovereigns acting in bad faith to politically create and deploy a special international court as a ploy to subvert the immunities of Liberia as a non-consenting state to the SCSL's jurisdiction. Such an attempt would not be legally sustainable because a handful of them could not come together to delegate powers to another body that they themselves do not possess (*nemo dat quod non habet*), with all the negative repercussions that might entail for immunities.

Besides the above justification, the SCSL Appeals Chamber appeared to have offered a second and more controversial reason for its denial of Taylor's immunity. Under this proposition, which some commentators have advanced, it has been submitted that the SCSL was asserting that it enjoyed Chapter VII powers.[236] This despite the lack of explicit reference in the operative part of Resolution 1315, the UN-Sierra Leone Agreement and its Statute to that basis of authority. This is arguably a misreading of the Appeals Chamber decision in Taylor for three simple reasons.

First, it had always been acknowledged by the SCSL judges in other decisions that the Tribunal did not possess Chapter VII powers.[237] Second, if we assume that this is what the judges were trying to do, we would have expected them to mount a robust defense of that position. Instead, they are said to have defended such a significant proposition by implication rather than explicitly. Third, the language of their Taylor decision and their prior rulings on the issue of the legal nature of the tribunal rules out that possibility. Even if this was what the Appeals Chamber was seeking to argue, albeit impliedly, a simple reading of its constitutive instruments and the context of the SCSL's establishment would have debunked it. It would quickly demonstrate that the SCSL was not a Chapter VII tribunal. Several factors are relevant here.

To start with, if we juxtapose the actual language used in Resolution 1315 from the language of the Chapter VII resolution authorizing the ICTY and ICTR, we will find that there are significant variations. The most obvious difference is that Resolution 955, which created the ICTR, and Resolution 827 establishing the ICTY, both *explicitly invoke* Chapter VII powers. They say so in unambiguous

---

[236] Zsuzsanna Deen-Racsmány, *Prosecutor v. Taylor: The Status of the Special Court for Sierra Leone and Its Implications for Immunity*, 18 LEIDEN J. INT'L L. 299, 317 (2005).

[237] *See*, in this regard, Prosecutor v. Norman Case No. SCSL-2004-14-AR72(E), SCSL-2004-15-AR72(E), SCSL-2004-16-AR72(E), Decision on Constitutionality and Lack of Jurisdiction (Mar. 13, 2004); Prosecutor v. Kallon, Case No. SCSL-2004-15-AR72(E), SCSL-2004-16-AR72(E), Decision on Challenge to Jurisdiction: Lomé Accord Amnesty, (Mar. 13, 2004).

terms in their preambles that the SC was "[a]cting under Chapter VII of the Charter of the United Nations."[238] The lack of any similar language in Resolution 1315 is instructive. It certainly lends credence to at least the initial assessment that the SCSL was operating outside of Chapter VII.

Second, the requests in Resolution 1315 have none of the force of the binding language we find in Resolutions 827 and 955. One should further recall that Article 25 of the UN Charter provides that the "Members of the United Nations agree to accept and carry out the decisions of the Security Council in accordance with the present Charter."[239] In addition, Article 24(1) requires the Member States to agree that the Security Council act on their behalf when maintaining international peace and security.[240] The traditional and widely-accepted understanding of these articles is that UNSC decisions are binding on the Member States.[241] The General Assembly, which has a secondary responsibility for the maintenance of international peace and security, ECOSOC or individual Member States, cannot prescribe the threats to international peace and security. Nor can they legally determine the actions that states must take for the amelioration thereof. That primary function is reserved for the Security Council. Thus, actions taken by the UNSC under Chapter VII are deemed generally binding upon all Member States, subject of course to the Security Council's exercise of its discretion to urge voluntary compliance. Further, these obligations would prevail over conflicting ones pursuant to Article 103 of the UN Charter.

Having said that, the language of Resolutions 827 and 955, separate and apart from the explicit invocation of Chapter VII powers in the preamble, indicate that the Security Council is acting in a binding capacity in the operative part of those resolutions. That would be more consistent with that body's established practice. Plainly, Resolutions 827 and 955 are animated by what the Security Council "decides," whereas the Council in Resolution 1315 is "requesting" and "recommending." More substantively, the ICTY and ICTR Resolutions specifically inform states of their obligation to facilitate the mission of the Tribunals, saying that the Security Council:

> Decides that all States shall cooperate fully with the International Tribunal and its organs in accordance with the present resolution and the Statute of the International Tribunal and that consequently all States shall take any measures necessary under their domestic law to implement the provisions of the present resolution and the Statute, including the obligation of States to comply with requests for assistance or orders issued by a Trial Chamber under Article 28 of the Statute [.][242]

Resolution 1315 on the other hand, contains no such imperatives. The thrust of it was the Security Council's request that the Secretary-General "negotiate an agreement

---

[238]   S.C. Res. 827, ¶ 2 (May 25, 1993); S.C. Res. 955 ¶ 2 (Nov. 8, 1994).
[239]   U.N. Charter art. 25.
[240]   U.N. Charter art. 24 (1).
[241]   Although, it should be noted, that any *ultra vires* act of the Security Council would not be subject to Article 25 since such an act would not be "in accordance with" the Charter.
[242]   S.C. Res. 955, ¶ 2 (Nov. 8, 1994).

with the Government of Sierra Leone to create an independent special court[.]"[243] Although some of the details are left for later action, the Security Council had reasons to avoid the use of Chapter VII authority in Resolution 1315. It wanted to be sure that Member States' contributions to the mission of the SCSL will be *voluntary*, not mandatory, in line with the preferences of some of its influential permanent members. Thus, it sought the Secretary-General's recommendation regarding "the amount of voluntary contributions, as appropriate, of funds, equipment and services to the special court, including through the offer of expert personnel that may be needed from States, intergovernmental organizations and nongovernmental organizations[.]"[244]

Third, as the SCSL discussed in the Taylor immunity decision, the Security Council has powers and responsibilities outside of Chapter VII. Thus, any automatic imputation of the use of such binding powers based on UNSC action would be misplaced. Specifically, it is obvious that Chapter VI ("Pacific Settlement of Disputes") entitles the Security Council to call upon parties to settle their disputes by "negotiation, enquiry, mediation, conciliation, arbitration, judicial settlement, resort to regional agencies or arrangements, or other peaceful means of their own choice";[245] recommend "appropriate procedures or methods" to resolve disputes pacifically;[246] and to do so as a preliminary matter if the parties agree.[247] It is therefore uncontroversial that the Security Council's role in the larger framework of the UN system contemplates both the conciliatory and more forceful types of actions to manage conflicts. This leaves open the strong possibility, as some have suggested, that it might have been relying on Chapter VI when it decided to authorize the establishment of the SCSL.[248]

Admittedly, after acknowledging the SCSL's lack of Chapter VII powers, the Chamber decision in Taylor proceeded to discuss portions of the UN Charter substantive articles that brought the SCSL as close to the most extraordinary powers of the Security Council, namely Articles 39, 41, and 48.[249] This, of course, was not necessary to prove that the Court was an international tribunal. So, even as it sought to navigate its way into the ICJ's "certain international criminal courts" category by riding on the blessings given to its creation by the Security Council, it did not in fact invoke that as the legal ground upon which to deny Taylor's immunity. Indeed, the Appeals Chamber constructed the opposite argument when it observed that while much has been read into the lack of a Chapter VII mandate, that such an "omission" by the Security Council was not determinative of the legal status of the Court.[250]

---

[243] S.C. Res. 1315, ¶ 1 (Aug. 14, 2000).

[244] *Id.* at ¶ 8(d).

[245] U.N. Charter art. 33.

[246] U.N. Charter art. 36.

[247] U.N. Charter art. 38.

[248] Deen-Racsmány, *supra* note 236, at 299, 317.

[249] Prosecutor v. Taylor, Case No. SCSL-03-01-A, Appeals Chamber, Decision on Immunity from Jurisdiction, ¶ 38 (May 31, 2004).

[250] *Id.*

This finding and the subsequent explication of the internationality of the SCSL might make more sense if construed in that way.

Ultimately, and this has been a widely and legitimately critiqued aspect of the decision, the judges ruled that the Agreement between the United Nations and Sierra Leone to create the SCSL was an agreement between *all* UN Member States and Sierra Leone. The judges have been faulted for failing to address the legal consequences that would follow from such a finding.[251] They are also rightly said to have ignored the separate independent legal personality of the UN from that of its Member States and would have affected the rights and obligations of third states.[252] It appears that they conflated and even collapsed the two. Nevertheless, although one can concede that the language used here was problematic, this line of reasoning is arguably another misunderstanding of what the judges were saying. A perhaps better view is more consistent with the argument above that the main justification that the SCSL has given to uphold the removal of immunity is the SCSL's international legal nature as evidenced by the international involvement in its creation. In fact, after making this statement about the basis of the SCSL in a bilateral treaty, the Appeals Chamber went on to explain that "this fact makes the Agreement an expression of the will of the international community"[253] and that "the Special Court established in such circumstances is truly international."[254]

Several commentators have taken issue with the SCSL ruling that the internationality of a tribunal, without more, is sufficient to enable the removal of immunities. One of them has argued that the SCSL's reasoning, which basically stretches *Yerodia* too far to insist that international law immunities can never be pleaded in proceedings before an international tribunal, oversimplifies the matter.[255] The main reason for this is that international law would require the consent or the waiver of the immunities by the state which enjoys the immunity in order to make them unavailable before a particular court. Deen-Racsmány has reached essentially the same conclusion, concluding that the ICJ's finding in Yerodia "cannot reasonably be read to imply the irrelevance of immunities before *all* international criminal courts."[256] Frulli,[257] Kress,[258] Nouwen,[259] and Cryer,

---

[251]   See Deen-Racsmány, *supra* note 236.
[252]   *Id.*
[253]   Prosecutor v. Taylor, Case No. SCSL-03-01-A, Appeals Chamber, Decision on Immunity from Jurisdiction, ¶ 38 (May 31, 2004).
[254]   *Id.*
[255]   Akande, *supra* note 165.
[256]   Deen-Racsmány, *supra* note 236.
[257]   See Frulli *supra* note 200.
[258]   Claus Kreß, *The International Criminal Court and Immunities under International Law for States Not Party to the Court's Statute*, in STATE SOVEREIGNTY AND INTERNATIONAL CRIMINAL LAW 65 (Morten Bergsmo & LING Yan eds., 2012) (claiming that the *truly international legal nature* argument and reasoning of the SCSL was fundamentally flawed; but also advancing a thoughtful claim essentially agreeing with the SCSL that modern customary international law does not recognize a claim to personal immunity when certain international crimes are being prosecuted).
[259]   See Nouwen, *supra* note 121.

Friman, Robinson, and Wilmshurst all express similar views.[260] In a nutshell, scholars appear near unanimous that it is not the international features or nature of a tribunal, as such, which is material to the question of extinguishment of immunities – as the Appeals Chamber implied. The present writer could not agree more.

In terms of legal reasoning, the better question the judges should have focused on might have been to, first, determine whether the statute of the Tribunal had removed the immunities (which was not controversial in the SCSL because of Article 6(2)), and second, whether the concerned state had explicitly or implicitly consented to the removal of that immunity (which was in issue because Taylor was president of Liberia which had no role in the creation of the SCSL). These concerns reflect a positivist view that gives primacy to the notion of consent of the state and its rights under international law. It is, of course, possible to advance an alternative reading that immunities could also be deemed unavailable before a particular international court if customary international law (which subsists independently of whether there was a treaty removal or waiver) rejects such a notion because of the wider community interest. Though I tend to join in this view, it may at this point well be a minority opinion.

In relation to the ICC, which is a treaty-based court similar in that respect to the SCSL, Article 27 removes the immunities of the officials of the States Parties. At the same time, Article 98 of the Rome Statute, which was not mentioned by the ICJ, presupposes that the non-applicability of immunities arises only in respect of the states that have become parties to the ICC. This is because Article 27 constitutes in effect a waiver of the immunities of their officials for the States Parties. In relation to third states, that are not party to the ICC Statute, Article 98(1) requires the ICC not to proceed with a request for surrender or assistance which would require the requested state to act inconsistently with its obligations under international law with respect to the *state* or *diplomatic immunity* of a person unless the ICC can first obtain the cooperation of that third state for the waiver of the immunity. In the SCSL, there was both an Article 27 equivalent and a subsequent implicit waiver of any immunity that would have benefited Taylor when Liberia requested Nigeria transfer him to the SCSL.

As to the ICTY and ICTR, which are not treaty-based, they had some legally binding character in relation to all UN Member States. This is because both were rooted in Chapter VII of the UN Charter and the binding nature of Security Council decisions on all states under Article 25. For that reason, in their respective charters, all states were obligated to cooperate with them in their investigation and prosecution of persons accused of international crimes. This included the duty to comply, without undue delay with any request for assistance or an order issued by a chamber, including the identification and location of persons, the taking of testimony, or arrest and detention of persons.

---

[260] See CRYER ET AL., *supra* note 90, at 561–64.

Fourth, although the Secretary-General's interpretation is not per se binding on the Appeals Chamber which was the final interpreter of its own statute, the drafting history shows that key participants in the creation of the SCSL were uncertain that it was the type of international court that could go so far as to remove the immunities of a sitting president. In his report to the Security Council, requested in Resolution 1315, then-Secretary General Kofi Annan explicitly acknowledged the special status of the SCSL:

> Unlike either the International Tribunals for the Former Yugoslavia and for Rwanda, which were established by resolutions of the Security Council and constituted as subsidiary organs of the United Nations, or national courts established by law, the Special Court, as foreseen, is established by an Agreement between the United Nations and the Government of Sierra Leone and is therefore a treaty-based sui generis court of mixed jurisdiction and composition.[261]

Furthermore, Annan explicitly pointed to the lack of Chapter VII powers and identified it as a weakness of the then proposed court's structure, specifically vis-à-vis a non-Sierra Leonean accused, a point that is broadly relevant vis-à-vis Taylor:

> The primacy of the Special Court, however, is limited to the national courts of Sierra Leone and does not extend to the courts of third States. Lacking the power to assert its primacy over national courts in third States in connection with the crimes committed in Sierra Leone, *it also lacks the power to request the surrender of an accused from any third State and to induce the compliance of its authorities with any such request.* In examining measures to enhance the deterrent powers of the Special Court, the Security Council *may wish to consider endowing it with* Chapter VII *powers* for the specific purpose of requesting the surrender of an accused from outside the jurisdiction of the Court.[262]

Facially, this could be read as yet another affirmation that the SCSL was not an international court at least for the purposes of removal of immunities enjoyed under customary law for a non-Sierra Leonean president. This seems to confirm, from the outset, that it was already clear to the judges that the Tribunal was not based in Chapter VII. Still, we can fairly criticize the Chamber for unnecessarily advancing unclear reasoning. The ambiguity could be read as an attempt to bring the SCSL into the ambit of Chapter VII – a position that could not evidentially be sustained. The unfortunate effect of all this was to open the SCSL to later academic criticism. In any case, the effect of its weak legal path was to obscure the correctness of what should have been the uncontroversial conclusion that the SCSL was an international court which was thereby capable of removing Taylor's immunities since *he was no longer head of state* entitled to immunities at the time of its decision.

---

[261] U.N. Secretary-General, *The Report of the Secretary-General on the establishment of a Special Court for Sierra Leone*, ¶ 9, U.N. Doc. S/2000/915 (Oct. 4, 2000).

[262] *Id.* at ¶ 10 (emphasis added).

8.7 THE *TAYLOR* CASE AND ITS EFFECT ON THE INTERNATIONAL CRIMINAL COURT

Notwithstanding concerns about aspects of the decision, the *Taylor* Appeals Chamber decision has been the subject of discussion in other international fora. This includes the principal subsidiary body responsible for assisting the UN General Assembly with its mandate to promote the progressive development of international law and its codification: the International Law Commission, where the issue of immunity of state officials from foreign criminal jurisdiction has been under study for several years. However, and unsurprisingly, the most important use of the *Taylor* ruling has been at the ICC which has been confronted with the question of the immunity of high officials from arrest and transfer to answer charges regarding international crimes before The Hague-based tribunal. The use of the decision is evident from several important decision relating to the request to arrest President Omar al-Bashir of Sudan who is wanted on charges of genocide and crimes against humanity in relation to crimes allegedly committed in Darfur.

8.7.1 Malawi *Decision*

In December 2011, Pre-Trial Chamber I of the ICC rendered two decisions in rapid succession. Both decisions were related to the pending ICC arrest warrant against the Sudanese president Omar Al-Bashir.[263] In the *Malawi* decision, the Chamber found that the Republic of Malawi had failed to comply with the cooperation requests issued by the ICC for the arrest and surrender of Al Bashir.[264] President Al Bashir had visited the Republic of Malawi to which the Registrar had sent a diplomatic note to the Embassy of the Republic of Malawi, reminding of Malawi's obligations under the Rome Statute and requesting its cooperation for the arrest and surrender of Al Bashir.[265] In its decision, the Chamber – which found no significance in Sudan's non-party Status of the Rome Statute – relied on among others the findings of the SCSL that "the principle seems now established that the sovereign equality of states does not prevent a Head of State from being prosecuted before an international criminal tribunal or court" when it concluded that the principle in international law is that neither former nor sitting heads of state can invoke immunity to prevent arrest and prosecution by an international Court.[266] Also, the Chamber referred to the "international prosecution" against Charles Taylor and a number of other leaders to show that the initiation of international prosecutions against heads of state has gained "widespread recognition as accepted practice."[267]

---

[263]   Prosecutor v. Al Bashir, ICC-02/05-01, Decision on the Prosecution's Application for a Warrant of Arrest against Omar Hassan Ahmad Al Bashir (Mar. 4, 2009).

[264]   Prosecutor v. Al Bashir, ICC-02/15-01/09, Corrigendum to the Decision Pursuant to Article 87(7) of the Rome Statute on the Failure by the Republic of Malawi to Comply with the Cooperation Requests Issued by the Court with Respect to the Arrest and Surrender of Omar Hassan Ahmad Al Bashir, ¶ 1 (Dec. 13, 2011).

[265]   *Id.* at ¶ 5.

[266]   *Id.* at ¶¶ 35–36; 42-43.

[267]   *Id.* at ¶ 39.

8.7.2 *The* Chad *Decision*

Following the *Malawi* decision, Pre-Trial Chamber I of the ICC rendered a separate, but a very similar decision. In 2013, reports surfaced that Mr Al-Bashir had visited both Chad and Libya. The Chamber found that the Republic of Chad, a State Party to the ICC, had failed to cooperate with the Court by failing to arrest and surrender Al Bashir.[268] In its decision, while noting that Security Council referrals to the ICC are only effective if follow-up action is taken with respect to non-compliance, the Chamber chose to refer to the *Malawi* decision where it pointed to, amongst other things, to the "international prosecution" against Charles Taylor to show that the initiation of international prosecutions against heads of state has gained "widespread recognition as accepted practice."[269]

8.7.3 *Judgment in the Jordan Al-Bashir Appeal*

The Judgment in the Jordan Al Bashir Appeal,[270] by the ICC's Appeals Chamber, is to date the most important example of the lasting legacy of the SCSL in general and the *Taylor* case in particular. The procedural background to the case is as follows: In March 2005 the Security Council of the United Nations adopted UN Security Council Resolution 1593, acting under Chapter VII of the UN Charter. The Resolution referred the situation in Darfur to the Prosecutor of the ICC.[271] The Resolution further stipulated that the Sudanese government and other parties to the conflict in Darfur were obliged to cooperate fully and provide any necessary assistance to the ICC and the Prosecutor.[272] Subsequently, in 2009, the Pre-Trial Chamber I issued an arrest warrant for Al-Bashir, the President of Sudan, upon the request of the Prosecutor.[273] In the following year, a second arrest warrant adding genocide to the crimes against humanity charges was issued.[274] In 2017, Jordan hosted the Summit of the Arab League, an event which Al-Bashir attended. During Al-Bashir's visit, Jordan did not arrest nor surrender him.[275]

---

[268]   Prosecutor v. Al Bashir, ICC-02/05-01/09, Decision pursuant to article 87(7) of the Rome Statute on the refusal of the Republic of Chad to comply with the cooperation requests issues by the Court with respect to the arrest and surrender of Omar Hassan Ahmad Al Bashir, p. 8 (Dec. 13, 2013).

[269]   *Id.* at ¶ 39.

[270]   Prosecutor v. Al Bashir, ICC-02/05-01/09 OA2, Judgment in the Jordan Referral re Al-Bashir Appeal (May 6, 2019).

[271]   S.C. Res. 1593, ¶ 1 (Mar. 31, 2005).

[272]   *Id.* at ¶ 2.

[273]   Prosecutor v. Al Bashir, ICC-02/05-01, Decision on the Prosecution's Application for a Warrant of Arrest against Omar Hassan Ahmad Al Bashir (Mar. 4, 2009).

[274]   Prosecutor v. Al Bashir, ICC-02/05-01/09, Second Decision on the Prosecution's Application for a Warrant of Arrest (July 12, 2010).

[275]   Prosecutor v. Al Bashir, ICC-02/05-01/09, Decision under article 87(7) of the Rome Statute on the non-compliance by Jordan with the request by the Court for the arrest and surrender or Omar Al Bashir, ¶ 8 (Dec. 11, 2017).

8.7.3.1 Jordan Pre-Trial Chamber Decision

The fact that Jordan omitted to execute the arrest warrant during Al Bashir's visit led the Pre-Trial Chamber II to issue the "Decision under article 87(7) of the Rome Statute on the non-compliance by Jordan with the request by the Court for the arrest and surrender o[f] Omar Al-Bashir" (Impugned Decision) wherein the Chamber found that Jordan had failed to comply with its obligations under the Rome Statute and that its non-compliance should be referred to the Security Council and the Assembly of States Parties.[276] Regarding the question of whether President Al-Bashir enjoyed immunity, the Pre-Trial Chamber came to the conclusion, with reference to Article 27(2) of the Rome Statute that stipulates that immunity shall not bar the Court's exercise of jurisdiction irrespective the official position of the person, and further that head of state immunity does not exist in a situation where the Court requests a state party to arrest and surrender the head of state of another State Party.[277] However, since Sudan had signed but not ratified the Rome Statute, it was not a State Party.[278] Further, since Sudan had been obligated by the Security Council's decision, the Pre-Trial Chamber found that the circumstances made it appropriate to refer Jordan to the Assembly of State Parties in respect of its non-compliance.[279]

In response to the Pre-Trial Chamber's decision, Jordan sought to appeal the decision. Jordan raised several grounds to appeal, arguing that the Pre-Trial Chamber conclusion on the effect that Article 27 had on Al-Bashir's immunity excludes the application of Article 98.[280] Second, Jordan argued, the Pre-Trial Chamber had erroneously concluded that Resolution 1593 affected Jordan's obligations under international law and customary international law to accord head of state immunity to Al-Bashir.[281] The final ground was that even if the Pre-Trial Chamber was correct in its finding that Jordan had failed to comply with the Court's request, the discretionary power to refer such failure to the Assembly of State Parties and the Security Council had been abused.[282]

---

[276] *Id.* at ¶¶ 21–22.

[277] *Id.* at ¶¶ 33–34.

[278] International Criminal Court, *The State Parties to the Rome Statute,* https://asp.icccpi.int/en_menus/asp/states%20parties/pages/the%20states%20parties%20to%20the%20rome%20statute.aspx (last visited Nov. 20, 2019).

[279] Prosecutor v. Al Bashir, ICC-02/05-01/09, Decision under article 87(7) of the Rome Statute on the non-compliance by Jordan with the request by the Court for the arrest and surrender or Omar Al Bashir, ¶¶ 51–55 (Dec. 11, 2017).

[280] Prosecutor v. Al Bashir, ICC-02/05-01/09, The Hashemite Kingdom of Jordan's Notice of Appeal of the Decision under Article 87(7) of the Rome Statute on the Non-Compliance by Jordan with the Request by the Court for the Arrest and Surrender of Omar Al-Bashir; or, in the Alternative, Leave to Seek Such an Appeal, ¶ 4 (Dec. 18, 2017).

[281] *Id.*

[282] *Id.*

8.7.3.2 The Appeals Chamber Ruling on Jordan's Appeal

In December 2017, the Appeals Chamber granted Jordan's request for appeal[283] and in May 2018 the Appeals Chamber invited competent authorities to files submissions.[284] Amongst those responding to the *amici curiae* was the African Union which concluded that "on account of Article 98 of the Statutes and the rules of customary law, there is no duty on Jordan or any other State to cooperate in the arrest and surrender of Mr Al Bashir" and that "neither UNSC resolution 1593 ... disturbs this legal position."[285] The basis for this argument was that although article 27(2) of the Statute excludes immunity before the Court, it does not affect immunity from foreign domestic jurisdiction, and that the duty to cooperate in the arrest and surrender does not apply to a head of state of a non-State Party by virtue of article 98 or, in other words, that Article 27 of the Statute removes the "vertical application of immunities," but that the "horizontal application" remains intact under Article 98 of the Rome Statute.[286] Furthermore, the African Union argued that customary international law has to be taken into account when interpreting the Statute and that when doing so, Article 98 provides for situations where there exists no duty for the state to cooperate with the Court.[287]

Finally, in relation to the Pre-Trial Chamber's impugned decision, the African Union asserted that United Nations Security Resolution 1593 and the subsequent referral under Article 13(b) of the Statute does not place a state that is not a party to the Statute in a situation comparable with that of a state party.[288]

In its decision, the Appeals Chamber relied heavily on both the Statute and the jurisprudence of the SCSL, especially the *Taylor* case. By reference to, amongst others, the Statute of the Special Court for Sierra Leone and it's Article 6(2) which stipulates that head of state immunity cannot be invoked when the SCSL exercise its jurisdiction and the fact that the SCSL finding in the *Taylor* case that there is an established principle that sovereign equality does not prevent the prosecution of a head of state before an international tribunal, the Appeals Chamber confirmed the absence of a rule of customary international law that recognizes head of state

---

[283] *Id.*

[284] Prosecutor v. Al Bashir, ICC-02/05-01/09 OA2, Order inviting submission in the Jordan Referral re Al-Bashir Appeal, p. 3 (Sept. 20, 2018).

[285] Prosecutor v. Al Bashir, ICC-02/05-01/09 OA2, The African Union's Submission in the "Hashemite Kingdom of Jordan's Appeal Against the 'Decision under Article 87(7) of the Rome Statute and the Non-Compliance by Jordan with the Request by the Court for the Arrest and Surrender [of] Omar Al-Bashir'", ¶ 83 (July 13, 2018).

[286] Prosecutor v. Al Bashir, ICC-02/05-01/09 OA2, Judgment in the Jordan Referral re Al-Bashir Appeal, ¶ 80 (May 6, 2019).

[287] *Id.* at ¶ 81.

[288] *Id.* at ¶ 82.

immunity before an international court.[289] This absence of immunity before an international tribunal, the Appeals Chamber concluded, does not only apply in the "vertical relationship" but also the "horizontal relationship," that is, between states when an international court requests the arrest and surrender of the head of state of another state, meaning that immunity cannot be invoked as a bar to cooperate with the Court.[290] The ICC Appeals Chamber went further than some might have expected in its finding in relation to the horizontal aspect.

As this chapter has shown, the SCSL, and in particular, the *Taylor* case, has had a considerable impact on the jurisprudence of the ICC, and its view on immunity *ratione personae*. In the jurisprudence of the ICC, the *Taylor* case has made several appearances. Starting with the *Malawi* decision, the Chamber referred both to the SCSL finding that sovereign equality does not prevent the prosecution of a head of state before an international criminal tribunal or court and that international prosecutions against heads of state have gained "widespread recognition as accepted practice." Finally, in the Jordan Appeals case the Chamber relied both on the Statute of the SCSL and its jurisprudence, arriving at the conclusion that there exists no norm in customary international law that prevents a head of state from being prosecuted before an international criminal tribunal and that this lack of immunity before an international criminal tribunal or court also applies to the "horizontal relationship," that is, between states.

The impact of the *Taylor* case can also be seen in the work of the International Law Commission, where the Special Rapporteur on the topic of Immunity of State officials from foreign criminal jurisdiction referred to the case to support the norm that immunity *ratione personae* does not constitute a bar from prosecution before an international criminal tribunal. The decision is also cited approvingly by some members of the ILC in their interventions. Also, the Special Rapporteur again turned to the jurisprudence of the SCSL for guidance in questions relating to procedural safeguards, such as the timing of the consideration of immunity. Further, one could make the argument that the very fact that an international criminal tribunal convicted a sitting head of state fed in to the overall sense that there is a trend whereby full and absolute immunity is being increasingly put into question, especially in the context of allegations of commission of core international crimes.

8.8 CONCLUSION

This chapter has determined that the SCSL decision in *Prosecutor v. Charles Taylor*, as the first judicial application of the *Yerodia* judgment by an international penal court, was an important addition to the evolution of the law of head of state immunity in modern international law. *Yerodia* resembled *Taylor* in at least four

[289] *Id.* at ¶¶ 108–13.
[290] *Id.* at ¶ 117.

ways: (1) both men were senior government officials in their home states when they were indicted (Taylor a president, Yerodia a foreign minister); (2) both were charged with the commission of crimes against humanity and war crimes; (3) both had their indictments and arrest warrants circulated through INTERPOL; and (4) both were holding office when they were charged, but perhaps because of their controversial activities, were no longer occupying their offices by the time the ICJ and the SCSL ruled on their cases. Despite these similarities, the Court reached the correct conclusion that the *Taylor* and *Yerodia* cases could be distinguished on the basis of the type of court that had issued their respective warrants: an *international court* (in this case one created by treaty by the UN and one of its Member States), before which immunities could not be pleaded, and in respect of the latter, a Belgian *domestic court* before which immunities are available.

In big picture terms, because of *Yerodia* and the decisions such as that of the SCSL in *Taylor*, customary immunities *ratione personae* and *ratione materiae* seem destined to follow two parallel tracks. With regard to national courts' attempts to exercise jurisdiction over foreign state officials, it appears that the customary immunities accorded to, at least the so-called troika of Ministers of Foreign Affairs, Heads of State, and Heads of Government will for the moment remain important sources of protecting the principle *par in parem non habet imperium*. It is also a way to ensure the continuation of stability in international affairs. However, the continued vitality of customary immunities before prosecutions taking place in international courts, seems to be more suspect. Here, immunities may be receding somewhat, its fate seemingly tied to the doctrine of sovereignty which is slowly being redefined by the emergence of human rights norms and the notion of sovereignty as non-absolute and as a corollary to responsibility.

I focused in this chapter on the assertion of immunity from prosecution by Liberian President Charles Taylor on the basis that he was entitled to annulment of his indictment because he enjoyed immunities as a serving head of state under customary international law. The judges rejected the claim, finding that while the rationale for the availability of immunities may be sound when it comes to regulating relations between states whose leaders are considered coequal sovereigns, it made little sense when it comes to proceedings carried out by an international penal court established by and with the blessings of the United Nations. This finding did not negate the necessity of advancing peaceful interstate interaction on the international level – a key rationale underpinning aspects of the modern law of immunity. Nor does it deny the fact that immunities are ordinarily available for incumbent presidents to block foreign criminal proceedings, within national courts, even where the suspect is accused of committing heinous international crimes. Far from creating a world of chaos, in the alternate view advanced by the Appeals Chamber, certain international criminal courts which exist and function above national courts could prioritize the emergence of an international rule of law by ignoring such technical legal obstacles to criminal prosecutions – at least in relation to the prosecution of core international offenses. Such a rule of law would emphasize, like domestic law, the equality of all persons before the law. It would at the same time recognize there is much common sense behind the rejection of immunities for those who wield the greatest amount of power, but who, for whatever reasons, choose to abuse that power by participating in the commission of atrocities with untold consequences for victims. It is therefore submitted that the SCSL Appeals Chamber made a useful jurisprudential contribution to the development of the law of head of state immunity.

On the other hand, the SCSL Appeals Chamber decision was rather vague on the applicability of the Yerodia exception to the president of a third state to the treaty between the UN and Sierra Leone which had created the SCSL. The judges attempted to resolve the problem by holding that immunities are not available to Taylor under customary international law. Thus, dispensing with the need for a treaty-based link through the UN Charter, the significant precedent determined that a leader accused of committing core international crimes by an international penal tribunal established with the support of the UN is prosecutable. This judicial reframing of the policy behind immunity, which here focused on the involvement of the international community in creating the court, essentially found that the rationale for immunities which applies *horizontally* between sovereigns has no place when it comes to the relationship between one of those sovereigns and an international tribunal operating at the *vertical* level. This was a much broader finding than that the ICJ had reached, and can be seen either as an expansion or a clarification of some of the confusion that remained after *Yerodia*.

But the case need not be overstated. The reason is that the current practice of some African States which now appear vociferous in their insistence on the sacrosanct nature of immunity to the point of even advocating its expansion within international penal courts would seem to undermine this argument. Against this backdrop, the principle that one sovereign must not exercise power over another, which traditionally undergirded immunity, will likely increasingly find little succor in future international tribunals. A key reason is that, as the SCSL has rightly offered and emphasized, such a doctrine does not deserve a meaningful place in trials conducted by independent international tribunals which do not act as organs of states but derive their mandate from the most representative body of the international community of states. Furthermore, these tribunals act solely to give effect to prohibitions against heinous international crimes condemned by international law in the name of all of humanity.

True, the SCSL ruling made some mistakes by reproducing some of the problems of the ICJ immunity stance. Still, it will likely in the future be remembered for teaching at least two key legal lessons. That is to say, first, that the involvement of the UN and its Security Council in creating an ad hoc tribunal could well offer a sound legal basis for the removal of immunities whether explicitly or by implication. This would be so even in respect of the leaders of third states, so long as they involve themselves in enabling conflicts in neighboring states that are then deemed by the Security Council as threats to the maintenance of international peace and security. The second SCSL legacy on the immunity issue that may well stand the test of time is methodical and is this: Future international courts should carefully study the purpose and rationale for immunities, and in the process, they might find that immunities are – or should be – irrelevant to prosecutions before international criminal courts supported by the international community. They can, on the latter point, rely on the *Taylor* case as at least a useful starting point for their analysis.

Before closing, one might observe that the confirmation that the SCSL is an international criminal court, though in the context of this chapter focused only on the legal consequences of that finding for Taylor's immunities, will also prove to be relevant to the next chapter. In the case discussed in that chapter, the SCSL was asked by other suspects to determine whether the Government of Sierra Leone could grant a *blanket amnesty* from prosecution to all the combatants, including those who committed serious violations of international law during the Sierra Leone conflict. The next chapter considers the Appeals Chamber's important ruling on that question and its own judicial contributions to the development of modern international criminal practice.

9

Amnesties

9.1 INTRODUCTION

Amnesty is one of the most well-known, and at the same time, one of the most controversial alternatives to criminal prosecutions in the aftermath of conflict. Amnesty, which has been defined as, "a sovereign act of oblivion for past acts, granted by a government to all persons (or to certain persons) who have been guilty of crime or delict, generally political offences, – treason, sedition, rebellion, – and often conditioned upon their return to obedience and duty within a prescribed time,"[1] was apparently a standard part of peace arrangements at certain points in history. Its use, along with pardons,[2] to help end political crises, wars, or dictatorships or even as part of festive occasions dates back several hundred years.[3] Similarly, in the modern context, states appear to see amnesties as part of the transitional justice menu from which they can choose in order to end civil wars, violence, and conflict in the hope of restoring peace, security, and stability. Amnesties have therefore been reportedly deployed in over 500 transitional justice situations ranging from Chile through to Cambodia, Colombia, East Timor, South Africa to Sierra Leone and further afield.[4]

The question which arises, and that the Special Court for Sierra Leone (SCSL) had to consider in several of its decisions, is whether unconditional grants of amnesties by a warring government can bar individual criminal prosecutions before an independent international criminal tribunal in respect of war crimes, crimes against humanity, and other serious violations of international humanitarian law.

[1] *Amnesty*, BLACK'S LAW DICTIONARY (5th ed. 1983).
[2] Amnesty is said to be abolition and forgetfulness of the offence; pardon is forgiveness. The first typically addresses crimes against the sovereignty of the nation, to political offences, the second condones infractions of the peace of the nation. *See* Knote v. U.S., 95 U.S. 149, 152 (1877); Burdick v. U.S., 236 U. S. 79 (1915).
[3] Prosecutor v. Kondewa, SCSL-2004-14-AR72(E), Decision on Lack of Jurisdiction/Abuse of Process: Amnesty Provided by the Lomé Accord (Separate Opinion of Justice Robertson), ¶¶ 15–17 (May 25, 2004).
[4] *See* LOUISE MALLINDER, AMNESTY, HUMAN RIGHTS AND POLITICAL TRANSITIONS: BRIDGING THE PEACE AND JUSTICE DIVIDE (2008).

9.2 PURPOSE AND STRUCTURE OF THIS CHAPTER

This chapter examines the controversial amnesty and pardon which, before the Sierra Leone Government changed its mind and sought United Nations assistance to establish a special court,[5] purported to grant all combatants and their collaborators involved with the Sierra Leonean conflict absolute freedom and pardon in respect of anything done by them in pursuit of their objectives during the course of the notoriously brutal civil war. Toward that end, though also discussed in Chapter 2, Section 9.3 of the Chapter briefly discusses the background to the Lomé Peace Agreement and its controversial amnesty clause which later supplied the legal basis for the defense argument that the SCSL's attempt to prosecute them, for alleged crimes that predated that accord, constituted an abuse of process. Section 9.4 analyzes the Appeals Chamber's main ruling on this question, issued on March 13, 2004, holding that the amnesty conferred by the national authorities of Sierra Leone could not prevent the defendants' prosecution for international crimes before the independent SCSL.[6] Section 9.5 engages in a critical assessment of the significance of the decision, as one of the first such rulings by an international criminal court, to discern what, if any contributions, the SCSL amnesty decision may be said to have bequeathed to international criminal law and practice. The last part (that is, Section 9.6) summarizes the key findings.

As with the overall thrust of my argument in the previous chapter on immunity, I aim to show that while the Appeals Chamber reached the right conclusion that the SCSL was not legally barred from prosecuting the various defendants before it because the amnesty conferred by Sierra Leone in the 1999 peace accord could not prohibit their trial before an independent international penal court, the judicial reasoning offered was sometimes muddled. Nonetheless, because the Tribunal added its voice to the emerging international practice frowning upon amnesties, its contribution has partly already been relied upon by, for instance, the Inter-American Court of Human Rights to invalidate or ignore self-serving amnesties for gross human rights violations such as those conferred by Brazil and Peru.[7] Overall, the judicial contribution and legacy of the SCSL ruling denying legal effect to Sierra Leone's blanket amnesty for war crimes, crimes against humanity, and other serious violations of the law of armed conflict is a useful addition to the normative development of international criminal law.

---

[5] Agreement between the United Nations and the Government of Sierra Leone on the Establishment of a Special Court for Sierra Leone, Jan. 16, 2002, 2178 U.N.T.S. 138 [hereinafter UN-Sierra Leone Agreement]. The Statute of the Special Court for Sierra Leone was annexed to the UN-Agreement and an integral part thereof [hereinafter SCSL Statute]. Both instruments are annexed to this work.

[6] Prosecutor v. Kallon, Case No. SCSL-2004-15-AR72 (E), SCSL-2004-16-AR72(E), Decision on Challenge to Jurisdiction: Lomé Accord Amnesty, ¶ 3 (Mar. 13, 2004) [hereinafter Lomé Amnesty Decision].

[7] See Gomes Lund et al. ("Guerrilha Do Araguaria") v. Brazil, Judgment, Inter-Am Ct. H.R. (ser. C) No. 219, ¶ 159 (Nov. 29, 2010) (citing the decision and statute of the SCSL as part of the evidence against amnesty; affirming the prior ruling in Barrios Altos v. Peru, Judgment, Inter-Am Ct. H.R. (ser. C) No. 75, ¶¶ 41–44 (Mar. 14, 2001).

9.3 THE ORIGINS OF THE AMNESTY DEBACLE
IN THE SIERRA LEONE CONFLICT

The Sierra Leone conflict began in March 1991, and as described in Chapter 2, led to the commission of numerous atrocities against the local population by all factions in the war especially the Revolutionary United Front (RUF) rebels and their collaborators. The Lomé Peace Agreement, provided the blueprint for the country's return to peace by January 2002.[8] It was brokered under the auspices of the Economic Community of West African States (ECOWAS) and was signed after months of intense negotiations in the Togolese capital in July 1999.

However, even before Lomé, there had been several other ultimately unsuccessful attempts to end the bitter conflict between the RUF and the Government of Sierra Leone (GoSL). In the Abidjan Accord, which was negotiated in November 1996 in the capital of Ivory Coast it was named after, the parties fashioned the precursor to the much-derided amnesty later agreed at Lomé. Article 14 of that first accord provided that no official or judicial action would be taken against any member of the RUF for anything done by them and mandated adoption of legislative and other measures to enable the return of exiles, combatants, and others to encourage full exercise of their civil rights and reintegrating them into society. They justified both on the ground that this was necessary in order to secure and "consolidate the peace" and "promote the cause of national reconciliation" in Sierra Leone.[9] But the RUF violated the key terms of the Abidjan cease-fire just days afterwards. This led to a resumption of hostilities between the two sides and the return to the bitter fighting, amputations, killings, and the other mayhem that had become associated with the Sierra Leone conflict.

The Lomé Peace Agreement, which was signed by Sierra Leone's President Ahmed Tejan Kabbah and the RUF leader Corporal Foday Sankoh, received the endorsement (so-called "moral guarantee") of several other personalities from ECOWAS, the United Nations, representatives of the Organization of African Unity, as well as the United States.[10] Article IX, which was entitled "Pardon and Amnesty," was a general provision which was controversial in the local civil society community both in the lead-up to the Togolese negotiations and afterwards. As it was the center of the later dispute about the implications of the amnesty at the SCSL, which we will study in this chapter, it is worth setting out in full. It provided as follows:

---

[8] Peace Agreement between the Government of the Republic of Sierra Leone and the Revolutionary United Front of Sierra Leone, U.N. Doc. S/1999/777 (July 7, 1999) [hereinafter Lomé Peace Agreement].

[9] Peace Agreement between the Government of the Republic of Sierra Leone and the Revolutionary United Front of Sierra Leone, at art. 14, U.N. Doc. S/1996/1034 (Nov. 30, 1996) [hereinafter Abidjan Accord].

[10] Several delegates signed the accord as witnesses. Nonetheless, the only parties to it were, on the one part, the Government of Sierra Leone as represented by President Ahmed Tejan Kabbah, and on the other, Foday Saybana Sankoh as Leader of the RUF.

1. In order to bring lasting peace to Sierra Leone, the Government of Sierra Leone shall take appropriate legal steps to grant Corporal Foday Sankoh absolute and free pardon.

2. After the signing of the present Agreement, the Government of Sierra Leone shall also grant absolute and free pardon and reprieve to all combatants and collaborators in respect of anything done by them in pursuit of their objectives, up to the time of the signing of the present Agreement.

3. To consolidate the peace and promote the cause of national reconciliation, the Government of Sierra Leone shall ensure that no official or judicial action is taken against any member of the RUF/SL, ex-AFRC, ex-SLA or CDF in respect of anything done by them in pursuit of their objectives as members of those organisations since March 1991, up to the signing of the present Agreement. In addition, legislative and other measures necessary to guarantee immunity to former combatants, exiles and other persons, currently outside the country for reasons related to the armed conflict shall be adopted ensuring the full exercise of their civil and political rights, with a view to their reintegration within a framework of full legality.[11]

Paragraph 1 of Article IX of the Lomé Agreement was imperative because Sankoh had been arrested and tried for treason and related offenses. He had been found guilty on August 25, 1998 and sentenced to death by the High Court of Sierra Leone. As his conviction was on appeal, the judicial authorities had to grant him bail before he could even travel to Togo to attend the peace negotiations. Everyone knew that, without his presence in Lomé and without his participation in the talks, there was very little hope for peace in Sierra Leone. His first demand, even before the negotiations began, was that he be cleared of his conviction and all charges. His position was therefore secured through this first government concession to subsequently take the requisite legal steps to pardon him – all in order to bring back "lasting peace" to Sierra Leone. This first act of good faith on the part of the national authorities seemed inevitable.

Paragraph 2, for its part, was a promise to grant "absolute and free pardon and reprieve to all combatants and collaborators." It is notable that this was a general pardon *for all the* actors and parties involved in the conflict. This included members of the government forces, paramilitary groups supported by the Kabbah Government such as the Civil Defense Forces (CDF), the mutinying elements of the Sierra Leone army who had carried out a coup d'état and formed a military junta in October 1997 known as the Armed Forces Revolutionary Council (AFRC), and of course, the RUF rebels. The broad formulation of the clause, which was drafted and agreed even before the substantive peace negotiations began, makes sense from the RUF perspective. But it seems striking because of its language anticipating wide coverage over "anything done by them in pursuit of their objectives."[12] This

---

[11]   Lomé Peace Agreement, *supra* note 8, at art. IX.
[12]   Solomon E. Berewa, A New Perspective on Governance, Leadership, Conflict and National Building in Sierra Leone 134 (2011).

effectively excluded from the reach of the local law any use of violence and possible domestic crimes such as murder, rape, arson, etc. The paragraph would also on its face bar civil claims for tortious conduct. The same provision was also apparently meant to capture, as part of the amnestied conduct, all the behavior that might have amounted to international crimes such as crimes against humanity and war crimes and other serious violations of the law of armed conflict.

Paragraph 3 was cut and paste verbatim from Article 14 of the Abidjan Accord. There were only slight modifications. The significant one was the expansion of the categories of combatants to whom the benefit of the amnesty and pardon will redound (that is, not just the RUF, but also to all the former AFRC, Sierra Leone Army (SLA) or CDF forces; the Abidjan formulation only benefited the RUF rebels). A key weakness, even on a quick reading of the clause, was the blanket scope of the amnesty and pardon. There were no conditions or criteria put in place in Article IX of the Lomé Agreement, or indeed the remainder of the peace accord, to qualify the receipt of the pardon or amnesty. Neither, looking forward, did the parties anticipate what would happen if any or both of the parties failed to abide by the peace accord's terms. This, in retrospect, was a big weakness of the agreement. It also did not reflect the more recent practice concerning amnesties, which would have contemplated both.

In a significant statement during his public testimony before the Sierra Leone Truth and Reconciliation Commission, on August 5, 2003, President Kabbah confirmed that the conferral of the amnesty was deliberate and part of his policy approach to ending the war.[13] It was not inadvertent, as his government had basically tried to trade amnesty to the RUF in return for securing the peace. The national authorities, which evidently were not negotiating from a position of military strength, felt that they had to incentivize the rebels to lay down their weapons. They had therefore sweetened the pot for them by agreeing to confer an unconditional amnesty. This was later supplemented by the power sharing arrangement, which included conferment of the *status* (evidently not the actual position) of Vice-President to Sankoh, as well as several senior government cabinet posts for the RUF and its AFRC collaborators. The president also explained that his government had been aware that they were asking war-weary Sierra Leoneans to "swallow a bitter pill"; and further that the amnesty was popularly perceived as the case of the perpetrators being "richly rewarded" while the population "got nothing at all."[14]

However, though in his view the RUF repudiated their end of the deal thereby forfeiting the generous amnesty, he felt that his government had no choice under the circumstances at the time.[15] His, at bottom, was an argument about exceptional

[13]   His Excellency the President Alhaji Dr. Ahmad Tejan Kabbah, Statement before the Truth and Reconciliation Commission ("TRC"), at ¶ 35, (Aug. 5, 2003) [hereinafter President Kabbah Speech to the TRC].

[14]   *Id.*

[15]   *Id.*

circumstances. In this regard, he interestingly affirmed before the Truth and Reconciliation Commission (TRC) that his government's initial goal was not to limit the amnesty to cover acts that might have been criminal under *domestic law*, but also to encompass all conduct that could also have been considered criminal under *international law*.[16] This seems significant because it offers a strong basis, if that was the understanding of the parties at the time, for what would be a robust argument that the SCSL was established in breach of that undertaking. President Kabbah was unapologetic, giving valuable insights into how state leaders might sometimes shove international law obligations to the background and assert national sovereignty for the sake of national interest, when they feel they have everything to lose. In his unequivocal words: "We had resisted the persuasion of the international community for the exclusion of war crimes, crimes against humanity and against international humanitarian law from the applicability of the amnesty provision in the Lomé Agreement. We did this *deliberately*."[17] The policy rationale, which bolsters the arguments favoring retention of the amnesty option in other conflicts in other parts of the world, was that restricting the operation of the amnesty and pardon would have given the RUF an excuse to refuse to sign the agreement and to resume the hostilities.[18] The country simply needed to bring the war to an end. It was clear that the president, who had run on a platform of bringing peace during the vote that led to his election, was keenly aware that many Sierra Leoneans were fed up with the long and brutal civil war. It did not seem to matter what immediate price they had to pay to get peace, even if it meant giving de facto impunity to the perpetrators of the atrocities. It can be presumed that it was also of little concern whether international law obligations owed by Sierra Leone under international law would be violated, considering that the country was a party to the 1949 Geneva Conventions and their Additional Protocols. Ironically, in many of his public speeches about the war, President Kabbah would insist on the RUF's lack of compliance with international humanitarian law.

But, perhaps reflecting potential concerns about the broad nature of the amnesty, the Special Representative of the United Nations Secretary-General Francis G. Okello who had signed the agreement as one of the witnesses, apparently scribbled a last minute note during the signing ceremony of the Lomé Peace Agreement.[19] That note, which has been described as a "reservation" but may be more accurately characterized as an "understanding" or perhaps even more aptly a "unilateral declaration or statement," was to the effect that "[t]he UN holds the understanding that the amnesty provisions of the Agreement shall not apply to international crimes

---

[16]   *Id.*
[17]   *Id.* (emphasis added).
[18]   *Id.*
[19]   U.N. Secretary-General, *Report of the Secretary-General on the Establishment of a Special Court for Sierra Leone*, ¶23, U.N. Doc. S/2000/915 (Oct. 4, 2000).

of genocide, crimes against humanity, war crimes and other serious violations of international humanitarian law."[20] This statement, which was unprecedented for the UN in relation to a peace agreement anywhere in the world, would later gain in significance in terms of its implications for the SCSL's judicial functioning. That said, the value of the statement might have been more for setting out UN policy, the reason being that it could not, in the context of the Sierra Leone fact pattern, offer more. This is because the UN representative was there as a *witness* to the signature of the accord. The UN was thus not a *party* to the substantive agreement. The position, by the representative of the Secretary-General, is also a view of that organ of the UN. It served to later influence the official negotiations, between the UN and the Sierra Leone government, and allowed for the inclusion of the clause not recognizing the amnesty clause but is ultimately not attributable to the UN Member States or the organization.

Sierra Leone's Parliament ratified the Lomé Agreement on July 22, 1999.[21] It thereby gave legal effect in national law to the Kabbah Government's commitments during the peace negotiations. For its part, the Security Council adopted a resolution in which it endorsed the agreement (though this is not to imply that it was in any case bound by it). [22] In the meantime, only weeks later, the RUF violated key terms of the peace accord. Following a brazen set of disturbing acts aimed at scuttling the peace process, which included the hostage taking of over 500 UN peacekeepers and the killing of unarmed civilian protesters in a May 2000 incident at Sankoh's house in Freetown the Sierra Leonean capital, the President requested UN support to create a "credible special court" to try the RUF and its accomplices arguing, inter alia, that they had "reneged" on the Lomé Agreement.[23] The circumstances of the creation of the SCSL have been discussed in detail in Chapters 3 and 4 of this book.

The Security Council adopted Resolution 1315 in which it, among other things, recalled and reaffirmed the amnesty disclaimer in the fifth preambulary paragraph. It thereafter requested the Secretary-General to negotiate an agreement with Sierra Leone to establish the SCSL.[24] That bilateral treaty, to which the Statute of the SCSL was an annex, explicitly stated in Article 10 that "an amnesty to any person falling with the jurisdiction of the Special Court in respect of crimes referred to in Articles 2 to 4 [that is, the international crimes] of the present Statute shall not be a

---

[20]   *Id.* at ¶ 23.

[21]   *See* Lomé Peace Agreement, *supra* note 8.

[22]   S.C. Res. 1260 (Aug. 20, 1999) (stressing the urgent need to promote peace and national reconciliation and to foster accountability and respect for human rights in Sierra Leone, and in that context, taking note of the Secretary-General's view that the Sierra Leonean people should be allowed the opportunity to realize their best and only hope of ending their long and brutal conflict).

[23]   *See* Permanent Rep. of Sierra Leone to the U.N., Letter date 9 August from the Permanent Rep. of Sierra Leone to the President of the Security Council, annex, U.N. Doc. S/2000/786 (Aug. 10, 2000).

[24]   S.C. Res. 1315 (Aug. 14, 2000).

bar to prosecution."[25] The Secretary-General's subsequent report discussing the legal framework of the Tribunal observed that, in the course of negotiating the agreement, the Sierra Leone Government had concurred with the UN's position that the terms of the Lomé Agreement did not preclude the prosecution of international crimes before the SCSL.[26]

He also recalled the entry of a "reservation" by his special representative during the conclusion of the peace agreement. In what might have been an exaggeration, and with the apparent intent to deny "legal effect" to the amnesty "to the extent of its illegality under international law," Annan asserted that "[w]hile recognizing that amnesty is an accepted legal concept and a gesture of peace and reconciliation at the end of a civil war or an internal armed conflict, the United Nations has *consistently maintained the position that amnesty cannot be granted in respect of international crimes*, such as genocide, crimes against humanity or other serious violations of international humanitarian law."[27] Yet, although the UN stance might have been a reference to other peace agreements, there was no real evidence of any UN opposition to the broad amnesty that had been included in the Abidjan Peace package between the Sierra Leone government and the RUF just three years before. That said, the fact that international law does not yet seem to prohibit amnesties does not mean that the UN is bound by any particular amnesty. Indeed, as argued above, the amnesty in Abidjan was only slightly narrower than that agreed at Lomé and explicitly also addressed Sankoh's position given his August 1998 conviction for treason.

Nonetheless, this being the first clear public statement by the UN opposing the use of amnesties in circumstances of commission of core international crimes in a contemporary armed conflict, it is an important contribution to the emerging international practice pertaining to amnesties. On the other hand, depending on one's views of the propriety of amnesties to end civil wars, it could be seen as a troubling development. Among the reasons is that such measures fail to account for the realities that such a rigid policy stance might mean for ending often unwinnable civil wars. This, of course, is not to suggest that such agreements reached by states could in any event bind the UN as an independent international organization with its own separate legal personality from that of its members. Nonetheless, it could be read as a positive development, a chink in the armor of impunity in favor of accountability given that many conflicts around the world have also demonstrated that conferrals of amnesties for international crimes may be counterproductive and even undermine the creation or restoration of peace and stability in a given post-conflict society.

---

[25] SCSL Statute, *supra* note 5, at art. 10.
[26] U.N. Secretary-General, *Report of the Secretary-General on the Establishment of a Special Court for Sierra Leone*, ¶24, U.N. Doc. S/2000/915 (Oct. 4, 2000).
[27] *Id.* (emphasis added).

9.4 CAN DEFENDANTS BENEFIT FROM THE LOMÉ AMNESTY TO AVOID PROSECUTION?

9.4.1 *SCSL Suspects Allege Abuse of Process to Prosecute Them*

One of the earliest SCSL motions, during the pre-trial phase, was filed by RUF defendants Morris Kallon and Brima Kamara and related to the question of amnesty.[28] Their application was later joined by several other accused who had also been charged for crimes allegedly committed before the conclusion of the Lomé Peace Agreement. In the main, the suspects argued that the SCSL could not try them for acts committed before July 1999 given the unconditional amnesty/ pardon that the Sierra Leone Government had conferred on them precluded their prosecution.[29] They further submitted that it would be an "abuse of process" to ignore that amnesty and seek to prosecute them.[30] They claimed that the Lomé Agreement was a treaty under international law and the obligations contained within it for the signatory government and rebel side could not be modified without the consent of all the parties to it. This modification was what the government had unilaterally undertaken through its bilateral treaty subsequently concluded with the UN which would establish the SCSL and purportedly withdrew the amnesty.[31]

The Prosecution replied that the SCSL was only bound by Article 10 of its Statute which rendered the amnesty irrelevant.[32] The Lomé Agreement, being a mere agreement between two national bodies rather than a treaty, was limited in its effect only to Sierra Leone. It did not extend to the SCSL which was an independent body with its own legal personality. It was, in any event, not intended that the amnesty would cover the type of international crimes within the Tribunal's jurisdiction such as to bar the prosecutions of the persons before the SCSL.[33] Furthermore, the prosecutors submitted that, given the gravity of the alleged crimes, the judges could not exercise discretion to grant a stay of proceedings on the ground that there had been abuse of process.[34]

9.4.2 *The Appeals Chamber Ruling*

Analytically, the Appeals Chamber ruling on the defense motion can be divided into three main steps. In the first step, according to the judges, they had to determine the legal character of the Lomé Agreement.[35] They discussed at length whether the

---

[28] Lomé Amnesty Decision, *supra* note 6.
[29] *Id.* at ¶¶ 1–2.
[30] *Id.* at ¶¶ 75, 77.
[31] *Id.* at ¶ 30.
[32] *Id.* at ¶ 32.
[33] *Id.* at ¶ 2.
[34] *Id.* at ¶ 36.
[35] *Id.* at ¶ 78.

accord could be deemed a binding instrument under international law.[36] They considered the nature of the Sierra Leone conflict as an internal, instead of international armed conflict, and the fact of involvement in the negotiations of a peace settlement by the United Nations, other international organizations and the representatives of states who subsequently signed it as "moral guarantors."[37] They found all these indications insufficient to reach the conclusion that the Lomé Agreement was an international agreement or instrument concluded under international law. They considered that international agreements created rights and obligations for the parties regulated by international law and found that this was not the case here. The agreement did not create obligations that are enforceable under international law. It did not matter that the national authorities chose to ratify the instrument, in compliance with their own domestic laws, since the classification of the transaction by Sierra Leone is not determinative of whether the agreement was concluded under international law and regulated by it.

Nonetheless, the Appeals Chamber conceded, "[t]hat [the Lomé Agreement] does not have that [international] character does not, however, answer the further question whether, as far as grave crimes such as are stated in Articles 2 to 4 of the Statute of the Court are concerned, it offer[ed] any promise that is permissible or enforceable in international law."[38] It therefore went further to address whether insurgents like the RUF had treaty-making capacity. After close analysis, the judges concluded that, though the law of armed conflict subjects armed opposition groups to the requirements to comply with at least the minimalistic provisions codified in Common Article 3 of the Geneva Conventions of 1949 which now amount to customary international law, that existence of a legal obligation to abide by the laws of armed conflict did not give them party status to the relevant treaties or confer any international legal personality on them.[39] Indeed, the status of the RUF organization was nothing more than that of an armed faction *within* Sierra Leone.[40]

---

[36]   *Id.* at ¶ 37. The Appeals Chamber uses the language of "international instrument," which is a broad term that captures many different types of documents, inclusive of both hard and soft law texts. This was necessitated by the reference to the defense counsel argument that the Lomé Accord had the status of an international(ized) instrument that was binding under international law because it had also been signed, in addition to the GoSL and the RUF, by the United Nations as well as foreign heads of states or their representatives. The judges rejected the argument on the basis that such signatures, to a negotiated settlement to end an internal armed conflict, could not create binding legal obligations for the moral guarantors that would then be enforceable under international law. For the opposite view, that such internationalized agreements as the peace accord do create international legal obligations which the SCSL considered and rejected, *see* P. H. Kooijmans, *The Security Council and Non-State Entities as Parties to Conflicts, in* INTERNATIONAL LAW: THEORY AND PRACTICE: ESSAYS IN HONOUR OF ERIC SUY 333–46 (K. Wellens ed., 1998). In a comment critical of the SCSL amnesty decision, another renowned jurist has concurred with Kooijmans. *See infra* footnotes 55–57 and accompanying text.

[37]   Lomé Amnesty Decision, *supra* note 6, at ¶¶ 6, 32, 41.

[38]   *Id.* at ¶ 42.

[39]   *Id.* at ¶ 47.

[40]   *Id.*

There was no evidence that the group had been recognized by any other states for the purposes of entering into any agreements with them.[41] It followed that the group had no rights enforceable under international law such as to permit it to claim that the government reneged on an undertaking that it had made to them under international law.

This argument may be criticized for missing the point. The real question was whether, as the Defense argued, Sierra Leone as a State accepted that an armed group in a non-international armed conflict can enter an international agreement with its own government and to what extent if any other states acquiesced in this decision. After all, in a non-international armed conflict third states will not have any interest in signing the peace agreement. But that does not prevent them from acknowledging that the agreement between Sierra Leone and the RUF as such can be a treaty that is regulated by the rules of international law (rather than a contract under domestic law). The situation was acknowledged to be different, by the SCSL itself, had the matter concerned a dispute concerning an international armed conflict. It may be that the Appeals Chamber was concerned about the consequences of accepting that there was a treaty between the GoSL and the rebels. This, however, would not have necessarily implied that the agreement between the two sides is valid for the purposes of retaining the amnesty, to the extent that it would not have been binding on the SCSL such as to prevent it from prosecuting the international crimes within its jurisdiction. The acceptance of some obligations under common Article 3 would seem to imply at least a narrow form of legal personality for the RUF, although the Lomé Agreement, not being a treaty, could also not as such serve to create legal personality for the RUF under international law.[42] The RUF being, for all intents and purposes, a mere faction within a state did not enjoy rights or obligations under its agreement with Sierra Leone on the basis of international law. The discussion of the Security Council's treatment of an agreement concerning UNITA and Angola, the so-called Lusaka Protocol, indicate that legal effects can flow from such agreements between insurgents and a state under international law. The difference, of course, is that the actions of the executive body of the UN itself would rest in its Chapter VII power under the Charter to take decisions that are binding on all UN Member States.

Turning to the second core issue, which is of special interest here, the Appeals Chamber considered whether international law would, in these circumstances, debar the SCSL from exercising jurisdiction over the defendants in regard to war crimes and crimes against humanity allegedly committed by them before the Lomé

---

[41] *Id.*

[42] *Id.*, at ¶ 49. A further point is that the reasoning of the Appeals Chamber could have been more precise. Even if one acknowledged the international legal personality of the RUF in the context of the discussion of common article 3, that does not in and of itself make any determination as to whether amnesties are allowed or not. That provision only prohibits engaging in certain actions, although the fear might have been that Additional Protocols still appear to be permissive towards amnesties.

Agreement. They rightly ruled that it would not. Furthermore, there was the additional issue whether adequate grounds had been pleaded to justify the exercise of judicial discretion to stay the proceedings based on the alleged abuse of process. They found this to not have been the case. Here, the judges distinguished the question of legal validity of the amnesty clause under the *municipal law* of Sierra Leone which was "not of prime importance in these proceedings"[43] since the challenge to jurisdiction based on the amnesty clause did not rest on its validity under Sierra Leone's domestic law.

In grappling with the "limits of amnesties," the Appeals Chamber first offered two working definitions of the concept of amnesty drawn from a dictionary and a US case.[44] The judges then went on to explain that grants of amnesties were based on the authority of the state exercising its sovereign powers which, in relation to offenses, is closely linked to the exercise of its criminal jurisdiction. However, where jurisdiction was for an "international crime"[45] and is universal in nature, a state such as Sierra Leone could not effectively deprive other states of their jurisdiction to prosecute the perpetrators through the grants of an amnesty. It is for this reason, according to the judges, that it was "unrealistic to regard as universally effective the grant of amnesty by a State in regard to grave international crimes in which there exists universal jurisdiction. A State cannot bring into oblivion and forgetfulness a crime, such as a crime against international law, which other States are entitled to keep alive and remember."[46]

This reasoning seems attractive, especially at the normative level, considering where international criminal law might need to go to fulfill the yearnings of victims for some justice. Indeed, it is hard to argue that one state should be able to take measures that would unilaterally permit it to defeat the protections conferred by international law in this case to the victims of armed conflict. At the same time, the analysis seems beg the question. The reason is that the crucial question is not whether an amnesty is effective, but whether there is legal power residing in the sovereign state purporting to grant it to grant it all. The point is that it is possible that there will be a limitation, under international law, for a state seeking to assert such an authority to grant an unconditional pardon. To the extent that it has obligations binding on it that renders such amnesty nugatory.

Recognizing that not all crimes within the competence of the SCSL were necessarily "susceptible to universal jurisdiction,"[47] the Appeals Chamber reasoned that the crimes under Sierra Leonean law in Article 5 of the SCSL Statute were excluded from the purview of Article 10, but that the remaining international crimes (specified in Articles 2 to 4 of the Statute) were grave crimes of an international

---

[43]   *Id.* at ¶ 50.
[44]   *Id.* at ¶ 66.
[45]   *Id.* at ¶¶ 67–68.
[46]   *Id.* at ¶ 67.
[47]   *Id.*

nature which attracted universal jurisdiction. Here, those crimes were being prosecuted by an international penal court. Accordingly, it went on to review international practice regarding the effectiveness or otherwise of amnesty granted by a state and noted the inconsistencies in state practice on the prohibition of amnesty for crimes against humanity.[48] Thereafter, the Appeals Chamber concluded that the amnesty granted by Sierra Leone cannot extend to cover crimes under international law given the nature of those crimes which are also subject to universal jurisdiction.[49] The main argument in favor was that Sierra Leone could not, as one state, sweep such crimes into oblivion which other states have a duty to remember and the jurisdiction to prosecute such crimes given that "the obligation to protect human dignity is a *peremptory norm* and has assumed the nature of obligation *erga omnes.*"[50] In this view, such a conferral of amnesty would not only be incompatible with international law, but also a clear violation of the superior character of *jus cogens* over other international legal norms as well as the obligation that a state may owe towards the international community as a whole.

It can be argued that much of this discussion was unnecessary as it seems doubtful that current state practice, which admittedly seems to be changing, supports an expansive or absolutist positions on conditional or qualified amnesties. The situation may be starkly different in relation to blanket amnesties. In any event, the concept of peremptory norms first and foremost concerns the question how to resolve normative superiority in conflicting treaty obligations. This will require that there be a duty on the part of Sierra Leone to protect human dignity, whatever that may mean, and as part of this prohibit those crimes and even put a mechanism in place to investigate and prosecute them. Though abhorrent, it is hard to justify at present that there is such a duty for states as a matter of positive obligation under international law. In fairness to the Appeals Chamber, the point does raise a question about the possible legal consequences of *jus cogens*. If such a duty exists, it could serve to essentially nullify any grant of amnesty by Article IX of the Lomé Agreement since, as a result of Articles 53 and 64 of the Vienna Convention on the Law of Treaties, it would be void and devoid of legal effects under international law. In addition, the *erga omnes* effect of peremptory obligations may allow for the invocation of state responsibility. Put differently, the *erga omnes* nature of such an obligation may entitle a state to invoke responsibility of another state under international law, meaning that other states might still retain the right to demand prosecution by the amnesty granting state. Or, if more plausibly if they so choose, they could assert their jurisdiction to investigate or prosecute the perpetrator of the international crime themselves if the offense is one that attracts universal jurisdiction.

[48]   *Id.* at ¶ 71.
[49]   *Id.*
[50]   *Id.* (emphasis added).

In the final step of its reasoning, the Appeals Chamber had one last issue to resolve, which was that whether the amnesty is unlawful under international law becomes a concern only if it were considering the question whether Article IX of the Lomé Agreement can constitute a legal bar to prosecution of the defendants by another state or by an independent international tribunal. This might have been the useful path to pursue from the outset, since they might have necessarily found the answer that there was no such limitation. As a result, the Appeals Chamber could have readily disposed of the question and the follow-on sub-issue whether the GoSL undertaking contained in Article IX was a valid ground for holding that the prosecution of the defendants was an abuse of process that should operate to stay the proceedings. Here, noting the fairness element underpinning the abuse of process doctrine, the Court agreed with the *amici curiae* that given the existence of a treaty obligation to prosecute or extradite the types of crimes before the SCSL, the amnesty was not effective especially vis-à-vis the right of other states or an international court to try them.[51]

Pursuant to Article 10 of the SCSL Statute, which was an express directive in the founding statute, stating that no amnesty granted to any person within the Tribunal's jurisdiction would bar his prosecution, the judges opined that it would be unlawful for the Court to ignore or circumvent the text of the clause under the guise of exercising an inherent discretionary power to block proceedings solely on the strength of such a purported amnesty.[52]

As regards the legality of amnesties, the judges accepted the Prosecution argument that though there was nothing under present international law prohibiting amnesties explicitly, there is a "crystallising international norm that a government cannot grant amnesty for serious violations of crimes under international law."[53] This position would appear to be correct, given that there is limited contradicting state practice granting amnesties to persons for grave crimes as a way to end conflicts. In any case, even if it is assumed that Sierra Leone may not have breached customary law in granting an amnesty, the Court would be entitled in the exercise of its *discretion* "to attribute little or no weight to the grant of such amnesty which is contrary to the *direction in which customary international law is developing* and which is contrary to the obligations in certain treaties and conventions the purpose of which is to protect humanity."[54]

It seems notable that the Appeals Chamber did not offer many examples of state practice to support its argument on the ultimate question. This seems instructive as it may be that what evidence there is, in terms of such practice regarding use or non-use of amnesties, might instead better support the (opposite) conclusion that states tend to grant amnesties even in respect of core international crimes as a way of

---

[51] *Id.* at ¶ 73.
[52] *Id.* at ¶ 80.
[53] *Id.* at ¶ 82.
[54] *Id.* at ¶ 84 (emphasis added).

settling or ending bitter conflicts. The irony is that this was in fact the attitude of the GoSL, which in the statement of President Kabbah discussed at the opening of this chapter, did not at all consider that Sierra Leone felt constrained in any way by international law to *not* give amnesty to the RUF and all combatants involved in the war for atrocity crimes. That, of course, was until President Kabbah ran into some trouble with the rebels due to their recalcitrance.

In summary, to recap the Appeals Chamber's key conclusions, the judges determined, first, that the invalidity of Article 10 of the Statute had not been successfully established by the defense for Kallon and Kamara. That clause contained an express statutory limitation on the discretion of the Court to decline jurisdiction on the sole ground that an amnesty had been granted to a particular defendant. Second, they ruled that whatever effect the amnesty granted in the Lomé Agreement may have on the prosecution of crimes under the national law of Sierra Leone, it was completely ineffective in removing the universal jurisdiction of others to prosecute persons accused of such offenses. Other states may have, by reason of the gravity and nature of the crimes, an interest in pursuing those crimes. They would continue to be free to do so. Moreover, and in any case, the defense argument was unhelpful in depriving an international penal tribunal such as the independent SCSL with its own separate legal personality of its jurisdiction. These are important contributions to the emerging norm against the availability of amnesties in international criminal tribunals.

9.5 THE SCSL'S CONTRIBUTION TO THE DEBATE ON THE LEGALITY OF AMNESTIES FOR INTERNATIONAL CRIMES UNDER INTERNATIONAL LAW

9.5.1 *Negative Scholarly Reactions to the SCSL's Amnesty Decision*

Scholarly reviews of the SCSL's decision on the amnesty have been mixed. As seems routine, when it comes to decisions of the Appeals Chamber on these types of weighty topics, some have applauded the findings while others have been more critical of them. I take what strikes me as a roughly representative sample of views. For instance, Schabas, a leading scholar in international criminal law, has lamented that rather than "promote incremental progress in this area," the Lomé Agreement decision is likely to be "dismissed as a superficial and exaggerated treatment" of the complex amnesty question.[55] But Schabas' skepticism about the weakness of the judicial conclusions and reasoning underpinning the amnesty decision, which he also described as using "extravagant language,"[56] is far from unique.

---

[55] William A. Schabas, *Amnesty, the Sierra Leone Truth and Reconciliation Commission and the Special Court for Sierra Leone*, U.C. DAVIS J. INT'L LAW & POL'Y 145, 163 (2004).

[56] *Id.*

Another renowned commentator, the now late Italian jurist Cassese, had argued that the SCSL "arrived at the right solution" on the amnesty issue.[57] However, he also equally concluded that the judicial reasoning "amassed disparate legal grounds, often without any apparent nexus between them, and in some respects even contradictory" points leading to the conclusion that rather than use the opportunity to clarify key principles of international law on a difficult topic resulted in "legally flawed reasoning" that was overall "obscure and unnecessarily tortuous."[58] In other words, he liked the result, but not the manner in which the judges got to it. Perhaps, in part for that reason and likely in anticipation of other scenarios in which the question of the international legal validity of amnesties will no doubt arise in the future, Cassese helpfully suggested an alternative path that the Appeals Chamber could have taken to more simply resolve the amnesty question.

He suggested four simpler steps towards resolution of the issue would have been to examine (1) whether the peace accord was a binding treaty under international law; (2) if it determined that it was not, consider whether nonetheless the passage of domestic law implementing the agreement could have any legal impact on the international proceedings, and in particular, whether it could in some way nullify Article 10 of the SCSL Statute; or (3) if alternatively it decided that the treaty was binding under international law, ask whether it subsequently became void or was cancelled either because the RUF ceased to exist or on any other valid legal ground; or (4) had it held that the accord had been terminated, whether it could still produce legal effects under national law of Sierra Leone as a result of the previous implementation law, and in any case, whether those domestic effects had any impact on Article 10.[59] This is a constructive approach, paving the way for other courts that may in the future be asked to rule on the issue to improve upon the reasoning of the SCSL Appeals Chamber.

9.5.2 *Scholarly Support for the SCSL's Amnesty Decision*

On the other hand, Sadat, another prominent international criminal law commentator, has praised the Appeals Chamber decision. She concludes that "a fundamental contribution" of the SCSL decision "was the specific linkage made between the universal nature of international crimes within the SCSL Statute and the ineffectiveness of amnesties therefore."[60] She observed that many discussions of amnesties "avoid the question of the legal status of the crimes in question" and lauded the SCSL for making that explicit connection.[61] Indeed, the appeals judges linked the

---

[57] Antonio Cassese, *The Special Court and International Law: The Decision Concerning the Lomé Agreement Amnesty*, 2(4) J. INT'L. CRIM. JUSTICE 1130 (2004).

[58] *Id.*

[59] *Id.* at 1140.

[60] Leila Sadat, *The Lomé Amnesty Decision of the Special Court for Sierra Leone, in* THE SIERRA LEONE SPECIAL COURT AND ITS LEGACY: THE IMPACT FOR AFRICA AND INTERNATIONAL CRIMINAL LAW 311–24 (Charles C. Jalloh ed., 2014).

[61] *Id.* at 314.

nature of the crimes and their condemnation under international law to the invalidity of the amnesty under international law.

Meisenberg, while also conceding that some of the statements of the Appeals Chamber were "controversial" and perhaps even too sweeping, has also gone further and claimed that the Lomé amnesty decision "is of critical importance for the development of international humanitarian law."[62] Nonetheless, towards the conclusion of his article, he caveated the earlier position by finding that it was merely "a step towards the abolition of the blanket amnesties for mass atrocities rather than a landmark in the development of international humanitarian law."[63] With such disparate assessments, on the negative (Schabas, Cassese) and positive sides (Sadat, Meisenberg), the challenge may be to seek the middle.

9.5.3 *Finding the Middle Ground: the SCSL Amnesty Ruling As a Modest Contribution*

For my part, I share in some of the skepticism expressed by Schabas and Cassese about the SCSL's legal reasoning on the question of the international legal validity of the amnesty contained in the Lomé Agreement. At the same time, like Sadat and Meisenberg, I tend to believe that the SCSL decision adds a new dimension to the amnesty debate, though I would not go so far as the Appeals Chamber did. In my view, much of what was said was unnecessary for the Appeals Chamber to address and dispose of the central question before it. That narrower question should have been whether, in view of the status of present international law, the blanket Lomé amnesty offered by the Sierra Leone Government in the July 1999 accord operated to potentially debar the subsequent proceedings before the SCSL. The Court can but perhaps did not need to pronounce on the wider issue beyond whether Article IX or amnesties more generally breached international law. This argument finds support from the reasons that Schabas and Cassese have given. It also finds a basis in the following additional considerations.

First, due in large part to the near unique fact pattern of the Sierra Leone conflict, the Appeals Chamber decision was among the first by an international criminal tribunal to tackle the question whether amnesties can be used to block the prosecution for core international crimes before an international criminal court. Indeed, although the ICTY had postulated somewhat on the status of amnesties in the *Furundzija* Judgment in the context of its discussion of the criminal prohibition of torture as entailing a duty to prosecute under universal jurisdiction and holding a *jus cogens* status,[64] that decision had been limited to amnesties pertaining specifically to

---

[62] *See generally* Simon M. Meisenberg, *Legality of Amnesties in International Humanitarian Law: The Lomé Amnesty Decision of the Special Court for Sierra Leone*, 86 INT'L REV. RED CROSS 837 (2004).

[63] *Id.* at 851.

[64] *See* Prosecutor v. Furundzija, Case No., IT-95-17/1-T, Judgment (Int'l Crim. Trib. for the Former Yugoslavia Dec. 10, 1998).

the crime of torture rather than the larger category of *serious international crimes* more broadly. The decision of the Appeals Chamber here drew a useful distinction between the applicability of amnesties and pardons to crimes under municipal law as a sovereign act of a state compared to the availability of that option when it comes to international offenses being prosecuted before an international penal tribunal. The SCSL judges emphasized that, whereas it may be entirely up to the national authorities to determine whether to prosecute rebels or not to do so, since there was no rule against rebellion in international law, a state does not have the same choice to "dispense with the prosecution of the alleged offenders"[65] who might have engaged in perpetrating international crimes. The idea that international law imposes duties that may limit the freedom of action of a state is not new. It is an idea that animated the work and judgment of the Nuremberg Tribunal. This point could perhaps be a useful point of departure to articulate for future analyses of these issues. It is therefore added value to discussions of amnesties in the context of internal armed conflicts.

Second, the Appeals Chamber decision clarified that even where a given jurisdiction (like Sierra Leone) decides to grant an unconditional or blanket amnesty, it does not follow that this is determinative in blocking the prosecution of grave crimes in a subsequent international tribunal established explicitly to prosecute. Surely this is correct, especially where such a tribunal enjoys the support of or is created by the international community. Nor would such actions bind another state wishing to assert universal jurisdiction in order to prosecute the perpetrators. This can be seen as an additional useful clarification given that the same states, such as Sierra Leone, could well have independent duties to prosecute or extradite persons who commit the types of grave crimes committed in the armed conflict. This not only goes to the lack of effectiveness of one state's choice when it decides to amnesty combatants for international crimes, it also raises a question of whether it would have violated its prior international legal duty to investigate, and if it has sufficient evidence, to prosecute by conferring the unconditional amnesty in the first place.

Another commentator has criticized the Appeals Chamber on the argument that it could have been more methodical in its approach to the amnesty issue and in that way added even greater value to the debate through its Lomé amnesty decision.[66] The present writer agrees. The reason is that, while it is evident that under the Geneva Conventions to which Sierra Leone was and is still bound there are "grave breaches" in respect of which the *aut dedere aut punire* (prosecute or extradite) obligation will arise, it is not entirely clear that this would be the same obligation given the specific war crimes (which are *not* considered grave breaches) that were the ones at issue in the SCSL Statute.[67] Grave breaches, of course, exist and are

[65] Lomé Amnesty Decision, *supra* note 6, at ¶ 20.

[66] *See* Meisenberg, *supra* note 62.

[67] Geneva Convention for the Amelioration of the condition of the wounded, sick and shipwrecked members of the armed forces at sea art. 49, Dec. 8, 1949, 75 U.N.T.S. 85; Geneva Convention for the

widely recognized in the context of international armed conflicts, and generally, the SCSL Statute did not include them. The judges had in a different decision ruled that the Sierra Leone conflict was a non-international armed conflict. The statute of the tribunal implicitly recognizes this because the codifications of war crimes pertain to those that would be serious violations applicable, as is the case of the ICTR, only in internal armed conflicts.

The legal question therefore arises whether the judges were making too much of a leap to universal jurisdiction. That connection presupposes in some treaty form or another customary law basis the prior existence of a war crime which is prosecutable regardless of geographic location or the nationality of the perpetrator or the victim. Indeed, it seems undisputed, as a matter of treaty law, that there is no prosecute or extradite provisions for serious violations of Common Article 3 to the Geneva Conventions and Additional Protocol II – the bulk of the codifications in Articles 3 and 4 of the SCSL Statute. This is why any such contraventions may not necessarily automatically be deemed universal jurisdiction offenses.

True, the Appeals Chamber cited *Eichmann*, the *Hostage* case, and *Arrest Warrant* for the dictum on universality to strengthen its legal position.[68] But the former two cases involved war crimes and crimes against humanity within the context of *international* armed conflicts. The latter, *Yerodia*, which is discussed in Chapter 8 of this book, addressed the different question of immunity from prosecution for international crimes of the foreign minister of the Democratic Republic of the Congo before the national courts of another state (Belgium). The International Court of Justice (ICJ), which has also been criticized for this methodology elsewhere, did not reach the question whether certain international crimes such as those codified in the SCSL Statute qualify as universal jurisdiction offenses.[69] Indeed, while discussing the existence of such a duty in relation to torture, the ICJ itself has since determined the similar question of the status of torture under the treaty provisions of the Convention Against Torture and found that the issue whether a duty to prosecute that would root universal jurisdiction exists under customary

Amelioration of the Condition of the Wounded and Sick in Armed Forces in the Field, art. 51, Dec. 8, 1949, 75 U.N.T.S. 31; Geneva Convention Relative to the Treatment of Prisoners of War, art. 130, Dec. 8, 1949 75 U.N.T.S. 135; Geneva Convention Relative to the Protection of Civilian Persons in Time of War art. 147, Dec. 8, 1949, 75 U.N.T.S. 287; are all considered *grave breaches* that are explicitly recognized as violations that would give rise to universal jurisdiction. It can be noted here that Additional Protocol I (1977) also introduced additional grave breaches. Whereas those under the Geneva Conventions are all considered as customary international law; the latter are not. The statutes of the ICTR, the SCSL, and the ICC all include various serious violations that are only applicable in non-international armed conflicts as part of their war crimes provisions. But, crucially for the argument here, these are not generally considered, at present, to be universal jurisdiction offenses.

[68] Lomé Amnesty Decision, *supra* note 6, at ¶ 70.
[69] Arrest Warrant of 11 April 2000 (Dem. Rep. Congo v. Belg.), Judgment, 2002 I.C.J. Rep. 3, at 63 ¶¶ 3–5 (Feb. 14) (separate opinion by Judges Higgins, Kooijmans, and Buergenthal) [hereinafter Arrest Warrant of 11 April 2000].

international law is a separate legal matter.[70] It follows that it is hard to accept the SCSL Appeals Chamber ruling under which it lumped all the war crimes within its jurisdiction with the grave breaches regime, which they are not, thereby erroneously labeling them all as universal jurisdiction offenses.[71]

But this argument, though seemingly fair, should not be overstated.[72] The Appeals Chamber reflected some awareness of this difficulty through its statement that "not every activity" that amounts to an international crime is "susceptible to universal jurisdiction."[73] Certainly, with that concession, the judges could have been more methodical in their decision on the existence of universal jurisdiction for the specific war crimes in the SCSL Statute. All the more so because some of the prohibitions apply only in respect of non-international (that is, internal) armed conflicts. By the same token, given the customary international law restatement of the International Committee of the Red Cross (ICRC), it can perhaps be argued in a good (not yet strong) defense of the Appeals Chamber of the SCSL that international law and practice now allows for the inclusion of serious violations of Common Article 3 to the Geneva Conventions and Additional Protocol II in the list of crimes subject to universal jurisdiction.[74]

Whatever the case, the Appeals Chamber might have also been more careful in separating the issue of the exercise of criminal jurisdiction whether or not rooted in universal jurisdiction as a basis for national prosecution by a state from the unavailability of an amnesty granted under that country's domestic law before an international criminal court like the SCSL. The idea of universal jurisdiction is, of course,

---

[70]   Questions Relating to the Obligation to Prosecute or Extradite (Belg. v. Sen.), Judgment, 2012 I.C.J. Rep. 422 ¶ 83 (July 20). For thoughtful commentary, see André Nollkaemper, *Wither Aut Dedere? The Obligation to Extradite or Prosecute after the ICJ's Judgment in Belgium v Senegal*, 4(3) J INT. DISP. SETTLEMENT 501 (2013) (examining the ICJ's pronouncement on the duty to prosecute or extradite alleged torturers and finding paradoxes arising from the implications of the ruling).

[71]   In fact, scholars remain divided as to whether there is a legal duty to prosecute war crimes, crimes against humanity and genocide which would give rise to valid assertions of universal jurisdiction. For prominent commentators in favor, see, Diane F. Orentlicher, *Settling Accounts: the Duty to Prosecute Human Rights Violations of a Prior Regime*, 100 YALE L. J. 2537, 2593 (1999); M. Cherif Bassiouni, *Crimes Against Humanity: The Case for a Specialized Convention*, 9 WASH. U. GLOBAL STUD. L. REV. 575, 588 (2010); Jordan J. Paust, *Genocide in Rwanda, State Responsibility to Prosecute or Extradite, and Nonimmunity for Heads of State and Other Public Officials*, 34 HOUS. J. INT'L L. 57, 66 (2011). For a sampling of others against, see Claus Kress, *Reflections on the Iudicare Limb of the Grave Breaches Regime*, 7 J. INT'L CRIM. J. 789, 809 (2009); Leila Nadya Sadat, *The Lomé Amnesty Decision of the Special Court for Sierra Leone, in* THE SIERRA LEONE COURT AND ITS LEGACY: THE IMPACT FOR AFRICA AND INTERNATIONAL CRIMINAL LAW 319–20 (Charles C. Jalloh ed., 2014) and Eveylon Mack, *Does Customary International Law Obligate States to Extradite or prosecute Individuals Accused of Committing Crimes Against Humanity?*, 24 MINN. J. INT'L L. 73, 96–97 (2015).

[72]   Prosecutor v. Tadić, Case No. IT-94-1-AR72, Judgment (Int'l Crim. Trib. for the Former Yugoslavia July 15, 1999) (effectively finding that there is a minimum standard of protection provided by the law of armed conflict and that the classification of the conflict may not be as material as might sometimes be assumed).

[73]   Arrest Warrant of 11 April 2000, *supra* note 69, at ¶ 68.

[74]   JEAN-MARIE HENCKAERTS & LOUISE DOSWALD-BECK, CUSTOMARY INTERNATIONAL HUMANITARIAN LAW 611 (2005).

relevant for the purposes of national prosecutions before national courts. The reason is that, if in such circumstances a national measure constitutes such an amnesty is endorsed as valid, it could preclude the potential prosecution of international crimes for which there might well be an international legal duty to prosecute. In this regard, it would indeed appear to be the case that depending on the status of the crime under discussion, a state may be prohibited from taking legal, administrative, or other measures such as granting an amnesty that would purport to absolve the perpetrators of the crime. Still, determining the jurisdictional basis for criminal prosecutions in relation to certain types of international crimes is something differ- ent from determining whether amnesties, conferred by another jurisdiction, would be legally recognized by another state. The latter assumes there was separately existent an international legal duty to prosecute the alleged perpetrator.

Put differently, the existence of universal jurisdiction for the crime could not be displaced by the choice of another jurisdiction to confer a domestic amnesty measure on the suspect. That would not in any event be binding on the jurisdiction asserting state.[75] On the other hand, on this same reasoning, it can be argued that the desire of the Sierra Leonean authorities to confer an amnesty on all the combatants engaged in atrocity crimes in exchange for peace could not plausibly have any legal effect on the mandate of the Tribunal. The Court had to follow its statute, and in an explicit provision, it had been told that anyone before it charged with the alleged commission of the offense is prosecutable. That there might have been an agree- ment, by two separate parties with independent legal personalities that were not before the court, was sufficient basis to deny effects to the immunity. A decision not to proceed would be purely discretionary.

Returning to the specific issue of serious violations, according to the ICRC, state practice already supports the conclusion that states are entitled to vest universal jurisdiction in their national courts over war crimes whether or not committed in international as well as non-international armed conflict.[76] The asserted proof of this is however apparently undermined by the fact that there are only a handful of trials carried out in national courts for war crimes committed in an internal armed conflict using universal jurisdiction. The effect of this is to perhaps devalue the claim that this is a position that can be sustained, even if one is wont to accept that there is some academic support for the ICRC position.[77]

---

[75] For a thoughtful account on the place of a duty to prosecute for core crimes and their relationship to amnesties, within the framework of the Rome Statute, *see* Darryl Robinson, *Serving the Interests of Justice: Amnesties, Truth Commissions and the International Criminal Court*, 14 EUR. J. INT'L L. 481, 483 (2003).

[76] WILLIAM SCHABAS, UNIMAGINABLE ATROCITIES 182–95 (2012) (setting out an argument challenging the plausibility of the ICRC's conclusion).

[77] Academics also seem torn on the issue. For example, Meron, who perceives a clear duty to prosecute for grave breaches but a right (not a duty), in relation to other serious violations of the Geneva Conventions. For more on this, see Theodor Meron, *Is International Law Moving Towards Criminalization*, 9 EUR. J. INT'L L. 18, 23 (1998). Conversely, because States have not as a general rule complied with this duty, the claim that it is customary law comes off as questionable. For more on

The third contribution of the Sierra Leone amnesty decision could well be illustrating how difficult it is to untangle fundamental legal questions such as the minefield about the validity of blanket amnesties under international law. The Appeals Chamber here added somewhat to the jurisprudence, but because its reasoning was convoluted, it ultimately undermined the weight of its findings. The judges, instead of considering whether the Lomé Agreement violated international law when it purported to offer an amnesty for international crimes and therefore not necessarily relevant to discussions about the possible culpability of the defendants before the SCSL, instead made two contradictory pronouncements.

In the first place, the Appeals Chamber seemingly rejected the Defense argument that amnesties are not, as of yet, unlawful under international law.[78] They could not therefore strike the amnesty on that basis. Instead, they found that, given the available state practice in the area, it is probably more accurate to say, as the Prosecution had argued, that there is a "crystallising international norm that a government cannot grant amnesty for serious violations of crimes under international law."[79] The appeals judges accepted the bare argument without a solid review of the state practice supporting this conclusion. According to the judges, in only a few paragraphs, evidence of this could be found in the duty to prosecute or extradite contained in a limited set of specific human rights treaties prohibiting genocide, torture, and war crimes, but also apparently in "quite a number" of the UN General Assembly and Security Council resolutions reaffirming the duty of states to prosecute such crimes.[80] The practice of the treaty bodies, for instance the Human Rights Committee, is said to offer additional support for the Appeals Chamber's position.[81] Not all these instances of practice seem convincing, or to fit the classical paradigm of conduct manifesting valid practice in relation to amnesties.

In the end, if the conclusion is correct that there is a rule against amnesties that is "emerging," it is unfortunate that, in the next step of its analysis, the Appeals Chamber assumed it rather than explicitly demonstrated it. A demonstration of it would have required a careful evaluation of the existence of (1) a general practice

---

this, *see* Antonio Cassese, *On the Current Trends towards Criminal Prosecution and Punishment of Breaches of International Humanitarian Law*, 9 EUR. J. INT'L. L. 2, 5 (1998) and M. CHERIF BASSIOUNI AND EDWARD M. WISE, AUT DEDERE AUT JUDICARE: THE DUTY TO EXTRADITE OR PROSECUTE IN INTERNATIONAL LAW 44–46 (1995).

[78]   Lomé Amnesty Decision, *supra* note 6, at ¶ 82.

[79]   *Id.*

[80]   *Id.*

[81]   As for amnesties, in General Comment No. 20 on art. 7 of the International Covenant on Civil and Political Rights, the Human Rights Committee opined as follows: "The Committee has noted that some States have granted amnesty in respect of acts of torture. Amnesties are generally incompatible with the duty of States to investigate such acts; to guarantee freedom from such acts within their jurisdiction; and to ensure that they do not occur in the future. States may not deprive individuals of the right to an effective remedy, including compensation and such full rehabilitation as may be possible." *See*, in this regard, the Compilation of General Comments and General Recommendations adopted by Human Rights Treaty Bodies, at 30, U.N. Doc. HRI\GEN\1\Rev. 1 (1994).

that is (2) accepted as law. In the assessment of state practice, a focus on the practices of states will have to be the primary emphasis, although in certain cases, the practice of international organizations and their organs such as the General Assembly might also be relevant. The judges decided to hold on the basis of references to a handful of treaties that were hardly applicable to the Sierra Leone situation. The claim followed that the international crimes stated in Articles 2 to 4 of its Statute and fact that there is universal jurisdiction for these crimes implied that the prosecution of such offenses reflects "the obligation to protect human dignity" which is "a peremptory norm and has assumed the nature of obligations *erga omnes*."[82] But this perhaps went a bit too far.

For one thing, the idea that there is a duty on states to protect human dignity is already broad enough and is of course widely known as a concept in the area of human rights law. Nevertheless, the assertion, in the context of an international criminal tribunal and process, is not carried much further by mounting it on the stilts of both *jus cogens* and *erga omnes* obligations. It was an apparent effort to boost its presumed validity. Furthermore, by its few rather inapposite examples, the entirety of the claim comes off as too simple. All the more so because, rather than prove their point, the tendency in the reported state practice might well be more that states – instead of rushing to prosecute hundreds of cases – choose to exercise universal jurisdiction rather selectively, even in respect of the most widely recognized of crimes such as genocide. In this wider context, it seems hard not to conclude that there might have been somewhat of a judicial misunderstanding of how customary international law is formed and how it intersects with treaty obligations. The difficult notions of peremptory or *jus cogens* norms have themselves, of course, been subject to considerable academic debate.[83] There also continues to be some questions about the legal consequences of *jus cogens* among jurists and states. This has even prompted the International Law Commission of the United Nations to open a study of the matter for which Dire Tladi of South Africa is Special Rapporteur. In the context of that work, the Commission has not examined the specific implications of characterizing any international crime as having a peremptory character.

Moreover, even if one were to accept for the sake of argument that these prohibitions to commit various crimes are all peremptory norms, it does not follow that the obligations to exercise (universal) jurisdiction to enforce those substantive obligations are *jus cogens* as well. The ICJ has recently confirmed as much when it maintained a distinction between substance and procedure.[84] Furthermore, as the

---

[82] Lomé Amnesty Decision, *supra* note 6, at ¶¶ 71, 84.

[83] *See, e.g.*, Anthony D'Amato, *It's a Bird, it's a Plane, it's Jus Cogens*, 6 CONN. J. INT'L L. 1 (1990); Gennady M. Danilenko, *International Jus Cogens: Issues of Law-Making*, 2 EUR. J. INT'L L. 42 (1991).

[84] Jurisdictional Immunities of the State (Ger. v. It., Greece Intervening), Judgment, 2012 ICJ Rep. 95 (Feb. 3) (explaining that a *jus cogens* rule is one from which no derogation is permitted but that the rules which determine the scope and extent of jurisdiction and when that jurisdiction maybe

ICJ confirmed, there is a wall separating substantive prohibitions and the procedural consequences that follow those. It might therefore be the case that the prohibition to commit these crimes (assuming this to be a peremptory norm) is not matched by a similar legal duty to assert the jurisdiction to entertain such claims. In fact, in a later paragraph of their decision, the judges determined that the grant of amnesty by Sierra Leone would not only be incompatible with but also amount to the breach of the obligation of the state towards the *international community as a whole*. The issue of obligations owed to the international community arises, for the most part, in the law of state responsibility; not the law of criminal responsibility.[85] This might have been another extraneous statement, since in any event, the chamber did not need to pronounce on it for the purposes of the limited motion before them.

Another troubling aspect of the SCSL amnesty ruling is that, besides the age-old challenge of deciding what would amount to accepted *jus cogens* norms, the purported duty to prosecute such crimes would hardly seem to fall in that special category of obligations.[86] The reason is that these new duties would have to be peremptory norms of general international law that are accepted and recognized by the international community of states as a whole as a norm from which no derogation is permitted. The widespread state practice relying on amnesties would seem to undermine such a conclusion.

To confound matters even further, having ruled that a norm towards the prohibition of amnesties is presently developing, the Appeals Chamber determined that

> even if the opinion is held that Sierra Leone may not have breached customary law in granting an amnesty, this court is entitled in the exercise of its discretionary power, to attribute little or no weight to the grant of such amnesty which is contrary to the direction in which customary international law is developing and which is contrary to the obligations in certain treaties and conventions the purpose of which is to protect humanity.[87]

It is of course for the Appeals Chamber to decide whether to exercise discretion in a given case. Nonetheless, as another commentator has argued, courts of law are meant to

---

exercised do not derogate from those substantive rules which possess *jus cogens* status, nor is there anything inherent in the concept of *jus cogens* which would require their modification of displace their application). The World Court has also upheld that approach even if the effect was that a means by which a peremptory rule might be enforced was rendered unavailable in Armed Activities on the Territory of the Congo (New Application: 2002) (Dem. Rep. Congo v. Rwanda), Jurisdiction and Admissibility, Judgment, 2006 I.C.J. Rep. 6, ¶¶ 52, 65, 125 (Feb. 3).

[85] Lomé Amnesty Decision, *supra* note 6, at ¶ 73.

[86] Questions relating to the Obligation to Prosecute or Extradite (Belg. v. Sen.), Judgment, 2012 I.C.J. Rep. 422 ¶¶ 94–95 (July 20) (holding that there was a duty on the part of Senegal, pursuant to art. 7(1) of the Convention Against Torture, to exercise its duty to prosecute an alleged torture the failure of which would engage its international responsibility; but noting that, while the treaty offers the option of extradition, this does not carry the same weight as it merely allows the State to relieve itself of the *aut dedere aut punire* obligation).

[87] Lomé Amnesty Decision, *supra* note 6, at ¶ 84.

apply the law as it exists today.[88] Not as *it might exist* tomorrow, or for that matter, the day or week or year or two from now. It further demands an answer to the vital question whether, if a norm is still developing as part of customary international law, something which the appeals court apparently conceded, the judges are free to exercise any "discretionary powers" to choose not to apply the existing law by attributing little if any weight to any grants of amnesties because the principle is "developing" in a particular "direction." The recent work of the International Law Commission (ILC) on custom serves to underscore both the twin-elements requiring both state practice accompanied by acceptance as law as the conduct of the state and the forms of practice and the evidence needed to establish the point.[89]

The preceding concern takes on a new significance considering that, rather than prohibit amnesties, there are only two references to *amnesty* in multilateral treaties and both of them appear to favor the concept or at least not condemn it. In the human rights context, under Article 6(4) of the International Covenant on Civil and Political Rights, it provides that "anyone sentenced to death shall have the right to seek pardon or commutation of the sentence. Amnesty, pardon or commutation of the sentence of death may be granted in all cases." Admittedly, this was used in a context of the possible application of the death penalty in a given jurisdiction and could be seen as a way to encourage its discontinuation by favoring the grants of amnesties or pardons in relation thereof.

More pertinently, however, Article 6(5) of Additional Protocol II to the Geneva Conventions and Relating to the Protection of Victims of Non-International Armed Conflict states that "[a]t the end of hostilities, the authorities in power shall endeavor to grant the broadest possible amnesty to persons who have participated in the armed conflict, or those deprived of their liberty for reasons related to the armed conflict, whether they are interned or detained."[90] Though there seems to be academic commentary as well as many recent rulings from human rights tribunals such as the Inter-American Court of Human Rights,[91] the European[92] and African Human Rights Courts

---

[88]   *See* Schabas, *supra* note 55, at 162.

[89]   *See*, in this regard, Michael Wood (Special Rapporteur on the Identification of Customary International Law), *Second Rep. on the Identification of Customary International Law*, U.N. Doc. A/CN.4/672 (May 22, 2014).

[90]   *See* Protocol Additional to the Geneva Conventions of 12 August 1949, and relating to the protection of victims of international armed conflict (Protocol I), Aug. 6, 1977, 1125 U.N.T.S. 3.

[91]   *See* Massacres of El Mozote and Nearby Places v. El Salvador, Merits, Reparations, and Costs, Judgment, Inter-Am. Ct. H.R. (ser. C) No. 252, ¶ 283, 296 (Oct. 25, 2012); Gomes Lund et al. ("Guerrilha Do Araguaia") v. Brazil, Preliminary Objections, Merits, Reparations, and Costs, Judgment, Inter-Am. Ct. H.R. (ser. C) No. 219, ¶ 148-49 (Nov. 24, 2010); Almonacid Arellano et al. v. Chile, Preliminary Objections, Merits, Reparations, and Costs, Judgment, Inter-Am. Ct. H.R. (ser. C) No. 154, ¶ 108, 110-11 (Sept. 26, 2006); Barrios Altos v. Peru, Merits, Reparations, and Costs, Judgment, Inter-Am. Ct. H.R. (ser. C) No. 75, ¶ 41 (Mar. 14, 2001); Gelman v. Uruguay, Merits and Reparations, Judgment, Inter-Am. Ct. H.R. (ser. C) No. 221 (Feb. 24, 2011).

[92]   *See* Marguš v. Croatia (No. 4455/10), Eur. Ct. H.R. 74 (2012); Abdülsamet Yaman v. Turkey, (No. 32446/96), Eur. Ct. H.R. 55 (2004); Okkah v. Turkey, (No. 52067/99), Eur. Ct. H.R. 76 (2006); Yesil and Sevim v. Turkey, (No. 34738/04), Eur. Ct. H.R. 38 (2007).

and Commissions,[93] the Extraordinary Chambers in the Courts of Cambodia,[94] the ICTY,[95] as well as the International Criminal Court,[96] which have in some decisions relied in part on the SCSL's Lomé Amnesty decision to find them incompatible with the rights of victims to receive justice, the Appeals Chamber did not even mention the Additional Protocol. Neither did it address how we should reconcile the presence of that permissive clause, which seems to rather be encouraging amnesty, with its holding that the principle may now be firmly established and admits of no exceptions because it is peremptory in nature. Nor, for that matter since they brought it up, did the judges consider the full implications of their position that states may not grant amnesties because it would give rise to a breach of obligations *erga omnes* (that is, those owed to the international community as a whole).

Perhaps even more significantly, the SCSL judges did not account for the empirical studies which suggest quite the opposite: That states have both historically and in the modern context continued to rely on amnesties to solve conflicts and other social schisms.[97] Indeed, it is regrettable that the Appeals Chamber, after having extensively quoted President Kabbah's statements and justifications for the grant of the amnesty under circumstances where the very survival of the State of Sierra Leone seemed to be at stake, failed to consider the wider policy impact of its ruling that sometimes amnesties are simply unavoidable as a way of ending armed conflicts. All the more so in circumstances where, as in Sierra Leone, the national authorities had failed to win the war, and, by pandering to the rebels, placed them in a stronger position to negotiate the terms of the peace agreement. In Liberia, as with South Africa, the promise of amnesty was integral to the conclusion of a peace

---

93   *See* Mouvement Ivoirien des Droits Humains (MIDH) v. Cote d' Ivoire, Communication 246/02, [Afr. Comm'n H.P.R.], ¶¶ 96–98 (July 29, 2008); Malawi African Association v. Mauritania, Communication 54/91, 61/91, 98/93, 164/97, 196/97, 210/98, [Afr. Comm'n H.P.R.], ¶¶ 81–83 (May 11, 2000); Zimbabwe Human Rights NGO Forum v. Zimbabwe, Communication 245/2002, [Afr. Comm'n H.P.R.], ¶¶ 196, 200 (May 15, 2006).

94   *See* Prosecutor v. Sary, Case No. 002/19-09-2007/ECCC/TC, Decision on Ieng Sary's Rule 89 Preliminary Objections (*Ne bis in idem* and Amnesty and Pardon) ¶¶ 40–51 (Nov. 3, 2011). *See also* Prosecutor v. Sary, Case No. 002/19-09-2007/ECCC/OCIJ (PTC75), Decision on Ieng Sary's Appeal against the Closing Order, ¶ 201 (Apr. 11, 2011).

95   *See* Prosecutor v. Erdemovic, Case No. IT-96-22-T, Sentencing Judgment, ¶ 28 (Int'l Crim. Trib. for the Former Yugoslavia Nov. 29 1996); Prosecutor v. Furundžija, Case No. IT-95-17/1-T, Judgment, ¶¶ 141, 155–56 (Int'l Crim. Trib. for the Former Yugoslavia Dec. 10, 1998).

96   *See* ICC-RoC46(3)-01/18-37, Decision on the Prosecution's Request for a Ruling on Jurisdiction under Article 19(3) of the Statute, ¶ 88 (Sept. 6, 2018) and ICC-01/11-01/11, Pre-Trial Chamber I, Decision on the Admissibility Challenge by Dr. Saif Al-Islam Gadafi pursuant to Articles 17(1)(c), 19 and 20(3) of the Rome Statute, ¶ 77, 61–76 (April 5, 2019) (citing several cases from the Inter-American, European and African Human Rights systems as well as the SCSL decision in *Kallon et al.* to conclude that "It follows that granting amnesties and pardons for serious acts such as murder constituting crimes against humanity is incompatible with internationally recognized human rights. Amnesties and pardons intervene with States' positive obligations to investigate, prosecute and punish perpetrators of core crimes. In addition, they deny victims the right to truth, access to justice, and to request reparations where appropriate.")

97   *See* MALLINDER, *supra* note 4.

accord which ended a long and bitter conflict. It may have helped to hasten Taylor's decision to step down and to accept not to be part of a future political dispensation in Liberia. In other situations in Africa, such as Uganda where the Lord's Resistance Army has been fighting the government for decades, it has been said that the involvement of the International Criminal Court without any willingness to yield any ground for a peace accord containing an amnesty may have led to the prolongation of one of Africa's longest running wars. In the Colombian context, the ICC – seized of the situation – has more or less looked the other way even as the country – a State Party – conferred an amnesty on the Revolutionary Armed Forces of Colombia (FARC) rebels. The difference is that a narrower and conditional amnesty seems to have been applied; something that might not have been the case in a world without the ICC looking over the national jurisdiction.

In short, while fully appreciating that these are now more policy-based rather than legal arguments, the SCSL took a strong legal position on amnesties that somewhat decontextualized its statements of law from the wider context in which they were formulated. The Sierra Leone TRC, on the other hand, did not take a similar stance. It did not, like the SCSL, try to wave its magic wand in order to impugn all amnesties not just in the specific situation before it but also internationally. Rather, the TRC carefully considered the pained circumstances in which Sierra Leone found itself in July 1999. It concluded in its final report that we can all recognize that it is generally desirable to prosecute perpetrators of serious human rights abuses especially where their gravity rises to the threshold of international crimes.[98] That was ideal in the typical scenario. At the same time, and I would submit that this is the better view, the TRC felt that it would be unwise to formulate a blanket rule that excludes *entirely* the potential availability of amnesties in the context of modern armed conflict as a way to end hostilities between warring parties. This would be unwise in scenarios where neither side is winning the war, and the commission of atrocities would otherwise continue.

One can appreciate the TRC position considering that, in South Africa for example, it would have been difficult – if not near impossible – for the inhumane system of apartheid to end were it not for some kind of political accommodation and amnesty compromise reached by Nelson Mandela and the racist apartheid government in Pretoria. This suggests that, at a normative level, the Appeals Chamber issued a decision that was not only legally hard to sustain, but also perhaps unwise in its potential application. For especially for the types of contemporary conflicts we see in Africa today, between states and non-state armed groups, it would seem fatalistic to take amnesties entirely off the table in peace negotiations on the basis that to do so would amount to a breach of international law.

---

[98] WITNESS TO TRUTH: REPORT OF THE SIERRA LEONE TRUTH AND RECONCILIATION COMMISSION, vol. 3B, ch. 6 at 4 (2004).

On balance then, and with the benefit of hindsight, it might have been more prudent for the SCSL Appeals Chamber to be more modest and hold that Article 10 of the SCSL Statute did not bar the prosecution of the specific defendants before the SCSL. The Tribunal, as an independent legal personality, was not legally obliged to give effect to the past decision of one of its founders (Sierra Leone) purporting to confer an unconditional amnesty on the rebels. It might have also been sounder had the judges considered the argument that President Kabbah made that the rebels in any event repudiated any gains they would have received from the accord because of forfeiture. This could have settled the matter without requiring an excursion into the intricacies of international law concepts such as universal jurisdiction or other far reaching legal propositions on the status of these as *jus cogens* or *erga omnes* obligations.

9.6 CONCLUSION

This chapter has examined the SCSL's decision on the legal effect of the Lomé amnesty under international law in light of the provisions of the SCSL Statute. It has considered the key reason that the Appeals Chamber advanced when it ruled, in effect, that amnesties are not available to national jurisdictions when it comes to the prosecution of international crimes. One can normatively agree with this part of this important SCSL decision. The judges were right that, taken to its logical conclusion, because of the principle of universality, one state such as Sierra Leone cannot hinder the ability of another state or an international criminal court like the SCSL to prosecute atrocities amounting to war crimes, crimes against humanity, and other serious violations of international humanitarian law. This finding assumes, of course, that there is a prior international law obligation to prosecute or extradite the concerned crimes. Viewed in this light, it can be said that the decision of the court in relation to the Lomé Agreement amnesty is generally a welcome addition to international criminal law case law. All the more so given the increasing tendency of some modern courts to find amnesties as generally incompatible with the human rights of individuals.

The difficulty is that the Appeals Chamber, in its decision, seemed to go well out of its way to pronounce itself on issues that were arguably a bit far removed from the immediate amnesty question with which it was confronted. They navigated their way into the choppy waters of treaty and customary international law in relation to amnesties and peremptory norms and obligations owed to the international community as a whole. Oscillating somewhat conveniently between the law as it is, and the law as it ought to be, the judges reframed the issues. They were able to simplify the difficult issues before them. They then arguably gave short shrift to sometimes strong defense counterarguments on the law. They also ignored the implications of their finding on significant issues of post-conflict policy. Seemingly fixated on the end goal that would justify the prosecution of the defendants before the SCSL, an end result with which I take no quarrel had they used a different and perhaps simpler route, they ignored the harder questions that would tend to contradict their judicial findings.

The irony was that this was contrary to the very fact pattern of the Sierra Leone conflict, which in the lead-up to the July 1999 peace accord reflects best the dangers of a hardline finding that amnesties can never be available to peace negotiators because international law *prohibits* them. Solid evidence of practice supporting such a conclusion was not given. One hopes that the position taken on this issue by the TRC, which was the other transitional justice mechanism that Sierra Leone had put in place (the first jurisdiction to have both mechanisms as discussed in Chapter 10), will be taken fully into account in future discussion of the pronouncements of the SCSL as the international community reconciles the compatibility of amnesties with the principle of individual criminal responsibility. Already, in the context of the work of other international bodies such as the ILC's draft convention on the prevention and punishment of crimes against humanity, the SCSL view frowning down upon amnesties has been invoked on several occasions. It seemed like a useful source within the context of discussions of the framing of obligation of states to investigate and prosecute crimes against humanity. It is likely that as the tide turns even more strongly against amnesties, even more reference will be made to the SCSL case law in the future, thereby amplifying its judicial legacy on the status of amnesties under international law.

Special Courts and Truth Commissions

10.1 INTRODUCTION

As we saw in the previous chapter, addressing the Special Court for Sierra Leone's (SCSL) treatment of amnesty for international crimes, societies emerging from civil and political unrest often face daunting challenges as they seek to transition from war to peace. A key consideration for such countries and the international community has been the question of how best to come to terms with the past while mapping out a viable route towards the future. The current panoply of judicial and non-judicial options range from criminal prosecutions to amnesties, reparations, institutional reforms, vetting, the establishment of truth and reconciliation commissions, and even the use of traditional justice mechanisms such as *gacaca* (Rwanda), *matu oput* (Uganda) and *palaver huts* (Liberia).[1] Often, some of these options on the "transitional justice"[2] menu are used in isolation in an attempt to address a legacy of past abuses. In a handful of situations, such as those in Sierra Leone, Rwanda, Central African Republic and Timor-Leste, a cocktail of more than one of these approaches have been tried simultaneously – as part of a broader attempt to help restore accountability and the rule of law.

Sierra Leone, which in January 2002 emerged from the brutal civil war notorious for its horrific violence and amputations discussed in Chapter 2, is a well-known example of a modern African state's struggle to address the devastating effects of conflict. The former British colony, located in West Africa, thus became a nerve center of experimentation with various transitional justice options. Initially, the government established a National Unity and Reconciliation Commission (NURC) in 1996 whose mandate was to identify the causes which alienated the citizens from the State and created conflict and division in the society.[3] The

---

[1] See M. C. Bassiouni, Introduction to International Criminal Law 938–39 (2nd rev. ed., 2013).

[2] By transitional justice, the reference is to "the full range of processes and mechanisms associated with a society's attempt to come to terms with a legacy of large-scale past abuses, in order to ensure accountability, serve *justice* and achieve reconciliation." See U.N. Secretary General, United Nations Approach to Transitional Justice: Guidance Note of the Secretary-General (Mar. 2010), www .un.org/ruleoflaw/files/TJ_Guidance_Note_March_2010FINAL.pdf.

[3] National Unity and Reconciliation Commission Act 1996 (Sierra Leone) [hereinafter NURC Act].

NURC was also tasked with investigating and reporting on injustices brought to its attention, including any "official violence"[4] to individuals as well as communities. It could recommend means of redress such as victim rehabilitation, reparation, and the conditions for the granting of amnesty to the culprits deemed responsible.[5]

But, just three years later, the government, as part of the "necessary price"[6] it was willing to pay to entice its adversaries to end their rebellion, agreed in the Lomé Peace Agreement signed in Togo in July 1999 to a pardon and amnesty for the Revolutionary United Front (RUF) leader Foday Sankoh.[7] It also conferred an unconditional amnesty, the legality of which was discussed in the immediately preceding chapter, on all other combatants, irrespective of which side they fought for, promising that no official or judicial action will be taken against them for anything that they had done in the pursuit of their objectives during the war.[8] To "sugar coat"[9] the "bitter pill,"[10] which it was asking the Sierra Leoneans to swallow, President Ahmed Tejan Kabbah instead advocated for a Truth and Reconciliation Commission (TRC or the Commission). The TRC, for which Parliament passed enabling legislation in February 2000,[11] was to be a forum for both victims and perpetrators to tell their stories. Victims were asked to forgive and forget. Perpetrators were urged to confess to their abuses. All for the sake of national peace and national reconciliation.

But the Kabbah Government's forgive and forget policy faltered not long after the controversial amnesty-laden and power-oversharing peace deal was signed. The RUF, which had apparent bargaining strength, took things for granted.[12] Members of its hawkish faction, which preferred to continue the fight instead of make peace, violated key terms of the peace agreement including by holding hostage 500 UN peacekeepers. Following demonstrations at the RUF Leader Foday Sankoh's house, in the capital Freetown in May 2000, over twenty-one unarmed demonstrators were killed. These two incidents angered the Kabbah government. It thereafter reversed

---

4   *See*, NURC Act, *supra* note 3, at § 6(2)(b).

5   *Id.*

6   Solomon E. Berewa, A New Perspective on Governance, Leadership, Conflict and Nation Building in Sierra Leone 143 (2011).

7   Lomé Peace Agreement Between the Government of Sierra Leone and the Revolutionary United Front of Sierra Leone art. IX (I), U.N. Doc. S/1999/777 (June 7, 1999) (granting Sankoh "absolute and free pardon") [hereinafter Lomé Peace Agreement].

8   *See Id.* at art. IX.

9   *See* William A. Schabas, *Foreword, in* The Sierra Leone Special Court and Its Legacy: The Impact for Africa and International Criminal Law xxv (Charles C. Jalloh ed., 2014).

10 His Excellency the President Alhaji Dr. Ahmad Tejan Kabbah, Statement before the Truth and Reconciliation Commission ("TRC") (Aug. 5, 2003).

11 Truth and Reconciliation Commission Act, Supplement to the Sierra Leone Gazette Vol. CXXXI, No. 9 (Feb. 10, 2000) (Sierra Leone) [hereinafter TRC Act].

12 Ahmed Tejan Kabbah, *Two Decades of Conflict and Democracy in Sierra Leone: A Personal Experience*, Institute for Security Studies: Situation Report (Apr. 13, 2012).

the forgive and forget policy in favor of punishment and retribution against the rebel leadership.[13]

In June 2000, President Kabbah sought United Nations assistance to establish an independent court to prosecute those responsible for the atrocities committed during the conflict, as set out in greater detail in Chapters 3 and 4 of this book.[14] The UN Security Council endorsed his request.[15] Thereafter, swift negotiations took place between the UN Secretary-General and the Government of Sierra Leone.[16] The parties signed a bilateral treaty in the Sierra Leonean capital Freetown in January 2002, to which was annexed the statute, in which the parties formally provided for the establishment of an independent Special Court for Sierra Leone (SCSL).[17] The SCSL's main purpose was to investigate and prosecute those bearing "greatest responsibility"[18] for war crimes, crimes against humanity, and other serious international humanitarian law violations perpetrated during the second half of the country's conflict. The Court's unique judicial contribution to our understanding of "greatest responsibility" personal jurisdiction in international criminal law was the subject of Chapter 5 of this work. The SCSL's legal legacy on the prosecution forced marriage as a crime against humanity and of child recruitment as a war crime were discussed in Chapters 6 and 7.

Sierra Leone domesticated the UN-SL agreement into national law with the adoption of the Special Court Agreement Ratification Act in April 2002, although it was also subsequently amended.[19] Secretary-General Kofi Annan appointed the judges, followed by the chief prosecutor and registrar in April and June 2002 respectively. Formal court operations commenced in July 2002. The majority of the Court's indictments were issued in March 2003. A handful of others followed in September 2003. Sierra Leonean authorities promptly arrested the suspects, nearly all of whom were in the country, and turned them over to the Tribunal for prosecution.[20] A number of others such as Sam Bockarie and Johnny Paul Koroma were not found.

The TRC, which was to be established within three months of the signature of the Lomé Peace Agreement, was delayed due to late passage of its implementing legislation. This finally occurred in Parliament in February 2000. It also encountered various

---

13   Permanent Rep. of Sierra Leone to the U.N., Letter dated 9 August 2000 from the Permanent Rep. of Sierra Leone to the United Nations addressed to the President of the Security Council, annex, U.N. Doc. S/2000/786 (Aug. 10, 2000).

14   *Id.*

15   *See* S.C. Res. 1315 (Aug. 14, 2000).

16   *See* U.N. Secretary-General, *Report of the Secretary-General on the Establishment of a Special Court for Sierra Leone*, U.N. Doc. S/2000/915 (Oct. 4, 2000) [hereinafter *U.N.S.G. Report*].

17   Agreement between the United Nations and the Government of Sierra Leone on the Establishment of a Special Court for Sierra Leone, Jan. 16, 2002, 2178 U.N.T.S. 138 [hereinafter UN-Sierra Leone Agreement]. The Statute of the Special Court for Sierra Leone was annexed to the UN-Agreement and an integral part thereof [hereinafter SCSL Statute].

18   SCSL Statute, *supra* note 17, at art. 1.

19   Special Court Agreement 2002 Ratification Act (Sierra Leone) [hereinafter Special Court Agreement Ratification Act].

20   *See* Geoffrey Robertson (President of the Special Court for Sierra Leone), *First Annual Report of the President of the Special Court for Sierra Leone* (Dec. 2, 2002 to Dec. 1, 2003), www.rscsl.org /Documents/AnRpt1.pdf.

funding, management, and other start-up problems. The TRC's interim secretariat was established in March 2002. Formal opening was inaugurated in July 2002. Statement taking began in December 2002 and ended in March 2003. The TRC continued investigations and held public hearings between April and August 2003.[21]

The TRC and the SCSL, which shared common but also distinctive objectives, were launched around the same time. Due to their coincidental timing, the two entities ended up working in parallel for slightly under two years. During their overlap, the TRC was holding its public hearings while the SCSL was undertaking investigations, issuing indictments, apprehending suspects, and addressing preliminary legal issues in preparation for trials. Each of the two institutions worked in tandem, and again in another coincidence, within close proximity to each other in central Freetown.

However, by the time the SCSL began trials in June 2004, the TRC had effectively completed its work and was in the early report preparation phase. The truth commission process seemed more efficient, though given the nature of the TRC's role, it might be unfair to compare it to the criminal justice processes of the SCSL. In any event, its lengthy report consisting of four volumes was issued in October 2004 providing what appears to be the most comprehensive narrative to date of the causes and consequences of the Sierra Leonean conflict. For its part, over the course of several years, the SCSL successfully completed eight trials in Freetown and one in The Hague. All nine of the accused were convicted as is further discussed in Chapter 4. The Court rendered its first judgment in June 2007 and its last in September 2013, closing finally its doors in December 2013.[22]

The concurrent operation of the TRC and the SCSL, two traditional alternatives for post-conflict situations, was an unprecedented development for Sierra Leone and the international community. It led to intense debates about the nature of these mechanisms, their pros and cons, as well as the potential and limitations of their simultaneous operation in a single situation country. For these and other related reasons, the Sierra Leone case study has generated considerable interest in the transitional justice literature. The experience of this West African country could prove to be relevant given that nearly half of the fifty-five African countries have established a truth commission in one form or another. Several African States, including Central African Republic and South Sudan, have established both types of mechanisms in an attempt to bring both justice and reconciliation for their people.

10.2 THE PURPOSE AND STRUCTURE OF THIS CHAPTER

This chapter considers the key issues arising from the SCSL–TRC interactions in Sierra Leone. In Section 10.3, I examine the wider context from which the two

---

[21] SIERRA LEONE TRUTH & RECONCILIATION REPORT, WITNESS TO TRUTH: REPORT OF THE SIERRA LEONE TRUTH AND RECONCILIATION COMMISSION, vol. 1, ch. 2 (Oct.4, 2004) [hereinafter SL TRC REPORT].

[22] *See* Prosecutor v. Brima, SCSL-04-16-T-628, Judgment (June 20, 2007); Prosecutor v. Taylor, SCSL-03-01A-1389, Judgment (Sept. 26, 2013).

bodies emerged and their disparate functions as truth and criminal justice bodies. Section 10.4 traces the implications of the distinct theoretical goals and practical challenges inherent in operating the two institutions based on their respective mandates.

Section 10.5 evaluates the two most controversial legal issues that drove a wedge between the two institutions. First, the issue whether, due to the silence and presumed ambiguities in their legislation, the SCSL had primacy over the TRC such as to order it to turn over confidential information it may have collected from perpetrators with guarantees of confidentiality. Second, whether the suspects held by the SCSL should be permitted to publicly testify before the TRC. This despite the significant potential for them to incriminate themselves and therefore imperil their fair trial rights before the Court. This section explains how although several of the detainees expressed a willingness to appear before the Commission to offer testimony, the SCSL's concerns about the wider implications of this for the integrity and fairness of the trial process and the fragile security situation in Sierra Leone led to a denial of public hearings. That decision led to an unfortunate public dispute between the TRC and the SCSL, which in my submission, could have been largely avoided.

Overall, I conclude that a key lesson we can derive from Sierra Leone's experimentation with transitional justice is that ad hoc criminal tribunals cannot work successfully with truth commissions where they function in parallel without formal clarity in their founding instruments or a formal relationship agreement between the two institutions. It is possible that they can coexist as was the case in Sierra Leone. I suggest that anticipating how best to coordinate their respective roles, whenever used simultaneously as occurred in this scenario, could enhance synergy for future post-conflict situations. This would more likely allow each to play its distinctive function and thus contribute to the wider struggle for peace, justice, and reconciliation in the aftermath of conflict and mass atrocity in the situation country. Road testing the operation of these two separate institutions in tandem, which first occurred in Sierra Leone, constitutes a valuable SCSL legacy and contribution to the development of international criminal law and justice.

10.3 THE TENSION IN THE MANDATE OF THE SCSL AND THE TRC

10.3.1 *The Conflicting Goals of Truth Commissions and Criminal Tribunals*

It seems established that truth commissions, when compared to criminal courts, are primarily reconciliatory instead of punitive institutions.[23] They focus on the health

---

[23] *See* MARK FREEMAN, TRUTH COMMISSIONS AND PROCEDURAL FAIRNESS 33–34 (2006); PRISCILLA HAYNER, UNSPEAKABLE TRUTHS: CONFRONTING STATE TERROR AND ATROCITY (2001).

and healing of a whole society by seeking to determine what happened, why, when, and how.[24] They do so both to document the past, but also often, as a way to look towards the future. The attempt is to reconcile victims with their tormentors and indeed the rest of society as a whole.[25] Truth commissions therefore typically collect evidence through the conduct of investigations, taking of statements, and holding of public and private hearings.

In many of the over thirty countries that have experimented with them, truth commissions are often associated with grants of amnesty, whether conditional or, as in the case of Sierra Leone, unconditional. The assumption is that the combination of uncovering the truth coupled with recommendations for change might, if adopted and implemented, help to avoid a repetition of the mistakes of the past. The theory is that confronting, rather than running away from the demons of the past, gives a better chance for individuals and a given society to get past bad acts and reconcile and move towards a more secure and a more stable future.

Criminal courts, on the other hand, aim primarily at punishment, retribution, deterrence, and incapacitation.[26] They try specific persons charged with specific offenses. Prosecutors carry the burden to prove the culpability of the suspect beyond a reasonable doubt before an independent and impartial tribunal. The process is typically highly adversarial. Truth commissions, on the other hand, are often said to be better at achieving certain wider goals such as reconciliation.[27] In contrast, at least in the short-term, criminal trials are usually expected to exacerbate differences between the victims and perpetrators and between them, their supporters, and the rest of the community.

For our purposes, a key point to emphasize is that the SCSL's very creation was a negation of the government's expectation that a process such as the TRC alone would be sufficient to end the war. The creation of the Court signaled a major policy shift to try those that had threatened the peacemaking process. The decision to prosecute was thus a repudiation of the amnesty and a downgrading of the emphasis on reconciliation in favor of punishment, incapacitation, and deterrence of the rebel leadership and their collaborators who had carried out heinous offenses in Sierra Leone with impunity. The official government tune seemed to change to insist that, instead of being treated as outright substitutes, peace and reconciliation would be better strengthened if supplemented with criminal trials and punishment of the worst perpetrators.

Yet, the mandates of the SCSL and the TRC overlapped in great respects. Both were aimed at helping to heal a wounded nation secure a fragile peace, in the short-term, and enhance respect for human rights in the long-term. Simultaneously, there was serious potential for conflict too that we are beginning to see also in other more

---

[24]   BASSIOUNI, *supra* note 1, at 938–39.
[25]   *See* HAYNER, *supra* note 23, at 599, 604.
[26]   ROBERT CRYER ET AL., AN INTRODUCTION TO INTERNATIONAL CRIMINAL PROCEDURE 22–36 (2nd ed., 2010).
[27]   *See generally* ALISON BISETT, TRUTH COMMISSIONS AND CRIMINAL COURTS (2012).

recent situations such as that of Central African Republic which has established both a Truth, Justice and Reparation and Reconciliation Commission and a Special Criminal Court. For instance, the way a TRC collects testimony and compiles evidence when documenting history is substantially different from the manner and purpose for which prosecutors collect such evidence to establish an accused person's guilt before independent judges at a criminal court like the SCSL. The TRC process emphasized cooperation and communal participation in public hearings, whereas the SCSL process was adversarial and focused on the individual charged. Suspects also enjoy certain legal and procedural safeguards, as required by international law. Truth commissions do not need to have such safeguards, as they are focused on voluntariness and consent when they cajole the perpetrator to face victims. Thus, both types of mechanism can be mechanisms through which to advance the grander goals of peace, justice, and reconciliation for Sierra Leone. Though these were the constant refrains of the UN, this was insufficient to resolve the key differences in the TRC and the SCSL's emphasis, methodologies, and ultimately the outcomes of their separate processes.

In sum, there were inherent differences in the legal mandates and priorities of the two institutions as well as the legal norms to which each had to adhere. These dissimilarities, which in the context of the Sierra Leone case study are briefly highlighted next, increased the potential for an operational clash between them. The prospects for conflict were further exacerbated because the founders of the SCSL (that is, Sierra Leone and the UN) neglected to explicitly consider and spell out how the various legal differences in their functions could impact their daily operations.

10.3.2 *Comparing the Legal Basis and Functions of the SCSL and TRC*

The legal basis of the SCSL, as an international criminal court with jurisdiction to prosecute serious international crimes, was necessarily distinct from that of the TRC. The Commission, unlike the Court, was a *national* body created under Sierra Leonean law. It was an outcome of the agreement reached by the government and a non-state armed group within its territory – the RUF – to end the war and establish the facts of what happened as a way of promoting peace and national reconciliation. Similarly, the SCSL was the result of the treaty concluded by Sierra Leone, as a sovereign state, with an international organization (the UN) to create an independent *international* penal court that functioned independently and in the realm of international law.

The Sierra Leone Parliament passed the TRC Act in February 2000 to give effect to the Kabbah Government's undertaking in Article XXVI of the Lomé Agreement.[28]

---

[28] That clause provided that "[a] Truth and Reconciliation Commission shall be established to address impunity, break the cycle of violence, provide a forum for both the victims and perpetrators of human

It essentially provided for the creation of a body corporate with a five-part mandate to: (1) create an impartial historical record of violations and abuses of human rights and international humanitarian law; (2) address impunity; (3) respond to the needs of victims; (4) promote healing and reconciliation; and (5) prevent a repetition of the violations and abuses suffered.[29] The same legislature would later pass the statute implementing the SCSL Agreement between Sierra Leone and the UN.

In discharging these functions, which William Schabas has rightly observed had both "fact finding" as well as "therapeutic dimensions,"[30] the TRC had wider room to maneuver than the SCSL. The Commission was to investigate and report on the causes, nature, and extent of the violations to the fullest degree possible; the context in which the violations occurred and why; as well as address the role of both internal and external factors and entities in fomenting war in Sierra Leone. It was to also help restore the human dignity of victims by providing a conducive climate for them to tell their stories; to allow an exchange with their abusers; and do whatever other things the TRC found necessary to contribute to achievement of its wider mandate to help Sierra Leoneans reconcile with each other.[31] By comparison, the SCSL was largely a retributive body charged with investigation and prosecution of a small group of persons deemed most responsible for war crimes, crimes against humanity, and other serious international humanitarian law violations in Sierra Leone. The Tribunal was more interested in determining the guilt or innocence of the suspects before it, rather than in answering the question regarding what led to the outbreak of a vicious conflict in a formerly peaceful country.

Although primarily a Sierra Leonean institution, in contrast to the SCSL, which was basically an international body with some national features, the TRC also had several international attributes. First, in its composition, four of its seven members were Sierra Leonean commissioners.[32] But, by legislation, the other three were to be "non-citizens."[33] This was essentially the reverse of the situation at the SCSL where the Sierra Leonean government appointees were in the minority in the trial and appeals chambers.[34] In a way, then, the argument could be made that the TRC was more representative of the views of Sierra Leone.

The TRC's second international feature related to its mode of funding, which took the form of "gifts or donations"[35] from international donors (that is, foreign governments, intergovernmental organizations, foundations, and NGOs) much like

---

rights violations to tell their story, get a clear picture of the past in order to facilitate genuine healing and reconciliation." *See* Lomé Peace Agreement, *supra* note 7.

[29] TRC Act, 2000, *supra* note 11, at §§ 6–7.

[30] William A. Schabas, *A Synergistic Relationship: The Sierra Leone Truth and Reconciliation Commission and the Special Court for Sierra Leone*, 15 CRIM. L. F. 3, 8 (2004) [hereinafter Schabas, *Synergistic Relationship*].

[31] *See* TRC Act, *supra* note 11, at §§ 6–7.

[32] *Id.* at § 3(1).

[33] *Id.*

[34] *See* SCSL Statute, *supra* note 17, at art. 2 and art. 12.

[35] TRC Act, *supra* note 11, at § 12(1)(a).

the SCSL's funding structure.[36] Perhaps partly because they would rely on the same pool of donors, and partly due to the obvious overlap in their respective mandates, both were generally underfunded. Although, on balance, the Court fared much better than the truth commission. The SCSL unsurprisingly costed more given the nature of the criminal justice process.[37]

Finally, in the operationalization of the TRC, the UN played a significant role especially its Office of the High Commissioner for Human Rights (OHCHR). That subsidiary entity was responsible for helping to secure "*technical assistance* from the international community."[38] Various other UN agencies, including some in Freetown, also supported the TRC's work. In contrast to the SCSL, which had the role of investigating, arresting, prosecuting, and punishing those suspected of crimes, the TRC did not have a punitive mandate. It did, however, have some overlaps with the Court which received international coordination support both from the UN (including its peacekeepers in Freetown and the Secretariat in New York) as well as a Management Committee comprised of third party states which provided policy and management oversight.

10.3.3 *The SCSL–TRC Subject Matter Jurisdiction*

The TRC's and the SCSL's subject matter jurisdiction overlapped with each other. Under the TRC Act, the former was tasked with examining "violations and abuses of *human rights* and *international humanitarian law*"[39] including creating an unbiased historical record. It was to also identify and report on the "causes, nature and extent" of the war.[40] The TRC did not make guilty findings, but in its report, apportioned responsibility to the factions in the conflict. This included the suspects that were being tried by the Court.[41] The prospect for the latter had been a concern for the SCSL with the judges seemingly worrying that any such TRC findings could create public expectations and anxieties among prospective witnesses and defendants and prove damaging to the criminal proceedings before the Court. As Judge Robertson of the SCSL Appeals Chamber observed, the "truth" functions described in Section 6(2)(a) of the TRC Act could also be interpreted as permitting findings about individual responsibility which of course was the heart of the SCSL's function.[42]

---

[36]   The SCSL was funded by donations from interested states rather than the UN budget. These features of the SCSL are discussed in Chapter 3 of this work.

[37]   The Court, which was supposed to be justice on the cheap, ended up spending over $200 million dollars whereas the TRC was forced to make do with less than the initially projected $7 million. This led to serious delays in the Commission's work and hampered its operations.

[38]   TRC Act, *supra* note 11, at § 12(2).

[39]   *Id.* at § 6(1) (emphasis added).

[40]   *Id.* at § 6(2)(a).

[41]   SL TRC REPORT, *supra* note 21, at vol. 2, ch. 2.

[42]   Prosecutor v. Norman, Case No. SCSL-2003-08-PT, Grounds of Appeal by the Truth and Reconciliation Commission ("TRC" or "The Commission") for Sierra Leone and Chief Samuel Hinga Norman JP Against the Decision of His Lordship, Mr. Justice Bankole Thompson ("The

According to one academic commentator, the enabling Sierra Leonean legislation did not specify further the meaning of *human rights* or *humanitarian* law.[43] The Lomé Agreement appeared to limit "human rights" to civil and political rights.[44] However, the TRC could adopt a more complete view of human rights as also encompassing the indivisible economic, social, and cultural rights in addition to civil and political rights.[45] I support this holistic approach and interpretation. With respect to the TRC's jurisdiction over abuses of *international humanitarian law*, there was substantial overlap with the Statute of the SCSL which also included adjudication over war crimes, crimes against humanity, and other serious international humanitarian law violations. For their part, the SCSL's constitutive documents emphasized the Court's jurisdiction over two categories of offences: "very serious crimes" and "serious violations of international humanitarian law."[46] The former was a wider category in which the latter could also plausibly fall. However, the specific offenses within the latter were narrowed down by the specification of particular crimes as spelled out in the Statute of the SCSL.

10.3.4 *The SCSL–TRC Temporal Jurisdiction*

The differences between the TRC and the SCSL and their purposes were very pronounced in respect of their temporal responsibilities. The TRC's mandate tasked it with preparing an "impartial historical record"[47] of the war, which dated back to March 1991, through to the conclusion of the Lomé Peace Agreement in July 1999. The Commission was also empowered to examine the nature, causes and extent of the violations. This included the precursors to the conflict. This allowed it to examine earlier periods.

By comparison, the SCSL, as a criminal court concerned with assessing the culpability of specific suspects, did not have the same flexibility to ignore the start date of its temporal jurisdiction which, as we saw in Chapter 3, began on November 30, 1996.[48] And, although the SCSL had no formal expiry date for its jurisdiction, like the TRC, the end point overlapped with that of the Commission in relation to the period between November 1996 and July 1999 (the latter being when the final peace accord was signed). A proposal by the Sierra Leonean Attorney-General to avoid temporal overlaps between the two institutions did not find support, at the UN, as described in Chapter 3. So was Sierra Leone's proposal to have the temporal jurisdiction coincide with the start of the war. That too was

Decision") Delivered on Oct. 30, 2003 to Deny the TRC's Request to Hold a Public Hearing with Chief Samuel Hinga Norman JP, ¶ 15 (Nov. 28, 2003).
[43] Schabas, *Synergistic Relationship, supra* note 30, at 10–11.
[44] *Id.*
[45] *Id.*
[46] SCSL Statute, *supra* note 17, at art. 1.
[47] TRC Act, *supra* note 11, at § 6(1).
[48] SCSL Statute, *supra* note 17, at art. 1.

rejected by the UN which wanted to have a narrower time frame that the SCSL would cover in order to keep the caseload and thus overall cost low.

10.3.5 *The SCSL–TRC Territorial Jurisdiction*

The SCSL's jurisdiction, under Article 1(1) of the Statute, was limited to crimes committed "in the territory of Sierra Leone."[49] The TRC was not so geographically restricted. The enabling domestic legislation did not narrow its scope to investigations of events which took place *within* Sierra Leone. The key constraint, under its statute, was that the violations and abuses be related to the *armed conflict*. In fact, as part of its work, the TRC visited several countries in the West Africa region. This included refugee camps in Guinea and Liberia. It even attempted to reach out to diaspora Sierra Leoneans living much farther afield and to include their views in its final report.[50]

10.3.6 *The SCSL–TRC Personal Jurisdiction*

The TRC could not and did not prosecute anyone because it was not a court of law. At best its process can be described as quasi-judicial. This implies, as one commentator has rightly argued, that it might be inappropriate to speak of its "personal jurisdiction."[51] In a loose sense, however, we can discuss the TRC's personal jurisdiction if we define that to mean the power of the commission to bring someone into its adjudicative processes.[52] If one accepts that argument, and although a "commission" is obviously not the same as the "court," it is notable that whereas the SCSL exercised jurisdiction over "persons" deemed to bear "greatest responsibility" for serious international and humanitarian law violations committed in Sierra Leone, the TRC's enabling legislation focused on three categories of actors: (1) "victims"; (2) "perpetrators" of "abuses and violations"; as well as (3) "interested parties."

The law enabled the Commission to implement special procedures to address the needs of particular victims such as children who had suffered sexual abuse. In the SCSL Statute, as in other ad hoc international courts (although not the ICC), victims were only scantily mentioned and only in reference to the prosecutor's taking testimony from them, hiring of staff with expertise in matters of sexual violence affecting them, and the provision of protective measures through a specialized unit of the Court. The Rules of Procedure and Evidence fleshed out

---

[49]   *Id.* at art. 1(1).
[50]   SL TRC Report, *supra* note 21, at ch. 4.
[51]   Schabas, *Synergistic Relationship, supra* note 30, at 10–11.
[52]   Charles C. Jalloh, *Prosecuting Those Bearing "Greatest Responsibility": The Lessons of the Special Court for Sierra Leone,* 96 Marq. L. Rev. 863, 864 (2013) [hereinafter Jalloh, *Greatest Responsibility*].

aspects of this for the facilitation of witness testimony and even addressed the possibility of compensation.[53]

The TRC mandate also covered "perpetrators," the general focus of the SCSL.[54] Of course, the types of perpetrators before the TRC could include everyone from the highest leaders to the foot soldiers. Whereas, in the SCSL, the limitation of personal jurisdiction to those bearing "greatest responsibility" implied that the Court was only to focus on the so-called "big fish." Yet, as already analyzed in Chapter 5, the phrase was interpreted by the judges to also capture what I have in that earlier chapter described as "killer-perpetrators"[55] who may not hold ranking positions but were particularly vicious in their criminal behavior. The potential for conflicts stemming from this jurisdictional overlap was high. The TRC saw its historical narrative as being incomplete if it did not contain the testimony of leaders in the war. It also wanted the public hearing to be a basis for participation towards reconciliation of Sierra Leoneans. It therefore sought the suspect's appearance before the Commission. Those leaders, in the custody of the SCSL, being the ones who were indicted by the Tribunal. This, as will be discussed later on, is what animated the request that provoked a major row between the two bodies.

10.3.7 *The Failure to Define the TRC–SCSL Relationship in the Founding Instruments*

Since the TRC preceded the establishment of the SCSL, and had an overlapping and potentially conflicting mandate, one might have expected that Sierra Leone and the UN would have attempted to formally clarify the legal relationship between the two institutions. They failed to do so in the two founding instruments that were the constitutional basis of the SCSL. In fact, besides withdrawing the Lomé Peace Agreement amnesty provision and providing for diversion of child soldiers from prosecutions to rehabilitation mechanisms including to the TRC, there was no mention of how the two entities were to interact. This significant omission laid the groundwork for the SCSL and the TRC to later clash with each other.

Two provisions included in the SCSL Statute were relevant. The first addressed the amnesty question. This was the only issue that the parties could not avoid and still establish the SCSL. Here, the Secretary-General and Sierra Leone agreed to include a clause denying legal effect to it in relation to the international (not domestic) offenses that would be prosecuted by the Tribunal. Thus, as discussed in Chapter 9 in greater detail, Article 10 of the SCSL Statute stated that an "amnesty granted to any person falling with the jurisdiction of the [SCSL] in respect of the crimes referred to in articles 2 to 4 [that is, war crimes, crimes against humanity, and

---

[53] Special Court for Sierra Leone Rules of Procedure and Evidence, 24, 69, 75, 105 (Mar. 7, 2003), http://hrlibrary.umn.edu//instree/SCSL/Rules-of-proced-SCSL.pdf.

[54] TRC Act, *supra* note 11, at § 2(b).

[55] Jalloh, *Greatest Responsibility, supra* note 52, at 882.

other serious violations of international humanitarian law] of the present Statute shall not be a bar to prosecution."[56] The parties justified this on the basis that, although the Kabbah Government had promised all combatants immunity from prosecution in Article IX of the Lomé Peace Agreement, the representative of the UN Secretary-General at the talks had entered a disclaimer clarifying the UN's "understanding that the amnesty provisions of the Agreement shall not apply to international crimes of genocide, crimes against humanity, war crimes and other serious violations of Sierra Leonean law."[57] This caveat, which the TRC sharply criticized in its report, had also been mentioned in Security Council Resolution 1315 authorizing the Secretary-General's negotiations with Sierra Leone to create the Court.[58] Article 10 later proved crucial for the SCSL Appeals Chamber.[59] It supplied the legal foundation to dismiss the applications by the accused who claimed that it would be an abuse of process to ignore the dictates of the promised amnesty in the Lomé Peace Agreement – as argued in the preceding chapter.[60]

Besides the amnesty, the SCSL's founding instruments contained only one other reference to the TRC in Article 15(5). That article outlined the prosecutor's powers. It also stated that "[i]n the prosecution of juvenile offenders, the Prosecutor shall ensure that the child-rehabilitation programme is not placed at risk and that, where appropriate, resort should be had to alternative truth and reconciliation mechanisms, to the extent of their availability."[61] Article 15(5) had been included in the Statute, upon the suggestion of the UN Secretary-General, as a compromise between the two camps that emerged on the "difficult moral dilemma"[62] of whether to prosecute child soldiers, who were largely seen as victims, for any atrocities that they might have committed during the Sierra Leone civil war.

Besides addressing these exceptions (that is, the amnesty and the diversion of children to alternative measures), the nature of the TRC–SCSL relationship was remarkably vague. Secretary-General Annan's report on the SCSL confirmed that he would "not address in detail specifics of the relationship between the Special Court and the national courts in Sierra Leone, or *between the Court and the National Truth and Reconciliation Commission*."[63] However, he urged that once the SCSL was established and its prosecutor appointed, arrangements regarding

---

[56]   SCSL Statute, *supra* note 17, at art. 10.

[57]   *See U.N.S.G. Report, supra* note 16, at ¶¶ 22–24.

[58]   SL TRC Report, *supra* note 21, at vol. 3B, ch. 6 at ¶¶ 5–26.

[59]   Prosecutor v. Kallon, Case No. SCSL-2004-15AR72 (E) &SCSL-2004–16-AR72(E), Decision on Challenge to Jurisdiction: Lomé Accord Amnesty (Mar. 13, 2004).

[60]   For thoughtful commentary, *see* Leila N. Sadat, *The Amnesty Decision of the Special Court for Sierra Leone, in* The Sierra Leone Special Court and Its Legacy: The Impact for Africa and International Criminal Law 311–24 (Charles Jalloh ed., 2014); William A. Schabas, *Amnesty, the Sierra Leone Truth and Reconciliation Commission and the Special Court for Sierra Leone*, 11 U.C. Davis J. Int'l. Law & Pol'y 145 (2004).

[61]   *See U.N.S.G. Report, supra* note 16, at ¶¶ 32–38.

[62]   *Id.* at ¶ 33.

[63]   *U.N.S.G. Report, supra* note 16, at ¶ 8 (emphasis added).

cooperation, assistance, and information sharing would be made including with the TRC.[64]

This, especially in retrospect, was a big mistake. Not only should the SCSL legal framework have included clarity from the parties on how they expected the Court to function alongside the TRC, its practical operation had the potential to also impact both the legal mandate and practical work of the TRC. This later occurred. In the TRC's final report, it addressed this concern, noting that it would "have been helpful for the [UN] and [Sierra Leone] to lay down guidelines for the simultaneous conduct of the two organisations."[65]

To their credit, various UN agencies attempted to step in to address the SCSL–TRC interaction. In two reports, and subsequent correspondence, the UN mission in Sierra Leone and the UN OHCHR underscored the complementarity and mutually reinforcing nature of each of their respective mandates. Similarly, in a January 2001 letter to the Security Council, the UN Secretary-General warned that care should be taken to ensure that the two bodies "operate in a complementary and mutually supportive manner, fully respectful of their distinct but related functions."[66] Essentially the same message that the two entities must ensure that they work in a "symbiotic manner yet respecting their related but varied mandates,"[67] kept being repeated by UN officials. Nevertheless, despite all these statements, and the explicit consideration of their relationship in advance of the SCSL's creation, the TRC and the SCSL did not ultimately provide for any legal framework addressing what specific shape the formal relationship between the two bodies should take.

Although the founders failed to formally establish rules regulating the relationship between the SCSL and the TRC, experts and NGOs tried to help. The US Institute of Peace and the International Human Rights Law Group, as well as the International Center for Transitional Justice, all convened expert meetings to anticipate and map out how the two institutions might relate to each other in a way that was mutually supportive.[68] A subsequent discussion also took place in November 2000 after the draft statute of the SCSL had been released. The United Nations Assistance Mission for Sierra Leone and the OHCHR also convened expert meetings, curiously without the commissioners present, in which they highlighted the need for an "amicable relationship between the two institutions that would

[64]   *Id.*

[65]   SL TRC Report, *supra* note 21, at vol. 3B, ch. 6 ¶ 46.

[66]   U.N. Secretary-General, Letter dated 12 Jan. 2001 from the Secretary-General addressed to the President of the Security Council, ¶ 9, U.N. Doc. S/2001/40 (Jan. 12, 2001).

[67]   U.N. High Comm'r for Human Rights, *Report of the United Nations High Commissioner for Human Rights on the Human Rights Situation in Sierra Leone*, ¶ 51, U.N. Doc. A/56/281 (Aug. 9, 2001).

[68]   *See* Marieke Wierda, Priscilla Hayner, & Paul van Zyl, *Exploring the Relationship Between the Special Court and the Sierra Leone Truth and Reconciliation Commission*, Int'l Ctr. for Transitional Justice (2002) [hereinafter *ICTJ Report*]; Human Rights Watch, *The Interrelationship Between the Sierra Leone Special Court and Truth and Reconciliation Commission* (Apr. 18, 2002).

reflect their roles."[69] Many rightly felt that because the two entities were each aimed at addressing issues of impunity and accountability, understood in their broadest senses, that their activities should naturally be coordinated.

Three vital points emerged from these discussions.[70] First, that although the two institutions were established at different times and had different legal bases and different legal mandates, they performed "complementary roles" in so far as they all provided for accountability, a meeting point for victims and perpetrators, national reconciliation, and even the possibility of reparations.[71]

A second principle was that, although the SCSL enjoyed concurrent jurisdiction with primacy over the national courts of Sierra Leone, that type of framework ought not to be employed to regulate its interactions with the TRC. The Secretary-General's and the Security Council's various statements that the two should operate in complementary and supportive ways respectful to their distinctive mandates bolstered this argument.[72] Primacy would apply only in respect of the formal courts.

Third, experts recommended that cooperation between the two bodies should be cemented in a formal agreement between the two, and as appropriate, in their respective rules of procedure and evidence. This was to emphasize the independence of each and their distinctive responsibilities to Sierra Leoneans.[73] In 2002, the UN's Planning Mission to Sierra Leone, which was dispatched to Freetown to prepare for the arrival of the Court, also underscored the imperative for the two to "perform complementary roles. . . mutually supportive and in full respect for each other's mandate."[74]

Some NGOs even went further to propose detailed relationship agreements. Unfortunately, all these deliberations resulted in no formal actions by the two concerned bodies. The two entities, once operations began, elected not to develop a formal relationship arrangement. It is not entirely clear from the final TRC report, which discussed this issue, why the UN and Sierra Leone failed to demarcate the relationship between the two institutions or why after they started their work the TRC and the SCSL themselves chose not to do so. It appears that there was a fear that this could lead to a "chilling effect"[75] whereby perpetrators would refuse to testify before the TRC. This would have certainly affected the work of the Commission; it would have found it difficult to execute its mandate without testimony. In fact, some local NGOs surveyed former combatants and reported

---

[69] Econ. & Soc. Council, Rep. of the High Commissioner for Human Rights pursuant to Commission on Human Rights Resolution 2001/20: Situation of human rights in Sierra Leone, ¶ 70, U.N. Doc. E/CN.4/2002/3 (Feb. 18, 2002).

[70] *Id.*

[71] *Id.*

[72] *Id.*

[73] *Id.*

[74] U.N. Secretary-General, *Report of the Planning Mission on the Establishment of the Special Court for Sierra Leone*, ¶¶ 49, 53, U.N. Doc. S/2002/246 (Mar. 8, 2002).

[75] SL TRC Report, *supra* note 21, at vol. 3B, ch. 6 ¶ 48.

many ex-combatant's fears about testifying. Rumors circulated that any evidence given to the TRC would be transferred to the SCSL which could then use it to prosecute them.[76] In the end, fortunately, both perpetrators and victims appeared before both the Commission and the Court. Nonetheless, as the TRC later looked back and concluded, the two entities should "have given more consideration to an arrangement or memorandum of understanding to regulate their relationship."[77]

In sum, as the discussion in the preceding sections demonstrate, there was a substantial overlap in the mandate of the SCSL and the TRC. This intersection was a function of the fact that the TRC had initially been created when the SCSL was not even thought of, let alone provided for. In fact, as argued earlier, the governmental preference for a truth commission was seen as foreclosing the idea of criminal prosecutions. This was partly because of the amnesty that had been agreed, even before the substantive peace talks began at Lomé. At its core, therefore, the TRC was meant to have occupied the justice field in Sierra Leone. When the SCSL was born, on top of being perceived as a repudiation of the Commission, it eclipsed the TRC. It thus had to consider, and ultimately, nullify the effects of the amnesty. The Court also reinserted the ascendancy of the idea of retribution over reconciliation. The stage, in other words, had been informally set for the two bodies to clash.

10.4 THE CONFLICTS BETWEEN THE SCSL AND THE TRC

10.4.1 *The Disclosure of Confidentially Obtained Information*

One of the most divisive issues in the numerous discussions about the "relationship" between the TRC and the SCSL related to *information sharing*. The concern was that, when the TRC began operations, as a way of encouraging perpetrators to come forward and testify, the Commission had stated publicly that it could receive statements or testimony from perpetrators and that it would hold those in confidence. The Sierra Leone Parliament had not contemplated any clauses addressing this issue, as had occurred in the South Africa truth commission for example, most likely because no trials were contemplated at the time the TRC Act was adopted in 2000. With the SCSL in place and given the TRC confidentiality policy, the controversy about "information sharing" continued, with many asking whether the Court could compel the TRC to produce confidentially received information to aid in its investigations and prosecutions. Some, especially some human rights NGOs such as the International Center for Transitional Justice (ICTJ), lined up behind the SCSL. They offered what Carsten Stahn and Larissa van den Herik have suggested

---

[76] *See* Post Conflict Reintegration Initiative for Development and Empowerment (PRIDE), Ex-Combatant Views of the Truth and Reconciliation Commission and the Special Court for Sierra Leone, at 7 (Sept. 12, 2002).
[77] SL TRC REPORT, *supra* note 21, at vol. 3B, ch. 6 ¶ 46.

was a "bold interpretation"[78] of the relevant provisions claiming that, as an international court, the Court had supremacy over nationally created institutions like the TRC which was purely a creature of domestic law.[79]

Others lined up behind the TRC, perhaps because they felt it could play a more constructive role after the war as a body dedicated to helping the people of the country reconcile with each other. The better view, at least theoretically, was that which the UN advanced insisting that the mandates of the two bodies were complementary and that each had a distinct and important contribution to make to post-conflict Sierra Leone. The issue though was not about advancing abstractions, but about how all this would work in practice. The reality was messy. In the absence of clarity in the basic law of the two institutions, on this question, how could the two bodies work in tandem without stepping on each other's toes?

10.4.2 *Primacy of the SCSL over the TRC As a Solution to the Problem?*

Some suggested that the answer to the SCSL–TRC difficulty would lie in the primacy principle. Primacy, of course, is a legal principle that regulates the relationship between courts exercising concurrent jurisdiction. The doctrine became relevant because of the ambiguity in certain domestic legislative provisions in each of the two bodies' enabling laws which seemed facially inconsistent. The primacy principle, which is articulated in the SCSL Statute, was the same as can be found in the International Criminal Tribunal for the former Yugoslavia (ICTY) and International Criminal Tribunal for Rwanda (ICTR) Statutes. Under Article 8(2) of the SCSL Statute, as with its equivalent in the Chapter VII tribunals, the Court enjoyed concurrent jurisdiction with but also priority over national courts. However, in the SCSL contrasted with the ICTY and ICTR, primacy only applied to Sierra Leonean courts.[80] As a consequence, the SCSL could request at any stage of the proceedings that a *national court* seized of the same matter defer to its competence through issuance of a judicial order to that effect. Any such order would take precedence and bind Sierra Leone.

Under Section 20 of the Special Court Agreement (Ratification) Act 2002, which domesticated the UN-SL Agreement, "for the purposes of execution, an order of the Special Court shall have the same force or effect as if it had been issued by a Judge, Magistrate or Justice of the Peace of a Sierra Leone court."[81] In the definitions section, an "order of the Special Court" was defined to mean

---

[78] Larissa van den Herik and Carsten Stahn, *'Fragmentation', Diversification and '3D' Legal Pluralism: International Criminal Law as the Jack-in-the-Box?, in* THE DIVERSIFICATION AND FRAGMENTATION OF INTERNATIONAL CRIMINAL LAW (Larissa van den Herik & Carsten Stahn eds., 2012).

[79] *ICTJ Report, supra* note 68.

[80] This obligation was enshrined in Sierra Leonean law by the Special Court Agreement Ratification Act, *supra* note 19, at §14 (requiring the Attorney-General to grant the SCSL request for a discontinuance of deferral of any proceedings if in his opinion there are sufficient grounds to do so).

[81] *Id.* at § 20.

"any order, summons, subpoena, warrant, transfer order or any other issued by a judge of the Special Court."[82] This was an extremely wide provision that could form the basis of a broad range of cooperation requests from the SCSL to a national court. Indeed, as part of this, the Court could request the national authorities' assistance with the identification and location of persons, service of documents, arrest or detention of persons, and even the arrest and transfer of suspects to the Court.[83] The challenge was that the TRC was not a Sierra Leonean court. At best, it was an independent quasi-judicial body. The question therefore arose whether this cooperation regime could apply to it to compel the disclosure of any evidence in the hands of the independent Commission.[84]

Some NGOs took the SCSL's primacy clause and read it together with Section 21(2) of the Special Court Agreement Ratification Act. That clause, which Marieke Wierda, Priscilla Hayner, and Paul van Zyl have aptly descried as a "blunt provision of wide scope,"[85] stated that ("[n]otwithstanding any other law, every natural person, corporation, or other body created by or under Sierra Leone law shall comply with any direction specified in an order of the Special Court."[86] This was perceived as a way out of the primacy dilemma, resolving it in favor of the SCSL. The reason seemed to be that the TRC was a legal body or corporation created under Sierra Leone's domestic law. And, on the literal meaning of that provision under this interpretation, especially the formulation "notwithstanding any other law," the TRC was enjoined to "comply" with any order emanating from the SCSL. Importantly as well, Section 21(2) covered a wide range of national bodies and contained no exceptions.

From the TRC perspective, this far-reaching interpretation could not be tenable since the Commission could also invoke Section 7(3) of its own TRC Act. Under that provision, "any person shall be permitted to provide information to the Commission on a confidential basis and the Commission shall not be compelled to disclose any information given to it in confidence."[87] This granted the TRC full powers to receive confidential information. It also assured that no one could demand it to divulge confidentially received information. This position held true in relation to all Sierra Leonean institutions. The challenge was that this argument contradicted a key clause in the national implementing legislation which subsequently incorporated the UN-Sierra Leone Agreement that had created the SCSL.

---

[82] *Id.* at § 1.
[83] *Id.* at §§ 23–29 (regulating arrest and delivery of persons).
[84] *Id.* at § 4.
[85] *ICTJ Report, supra* note 68, at 5.
[86] Special Court Agreement Ratification Act, *supra* note 19, at § 21(2).
[87] TRC Act, *supra* note 11, at § 7(3).

10.4.3 *The Kabbah Government Established Primacy for the SCSL*

How then to reconcile these two apparently contradictory laws, on the one hand seemingly giving stronger powers to the SCSL (Section 21), and on the other, circumscribing the initially wide powers of the TRC in relation to protection of confidential information (Section 7)? In Part IV of the Special Court Agreement Ratification Act, in effect, the Kabbah government had implicitly determined that, in a Section 21–7 conflict, Section 21 would win out. The TRC was required to cooperate with the SCSL and to comply with any of the Court's cooperation requests. It went on to state this explicitly, although the TRC would later reject this interpretation and even sharply criticize it in its final report.

In January 2002, the Ministry of Justice released a "briefing paper" in which it stated the official policy unequivocally: "The legal relationship between the Special Court and the Truth and Reconciliation Commission is clear. The Special Court is an international judicial body whose requests and orders require no less than full compliance by the Truth and Reconciliation Commission, as by all Sierra Leonean national institutions, in accordance to the international obligations agreed to by Sierra Leone."[88] It is true that this policy, as Alpha Sesay has noted, was prepared by Sierra Leone's Attorney-General and therefore not an act of parliament like the TRC Act or the Special Court Agreement Ratification Act. Nevertheless, this policy position was important because it confirmed the Sierra Leonean government's official view regarding the hierarchy in the legal relationship between the two bodies in the event of a conflict. In this statement of government, advanced by the chief legal adviser to Sierra Leone, the SCSL as an international tribunal was intended to enjoy primacy over the TRC, which had been a national body, created under national law. It also reflects the views and carries the weight of the executive branch of the Sierra Leonean government.

10.4.4 *The TRC Rejects Subordination to the SCSL*

But one international lawyer, and later the TRC itself, each contested the government's official position. Schabas opined that any interpretation that would have subordinated the TRC to the SCSL seemed "far-fetched and manifestly incorrect."[89] He offered several reasons for this. I examine the main ones critically in the subsequent sections given the weight of his views as a prominent author in international criminal law; and also importantly, because his position naturally shaped the TRC's official take on the issue. This should not be surprising because Schabas was one of the three non-Sierra Leonean commissioners who served on the

---

[88] OFF. OF THE ATT'Y GEN.& MINISTRY OF JUST. SPECIAL CT. TASK FORCE, *Briefing Paper on the Relationship Between the Special Court and the Truth and Reconciliation Commission, Legal Analysis and Policy Considerations of the Government of Sierra Leone for the Special Court Planning Mission* 9 (2002) [hereinafter *Att'y Gen. Briefing Paper*].

[89] Schabas, *Synergistic Relationship, supra* note 30, at 37.

TRC. Both the Commission and Schabas were motivated by an admirable desire to ensure the success of the Sierra Leone experiment both for the sake of the country and other transitional justice situations that might in the future go down this path of deploying a TRC and a court at the same time. There have already been countries such as the Central African Republic currently pursuing this. The issue therefore needed to be addressed. But, in my view, their arguments – which effectively circumvented the legislative intent of Parliament and at the least rejected explicit government policy – were unconvincing.

First, in a stance that the TRC later echoed in its report, Schabas cited the "golden rule" of statutory interpretation. He argued that a literal reading of Section 21(2) leads to a "patent absurdity" because it would imply that an SCSL order "would override any previous legislative provision or common law rule"[90] that was facially inconsistent with it. This argument initially seems attractive. However, its key problem is that it carries with it a presumption that is rebuttable. Under that rule, which the House of Lords developed in *Grey v. Pearson*, Lord Wensleydale famously explained that "the grammatical and ordinary sense of the words [of a statute] is to be adhered to, unless that would lead to some absurdity, or some repugnance or inconsistency with the rest of the instrument, in which case the grammatical and ordinary sense of the words maybe modified, so as to avoid that absurdity and inconsistency, but no farther."[91]

But, in my view, the grammatical and ordinary meaning of the words in the Special Court Agreement Ratification Act is precise. They are unambiguous. They demonstrated the clear intention of the Sierra Leonean Parliament as the lawgiver. Thus, there was no issue, absurdity, or repugnance or inconsistency in Section 21(2) with the rest of the instrument (that is, the rest of the Special Court Agreement Ratification Act) and vis-à-vis the TRC Act. Indeed, the tenor of the rest of the act undermines the absurdity argument since the remainder of the legislation, read as a whole and contextually, focused on ensuring that all Sierra Leonean institutions cooperate with the Court when requested to do so. The ordinary meaning is clear that "notwithstanding any other law," any natural person, corporation, or other body created by or under Sierra Leonean law was required to comply with the SCSL's order. It follows that, on a plain reading of its express terms, the TRC being a body created by and under Sierra Leonean law was simply asked, if required to do so, to comply with any orders of the SCSL.

It should be clear, if my reasoning is correct, that Section 21(2) of the Special Court Agreement Ratification Act did not reduce the TRC's powers to ensure and protect the confidentiality of information it received vis-à-vis other *Sierra Leonean* (that is, *national*) institutions. Again, returning to the language of the TRC's own founding legislation, any Sierra Leonean person (presumably including both

---

[90]   *Id.* at 37–38.
[91]   Grey v. Pearson, [1857] 6 HLC 61, 106 (Eng.). That rule was expounded in an earlier case.

natural and legal persons) was permitted to provide information to the Commission confidentially. The TRC was not compellable to disclose any information given to it in such circumstances. My narrower claim here is that this TRC power to assure confidentiality of information did not extend to the SCSL itself because of the latter's own implementing legislation which had superseded that of the Commission – to the extent of the inconsistency.

The TRC was created by an earlier law and was a body whose establishment had been agreed at Lomé and subsequently incorporated into domestic law by Sierra Leone's Parliament. Notably, the SCSL was created by Sierra Leone's agreement with the UN after the forgive and forget policy behind the TRC was seen as having failed. In that scenario, in which legislators gave effect to the international obligations the executive branch had assumed as per the Constitution, it was apparent in the Special Court Agreement Ratification Act what the goal was: To ensure that the SCSL would enjoy in Sierra Leonean law every power necessary for it to exercise its unfettered jurisdiction. This, to the government, seemed to have required passage of a far-reaching law that would bind all national institutions to cooperate in the event that the Court sought their assistance. As absurd as it might initially have sounded to Schabas, the ordinary text of the law showed the clear intention of a sovereign Sierra Leonean Parliament to subordinate all other institutions in the country to the SCSL. This result, as normatively undesirable as it might have been, was the consequence of the ordinary meaning of the text because it left no ambiguity in specifying the hierarchy between the two contradictory statutes.

In seeking to establish the absurdity of a plain reading of the SCSL implementing law, which then allowed a resort to an alternative theory like purposive interpretation, Schabas suggested that consideration of other circumstances in which the SCSL could have theoretically asked other persons or entities to breach confidentiality in Sierra Leone would be instructive. He cited cabinet confidences, notes of judicial deliberations of appellate and supreme court judges, and the immunities of diplomats, all of which he rightly contended would ordinarily be protected under the country's laws, the common law, or international law.[92] In the TRC's final report, the same argument was repeated albeit with the additional illustrations of doctor-patient and solicitor-client relationships which are traditionally treated as privileged as well.[93] Both the TRC report and Schabas concluded that it was unlikely that all these forms of privilege would have been implicitly repealed by the SCSL's implementing legislation. Or, for that matter, that Parliament would have intended such a far-reaching result since this would have effectively cancelled all privileges and confidentiality protected under Sierra Leonean law.[94]

But the examples Schabas gave of possible SCSL breaches of confidentiality through orders for production of files in the United States Embassy or the UN

---

[92]   Schabas, *Synergistic Relationship, supra* note 30, at 38.
[93]   SL TRC Report, *supra* note 21, at vol. 3B, ch. 6 at ¶ 66.
[94]   *Id.*

Secretary-General's Representative were not apposite. Both US and the UN diplomats enjoy diplomatic immunity, from the criminal processes of the host State (Sierra Leone), and neither could be compelled either to testify or to produce any documents by the SCSL based on Section 21 of the Special Court Agreement Ratification Act because neither entity was "created by or under" Sierra Leonean law. Thus, the US and UN examples were of no help, as there was simply no issue by the terms of the Special Court Agreement Ratification Act that they could be required "to comply with any direction specified in an order of the Special Court."[95]

Relatedly, Schabas has argued that even if the effect of Section 21(2) of the Special Court Agreement Ratification Act is cabined to being a reference that only "targets the TRC, rather than all privileges and immunities" more widely, that argument too would be unsustainable.[96] He observes that Section 21(2) did not in fact mention the TRC, which was a body independent of the Sierra Leone government, and suggested that if that was Parliament's goal, "it would have said so more explicitly"[97] instead of implicitly repealing so many other laws including those that might be protecting other privileges.

This argument too seems unpersuasive. Surely, it would have been preferable for Parliament to explicitly mention its intent to limit the TRC's confidentiality provisions. But it may be that there were other legitimate reasons why the legislature might want to achieve the same result, implicitly, without stating them explicitly. I suggest that there were several. For one thing, given that the Kabbah government was in a delicate dance with the RUF in which it was purporting to abrogate the amnesty and getting heat for that domestically, it was politically very difficult for it to actually present legislation to Parliament that would openly withdraw the TRC's initially conferred powers. To do so would have surely generated opposition.

Even more importantly, perhaps, one recalls that the remainder of the peace accord, which required the establishment of the truth commission, was being applied in country in order to demobilize combatants and was also being implemented in respect of power sharing and other fundamental aspects. The same agreement had in fact been incorporated into Sierra Leonean law, thereby creating legal duties for the Kabbah Government. Because the Lomé Peace Accord's continued existence was no longer in doubt, at the point the SCSL was established, it was plausible that a vague provision would have been selected on the issue of hierarchy since the government was near desperate to not do anything, including in Parliament, to scuttle the restoration of peace to Sierra Leone. The latter required continued adherence to the other components of the fragile accord even if the amnesty had effectively been unilaterally withdrawn. Taking all these factors into account, one can appreciate why there might *not* have been any explicit statements in relation to the TRC given the high stakes facing the government.

---

[95] Special Court Agreement Ratification Act, *supra* note 19, at § 21(2).
[96] Schabas, *Synergistic Relationship*, *supra* note 30, at 38.
[97] *Id.*

This debate, however, does not end there. Schabas has also questioned the applicability of the stated source of the government's obligation, which came from Article 17 of the UN-Sierra Leone Agreement, to the TRC. Under that provision, "the Government" was required to cooperate with all organs of the Court and to comply without undue delay with any of its "directions" specified in the orders of the chambers of the tribunal.[98] The TRC has advanced the same position.[99] However, this argument also ignores other important factors. First, it was true that Article 17 of the UN-Sierra Leone Agreement and Section 21(2) of the implementation law did not mention the TRC, only the *government*. By the same token, these same instruments did not mention any other organs of the Sierra Leone Government such as the Ministry of Justice or the Sierra Leone Police. Yet, both of those entities had crucial roles to play in giving effect to the country's obligations to cooperate with the SCSL. This included enforcing arrest warrants and collecting evidence. The wide scope of the obligation and the very many national bodies that could be implicated by the Court's requests required broader language than one which identified specific institutions. This despite that the TRC would have been among the more important ones in that regard.

In any event, and going beyond this claim, what exactly does the term "government" encompass? In his policy paper, the Sierra Leonean Minister of Justice and Attorney-General addressed this point in clear terms which held implications for the TRC position:

> The fact that the obligation [in Article 17 of the SCSL Statute] is imposed on the "Government" should not be misinterpreted to mean that the obligation is only imposed with respect to *governmental institutions*. Rather, the obligation is imposed on the State of Sierra Leone, represented by Government, *and subsists in respect of all institutions and bodies established under Sierra Leone law, whether that be by the Constitution, by Act of Parliament or otherwise.*[100]

In this view, according to this official explanation, even though the TRC was intended to act independently of the government, it still formed part of "government" in the sense that it was a body or institution created by or established by the State of Sierra Leone via an act of the country's parliament. A creature can be established under national law and still function independently of its founders, much in the same way that the SCSL itself was created jointly by a treaty between the UN and Sierra Leone but at the same time also enjoyed a separate legal personality and functional independence from its creators. This position is hardly unique. In my view then, taking Sierra Leone's official interpretation of "government," as reflective of the State of Sierra Leone, the mere fact that Article 17 did not mention the TRC is by itself not dispositive of whether there might have been a duty

---

[98]   Schabas, *Synergistic Relationship, supra* note 30, at 36.

[99]   SL TRC REPORT, *supra* note 21, at vol. 3B, ch.6, at ¶ 66.

[100] *Att'y Gen. Briefing Paper, supra* note 88, at ¶ 7 (emphasis added).

on the part of the Commission to obey disclosure orders should such have come from the SCSL judges.

Moreover, that the government read its obligations to provide for the disclosure of whatever was needed to facilitate the SCSL's work so widely that it implicitly revoked the confidentiality clauses of the TRC can be found in another part of the same legislation which even compelled the Attorney-General to turn over evidence that "maybe prejudicial to the national security."[101] The foregoing is a far-reaching clause for Sierra Leone's sovereignty. Reading the entirety of the implementing legislation in the circumstances from which the SCSL was created goes to show the government's deep respect for international law, or more plausibly, its policy preference by that point for the SCSL to have whatever power it needed to carry out its mandate (that is, investigate and prosecute and punish the adversaries in the RUF with whom it had been struggling for years), even if that meant sacrificing or subordinating other core national priorities such as national security. The TRC, which initially had been created to promote forgiveness and reconciliation, could not have been exempted from such sentiments. It might have even been the more direct focus of such a policy given the disdain that the governmental leadership held at that point towards the unreliable RUF leadership.

Furthermore, under Sierra Leonean law, one act of Parliament could be over-ridden by a later act of Parliament. This is the same in other Commonwealth jurisdictions. It follows that, because the TRC's enabling legislation was adopted before the SCSL was contemplated, a later statute such as the Special Court Agreement Ratification Act could override the earlier law especially given the similarity of the mandates of the two institutions and their overlapping subject matter. This assumes, of course, that rules of statutory interpretation could not be found to resolve and harmonize the ambiguity created by the two laws. I submitted above that this did not even arise as there was in fact no ambiguity in the plain text of the law implementing the SCSL vis-à-vis the TRC. In any event, Parliament could implicitly repeal any legislation. Support for this argument can be found in the doctrine of implied repeal, which is recognized not only in Sierra Leonean law but also other commonwealth jurisdictions with which it shares a common legal heritage. Under that doctrine, one parliament cannot bind its successors because each parliament is sovereign.

Whatever the merits of the arguments by the TRC and Schabas, they certainly deserve commendation for a good faith commitment to addressing the messy situation that Sierra Leone found itself in as it sought to transition from war to peace. Still, as I have hopefully shown in the foregoing analysis, it was fortunate that the much speculated legal clash that would have come from an SCSL request for evidence that might have been confidentially taken by the TRC did not directly come to pass in practice. If that had occurred, it is not clear to me that the TRC

---

[101]   Special Court Agreement Ratification Act, *supra* note 19, at § 18(4).

would not have been required to comply. It is also not clear that there might not have been ways to address such orders without imperiling its own undertakings to those that shared evidence with it. The good news is that any such concerns should have eased, as Judge Robertson put it, when the SCSL's first prosecutor, David Crane, made public announcements in September 2002 indicating that he had no interest in seeking evidence collected or heard by the TRC.[102] That seemed to be a wise decision.

In the final analysis, the end result was that the TRC was never asked to produce any documents before the SCSL. This meant that the question of whether the latter could be compelled by the former to turn over evidence was never formally tested, although in an interesting twist, the TRC did seek to secure public evidence from detainees in SCSL custody that might have been more easily secured from them if it had been taken confidentially or at least in private.

10.5 SCSL–TRC DISPUTE OVER WHETHER DETAINEES MAY TESTIFY

Besides the question of primacy and the SCSL's legal ability to compel confidential evidence from the TRC, which did not come to pass, the real significance of the absence of clarity in the legal relationship between the SCSL and the TRC when they operated concurrently was felt in a public dispute that occurred between the two bodies towards the completion of the TRC's mandate. This involved three different applications by three different defendants who were in SCSL custody when they sought to appear in public to give testimony before the TRC.

Below, I focus on the most widely known of those disputes. It concerned Sam Hinga Norman, the former deputy minister in Kabbah's government charged on eight counts of war crimes, crimes against humanity, and other serious international humanitarian law violations, who offered to testify in a public hearing before the TRC. The decision in that case drove the result of all the others. It is therefore the most pertinent.

10.5.1 *The TRC Application for Norman to Testify in Public*

In June 2003, just months after the arrest of the bulk of the SCSL indictees but before the start of SCSL trials, the TRC approached the Court seeking access to some of them. Many of their names had frequently come up in its investigations. The TRC asked the indictees who were in pre-trial custody at the SCSL to participate in its "information gathering activities, including public hearings."[103] However, due to

---

[102]   Thierry Cruvellier & Marieke Wierda, *The Special Court for Sierra Leone: The First Eighteen Months*, 12 Int'l Ctr. for Transitional Just. (ICTJ) Case Stud. Series (Mar. 2004).

[103]   SL TRC Report, *supra* note 21, at vol. 3B, ch. 6 ¶ 74.

concerns about self-incrimination, defense counsel advised them against appearing before the TRC prior to their trials before the SCSL.

On August 26, 2003, Norman decided to ignore legal advice. He instead indicated in writing his "willingness to appear and testify before the TRC without any further delay."[104] For its part, the TRC, which had wanted to interview Norman since June 2003, sought to facilitate it.[105] The SCSL decided to adopt a Practice Direction to create a regime that would permit the TRC or any other body to apply to an SCSL judge for access to a Court detainee. The protocol sought to balance the interests of the party seeking access and the fair trial rights of the accused persons, consistent with their status as detainees being held in pre-trial detention and the presumption of innocence. It required that specific questions be provided in advance, for a court legal officer to be present to "supervise" the interview, and permitted the recording and transcribing of the interview and the transmission of the transcripts to the Prosecutor.[106]

The TRC reacted negatively to the SCSL guidelines.[107] It took particular issue with the suggestion that information from the interview could be turned over to prosecutors which it considered would violate the fair trial rights of the suspects.[108] The Commission, inter alia, also warned of the consequence that this might create a "chilling effect"[109] on detainees who wished to appear before the TRC.

On October 4, 2003, the SCSL adopted a revised directive, which tried to reflect some of the TRC's concerns while preserving the rights of the accused.[110] A major element of the new directive was the presumption created in favor of granting such requests under Rule 5 of the Practice Direction and the decision to place under seal any evidence received in such circumstances.[111] The exceptions were that the presiding judge could reject an application if a refusal was "necessary in the interest of justice or to maintain the integrity of the proceedings of the Special Court."[112]

The TRC submitted joint applications for public instead of private hearings with Norman and another detainee (Gbao) on October 7 and 10, 2003 respectively.[113] Judge Bankole Thompson, the presiding judge of the trial chamber that had been assigned to hear the *Norman* case, issued a ruling on the joint application on

---

[104] *Id.* at ¶ 75.

[105] *Id.* at ¶¶ 78, 81.

[106] Registrar of the Special Court for Sierra Leone, *Practice Direction on the procedure following a request by a State, the Truth and Reconciliation Commission, or other legitimate authority to take a statement from a person in the custody of the Special Court for Sierra Leone*, ¶ 5 (Sept. 9, 2003) (amended Oct. 4, 2003) [hereinafter *Registrar of SCSL Practice Direction*].

[107] SL TRC REPORT, *supra* note 21, at vol. 3B, ch. 6 at ¶ 87.

[108] *Id.*

[109] *Id.*

[110] *Id.*, at vol. 3B, ch. 6 at ¶¶ 99–102.

[111] *Registrar of SCSL Practice Direction*, *supra* note 106.

[112] *Id.*

[113] SL TRC REPORT, *supra* note 21, at vol. 3B, ch. 6 at ¶¶ 97–98.

October 29, 2003.[114] He determined that he had only two choices under the directive: (1) to approve the TRC request; or (2) refuse the application on one or both exceptional grounds.[115] Judge Thompson concluded that the presumption of innocence, which was guaranteed in Article 17 of the Statute of the SCSL, would be violated if Norman who had been accused of a crime before the Court was given license to incriminate himself in another forum where he would not be afforded such protections.[116] He purported to find language proving this, such as the description of Norman in the TRC application categorically stating that he "did play a central role in the conflict in Sierra Leone."[117] Judge Thompson implied that his reasoning would have been different had Norman, who was an indictee, confessed to his crimes rather than contested the charges; in the former scenario, it could have been appropriate for him to have a public hearing and at the same time to participate in the TRC process which was for self-confessed perpetrators to face their victims and seek atonement.[118] In circumstances where that was not the case, the risk of self-incrimination raised special concern for both the actual and perceived fairness of Norman's trial.

Interestingly, both Norman and the TRC appealed Judge Thompson's negative decision. In a brief filed on November 4, 2003, the appellants essentially raised questions of law and challenged this interpretation before the SCSL President. They argued in the main, as the TRC later summarized them: (1) that he had failed to appreciate the proper role of the TRC vis-à-vis the SCSL especially his tendency to treat the former as a court of law; (2) that he did not do any proportionality analysis of the various interests at stake in the application when he expressed that the accused interests should trump those of the TRC; and (3) that he had erred in developing novel arguments about the fair trial rights of the accused for which the SCSL was guardian.[119] The prosecution opposed the appeal. They countered, much as they had argued before Judge Thompson, that allowing the testimony could undermine the integrity of the Court, imperil the security situation of Sierra Leone, and perhaps even lead to intimidation of prospective witnesses in Norman's trial.

In his November 28, 2003 decision, Judge Robertson explained that since it was normally inappropriate for one judge to review another judge's exercise of discretion, he would treat the application "as a fresh hearing."[120] That enabled him to

---

[114] Prosecutor v. Norman, Case No. SCSL-2003–08-PT, Decision on the Request by the Truth and Reconciliation Commission of Sierra Leone to Conduct a Public Hearing with Samuel Hinga Norman, ¶¶ 1, 2 (Oct. 29, 2003).

[115] *Id.* at ¶ 8.

[116] *Id.* at ¶ 12.

[117] *Id.*

[118] Prosecutor v. Norman, Case No. SCSL-2003–08-PT, Decision on the Request by the Truth and Reconciliation Commission of Sierra Leone to Conduct a Public Hearing with Samuel Hinga Norman, ¶ 12 (Oct. 29, 2003).

[119] SL TRC Report, *supra* note 21, at vol. 3B, ch. 6 ¶ 142.

[120] Prosecutor v. Norman, Case No. SCSL-2003–08-PT, Decision on Appeal by the Truth and Reconciliation Commission for Sierra Leone ("TRC" or "The Commission") and Chief Samuel Hinga Norman JP Against the Decision of His Lordship, Mr. Justice Bankole Thompson Delivered

"explore alternative solutions" and to bring a "broader view about an indictees contacts with third parties and institutions."[121] In other words, he did not want to be limited to the two options within the Practice Direction that apparently informed Judge Thompson's reasoning. He took a wider perspective that attempted to balance the interests of the TRC in seeking evidence from indictees and the interests of the SCSL in maintaining its integrity and ensuring that the fair trial rights of the accused are protected. He flagged the significance of the question before him, noting that it was a "novel question" that had not yet arisen elsewhere but would likely recur "for other indictees and in other post-war situations where the local or international community considers that the establishment of both a Special Court and a Truth Commission will assist in the restoration of peace and justice."[122]

However, despite what seemed to have been a good faith attempt to balance the interests of the two institutions on his part, Judge Robertson ultimately did what he felt was necessary in order to maintain the integrity of the trials before the SCSL. Though, from the TRC perspective, this might have been perceived as coming at its expense. In fact, as Schabas, himself a TRC commissioner, has thoughtfully observed, while some in the Commission later saw Robertson's decision as a major blow, "he sought to reconcile conflicting concerns and to allow the operation of both bodies to proceed."[123] Evidence of this effort can be found throughout his decision; he attempted to walk a tight rope minimizing the tension between truth commissions and criminal courts.

First, as Judge Robertson clarified, the practice direction aimed to ensure that detainees who wished to testify before the TRC "knew what they were letting themselves in for if they gave interviews to the TRC, and to ensure that in that event they would be given every reasonable protection against self-incrimination."[124] That is what explained the various requirements that the TRC commissioners might have seen as unnecessary obstacles, among which, (1) why a detainee had to agree to testify in writing, (2) required confirmation of an attorney who had advised him, (3) was to be given an advance list of written questions and be advised that he could invoke the right to silence not to answer any particular one if he did not so wish, (4) that he was aware that any answers could be used against him by the prosecution, and (5) that no conclusion or finding on his guilt by the TRC, which might find its way into the final report, would sway the views of the three professional judges who

---

on 30 October 2003 to Deny the TRC's Request to Hold a Public Hearing with Chief Samuel Hinga Norman JP, ¶ 3 (Nov. 28, 2003).

[121] *Id.*

[122] *Id.* at ¶ 2.

[123] Schabas, *Synergistic Relationship, supra* note 30, at 50.

[124] Prosecutor v. Norman, Case No. SCSL-2003–08-PT, Decision on Appeal by the Truth and Reconciliation Commission for Sierra Leone ("TRC" or "The Commission") and Chief Samuel Hinga Norman JP Against the Decision of His Lordship, Mr. Justice Bankole Thompson Delivered on 30 October 2003 to Deny the TRC's Request to Hold a Public Hearing with Chief Samuel Hinga Norman JP, ¶ 20 (Nov. 28, 2003).

were the sole persons obligated to rule on guilt or innocence following the conclusion of the SCSL trials (which were pending at the time). Similarly, the presence of a registry lawyer and counsel for the indictee were all meant to offer additional protections to the defendant, as this could ensure he was able to stop the interview if there was a risk of self-incrimination.

These requirements essentially tracked the fair trial rights contained in Article 17 of the SCSL Statute. In any event, as the judge observed in his decision, there was nothing in principle that prevented Norman or any of the other SCSL detainees from "volunteering or communicating information to the TRC in writing, either directly or through his lawyers."[125] Indeed, Judge Robertson underscored that, in a way that overturned Judge Thompson's decision on the point, all that was denied was a public (not private) hearing which would have been preferable in the circumstances.

Second, Judge Robertson compared the TRC and SCSL's mandate noting in particular that the latter was not expected when the former was statutorily created. The TRC Act, at the time of its adoption, did not envisage that detainees might wish to testify before it or the basis upon which they might do so. He therefore asserted that the Tribunal, which had jurisdiction to prosecute, had "primacy over the national courts of Sierra Leone (and, by implication, over national bodies like the TRC)"[126] – a point that this author had also essentially agreed with in Section 10.3 of this chapter. He, though looking out for the interests of the Court, considered that it had an "overriding duty to prosecute," which in his view gave victims "the most effective remedy" compared to the TRC and its focus on "truth," he found nothing in its founding instruments requiring it to defer to local courts or national institutions.[127]

Third, even though Judge Robertson's solution was not welcomed by the TRC, it is clear that the reason for the denial of a hearing related more to concerns about the dangers of doing so for the presumed fragile security situation in Sierra Leone. He accepted that the Court could not block Norman from giving testimony, if he chose to do so, but insisted that had to be done "in a manner that reduces to an acceptable level any danger that it will influence witnesses (whether favourably or adversely) or affect the integrity of court proceedings or unreasonably affect co-defendants and other indictees."[128] This makes sense since it is hard to argue against an accused person who had decided to waive his or her fair trial rights, even if that could lead to the risk of self-incrimination. In the final analysis, Judge Robertson saw the decision as an attempt to facilitate the work of the TRC so it could achieve it statutory mandate while also protecting the rights of the accused and the integrity of the SCSL proceedings. This seemed like a good attempt to find a middle ground, which

[125] *Id.* at ¶ 21.
[126] *Id.* at ¶ 4.
[127] *Id.* at ¶¶ 4, 33.
[128] *Id.* at ¶ 41.

the TRC might have given greater consideration rather than reacted negatively to. Ultimately, each institution had its interest; and in the power balance, the SCSL held most of the cards. Part of this stemmed from the factual reality that it had the accused in its custody and could decide one way or another.

Finally, and importantly, he accepted that the TRC and the SCSL were "complementary and each must accommodate the existence of the other."[129] Robertson opined that the objectives of truth commissions and criminal courts, being so distinct, "are separate and severable."[130] He emphasized that the "Special Court respects the TRC's work and will assist it as far as possible and proper, subject only to our overriding duty to serve the interests of justice without which there may not be the whole truth and there is unlikely to be lasting reconciliation."[131]

Nonetheless, ultimately, it seems that it would have been inappropriate for the TRC to apply its reconciliation process of public hearings, confrontation with victims, live broadcasts and so on with SCSL detainees who had not pleaded guilty. At least from a criminal lawyer's perspective. In addition, this carried potential to confuse the public in Sierra Leone about what were in essence two separate processes with two different implications for the participants: jail if convicted (SCSL), and public absolution if forgiven (TRC). After the Robertson ruling, Norman, who apparently harbored political reasons why he wanted only a public hearing, decided that he would no longer cooperate with the TRC. The latter decision suggests, at least to a degree, that he might have been seeking to weaponize the public hearing process for his political gain.

10.5.2 *Criticisms of the SCSL Decision Points to Deeper Problem*

The decision of the SCSL in relation to Norman generated national discussions. Some actors, especially from civil society, expressed disappointment at the SCSL's refusal to allow the TRC public hearings with the detainees. A coalition of Sierra Leonean civil society groups, which supported the work of the TRC, argued that the decision not to permit Norman to testify created a "high risk of incomplete historical memory and denial of Right to Truth."[132] The SCSL, for its part, emphasized in its press materials that it had sought to ensure each of it and the TRC would do its job without affecting the other. This should have been the end of the fight. In a sign of continuation, the TRC issued a press statement forcefully rejecting such views and dramatically insisting that the SCSL had "dealt a serious blow to the cause of truth

---

[129] *Id.* at ¶ 33.
[130] *Id.* at ¶ 44.
[131] *Id.*
[132] Abdoulaye W. Dukulé, *West Africa: Taylor at Accra Peace Talks: "Honourable Exit or Extended Mandate?"*, ALLAFRICA (June 4, 2003), http://allafrica.com/stories/200306040021.html.

and reconciliation in Sierra Leone."[133] The TRC also expressed worries about the rights of the detainees who were not allowed to testify. And, in its final report, it recounts in great detail the saga between it and the SCSL; which at the time was just beginning its trials.

In the end, the irony is that Norman, though not convicted, was able to subsequently give lengthy testimony before the SCSL. His time on the stand carried daily headlines in Sierra Leone's newspapers about his role in the conflict as leader of the Civil Defense Forces (CDF). This was before he fell ill and died, before the rendering of the Court's judgment on his guilt or innocence. In a way then, presumably the same evidence that would have been captured by the TRC report is now available in the public record in Sierra Leone. Perhaps the lesson, if we can draw one from a single instance, is that it would be better for sworn testimony to be taken in the criminal tribunal process before the truth commission process follows it.

10.6 CONCLUSION

Sierra Leone's attempt to blend a cocktail of truth and reconciliation with criminal prosecutions in an ad hoc criminal court established solely for such a purpose was unique. That much was made clear by this chapter. Even though, it was more of an accidental development, rather than a deliberate policy choice, which ended up generating practical complications of its own. The Sierra Leone transitional justice experiment raised important questions about whether a criminal court or a truth commission should have primacy over the other, whether confidential information could be subpoenaed from the TRC, and in the case of accused in the Court's custody who wanted to testify in public hearings, whether they could do so in light of their right not to be compelled to testify or to incriminate themselves. These were thorny issues which affected the SCSL's decisions on the TRC's request for access to the high-profile detainees that were in its custody. Whether the manner in which the Court and the TRC resolved the confrontation was successful is open to some doubt. And, as with many other things, the answer to the question might turn on whether one sees the glass of transitional justice as half-empty rather than half-full. It might also depend on whether one has a normative preference for truth telling over criminal trials, or a preference for determinations of individual culpability for persons most responsible for them and punishment over reconciliation.

My main conclusion is that a key contribution we can derive from Sierra Leone's fiddling with having a truth commission coupled with amnesty, which then failed and gave rise to prosecutions and criminal accountability, is that two such bodies cannot work productively with each other in the absence of legal clarity in their founding instruments or at least in a relationship agreement between the two

---

[133] Press Release, Truth and Reconciliation Commission, Special Court Denies Hinga Norman's Right (and that of the other detainees) to Appear Publicly Before the TRC, www.sierraleonetrc.org/images/docs/hinganorman/2003–12-01_FINAL_TRC_PRESS_RELEASE.pdf (Dec. 1, 2003).

institutions. Although an agreement is a necessary, but not by itself a sufficient condition for harmonious coordination between such entities, I have contended that the origins, mandate, and concurrent operation of the two mechanisms in Sierra Leone (that is, the truth commission and the SCSL) demonstrate what happens when coordination only occurs at an informal level or during a moment of crisis in which each side dug its heels and naturally tried to do what it could to prioritize its own role, even if this came at the expense of the other institution or the greater good of the situation country. On the other hand, it would be an exaggeration to claim that the process was a failure. For the most part, the two entities functioned separately and did not cross paths with each other.

In sum, through this analysis, this chapter has shown that it would be wise in the future whenever two such institutions are expected to operate alongside each other to delimit the nature of the legal relationship between the bodies. Failure to specify and clarify things in advance should not be the end of the matter. If all else fails, there is still the possibility of a negotiated relationship agreement between the two bodies. We saw that, in Sierra Leone, doing so would have allowed each institution to better achieve its own separate but equally important mandate. In the absence of such formal arrangements, the leadership of such concurrently operating institutions should build on the lessons of Sierra Leone to identify a way forward. This lesson is a useful legacy item for other transitional justice situations in Africa such as the Central African Republic which, at the time of writing, had both types of process and the questions similar to those that arose in Sierra Leone are now confronting it. This lesson, as much as it could have been avoided, is a vital contribution to the development of international criminal practice.

11

Conclusion

11.1 GENERAL REMARKS ON THE LEGAL LEGACY OF THE SPECIAL COURT

The Special Court for Sierra Leone (SCSL) was established in 2002 in an unprecedented type of partnership between the United Nations and one of its Member States (Sierra Leone). The SCSL became the first ad hoc criminal tribunal created through a bilateral treaty instead of as a Security Council imposition. It followed in the footsteps of the International Tribunals for the former Yugoslavia (ICTY) and Rwanda (ICTR), which were established by the UN Security Council in 1993 and in 1994, as measures aimed to restore international peace and security under Chapter VII of the Charter of the United Nations. This book has examined the SCSL's main judicial legacy, as the third major ad hoc international criminal tribunal, and its attempt to chart a new path for international justice by drawing on the experiences of its two predecessors, the ICTY and ICTR, while also improving upon certain aspects of their work in relation to the pace, cost and efficiency of their trials.

In this regard, when it was created, the SCSL model's main selling points included its duality in terms of the mix between the *national* and *international* crimes within its subject matter jurisdiction, its mixed national and international staff composition, and perhaps most radically compared to the Chapter VII tribunals, the opportunities for the requesting state to claim some type of local ownership of the project through the appointment of some of its principal officials. The latter included the appointment of a minority of its judges for each chamber along with the deputy prosecutor and the deputy registrar. From the perspective of the UN, at least the Security Council, the donations-based funding structure of the SCSL seemed particularly attractive. It portended a new type of institutional framework for the enforcement of the proscriptions of international humanitarian law without imposing the same financial burden on the UN as an organization which is what would have been required if it were, like the Chapter VII courts, a subsidiary body established by the Security Council. Although the uncertain funding structure proved to be a bad decision, an issue that had in fact initially been flagged as a concern for the Secretary-General who lost the argument to the preference of the Security Council, the SCSL model at inception sought to combine the best of two worlds by drawing inspiration from both Sierra Leone and the international community. The hybrid model has, perhaps unsurprisingly, already been replicated elsewhere with the creation of a similarly structured and funded Special Tribunal for Lebanon, for example.

The SCSL also distinguished itself in several other ways. It was the first modern international criminal court to sit in the country where the crimes were committed, the first to use an entirely donations-based funding scheme to pay for its core operations, and the first to create a management committee comprised of third states providing operational oversight for the non-judicial aspects of its work. The Court, which was based in the Sierra Leonean capital Freetown, was initially expected to operate only for three years. In reality, it functioned on a shoestring budget for about eleven years, between the years 2002 and 2013. It exceeded by about four times the initially envisaged timeline for its trials. It also cost more money than had been anticipated during its establishment. In hindsight, the cost proved not to be a significant improvement on the record of the Chapter VII tribunals for the former Yugoslavia and Rwanda.

During its existence, the SCSL issued a total of thirteen international crime indictments targeting all the factions involved with the Sierra Leone conflict. But, due to the deaths of some of the suspects and some circumstances outside its control, the SCSL only completed a total of nine cases of some key military and political leaders deemed to be among those most responsible for the war crimes, crimes against humanity and other serious violations of international humanitarian law committed in the West African nation between November 1996 and January 2002. One indictment was held in abeyance because the suspect disappeared. He has not yet been found as of this writing. It is rumored that he was killed in Liberia on the orders of then President Charles Taylor's orders. There has been no official confirmation of his death. Plans have therefore been made for his trial, should he surface at some future point, through the Residual Special Court for Sierra Leone (RSCSL).

The RSCSL replaced the SCSL when it closed down in December 2013 and began operations in January 2014. The RSCSL today sits in The Hague, an odd political choice, when the branch office would then have to be the former actual seat of the SCSL in a much more stable and conflict-free Freetown. The irony cannot be lost on Sierra Leoneans that at a time when the country was more vulnerable to conflict, it was seen as capable of hosting the tribunal. And so it successfully did with only one of the SCSL's trials controversially taken outside the country to the heart of Europe. Now, when the country is out of conflict and peace has returned and the work is essentially complete, the documentary archives and history of the whole process is moved outside the country. The sensitive point of the nation's recorded history being properly preserved could have surely been addressed and the relevant facilities built in the country. That there is a copy of the materials in a museum on site where the SCSL used to be only serves to underscore not detract from this point.

Viewed against this wider context, and as discussed in Chapter 1, the principal aim of this study has been to examine the SCSL's main judicial legacy and contributions to the development of public international law. The analysis had to be limited to key legal issues. The selected issues are those generally agreed to be of potential wider significance for other post-conflict justice discussions and the development of the nascent field of international criminal law. The research shows that, through its establishment but most significantly its jurisprudence on specific legal issues, the SCSL made some important contributions to the emerging corpus of international criminal law and practice.

11.1.1 *Summary of Chapter 2*

To recap, Chapter 2 briefly introduced the origins and key features of the Sierra Leone conflict. Drawing on authoritative sources, including the SCSL judgments and the official report of the Sierra Leone Truth and Reconciliation Commission (TRC), it explained the main parties to the conflict. Their roles are relevant to understanding the charges issued by the Tribunal against certain persons as well as the limited trials that were subsequently carried out. It will be recalled that the main actors in the Sierra Leone conflict were the Revolutionary United Front (RUF) rebels, that being the group that started a rebellion purportedly aimed at unseating the government in 1991. The other protagonist, on the opposite side, was the Sierra Leone Army which had the constitutional responsibility to defend the nation. It is shown that there is no doubt that there were complex internal and external factors which gave rise to the horrific conflict that took place in the West African nation until 2002. These included years of poor governance, economic decay, widespread corruption and extreme poverty.

What was also equally significant was the motivation of the deeply disenchanted Sierra Leonean youth who saw opportunity in the plunder of diamonds and other economic assets as a way to improve their otherwise blighted lives. In the end, the bad governance and related internal factors seemed to be the primary reasons behind the war. But some external factors also contributed to fueling or sustaining the conflict which, considering the poor state of affairs of the country in 1991, seemed nearly inevitable. These included the support received from Libya, under the self-described revolutionary leader Muamar Gaddafi, where many of the initial RUF invasion forces received free military training. They, and other revolutionary aspirants from West African countries like Liberia and the Gambia, had gone to Libya in the hope of returning home to effect regime change. They all claimed to be carrying out a people's revolution. This, to be clear, is not justification in any way for the atrocities that they would subsequently carry out. It is only to recognize that there were some legitimate grievances that should have been long addressed instead of allowed to fester into outright hostilities.

The analysis in Chapter 2 also demonstrated that the RUF initially enjoyed the support of the National Patriotic Front of Liberia (NPFL) from neighboring Liberia, from where the invasion into eastern Sierra Leone took place in March 1991. They received the help from an estimated 2,000 NPFL forces as well as other Liberian fighters associated with NPFL rebel leader Charles Taylor. The RUF later parted company with their main supporters from neighboring Liberia. They fell out, among other reasons, over the extreme means and methods of warfare used in the conflict, including allegations of cannibalism. They also bickered over who would have ultimate control of the diamond-rich areas that they conquered and plundered. Be that as it may, in the course of a decade of appalling brutality against ordinary civilians, the world witnessed unspeakable acts of terror in Sierra Leone. Most of the behavior by the rebels seemed aimed at intimidating, rather than actually liberating, the defenseless civilian population.

Gross humanitarian law violations included forced displacement, indiscriminate amputations, kidnappings for the use of children as combatants, acts of rape and other types of sexual violence against women and girls, wanton killings and the total destruction of many villages and towns through arson and pillage. The Sierra Leonean rebels would later form a coalition with the mutinying ex-soldiers from the national army. The latter had staged a coup in 1997 and seized power from the elected government of President Ahmed Tejan Kabbah. They dubbed themselves the Armed Forces Revolutionary Council (AFRC). The AFRC-RUF alliance briefly ruled Sierra Leone under the leadership of Major Johnny Paul Koroma (the only person charged by the SCSL that has not been arrested). The AFRC-RUF were eventually dislodged from power by West African peacekeepers deployed under the auspices of the Economic Community of West African States (ECOWAS) which sought to help restore democracy back to Sierra Leone. The tussle for the capital between ECOWAS forces and the AFRC-RUF culminated in the infamous attack on Freetown, the seat of the central government in January 1999, in which the rebels and their collaborators killed and injured thousands of people in a scorched earth campaign as they retreated under fire from the city.

Sierra Leonean President Kabbah, who had assumed power after winning elections conducted in 1996, was ready to do whatever was necessary to end the war. But, because his army was not loyal, he later helped to formalize the status of a civilian-run paramilitary group of traditional hunters known as the Civil Defense Forces (CDF). The CDF, comprised of vigilante volunteers, was tasked to help restore public order. The Kabbah administration's commitment to returning Sierra Leone to peace as a way of ending a particularly nasty conflict, alongside international pressure to end the war, also led him to concede a blanket amnesty on all combatants first in a November 1996 peace accord and then again in another one signed in July 1999. The peace agreements purported to give all combatants a free pass, assuring them that no judicial or legal or other official action would be taken against them by the Sierra Leone government.

In return, the RUF and other combatants were to lay down their weapons, share political power and accept to express their dissent through democratic means in the form of the RUF Party. The unconditional amnesty, which could also be understood as a reflection of the stark choice that often faces countries on the brink of collapse under the weight of a modern type of guerrilla-driven civil war that is often impossible to win, put Sierra Leone initially on the side of those states that would choose peace over justice – if peace is understood narrowly as a silencing of the guns, and justice as no criminal liability for those who perpetrated atrocity crimes in the country. The main concern at that stage seemed to be the continued viability of the state, the desire to stem the further commission of atrocity crimes and the need to help the country turn over a difficult chapter of its history. These rationales animated the initial official policy of forgive and forget.

The Sierra Leone government, driven by the pragmatism of these goals, naturally downplayed the idea of criminal investigations and trials. It was not the first government; nor the last one that will do so, as history and other contemporary conflicts confirm. It instead settled on the idea of a *national unity commission* and passed domestic legislation to that effect. That notion later matured into a proposal for a *national truth and reconciliation commission* (TRC). The focus of the former had been to forge national cohesion while that of the TRC was to help promote peace and national reconciliation. The TRC had a fact-finding role and no authority to punish any of the perpetrators.

But this luxury package, which reflected a preference towards alternative instead of punitive mechanisms, could not hold for long. It has not held up in many other conflicts. In fact, it quickly fell apart due to non-compliance by the rebels. The RUF and AFRC continued to kill, rape and maim, as if they did not know when or how to stop. The fact that they were offered key cabinet posts in government, alongside the generous amnesty, did not win over the hawks in the rebel camp who seemed convinced that they had more to gain from continuing the war instead of ending it. A key lesson derived from the Sierra Leone case study then was that, while governments that face protracted civil wars sometimes choose to silence the guns at all cost, such remains a risky gamble. Peace may come. But, in other cases, peace could prove to be elusive. The very decision to immunize from prosecution all the perpetrators, without requiring their fulfillment of any conditions for its receipt (as per the South Africa amnesty for instance), seemed only to embolden them.

11.1.2 *Summary of Chapter 3*

In Chapter 3, we turned from these circumstances that led to the creation of the SCSL. The Court was President Kabbah's brainchild. It originated from his repeated disappointments with the RUF leadership. They, and their collaborators in Liberia and elsewhere, could simply not be trusted as genuine partners for peace over a three-year period. From the first ceasefire he signed with them in Ivory Coast in November 1996 through to the one in Togo in July 1999, they demonstrated bad faith, saying one thing during the negotiations and winning concessions, then doing something completely different afterwards. A fed-up President Kabbah would later seek United Nations support to prosecute the RUF and their accomplices and collaborators. The government was at that point unwilling to countenance the rebels' violations of the key terms of the July 1999 Lomé Accord. Foremost among these was the killing of peaceful unarmed demonstrators in Freetown at the RUF rebel leader's house. It was a new low in a country that had become so fed up with the irrational killings and impact of the war.

The cold-blooded murder of innocent Sierra Leoneans, as well as foreign UN peacekeepers in May 2000, became a source of shame for the national authorities. It angered the international community into action. The Sierra Leonean president's call for help to establish a tribunal to prosecute them was propitious. It came at a time when there was now new resolve in New York to rally to the aid of the Sierra Leonean government to call the RUF bluff and perhaps even put them in their place. The previous plea for a truth commission process became a plea for a retributive criminal prosecutions process. But the TRC was not disbanded either. It still had contributions to make since the trials would be limited to a handful of leaders. Everyone knew that the majority of the combatants would never face any form of legal accountability elsewhere. Thus, the two transitional justice bodies were asked to work with each other in parallel; each towards its distinctive set of goals. This would eventually put Sierra Leone on the map for its deployment of two such justice mechanisms: One aimed solely at advancing truth and reconciliation; the other directed principally at punishing those found most culpable for carrying out atrocity crimes.

While President Kabbah's case for creation of an international court was success-ful, the hitch was that the Security Council was hardly ready to support another expensive ad hoc tribunal that would be created as a subsidiary organ of the UN. The same body had, only a few years prior, imposed such a court as a way to help end the conflicts in the former Yugoslavia and Rwanda. The Sierra Leone government's hopes were high it would get the same. However, the experience from the processes relating to the creation of those courts had taught the wealthier members, especially some of the Permanent Five in the Security Council, that such tribunals could last for years, potentially cost billions of dollars, and ultimately, be difficult to shut down. In other words, they would take on a life of their own, ticking at their own slow judicial pace instead of the frenetic stride that New York is renowned for as it seeks to put out one conflict after another.

This chapter also evaluated the jurisdiction and organizational form of the SCSL. It revealed that, though some support was given, the Security Council wanted a court with a severely restricted personal and temporal jurisdictional reach. This was in contrast to having a tribunal with a time unconstrained mandate covering the entire span of the Sierra Leonean civil war, as the Sierra Leonean authorities had proposed. Some of the members of the Security Council also envisioned a court that would be paid for by donations from UN Member States rather than through so-called assessed contributions (that is, indirectly out of their own pockets). The end result was that the special court created for Sierra Leone, and entrusted with the mandate of prosecuting those bearing greatest responsibility, was in reality a shoestring court. It was to have a short timeline which selectively excluded up front about half of the atrocities that had been carried out during the first part of a decade-long war. Here, contrary to what has been witnessed in some other conflicts, the national government was not dragging its feet. Nor, perhaps because it thought it was only going after its enemies, did it seek to limit trials to a mere handful of cases. Rather, we experienced the unusual situation whereby the local government would actively but ultimately unsuccessfully lobby for a more robust full-fledged international special court with a much wider competence rooted in the mandatory Chapter VII authority. Yet, the Security Council, which is vested with enforcement of the norms of the international community, refused to budge. The august body, of course, had its way. It was a David versus Goliath Situation. Only that, in this instance, Goliath always won.

11.1.3 *Summary of Chapter 4*

Chapter 4 turned to the subject matter, temporal, personal and territorial jurisdiction of the SCSL. The Court's *ratione materiae* jurisdiction mostly concerned core international crimes (that is, war crimes, crimes against humanity and other serious international humanitarian law violations). But it also (almost merely symbolically) incorporated a handful of offenses drawn from domestic (that is, Sierra Leonean) law. These additions were meant to plug gaps perceived in the law. They were also to help anticipate specific features of the conflict that were deemed to be inadequately regulated under international law. Nonetheless, the inclusion of the crimes of arson, the sexual abuse of minors and the wanton destruction of property did not have much value or impact in practice. In fact, no cases were charged using those national crimes. The jurisdiction of the SCSL prioritized those holding leadership positions. It was also limited temporally, due to funding limitations. There was no mandate for the Court to prosecute the offenses that had occurred during the first half of the war. This attracted strong objections from the Sierra Leonean government. But, in the end, that type of selectivity seemed unavoidable. For similar reasons, the territorial ambit of the court only extended to the crimes committed within Sierra Leone, instead of also including those crimes in neighboring states related to the same conflict – as was the case for the ICTR.

11.2 LEGAL LEGACY ON GREATEST RESPONSIBILITY PERSONAL JURISDICTION

In Chapter 5, which is in some respects the first substantive chapter, I examine the by now most popular way of describing personal jurisdiction in international law which was first introduced by the SCSL Statute, I analyzed Article 1(1) which endowed the Court with the competence to "prosecute persons bearing greatest reasonability" for the various crimes within its jurisdiction. I demonstrated, through a detailed analysis, that this way of framing personal jurisdiction was deeply problematic because it raised all kinds of practical questions during the Freetown trials. There was a lack of clarity as to what kinds of persons could be considered as falling within that type of personal jurisdiction. The prosecution and defense were divided on the answer. So were the judges who proved to also be split on the question between the two separate trial chambers. The Appeals Chamber pronounced on the issue. Rather than clarify things, as one might expect, its appellate decisions seemingly confused things further by reaching the right conclusion but using the wrong reasoning. This led to the concrete general suggestion that international criminal lawyers might as well abandon this type of troubling phrasing in future iterations of personal jurisdiction for any ad hoc international penal tribunals that might be created jointly by the UN and one of its Member States.

Five specific recommendations constituted the takeaway from the analysis offered here. First, in taking up a largely ignored topic in the literature about the best way to interpret and apply greatest responsibility personal jurisdiction, the analysis demonstrated that it is imperative for the creators of future international criminal tribunals to be alive to this concern and take steps to properly delineate their personal jurisdiction. The greatest responsibility concept used at the SCSL was born out of political and practical convenience. For one thing, though the Security Council appeared keen to help Sierra Leone mete out some justice, it was only enthusiastic about this to the extent that the whole project would be relatively cheap and time limited and focused only on a few of the worst perpetrators. Nonetheless, as I have sought to show through this original contribution to the literature, without further specificity, these types of general statements of personal jurisdiction in reality raise important problems of interpretation and application in the context of concrete trials. Ambiguous terminology is always problematic, but especially in a criminal tribunal statute. It undermines legal certainty and predictability, and may even raise issues of fairness towards the defendants.

Second, the type of "greatest responsibility" clause found in Article 1(1) of the SCSL Statute (which displaced the standard language of "persons responsible" traceable back to the Nuremberg IMT) should be avoided whenever possible. I advocate, based on the careful analysis in Chapter 5, a return to the original and more flexible Nuremberg, ICTY and ICTR approach to framing jurisdiction *ratione personae* for such courts. On the other hand, if for political and pragmatic reasons such problematic text must be used in the statute of a future ad hoc international court, it would be prudent to define what it means to say that a court shall prosecute those "bearing greatest responsibility." The lesson of Sierra Leone is that there will be ambiguity as to the practical import of the phrase for prosecutorial decision-makers. Here, one might highlight that, though it did not come to pass for different reasons having to do with the domestic attempt to evade accountability by some of that country's elite, an effort was indeed made in at least one instance to remedy the greatest responsibility personal jurisdiction conundrum when a draft statute was prepared for an ad hoc Special Tribunal for Kenya. This was encouraging to see.

Interestingly, taking a page out of the case law of the SCSL discussed in this work, the Kenyan drafters sought to specify that the phrase should be treated as an explicit directive to the court to focus on investigating and prosecuting the leaders in positions of authority and influence as well as those whose conduct was particularly egregious in the course of carrying out their crimes. The other factors, which were to be taken into account in addition to the level or authority or influence of the person concerned were the gravity, severity, seriousness or scale of the relevant offenses. The drafters of this new version of the greatest responsibility clause would have in that way resolved the thorny issues that led to much debate and litigation about that phraseology at the SCSL. The Kenyan terminology, which learns from the Sierra Leone experience, would be helpful in any future deliberations about this type of personal jurisdiction in international criminal law. This underscores the added value of some of the judicial contributions from the Sierra Leone Tribunal for other African situations that might be faced with the question of how best to address the question of impunity.

Third, and flowing from the preceding point, this study also clarified that future ad hoc tribunal statutes should state whether such a phrase was intended to be (or not be) a jurisdictional hurdle that prosecutors must clear beyond a reasonable doubt or a simple guideline for the exercise of discretion. From Chapter 5, it would seem to make sense that jurisdiction over persons bearing greatest responsibility must not be treated as a jurisdictional threshold. Otherwise, the prosecutions of concrete cases would be difficult, if not impossible. This is a key lesson from the SCSL, which struggled throughout its trials from the earliest through to the last of its cases, to settle the same point that the focus on the investigation and prosecution of persons in leadership positions would not mean that those of a lower rank, in effective control or with greater amount of blood on their hands, could not also be pursued by an international criminal court merely because its jurisdiction is defined as covering only those bearing "greatest responsibility" for the commission of crimes.

Fourth, if greatest responsibility is also used in the standard clauses describing the powers of the chief prosecutor, the purpose of such a statement would also ideally be clarified. If the goal is to use such language to limit the scope of prosecutorial discretion, that should be stated expressly. On the other hand, though highly unlikely, if the goal is to establish an additional jurisdictional requirement, that too should be made explicit. In either case, as argued in the chapter itself, it might be wiser to adopt within such a provision some stance on the relationship and link between the personal jurisdiction article (in the opening of the statute) and the limitations to the prosecutorial mandate (in the clause setting out the prosecutor's functions/responsibilities). The consequence would be to undercut future claims that suspects might otherwise make that the prosecutor lacks the power to make choices as to which persons to prosecute from a large pool of potential perpetrators.

The final recommendation from Chapter 5, which is worth highlighting in the present Conclusion, is that the drafters of ad hoc tribunal instruments, especially the lawyers from the UN Office of Legal Affairs, should attend to these issues from the Sierra Leone case law. They would likely then be better placed to address the legal consequences of a judicial finding that personal jurisdictional requirements had either been fulfilled, or not fulfilled, within the framework of a particular statute. Given the SCSL's own application of this novel phrase, as elucidated in depth in this work, it might also be good practice to specify whether any such determinations would require factual assessments of evidence or are purely procedural or legal questions to be considered by the judges even before the Prosecution calls any witnesses. If factual assessments are required, then the stage of the trial at which the challenge to greatest responsibility jurisdiction should be made must also account for which of the parties bears the burden of proof and what they must show to meet it. Some of these important concerns will need some answers. The SCSL's jurisprudence, whether to resolve them in the statute or even during the drafting of the future tribunal instrument, would serve as a useful starting point in that discussion.

11.3 LEGAL LEGACY ON FORCED MARRIAGE AS A CRIME AGAINST HUMANITY

Chapter 6 of the book examined forced marriage, which was prosecuted for the first time in international law at the SCSL, after being found to fulfill the criteria for inclusion in the residual category of other inhumane acts as crimes against humanity. The chapter begins with a discussion of the gender critique of international law generally and international criminal law in particular. It shows that, while modern efforts to ensure that the gendered burden borne by women and girls in armed conflict was also prevalent in Sierra Leone, the efforts to give expressive recognition to condemn such behavior continues.

In this regard, several ICTY and ICTR cases are reviewed before delving into the discussions of the SCSL prosecutors' attempt to charge the defendant with a novel crime against humanity of forced marriage alleged to constitute part of the other inhumane acts. The chapter shows that the Sierra Leone case study follows a similar pattern of the other tribunals, where predominantly male prosecutors fail to charge defendants with gendered crimes until after the proceedings began. The trial chambers, tasked with determining whether to amend the indictments, then had the difficult task of determining whether to approve the new charges in light of the rights of the defendants. The judges in separate chambers reached different results. Yet, in the end, the appeals court upheld the existence of the crime.

11.4 LEGAL LEGACY ON CHILD RECRUITMENT
AS A WAR CRIME

Chapter 7 of the book is particularly important given the notorious use of child soldiers during the Sierra Leone civil war by all parties to the conflict. While children have been part of armed conflict, whether as victims or as perpetrators for a large part of history, it was only during the negotiations of the Statute of the International Criminal Court at Rome in the summer of 1998 that the conduct became criminal under international law with the inclusion of the conduct as a war crime. It would take a few years for the ICC treaty to enter into force, on July 2002, and thereafter several more years before a defendant was brought before the tribunal. This meant that the SCSL became the first international criminal court to invoke the crime in charges against an accused person, and even more importantly, to interpret and apply the crime. With the arrival of the first case at the ICC, the turn to SCSL case law was inevitable for ICC prosecutors and judges. This was, after all, the maiden case which was also only based on the war crime of child recruitment even though there is no formal relationship between the ICC and the SCSL. This enabled the SCSL's interpretation of the elements of the crime to be used by the ICC judges thereby impacting the development of the crime and its wider application in international criminal law.

11.5 LEGAL LEGACY ON THE LAW OF HEAD
OF STATE IMMUNITY

Chapter 8 of this book, which unsurprisingly was the longest, evaluated head of state immunity in the context of international criminal proceedings. Specifically, it asked the question whether Charles Taylor, who was incumbent president of Liberia, could be indicted by the SCSL given the immunities he claimed to enjoy by virtue of his exalted presidential office under customary international law. The judges ruled, contrary to Taylor's submissions, that immunities *are not* available under customary international law to persons accused of certain offenses before certain international courts supported by the international community. The *Taylor* case was significant for being the first judicial application of the leading International Court of Justice precedent on head of state immunity. I submitted that, overall, the SCSL approach made an important contribution to the normative development of the law of immunity under customary international law. It did so by fashioning, in an admittedly controversial decision, a limited international crimes exception to the doctrine of head of state immunity under customary international law in relation to international courts enjoying significant international community (that is, UN) involvement in their creation. Interestingly, we have already begun to see the possible effects of the Taylor holding on immunity rulings regarding heads of state or former heads of state in other tribunals such as The Hague-based permanent

International Criminal Court in the situation concerning Jordan's failure to arrest President Omar Al Bashir of Sudan.

On the other hand, the SCSL Appeals Chamber decision on Taylor's immunity has been criticized as vague on how the international criminal courts exception applied to the head of state of a *third country* to the treaty between the UN and Sierra Leone which established the SCSL and had statutorily removed immunities. The judicial route around this problem was to find that immunities are not available to Taylor, under *customary international law*, to the extent that he was alleged to have committed certain internationally condemned offenses before an internationally supported court. Through this holding, the Appeals Chamber considered but rejected the classical rationale for immunities which traditionally applied at the *horizontal* level between co-equal sovereigns. They determined that such justifications do not have any relevance when it comes to proceedings arising from the *vertical* relationships that exist between national and international criminal jurisdictions enjoying the blessings of the international community.

The chapter further demonstrated that because of the ICJ and SCSL rulings, the customary law immunities *ratione personae* and *ratione materiae* now appear to cement two important tracks. The first, at the national or municipal level, accepts the applicability of immunities and serves to prevent one state from asserting jurisdiction over important foreign state officials. In this regard, heads of state and heads of government, along with Ministers of Foreign Affairs, enjoy personal immunity based on the maxim *par in parem non habet imperium*. Nonetheless, whether customary immunities will apply before international courts remains doubtful. Immunities, though they are still important for the promotion of peaceful conduct of international relations, are being redefined by the ascendancy of human rights norms as well as the notion of sovereignty as responsibility. If this view comes across as too optimistic, one only has to remember that the current debate about the place of immunity is manifestly different today than it was before the first international trials started at Nuremberg. That legacy, which expressed a radical idea that a leader can be prosecuted, had only developed strong feet around 1919. Yet, it morphed into a norm that was applied at Nuremberg and Tokyo and that has since been handed down through to the provision finding capacity irrelevant in the statutes of tribunals sitting in The Hague, Arusha and now Freetown. This principle seems set to continue to blossom as international criminal law matures. At the moment, immunity has come under fire, with the voices of those states and others who like it seemingly louder than those who oppose it.

To conclude on this chapter, the SCSL case law on Taylor's contentious immunity challenge can be said to offer two additional contributions. First, the involvement of the UN and its Security Council in creating an ad hoc international court may provide a sufficient legal basis for removal of immunities whether this is done explicitly or by implication. This would be so even for the incumbent or former heads of *third* states. This now stands as a sort of warning to the leaders of third countries who meddle in the affairs of their neighbors. The precedent now exists that they too could be prosecuted by an ad hoc international criminal tribunal, including one to which they have not directly consented, so long as they choose to involve themselves in fueling conflicts in which international crimes are committed. The UN determination that such conflicts amount to threats to the maintenance of international peace and security may offer some of the safeguards to stem unilateral action by states which might otherwise seek to manipulate such judicial processes for selfish reasons of national interest.

The second takeaway from the SCSL immunity ruling is that, in the future, other international penal courts should carefully scrutinize the rationale for immunities in cases where they are invoked by a particular defendant. In doing so, they might discover that immunities can be construed as either relevant or irrelevant to prosecutions before certain types of international courts created by the international community. Those established by or with the support of the United Nations may well have greater claim to removal of such immunities. In the case of the latter, they would find useful the Taylor precedent, which offers at least a starting point for their analysis.

11.6 LEGAL LEGACY ON AMNESTIES IN INTERNATIONAL LAW

Shifting from the controversial topic of immunity to a summary of the findings on the controversial topic of amnesty, in Chapter 9, this work evaluated the judicial contribution of the SCSL's decision on the status of amnesties and their relationship to international crimes under international law. The Appeals Chamber determined that national authorities, such as the Sierra Leone government, are unable to confer an unconditional amnesty on the perpetrators of certain types of internationally condemned crimes. On a normative level, this part of the SCSL judicial contribution on amnesty may not be too problematic. It is arguably even a positive step forward in the global struggle against impunity. Surely one state, like Sierra Leone, should not hinder the ability of other states or international criminal courts like the SCSL to investigate or prosecute war crimes, crimes against humanity and other serious violations of international humanitarian law. This position nonetheless assumes that there is in fact an explicit international law duty to prosecute or extradite all the concerned crimes. Viewed in this light, the decision of the court in relation to the Lomé Agreement amnesty constitutes an addition to the normative development of international criminal law.

Conversely, this chapter also showed that the Appeals Chamber's amnesty ruling could be perceived as showing a lack of appreciation of the present state of customary international law on amnesties. Custom is made up of *state practice* and *opinio juris*. State practice, which continues to confer amnesties, appears to undercut the SCSL's definitive conclusions. The belief of the legality of municipal amnesties for atrocity crimes may, however, be in the process of changing, especially in our post–ICC world.

Similarly, turning to aspects of their reasoning, it may be argued that the SCSL judges confused amnesties and the concepts of peremptory norms and obligations owed to the international community as a whole. All these were mentioned in the ruling but were hardly needed to support the Court's ultimately correct conclusion that amnesties were unavailable to the specific defendants before the SCSL by dint of the provisions of its statute. Through its broad ruling, the Appeals Chamber ran the risk of being labelled an activist court that oscillated between stating the law *as it is* and the law *as it wanted it to be*.

Indeed, it could be that the Appeals Chamber of the SCSL reframed and over-simplified the complex legal and policy issues before them. They arguably did this through, among other things, sweeping statements that left little if any room for other considerations. The irony is that this was contrary to the experience of Sierra Leone itself. That situation, in the lead up to the July 1999 peace accord, reflected the dangers of adopting too rigid a rule insisting that amnesties can never be available to peace negotiators because international law *prohibits* them virtually under all circumstances. Solid evidence of the practice supporting such a conclusion was not offered by the SCSL. It is hoped that, in the final analysis, the experience of Sierra Leone both during the war and in the judicial rulings regarding the validity of amnesty at the SCSL will be taken into account in future international community assessments of the compatibility of amnesties with the principle of individual criminal responsibility.

A key and uncontroversial benefit from this Sierra Leone case study was the UN's subsequent explicit adoption of a formal policy barring the conferral of amnesties for international crimes. Under that approach, the UN no longer recognizes peace agreements that endorse amnesties for genocide, crimes against humanity or war crimes. That official stance, which pushes states towards a prohibition that the SCSL wanted them to have, can be properly credited to Sierra Leone. It helps to solidify the Tribunal's contributions to the evolution of the law and policy on amnesties for atrocity crimes.

11.7 LEGAL LEGACY ON THE RELATIONSHIP BETWEEN SPECIAL COURTS AND TRUTH COMMISSIONS

In Chapter 10, I demonstrated that the attempt to simultaneously blend some truth with some reconciliation, on the one hand, and criminal prosecutions and indivi-dual criminal responsibility on the other, was unique and a first when it occurred in Sierra Leone. Though this was a result of how the conflict unfolded, instead of a deliberate choice, the Sierra Leone transitional justice experiment exposed impor-tant legal and policy issues about whether a criminal court or a truth commission can coexist and operate in a way that is complementary rather than antagonistic.

Several questions had to be resolved. The debates turned on which of the criminal court or the truth commission should have primacy over the other, whether confidential information could be subpoenaed from the TRC for use in the criminal prosecutions, and in the case of accused in the Court's custody who wished to appear in public hearings to tell their stories, whether they could be permitted to do so given their right not to incriminate themselves in relation to the proceedings pending before the special criminal tribunal. These were thorny issues. They impacted the SCSL's decisions which effectively blocked the TRC's access to the high-profile detainees in its custody. The Court and TRC confronted each other in an unfortunate public row that might have been avoidable.

A key contribution, from the SCSL-TRC transitional justice experiment, is that criminal trials will not easily reconcile with truth commissions where they operate concurrently. This is especially so where there is no legal clarity in their founding instruments or some type of formal relationship agreement between the two institutions. Although an agreement would seem to be a necessary, but not by itself a sufficient condition for harmonious coordination, I showed that the origins, mandate and operation of the two mechanisms in Sierra Leone (that is, the truth commission and the SCSL) illustrate what happens when coordination only occurs at an informal level or during a moment of tension or crisis. Each side would have the natural tendency to dig its heels and to do what it could to prioritize its own mandate, even if at the expense of the other institution, and perhaps even the greater good of the country under examination.

In the end, the added value of the last substantive part of this study boils down to this. That is, in the future, whenever the international community contemplates having two such institutions (as happened in East Timor and more recently Central African Republic), it is better to work out in advance how the commission and special tribunal can best coordinate and complement their respective roles. It is in this way that we can better assist to resolve a given society's bigger struggle, in which truth and justice can each play its role, to come to terms with a violent past and build a stable and more secure rule of law-based future. Each could live and let the other live. Each can have a useful place to play in the transition from war to peace. It would be counterproductive to ignore this reality or to let things play out on an ad hoc basis. That was mistake made in Sierra Leone. It can be avoided in other conflict or post-conflict situations. So it ought not to be repeated elsewhere.

11.8 FINAL REMARKS ON THE LEGAL LEGACY OF THE SCSL

In closing, as this research has shown through examination of the meaning of greatest jurisdiction, forced marriage as a crime against humanity, child recruitment as a war crime, the immunity of sitting heads of state, the legality of unconditional domestic amnesties for international crimes and the relationship between criminal tribunals and truth commissions, the SCSL can be said to have made substantial judicial contributions to the development of international criminal justice. It is therefore befitting to note that the impact of the SCSL has already been felt well outside Sierra Leone. It will continue to do so. The Court has, while executing its mandate to hold credible trials to prosecute the most responsible perpetrators of certain international crimes, been able to contribute to the larger projects of international law and international community. Indeed, as the now late Sierra Leonean President Ahmad Tejan Kabbah presciently suggested at the opening ceremony of the SCSL courthouse in Freetown in March 2004, the "Special Court" was not only a "symbol of rule of law and an essential element in the pursuit of peace, justice, and national reconciliation for the people of Sierra Leone," that it would "certainly contribute to the jurisprudence of international humanitarian law, and enhance the promotion and protection of the fundamental rights of people everywhere," it was

> also a Special Court for the international community, a symbol of the rule of international law, especially at a time when some State and non-State actors are increasingly displaying, shamelessly, contempt for the principles of international law, including international humanitarian law and human rights law. This Special Court [was] good for Sierra Leone. It [was] also good for the world today.[1]

---

[1]   www.sierra-leone.org/Speeches/kabbah-031004.html.

Appendices

UN SECURITY COUNCIL RESOLUTION 1315 (2000) *

The Security Council

Deeply concerned at the very serious crimes committed within the territory of Sierra Leone against the people of Sierra Leone and United Nations and associated personnel and at the prevailing situation of impunity,

Commending the efforts of the Government of Sierra Leone and the Economic Community of West African States (ECOWAS) to bring lasting peace to Sierra Leone,

Noting that the Heads of State and Government of ECOWAS agreed at the 23rd Summit of the Organization in Abuja on 28 and 29 May 2000 to dispatch a regional investigation of the resumption of hostilities,

Noting also the steps taken by the Government of Sierra Leone in creating a national truth and reconciliation process, as required by Article XXVI of the Lomé Peace Agreement (S/1999/777) to contribute to the promotion of the rule of law,

Recalling that the Special Representative of the Secretary-General appended to his signature of the Lomé Agreement a statement that the United Nations holds the understanding that the amnesty provisions of the Agreement shall not apply to international crimes of genocide, crimes against humanity, war crimes and other serious violations of international humanitarian law,

Reaffirming the importance of compliance with international humanitarian law, and *reaffirming further* that persons who commit or authorize serious violations of international humanitarian law are individually responsible and accountable for those violations and that the international community will exert every effort to bring those responsible to justice in accordance with international standards of justice, fairness and due process of law,

Recognizing that, in the particular circumstances of Sierra Leone, a credible system of justice and accountability for the very serious crimes committed there would end impunity and would contribute to the process of national reconciliation and to the restoration and maintenance of peace,

Taking note in this regard of the letter dated 12 June 2000 from the President of Sierra Leone to the Secretary-General and the Suggested Framework attached to it (S/2000/786, annex),

Recognizing further the desire of the Government of Sierra Leone for assistance from the United Nations in establishing a strong and credible court that will meet the objectives of bringing justice and ensuring lasting peace,

Noting the report of the Secretary-General of 31 July 2000 (S/2000/751) and, in particular, *taking note* with appreciation of the steps already taken by the Secretary-General in response to the request of the Government of Sierra Leone to assist it in establishing a special court,

Noting further the negative impact of the security situation on the administration of justice in Sierra Leone and the pressing need for international cooperation to assist in strengthening the judicial system of Sierra Leone,

Acknowledging the important contribution that can be made to this effort by qualified persons from West African States, the Commonwealth, other Member States of the United Nations and international organizations, to expedite the process of bringing justice and reconciliation to Sierra Leone and the region,

Reiterating that the situation in Sierra Leone continues to constitute a threat to international peace and security in the region,

1. *Requests* the Secretary-General to negotiate an agreement with the Government of Sierra Leone to create an independent special court consistent with this resolution, and *expresses* its readiness to take further steps expeditiously upon receiving and reviewing the report of the Secretary-General referred to in paragraph 6 below;

2. *Recommends* that the subject matter jurisdiction of the special court should include notably crimes against humanity, war crimes and other serious violations of international humanitarian law, as well as crimes under relevant Sierra Leonean law committed within the territory of Sierra Leone;

3. *Recommends further* that the special court should have personal jurisdiction over persons who bear the greatest responsibility for the commission of the crimes referred to in paragraph 2, including those leaders who, in committing such crimes, have threatened the establishment of and implementation of the peace process in Sierra Leone;

4. *Emphasizes* the importance of ensuring the impartiality, independence and credibility of the process, in particular with regard to the status of the judges and the prosecutors;

5. *Requests*, in this connection, that the Secretary-General, if necessary, send a team of experts to Sierra Leone as may be required to prepare the report referred to in paragraph 6 below;

6. *Requests* the Secretary-General to submit a report to the Security Council on the implementation of this resolution, in particular on his consultations and

negotiations with the Government of Sierra Leone concerning the establishment of the special court, including recommendations, no later than 30 days from the date of this resolution;

7. *Requests* the Secretary-General to address in his report the questions of the temporal jurisdiction of the special court, an appeals process including the advisability, feasibility, and appropriateness of an appeals chamber in the special court or of sharing the Appeals Chamber of the International Criminal Tribunals for the Former Yugoslavia and Rwanda or other effective options, and a possible alternative host State, should it be necessary to convene the special court outside the seat of the court in Sierra Leone, if circumstances so require;

8. *Requests* the Secretary-General to include recommendations on the following:
   (a) any additional agreements that may be required for the provision of the international assistance which will be necessary for the establishment and functioning of the special court;
   (b) the level of participation, support and technical assistance of qualified persons from Member States of the United Nations, including in particular, member States of ECOWAS and the Commonwealth, and from the United Nations Mission in Sierra Leone that will be necessary for the efficient, independent and impartial functioning of the special court;
   (c) the amount of voluntary contributions, as appropriate, of funds, equipment and services to the special court, including through the offer of expert personnel that may be needed from States, intergovernmental organizations and nongovernmental organizations;
   (d) whether the special court could receive, as necessary and feasible, expertise and advice from the International Criminal Tribunals for the Former Yugoslavia and Rwanda;

9. *Decides* to remain actively seized of the matter.

AGREEMENT BETWEEN THE UNITED NATIONS AND THE GOVERNMENT OF SIERRA LEONE ON THE ESTABLISHMENT OF A SPECIAL COURT FOR SIERRA LEONE[*]

Whereas the Security Council, in its resolution 1315 (2000) of 14 August 2000, expressed deep concern at the very serious crimes committed within the territory of Sierra Leone against the people of Sierra Leone and United Nations and associated personnel and at the prevailing situation of impunity;

Whereas by the said resolution, the Security Council requested the Secretary-General to negotiate an agreement with the Government of Sierra Leone to create an independent special court to prosecute persons who bear the greatest responsibility for the commission of serious violations of international humanitarian law and crimes committed under Sierra Leonean law;

Whereas the Secretary-General of the United Nations (hereinafter "the Secretary-General") and the Government of Sierra Leone (hereinafter "the Government") have held such negotiations for the establishment of a Special Court for Sierra Leone (hereinafter "the Special Court");

Now therefore the United Nations and the Government of Sierra Leone have agreed as follows:

Article 1 *Establishment of the Special Court*

1. There is hereby established a Special Court for Sierra Leone to prosecute persons who bear the greatest responsibility for serious violations of international humanitarian law and Sierra Leonean law committed in the territory of Sierra Leone since 30 November 1996.
2. The Special Court shall function in accordance with the Statute of the Special Court for Sierra Leone. The Statute is annexed to this Agreement and forms an integral part thereof.

Article 2 *Composition of the Special Court and appointment of judges*

1. The Special Court shall be composed of a Trial Chamber and an Appeals Chamber with a second Trial Chamber to be created if, after the passage of at least six months from the commencement of the functioning of the Special Court, the Secretary-General, or the President of the Special Court so request. Up to two alternate judges shall similarly be appointed after six months if the President of the Special Court so determines.
2. The Chambers shall be composed of no fewer than eight independent judges and no more than eleven such judges who shall serve as follows:

---

[*] Signed in Freetown, Sierra Leone on 16 January 2002; entered into force on 12 April 2002.

(a) Three judges shall serve in the Trial Chamber where one shall be appointed by the Government of Sierra Leone and two judges appointed by the Secretary-General, upon nominations forwarded by States, and in particular the member States of the Economic Community of West African States and the Commonwealth, at the invitation of the Secretary-General;

(b) In the event of the creation of a second Trial Chamber, that Chamber shall be likewise composed in the manner contained in subparagraph (a) above;

(c) Five judges shall serve in the Appeals Chamber, of whom two shall be appointed by the Government of Sierra Leone and three judges shall be appointed by the Secretary-General upon nominations forwarded by States, and in particular the member States of the Economic Community of West African States and the Commonwealth, at the invitation of the Secretary-General.

3. The Government of Sierra Leone and the Secretary-General shall consult on the appointment of judges.

4. Judges shall be appointed for a three-year term and shall be eligible for re-appointment.

5. If, at the request of the President of the Special Court, an alternate judge or judges have been appointed by the Government of Sierra Leone or the Secretary-General, the presiding judge of a Trial Chamber or the Appeals Chamber shall designate such an alternate judge to be present at each stage of the trial and to replace a judge if that judge is unable to continue sitting.

Article 3 Appointment of a Prosecutor and a Deputy Prosecutor

1. The Secretary-General, after consultation with the Government of Sierra Leone, shall appoint a Prosecutor for a three-year term. The Prosecutor shall be eligible for reappointment.

2. The Government of Sierra Leone, in consultation with the Secretary-General and the Prosecutor, shall appoint a Sierra Leonean Deputy Prosecutor to assist the Prosecutor in the conduct of the investigations and prosecutions.

3. The Prosecutor and the Deputy Prosecutor shall be of high moral character and possess the highest level of professional competence and extensive experience in the conduct of investigations and prosecutions of criminal cases. The Prosecutor and the Deputy Prosecutor shall be independent in the performance of their functions and shall not accept or seek instructions from any Government or any other source.

4. The Prosecutor shall be assisted by such Sierra Leonean and international staff as may be required to perform the functions assigned to him or her effectively and efficiently.

Article 4 Appointment of a Registrar

1. The Secretary-General, in consultation with the President of the Special Court, shall appoint a Registrar who shall be responsible for the servicing of the Chambers and the

Office of the Prosecutor, and for the recruitment and administration of all support staff. He or she shall also administer the financial and staff resources of the Special Court.

2. The Registrar shall be a staff member of the United Nations. He or she shall serve a three-year term and shall be eligible for re-appointment.

Article 5 Premises

The Government shall assist in the provision of premises for the Special Court and such utilities, facilities and other services as may be necessary for its operation.

Article 6 Expenses of the Special Court

The expenses of the Special Court shall be borne by voluntary contributions from the international community. It is understood that the Secretary-General will commence the process of establishing the Court when he has sufficient contributions in hand to finance the establishment of the Court and 12 months of its operations plus pledges equal to the anticipated expenses of the following 24 months of the Court's operation.

It is further understood that the Secretary-General will continue to seek contributions equal to the anticipated expenses of the Court beyond its first three years of operation. Should voluntary contributions be insufficient for the Court to implement its mandate, the Secretary-General and the Security Council shall explore alternate means of financing the Special Court.

Article 7 Management Committee

It is the understanding of the Parties that interested States will establish a management committee to assist the Secretary-General in obtaining adequate funding, and provide advice and policy direction on all non-judicial aspects of the operation of the Court, including questions of efficiency, and to perform other functions as agreed by interested States. The management committee shall consist of important contributors to the Special Court. The Government of Sierra Leone and the Secretary-General will also participate in the management committee.

Article 8 Inviolability of premises, archives and all other documents

1. The premises of the Special Court shall be inviolable. The competent authorities shall take appropriate action that may be necessary to ensure that the Special Court shall not be dispossessed of all or any part of the premises of the Court without its express consent.

2. The property, funds and assets of the Special Court, wherever located and by whomsoever held, shall be immune from search, seizure, requisition, confiscation, expropriation and any other form of interference, whether by executive, administrative, judicial or legislative action.

3. The archives of the Court, and in general all documents and materials made available, belonging to or used by it, wherever located and by whomsoever held, shall be inviolable.

Article 9 *Funds, assets and other property*

1. The Special Court, its funds, assets and other property, wherever located and by whomsoever held, shall enjoy immunity from every form of legal process, except insofar as in any particular case the Court has expressly waived its immunity. It is understood, however, that no waiver of immunity shall extend to any measure of execution.

2. Without being restricted by financial controls, regulations or moratoriums of any kind, the Special Court:

   (a) May hold and use funds, gold or negotiable instruments of any kind and maintain and operate accounts in any currency and convert any currency held by it into any other currency;

   (b) Shall be free to transfer its funds, gold or currency from one country to another, or within Sierra Leone, to the United Nations or any other agency.

Article 10 *Seat of the Special Court*

The Special Court shall have its seat in Sierra Leone. The Court may meet away from its seat if it considers it necessary for the efficient exercise of its functions, and may be relocated outside Sierra Leone, if circumstances so require, and subject to the conclusion of a Headquarters Agreement between the Secretary-General of the United Nations and the Government of Sierra Leone, on the one hand, and the Government of the alternative seat, on the other.

Article 11 *Juridical capacity*

The Special Court shall possess the juridical capacity necessary to:

(a) Contract;
(b) Acquire and dispose of movable and immovable property;
(c) Institute legal proceedings;
(d) Enter into agreements with States as may be necessary for the exercise of its functions and for the operation of the Court.

Article 12 Privileges and immunities of the judges,
the Prosecutor and the Registrar

1. The judges, the Prosecutor and the Registrar, together with their families forming part of their household, shall enjoy the privileges and immunities, exemptions and facilities accorded to diplomatic agents in accordance with the 1961
   Vienna Convention on Diplomatic Relations. They shall, in particular, enjoy:

   (a) Personal inviolability, including immunity from arrest or detention;
   (b) Immunity from criminal, civil and administrative jurisdiction in conformity
       with the Vienna Convention;
   (c) Inviolability for all papers and documents;
   (d) Exemption, as appropriate, from immigration restrictions and other alien
       registrations;
   (e) The same immunities and facilities in respect of their personal baggage as
       are accorded to diplomatic agents by the Vienna Convention;
   (f) Exemption from taxation in Sierra Leone on their salaries, emoluments and
       allowances.

2. Privileges and immunities are accorded to the judges, the Prosecutor and the
   Registrar in the interest of the Special Court and not for the personal benefit of
   the individuals themselves. The right and the duty to waive the immunity, in any
   case where it can be waived without prejudice to the purpose for which it is
   accorded, shall lie with the Secretary-General, in consultation with the
   President.

Article 13 Privileges and immunities of international
and Sierra Leonean personnel

1. Sierra Leonean and international personnel of the Special Court shall be
   accorded:

   (a) Immunity from legal process in respect of words spoken or written and all
       acts performed by them in their official capacity. Such immunity shall
       continue to be accorded after termination of employment with the Special
       Court;
   (b) Immunity from taxation on salaries, allowances and emoluments paid to
       them.

2. International personnel shall, in addition thereto, be accorded:

   (a) Immunity from immigration restriction;
   (b) The right to import free of duties and taxes, except for payment for services,
       their furniture and effects at the time of first taking up their official duties in
       Sierra Leone.

3. The privileges and immunities are granted to the officials of the Special Court in the interest of the Court and not for their personal benefit. The right and the duty to waive the immunity in any particular case where it can be waived without prejudice to the purpose for which it is accorded shall lie with the Registrar of the Court.

Article 14 *Counsel*

1. The Government shall ensure that the counsel of a suspect or an accused who has been admitted as such by the Special Court shall not be subjected to any measure which may affect the free and independent exercise of his or her functions.
2. In particular, the counsel shall be accorded:
   (a) Immunity from personal arrest or detention and from seizure of personal baggage;
   (b) Inviolability of all documents relating to the exercise of his or her functions as a counsel of a suspect or accused;
   (c) Immunity from criminal or civil jurisdiction in respect of words spoken or written and acts performed in his or her capacity as counsel. Such immunity shall continue to be accorded after termination of his or her functions as a counsel of a suspect or accused.
   (d) Immunity from any immigration restrictions during his or her stay as well as during his or her journey to the Court and back.

Article 15 *Witnesses and experts*

Witnesses and experts appearing from outside Sierra Leone on a summons or a request of the judges or the Prosecutor shall not be prosecuted, detained or subjected to any restriction on their liberty by the Sierra Leonean authorities. They shall not be subjected to any measure which may affect the free and independent exercise of their functions. The provisions of article 14, paragraph 2(a) and (d), shall apply to them.

Article 16 *Security, safety and protection of persons referred to in this Agreement*

Recognizing the responsibility of the Government under international law to ensure the security, safety and protection of persons referred to in this Agreement and its present incapacity to do so pending the restructuring and rebuilding of its security forces, it is agreed that the United Nations Mission in Sierra Leone shall provide the necessary security to premises and personnel of the Special Court, subject to an appropriate mandate by the Security Council and within its capabilities.

Article 17 Cooperation with the Special Court

1. The Government shall cooperate with all organs of the Special Court at all stages of the proceedings. It shall, in particular, facilitate access to the Prosecutor to sites, persons and relevant documents required for the investigation.
2. The Government shall comply without undue delay with any request for assistance by the Special Court or an order issued by the Chambers, including, but not limited to:
   (a) Identification and location of persons;
   (b) Service of documents;
   (c) Arrest or detention of persons;
   (d) Transfer of an indictee to the Court.

Article 18 Working language

The official working language of the Special Court shall be English.

Article 19 Practical arrangements

1. With a view to achieving efficiency and cost-effectiveness in the operation of the Special Court, a phased-in approach shall be adopted for its establishment in accordance with the chronological order of the legal process.
2. In the first phase of the operation of the Special Court, judges, the Prosecutor and the Registrar will be appointed along with investigative and prosecutorial staff. The process of investigations and prosecutions of those already in custody shall be initiated.
3. In the initial phase, judges of the Trial Chamber and the Appeals Chamber shall be convened on an ad hoc basis for dealing with organizational matters, and serving when required to perform their duties.
4. Judges of the Trial Chamber shall take permanent office shortly before the investigation process has been completed. Judges of the Appeals Chamber shall take permanent office when the first trial process has been completed.

Article 20 Settlement of Disputes

Any dispute between the Parties concerning the interpretation or application of this Agreement shall be settled by negotiation, or by any other mutually agreed-upon mode of settlement.

Article 21 *Entry into force*

The present Agreement shall enter into force on the day after both Parties have notified each other in writing that the legal requirements for entry into force have been complied with.

Article 22 *Amendment*

This Agreement may be amended by written agreement between the Parties.

Article 23 *Termination*

This Agreement shall be terminated by agreement of the Parties upon completion of the judicial activities of the Special Court.

IN WITNESS WHEREOF, the following duly authorized representatives of the United Nations and of the Government of Sierra Leone have signed this Agreement.

Done at Freetown, on 16 January 2002 in two originals in the English language.

For the United Nations Hans Corell, Under-Secretary-General for Legal Affairs

For the Government of Sierra Leone Solomon Berewa, Attorney General and Minister of Justice

---

STATUTE OF THE SPECIAL COURT FOR SIERRA LEONE[*]

Having been established by an Agreement between the United Nations and the Government of Sierra Leone pursuant to Security Council resolution 1315 (2000) of 14 August 2000, the Special Court for Sierra Leone (hereinafter "the Special Court") shall function in accordance with the provisions of the present Statute.

Article 1 *Competence of the Special Court*

1. The Special Court shall, except as provided in subparagraph (2), have the power to prosecute persons who bear the greatest responsibility for serious violations of international humanitarian law and Sierra Leonean law committed in the territory of Sierra Leone since 30 November 1996, including those leaders who,

---

[*] Note: This statute was annexed to the preceding agreement between the UN and Sierra Leone which provided for the establishment the SCSL. Under Article 8(2), it formed an integral part thereof.

in committing such crimes, have threatened the establishment of and implementation of the peace process in Sierra Leone.

2. Any transgressions by peacekeepers and related personnel present in Sierra Leone pursuant to the Status of Mission Agreement in force between the United Nations and the Government of Sierra Leone or agreements between Sierra Leone and other Governments or regional organizations, or, in the absence of such agreement, provided that the peacekeeping operations were undertaken with the consent of the Government of Sierra Leone, shall be within the primary jurisdiction of the sending State.

3. In the event the sending State is unwilling or unable genuinely to carry out an investigation or prosecution, the Court may, if authorized by the Security Council on the proposal of any State, exercise jurisdiction over such persons.

Article 2 Crimes against humanity

The Special Court shall have the power to prosecute persons who committed the following crimes as part of a widespread or systematic attack against any civilian population:

a. Murder;
b. Extermination;
c. Enslavement;
d. Deportation;
e. Imprisonment;
f. Torture;
g. Rape, sexual slavery, enforced prostitution, forced pregnancy and any other form of sexual violence;
h. Persecution on political, racial, ethnic or religious grounds;
i. Other inhumane acts.

Article 3 Violations of Article 3 common to the Geneva Conventions and of Additional Protocol II

The Special Court shall have the power to prosecute persons who committed or ordered the commission of serious violations of article 3 common to the Geneva Conventions of 12 August 1949 for the Protection of War Victims, and of Additional Protocol II thereto of 8 June 1977. These violations shall include:

a. Violence to life, health and physical or mental well-being of persons, in particular murder as well as cruel treatment such as torture, mutilation or any form of corporal punishment;
b. Collective punishments;

c. Taking of hostages;
d. Acts of terrorism;
e. Outrages upon personal dignity, in particular humiliating and degrading treatment, rape, enforced prostitution and any form of indecent assault;
f. Pillage;
g. The passing of sentences and the carrying out of executions without previous judgment pronounced by a regularly constituted court, affording all the judicial guarantees which are recognized as indispensable by civilized peoples;
h. Threats to commit any of the foregoing acts.

Article 4 *Other serious violations of international humanitarian law*

The Special Court shall have the power to prosecute persons who committed the following serious violations of international humanitarian law:

a. Intentionally directing attacks against the civilian population as such or against individual civilians not taking direct part in hostilities;
b. Intentionally directing attacks against personnel, installations, material, units or vehicles involved in a humanitarian assistance or peacekeeping mission in accordance with the Charter of the United Nations, as long as they are entitled to the protection given to civilians or civilian objects under the international law of armed conflict;
c. Conscripting or enlisting children under the age of 15 years into armed forces or groups or using them to participate actively in hostilities.

Article 5 *Crimes under Sierra Leonean law*

The Special Court shall have the power to prosecute persons who have committed the following crimes under Sierra Leonean law:

a. Offences relating to the abuse of girls under the Prevention of Cruelty to Children Act, 1926 (Cap. 31):
   i. Abusing a girl under 13 years of age, contrary to section 6;
   ii. Abusing a girl between 13 and 14 years of age, contrary to section 7;
   iii. Abduction of a girl for immoral purposes, contrary to section 12.

b. Offences relating to the wanton destruction of property under the Malicious Damage Act, 1861:
   a. Setting fire to dwelling – houses, any person being therein, contrary to section 2;
   b. Setting fire to public buildings, contrary to sections 5 and 6;
   c. Setting fire to other buildings, contrary to section 6.

Article 6 Individual criminal responsibility

1. A person who planned, instigated, ordered, committed or otherwise aided and abetted in the planning, preparation or execution of a crime referred to in articles 2 to 4 of the present Statute shall be individually responsible for the crime.
2. The official position of any accused persons, whether as Head of State or Government or as a responsible government official, shall not relieve such person of criminal responsibility nor mitigate punishment.
3. The fact that any of the acts referred to in articles 2 to 4 of the present Statute was committed by a subordinate does not relieve his or her superior of criminal responsibility if he or she knew or had reason to know that the subordinate was about to commit such acts or had done so and the superior had failed to take the necessary and reasonable measures to prevent such acts or to punish the perpetrators thereof.
4. The fact that an accused person acted pursuant to an order of a Government or of a superior shall not relieve him or her of criminal responsibility, but may be considered in mitigation of punishment if the Special Court determines that justice so requires.
5. Individual criminal responsibility for the crimes referred to in article 5 shall be determined in accordance with the respective laws of Sierra Leone.

Article 7 Jurisdiction over persons of 15 years of age

1. The Special Court shall have no jurisdiction over any person who was under the age of 15 at the time of the alleged commission of the crime. Should any person who was at the time of the alleged commission of the crime between 15 and 18 years of age come before the Court, he or she shall be treated with dignity and a sense of worth, taking into account his or her young age and the desirability of promoting his or her rehabilitation, reintegration into and assumption of a constructive role in society, and in accordance with international human rights standards, in particular the rights of the child.
2. In the disposition of a case against a juvenile offender, the Special Court shall order any of the following: care guidance and supervision orders, community service orders, counseling, foster care, correctional, educational and vocational training programmes, approved schools and, as appropriate, any programmes of disarmament, demobilization and reintegration or programmes of child protection agencies.

Article 8 Concurrent jurisdiction

1. The Special Court and the national courts of Sierra Leone shall have concurrent jurisdiction.
2. The Special Court shall have primacy over the national courts of Sierra Leone. At any stage of the procedure, the Special Court may formally request a national court to defer to its competence in accordance with the present Statute and the Rules of Procedure and Evidence.

Article 9 Non bis in idem

1. No person shall be tried before a national court of Sierra Leone for acts for which he or she has already been tried by the Special Court.
2. A person who has been tried by a national court for the acts referred to in articles 2 to 4 of the present Statute may be subsequently tried by the Special Court if:
   a. The act for which he or she was tried was characterized as an ordinary crime; or
   b. The national court proceedings were not impartial or independent, were designed to shield the accused from international criminal responsibility or the case was not diligently prosecuted.
3. In considering the penalty to be imposed on a person convicted of a crime under the present Statute, the Special Court shall take into account the extent to which any penalty imposed by a national court on the same person for the same act has already been served.

Article 10 Amnesty

An amnesty granted to any person falling within the jurisdiction of the Special Court in respect of the crimes referred to in articles 2 to 4 of the present Statute shall not be a bar to prosecution.

Article 11 Organization of the Special Court

The Special Court shall consist of the following organs:

a. The Chambers, comprising one or more Trial Chambers and an Appeals Chamber;
b. The Prosecutor; and
c. The Registry.

Article 12 *Composition of the Chambers*

1. The Chambers shall be composed of not less than eight (8) or more than eleven (11) independent judges, who shall serve as follows:
   a. Three judges shall serve in the Trial Chamber, of whom one shall be a judge appointed by the Government of Sierra Leone, and two judges appointed by the Secretary-General of the United Nations (hereinafter "the Secretary-General").
   b. Five judges shall serve in the Appeals Chamber, of whom two shall be judges appointed by the Government of Sierra Leone, and three judges appointed by the Secretary-General.

2. Each judge shall serve only in the Chamber to which he or she has been appointed.
3. The judges of the Appeals Chamber and the judges of the Trial Chamber, respectively, shall elect a presiding judge who shall conduct the proceedings in the Chamber to which he or she was elected. The presiding judge of the Appeals Chamber shall be the President of the Special Court.
4. If, at the request of the President of the Special Court, an alternate judge or judges have been appointed by the Government of Sierra Leone or the Secretary-General, the presiding judge of a Trial Chamber or the Appeals Chamber shall designate such an alternate judge to be present at each stage of the trial and to replace a judge if that judge is unable to continue sitting.

Article 13 *Qualification and appointment of judges*

1. The judges shall be persons of high moral character, impartiality and integrity who possess the qualifications required in their respective countries for appointment to the highest judicial offices. They shall be independent in the performance of their functions, and shall not accept or seek instructions from any Government or any other source.
2. In the overall composition of the Chambers, due account shall be taken of the experience of the judges in international law, including international humanitarian law and human rights law, criminal law and juvenile justice.
3. The judges shall be appointed for a three-year period and shall be eligible for reappointment.

Article 14 *Rules of Procedure and Evidence*

1. The Rules of Procedure and Evidence of the International Criminal Tribunal for Rwanda obtaining at the time of the establishment of the Special Court shall be applicable *mutatis mutandis* to the conduct of the legal proceedings before the Special Court.

2. The judges of the Special Court as a whole may amend the Rules of Procedure and Evidence or adopt additional rules where the applicable Rules do not, or do not adequately, provide for a specific situation. In so doing, they may be guided, as appropriate, by the Criminal Procedure Act, 1965, of Sierra Leone.

Article 15 *The Prosecutor*

1. The Prosecutor shall be responsible for the investigation and prosecution of persons who bear the greatest responsibility for serious violations of international humanitarian law and crimes under Sierra Leonean law committed in the territory of Sierra Leone since 30 November 1996. The Prosecutor shall act independently as a separate organ of the Special Court. He or she shall not seek or receive instructions from any Government or from any other source.
2. The Office of the Prosecutor shall have the power to question suspects, victims and witnesses, to collect evidence and to conduct on-site investigations. In carrying out these tasks, the Prosecutor shall, as appropriate, be assisted by the Sierra Leonean authorities concerned.
3. The Prosecutor shall be appointed by the Secretary-General for a three-year term and shall be eligible for re-appointment. He or she shall be of high moral character and possess the highest level of professional competence, and have extensive experience in the conduct of investigations and prosecutions of criminal cases.
4. The Prosecutor shall be assisted by a Sierra Leonean Deputy Prosecutor, and by such other Sierra Leonean and international staff as may be required to perform the functions assigned to him or her effectively and efficiently. Given the nature of the crimes committed and the particular sensitivities of girls, young women and children victims of rape, sexual assault, abduction and slavery of all kinds, due consideration should be given in the appointment of staff to the employment of prosecutors and investigators experienced in gender-related crimes and juvenile justice.
5. In the prosecution of juvenile offenders, the Prosecutor shall ensure that the child-rehabilitation programme is not placed at risk and that, where appropriate, resort should be had to alternative truth and reconciliation mechanisms, to the extent of their availability.

Article 16 *The Registry*

1. The Registry shall be responsible for the administration and servicing of the Special Court.

2. The Registry shall consist of a Registrar and such other staff as may be required.
3. The Registrar shall be appointed by the Secretary-General after consultation with the President of the Special Court and shall be a staff member of the United Nations. He or she shall serve for a three-year term and be eligible for re-appointment.
4. The Registrar shall set up a Victims and Witnesses Unit within the Registry. This Unit shall provide, in consultation with the Office of the Prosecutor, protective measures and security arrangements, counseling and other appropriate assistance for witnesses, victims who appear before the Court and others who are at risk on account of testimony given by such witnesses. The Unit personnel shall include experts in trauma, including trauma related to crimes of sexual violence and violence against children.

Article 17 Rights of the accused

1. All accused shall be equal before the Special Court.
2. The accused shall be entitled to a fair and public hearing, subject to measures ordered by the Special Court for the protection of victims and witnesses.
3. The accused shall be presumed innocent until proved guilty according to the provisions of the present Statute.
4. In the determination of any charge against the accused pursuant to the present Statute, he or she shall be entitled to the following minimum guarantees, in full equality:
   a. To be informed promptly and in detail in a language which he or she understands of the nature and cause of the charge against him or her;
   b. To have adequate time and facilities for the preparation of his or her defence and to communicate with counsel of his or her own choosing;
   c. To be tried without undue delay;
   d. To be tried in his or her presence, and to defend himself or herself in person or through legal assistance of his or her own choosing; to be informed, if he or she does not have legal assistance, of this right; and to have legal assistance assigned to him or her, in any case where the interests of justice so require, and without payment by him or her in any such case if he or she does not have sufficient means to pay for it;
   e. To examine, or have examined, the witnesses against him or her and to obtain the attendance and examination of witnesses on his or her behalf under the same conditions as witnesses against him or her;
   f. To have the free assistance of an interpreter if he or she cannot understand or speak the language used in the Special Court;
   g. Not to be compelled to testify against himself or herself or to confess guilt.

Article 18 Judgement

The judgement shall be rendered by a majority of the judges of the Trial Chamber or of the Appeals Chamber, and shall be delivered in public. It shall be accompanied by a reasoned opinion in writing, to which separate or dissenting opinions may be appended.

Article 19 Penalties

1. The Trial Chamber shall impose upon a convicted person, other than a juvenile offender, imprisonment for a specified number of years. In determining the terms of imprisonment, the Trial Chamber shall, as appropriate, have recourse to the practice regarding prison sentences in the International Criminal Tribunal for Rwanda and the national courts of Sierra Leone.
2. In imposing the sentences, the Trial Chamber should take into account such factors as the gravity of the offence and the individual circumstances of the convicted person.
3. In addition to imprisonment, the Trial Chamber may order the forfeiture of the property, proceeds and any assets acquired unlawfully or by criminal conduct, and their return to their rightful owner or to the State of Sierra Leone.

Article 20 Appellate proceedings

1. The Appeals Chamber shall hear appeals from persons convicted by the Trial Chamber or from the Prosecutor on the following grounds:
   a. A procedural error;
   b. An error on a question of law invalidating the decision;
   c. An error of fact which has occasioned a miscarriage of justice.

2. The Appeals Chamber may affirm, reverse or revise the decisions taken by the Trial Chamber.
3. The judges of the Appeals Chamber of the Special Court shall be guided by the decisions of the Appeals Chamber of the International Tribunals for the former Yugoslavia and for Rwanda. In the interpretation and application of the laws of Sierra Leone, they shall be guided by the decisions of the Supreme Court of Sierra Leone.

Article 21 Review proceedings

1. Where a new fact has been discovered which was not known at the time of the proceedings before the Trial Chamber or the Appeals Chamber and which could have been a decisive factor in reaching the decision, the convicted person or the Prosecutor may submit an application for review of the judgment.

2. An application for review shall be submitted to the Appeals Chamber. The Appeals Chamber may reject the application if it considers it to be unfounded. If it determines that the application is meritorious, it may, as appropriate:
   a. Reconvene the Trial Chamber;
   b. Retain jurisdiction over the matter.

Article 22 Enforcement of sentences

1. Imprisonment shall be served in Sierra Leone. If circumstances so require, imprisonment may also be served in any of the States which have concluded with the International Criminal Tribunal for Rwanda or the International Criminal Tribunal for the former Yugoslavia an agreement for the enforcement of sentences, and which have indicated to the Registrar of the Special Court their willingness to accept convicted persons. The Special Court may conclude similar agreements for the enforcement of sentences with other States.
2. Conditions of imprisonment, whether in Sierra Leone or in a third State, shall be governed by the law of the State of enforcement subject to the supervision of the Special Court. The State of enforcement shall be bound by the duration of the sentence, subject to article 23 of the present Statute.

Article 23 Pardon or commutation of sentences

If, pursuant to the applicable law of the State in which the convicted person is imprisoned, he or she is eligible for pardon or commutation of sentence, the State concerned shall notify the Special Court accordingly. There shall only be pardon or commutation of sentence if the President of the Special Court, in consultation with the judges, so decides on the basis of the interests of justice and the general principles of law.

Article 24 Working language

The working language of the Special Court shall be English.

Article 25 Annual Report

The President of the Special Court shall submit an annual report on the operation and activities of the Court to the Secretary-General and to the Government of Sierra Leone.

Selected Bibliography

ACADEMIC LITERATURE

Books

Akinmuwagun, T.L. and Vormbaum, M., Africa and the International Criminal Court (Gerhard Werle, Lovell Fernandez, and Moritz Vormbaum eds., 2014).

Alvarez, Jose E., *The Main Functions of International Adjudication, in* The Impact of International Organizations on International Law (2017).

Aptel, Cecile, *Unpunished Crimes: The Special Court for Sierra Leone and Children, in* The Sierra Leone Special Court and Its Legacy: The Impact for Africa and International Criminal Law (Charles C. Jalloh ed., 2014).

Bassiouni, M. C., Introduction to International Criminal Law (2nd. rev. ed., 2013).

Bassiouni, M. C. and Wise, Edward M., Aut Dedere Aut Judicare: The Duty to Extradite or Prosecute in International Law (1995).

Bisett, Alison, Truth Commissions and Criminal Courts (2012).

Bix, Herbert P., Hirohito and the Making of Modern Japan (2000).

Berewa, Solomon E., *Addressing Impunity using Divergent Approaches: The Truth and Reconciliation Commission and the Special Court, in* Truth and Reconciliation in Sierra Leone (1999).

Berewa, Solomon E., A New Perspective On Governance, Leadership, Conflict and Nation Building in Sierra Leone (2011).

Brownlie, Ian, Principles of Public International Law (7th ed., 2008).

Cartwright, John R., Politics in Sierra Leone 1947–1967 (1970).

Cassese, Antonio, International Criminal Law (2008).

Cassese, Antonio, *The Role of Internationalized Courts and Tribunals in the Fight Against International Criminality, in* Internationalized Criminal Courts: Sierra Leone, East Timor, Kosovo, and Cambodia (Cesare Romano, et al. eds., 2004).

Combs, Nancy, Fact Finding Without Facts : The Uncertain Evidentiary Foundations of International Criminal Convictions (2013).

Crawford, James, The International Law Commission's Articles on State Responsibility: Introduction, Text and Commentaries (2002).

Cryer, Robert et al., An Introduction to International Criminal Procedure (2nd ed., 2010).

CRYER, ROBERT ET AL., AN INTRODUCTION TO INTERNATIONAL CRIMINAL LAW AND PROCEDURE (3rd ed., 2014).

Cryer, Robert, *Special Proclamation – Establishment of an IMT, in* DOCUMENTS ON THE TOKYO INTERNATIONAL MILITARY TRIBUNAL: CHARTER INDICTMENT AND JUDGMENTS (Neil Boister and Robert Cryer eds., 2008).

Cullen, Anthony, *The Characterization of Armed Conflict in the Jurisprudence of the ICC, in* THE LAW AND PRACTICE OF THE INTERNATIONAL CRIMINAL COURT (2015).

De Bertodano, Sylvia, *East Timor: Trials and Tribulations, in* INTERNATIONALIZED CRIMINAL COURTS: SIERRA LEONE EAST TIMOR, KOSOVO, AND CAMBODIA (Cesare Romano, et al. eds., 2004).

DEMBOUR, MARIE-BÉNÉDICTE, *Critiques [in] International Human Rights Law, in* INTERNATIONAL HUMAN RIGHTS LAW (Daniel Moeckli, et al. eds., 3d ed. 2017).

DRUMBL, MARK A., REIMAGINING CHILD SOLDIERS IN INTERNATIONAL LAW AND POLICY (2012).

DUBLER SC, ROBERT AND KALYK, MATTHEW, CRIMES AGAINST HUMANITY UNDER CUSTOMARY INTERNATIONAL LAW AND THE ICC: THE CHAPEAU ELEMENTS (2018).

Etcheson, Craig, *Politics of Genocide Justice in Cambodia, in* INTERNATIONALIZED CRIMINAL COURTS: SIERRA LEONE, EAST TIMOR, KOSOVO, AND CAMBODIA (Cesare P.R. Romano et al. eds., 2004).

FOX, HAZEL AND WEBB, PHILIPPA, THE LAW OF STATE IMMUNITY (3rd ed., 2013).

FREEMAN, MARK, TRUTH COMMISSIONS AND PROCEDURAL FAIRNESS (2006).

Frulli, Micaela, *Piercing the Veil of Head of State Immunity: The Taylor Trial and Beyond, in* THE SIERRA LEONE SPECIAL COURT AND ITS LEGACY: THE IMPACT FOR AFRICA AND INTERNATIONAL CRIMINAL LAW (Charles C. Jalloh ed., 2014).

Gell, Annie, *Lessons from the Trial of Charles Taylor at the Special Court for Sierra Leone, in* THE SIERRA LEONE SPECIAL COURT AND ITS LEGACY: THE IMPACT FOR AFRICA AND INTERNATIONAL CRIMINAL LAW (Charles Chernor Jalloh ed., 2014).

Grant, Andrew J., *Salone's Sorrow: The Ominous Legacy of Diamonds in Sierra Leone, in* RESOURCE POLITICS IN SUB-SAHARAN AFRICA (Matthias Basedau and Andreas Mehler eds., 2005).

HAYNER, PRISCILLA, UNSPEAKABLE TRUTHS: CONFRONTING STATE TERROR AND ATROCITY (2001).

HENCKAERTS, JEAN-MARIE AND DOSWALD-BECK, LOUISE, CUSTOMARY INTERNATIONAL HUMANITARIAN LAW (2005).

Jalloh, Charles C., *Assessing the Legacy of the Special Court for Sierra Leone, in* THE SIERRA LEONE SPECIAL COURT AND ITS LEGACY: THE IMPACT FOR AFRICA AND INTERNATIONAL CRIMINAL LAW (Charles C. Jalloh ed., 2014).

Jalloh, Charles C., *Charles Taylor, in* CAMBRIDGE COMPANION TO INTERNATIONAL CRIMINAL LAW (William A. Schabas ed., 2016).

Jalloh, Charles C., *Conclusion, in* THE SIERRA LEONE SPECIAL COURT AND ITS LEGACY: THE IMPACT FOR AFRICA AND INTERNATIONAL CRIMINAL LAW (Charles C. Jalloh ed., 2014).

Jalloh, Charles, Consolidated Legal Texts for the Special Court for Sierra Leone (2007).

JALLOH, CHARLES C., THE SIERRA LEONE SPECIAL COURT AND ITS LEGACY: THE IMPACT FOR AFRICA AND INTERNATIONAL CRIMINAL LAW (2014).

KARGBO, MICHAEL S., BRITISH FOREIGN POLICY AND THE CONFLICT IN SIERRA LEONE, 1991 (Peter Lang AG ed., 2006).

KEEN, DAVID, CONFLICT AND COLLUSION IN SIERRA LEONE (2005).

KELSALL, TIM, CULTURE UNDER CROSS EXAMINATION: INTERNATIONAL JUSTICE AND THE SPECIAL COURT FOR SIERRA LEONE (2013).

Kooijmans, P. H., *The Security Council and Non-State Entities as Parties to Conflicts, in* INTERNATIONAL LAW: THEORY AND PRACTICE: ESSAYS IN HONOUR OF ERIC SUY (K. Wellens ed., 1998).

Kreß, Claus, *The International Criminal Court and Immunities under International Law for States Not Party to the Court's Statute, in* STATE SOVEREIGNTY AND INTERNATIONAL CRIMINAL LAW (Morten Bergsmo and LING Yan eds., 2012).

Kwakwa, Edward, *The International Community, International Law and the United States: Three in One, Two against One, or One and the Same, in* UNITED STATES HEGEMONY AND THE FOUNDATIONS OF INTERNATIONAL LAW (Michael Byers and Georg Nolte eds., 2008).

LEVITT, JEREMEY I., ILLEGAL PEACE IN AFRICA: AN INQUIRY INTO THE LEGALITY OF POWER SHARING WITH WARLORDS, REBELS, AND JUNTA (2012).

LINCOLN, JESSICA, TRANSITIONAL JUSTICE, PEACE AND ACCOUNTABILITY: OUTREACH AND THE ROLE OF INTERNATIONAL COURTS AFTER CONFLICT (2011)

LIPMAN, JANNA, CHARLES TAYLOR'S CRIMINAL NETWORK: EXPLOITING DIAMONDS AND CHILDREN (Louise Shelley ed., 2009).

MALLINDER, LOUISE, AMNESTY, HUMAN RIGHTS AND POLITICAL TRANSITIONS: BRIDGING THE PEACE AND JUSTICE DIVIDE (2008).

MAGA, TIMOTHY P., JUDGMENT AT TOKYO: THE JAPANESE WAR CRIMES TRIALS (2001).

MANI, RAMA, SEEKING JUSTICE IN THE SHADOWS OF WAR (2002).

Marong, Alhagi B. M., *Fleshing Out the Contours of the Crime of Attacks against United Nations Peacekeepers – The Contribution of the Special Court for Sierra Leone, in* THE SIERRA LEONE SPECIAL COURT AND ITS LEGACY: THE IMPACT FOR AFRICA AND INTERNATIONAL CRIMINAL LAW (Charles C. Jalloh ed., 2014).

MERON, THEODOR, WAR CRIMES LAW COME OF AGE (1998).

METTRAUX, GUÉNAËL, INTERNATIONAL CRIMES AND THE AD HOC TRIBUNALS (2005).

MCBRIDE, JULIE, THE WAR CRIME OF CHILD SOLDIER RECRUITMENT (2014).

Mochochoko, Phakiso and Tortora, Giorgia, *The Management Committee for the Special Court for Sierra Leone, in* INTERNATIONALIZED CRIMINAL COURTS: SIERRA LEONE, EAST TIMOR, KOSOVO, AND CAMBODIA (Cesare Romano, et al. eds., 2004).

MORRIS, VIRGINIA AND SCHARF, MICHAEL P., AN INSIDER'S GUIDE TO THE INTERNATIONAL CRIMINAL TRIBUNAL FOR THE FORMER YUGOSLAVIA (1995).

MUGWANYA, GEORGE, THE CRIME OF GENOCIDE IN INTERNATIONAL LAW: APPRAISING THE CONTRIBUTION OF THE U.N. TRIBUNAL FOR RWANDA (2007).

NJIKAM, OUSMAN, THE CONTRIBUTION OF THE SPECIAL COURT FOR SIERRA LEONE TO THE DEVELOPMENT OF INTERNATIONAL HUMANITARIAN LAW (2013).

Nollkaemper, Andre et al., *Preface, in* SYSTEM CRIMINALITY IN INTERNATIONAL LAW (Harmen van der Wilt and André Nollkaemper eds., 2009).

ORENTLICHER, DIANE F., SHRINKING THE SPACE FOR DENIAL: THE IMPACT OF THE ICTY IN SERBIA (2008).

Oosterveld, Valerie, *Evaluating the Special Court for Sierra Leone's Gender Jurisprudence, in* THE SIERRA LEONE SPECIAL COURT AND ITS LEGACY: THE IMPACT FOR AFRICAN AND INTERNATIONAL CRIMINAL LAW (Charles Chernor Jalloh ed., 2013).

PENFOLD, PETER, ATROCITIES, DIAMONDS AND DIPLOMACY: THE INSIDE STORY OF THE CONFLICT IN SIERRA LEONE (2012).

Penfold, Peter, *International Community Expectations of the Special Court for Sierra Leone, in* THE SIERRA LEONE SPECIAL COURT AND ITS LEGACY: THE IMPACT FOR AFRICA AND INTERNATIONAL CRIMINAL LAW (Charles C. Jalloh ed., 2014).

Rapp, Stephen J., *The Challenge of Choice in the Investigation and Prosecution of International Crimes in Post-Conflict Sierra Leone, in* THE SIERRA LEONE SPECIAL COURT AND ITS LEGACY: THE IMPACT FOR AFRICA AND INTERNATIONAL CRIMINAL LAW (2014).

Reydams, Luc, Wouters. Jan and Odermatt, Jed, *Mandate and Jurisdiction, in* INTERNATIONAL PROSECUTORS (Luc Reydams et al. eds., 2012).

ROMANO, CESARE ET AL., INTERNATIONALIZED CRIMINAL COURTS: SIERRA LEONE, EAST TIMOR, KOSOVO, AND CAMBODIA (CESARE P.R. ROMANO, ET AL. EDS., 2004).

Sadat, Leila, *The Lomé Amnesty Decision of the Special Court for Sierra Leone, in* THE SIERRA LEONE SPECIAL COURT AND ITS LEGACY: THE IMPACT FOR AFRICA AND INTERNATIONAL CRIMINAL LAW (Charles C. Jalloh ed., 2014).

Schabas, William A., *A Synergistic Relationship: The Sierra Leone Truth and Reconciliation Commission and the Special Court for Sierra Leone, in* TRUTH COMMISSIONS AND COURTS: THE TENSION BETWEEN CRIMINAL JUSTICE AND THE SEARCH FOR TRUTH (William Schabas et al. eds., 2004).

Schabas, William A., *Foreword, in* THE SIERRA LEONE SPECIAL COURT AND ITS LEGACY: THE IMPACT FOR AFRICA AND INTERNATIONAL CRIMINAL LAW (Charles C. Jalloh ed., 2014).

SCHABAS, WILLIAM, THE TRIAL OF THE KAISER (2018).

SCHABAS, WILLIAM A., THE UN INTERNATIONAL CRIMINAL TRIBUNALS (2006).

SCHABAS, WILLIAM, THE UN INTERNATIONAL CRIMINAL TRIBUNALS: THE FORMER YUGOSLAVIA, RWANDA AND SIERRA LEONE (2006).

SCHABAS, WILLIAM, UNIMAGINABLE ATROCITIES (2012).

SCHEFFER, DAVID J., ALL THE MISSING SOULS: A PERSONAL HISTORY OF THE WAR CRIMES TRIBUNALS (2012).

SHAW, MALCOLM N., INTERNATIONAL LAW (6th ed., 2008).

Shraga, Daphna, *The Second Generation UN-Based Tribunals: A Diversity of Mixed Jurisdictions, in* INTERNATIONALIZED CRIMINAL COURTS: SIERRA LEONE EAST TIMOR, KOSOVO, AND CAMBODIA (Cesare Romano, et al. eds., 2004).

SHUTE, STEPHEN AND HURLEY, S. L., ON HUMAN RIGHTS: THE OXFORD AMNESTY LECTURES 1993 (1993).

Sluiter, Göran, *Procedural Lawmaking at the International Criminal Tribunals, in* JUDICIAL CREATIVITY AT THE INTERNATIONAL CRIMINAL TRIBUNALS (Shane Darcy and Joseph Powderly eds., 2010).

Sluiter, Göran, *The Legal Assistance to Internationalized Criminal Courts and Tribunals, in* INTERNATIONALIZED CRIMINAL COURTS: SIERRA LEONE, EAST TIMOR, KOSOVO, AND CAMBODIA (Cesare Romano, et al. eds., 2004).

Smeulers, Alette, Hola, Barbara and Van den Berg, Tom, "Sixty-Five Years of International Criminal Justice: The Facts and Figures", in The Realities of International Criminal Justice (2003).

SMILLIE, IAN ET AL., THE HEART OF THE MATTER- SIERRA LEONE, DIAMONDS AND HUMAN SECURITY (2000).

STEINBERG, RICHARD, ASSESSING THE LEGACY OF THE ICTY (2011).

SWART, BERT ER AL. LEGACY OF THE INTERNATIONAL CRIMINAL TRIBUNAL FOR THE FORMER YUGOSLAVIA (2011).

Tejan-Cole, Abdul, *A Big Man in a Small Cell: Charles Taylor and the Special Court for Sierra Leone, in* PROSECUTING HEADS OF STATE (Ellen L. Lutz and Caitlin Reiger eds., 2009).

THE AFRICAN COURT OF JUSTICE AND HUMAN AND PEOPLES' RIGHTS IN CONTEXT: DEVELOPMENT AND CHALLENGES (Charles C. Jalloh et al. eds., 2019).

THE INTERNATIONAL CRIMINAL COURT AND AFRICA (Charles Jalloh and Ilias Bantekas eds., 2017).

THE SIERRA LEONE SPECIAL COURT AND ITS LEGACY: THE IMPACT FOR AFRICA AND INTERNATIONAL CRIMINAL LAW (Charles C. Jalloh ed., 2014).

TRUTH & RECONCILIATION COMMISSION, REPUBLIC OF LIBER., CONSOLIDATED FINAL REPORT (2009).

TRUTH AND RECONCILIATION COMMISSION OF SOUTH AFRICA REPORT (2001).

VAN DEN HERIK, GEORGE, THE CRIME OF GENOCIDE IN INTERNATIONAL LAW: APPRAISING THE CONTRIBUTION OF THE UN TRIBUNAL FOR RWANDA (2007).

VAN DEN HERIK, LARISSA J., THE CONTRIBUTION OF THE RWANDA TRIBUNAL TO THE DEVELOPMENT OF INTERNATIONAL LAW (2005).

VAN DEN HERIK, LANSANA, A DIRTY WAR IN WEST AFRICA: THE RUF AND THE DESTRUCTION OF SIERRA LEONE (2005).

Van Den Herik, Larissa and Stahn, Carsten, 'Fragmentation', Diversification and '3D' Legal Pluralism: International Criminal Law as the Jack-in-the-Box?, in THE DIVERSIFICATION AND FRAGMENTATION OF INTERNATIONAL CRIMINAL LAW (Larissa van den Herik and Carsten Stahn eds., 2012).

Von Hebel, Herman, Foreword, in CONSOLIDATED LEGAL TEXTS FOR THE SPECIAL COURT FOR SIERRA LEONE (Charles C. Jalloh ed., 2007).

WERLE GERHARD AND JESSBERGER, FLORIAN, PRINCIPLES OF INTERNATIONAL CRIMINAL LAW (3rd ed. 2014).

WERLE GERHARD ET AL., AFRICA AND THE INTERNATIONAL CRIMINAL COURT (Gerhard Werle, et al. eds., 2014).

Articles in Academic Journals

Akande, Dapo, International Law Immunities and the International Criminal Court, 98 AM. J. INT'L L. 420 (2004).

Akande, Dapo, The Legal Nature of Security Council Referrals to the ICC and its Impact on Al Bashir's Immunities, 7 J. INT'L. CRIM. JUST. 333 (2009).

Akande, Dapo and Shah, Sangeeta, Immunities of State Officials, International Crimes, and Foreign Domestic Courts, 21 EUR. J. INT'L L. 815 (2010).

Amann, Diane M., Calling Children to Account: The Proposal for a Juvenile Chamber in the Special Court for Sierra Leone, 29 PEPP. L. REV. 167 (2001).

Bald, Stephanie, Searching for a Lost Childhood: Will the Special Court for Sierra Leone Find Justice for Its Children?, 18 AM. U. INT'L L. REV. 537 (2002).

Bangura, Mohamed, Prosecuting the Crime of Attack on Peacekeepers: A Prosecutor's Challenge, 23 LEIDEN J. INT'L L. 165 (2010).

Bassiouni, Cherif M., Crimes Against Humanity: The Case for a Specialized Convention, 9 WASH. U. GLOBAL STUD. L. REV. 575 (2010).

Begley, Tracey, The Extraterritorial Obligation to Prevent the Use of Child Soldiers, 27 AM. U. INT'L L. REV. 613 (2012).

Bélair, Karine, Unearthing the Customary Law Foundations of "Forced Marriages" During Sierra Leone's Civil War: The Possible Impact of International Criminal Law on Customary Marriage and Women's Rights in Post-Conflict Sierra Leone, 15 COLUM. J. GENDER & L. 551 (2006).

Beresford, Stuart, Child Witnesses and the International Criminal Justice System: Does the International Criminal Court Protect the Most Vulnerable?, 3 J. INT'L CRIM. JUST. 721 (2005).

Beresford, Stuart and Muller, A. S., The Special Court for Sierra Leone: An Initial Comment, 14 LEIDEN J. INT'L L. 635 (2001).

Bolten, Catherine E., The Memories They Want. Autobiography in the Chaos of Sierra Leone, 44 ETHNOLOGIE FRANCAISE 429 (2014).

Bunting, Annie and Ikhimiukor, Izevbuwa Kehinde, The Expressive Nature of Law: What We Learn from Conjugal Slavery to Forced Marriage in International Criminal Law, 18 INT'L CRIM. L. R. 331 (2018).

Cassese, Antonio, *On the Current Trends towards Criminal Prosecution and Punishment of Breaches of International Humanitarian Law*, 9 EUR. J. INT'L. L. 2 (1998).

Cassese, Antonio, *The Special Court and International Law: The Decision Concerning the Lomé Agreement Amnesty*, 4 J. INT'L. CRIM. JUST. 2 (2004).

Cerone, John, *The Special Court for Sierra Leone: Establishing a New Approach to International Criminal Justice*, 8 ILSA J. INT'L & COMP. L. 379 (2002).

Charlesworth, Hilary, *Not Waiving but Drowning – Gender Mainstreaming and Human Rights*, 18 HARV. HUM. RTS. J. 1 (2005).

Charlesworth, Hilary, Chinkin, Christine and Wright, Shelley, *Feminist Approaches to International Law*, 85 AM. J. INT'L L. 615 (1991).

Chinkin, Christine, *United Kingdom House of Lords: Regina v. Bow Street Stipendary Magistrate, Ex Parte Pinochet Ugarte*, 93 AM. J. INT'L L. 703 (1999).

Cohen, David, *"Hybrid" Justice in East Timor, Sierra Leone, and Cambodia: "Lessons Learned" and Prospects for the Future*, 43 STAN. J. INT'L L. 1 (2007).

Cohn, Ilene, *The Protection of Children and the Quest for Truth and Justice in Sierra Leone*, 55 J. INT'L AFF. 1 (2001).

Corriero, Michael, *The Involvement and Protection of Children in Truth and Justice-Seeking Processes: The Special Court for Sierra Leone*, 18 N.Y.L. SCH. J. HUM. RTS. 337 (2002).

Cruvellier, Thierry and Wierda, Marieke, *The Special Court for Sierra Leone: The First Eighteen Months*, 12 INT'L CTR. FOR TRANSITIONAL JUST. (ICTJ) CASE STUD. SERIES (Mar. 2004).

Cryer, Robert, A *"Special Court" for Sierra Leone*, 50 INT'L & COMP. L. Q. 435 (2001).

Custer, Michael, *Punishing Child Soldiers: The Special Court for Sierra Leone and the Lessons to be Learned from the United States' Juvenile Justice System*, 19 TEMP. INT'L & COMP. L. J. 449 (2005).

D'Amato, Anthony, *It's a Bird, it's a Plane, it's Jus Cogens*, 6 CONN. J. INT'L L. 1 (1990).

Damaska, Mirjan, *What Is the Point of International Criminal Justice*, 83 CHI.-KENT. L. REV. 329 (2008).

Danilenko, Gennady M., *International Jus Cogens: Issues of Law-Making*, 2 EUR. J. INT'L L. 42 (1991).

Davies, Pamela O., *Marriage, Divorce and Inheritance Laws in Sierra Leone and Their Discriminatory Effects on Women*, 12 HUM. RTS. BRIEF 17 (2005).

Deen-Racsmány, Zsuzsanna, *Prosecutor v. Taylor: The Status of the Special Court for Sierra Leone and Its Implications for Immunity*, 18 LEIDEN J. INT'L L. 299 (2005).

De Wet, Erika, *The Implications of President Al-Bashir's Visit to South Africa for International and Domestic Law*, 13 J. INT'L. CRIM. JUST. 1049 (2015).

Dickinson, Laura A., *The Promise of Hybrid Courts*, 97 AM. J. INT'L L. 295 (2003).

Dorman, *Contributions by the Ad Hoc Tribunals for the former Yugoslavia and Rwanda to the Ongoing Work on Elements of Crime for the ICC*, 94 PROC. ANN. MEETING AM. SOC'Y INT'L L. 284 (2000).

Ejigu, Mersie, *Post Conflict Liberia : Environmental Security as a Strategy for Sustainable Peace and Development* (Foundation for Environmental Security and Sustainability, Working Paper No. 3, 2006).

Ferme, Mariane C., *"Archetypes of Humanitarian Discourse": Child Soldiers, Forced Marriage, and the Framing of Communities in Post-Conflict Sierra Leone*, 4 HUMANITY: AN INT'L J. HUM. RTS., HUMAN'ISM, DEV. 49 (2013).

Fritz, Nicole and Smith, Alison, *Current Apathy for Coming Anarchy: Building the Special Court for Sierra Leone*, 25 FORDHAM J. INT'L L. 391 (2001).

Frulli, Micaela, *Advancing International Criminal Law: The Special Court for Sierra Leone Recognizes Forced Marriage as a "New" Crime Against Humanity*, 6 J. INT'L CRIM. JUST. 1033 (2008).

Frulli, Micaela, *The Special Court for Sierra Leone: Some Preliminary Comments*, 11 EUR. J. INT'L. L. 857 (2000).

Gaeta, Paola, *Does President Al Bashir Enjoy Immunity from Arrest?*, 7 J. INT'L. CRIM. JUST. 315 (2009).

Gekker, Elena, *Rape, Sexual Slavery, and Forced Marriage at the International Criminal Court: How Katanga Utilizes A Ten-Year-Old Rule but Overlooks New Jurisprudence*, 25 HASTINGS WOMEN'S L.J. 105 (2014).

Gong-Gershowitz, Jennifer, *Forced Marriage: A "New" Crime Against Humanity?*, 8 NW. U. J. INT'L HUM. RTS. 53 (2009).

Goodfellow, Nicholas Azadi, *The Miscategorization of "Forced Marriage" as a Crime Against Humanity by the Special Court for Sierra Leone*, 11 INT'L CRIM. L. REV. 831 (2011).

Happold, Matthew, *International Humanitarian Law, War Criminality and Child Recruitment: The Special Court for Sierra Leone's Decision in Prosecutor v. Samuel Hinga Norman*, 18 LEIDEN J. INT'L L. 283 (2005).

Hoffmann, Michael, *May We Hold Them Responsible? The Prosecution of Child Soldiers by the Special Court for Sierra Leone*, 14 INT'L CHILD. RTS. MONITOR 23 (2001).

Jain, Neha, *Forced Marriage as a Crime Against Humanity: Problems of Definition and Prosecution*, 6 J. INT'L CRIM. JUST. 1013 (2008).

Jalloh, Charles, *Immunity from Prosecution for International Crimes: The Case of Charles Taylor at the Special Court for Sierra Leone*, 8 AM. SOC'Y INT'L L. INSIGHT 21 (2004).

Jalloh, Charles C., *Prosecuting Those Bearing "Greatest Responsibility": The Lessons of the Special Court for Sierra Leone*, 96 MARQ. L. REV. 863 (2013).

Jalloh, Charles, *Regionalizing International Criminal Law?*, 9 INT'L. CRIM. L. REV. 445 (2009).

Jalloh, Charles C., *Special Court for Sierra Leone: Achieving Justice?*, 32 MICH. J. INT'L L. 395 (2011).

Jalloh, Charles C. *The Contribution of the Special Court for Sierra Leone to the Development of International Law*, 15 AFR. J. INT'L & COMP. L. 165 (2007).

Jalloh, Charles C., *The Law and Politics of the Charles Taylor Case*, 43 DENV. J. INT'L L. & POL'Y 229 (2014).

Jalloh, Charles C., *The Special Tribunal for Lebanon: A Defense Perspective*, 47 VAND. J. TRANSNAT'L L. 765 (2014).

Jalloh, Charles and Marong, Alhagi, *Ending Impunity: The Case for War Crimes Trials in Liberia*, 2 AFR. J. LEGAL STUD. 53 (2005).

Jalloh, Charles C. and Nmehielle, Vincent, *The Legacy of the Special Court for Sierra Leone*, 30 FLETCHER F. WORLD AFF. 107 (2006).

Jones, John R. W. D. et al., *The Special Court for Sierra Leone: A Defense Perspective*, 2 J. INT'L CRIM. JUST. 211 (2004).

Kabbah, Ahmed Tejan, *Two Decades of Conflict and Democracy in Sierra Leone: A Personal Experience*, Institute for Security Studies: Situation Report (Apr. 13, 2012).

Klingberg, Vanesa, *(Former) Heads of State before International(ized) Criminal Courts: The Case of Charles Taylor before the Special Court for Sierra Leone*, 46 GERMAN Y.B. INT'L L. 537 (2004).

Kress, Claus, *Reflections on the Iudicare Limb of the Grave Breaches Regime*, 7 J. INT'L CRIM. JUST. 789 (2009).

Konge, Paola, *International Crimes and Soldiers*, 16 SW. J. INT'L L. 41 (2010).

Leveau, Fanny, *Liability of Child Soldiers Under International Criminal Law*, 4 OSGOODE HALL REV. L. & POL'Y 36 (2013).

Linton, Suzannah, *Cambodia, East Timor and Sierra Leone: Experiments in International Justice*, 12 CRIM. L. FOR. 185 (2001).

Lisk, Ida E. P. and Williams, Bernadette L., *Marriage and Divorce Regulation and Recognition in Sierra Leone*, 29 FAM. L. Q. 655 (1995).

Mack, Eveylon. *Does Customary International Law Obligate States to Extradite or Prosecute Individuals Accused of Committing Crimes Against Humanity?*, 24 MINN. J. INT'L L. 73 (2015).

Marchuk, Iryna, *Confronting Blood Diamonds in Sierra Leone: The Trial of Charles Taylor*, 4 YALE J. INT'L AFF. 87 (2009).

McDonald, Avril, *Sierra Leone's Shoestring Special Court*, 84 INTL'L REV. R.C. 121 (2002).

Meisenberg, Simon M., *Legality of Amnesties in International Humanitarian Law: The Lomé Amnesty Decision of the Special Court for Sierra Leone*, 86 INT'L REV. RED CROSS 837 (2004).

Meron, Theodor, *Is International Law Moving Towards Criminalization*, 9 EUR. J. INT'L. L. 18 (1998).

Miglin, James L., *From Immunity to Impunity: Charles Taylor and the Special Court for Sierra Leone*, 16 DALHOUSIE J. LEGAL STUD. 21 (2007).

Moreno-Ocampo, Luis, *The International Criminal Court : Seeking Global Justice*, 40 CASE W. RES. J. INT'L L. 215 (2008).

Morini, Claudia, *First Victims then Perpetrators: Child Soldiers and International Law*, 3 ANUARIO COLOMBIANO DE DERECHO INTERNACIONAL 187 (2010).

Morrison, Sean, *Extraordinary Language in the Courts of Cambodia: Interpreting the Limiting Language and Personal Jurisdiction of the Cambodian Tribunal*, 37 CAP. U. L. REV. 583 (2009).

Møse, Erik, *Main Achievements of the ICTR*, 3 J. INT'L CRIM. JUST. 920 (2005).

Murphy, Sean D., *Contemporary Practice of the United States Relating to International Law*, 94(2) AM. J. INT'L L. 482 (2002).

Murphy, Sean D., *State Department Views on the Future of War Crimes Tribunals*, 96(2) AM. J. INT'L L. 482 (2002).

Nicol-Wilson, Melron C., *Accountability for Human Rights Abuses: The United Nations' Special Court for Sierra Leone*, AUSTL. INT'L L. J. 159 (2001)

Nmehielle, Vincent O., *Position Paper on the Independence of the Office of the Principal Defender at the Special Court for Sierra Leone* (Submitted to the Management Committee of the SCSL by Principal Defender) (on file with the author).

Nollkaemper, André, *Wither Aut Dedere? The Obligation to Extradite or Prosecute after the ICJ's Judgment in Belgium v Senegal*, 4 J INT. DISP. SETTLEMENT 3 (2013).

Nouwen, Sarah M. H., *The Special Court for Sierra Leone and the Immunity of Taylor: The Arrest Warrant Case Continued*, 18 LEIDEN J. INT'L. L. 645 (2005).

Novogrodsky, Noah, *Litigating Child Recruitment Before the Special Court for Sierra Leone*, 7 SAN DIEGO INT'L L.J. 421 (2006).

O'Connell, Jamie, *Here Interest Meets Humanity: How to End the War and Support Reconstruction in Liberia, and the Case for Modest American Leadership*, 17 HARV. HUM. RTS. J. 207 (2004).

O'Keefe, Roger, *An "International Crime" Exception to the Immunity of State Officials from Foreign Criminal Jurisdiction: Not Currently, Not Likely*, 109 AM. J. INT'L L. UNBOUND 167 (2015).

Oosterveld, Valerie, *Gender and the Charles Taylor Case at the Special Court for Sierra Leone*, 19 WM & MARY J. WOMEN & L. 7 (2012).

Oosterveld, Valerie, *Lessons from the Special Court for Sierra Leone on the Prosecution of Gender-Based Crimes*, 17 AM. U.J. GENDER SOC. POL'Y & L. 407 (2009).

Oosterveld, Valerie, *The Gender Jurisprudence of the Special Court for Sierra Leone: Progress in the Revolutionary United Front Judgments*, 44 CORNELL INT'L L. J. 49 (2011).

Oosterveld, Valerie, *The Special Court for Sierra Leone, Child Soldiers, and Forced Marriage: Providing Clarity or Confusion?*, 45 CAN. Y.B. INT'L L. 131 (2007).

Orentlicher, Diane F., *Settling Accounts: The Duty to Prosecute Human Rights Violations of a Prior Regime*, 100 YALE L. J. 2537 (1999).

Paust, Jordan J., *Genocide in Rwanda, State Responsibility to Prosecute or Extradite, and Nonimmunity for Heads of State and Other Public Officials*, 34 HOUS. J. INT'L L. 57 (2011).

Pellet, Alain, *Response to Koh and Buchwald's Article: Don Quixote and Sancho Panza Tilt at Windmills*, 109(3) AM. J. INT'L L. 557 (2015).

Prosper, Pierre-Richard and Newton, Michael A., *The Bush Administration View of International Accountability*, 36 NEW ENG. L. REV. 891 (2002).

Romano, Cesare and Nollkaemper, André, *The Arrest Warrant Against the Liberian President Charles Taylor*, 8 AM. SOC'Y INT'L L. INSIGHTS 16 (2003).

Sainz-Pardo, Pilar Villanueva, *Is Child Recruitment as a War Crime Part of Customary International Law*, 12 INT'L J. HUM. RTS. 555 (2008).

Schabas, William A., *Amnesty, the Sierra Leone Truth and Reconciliation Commission and the Special Court for Sierra Leone*, U.C. DAVIS J. INT'L LAW & POL'Y 145 (2004).

Schabas, William A., *Genocide Trials and Gacaca Courts*, 3 J. INT'L CRIM. JUST. 879 (2005).

Schabas, William A., *Victor's Justice: Selecting "Situations" at the International Criminal Court*, 43 J. MARSHALL L. REV. 535 (2010).

Scharf, Bridgette, *What Is Forced Marriage? Towards a Definition of Forced Marriage as a Crime Against Humanity*, 19 COL. J. GENDER & L. 539 (2010).

Scharf, Michael and Mattler, Suzanne, *Forced Marriage: Exploring the Viability of the Special Court for Sierra Leone's New Crime against Humanity, Case Research Paper Series in Legal Studies*, (Case Law Sch. Case Research Paper Series in Legal Studies, Working Paper 05–35 2005).

Schocken, Celina, *The Special Court for Sierra Leone: Overview and Recommendations*, 20 BERKELEY J. INT'L L. 436 (2002).

Slater, Rachel, *Gender Violence or Violence Against Women? The Treatment of Forced Marriage in the Special Court for Sierra Leone*, 13 MELBOURNE J. INT'L L. 1 (2012).

Sluiter, Göran, *The Surrender of War Criminals to the International Criminal Court*, 25 LO. L. A. INT'L. & COMP. L. REV. 605 (2003).

Smith, Alison, *Child Recruitment and the Special Court for Sierra Leone*, 4 J. INT'L CRIM. JUST. 1141 (2004).

Sunga, Lyal, *The Commission of Experts on Rwanda and the Creation of the International Criminal Tribunal for Rwanda*, 16 HUM. RTS. L. J. 121 (1995).

Tejan-Cole, Abdul, *The Special Court for Sierra Leone: Conceptual Concerns and Alternatives*, 1 AFR. HUM. RTS. L. J. 107 (2001).

Tladi, Dire, *The Duty on South Africa to Arrest and Surrender President Al-Bashir under South African and International Law*, 13 J. INT'L. CRIM. JUST. 1027 (2015).

Thompson, Alison and Staggs, Michelle, *The Defense Office at the Special Court for Sierra Leone: A Critical Perspective*, WAR CRIMES STUD. CTR. UNIV. CAL. BERKLEY (2007).

Van Der Wilt, Harmen, *The Continuing Story of the International Criminal Court and Personal Immunities* (2016)(Amsterdam Law School Research Paper No. 2015–48)(on file with Amsterdam Center for International Law, University of Amsterdam).

Van Schaack, Beth, *Engendering Genocide: The Akayesu Case Before the International Criminal Tribunal for Rwanda*, Santa Clara Law Digital Commons (2008).

Ward, Kathy, *Might vs. Right: Charles Taylor and the Sierra Leone Special Court*, 11 Hum. Rts. Brief 8 (2003).

Wharton, Sara, *The Evolution of International Criminal Law: Prosecuting "New" Crimes Before the Special Court for Sierra Leone*, 11 Int'l Crim. L. Rev. 217 (2011).

Wierda, Marieke, Hayner, Priscilla and van Zyl, Paul, *Exploring the Relationship Between the Special Court and the Sierra Leone Truth and Reconciliation Commission*, Int'l Ctr. for Transitional Justice (2002).

Yuvaraj, Joshua, *When Does a Child "Participate Actively in Hostilities" under the Rome Statute? Protecting Children from Use in Hostilities after Lubanga*, 32 Utrecht J. Int'l & Euro. L. 69 (2016).

Zack-Williams, A. B., *Child Soldiers in the Sivil war in Sierra Leone*, 28 Rev. Afr. Pol. Econ. 73 (2001).

NEWSPAPER PUBLICATIONS

Chronology of Sierra Leone: How Diamonds Fuelled the Conflict, Afr. Confidential (Apr. 1998), www.africa-confidential.com/special-report/id/4/Chronology_of_Sierra_Leone.

Dukulé, Abdoulaye W. *West Africa: Taylor at Accra Peace Talks: "Honourable Exit or Extended Mandate?"*, AllAfrica (June 4, 2003), http://allafrica.com/stories/200306040021.html.

Goodwin, Jan *Sierra Leone Is No Place To Be Young*, N.Y. Times, Feb. 14, 1999, § 6 at 48.

Maharaji, Davan *Liberian President is Sought on War Crimes Indictment*, L.A. Times (June 5, 2003), http://articles.latimes.com/2003/jun/05/world/fg-indict5.

Roy-Macaulay, Clarence *Sierra Leone Court Indicts Liberia Leader*, Guardian (June 4, 2003), www.globalpolicy.org/component/content/article/163/29115.html.

The Standard Times (Freetown), AllAfrica (Nov. 4, 2003), http://allafrica.com/stories/200311050809.html.

Tran, Mark, *US-UK split halts bid for Sierra Leone war crimes court*, The Guardian (July 19, 2000), www.theguardian.com/world/2000/jul/19/sierraleone.

SPEECHES

Federal Government of Nigeria, Statement, Former President Charles Taylor to the transferred to the custody of the Government of Liberia (Mar. 25, 2006).

His Excellency the President Dr. Ahmad Tejan Kabbah, Address at the Start of Public Hearings
of the Truth and Reconciliation Commission (Apr. 14, 2003), www.sierra-leone.org /Speeches/kabbah-041403.html.

His Excellency the President Alhaji Dr. Ahmad Tejan Kabbah, Statement before the Truth and Reconciliation Commission ("TRC") (Aug. 5, 2003).

President Ahmad Tejan Kabbah, Address Opening of The Fourth Session of The First Parliament of The Second Republic (June 16, 2000).

Scheffer, David J., Ambassador at Large for War Crime Issues, Challenges Confronting International Justice Issues, Address before the New England School of Law (Jan. 14, 1998), *in* 4 New Eng. J. Int'l & Comp. L. 1 (1998).

ADDITIONAL SOURCES

Amnesty, BLACK'S LAW DICTIONARY (5th ed. 1983).

Ratione Personae Jurisdiction, BLACK'S LAW DICTIONARY (9th ed. 2009).

Person, OXFORD ENGLISH DICTIONARY (2nd ed., 1989).

Who, OXFORD ENGLISH DICTIONARY (2nd ed., 1989).

Bear, OXFORD ENGLISH DICTIONARY (2nd ed., 1989).

Greatest, OXFORD ENGLISH DICTIONARY (2d ed. 1989).

Responsibility, OXFORD ENGLISH DICTIONARY (2d ed. 1989).

Of one's own accord, BLACK'S LAW DICTIONARY (9th ed. 2009).

BRITANNICA ACADEMIC ENCYCLOPEDIA, "SIERRA LEONE", academic-eb-com.ludwig.lub.lu.se/levels/collegiate/article/Sierra-Leone/110795 (last visited Aug. 5, 2019).

Jennifer Easterday, Trial Charles Taylor, INT'L JUST. MONITOR, *Parties in Taylor Trial Make Appeals Submissions* (Jan. 22, 2013), www.charlestaylortrial.org/2013/01/22/parties-in-taylor-trial-make-appeals-submissions/.

Index

CPSIA information can be obtained
at www.ICGtesting.com
Printed in the USA
LVHW012333020820
662197LV00005B/99